STRENGTHS-BASED GENERALIST PRACTICE

A Collaborative Approach

STRENGTHS-BASED GENERALIST PRACTICE

A Collaborative Approach

THIRD EDITION

John Poulin

Widener University

with Contributors

WADSWORTH
CENGAGE Learning

Australia • Brazil • Japan • Korea • Mexico • Singapore • Spain • United Kingdom • United States

WADSWORTH
CENGAGE Learning™

**Strengths-Based Generalist Practice:
A Collaborative Approach
Third Edition
John Poulin with Contributors**

Publisher: Marcus Boggs

Acquisitions Editor, Counseling, Social Work, and Human Services: Seth Dobrin

Assistant Editor: Diane Mars

Editorial Assistant: Rachel McDonald

Technology Project Manager:

Senior Marketing Manager: Trent Whatcott

Marketing Associate: Darlene Macanan

Content Project Management: Pre-PressPMG

Creative Director: Rob Hugel

Art Director: Caryl Gorska

Print Buyer: Judy Inouye

Permissions Editor: Mardell Glinski-Schultz

Production Service: Pre-PressPMG

Photo Researcher: Pre-PressPMG

Copy Editor: Maria Cusano

Cover Designer: Cheryl Carrington

Cover Image: Richard Cook/Getty Images

Compositor: Pre-PressPMG

For product information and technology assistance contact us at **Cengage Learning Academic Resource Center
1-800-423-0563**

For permission to use material from this text or product, submit all requests online at **www.cengage.com/permissions**
Further permissions questions can be e-mailed to
permissionrequest@cengage.com

Library of Congress Control Number: 2009920923

Student Edition:
ISBN-13: 978-0-495-11587-8
ISBN-10: 0-495-11587-8

Wadsworth, Cengage Learning
10 Davis Drive
Belmont, CA 94002-3098
USA

Cengage Learning products are represented in Canada by Nelson Education, Ltd.

For your course and learning solutions, visit
academic.cengage.com.

Purchase any of our products at your local college store or at our preferred online store **www.ichapters.com.**

Printed in the United States of America
1 2 3 4 5 6 7 13 12 11 10 09

CONTENTS

PREFACE   xxi

ABOUT THE CONTRIBUTORS   xiii

PART I | GENERALIST SOCIAL WORK PRACTICE

CHAPTER 1   PRINCIPLES AND CONCEPTS OF GENERALIST PRACTICE   1

Strengths-Based Generalist Social Work Practice   2
Definition of Generalist Practice   3
Types of Generalist Social Work Interventions   3
Use of Self   6

Social Work Clients   8
Types of Clients   9

The Reluctant Client   11
The Experience of Being a Client   11
Prior Experiences with Helping Professionals   12
Expectations about the Helping Experience   13
Cultural and Ethnic Diversity   13
Client Skills and Knowledge   15

Social Work Values and Ethics   16
Core Social Work Values   16
   Service to Others   16
   Social Justice   16
   Human Dignity and Self-Worth   17
   Importance of Human Relationships   18

Ethical Standards   19
Ethical Dilemmas   19

Summary   22

Case Example   23
Discussion Questions   25
References   25

CHAPTER 2   **THEORETICAL AND CONCEPTUAL FRAMEWORKS FOR GENERALIST PRACTICE   28**

Modern and Postmodern Perspectives   29

Ecosystems Perspective   31

Strengths Perspective   33
Principles of Strengths-Based Practice   34
Principle 1: Every individual, group, family, and community has strengths   35
Principle 2: Trauma, abuse, illness, and struggle may be injurious, but they may also be sources of challenge and opportunity   35
Principle 3: Assume that you do not know the upper limits of the capacity to grow and change, and take individual, group, and community aspirations seriously   35
Principle 4: We best serve clients by collaborating with them   35
Principle 5: Every environment is full of resources   36
Principle 6: Caring, caretaking, and context are important   36
Attachment Theory   36
Critical Thinking and Generalist Social Work Practice   38
Evidence-Based Practice   39

Summary   39

Case Example   40
Discussion Questions   42
References   43

CHAPTER 3   **THE COLLABORATIVE MODEL PRINCIPLES AND CONCEPTS   45**

Theoretical Propositions   46
Proposition 1: Disadvantaged and oppressed (reluctant) clients often mistrust helping professionals   47
Proposition 2: Client change occurs through a collaborative helping relationship   47
Proposition 3: Relationships are built on trust   49

Practice Principles   51
Practice Principle 1: Focus on client strengths   51
Practice Principle 2: Put clients in charge of the helping process   53
Practice Principle 3: Continually evaluate your work and the client's progress   54

Strengths-Based Assessment   56

Assessment versus Diagnosis   56
Assessing Client Strengths   56
Identifying and Analyzing Person-in-Environment Factors   58

The Collaborative Model   59
Phases   61
Inputs   61
Skills   62
Outputs   62
Assessing the Helping Relationship   62
Scoring the HRI   62
Applications of the HRI for Social Work Practice   64

Summary   65

Case Example   66
Discussion Questions   68
References   69

CHAPTER 4   **EVALUATION AND GENERALIST SOCIAL WORK PRACTICE   72**

Measurement Guidelines   74

Measurement Tools   79
Client Logs   80
Behavioral Observations   81
Rating Scales   84
Goal Attainment Scales   86
Standardized Measures   88

Designing the Evaluation   89
Components of Single-System Designs   90
Establishing Baselines   91
Making Comparisons   91

Analyzing Single-System Data   93
Clinical Significance   94
Visual Significance   94
Statistical Significance   97

Summary   99

Case Example   100
Discussion Questions   102
References   103

CHAPTER 5   **THE COLLABORATIVE MODEL TASKS, INPUTS, AND PRACTICE SKILLS   105**

Pre-Engagement Phase of Collaborative Social Work   107
Task 1: Studying Your Client's Culture, Values, Beliefs, and Environment   107
Inputs: Understanding and Sensitivity   107

Practice Skills: Information Retrieval and Resource
Identification   108
Outputs: Increased Knowledge and Competence   109
Task 2: Asking Your Client to Tell His or Her Story   109
Inputs: Respect and Acceptance   110
Elaboration Practice Skills   111
Outputs: Identification of Needs, Concerns, Strengths,
and Coping Skills   114
Task 3: Listening for Meaning and Feelings   114
Inputs: Understanding and Empathy   115
Empathic Skills   116
Outputs: Identification of Feeling Content and Validation   117
Task 4: Clarify How You and the Client Will Work Together   118
Inputs: Cooperative Intentions   119
Outputs: Mutual Understanding and Collaboration   119

The Intervention Phase of Collaborative Social Work   120
Task 5: Articulate Your Focus and Plan of Action   120
Inputs: Hopefulness and Partnership   120
Contracting Skills   121
Outputs: Change Goals, Action Plan, and Evaluation Plan   124
Task 6: Persevere in Carrying Out Your Work Together   124
Inputs: Support and Commitment   125
Intervention Skills   126
Output: Client Change   129

The Disengagement Phase of Collaborative Social Work   129
Task 7: Solidifying the Changes Achieved   129
Input: Confidence   130
Ending Skills   130
Outputs: Evaluation, Generalization, and Aftercare   133

Summary   133
Case Example   133
DVD Exercises   134
References   134

CHAPTER 6   GENERALIST PRACTICE WITH INDIVIDUALS   135
Pre-Engagement   136
Assessing Individual Client Systems   137
Demographic Characteristics   137
Ethnicity and Culture   138
Personal Characteristics   138
Life Experiences   139
Assessment Forms   139
Strengths-Based Assessment Worksheets   139
Biopsychosocial Assessment Form   140
Mental Status Evaluation   142

Appearance 142
Speech 143
Emotions 143
Thought Process 143
Sensory Perceptions 143
Mental Capacities 143
Attitude 144

Input and Output Checklist 144

Graphic Displays 145
Strengths and Obstacles Plot Form 145
Ecomaps 146

Engagement 147

Determining Goals 147
Purpose of Goals 148
Goals and Objectives 148
Selecting and Defining Objectives 149
Goals, Objectives, and the Helping Relationship 151
Developing the Intervention and Evaluation Plan 152
Generalist Practice Interventions with Individual Clients 153
Counseling 154
    Supportive Counseling 154
    Problem-Solving Therapy 157
    Education and Training 159
Case Management 159
    Service Linkage 159
    Service Coordination 160
    Service Negotiation 161
    Resource Mobilization 161

Disengagement 163
Types of Termination 164
    Planned Endings 164
    Unanticipated Endings 165
Clients' Reactions to Termination 165

Summary 166

Case Example 167
Discussion Questions 170
References 170

CHAPTER 7 **GENERALIST PRACTICE WITH FAMILIES 184**

What Is a Family? 186
Family Diversity: Types of Families 186

From Interdependence to Individualism 187

Working with Family Strengths 190
    Strengths-Based/Assets-Based Approach 190

Developing and Working on Plans with Families   190
Family Involvement   191
Cultural Competence   191

When to Focus on the Family   191
When Families Have Multiple Challenges   192
Family Group Conferences   193
Family-Centered Programs   194
Family Systems Approach   196

Doing Assessment with Families   198

Family Development Plan   199

Family Systems Assessment   203

Family Subsystems Assessment   203
Structure   204
Authority   204
Relationship Subsystems   205
Ethnicity and Culture   205
Culture-Based Rules   206
Life-Cycle Stage   206
Emotional Climate   208
Communication Patterns   209
Boundaries   211

Summary: Engaging in a Helping Partnership
with Families   213

Case Example   213
Discussion Questions   217
References   217

CHAPTER 8   GENERALIST SOCIAL WORK PRACTICE WITH GROUPS   219

Generalist Practice with Groups   220
Types and Purposes of Groups   221

Group Membership   221
Group Resistance   221
Successful Group Work   222
The Need to Be Seen, Heard, and Known   223
Reducing Group Anxiety   225
Defense Mechanisms Function in the Group   226
Pre-Engagement, Engagement, and Disengagement   227

Group Leaders/Facilitators   227

Group Dynamics   229
An Introduction to Group Dynamics   229
Group Influences   230
Pseudocommunity/Initiation Stage   231
Chaos/Struggle Stage   231

Emptying/Resolution Stage   232
Community/Working Stage   232
Resist the Urge to Control the Group   234
Process versus Content   235
Termination   235

Tools for Group Leaders/Facilitators   236
Setting the Stage   236
Process versus Content   236
Examples of Useful Tools   237
Talking Paper   238
Common Ground Process   239
*An Example of Integration of Group Process and Common
Ground Process   241*
Group Intervention Models   244

Summary   247

Case Example   247
Discussion Questions   251
References   251

CHAPTER 9   **GENERALIST PRACTICE WITH ORGANIZATIONS   254**

Pre-Engagement   257

Assessment   259
The Starting Point—Something's Wrong   259
What to Assess   260
Organizational Identity   260
Internal Organizational Considerations   263
    Foundation Policies   263
    Internal Structure   264
    Internal Processes   266
    Organization Environmental Considerations   270
Legal/Policy Environment   272
Other Environmental Considerations   273
Organizational Assessment: How to Assess and What Tools to Use   273
Focus Groups   274
Observational Performance Ratings   274

Engagement   278
Setting Goals   278

Interventions   282
Developing the Intervention and Evaluation Plan   282
Productivity Improvements   283
Staff Development: Education and Training   284
Program Planning and Development: Strategic Planning   285
Resource Development   286
Grant Writing   286

Evaluation and Termination   290

Termination   290
Evaluation   291

Case Example   293
   Discussion Questions   295
   References   296

PART II | **GENERALIST PRACTICE WITH SPECIAL POPULATIONS**

CHAPTER 10   **GENERALIST PRACTICE WITH COMMUNITIES   322**

Social Work Practice with Communities   323
   Ethnicity and Culture   324
   Community Conditions   324
   Community Services and Resources   324
   Perspectives in Working with Communities   325
   Deficit Approach to Addressing Community Problems   325
   Empowerment Approach to Assessing Community Needs   326

The Collaborative Model and Community Practice   326

Pre-Engagement   327
   Needs Assessments   329
     Steps in the Needs Assessment Process   329
   Research Literature   331
   Population and Resource Data   331
   Observation   332
   Surveys   333
     Key Informant Surveys   334
     Community Surveys   334
     Client Satisfaction Surveys   334
   Focus Groups   334
   Data Collection   335
     Sensitive Issues   335
     Confidentiality and Informed Consent   337
   Assets Assessment   338
     Asset Mapping   339
   Individual Capacity Assessment   340
   Organizational Capacity Assessment   340
   Resource Mapping   340
   Geographic Information System (GIS)   341

Engagement   343
   Community Interventions   343
   Community Development   343
     Coalition Building   343
     Advocacy   344
   Education and Training   344

Program Planning   344
Evaluation and Termination   347

Summary   349

Case Example   350
Discussion Questions   353
References   353

CHAPTER 11   **GENERALIST PRACTICE WITH ECONOMICALLY DISADVANTAGED PEOPLE AND COMMUNITIES   372**

The Problem of Poverty and the Welfare Response   374
The Problem of Poverty   374
Measuring Poverty   376
Welfare   378

The Causes and Consequences of Poverty   379
Theories of Causation on the Micro Level (Individuals and Families)   379
Individual Deficits   380
Social and Structural Causes   380
Individual–Social Linkages   383
Employment and Income   384
Summary   388
Poverty Causation on the Macro Level—Communities and Larger Systems   388
Economic Issues   388
Political Power   389
Broken Windows   389
Client Needs: The Consequences of Poverty for Individuals and Families   390
Hunger and Nutrition   390
Shelter   391
Other Consequences   392
The Consequences of Community Poverty   392

Policy Issues   393
Health Policy   394
Cash Assistance   395
Social Security Old Age, Survivors, and Disability Insurance (OASDI)   395
Old Age   396
Survivors   396
Disability   396
Unemployment Insurance   396
Supplemental Security Income   397
Temporary Assistance for Needy Families (TANF)   397
Food and Nutrition Programs   398
Food Stamps   398
Housing and Energy   399
Public Housing & Section 8   399
Tax Policy   400

Practice Issues   400
Pre-engagement   400
The Bottom Line: What to Assess   400

Engagement   401
The Range of Target Problems and Goal Setting   401
*Collaboration, Coalition-Building,
and the Importance of Relationships   403*

Summary   405

Case Examples   406
Discussion Questions   410
References   410

CHAPTER 12   GENERALIST PRACTICE WITH PEOPLE AFFECTED BY ADDICTIONS   415

Addiction Overview   417

Classification of Drugs and Their Effects   418

Assessment   422
Use, Abuse, Dependence, and Addiction   422

Adolescence and Addictions   426
Teenagers at Risk   426

What is Addiction?   427

Neurobiology   429
The Pleasure or Reward Circuit   429

The Addiction Cycle   431

Different Theoretical Models   432
The Moral Model   432
The Sociocultural Model   433
Disease Model/Psychological Model   433

Interventions   434

Motivational Interviewing   436
The Motivational Stages of Change   437

Types of Treatment   438
Detoxification   438
Agonist Maintenance Treatment   439
Court-Mandated Treatment   439
Residential Treatment Programs   439
Therapeutic Communities   440
Outpatient Treatment   441
Counseling   441
Self-Help Groups   442
Online Support   442
Nonstep Support Groups   443

Adolescent Treatment (Teen Programs)   443

Summary   444
Discussion Questions   447
References   447

CHAPTER 13   GENERALIST SOCIAL WORK PRACTICE WITH THE ELDERLY   449

Demographics in Aging   450

Policy Issues   453

Generalist Social Work practice with Elderly Clients   455

Assessment   461
Resources   469

Interventions   478
Engagement Strategies   478
Advocacy   480
Case Management   482
Life Review   483
Supportive Counseling   484
Cognitive-Behavioral Therapy   485

Summary   486

Case Example   486
Discussion Questions   488
References   488

CHAPTER 14   GENERALIST PRACTICE WITH GAY, LESBIAN, BISEXUAL, AND TRANSGENDER PEOPLE   491

Client Population Needs and Circumstances   492
Sexual Orientation   493
Forces of Oppression   493
   Homophobia   493
   Heterosexism   493
   Bi-negativity   494
Orientation–Behavior–Identity   494
The Kinsey Scale   495
GLB Identity Development   496
   Gender Identity   498
   Forces of Oppression   501
Transgender Identity Development   501

Specific Populations in the GLBT Community   501
GLBT Youth   501
GLBT People of Color   502
Lesbian and Gay Parents and their Children   504
   Lesbian and Gay Parents   504
   Children of Gay and Lesbian Parents   504
GLBT Older Adults   505

Social Policy Issues   505
   Marriage Equity   505
   Nondiscrimination Policies   506
      A Policy Example   507

Practice Issues and Best Practice Recommendations   508
   Oppression in Practice   508
   Gay and Lesbian Clients   508
   Bisexual Clients   509
   Transgender Clients   510
   Practice Recommendations: A Strengths Perspective   510
      Affirmative Practice   512
   Best Practice Recommendations for Working with GLBT Clients   515
   Guidelines for Working with Transgender Clients   516

Evidence-Based Practice   516
   Cognitive-Behavioral Interventions   516
      Assessment and Interventions   517
   Gay–Straight Alliances   518

Summary   519

Case Example   519
   Discussion Questions   520
   References   521

CHAPTER 15   GENERALIST PRACTICE WITH ABUSED AND NEGLECTED CHILDREN AND THEIR FAMILIES   526

Child Welfare as a Field of Practice   528
   Child Maltreatment Defined   528
   Prevalence of Child Maltreatment   529

The Evolution of Child and Family Welfare Policy   530
   Children as Property (1600s–1700s)   530
   Emergence of Public Concern for Children (1800s)   531
   *The Federal Mandate to Protect Children
   in the 20th Century (1900s)   532*
   Child Welfare in the 21st Century (2000s)   537

Child Welfare: Generalist Practice Skills   538
   Strengths-Based Practice—An Overarching Paradigm   538
   Critical Thinking   539
   Solution-Focused Approaches   540
   Engagement: Working with the Involuntary or Mandated Client   541

Child Welfare: Generalist Practice Functions   545
   Safety and Risk Assessment   545
   The Planning Phase   552
   The Family Service Plan   556

Child Welfare Services   560
   In-home Family Services   560

Foster Care   563
Promising Approaches in Addressing the Challenges
of Foster Care   565
Supporting Children in Temporary Foster Care   567

Summary   569
  Discussion Questions   572
  References   572

CHAPTER 16   **GENERALIST PRACTICE WITH PEOPLE WHO HAVE EXPERIENCED TRAUMA   574**

Psychological Trauma   576
  Type I and Type II Traumas   576

Diagnostic Categories in the DSM-IV-TR
(Diagnostic and Statistic Manual)   576
  An Expanded Diagnosis: Complex PTSD   579
  The Plastic Brain: The Neurobiology of Attachment versus
  Neglect   580
    The Neurobiology of Attachment   580
    Nurturing Attunement   580
    Neglect, a Lack of Attunement   581
    Plastic throughout Life: The Impressionable Brain   581
    Neuroplastic Implications   582
  State-Dependent Learning   582

Symptoms of Trauma   584
  The Biological Impact of Trauma
  on the Brain and Body   584
    The Survival Response: Flight, Fight, and Freeze   584
    Biological Changes and Trauma Symptoms   585

Recovery from Trauma   595
  Phase 1—Stabilization and Skill Building   596
    Restoration of Safety   596
    Assessment   597
    Building a Relationship   597
  Nadia, Phase 1: Assessment   599
    Psychoeducation and Skill Building   599
    Self-Care and Self-Soothing Exercises   601
    Managing Self-Injurious Behaviors   603
    Dialectical Behavior Therapy   604
    Other Cognitive Therapy Approaches   606
  Phase 2—Remembering   607
    Safely Telling the Trauma Story   608
    EMDR   608
  Nadia, Phase 2: Remembering   609
  Phase 3—Reconnection   610
  Nadia, Phase 3: Reconnection and Transformation   610

Substance Abuse and PTSD 611
Trauma Interventions for Children 611
Play Therapy 613

Psychological First Aid: Immediate Posttrauma Interventions 615
Group Work 617
Screening and Preparing Potential Members 618
Tips Specific to Running a Trauma Group 619

War Veterans 621

The Rewards and Challenges of Working with Trauma Survivors 622
Definition of Vicarious Traumatization 622
Signs of Vicarious Traumatization 622
Strategies to Minimize Vicarious Traumatization 623
Self-Care 623
Physical Self-Care 623
Emotional Self-Care 624
Spiritual Self-Care 625
Professional Self-Care 625
Guidelines for the Workplace 625

Summary 626

Case Example 627
Discussion Questions 629
References 629

Web Resources 634

INDEX 635

PREFACE

The third edition of *Collaborative Social Work* is substantially different from the second edition in a number of ways. The book has several new chapters. Among those are separate chapters on generalist practice with individuals, families, groups, organizations and communities. These five new chapters substantially increased coverage of generalist social work practice with each client system.

Coverage of generalist practice with client groups has also been expanded significantly. A new chapter on practice with persons who have experienced trauma has been added to this edition. In addition, the chapters on generalist practice with LGBT clients, people affected by addictions, elderly persons and abused and neglected children and their families have been completely re-written. The chapter on generalist practice with people on welfare has been substantially revised and up-dated. In this edition, the focus of the population chapters is much more on assessment and intervention with the specific client population than they were in earlier editions.

New content on attachment theory, critical thinking and evidence-based approaches has been added to the chapter on theoretical and conceptual frameworks. Coverage of evidenced-based interventions has increased substantially. Almost all of the client system and special population chapters incorporate evidenced-based interventions into the chapter.

In addition to the above changes, Part I of the book has been reorganized so that the reader is introduced to generalist practice, theory and frameworks in the first two chapters. Chapter three presents the collaborative model while chapter 4 focuses on evaluation. The final chapter in Part I covers the interpersonal skills associated with the collaborative model of generalist social work practice. The book's accompanying DVD illustrates the use of interpersonal skills during three phases of the helping relationship.

Part II of the book now contains comprehensive chapters on the five major client systems of generalist social work practice. In my opinion, the new chapters on practice with individual, family, group, organization and community client systems improves the book's balance in terms of the coverage of micro and macro practice and make this edition a much stronger generalist practice text.

Collaborative Social Work: Strengths-Based Generalist Practice differs from other generalist practice texts in several ways. It integrates the strengths-based collaborative approach to working with client systems. The book operationally defines the helping relationship and emphasizes its use throughout the helping process. It also provides detailed coverage of client groups that generalist social workers often encounter in their practice. These chapters provide the context and knowledge base needed to be an effective generalist social worker in a variety of settings with different client populations.

Collaborative Social Work: Strengths-Based Generalist Practice is suitable for use in senior BSW generalist practice courses and for the first foundation practice course in an MSW curriculum. It is designed as a comprehensive introduction to generalist social work practice. It presents concepts in an accessible manner, using straightforward language that is relatively free of jargon. There are numerous case examples throughout, and each chapter concludes with a detailed case study and discussion questions.

ACKNOWLEDGMENTS

Many people contributed to this book. I want to especially thank my colleagues at Widener University, Marina Barnett, Beth Barol, Betsy Crane, Donald Dyson, Barbara Gilin, John Giugliano, Stephen Kauffman, Brent Satterly, Paula Silver and Mimi Sullivan, for their excellent chapters. Their chapters greatly strengthen the book.

I am grateful to the following Widener MSW students and graduates who contributed case examples for this edition: Jill Albright, Denise Bubel, Leslie Freas, Sandra Fowkes, Kristina Kennedy, Pat Mullen, Heather Witt, Julia Wolfson and Rick Vukmanic. A special thanks to my friend and former faculty colleague, Hussein Soliman, for also contributing a case example. I also want to thank Ann Bailey, Michelle McCann, Pat Mullen and Cheryl Sadeghee for being such excellent social work supervisors and role models for the SWCS student interns.

Finally, I thank my wife, Anne, for her love, patience, and encouragement, and the "kids" - Katherine, Adam, Jessica, Claire and Mike for making me feel proud everyday.

ABOUT THE CONTRIBUTORS

John Poulin is a Professor at Widener University's Center for Social Work Education, where he has taught generalist practice, research and policy courses. He received a BA from the University of Southern Maine, an MSW from the University of Michigan, and a Ph.D. from the University of Chicago's School of Social Service Administration. The former director of Widener's BSW program, he founded its MSW program and served as the dean and director for seven years. He is currently the executive director of Social Work Consultation Services (SWCS), an innovative community based field placement agency developed by the school of social work in collaboration with a local community human service organization. SWCS (www.swcs-cef.org) provides a wide range for free social work services to low income community residents as well as free capacity building services to under-resourced community based human service organizations. His current practice and research focuses on the helping social work colleagues at Chongqing Technology and Business University, Chongqing, China strengthen their undergraduate social work curriculum and establish a community-based social work NGO that will provide disaster relief services to community residents.

Marina Barnett an Associate Professor in Widener University's Center for Social Work Education. Dr. Barnett received her Bachelors of Arts Degree from Clarion University, a Masters in Social Work from the University of Michigan and a Doctorate in Social Work from the University of Pennsylvania. Dr. Barnett teaches Social Welfare Policy, Organizational Practice and Grant Writing and Community Organization at the BSW, MSW and Ph.D. levels. In addition to her teaching experience, Dr. Barnett has fifteen years of organizational and community development expertise. Dr. Barnett has served in the Philadelphia and Chester communities as a consultant to numerous community-based organizations and government offices. Her expertise includes working with community based organizations to develop organizational capacity, engage in strategic planning, and grant writings. In addition, Dr. Barnett also works with local organizations to map community resources and conduct asset assessments. Her research interests include conducting Community Based Participatory Research, using GIS software to map community assets, and developing a model to train community residents to understand and conduct research in their own communities.

Beth I. Barol is an Assistant Professor at Widener University's Center for Social Work Education where she teaches generalist practice, child welfare, group dynamics, and several courses on social work with people with intellectual and developmental disabilities. She received a BA from Temple University and an MSS and a Ph.D. from the Graduate School of Social Work and Social Research at Bryn Mawr College. She directs the Center's Certificate in Intellectual and Developmental Disabilities, as well as the free, community based clinic for people with challenging behaviors and those who support them. Dr. Barol has over thirty years of experience in working in the field of Intellectual and Developmental Disabilities. Her practice spans from work with individuals in crisis, to families and caregivers struggling to support individuals with challenging behaviors and concurrent diagnoses, to work with agencies and governments for systemic reform towards a culture of positive practice. She consults regularly nationally and internationally. Her research interests include group process and power-sharing leadership, trauma, and the importance of the biographical context in developing a empathic helping relationship with direct supporters.

Betsy Crane is a Professor of Education and Director of Graduate Programs in Human Sexuality at Widener University. She was co-developer at Cornell University of the Family Development Credential (FDC) training program from 1994–2000, and primary author of the first instructor's manual. She works with the Community Action Association of PA on implementation and evaluation of the FDC program in Pennsylvania, and is currently co-chair of the FDC PA Advisory Council. She received a BS in Sociology from Nazareth College of Rochester, an MA in Communications with a concentration in Mental Health Education from the University of Texas and a Ph.D. in Human Service Studies from Cornell University. Her research agenda encompasses democratizing influences in helping services and in the areas of gender and sexuality. She credits nearly 25 years of experience in community education in the areas of mental health and sexuality as teaching her how important it is for people to join hands, respect each other, and work together to effect a world where power is shared more equitably.

Don Dyson is an Assistant Professor in the Widener University Program in Human Sexuality, and serves as the Director of Doctoral Studies in the Center for Education. He also serves as an adjunct faculty member at Widener's Center for Social Work Education. Prior to that, he was the coordinator of STD prevention education for the State of New Jersey's Department of Health. He specializes in the training of sexuality professionals, the intersect between Social Work and Human Sexuality, and has specific interest in the areas of ethics, multiculturalism, and reproductive health. Research includes work on best practices in training sexologists, motivation and unsafe sexual behaviors and emotional literacy. He is the recent recipient of awards from SSSS (Emerging Professional, 2007) and AASECT (Schiller Award, 2008).

Barbara Gilin is a licensed clinical social worker and an Associate Clinical Professor at Widener University's Center for Social Work Education, where she teaches courses in Practice with Individuals, Practice with Groups, Practice with Families, and Treating Trauma. She received her B.A. in Psychology from Michigan State University and an MSW from the University of Pennsylvania. She is a Clinical Member of the American Association for Marital and Family Therapy and is a graduate of the Family Institute of Philadelphia, a 3-year post graduate training program. She has worked in outpatient and inpatient mental health settings and she currently maintains a private practice where she specializes in helping trauma survivors. In addition to providing individual and family therapy, she has also run groups for survivors of child sexual abuse and for survivors of domestic violence. She co-authored a manual entitled: *A group manual for survivors of domestic violence: Integration of feminist and social group work theories.* Most recently, she has been certified in EMDR, a treatment approach for trauma survivors.

John Giugliano is a licensed clinical social worker practicing psychotherapy in Philadelphia and Bala Cynwyd, Pennsylvania. He specializes in the treatment of persons with sex addiction, trauma, gay /lesbian and bisexual issues, and relational/intimacy disorders. Dr. Giugliano obtained his BA from Villanova University (Salutatorian), MSW from UCLA (Summa Cum Laude) and his PhD from Smith College (With Honors). He sits on the SASH (The Society for the Advancement of Sexual Health) Board of Directors. His major area of scholarly research is on the subject of problematic sexual behavior. He has lectured and published nationally and internationally on the subject of sex addiction. He has been regionally and nationally awarded for his community service and for his academic contributions. Dr. Giugliano is an Assistant Professor at Widener University where he teaches practice, HBSE, and clinical theory in Widener's MSW and Doctoral programs.

Stephen Kauffman, Ph.D. is an Associate Professor at Widener University's Center for Social Work Education, where he has taught social policy, community practice, program evaluation, and research since 1991. Dr. Kauffman received his MSW from the George Warren Brown School of Social Work at Washington University in 1987, and his Ph.D. from the Graduate School of Social Work and Social Research at Bryn Mawr College in 1992. The two major areas of his scholarly research are citizen participation, and the role of ideology in policy, and he has widely published in these subjects. Since arriving at Widener, he has consulted with several community organizations to evaluate the effectiveness of their programs in education, housing, lead poisoning prevention, and teenage pregnancy prevention. Dr. Kauffman has also served as the evaluator for two HOPE VI projects implemented by the Chester Housing Authority. The HOPE VI evaluation projects, funded by the US Department of Housing and Urban Development research at Chatham Estates, are widely cited as models for housing project evaluations.

Cheryl Seaman Sadeghee is a Licensed Clinical Social Worker and educator based in Delaware. She is currently Assistant Director of Social Work Consultation Services in Chester, Pennsylvania and Adjunct Faculty at Widener University, where she received her MSW degree. Previously she was the Supervisor of Senior Services at SWCS, and the Director of Social Services at Manor Care of Delaware, where she provided supportive services for individuals and families in hospice care. Cheryl has presented workshops in communication and conflict resolution, suicide prevention and critical incident stress management. She has co-presented workshops for the Hartford Geriatric Social Work Initiative, which aims to infuse geriatric content into social work courses and to encourage social work students to work in the field of gerontology.

Brent A. Satterly is an Associate Professor and the Director of the BSW Program at Widener University's Center for Social Work Education. He received his Masters of Social Service from Bryn Mawr College and a Doctorate in Human Sexuality Education from the University of Pennsylvania. With over 15 years clinical experience, Dr. Satterly is a Licensed Clinical Social Worker in the state of Pennsylvania and a Certified Sexuality Educator through the American Association of Sexuality Educators, Counselors, and Therapists. His areas of expertise include clinical work with Gay, Lesbian, Bisexual and Transgender (GLBT) populations, GLBT professional identity management, human sexuality and social work pedagogies, and HIV/AIDS. His published works have appeared in the *Journal of Social Work Education*, *Teaching in Social Work*, the *Journal of Gay and Lesbian Social Services* and *Families in Society*.

Paula Silver is the Director of Widener University's Center for Social Work Education and Professor of Social Work. She received a BA from the University of Chicago, MSW from University of Pennsylvania and Ph.D. from Bryn Mawr College's School of Social Work and Social Research. She teaches social work practice with individuals, families and groups and child welfare practice and research. She has served as a consultant to public child welfare agencies in Washington, D.C. and Pennsylvania. Prior to becoming a social work educator, Dr. Silver spent 15 years in child welfare practice, both in the public and private sectors. Dr. Silver's current research focus is social work pedagogy, including teaching strategies for promoting empathy and strengths-based practice among undergraduate and graduate social work students, and international social work. She has presented invited lectures at Chongqing Technology and Business University (CTBU) in Chongqing, China. Currently, Dr. Silver is coordinating an on-going collaboration between Widener and CTBU for student and faculty exchange and technical assistance for CTBU in developing its social work curriculum.

Mimi Sullivan is a private practice licensed clinical social worker in Haddonfield, NJ. She specializes in trauma treatment, and is currently a PhD student at Widener University's Center for Social Work Education where she has also been adjunct assistant professor. She received an MSW from Widener University. Ms. Sullivan has worked as a dual diagnosis (mental health and addiction) intensive outpatient primary therapist for the University Medical Center at Princeton, and as a clinical supervisor and therapist for the Burlington County New Jersey domestic abuse agency. Within the trauma treatment field, her particular areas of study are the neurobiology of trauma and the problem of domestic abuse.

PRINCIPLES AND CONCEPTS OF GENERALIST PRACTICE

CHAPTER 1

Michelle D. Bridwell/PhotoEdit

Robin P. is a first-year Masters in Social Work (MSW) student with a field placement in a public child welfare agency. She is assigned to a unit that provides case management services for adolescents in foster care, their birth parents, and their foster parents. In her role as case manager, Robin monitors clients' service plans, provides supportive counseling for adolescents, helps link clients to other services and resources, and advocates for clients who need help from various systems and organizations.

Robin is pleased with her field placement because she is getting experience in working with individual clients and families. However, because the first-year placement is supposed to be a generalist one, Robin is concerned that all her tasks are micro-practice activities. She decides to talk to Mary C., her field instructor, about adding some macro-practice activities to her placement responsibilities.

As she prepares for her meeting with Mary, Robin realizes that she is not sure what constitutes macro practice. What do generalist social workers do that is considered macro practice? How do they work with an organizational or community client system? What functions do generalist social workers perform at the organizational or community level? What is the purpose of the helping relationship when one is working with organizations and communities? How do macro-practice activities differ from micro-practice activities? How are they similar?

This chapter provides an introduction to generalist social work practice. The chapter begins with a definition of strengths-based generalist practice and then describes the various generalist interventions and roles. The chapter concludes with a review of social work client systems and the factors that influence clients' willingness to engage in a helping relationship.

By the end of this chapter, you should be able to help Robin

1. Understand the purpose of the helping relationship in working with individual, family, group, organizational, and community client systems
2. Identify micro-level generalist interventions
3. Understand the role that the "self" of the social worker plays in generalist social work practice
4. Identify macro-level generalist interventions
5. Clarify the differences among the terms **client system level**, **client system**, and **target system**
6. Classify clients by type and identify factors that might affect their willingness to develop a helping relationship and engage in the helping process
7. Describe the core values of the social work profession. Assess and resolve any ethical dilemmas that Robin faced

STRENGTHS-BASED GENERALIST SOCIAL WORK PRACTICE

Traditional agency-based social work practice is problem focused. Clients tend to be viewed as having deficits and pathologic problems that need to be overcome to improve functioning (Saleebey, 2002). The strengths-based approach, on the other hand, focuses on the client's inherent strengths, resources, and coping abilities. Clients are viewed as being capable of change. They are partners and active participants in the change process. The social worker is not the problem-solver; the client is the problem-solver. The generalist social worker's primary function is to help clients recognize, marshal, and enhance their inherent strengths and abilities (Weick et al., 1989). In the strengths-based approach, the client is the expert with the knowledge and ability to accomplish the needed changes. Social work practice focuses on empowering clients and establishing collaborative helping relationships.

In strengths-based generalist social work practice, a collaborative helping relationship is formed between a professional and an individual, a family, a group, an organization, or a community for the purposes of empowerment and promotion of social and economic justice. The relationship may involve direct work with client systems of all sizes as well as indirect work on behalf of client systems. The professional collaborates with the client or with systems that may benefit the client, all the while focusing on client strengths and resources.

DEFINITION OF GENERALIST PRACTICE

Generalist social work practitioners work with individuals, families, groups, communities, and organizations in a variety of social work and host settings. Generalist practitioners view clients and client systems from a strengths perspective in order to recognize, support, and build upon the innate capabilities of all human beings. They use a professional problem-solving process to engage, assess, broker services, advocate, counsel, educate, and organize with and on behalf of clients and client systems. In addition, generalist practitioners engage in community and organizational development. Finally, generalist practitioners evaluate service outcomes in order to continually improve the provision and quality of services most appropriate to client needs.

Generalist social work practice is guided by the National Association of Social Workers (NASW) Code of Ethics and is committed to improving the well being of individuals, families, groups, communities, and organizations and to furthering the goals of social justice (BPD, 2006).

TYPES OF GENERALIST SOCIAL WORK INTERVENTIONS

A classification of generalist social work practice interventions is shown in Table 1.1. In this conceptualization, intervention tasks are categorized by system level (individual, family, group, organization, or community). Generalist practice often requires simultaneous interventions on multiple levels. In any case situation, you and your client might be involved in a number of individual, family, group, organizational, or community change activities.

As Table 1.1 indicates, generalist social work practice entails micro-level and macro-level work. **Micro social work practice** is interventions with individuals, couples, and families (Hepworth, Rooney, and Larsen, 2002). Practice with these client systems is also referred to as **direct practice** or **interpersonal practice** (Garvin and Seabury, 1997). Some authors classify social work practice with small groups as **mezzo-level interventions** (Miley, O'Melia, and DuBois, 1998) and others as **micro-level direct practice** (Hepworth, Rooney, and Larsen, 2002; Pinderhughes, 1995; Shulman, 1999). Because helping relationships with individual, family, and

TABLE 1.1 | MAIN ASPECTS OF MICRO AND MACRO CLIENT SYSTEMS

System Level	Client System	Purpose of Helping Relationship	Use of Self	Interventions

Micro
Individual
 	
Family
 	
Group
	Individuals
	
	Couples
	Families
	
	Small groups
		Enhance
		  functioning
		Empowerment
			Understanding
			Sensitivity
			Respect
			Acceptance
			Empathy
			Cooperative
			  intentions
			Hopefulness
			Partnership
			Support
			Commitment
			Confidence
				Counseling
				Supportive
				  counseling
				Education and
				  training
				Case management
				Service linkage
				Service coordination
				Service negotiation
				Resource mobilization
				Client advocacy

Macro
Organization
 	
Community
	Agency leaders
	Agency task
	  forces
	Agency
	  committees
	
	Professional
	  task forces
	Community
	  coalitions
	Neighborhood
	  groups
		Improve
		  organization
		Improve services
		Develop services
		
		Improve commu-
		  nity conditions
		Empower
		  residents
		Develop commu-
		  nity resources
		Increase citizen
		  awareness
		Mobilize citizens
			Same as for
			  micro systems
				Education and
				  training
				Program planning
				Community
				  development

small group client systems share common purposes, this book treats social work practice with small groups as a form of micro practice. Regardless of the client system, the purpose of micro-level practice is to enhance functioning and empower the client. These two related purposes apply to work with individual clients, couples, families, and small groups.

Generalist social workers engage in a wide range of client system change activities with individuals, families, and small groups. Micro interventions commonly used by generalist social workers are divided into two broad groups, counseling and case management. Counseling interventions include supportive counseling and education and training. Case management includes service linkage, service coordination, service negotiation, resource mobilization, and client advocacy. These interventions are discussed in detail in Chapter 6. Table 1.2 briefly describes the more common micro generalist interventions.

Macro-level interventions focus on organizational and community change. Some authors include societal change in the macro practice category and place organizational change at the mezzo level (Miley, O'Melia, and DuBois, 1998). The more restricted definition of macro practice as work with community groups and

TABLE 1.2 | COMMON MICRO-GENERALIST INTERVENTIONS

Intervention	Description
Counseling	
Supportive counseling	The social worker and client engage in a collaborative therapeutic or counseling process. The purpose of the intervention is to help the client resolve concerns and challenges, enhance coping, and improve functioning.
Education and training	The social worker helps the client learn and master new concepts and skills.
Case management	
Service linkage	The social worker helps the client identify and contact other programs and services.
Service coordination	The social worker coordinates the various services and professionals involved in the client's life to ensure that services are integrated and have common goals.
Service negotiation	The social worker helps clients overcome difficulties they encounter with other programs and services.
Resource mobilization	The social worker helps the client obtain needed resources, such as housing, clothing, food, funiture, financial support, or health care.
Client advocacy	The social worker educates clients about their rights, teaches them advocacy skills, and applies pressure to make agencies and resources respond to client needs.

organizations; program planning and development; and the implementation, administration, and evaluation of programs (Connaway and Gentry, 1988; Kirst-Ashman and Hull, 1993; Specht, 1988) more realistically describes what most generalist social workers do in actual practice.

Typical client systems at the organizational level are organizational leaders, task forces, and committees. The system level is the organization, and the client systems that the social worker engages are the decision-makers and decision-making structures of the organization. The worker usually participates in formally organized work groups, such as agency task forces or committees. The client system might also be the organization's decision-makers, that is, administrators and supervisors. Thus, a generalist social worker seeking to change an organization views the decision-makers or the decision-making structures as the client system.

At the organizational level, the purpose of macro-level practice is to improve the functioning of the organization, improve services and service delivery, or develop new services. All three purposes involve change of the organization or agency. Generalist social workers tend to be agency based and work within an organizational framework.

This does not mean that organizational change from outside the system is impossible (Chavis, Florin, and Felix, 1993). There is a long-standing tradition in social work practice of working for change from the outside. This tradition dates back to the early days of social work and the social reformers of the progressive era (Haynes and Mickelson, 1991; Reeser and Epstein, 1990).

Typical client systems at the community level are professional task forces, community coalitions, and neighborhood or community citizens' groups. Often the

TABLE 1.3 | THREE MACRO INTERVENTIONS

Intervention	Description
Education and training	The social worker sets up organizational and community training meetings, workshops, and seminars.
Program planning	The social worker helps in the development, expansion, and coordination of social services and social policies.
Community development	The social worker helps improve community conditions and empowers residents to seek community change.

purpose of community practice is to improve community or neighborhood conditions, empower residents, develop resources, increase community awareness of social and economic problems, and mobilize people to advocate for needed resources and changes. Generalist social workers engaged in community change usually work with professional or community groups. Some groups have both professional and citizen members. Social workers engaged in community practice view the group they are working with as the client system. In other words, the client system is the professional task force, neighborhood group, or community coalition that is seeking to change or improve the community.

Generalist social workers engage in a range of organizational and community interventions. As shown in Table 1.3, macro interventions commonly used by generalist social workers include education and training, program planning, and community development. These interventions are discussed in detail in Chapters 9 and 10.

USE OF SELF

Use of self refers to the social worker's interpersonal skills and interactions with the client system (Goldstein, 1995; Northen, 1995). Social workers intervene by means of the helping relationship to assist client systems in achieving identified change goals. Research studies have consistently found that the strongest predictor of client change is the helping relationship (Marziali and Alexander, 1991; Russell, 1990). It is through the helping relationship that change takes place. When the social worker interacts with the client system, the quality of the interaction facilitates client change. The social worker uses himself or herself to communicate

- Understanding
- Sensitivity
- Respect
- Acceptance
- Empathy
- Cooperative intentions

- Hopefulness
- Partnership
- Support
- Commitment
- Confidence

Use of self is traditionally associated with micro-level practice: the social worker's interactions with individual, couple, family, and group client systems. However, the characteristics described above also apply to work at the macro level. A generalist social worker can provide support and foster hope and understanding through interactions at the organizational level with agency task forces and

CASE 1.1	PROFILES OF GENERALIST SOCIAL WORKERS

Gina B.

Gina had her first-year field placement at Social Work Consultation Services (SWCS), an innovative agency developed by her graduate school of social work and a community-based agency. SWCS provided generalist social work learning experiences for student interns and social work and capacity-building services for the residents and organizations of an economically disadvantaged community.

At SWCS Gina undertook a range of generalist social work tasks and activities. As a member of the senior services team, Gina provided counseling and case management services for elderly residents of a senior housing facility. Gina met with her senior clients weekly. For some, she provided **supportive counseling** addressing a variety of concerns, such as family relationships, isolation, depression, and a host of loss issues. For other clients, she served as a case manager. She referred clients to other service providers (**service linkage**), negotiated on their behalf with other service providers (**service negotiation**), obtained resources for them (**resource mobilization**), and advocated for them in any way she could (**client advocacy**).

Gina's work on the senior team also entailed a number of macro-practice activities. Gina and two of the senior team interns established a one-day-a-week drop-in center at the senior housing facility (**program planning**) and began holding monthly meetings with local providers who served elderly clients to share information, reduce service duplication, and increase coordination (**service coordination**). Gina helped develop programs and monthly group activities for residents and organized two ongoing support groups. Gina and her team also organized a community service day that targeted elderly community residents (**community development**). The student volunteers provided cleaning and chore services for 125 elderly people. The senior team provided follow-up and case management services for community residents who required additional services.

Gina also organized a three-day community and university event designed to promote awareness of violence against women (**education and training**). Gina and two other student interns planned, organized, obtained funding for, and implemented the event.

Approximately 200 community residents, students, faculty, and staff participated in the program.

During the year Gina wrote a grant proposal (program planning) for additional funding for the SWCS program. She also helped produce the agency's newsletter, developed new program brochures, helped conduct a program evaluation (program planning), conducted a series of training workshops for another agency's case managers (education and training), served on the agency's executive and recognition committees (program planning), and cofacilitated the agency's monthly staff meeting on two occasions.

Art D.

Art had his second-year placement at SWCS. His primary assignment was with the functional family therapy (FFT) team. FFT is an intensive model of social work practice for troubled adolescents and their families. Art participated in an extensive FFT training program and worked with five families (supportive counseling). He met with the families once or twice a week for about two hours at a time.

In addition to his work on the FFT team, Art, in collaboration with another student intern, developed an eight-week anger management group for adult residents of a local shelter (program planning and supportive counseling). Art researched anger management training programs, developed a curriculum for eight sessions, recruited the participants, and cofacilitated the sessions. Art and the other intern also opened a one-day-a-week drop-in day program for homeless adults at a local church (program planning). The program provided a warm place for the homeless to spend the day as well as case management services. Art was also a member of the agency's executive committee (program planning) and cofacilitated the agency's monthly staff meeting on two occasions.

Dianna P.

Dianna had her first-year placement at SWCS. Her primary assignment was the school team, which developed programs and services for schoolchildren and their families. Dianna, in collaboration with a local wellness center, helped expand a peer leadership

(Continued)

CASE 1.1 | *Continued*

program for high school students (program plan-ning). In this capacity, she conducted a number of training workshops (education and training) for about 70 high school peer leaders and assisted the peer leaders in implementing the program.

Dianna also became a member of a community task force that was formed to address the problem of teenage pregnancy and promote pregnancy preven-tion (community development). Dianna helped define the mission of the group and assisted in preparing a grant proposal (program planning) to help fund the prevention program.

Dianna recognized early in the year that the mid-dle schools lacked a referral system for children who needed counseling and case management services. Af-ter meeting with school officials and human services

providers, Dianna developed a referral system that was implemented in the school district (program planning).

Dianna also cofacilitated a series of workshops for case managers designed to increase their relationship and case management skills (education and training). She was a member of the team that organized the university-community violence prevention event (edu-cation and training), chaired the agency's recognition committee (program planning), and cofacilitated the agency's monthly staff meeting on two occasions. In addition to the above-mentioned macro-practice ac-tivities, Dianna provided **counseling** and **case man-agement** services for seven community residents who were referred directly to SWCS for social work services.

committees and at the community level with professional task forces, community coalitions, and neighborhood groups. Carrying out the various intervention tasks involves the use of self and system change activities. The worker must be skilled in the use of self when working with any system level. Effective interpersonal skills are needed to facilitate change at the individual, family, group, organizational, and community levels of generalist social work practice.

SOCIAL WORK CLIENTS

Generalist practice involves work with client systems of all sizes. The primary client system could be an individual, a family, a small group, an organization, or a com-munity. The primary client system is unlikely to be the only client system being helped or targeted for change. Typically, generalist practice involves working with multiple interrelated client systems.

Strengths-based generalist social work practice uses an ecosystems perspec-tive. This perspective focuses assessment and intervention on problematic transac-tions between individuals and their environment. These problematic transactions become the target systems that the client and worker seek to change (Pincus and Minahan, 1973). A target system can be an individual client or another individ-ual, family, group, organizational, or community system within the client's person-in-environment system. Any and all systems in a client's environment are potential target systems in the helping process.

Case 1.2 illustrates the person-in-environment perspective, client systems, and target systems in generalist social work practice. In this example, if Alice agrees to work with the social worker, she will be the primary client system. She needs help in assessing her options and deciding on a course of action. Depending on what she

CASE 1.2	I CAN'T TELL MY PARENTS

Alice C. is seventeen. She has been pregnant with her first child for two months. She is unmarried and very committed to her relationship with the teenage father of the child. They are both seniors in high school and plan to attend college in the fall. Alice's parents are devout Catholics, who follow the teachings of the church. Although quite strict, they have always been loving, and encouraged and supported their only adopted daughter.

Alice is afraid to talk to her parents about her situation. She is concerned about disappointing them and about the shame she will bring to the family. She has not told her boyfriend about the pregnancy, either. She is unsure how he will react.

Alice does not know what to do. She is unwilling to confide in her family and friends, so she contacts the school social worker for help.

decides to do, her parents, her boyfriend, and the school are all possible target systems.

If Alice decides, for instance, that she wants to keep the baby and ask her parents to help her care for the child, the transaction between Alice and her parents becomes the focus of the intervention and the target system. In this situation, the key to successfully assisting Alice is to help her parents respond supportively to her situation. The social worker would probably help Alice prepare for the meeting with her parents, might attend the meeting with her, and might offer to help the parents adjust to and cope with their daughter's pregnancy and the pending birth. In this case, Alice is the client system and her parents are a target system.

It is also possible for the school to become a target system. If, for example, the school has a policy prohibiting students in the third trimester from attending classes, Alice and her social worker might ask the school to develop an alternative plan for Alice to complete high school or even to change the existing policy. The school system would become a target system in the process of helping Alice carry out her plan to keep the baby.

Another possibility is that none of the systems within Alice's environment would become target systems. If Alice decides, for example, to have an abortion and not tell anyone about it, neither her parents, boyfriend, nor school become target systems. Alice would be both the client system and the target system.

In any given client situation, all systems within the client's person-in-environment system are potential target systems. Whether or not a system becomes a target system for intervention depends on the specifics of the case and focus of the work.

TYPES OF CLIENTS

A potential client becomes a client only if and when there is an explicit agreement between the person and the social worker about the purpose of their work together. **Clients** are people who agree to work with you to achieve a specified outcome. There are three types of clients: voluntary, nonvoluntary, and involuntary (Garvin and Seabury, 1997).

Voluntary clients seek out the services of a social worker or social agency on their own because they want help with some aspect of their lives. A young mother who recognizes that she has a drinking problem and seeks help from a professional social worker is an example of a voluntary client. She has made a decision to get professional help and is voluntarily entering into a helping relationship with the social worker.

Nonvoluntary clients are being pressured to seek help by someone they know personally. They have not been given a mandate by a court of law or social agency to receive help. A friend, relative, or acquaintance believes they have problems; they themselves may or may not agree. Even if they acknowledge the existence of problems, they are not seeking help under their own volition. Someone in their life is forcing them to seek help. They come to a social worker because "they may suffer unpleasant consequences if they refuse" (Garvin and Seabury, 1997, p. 132). A young mother who is being pressured by her husband to get help for her drinking problem is an example of a nonvoluntary client. She is meeting with a social worker only because her husband has threatened to leave her and seek custody of their child. She is essentially being forced by her husband to get professional help with her drinking problem and is complying with his wishes to prevent him from leaving her and possibly getting custody of their child.

Involuntary clients have a legal mandate to receive services. They have no choice in the matter. If the young mother with a drinking problem is arrested for drunken driving, part of her sentence might be a court order requiring her to participate in a 20-week counseling program. In this situation she is an involuntary client.

Regardless of whether prospective clients are voluntary, nonvoluntary, or involuntary, they must make some sort of contract or agreement with the social worker in order to become clients. They must knowingly and willingly participate in the helping process. Clearly, it is easier to reach an agreement with voluntary clients than with nonvoluntary or involuntary clients. Voluntary clients are motivated to seek help. The others, at the point of initial contact, have probably not made a decision to seek help and engage in a collaborative helping process.

Clients progress through five stages in self-initiated, professionally assisted change: precontemplation, contemplation, preparation, action, and maintenance. "**Precontemplation** is the stage at which there is no intention to change in the foreseeable future" (Prochaska, DiClemente, and Norcross, 1992, p. 1103). Clients at this stage are often unaware of their problems and are not seriously considering getting help. They are reluctant participants in the helping process. They have not chosen to seek help and probably are unhappy about the prospect of being helped. "**Contemplation** is the stage in which clients are aware that a problem exists and are seriously thinking about overcoming it but have not yet made a commitment to take action" (p. 1103). The key here is the lack of commitment to change. Many clients recognize the need to address concerns or problems but need help in making a genuine commitment to bring the change about. "**Preparation** is the stage that combines intention and behavioral criteria" (p. 1104). Clients at this stage have started to address the problem and are motivated to make the necessary changes. "**Action** is the stage in which individuals modify their behavior, experiences, or environment in order to overcome their problems" (p. 1104). During the action stage, clients are engaged in the helping process and are taking necessary steps to achieve the desired changes. "**Maintenance** is the stage in which people work to prevent relapse and consolidate the gains attained during action" (p. 1104). In a way, maintenance is a continuation of the action phase. The client is actively trying to prevent a relapse.

The five stages of change highlight client differences in readiness to engage in the helping process. It is important to recognize these individual differences. Not all potential clients have reached the stage of contemplation or action. Many clients who are referred or have a mandate for service are in the precontemplation or contemplation stage. To become true clients, they must make a commitment to change. In the end, only those who willingly agree to work with the social worker to achieve a specified outcome can engage in a collaborative helping relationship. Nonvoluntary and involuntary clients might go through the motions because they are required to do so, but they will not truly become clients until they decide on their own to engage in a helping relationship.

THE RELUCTANT CLIENT

Social workers often work with clients who are in the precontemplation stage and are not interested in getting help. In the past, these clients were viewed as "resistant" and often blamed for not cooperating with their social workers (Anderson and Stewart, 1983). The strengths perspective views resistance as a natural and understandable coping mechanism. Many clients, at best, are going to be reluctant to engage in a helping relationship (Rooney, 1992). The following discussion reviews some factors that affect clients' willingness and ability to move beyond the precontemplation stage in the helping process.

THE EXPERIENCE OF BEING A CLIENT

A number of factors associated with clienthood affect the helping process. Understanding these factors and the way a person feels about being a client can facilitate the helping process and the development of a collaborative helping relationship. Understanding the client's feelings about needing and asking for help as well as his or her perceptions of what it means to be a client can facilitate the process of reaching an explicit agreement about the purpose of working together. Whether the individual arrives on a voluntary, nonvoluntary, or involuntary basis, the worker's sensitivity to his or her feelings about clienthood is critical to having that individual become a client.

Beliefs and feelings about receiving help from a professional are related to cultural mores. The dominant culture in American society has a strong tradition of individualism (Billups, 1992). Individuals who need psychological or social services are stigmatized and viewed negatively in American society because they are perceived as not living up to the cultural mandates of individual responsibility and self-reliance. This stigma keeps many who need the services provided by social workers from seeking them. Only after everything else has failed are they willing to get professional help.

Most clients have mixed feelings about getting help (Maluccio, 1979). People are uncomfortable about involving themselves in a helping relationship and admitting that they have failed or are unable to resolve their difficulties on their own. Clients may feel shame and embarrassment. They are concerned about what the social worker will think of them and what friends and family will think. Asking for help also raises negative feelings about themselves because they may view receiving professional help as a personal failure. Obviously, the intensity of these feelings varies greatly. However, it is probably safe to assume that every person is feeling some degree of discomfort when he or she asks for help and goes through the stages of becoming a client.

Clients are often afraid of the possibilities of change. Nevertheless, even the most reluctant nonvoluntary or involuntary client has the power to bounce back. The worker uses this resilience to infuse some degree of hopefulness and expectation about positive outcomes. At some level, all clients have what it takes to make changes. They may not know it, but we, as social workers, know it, and that is why we passionately look for a person's strengths when he or she is involved in difficult life situations. Clients may not be aware of their resilience because they are overwhelmed by feelings of failure and stigmatization.

It is only realistic to expect that clients have ambivalent feelings about working with the social worker and receiving professional help. The first interactions will probably determine whether clients decide to engage in the helping process or drop out. During initial meetings, it is critical for the worker to decrease the client's negative feelings and increase positive feelings about seeking help and engaging in the helping process. Empowerment starts during the first interview with the client.

PRIOR EXPERIENCES WITH HELPING PROFESSIONALS

Most clients who come to you will have received social services in the past and have had numerous prior contacts with helping professionals. Ignoring the possibility of prior negative experiences or assuming that all prior experiences were positive is a mistake. Clients' expectations about receiving help from a professional are influenced by their past experiences (Gambrill, 1997). Were they treated with respect? Were they given a voice in the decision-making process? Were the services helpful? Were their prior experiences with helping professionals satisfactory or unsatisfactory? Clients whose prior experiences were negative may expect more of the same and approach your work together with reservations, whereas those who enjoyed more positive experiences might be much more willing to engage in the helping process.

Early in the working relationship, preferably during the initial meeting, the social worker should explore the client's perceptions of prior experiences. The worker may not change these perceptions, but recognizing them and learning what clients liked and did not like about earlier experiences is an important step in the helping process.

Clients' perceptions of the agency may also influence their approach to service (Garvin and Seabury, 1997). Does the agency have a negative or positive reputation in the community? Does the agency communicate respect for clients and their cultures in its physical appearance and decor? Are clients greeted at the agency in a courteous and respectful manner? Is the waiting area pleasant and comfortable? Negative agency perceptions can impede the development of a helping relationship and the client's receptiveness to the helping process.

Understanding clients' perceptions of their prior experiences with helping professionals and their expectations for upcoming experiences with the agency is a critical step in the engagement process. Being sensitive to the possibilities of both positive and negative prior experiences enables you to directly address concerns. Communicating empathy about negative experiences and perceptions validates clients' experiences and perceptions. This validation begins the process of coconstructing a more positive mind-set regarding the helping process and a willingness to engage in a collaborative helping relationship.

EXPECTATIONS ABOUT THE HELPING EXPERIENCE

Social workers also need to be sensitive to clients' expectations about the helping process and their role as client. "Ignoring or misunderstanding client expectations may result in premature drop out" (Gambrill, 1997, p. 22). Research findings show that clarification of the client role is associated with better outcomes (Orlinsky, Grawe, and Parks, 1994; Yalom, 1995). Client expectations about changes or outcomes should match those of their helpers. Different expectations will affect outcome and client retention.

Clients come to the helping process with various expectations. Some may have little or no hope of making any meaningful change in their lives whereas others may expect a miracle. Some might be aware of the collaborative nature of the helping process, and others might expect the social worker to fix the problem. Early in your work together, although not necessarily during your first meeting, you need to discuss how you will work together and what your respective roles will be. Clients need to clearly understand the helping process as well as their roles and responsibilities in it. Inappropriate expectations and misunderstandings about how the work will proceed can lead to disillusionment and dissatisfaction. It is important to share your vision of the helping process. It is probably wise to assume that you and your clients have different visions and expectations. These differences need to be reconciled before meaningful work can begin.

CULTURAL AND ETHNIC DIVERSITY

American society is characterized by cultural and racial diversity. Therefore, it is no surprise that social work clients have diverse cultural backgrounds and beliefs. Values and beliefs of different cultural groups might conflict with the values of the dominant culture or with the worker's values and beliefs. Even though social workers and clients often have a great deal in common, the expectation should be one of diversity and heterogeneity. Expect your clients to be unique individuals with different beliefs and values, and expect them to have a belief system that differs from yours in important ways.

The cultural or ethnic background of individuals may influence whether they become clients. Perceived similarities lead to understanding, empathy, and trust. Perceived differences may hinder the development of mutual understanding and trust (Miley, O'Melia, and DuBois, 1998). Perceived differences are barriers to clients' willingness to develop helping relationships. Most people seek out others with whom they feel a connection, a sameness, a likeness. Individuals tend to trust those they perceive as similar and distrust those they perceive as different. The tendency to distrust those who are different makes the task of overcoming cultural and ethnic differences a challenge for all social workers.

The number of potential differences between you and your client is infinite. Differences in values, perspectives, and experiences create barriers to communication and trust. It is your responsibility, as the professional helper, to acknowledge differences directly and to communicate respect for your clients' values and beliefs. Rather than viewing cultural differences as threatening, view them as a resource that adds perspectives and options to your relationship with your client (Miley, O'Melia, and DuBois, 1998). Overcoming client–worker differences requires that you acknowledge the differences as well as communicate your understanding of the clients' values, perceptions, and beliefs. Value your clients' differences. Show respect and appreciation of diversity. The differences will remain; what will change is the perception that they are barriers to communication and trust. Directly acknowledging differences early in the helping process increases the likelihood that the individual will become a client. Ignoring cultural and ethnic differences tends to exacerbate the magnitude of differences and hinder the development of trust.

In working with people of color, women, gays and lesbians, and other oppressed populations, it is important to acknowledge that their perceptions and experiences have been subjugated by the dominant culture (Anderson, 2000; Collins, 1990). To understand the experiences of clients, ask questions from a position of not knowing. Be curious, and show a genuine interest in what the client has to say. The client, not the worker, is the expert on his or her perceptions and experiences (Pray, 1991). Client expertise also encompasses cultural, ethnic, and racial experiences and perceptions.

Hartman points out that "in our attempt to become more skilled and more sensitive in our work with people of color, we have sought to gather information about cultures, to learn about difference, to become experts" (1994, p. 29). This approach leads to stereotyping and assumptions that all members of an oppressed group are alike. A better approach is to "abandon our expert role and really listen to our clients and believe and trust their experience" (Hartman, 1994, p. 29). If we listen to our clients, are open to their experiences, and take the position of learning with them and of not knowing, the chances of overcoming our differences are greatly improved.

Another important factor in cross-cultural practice is awareness of self and one's own cultural and ethnic heritage (Greene, Jensen, and Jones, 1996). Being aware of your own ethnic and cultural identity will increase your comfort level in working with clients from different ethnic and cultural backgrounds (Pinderhughes, 1983; Thomas, 2000). A culturally self-aware person is capable of recognizing and acknowledging differences. Social workers who are not aware of their own cultural beliefs and values are more likely to impose their values and beliefs on their clients and to feel threatened by their clients' differences. The more you know about yourself, the more likely you are to want to learn about your clients.

CLIENT SKILLS AND KNOWLEDGE

Clients often seek professional help only after they attempt to resolve problems on their own, with assistance from friends, family, or informal community organizations, or with other helping professionals. First meetings with new clients usually occur after clients have made numerous attempts to cope with their situations. They have a wealth of experience in dealing with their problems. They know what has worked and what has not worked. They probably have ideas about what is making the issue difficult to resolve and what they need to do to successfully resolve it. Be open to and use this knowledge.

Clients bring unique skills to the relationship. Each client has interpersonal skills and competencies. Clients have developed coping strategies and have found ways to get by in spite of pressing life demands and circumstances. They have developed unique ways of adapting to their life experiences. They have been successful, at some level, in coping with their difficulties. They are struggling and need help, but they have managed to survive and cope with challenging situations. All clients bring strengths and skills to the helping relationship.

Clients are empowered when the social worker acknowledges their strengths, knowledge, and skills. They are also encouraged. Clients are given hope when they are viewed as capable and competent individuals. Miley, O'Melia, and DuBois point out that clients' ability to "articulate thoughts and feelings; skills in thinking, planning, and organizing; competencies in giving and receiving support—all are general skills for living that may have relevance for overcoming any challenging situation" (1998, p. 127). Regardless of their level of functioning, irrespective of the severity of their life circumstances, and in spite of the magnitude of the problems that need to be overcome, clients' knowledge and skills can contribute to the resolution of their problem situations. Look for strengths and abilities and expect to find them. It is your job to help clients identify and articulate the knowledge and skills that they bring to the helping process. Recognizing these strengths helps foster collaborative worker–client relationships by increasing clients' willingness to engage in the helping process.

No matter whether a client is voluntary, nonvoluntary, or involuntary, and regardless of the circumstances that bring a client into contact with a generalist social worker, the client has to choose to participate in the helping process. For this to occur, the client has to have progressed at least to the preparation stage of change. The challenge for generalist social workers is to help clients move beyond the precontemplation and contemplation stages, so that clients do not drop out or go through the motions of changing without truly engaging in the helping process.

A number of factors influence clients' ability to engage in helping relationships. One factor is their feelings about getting help and the stigma they feel about asking for help from a stranger. Cultural values and beliefs as well as prior experiences with helping professionals influence these feelings. At best, most clients have mixed feelings about working with a social worker. The social worker must communicate understanding of these feelings and create an expectation that change is possible in order for clients to engage in the helping process. Being sensitive to clients' expectations and their role in the helping process and clarifying the collaborative nature of your work together also help promote client participation.

SOCIAL WORK VALUES AND ETHICS

The practice of social work is based on a number of value positions and principles that guide the work with clients irrespective of the approach used, the presenting client problem, the client population, or the setting in which services are provided. These values and principles apply to all forms of social work practice.

CORE SOCIAL WORK VALUES

Social work is a value-based profession (Beckett and Maynard, 2005; Reamer, 1990). Values provide the basis for professional social work practice (Gumpert and Black, 2006; Loewenberg, Dolgoff, and Harrington, 2000). They guide the actions we take and our evaluations of what is "good" (DuBois and Miley, 1999). Values represent "a constellation of preferences concerning what merits doing and how it should be done" (Levy, 1976, p. 234).

Social work has a rich tradition of principles and beliefs. The heart of these is reflected in the 1997 NASW Code of Ethics. The Code of Ethics identifies core social work values and associated ethical principles. Four of these values—service to others, social justice, dignity and worth of the person, and importance of human relationships—play a critical role in generalist practice.

Service to Others.   The first ethical principle states that "social workers' primary goal is to help people in need and to address social problems" (NASW, 1996, p. 5). Service to others is placed above self-interest.

Social work is a service profession dedicated to providing help to individuals, families, and groups in need and to improving community and social conditions. This commitment to service is reflected in the goals of the profession:

- To enhance social functioning of individuals, families, groups, organizations, and communities
- To link client systems with needed resources
- To improve the operation of social service programs and service delivery systems
- To promote social and economic justice through advocacy and policy development (DuBois and Miley, 1999, p. 11)

Inherent in each of these goals is service to others. All four goals focus on helping others directly by enhancing their capacities to resolve problems and indirectly by linking clients with resources, improving service delivery systems, and developing social programs and policies.

Social Justice.   Social justice has long been valued in social work. Concern with social justice and inequality in the profession goes back to the advocacy efforts of Jane Addams and the settlement house movement of the early 1900s (Mickelson, 1995).

The Code of Ethics identifies social justice as a core social work value and states that challenging social injustice is an ethical principle of the profession:

> Social workers pursue social change, particularly with and on behalf of vulnerable and oppressed individuals and groups of people. Social workers' social change efforts are focused primarily on issues of poverty, unemployment, discrimination and other forms of social injustice. . . . Social workers strive to ensure access to needed information, services, and resources; equality of opportunity; and meaningful participation in decision making for all people. (NASW, 1996, p. 5)

Beverly and McSweeney define "justice as fairness in the relationships between people as these relate to the possession and/or acquisition of resources" (1987, p. 6). Social workers traditionally work with people who are victims of discrimination and prejudice. Many of our clients are unemployed or underemployed, have limited access to resources, received inadequate education and training, and are among the most disadvantaged members of society. They often face prejudicial attitudes and are "identified as 'lesser'—less capable, less productive, and less normal" (DuBois and Miley, 1999, p. 148). Social injustice is manifested in discrimination on the basis of race, gender, social class, sexual orientation, age, and disability. Prejudicial attitudes provide justification for "social structures that provide fewer prospects—fewer opportunities, fewer possibilities, and fewer resources—for those with lower status" (DuBois and Miley, 1999, p. 148).

Social workers' commitment to social justice is based on concern about the negative effect of discrimination and prejudice on disadvantaged populations. We often work with clients who have been denied basic rights and opportunities. We are called on to challenge social injustice and to increase the opportunities, possibilities, and resources of our clients. We have an ethical responsibility to address the social, physical, and economic needs of our clients as well as their psychological needs (Dodd and Jansson, 2004).

Human Dignity and Self-Worth.   A third core value is to treat our clients in a caring and respectful fashion, being mindful of individual differences and cultural and ethnic diversity (Saxon, Jacinto, and Dziegielewski, 2006). The underlying assumption of this value is that "all human beings have intrinsic worth, irrespective of their past or present behavior, beliefs, lifestyle, race, or status in life" (Hepworth, Rooney, and Larsen, 2002, p. 59). As a social worker, you are expected to treat your clients with respect and dignity. They deserve respect by virtue of their humanness. This does not mean that you have to agree with your clients' life choices or decisions. It does mean that you should strive to affirm their dignity and self-worth. Not doing so can have profound negative effects on the helping process.

Hepworth, Rooney, and Larsen point out that "before people will risk sharing personal problems and expressing deep emotions, they must first feel fully accepted and experience the good-will and helpful intent of practitioners" (2002, p. 59). This attitude is more important when clients' problematic behaviors involve moral, social, or legal infractions. A client whose behavior has violated social and cultural norms is not likely to engage in a collaborative helping relationship with a professional who communicates disapproval and condemnation.

Closely associated with respect for the individual is a nonjudgmental attitude. The social worker must not blame the client in attitude or behavior (Biestek, 1957). You should focus on understanding clients and their difficulties and on helping them find solutions or alternative ways of behaving. If you blame them for their difficulties and assign pejorative labels, most will become defensive and unwilling to trust you. The more you understand the life experience of your clients, no matter how personally distressing their behavior or beliefs may be, the more likely it is that you will be able to accept them as human beings who may have "suffered various forms of deprivation and have themselves been victims of harsh, abusive, rejecting, or exploitative behavior" (Hepworth, Rooney, and Larsen, 2002, p. 60).

Many of our clients' behaviors conflict with our personal values and beliefs. More often than not, there will be a clash of values between you and your clients. These differences should be viewed as a normal part of generalist social work practice. Expect them and accept them. There are going to be differences; in fact, there are going to be major differences. If you focus on your values and assign blame to clients for adopting behaviors or attitudes with which you disagree, you will not be able to help them.

Adopting nonjudgmental attitudes is a prerequisite for developing effective working relationships (Perlman, 1979). The challenge is to maintain your own values without imposing them on others and without judging those whose behavior and beliefs are in conflict with your belief system. To accomplish this, you need to be open to others and treat everyone with respect and dignity. This is difficult when you have negative feelings about your client. You are human, and you will have negative feelings about some clients. Pretending that you do not have these feelings will not work; clients will sense insincerity and negative reactions. The best approach is to try to understand your client and communicate that understanding to him or her in a caring and nonjudgmental manner. Clients are not seeking your approval; they are seeking your help. They need to feel that they have been heard and that you understand them and their situations. They need to feel that you care and that you want to work with them. Communicating care and concern facilitates the helping process. If clients perceive you as judging and blaming them, they are not likely to accept help from you.

Importance of Human Relationships.   A fourth core value of social work is the importance of human relationships (Dietz and Thompson, 2004). "Positive social exchanges may be the strongest elements shaping and enriching human life; adverse and coercive social exchanges are among the deepest sources of human pain" (Mattaini, 1997, p. 120). The Code of Ethics states that "social workers seek to strengthen relationships among people in a purposeful effort to promote, restore, maintain, and enhance the well-being of individuals, families, social groups, organizations, and communities" (NASW, 1996, p. 6). Focusing on the relationship issues of clients is common in generalist social work. Many clients need help in improving their human relationships and interpersonal interactions. "Deficits and excesses in social behavior often result in severe isolation (and loneliness), and many clients seen individually identify improvements in relationships among their most important goals" (Mattaini, 1997, p. 120).

Historically, the helping relationship has been given a central role in the helping process (Biestek, 1957; Perlman, 1979). The Code of Ethics states that "social workers engage people as partners in the helping process" (NASW, 1996, p. 6). Relationship implies that there is a reciprocal interactive process between two people. In social work, the helping relationship is a partnership. You and the client both have input and make decisions together. You are joint participants. Social workers do not solve problems for their clients; they work with clients and help them solve their own problems.

Beginning social workers often feel that unless they are doing something specific and concrete for their clients, they are not being helpful. You will be tempted to do things for clients, using your skills and abilities to get the task done and hand over the results to clients. It will make you feel useful and productive. Avoid the temptation, because it is a trap. More often than not, clients will not appreciate your generous efforts on their behalf. By doing work for them, you will put them in a dependent position, highlighting their inability to manage their lives. No one likes feeling incompetent and dependent. Rather than making your clients dependent on you, empower them. Help them help themselves. Help them do whatever they need to do to manage their own lives as best they can. Ultimately, your clients must become confident and learn to do tasks for themselves. The helping relationship in social work is a collaborative partnership. Social workers do not work for clients; rather they work with clients.

ETHICAL STANDARDS

The core social work values and ethical principles embody the ideals to which all social workers should aspire. The Code of Ethics sets specific standards and explains how the core values and principles influence the actions of professional social workers. "Values are concerned with what is good and desirable, while ethics deal with what is right and correct" (Loewenberg, Dolgoff, and Harrington, 2000, p. 22). The standards spell out social workers' ethical responsibilities to clients, to colleagues, in practice settings, as professionals, to the social work profession, and to the broader society (NASW, 1997, p. 7). They are detailed, comprehensive guidelines for professional conduct (Palmer and Kauffman, 2003). For example, the standards for ethical responsibilities to clients cover sixteen areas, including commitment to clients, self-determination, informed consent, and competence (see Table 1.4). A detailed discussion of each ethical standard in the six professional practice areas may be found in the Code of Ethics.

The guidelines in the ethical standards section of the Code of Ethics provide a basis for formulating judgments regarding unethical behavior and help resolve value conflicts. It is your responsibility as a professional social worker to be familiar with the Code of Ethics and follow it in your professional practice.

ETHICAL DILEMMAS

Social workers frequently have ethical obligations to several parties at the same time. For example, we have ethical obligations to both our clients and our employing organizations. This creates the possibility of conflict, or ethical dilemmas.

TABLE 1.4 | OUTLINE OF ETHICAL STANDARDS

Social workers' ethical responsibilities to clients

Commitment to clients	Self-determination	Informed consent
Competence	Cultural competence	Conflicts of interest
Confidentiality	Access to records	Sexual relationships
Physical contact	Sexual harassment	Derogatory language
Payment for services	Decision-making capacity	Interruption of services
Termination of services		

Social workers' ethical responsibilities to colleagues

Respect	Confidentiality	Interdisciplinary collaboration
Disputes involving colleagues	Consultation	Referral for services
Sexual relationships	Sexual harassment	Impairment of colleagues
Incompetence of colleagues	Unethical conduct of colleagues	

Social workers' ethical responsibilities in practice settings

Supervision and consultation	Education and training	Performance evaluation
Client records	Billing	Client transfer
Administration	Staff development	Commitments to employers
Labor–management disputes		

Social workers' ethical responsibilities as professionals

Competence	Discrimination	Private conduct
Dishonesty, fraud, and deception	Impairment	Misrepresentation
Solicitations	Acknowledging credit	

Social workers' ethical responsibilities to the social work profession

Integrity of the profession, evaluation, and research

Social workers' ethical responsibilities to the broader society

Social welfare	Public participation
Social and political action	Public emergencies

"An ethical dilemma occurs when you cannot simultaneously meet your obligations to two different parties in the role set without violating your ethical commitment to one or the other" (Compton and Galaway, 1994, p. 240). In these situations, you are forced to "choose between two apparent goods or to avoid two equally undesirable courses of action" (McGowan, 1995, p. 35). Because we have ethical responsibilities to our clients, our colleagues, our practice settings, the profession, and the broader society, value conflicts and ethical dilemmas occur often within and between the six areas of professional responsibilities outlined in Table 1.4.

Resolving ethical dilemmas is never easy or straightforward. Rarely is there a clear-cut right or wrong choice. The choice is between two seeming "rights"; the task is to determine which "right" is more so given the circumstances.

The first step in addressing ethical dilemmas is to refer to the Code of Ethics for clarification of the standards of practice. The Code, however, does not offer bases for choosing between two or more conflicting standards. A number of guidelines have been developed to help resolve ethical dilemmas. A hierarchy of

TABLE 1.5	ETHICAL GUIDELINES

1. The rights to life, health, well-being, and necessities of life are superordinate and take precedence over rights to confidentiality and opportunities for additive "goods" such as wealth, education, and recreation.
2. An individual's basic right to well-being takes precedence over another person's right to privacy, freedom, or self-determination.
3. People's right to self-determination takes precedence over their right to basic well-being, provided they are competent to make informed and voluntary decisions with consideration of relevant knowledge and so long as the consequences of their decisions do not threaten the well-being of others.
4. People's rights to well-being may override laws, policies, and arrangements of organizations (Hepworth, Rooney and Larsen, 2002, pp. 77–78, based on Reamer, 1990).

value assumptions is the basis for decision making (Loewenberg, Dolgoff, and Harrington, 2000; Reamer, 1990; Rhodes, 1991). One such hierarchy is shown in Table 1.5.

The first guideline in Table 1.5 proposes that a person's right to health and well-being takes precedence over the right of confidentiality. If you had to choose between protecting a person's health and well-being and violating a client's confidentiality, you would choose health and well-being. For example, the right of neglected and abused children to protection takes precedence over their parents' rights to confidentiality.

The second guideline proposes that a person's right to health and well-being takes precedence over another person's right to privacy, freedom, or self-determination. When you must choose between protecting a person's freedom and protecting another person from harm, the choice is to protect the person from harm. For example, if a client reveals plans to seek physical revenge on his or her former spouse, you should warn the former spouse.

The third guideline states that a person's right to self-determination takes precedence over his or her own right to well-being. That is, an individual's self-determination supersedes that person's well-being. The principle promotes freedom to choose and possibly fail or make mistakes. It protects the right of people to carry out actions that do not appear to be in their own best interests, as long as they are competent to make informed and voluntary decisions. However, the first guideline takes precedence if the individual's decision might result in death or serious harm. For example, you must take action to protect a client who is at risk of committing suicide.

The final guideline proposes that the right to well-being may override agency policies and procedural rules. Social workers are obligated to follow the policies and procedures of social work agencies, voluntary associations, and organizations. When agency policy has a negative effect on a client's well-being, however, violating the policy or procedure may be justified. "It would be permissible, for example, for a social worker who is prohibited from treating clients outside of the agency to counsel a suicidal client who has called from home to request assistance" (Reamer, 1983, pp. 34–35).

The guidelines described above—or any other guidelines—will not provide "unambiguous and commonly accepted solutions to ethical dilemmas" (Reamer, 1983, p. 35). Guidelines prioritize values to help clarify your thinking about ethical issues. Resolving ethical dilemmas almost always entails making value judgments and subjective interpretations. For example, the third guideline states that a person's right to self-determination takes precedence over his or her right to basic well-being, provided he or she is competent to make an informed decision. A social worker may have to apply this guideline to a person who is mentally ill and homeless, who prefers to remain on the street, and who has little or no interest in participating in a treatment program. Does this person have the right to refuse treatment as well as the right to live wherever he or she wants? The complicating factor in this situation is determining the person's competence and the degree of physical or mental harm that is likely to ensue. Can a person who is mentally ill, delusional, and exhibiting psychotic behavior make informed decisions? At what point does refusing shelter or treatment create a serious risk of physical and mental harm? Clearly, the answers to these questions are subjective and open to value judgments.

In attempting to resolve ethical dilemmas, always invoke the concept of shared responsibility and decision making. Do not make the decision on your own; enlist others in the process. Get your supervisor's or administrator's advice and approval before you take action on an ethical dilemma. Case 2.2 illustrates the difficult decisions involved in resolving ethical dilemmas.

Jill is faced with an ethical dilemma. She has been told by her supervisor to follow an agency policy that she believes is not in the best interests of her clients. What are Jill's options? Is it advisable for her to apply guideline 4 and disregard agency policy? What might be the consequences of such an action? How should she attempt to resolve her dilemma?

SUMMARY

Generalist social work practice involves a wide range of practice skills and interventions. It entails micro-level and macro-level work. Micro interventions focus on individuals, couples, families, and small groups. Macro interventions focus on agency task forces and committees, professional task forces, community coalitions, and neighborhood groups.

The helping relationship in micro interventions is directed toward the enhanced functioning and empowerment of the client systems. The helping relationship in macro interventions at the organizational level focuses on improving organizations and their services as well as developing new services. At the community level, the focus is on improving community conditions, empowering residents, developing resources, increasing awareness, and mobilizing citizens.

Generalist social workers must be skilled in the use of self regardless of the system level of the intervention. The use of self to help individuals, families, and small groups is widely regarded as a fundamental part of direct (micro) practice. It is also a critical component of macro practice. The ability to provide support, increase motivation, foster hope, strengthen commitment, mobilize energy, increase understanding, and facilitate communication is important regardless of the size of the client system. The helping process with individuals, families, groups, organizations, and communities requires generalist social workers who can use the self to help the client make changes.

Generalist practice takes place with individual, family, small group, organization, and community client systems. Thus, generalist social workers are prepared to address both micro-level and macro-level concerns. In addition to working with client systems of various sizes, generalists often work with multiple client systems. Typically, generalists work with a number of different client systems simultaneously. For example, generalist social work with individual clients often entails work with the family system as well as with organizations and community groups within the individual's environmental system. The target systems are those within the client's systems environment that are targeted for change or intervention.

Clients can be voluntary, nonvoluntary, or involuntary. Regardless of the circumstances that bring a client into contact with a generalist social worker, the client has to choose to participate in the helping process. For this to occur, the client must have progressed to at least the preparation stage of change. The challenge for generalist social workers is to help clients move beyond the precontemplation and contemplation stages so that clients do not drop out or merely go through the motions of the helping process.

A number of factors influence clients' ability to engage in helping relationships. One factor is how they feel about getting help, and how great a stigma they feel about needing to go to a stranger for assistance plays a role. Cultural values and beliefs as well as prior experiences with helping professionals influence these feelings. At best, most clients have mixed feelings about working with a social worker. Communicating understanding of these feelings and creating an expectation that change is possible are critical to having clients engage in the helping process. Being sensitive to clients' expectations and their role in the helping process and clarifying the collaborative nature of your work together also help promote client participation.

Strengths-based generalist practice is consistent with the core values of social work. The social work profession and strengths-based generalist practice both emphasize service to others, social justice, human dignity and self-worth, and the importance of human relationships. Generalist social workers incorporate these core values into their work with clients and use the ethical principles described in the profession's Code of Ethics to help resolve issues related to clients, colleagues, agencies, the profession, and the broader society. Ethical dilemmas occur when an individual has to choose between two or more conflicting ethical standards. Ethical dilemmas can be resolved by using a hierarchical decision-making approach. This approach is useful when a social worker is faced with a choice between two apparent goods or two equally undesirable courses of action.

CASE EXAMPLE

The final case in this chapter was written by Leslie Freas, a first-year MSW student placed in an adult partial hospitalization program. The case illustrates the termination process with an individual client who did not want to end the relationship.

CASE 1.3	BUT I'M NOT READY TO LEAVE

By Leslie Freas

The Senior Care Center is a 16-week partial hospitalization program for individuals aged 65 and over who are experiencing a mental illness. The majority of clients are experiencing depression, often following the onset of a medical condition (i.e., Parkinson's disease, cancer, a stroke) and/or following the loss of a spouse or loved one. Some clients have a long history of mental illness, including major depression, bipolar

(Continued)

CASE 1.3 | *Continued*

disorder, schizophrenia, etc. Many of the clients of the Center are either coming out of psychiatric hospitalization or are placed in this program to prevent hospitalization. There are others, however, who are referred by their outpatient psychiatrist or primary physician, or make a self-referral.

The Senior Care Center provides individual and group therapy. The groups consist of psychoeducation, music and art therapy, discharge planning, relapse prevention, and more intense psychotherapy groups. Clients also meet weekly with their social worker for supportive counseling. In addition, the social worker oversees the treatment plan and is responsible for developing the discharge plan.

Mrs. K. is a 77-year-old white woman with a 43-year history of depressive episodes, and has been diagnosed with both major depressive disorder and bipolar disorder. In late 1994, Mrs. K. was diagnosed with Parkinson's disease. Shortly after that she was admitted to the hospital's inpatient psychiatric ward where she received ECT. Following her discharge from the hospital, Mrs. K. was referred to the Senior Care Center for continued mental health treatment and therapy.

After attending the Center for over 3 years, Mrs. K. was told several weeks ago that she is being discharged at the end of March. When she entered the program there was no set time limit on how long a client could stay in the program. Recently the Center was informed by the managed care company that the maximum length of stay would be approximately 16 weeks per client.

Mrs. K.'s biggest obstacle is her physical health. Her Parkinson's has limited her ability to function independently, and it has also started to impair her cognitive abilities, including her memory. In addition, she is suffering from depression. With her medication and the benefits of the Senior Care Center, Mrs. K. has been coping with her depression very well. The concern is that she will fall back into her depression once she is no longer attending the Center.

Mrs. K. still needs to improve her ability to be assertive regarding her needs and wishes. She acknowledges this in her individual sessions with her social worker and realizes that she especially needs to work on this around the time of her discharge.

Mrs. K., fortunately, also has many strengths. She is a genuinely caring and optimistic person. She is also intelligent and has a wonderful sense of humor. In addition, Mrs. K. is determined to stay active and fight the effects of having Parkinson's disease. She rarely misses her scheduled days at the Center and states that she cannot stand to sit around the house and do nothing. Mrs. K. has a caring, supportive husband and son.

Given her current level of functioning, the treatment team does not feel that her continued participation in the program is justified given the new reimbursement guidelines and policies. Mrs. K., her husband, and their son are upset about her pending discharge. They all feel that she benefits from the treatment she receives at the Center and that after 3+ years the Center has become an important part of her life.

I explored with Mrs. K. her feelings about termination. She was very clear that she did not want to stop coming to the Center every day. She was very fearful of getting depressed again and also fearful about her health deteriorating. I acknowledged her feelings about the termination. Although I could not justify keeping Mrs. K. in the program based on the new guidelines, I felt that Mrs. K. needed the support and stability the program offered. Together we developed the following termination plan:

- Mrs. K., in coordination with her case manager, will enroll in the aftercare group at the hospital and attend outpatient therapy at the Center.
- Leslie would investigate the possibility of Mrs. K. receiving physical and/or occupational therapy for Parkinson's through the hospital.
- Mrs. K. will begin attending a Senior Activities Center once a week.
- Mrs. K. would continue to verbalize feelings about being discharged during individual counseling with Leslie and at home with her family members.
- Mrs. K. will verbalize her needs and wishes regarding her discharge to the Center staff and her family members.

Discussion Questions

1. Discuss the ethics of discharging Mrs. K. and whether or not Leslie is facing an ethical dilemma. What benefits do you see in having Mrs. K. stay in the program? What are the benefits of termination? What are the negatives of staying and leaving? What would you do if you were Leslie?

2. Critique Mrs. K.'s discharge plan. What additional aftercare services need to be added to the plan? Would assertiveness training be appropriate for Mrs. K.? (For information on assertiveness training, see Schroeder and Black (1985) and Alberti and Emmons (2001).)

3. List the types of activities you perform in your field placement. For each activity, identify the client system level and client systems. Assess the extent to which your field placement provides micro- and macro-practice experiences.

4. How do the purpose of the helping relationship, the use of self, and the system change activities vary between micro and macro interventions? In what ways are micro interventions similar to macro interventions? In what ways are they different?

5. What social work values appear to have a bearing on this case? Are there any ethical dilemmas that you would want to address? If so, how would you resolve them?

References

Alberti, R. E., and Emmons, M. (2001). *Your perfect right: Assertiveness and equality in your life and relationships* (8th ed.). Atascadeno, CA: Impact Publishers, Inc.

Anderson, C. M., and Stewart, S. (1983). *Mastering resistance: A practical guide to family therapy.* New York: Springer.

Anderson, F. S. (2000). Generalist practice with gay and lesbian clients. In J. Poulin, *Collaborative social work: Strengths-based generalist practice* (pp. 357–384). Itasca, IL: F. E. Peacock Publishers, Inc.

Association of Baccalaureate Program Directors (2006). Definition of generalist practice. Retrieved from www.bpdonline.org on June 2, 2008.

Barber, J. G. (1995). Politically progressive casework. *Families in Society,* 76, 30–37.

Beckett, C., and Maynard, A. (2005). *Values and ethics in social work.* London: Sage.

Beverly, D. P., and McSweeney, E. A. (1987). *Social welfare and social justice.* Englewood Cliffs, NJ: Prentice-Hall.

Biestek, F. (1957). *The casework relationship.* Chicago: Loyola University Press.

Billups, J. O. (1992). The moral basis for a radical reconstruction of social work. In P. N. Reid and P. R. Popple (Eds.), *The moral purposes of social work: The character and intentions of a profession* (pp. 100–119). Chicago: Nelson-Hall.

Chavis, D. M., Florin, P., and Felix, M. R. J. (1993). Nurturing grassroots initiatives for community development: The role of enabling systems. In T. Mizrahi and J. D. Morrison (Eds.), *Community organization and social administration* (pp. 41–67). New York: Haworth Press.

Collins, P. H. (1990). *Black feminist thought.* New York: Routledge.

Compton, B. R., and Galaway, B. (1994). *Social work processes* (5th ed.). Pacific Grove, CA: Brooks/Cole.

Connaway, R., and Gentry, M. (1988). *Social work practice.* Englewood Cliffs, NJ: Prentice-Hall.

Dietz, C., and Thompson, J. (2004). Rethinking boundaries: Ethical dilemmas in the social worker-client relationship. *Journal of Progressive Human Services, 15*(2), 1–24.

Dodd, S., and Jansson, B. (2004). Expanding the boundaries of ethics education: Preparing social workers for ethical advocacy in an organizational setting. *Journal of Social Work Education, 40*(3), 455–465.

Dorfman, R. (1996). *Clinical social work: Definition, practice, and vision.* New York: Brunner/Mazel.

DuBois, B., and Miley, K. K. (1999). *Social work: An empowering profession* (3rd ed.). Boston: Allyn and Bacon.

Ezell, M. (1994). Advocacy practice of social workers. *Families in Society,* 75, 36–46.

Freire, P. (1990). *Pedagogy of the oppressed.* New York: Continuum.

Freud, S. (1987). Social workers as community educators: A new identity for the profession. *Journal of Teaching in Social Work, 1,* 111–126.

Gambrill, E. (1997). *Social work practice: A critical thinker's guide.* New York: Oxford University Press.

Garvin, C. D., and Seabury, B. A. (1997). *Interpersonal practice in social work: Promoting competence and social justice* (2nd ed.). Boston: Allyn and Bacon.

Goldstein, E. (1995). *Ego psychology and social work practice* (2nd ed.). New York: Free Press.

Greene, G. J., Jensen, C., and Jones, D. H. (1996). A constructivist perspective on clinical social work practice with ethnically diverse clients. *Social Work, 41,* 172–180.

Gumpert, J., and Black, P. (2006). Ethical issues in group work: What are they? How are they managed? *Social Work with Groups, 29*(4), 61–74.

Hardcastle, D. A., Wenocur, S., and Powers, P. R. (1997). *Community practice: Theories and skills for social workers.* New York: Oxford University Press.

Hartman, A. (1994). Social work practice. In F. G. Reamer (Ed.), *The foundations of social work knowledge* (pp. 13–50). New York: Columbia University Press.

Haynes, K. S., and Mickelson, J. S. (1991). *Affecting change: Social workers in the political arena* (2nd ed.). New York: Longman.

Hepworth, D., Rooney, R., and Larsen, J. (2002). *Direct social work practice: Theory and skills* (6th ed.). Pacific Grove, CA: Brooks/Cole.

Kirst-Ashman, K., and Hull, G. (1993). *Understanding generalist practice.* Chicago: Nelson-Hall.

Kurzman, P. (1985). Program development and service coordination as components of community practice. In S. H. Taylor and R. W. Roberts (Eds.), *Theory and practice of community social work* (pp. 59–94). New York: Columbia University Press.

Lantz, J., and Lenahan, B. (1976). Referral fatigue therapy. *Social Work, 12,* 239–240.

Lauffer, A. (1981). The practice of social planning. In N. Gilbert and H. Specht (Eds.), *Handbook of the social services* (pp. 583–597). Englewood Cliffs, NJ: Prentice-Hall.

Levy, C. (1976). *Social work ethics.* New York: Human Sciences Press.

Lewis, E. (1991). Social change and citizen action: A philosophical exploration for modern social group work. *Social Work with Groups, 14,* 23–34.

Loewenberg, F. M., Dolgoff, R., and Harrington, D. (2000). *Ethical decisions for social work practice* (6th ed.). Itasca, IL: F. E. Peacock Publishers, Inc.

Maluccio, A. (1979). Perspectives of social workers and clients on treatment outcome. *Social Casework, 60,* 394–401.

Mattaini, M. A. (1997). *Clinical practice with individuals.* Washington, DC: NASW Press.

Marziali, E., and Alexander, L. (1991). The power of the therapeutic relationship. *American Journal of Orthopsychiatry, 61,* 383–391.

McGowan, B. (1995). Values and ethics. In C. H. Meyer and M. A. Mattaini (Eds.), *The foundations of social work practice: A graduate text* (pp. 28–41). Washington, DC: NASW Press.

Mickelson, J. S. (1995). Advocacy. *Encyclopedia of social work.* Washington, DC: NASW Press.

Middleman, R., and Wood, G. (1990). From social group work to social work with groups. *Social Work with Groups, 13,* 3–20.

Miley, K., O'Melia, M., and DuBois, B. L. (1998). *Generalist social work practice: An empowering approach* (2nd ed.). Boston: Allyn and Bacon.

Moxley, D. P. (1997). *Case management by design: Reflections on principles and practices.* Chicago: Nelson-Hall.

National Association of Social Workers (1996). *Code of ethics.* Silver Spring, MD: National Association of Social Workers.

Northen, H. (1995). *Clinical social work* (2nd ed.). New York: Columbia University Press.

Orlinsky, D., Grawe, K., and Parks, B. (1994). Process and outcome in psychotherapy-noch einmal. In A. Bergen and S. Garfield (Eds.), *Handbook of psychotherapy and behavior change* (4th ed., pp. 270–376). New York: John Wiley.

Palmer, N., and Kauffman, M. (2003). The ethics of informed consent: Implications for multicultural practice. *Journal of Ethnic & Cultural Diversity in Social Work, 12*(1), 1–26.

Perlman, H. (1979). *Relationship: The heart of helping people.* Chicago: University of Chicago Press.

Pincus, A., and Minahan, A. (1973). *Social work practice: Model and method.* Itasca, IL: F. E. Peacock Publishers, Inc.

Pinderhughes, E. (1983). Empowerment for our clients and for ourselves. *Social Casework, 64,* 331–338.

Pinderhughes, E. (1995). Direct practice overview. In R. Edwards (Ed.), *Encyclopedia of social work* (19th ed.). Silver Spring, MD: NASW Press.

Pray, J. (1991). Respecting the uniqueness of the individual: Social work practice within a reflective model. *Social Work, 36,* 80–85.

Prochaska, J. O., DiClemente, C. C., and Norcross, J. C. (1992). In search of how people change: Applications to addictive behaviors. *American Psychologist, 47,* 1102–1114.

Reamer, F. G. (1990). *Ethical dilemmas in social service* (2nd ed.). New York: Columbia University Press.

Reeser, L. C., and Epstein, I. (1990). *Professionalism and activism in social work: The sixties, the eighties, and the future.* New York: Columbia University Press.

Rhodes, M. L. (1991). *Ethical dilemmas in social work practice.* Milwaukee: Family Service America.

Rooney, R. H., (1992). *Strategies for work with involuntary clients.* New York: Columbia University Press.

Rothman, J., and Sager, J. S. (1998). *Case management: Integrating individual and community practice* (2nd ed.). Boston: Allyn and Bacon.

Rubin, H. J., and Rubin, I. S. (1992). *Community organizing and development* (2nd ed.). New York: Macmillan.

Russell, M. (1990). *Clinical social work: Research and practice.* Newbury Park, CA: Sage.

Saleebey, D. (2002). *The strengths perspective in social work practice* (3rd ed.). Boston: Allyn and Bacon.

Saxon, C., Jacinto, G., and Dziegielewski, S. (2006). Self-determination and confidentiality: The ambiguous nature of decision-making in social work practice. *Journal of Human Behavior in the Social Environment, 13*(4), 55–72.

Schroeder, H. E., and Black, M. J. (1985). Unassertiveness. In M. Hersen and A. S. Bellack (Eds.), *Handbook of clinical behavior therapy with adults* (pp. 509–530). New York: Plenum Press.

Shulman, L. (1999). *The skills of helping individuals, families, groups and organizations* (4th ed.). Itasca, IL: F. E. Peacock Publishers, Inc.

Specht, H. (1988). *New directions for social work.* Englewood Cliffs, NJ: Prentice-Hall.

Staples, L. (1990). Powerful ideas about empowerment. *Administration in Social Work, 14,* 29–42.

Thomas, N. D., (2000). Generalist practice with people of color. In J. Poulin, *Collaborative social work: Strengths-based generalist practice* (pp. 295–326). Itasca, IL: F.E. Peacock Publishers, Inc.

Weick, A., Rapp, C., Sullivan, W., and Kisthardt, S. (1989). A strengths perspective for social work practice. *Social Work, 34,* 350–354.

Weil, M. O., and Gamble, D. N. (1995). Community practice models. In R. Edwards (Ed.), *Encyclopedia of social work* (19th ed.). Silver Spring, MD: NASW Press.

Weissman, A. (1976). Industrial social service: Linkage technology, *Social Casework, 57,* 50–54.

Woodside, M., and McClam, T. (1998). *Generalist case management: A method of human service delivery.* Pacific Grove, CA: Brooks/Cole.

Yalom, I. D. (1995). *Theory and practice of group psychotherapy* (4th ed.). New York: Basic Books.

2

THEORETICAL AND CONCEPTUAL FRAMEWORKS FOR GENERALIST PRACTICE

Michael Newman/PhotoEdit

Karen L. was a senior MSW student who would soon graduate from college. She had had no prior social work experience when she reported for her first day of field placement at a drug and alcohol treatment program. Karen was excited about beginning her social work career but nervous about working with clients.

The field instructor gave Karen a brief tour of the facility and introduced her to the staff. He then told her that the best way to begin was to "jump right in." He handed her three case files and copies of the agency's assessment form and told her that she was scheduled to conduct assessments of three new residents that morning. Karen felt stunned and overwhelmed as she went to meet her first client.

During the interviews, Karen felt completely lost. She was not sure how to proceed with the interviews. She was unfamiliar with many of the terms on the form. The form used open-ended questions. Karen had to ask clients about their ecosystems, target systems, system strengths and challenges, and factors that might influence their capacity to engage in a helping relationship. Karen did not see her field instructor again that day, and she left feeling discouraged and confused.

Karen's experience is every beginning social work student's worst nightmare. It raises a number of questions and issues. Generalist social workers deal with a wide range of problems in a variety of practice settings (Pinderhughes, 1995). Generalists define client issues, collect and assess data, and plan interventions. Once a problem has been identified and the intervention planned, the generalist selects and implements an appropriate course of action, monitors and evaluates outcomes, and plans termination (Baker, 1995).

This chapter begins with a review of the two major paradigms in social work. It continues with a discussion of the ecosystem and strengths perspectives. The chapter concludes with a review of critical thinking and empirical-based practice. By the end of this chapter, you should be able to help Karen

1. Summarize the differences between modern and postmodern approaches to social work practice
2. Describe the ecosystem perspective and its role in generalist social work practice
3. Interpret the major principles of strengths-based generalist social work practice and understand how strengths-based practice differs from the traditional problem-solving model of practice
4. Summarize the principles of attachment theory
5. Describe the role critical thinking plays in generalist social work practice
6. Define empirical-based practice

All academic disciplines have philosophical and theoretical frameworks. Upon these frameworks are built practice models. The model of strengths-based generalist practice presented here integrates two very different conceptual frameworks: logical positivism and postmodernism.

MODERN AND POSTMODERN PERSPECTIVES

"The social work profession is deeply rooted in the Enlightenment of the 18th century and its modernist frames of reference" (Irving and Young, 2002). Until recently, empiricism and the scientific approach have dominated the social work profession (Reid, 1994; Weick and Saleebey, 1995, 1998): "the history of the social work profession has been consistently marked by both its adherence to and its attempt to maximize its linkage to a scientific model of knowledge" (Weick, 1993, p. 15). Logical positivism calls for empiricism, objectivity, and neutrality (Allen, 1993). In this tradition, the social worker is an expert who helps clients resolve their problems. The social worker is expected to be a neutral, value-free participant, and the relationship is expected to be hierarchical. There is a power differential between the social worker and the client. Client assessment and diagnosis are based on the superior knowledge of the social worker:

> It was the social worker who determined what the problem was, giving rise to sophisticated and widely varied diagnostic catalogs. It was the social worker who orchestrated the course of treatment, presumably based on the diagnosis. The social worker took the role of actor and organizer; the client took the role of obedient recipient. (Weick, 1993, p. 16).

Social work's adherence to the scientific method began with the publication of Mary Richmond's *Social Diagnosis* in 1917. Richmond viewed "social diagnosis" as a scientific process of gathering facts and testing hypotheses about clients' social functioning. The psychoanalytic-oriented casework movement that began in the 1920s was also based on scientific principles of study, diagnosis, and treatment (Reid, 1994). The psychosocial and psychodynamic approaches that evolved out of the psychoanalytic tradition have dominated social work practice theory from the 1940s to the present.

In the 1960s, the **empirical practice movement** evolved (Reid, 1994). The empirical practice movement stresses the application of research methods to practice with individuals, families, and groups. The distinguishing characteristic of empirical social work is the use of the scientific method in assessing client situations, specifying goals, formulating solution-focused interventions, and evaluating effectiveness (Reid, 1994). Empirical social workers focus on the assessment of relevant facts, the specification of the problem in measurable terms, and the objective assessment of outcomes (Fischer, 1981; Hudson, 1982; Reid, 1994). **Logical positivism** and empirical practice

- Assume the existence of an objective reality that can be measured
- Emphasize the expertise of the helping professional and attribute less importance to the client's own knowledge and experience
- Place knowledge and power in the hands of the objective expert social worker
- Stress the application of research methods in practice
- Require clear specification of client problems
- Involve developing measurable goals and objectives
- Require measuring client progress and outcomes

"Although social work has been slow, even reluctant and resistant at times, to embrace the postmodern cultural surround, a considerable body of writing from the perspective of postmodernism has been accumulating" (Irving and Young, 2002). Thus, logical positivism's dominance in social work is being challenged (Dean, 1993; Greene and Blundo, 1999; Weick, 1987).

Postmodernism is based on the assumption that language is used to construct our perceptions of reality (Greene, Jensen, and Jones, 1996). "Constructivism is the belief that we cannot know an objective reality apart from our views of it.... Knowledge is not so much discovered as created" (Dean, 1993, p. 58). With postmodernism, the emphasis is on the experiences of individuals and their perceptions of experiences, as well as on the social aspects of knowing and the influence of cultural, historical, political, and economic conditions (Dean, 1993). The interpersonal and interactional aspects of an individual's experiences are stressed. Individuals' perceptions are influenced by their communities and social environment. The individual cannot be separated from his or her interactions with others.

In sharp contrast to logical positivists, postmodernists argue that it is impossible to distinguish facts from values. "Reality is invented, constructed largely out of meanings and values of the observer" (Allen, 1993, p. 32). The constructivist perspective is not value free; rather, it is value based (Murphy, 1989). Values, not objective facts, become the central issue of treatment (Allen, 1993; Dean, 1992). The values and attitudes of both the client and the social worker determine what facts are relevant and how they are interpreted. This perspective explicitly recognizes the importance of values in the helping process and encourages their exploration.

Social workers operating under the postmodernist perspective recognize that understanding comes through dialogue and communication with the client. The client is the expert who is most knowledgeable about his or her life situation. The social worker also recognizes that he or she is a coparticipant in the quest for meaning. Worker–client interactions are characterized as collaborative conversations designed to create mutual understanding of the client's life events and issues. "For clients, participating in a dialogue with workers can be both empowering and self-determining..." (Irving and Young, 2002). The exploration of each participant's values and beliefs and the process of hearing the client's story are the basis on which the worker–client relationship is developed. Postmodernism

- Highlights the importance of clients' subjective perceptions of their experiences
- Places clients in the role of expert about their life experiences and potential solutions
- Recognizes that clients' perceptions of their experiences are shaped by their culture and social environment
- Views the ongoing dialogue between the social worker and the client as fundamental to the change process
- Requires an open discussion of the social worker's and client's values and beliefs
- Recognizes that meaning is developed through the process of interaction between the worker and the client
- Stresses the collaborative aspects of the worker–client relationship

ECOSYSTEMS PERSPECTIVE

The ecosystems perspective has been widely adopted as one of the primary conceptual bases of social work practice (Compton and Galaway, 1994; Meyer, 1988). Indeed, one could easily argue that it has been the dominant framework of social work practice since the mid-1970s. The ecosystems perspective fits in well with social work's long-standing mission to address the situational and environmental factors that negatively affect disadvantaged persons.

The heart of the ecosystems perspective is the **person-in-environment concept,** which views individuals and their environments as an interrelated whole (Germain and Gitterman, 1980). "Individuals are perceived as a system composed of biological, psychological (including cognitive), and emotional dimensions. Also, individuals are perceived as interacting with a variety of external systems, such as immediate family, extended family, peers, work or school, and community" (Jordan and Franklin, 1995, p. 5).

The person-in-environment perspective recognizes the interdependence of these various systems. The relationship between individuals and their social environment is reciprocal, with each component in the client's system affecting and being affected by the others. The social environment influences individuals' perceptions of themselves and their interactions with others. Individuals, in turn, influence their social environment (Sullivan, 1992).

In the ecosystems perspective, "understanding the nature of the ecological level of fit between a person's needs, capacities, and aspirations, on the one hand, and environmental resources and expectations, on the other, is the core task in assessing individuals' and collectives' life situations" (Gitterman, 1996, p. 475). The ecosystem perspective "helps the practitioner to see that all aspects of an individual's problem involve circular connections between the individual and environment, leading to a 'transactional focus' for practice that is consistent with social work's dual concern with person and environment" (Wakefield, 1996, p. 6).

A defining characteristic of social work practice, and one that sets it apart from most other helping professions, is the importance given to improving clients' person-in-environment transactions to facilitate their growth, health, and social functioning (Gordon, 1981):

> In attempting to understand a problem in social functioning, you cannot achieve understanding by adding together, as separate entities, the assessment of the individual and the assessment of the environment. Rather you must strive for a full understanding of the complex interactions between client and all levels of social systems as well as the meaning the client assigns to these interactions. (Compton and Galaway, 1994, p. 118)

The ecosystems perspective recognizes the role of the worker in the client's environmental system (Germain and Gitterman, 1980). Worker–client transactions are viewed as a component of the client's ecological system (Figure 2.1). Interactions between the worker and the client and between the worker and the client's social environment become part of the client's dynamic person-in-environment system. Shulman (1991) portrayed the social worker as "in the middle," between the client and the systems he or she must negotiate. However, this puts the client in "a reactive, secondary role vis-à-vis the worker" (Petr, 1988, p. 624) and portrays the worker as intervening on behalf of the client and responsible for effecting change in the client. In this respect, mutuality and reciprocity do not characterize the worker–client relationship. The interaction is, instead, unidirectional, flowing from worker to client. This is not the case in strengths-based generalist practice.

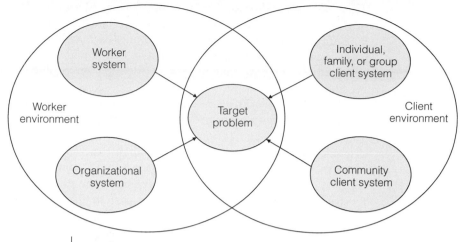

FIGURE 2.1 | PERSON-IN-ENVIRONMENT ASSESSMENT

STRENGTHS PERSPECTIVE

The idea of building on clients' strengths received a lot of attention during the 1990s. It is still fashionable to claim adherence to "the strengths perspective." However, as Saleebey put it:

> Many of these calls to attend to the capacities and competencies of clients are little more than professional cant. So let us be clear: The strengths perspective is a dramatic departure from conventional social work practice. Practicing from a strengths orientation means this—everything you do as a social worker will be predicated, in some way, on helping to discover and embellish, explore and exploit clients' strengths and resources. (2002, p. 1)

The strengths perspective is a dramatic departure from the traditional approach, which focuses primarily on client problems and history taking (Hepworth, Rooney, and Larsen, 2002, p. 198). Social work has a long history of helping disadvantaged clients overcome individual problems and problem situations. Clients come to us with problems, and there is a natural tendency to attempt to resolve the problems and to view the clients from a deficit perspective. Maluccio (1979) found that social workers' perceptions were in stark contrast with their clients' self-perceptions. The clients viewed themselves as proactive, autonomous human beings who were using counseling services to enhance their functioning and competence. In contrast, social workers tended to underestimate clients' strengths, focusing on their problems, underlying weaknesses, and limited potential.

When social workers focus on problems, they tend to perceive clients in essentially negative terms, as a collection of problems and diagnostic labels. This negative perception may lower expectations for positive change. More likely than not, clients are seen as diagnostic categories or their presenting problems, or both. These labels may create distance between clients and helpers (Saleebey, 2002, p. 5).

They also create pessimism in both parties. Negative labels and expectations obscure the unique capabilities of clients. The social worker's ability to recognize and promote a client's potential for change is markedly reduced. The focus is on what is wrong and the client's inability to cope with his or her life situation. Saleebey (2002) suggests that instead of focusing on problems, we should focus on possibilities.

The pathologic problem approach searches the past for causes. How did the client get into this situation? Why is the client experiencing these difficulties? The search for causes and rational explanations assumes a direct link between cause, disease, and cure (Saleebey, 2002). Human experience is rarely that simple. More often than not, it is uncertain and tremendously complex. In addition, looking to the past diverts attention away from exploring the present. The shift from problems to strengths moves the focus from the past to the present and future. Strengths-oriented social workers seek to discover the resources clients currently have that can be used to change their futures. The past cannot be completely dismissed, because it provides a context for the present. However, in strengths-based practice the focus is on the present and the future.

Social work has a long tradition of dealing with problems as ordinary aspects of human life. The profession's early efforts in charity organizations and settlement houses developed "family-oriented and community-oriented strategies to help those who were caught in the tide of major social upheaval" (Weick and Chamberlain, 1997, p. 40). However, during the 1940s, social problems and problems of everyday life were redefined as complex intrapsychic pathologic factors. "Psychological and psychiatric theories made human actions mysterious, complex, and rarely what they seemed" (Weick and Chamberlain, 1997, p. 41). Psychological definitions of problems and the focus on why a pathologic situation occurred have become the dominant perspective in social work, diverting attention from the "profession's historic commitment to working with people in the midst of their daily lives" (Weick and Chamberlain, 1997, p. 42).

Rather than focusing on why clients are having problems, social workers who have adopted a strengths perspective ask these questions:

> What do clients want? What do they need? How do they think they can get it? How do they see their situation—problems as well as possibilities? What values do they want to maximize? How have they managed to survive thus far? (Saleebey, 2002, p. 6)

These and similar questions will help you and your clients identify, use, build, and reinforce clients' strengths, resources, and abilities.

PRINCIPLES OF STRENGTHS-BASED PRACTICE*

Six principles guide strengths-based generalist practice (Saleebey, 2002). They also link the strengths perspective to the core values of the profession. "Social work practice is not only about whether and how to intervene or about skills and

---

*From Saleebey, Dennis (Ed.). Strengths Perspective in Social Work Practice, 3rd ed. Published by Allyn and Bacon, Boston, MA. Copyright © 2002 by Pearson Education. Reprinted by permission of the publisher.

techniques, but also about our entire attitude and stance toward the world, others, and human relations..." (Irving and Young, 2002).

Principle 1: Every individual, group, family, and community has strengths.
Regardless of the situation, every person, family, and community possesses assets, resources, wisdom, and knowledge that you need to discover (Saleebey, 2002). To become aware of these strengths, you need to be genuinely interested in your clients and respectful of their perceptions of their own experiences:

> In the end, clients want to know that you actually care about them, that how they fare makes a difference to you, that you will listen to them, that you will respect them no matter what their history, and that you believe that they can build something of value with the resources within and around them. But most of all, clients want to know that you believe they can surmount adversity and begin the climb toward transformation and growth. (Saleebey, 2002, p. 14)

The ultimate key to identifying client strengths is your belief in the client and his or her possibilities. Adopting a strengths perspective requires you to view your clients as underused sources of knowledge and untapped resources.

Principle 2: Trauma, abuse, illness, and struggle may be injurious, but they may also be sources of challenge and opportunity.
Dwelling on clients' pasts and hardships promotes "an image of themselves as helpless in the past, which then [becomes] the basis for fault-finding and continued helplessness in the present" (Wolin and Wolin, 1993, p. 14). Focusing on past hurts and deficits leads to discouragement, pessimism, and what Wolin and Wolin (1993) call the "victim trap." What is more extraordinary is that your clients have survived and that they are working with you to bring about changes in their lives. There is dignity and affirmation in having prevailed over trauma, abuse, illness, and other difficult situations. The strength of having survived and coped with numerous obstacles is often lost on clients who are struggling to meet life's daily challenges. A strengths approach recognizes clients' inherent competencies, resilience, and resourcefulness in having survived past difficulties as well as their current motivation for growth and development.

Principle 3: Assume that you do not know the upper limits of the capacity to grow and change, and take individual, group, and community aspirations seriously.
Simply put, this means that you should set high expectations for your clients and help expand their hopes, visions, and aspirations. The strengths perspective is the perspective of hope and possibilities. Believe in clients' capacities for change, growth, and self-actualization. If you do not believe in their abilities and motivation, you really do not believe in the possibility of change. Creating hope where there is little to hope for, strengthening belief when there is little to believe in, and creating aspirations where there are none are the essence of social work practice from a strengths perspective.

Principle 4: We best serve clients by collaborating with them.
The strengths perspective calls for a partnership characterized by reciprocity and mutual respect

between you and your client. There should be a sharing of knowledge and resources. You are not the sole expert or the only one with specialized information; your client is the expert who knows more about coping with his or her situation than you do:

> A helper may best be defined as a collaborator or consultant: an individual clearly presumed, because of specialized education and experience, to know some things and to have some tools at the ready but definitely not the only one in the situation to have relevant, even esoteric, knowledge and understanding. (Saleebey, 2002, p. 16)

Take advantage of the wisdom, insights, and understanding your clients bring to the helping process by entering into a collaborative partnership with them. The strengths approach to social work practice requires it. Work with your clients in partnership. Do not presume to work on your clients or to do the work for them.

Principle 5: Every environment is full of resources.   No matter how deprived a client's community, neighborhood, or family system, each has an abundance of untapped resources. "In every environment, there are individuals, associations, groups, and institutions who have something to give, something that others may desperately need: knowledge, succor, an actual resource or talent, or simply time and place" (Saleebey, 2002, p. 17). Looking to these untapped resources does not negate our responsibility to work for social and economic justice, and it does not mean that we accept the notion that a disadvantaged person should assume sole responsibility for his or her situation and its amelioration. It does mean, however, that the possibilities for identifying and arranging needed resources for clients from within their own environment are more numerous than you would expect.

Principle 6: Caring, caretaking, and context are important.   Caring for others and being cared for is a basic human right. "Families must be permitted and assisted in caring for their members" (Saleebey, 2002, p. 17, citing Stone, 2000). Caring strengthens our social web, our interconnectedness. Social work is a caring profession, and the strengths perspective recognizes and embraces our dependence upon others for our well-being.

Case 2.1 illustrates how Dawn W., a first-year social work student, built on her client's strengths to further his treatment goals.

ATTACHMENT THEORY

Attachment theory is one of the most empirically tested theories of human behavior (Rholes and Simpson, 2004). Bowlby (1982, 1988) proposed that infants have innate needs for closeness with others. Infants' need for closeness is related to their feeling safe and protected. Bowlby proposed that a secure attachment with an adult enabled the infant to explore the world, learn and grow, and return to a secure base when threatened or frightened. Ainsworth (1989) extended attachment theory to adult relationships. "Both Bowlby (1988) and Ainsworth (1989) believed that attachments formed in childhood influence one's inclination and ability to establish close and mature relationships throughout the lifespan" (Bennett, Mohr, BrintzenhofeSzoc, and Saks, 2008, p. 76).

CASE 2.1 | NO TIME FOR ME

John R. is an 11-year-old boy with behavior management problems. He has attention deficit hyperactivity disorder and has a great deal of difficulty controlling his impulses. He is socially immature. His peers usually make fun of him and reject him. He usually plays with much younger children. In addition to his behavior problems, he has a very difficult family situation. His mother lives out of state. He lives with his father, stepmother, and 18-month-old stepsister. His stepmother resents his presence in the family and the difficulties he causes her.

John is a student at an alternative school, where he is in a special behavior modification program. Dawn W. is John's social worker at the school and is also assigned to work with the family. The behavior management program is working well, but John's relationship with his stepmother is undermining his progress at home. The stepmother refuses to follow the treatment plan and is very rejecting. In fact, she openly tells John that he is bad and that she does not want him anywhere near his stepsister. While at home, John is generally either being punished or is alone in his room.

One of the treatment goals is to improve the relationship between John and his stepmother. Dawn recognized that one of John's strengths is that he is very good with young children. He is thoughtful and caring and has a nice way of engaging them in play. Dawn suggests to John's stepmother that she allow him to take care of his little sister for one hour a day. The plan is to have Dawn supervise John for the first week or until the stepmother is comfortable with John's ability to care for his sister.

The intervention is successful. John takes care of his little sister well, and his appreciation of being allowed to play with and care for her is evident. His stepmother's confidence in and patience with him improves. John's self-esteem appears to improve, as does his overall relationship with his stepmother. By recognizing one of John's strengths and enlisting that strength in the case plan, Dawn ensures progress on a critical treatment goal.

Bowlby (1988) viewed attachment as an evolutionary need to bond with other human beings for the purpose of survival. The child's early relationship experiences become an "internal working model" of attachment based upon internalized conceptualizations of the quality of the relationship (Marvin, Cooper, Hoffman, and Powell, 2002). "A child who has a 'secure' model of attachment has an internal representation of a sensitively attuned and secure caregiver who has enabled the child to feel worthy of care and able to depend on significant others. However, a child with an attachment figure who is dismissing, unpredictable, or frightening develops an 'insecure' working model, defined as an 'avoidant', 'resistant', or 'disorganized' model of attachment" (Bennett, 2008, p. 98).

Attachment theory postulates that attachment process lie at the center of the human experience throughout the life span (Schore and Schore, 2008). The innate need to bond with others makes human relationships central (Ecke, Chope, and Emmelkamp, 2006). "Attachment theorists postulate that people with secure attachment tend to more easily engage in intimate relationships than people with anxious or fearful attachment" (Johnson, Ketring, Rohacs, and Brewer, 2006, p. 206). "Bowlby (1988) noted that an infant's 'secure base' with an attachment figure triggers the infant's exploration of the wider world, and similarly, a client's secure base with a therapist facilitates exploration within the therapeutic process" (Bennett, 2008, p. 97). Thus, attachment theory is central to the helping relationship and generalist social work practice with individuals, families, and small groups (Dozier, Cue, and Barnett, 1994; von Sydow, 2002). It also has relevance for social work practice with organizations and communities indirectly through the need to develop relationships with organizational and community stakeholders.

Ainsworth, Belhar, Waters, and Wall (1978) identified four forms of childhood attachment: Secure, Insecure Avoidant, Insecure Anxious Resistant, and Disorganized. The four commonly used classifications of adult patterns of attachment are Secure, Dismissive, Preoccupied, and Unresolved (George and West, 2001). A number of measures have been developed to assess adult attachment. *The Handbook of Attachment* (Cassidy and Shaver, 1999) discusses them in detail and is an excellent source for finding measures that can be used in practice with clients. Most measures are self-report instruments that assess the respondents' perceptions of attachment. The Attachment History Questionnaire (Pottharst, 1990) and the Reciprocal Attachment Questionnaire for Adults (West and Sheldon-Keller, 1992) can be easily incorporated in the assessment of adult clients' attachment patterns.

CRITICAL THINKING AND GENERALIST SOCIAL WORK PRACTICE

Critical thinking is more than a rational step-by-step problem solving process (Gibbons and Gray, 2004). It involves an intuitive process as well as disciplined evaluation and analysis (Dean, 1993). Thinking critically includes the synthesis, comparison and evaluation of ideas from a variety of sources, such as texts, direct observation and experience and social dialogue (Gibbons and Gray, 2004). A critical thinking social worker attempts to understand the client systems' perception of their reality and how their perceptions inform their work together. Critical thinking in social work practice is "the process of figuring out what to believe or not about a situation, phenomenon, problem or controversy for which no single definitive answer exists" (Mumm and Kersting, 1997, p. 75). Social work practice is by definition a process in which there is no definitive answer. Effective social work practice requires critical thinking. A key component of generalist social work practice is formulating hypotheses and critically assessing them to better understand the client system. Practice interventions and/or strategies flow out of our understanding of the client's perception of their situation and social reality. Critical thinking is the open-minded search for understanding, rather than the discovery of a necessary conclusion (Mumm and Kersting, 1997, p. 75).

Heron (2006) identified key features of critical thinking. "Instead of viewing critical thinking as having separate features, it may be more useful to present them as being linked and cyclical in nature" (p. 221). Critical thinking is a process with the center of the cycle focused on explaining the why. Heron's (2006) conceptualization focuses on an explanation of why a phenomenon is significant. The process includes "providing evidence, examining the implications of the evidence, recognizing any potential contradictions and examining alternative explanations" (p. 221). The four components—**evidence**, **implications**, **contradictions**, and **alternative explanations**—are linked, and the critical thinking process can begin with any one of the four components.

EVIDENCE-BASED PRACTICE

Associated with critical thinking is the process of considering evidence when making decisions (Gambrill, 2003). **Evidence-Based Practice** (EBP) broadly defined is the use of current best evidence in making decisions about social work practice with clients (Gibbs and Grambrill, 2002). Gossett and Weinman (2007) state that "in an era in which social workers must defend their domain from encroaching disciplines, adding the role of evidence-based practitioner to the plethora of other social work roles is fundamental" (p. 147). Clearly, EBP has become a critical component of generalist social work practice.

Walker, Briggs, Koroloff, and Friesen (2007) point out that there are two kinds of knowledge that social workers must balance in making informed decisions about their work with clients. The first is "empirically based knowledge generated through the scientific method" (p. 361). The second is "knowledge that is acquired through relationships with unique individuals (or unique groups like families, communities and organizations)" (pp. 361–362). Balancing of the two types of knowledge allows social workers to move forward and make decisions with "reasonable confidence while also acknowledging uncertainty" (p. 362). Currently, there are a number of variations in terms of how EPB is defined. Rubin and Parrish (2007) offer the five-step model. The steps include:

1. Formulating an answerable question regarding practice needs
2. Tracking down the best evidence available to answer the question
3. Critically appraising the scientific validity and usefulness of the evidence
4. Integrating the appraisal with one's clinical expertise and client values and circumstances, and then applying it to practice decisions
5. Evaluating outcomes (with the use of single-case designs if feasible) (p. 407)

It is important to differentiate the five-step EBP definition from the more narrowly defined term of **empirically supported treatment** (EST) (Walker, Briggs, Koroloff, and Friesen, 2007). EBP represents a process of approaching your work with clients that incorporates critical thinking and the use of best available evidence to make practice decisions. EST refers to the use of empirically tested treatment interventions. Social workers employing EBP may or may not incorporate EST in their work with clients. The use of EST is based upon a critical assessment of client need, worker training, skill level, and the availability of an appropriate EST. A number of ESTs are described in Parts II and III of this book.

SUMMARY

The ecosystems perspective is one of two primary frameworks guiding the model of generalist social work practice presented in this book. The heart of the ecosystems perspective is the person-in-environment concept. Clients are not viewed in isolation but rather within the context of their environments. The focus is on the level of fit between the client system and the environment and on improving person-in-environment transactions to facilitate growth, empowerment, health, and social and economic justice. The strengths perspective is the second framework or philosophical perspective guiding the model of generalist social work practice presented in this book. The strengths perspective provides a lens for viewing client situations that is very different

CASE 2.2   DON'T ROCK THE BOAT

Jill is a first-year MSW student who has been placed in an after-school program for emotionally disturbed children. The program is run by a comprehensive mental health agency that offers a wide range of services for children and adults. The agency is a subsidiary of a larger organization that owns and operates a large number of inpatient and outpatient mental health facilities. The after-school program has two full-time social workers, a case aide, a half-time supervisor, and a quarter-tie program administrator. Approximately 20 children with emotional and behavioral problems are provided with on-site services five days a week and in-home services once a week.

Because of a technicality, the program lost its primary source of funding and was slated to close. Jill found out about the pending closing of the program from her supervisor. She was told not to tell the other staff or the children. The program administrator had decided that it was best for the children, their parents,

and the staff not to know in advance about the closing.

Jill was concerned about the children's need to have enough time to deal with their feelings about leaving the program and about the parents' needs to have time to make other arrangements for the treatment and after-school care of their children. She also wondered how the lack of process about closing the program would affect the staff and their morale.

Jill believed that the well-being of the children was being subjugated to the perceived needs of the agency. She suspected that the agency administrator felt that telling the children and their parents would upset them and that the children would act out more than usual during the time remaining in the program. She also suspected that he wanted to avoid having the parents put pressure on the agency to continue the program. It appeared to her that the closing policy was designed to protect the agency from disruption at the expense of the children and their parents.

---

from the traditional problem-focused approaches to social work practice. From the strengths perspective, the helping process emphasizes client strengths and resources as opposed to limitations and deficits. The client rather than the social worker is recognized as the expert. The focus of strengths-based generalist practice is on developing partnerships, empowerment, and collaboration.

Attachment theory is one of the most empirically tested theories of human behavior. Attachment theory postulates that the attachment process lie at the center of the human experience throughout the life span. The innate need to bond with others makes human relationships central to

the human experience and generalist social work practice with individuals, families, small groups.

Thinking critically includes the synthesis, comparison, and evaluation of ideas from a variety of sources, such as texts, direct observation and experience, and social dialogue. A critical thinking social worker attempts to understand the client systems' perception of their reality and how their perceptions inform their work together. Evidence-Based Practice (EBP) broadly defined is the use of current best evidence in making decisions about social work practice with clients. EBP involves a five-step process that can or cannot include the use of Evidence-Supported Treatment.

CASE EXAMPLE

The final case in this chapter (Case 2.3) was written by Daniel Lafferty when he was a first-year MSW student. It describes one client with whom he worked in his field placement. The case illustrates the differences between a strengths-based approach and the traditional deficit approach.

CASE 2.3 | **UNDER A CLOUD**
by Daniel Lafferty

Practice Setting

The Parents and Children Together (PACT) program functions as a family preservation agency whose main mission is to support family well-being, prevent child abuse and neglect, and promote optimal child development. This mission is carried out via parenting skills training, family needs assessments, and assisting clients to assess needed resources. Clients are referred to the program through Children and Youth Services (CYS), the county public child welfare agency. The referral objectives are to prepare parents to be reunited with children that have been placed in foster care due to abuse or neglect or to prevent the removal of at-risk children from their homes by helping their parents to learn better parenting skills. PACT clients are expected to participate in agency-based parenting skills training every other week. In addition, home visits are scheduled for nonprogram weeks, so that clients can demonstrate learned parenting skills in the family's natural environment.

Problem Situation

Mr. J. is a 34-year-old single white man who works part-time as a construction worker. He was referred to the PACT program by CYS following his daughter's placement in foster care due to neglect. Mr. J.'s daughter was three years old and living with her mother at the time of placement. Since then, Mr. J. has made it known that he intends to seek custody of his daughter. Mr. J. has been working with the staff at PACT, attending parenting classes, and meeting with his daughter for one-hour supervised home visits every two weeks in preparation for this goal. Because Mr. J. was separated from his daughter during the years prior to her foster care placement, he is interested in building a father–daughter relationship with her that can result in his being awarded full custody of his daughter.

History of Problem Situation

Mr. J. states that in 1992 he became involved in an intimate relationship. After a few months, his paramour informed him that she was pregnant. The couple continued to live together after their daughter was born. Three months after the birth of their daughter, Mr. J.'s paramour took their daughter and left to live with her parents because Mr. J. "refused to become a born-again Christian." Following this separation,

Mr. J. had only sporadic involvement with his daughter. For the first three years of his daughter's life, the girl's mother reportedly denied him contact for religious reasons.

Mr. J. states that when he attempted to have contact with his daughter, he noticed that she was being neglected by her mother. He claims that on several occasions he made reports to CYS about his concerns, but none of the agency's investigations established a case of neglect until the last one, in February, 1997. At that time, his daughter was found to be extremely developmentally delayed and showed signs of emotional and medical neglect. Mr. J.'s daughter was placed in foster care as a result of these findings. Since that time, she has made remarkable progress. The mother is described as suffering from a serious mental illness. She has not made any attempts to regain custody of her daughter to date.

Following his daughter's placement in foster care, Mr. J. began working with CYS and the PACT program in an attempt to gain custody. Due to the early and lengthy separation between Mr. J. and his daughter, it was decided that they needed time to form a parent–child relationship before custody could be considered. Although progress has been made in this regard, Mr. J. believes the process has been slower than necessary because of restrictive handling of his case by CYS.

There are several reasons why the CYS staff appears to be reluctant about Mr. J. gaining custody of his daughter. Mr. J. has a significant substance abuse history (about 20 years of marijuana abuse), and questions have been raised about his mental health. Over six months ago, Mr. J. decided to seek treatment for his marijuana use. Recently, he completed a residential rehabilitation program and subsequent outpatient substance abuse treatment. He claims to have abstained from all substance abuse since entering rehab.

At the present time, questions about Mr. J's mental health status remain unanswered. Psychiatric assessments have been conflicting. Mr. J.'s substance use at the time of some of these evaluations may have contributed to the findings. The CYS worker assigned to the case has serious concerns about his mental health. The general opinion of the PACT staff is that Mr. J. does not suffer from a major mental

(Continued)

CASE 2.3 | *Continued*

disorder, although at times he does exhibit character traits consistent with a dependent personality disorder. The CYS worker is also concerned about his employment situation and his ability to provide full-time care for his daughter.

Current Situation

Mr. J. has been consistent in visiting his daughter. He has attended all of the scheduled parent training classes and has met with his PACT social worker weekly. He is very motivated to establish a strong parent–child relationship and obtain custody of his daughter. He is looking for a full-time job, but the parenting classes and visitation schedule make it difficult for him to do so.

Mr. J.'s interactions with his daughter at the PACT program and during their visits are appropriate. His daughter appears to be comfortable with him, and their relationship is growing stronger. She seems to enjoy the visits and talks positively about going to live with her father.

The CYS worker continues to have concerns about Mr. J.'s suitability as a full-time parent and is very reluctant to increase his visitation privileges. The foster mother has become very attached to the daughter and has indicated that she wants to adopt her if possible. The foster mother does not seem to approve of having Mr. J. visit his daughter. She claims that it upsets the child and that she has no interest in visiting with her father. The foster mother frequently finds excuses to cancel the scheduled visits.

Client System Obstacles and Strengths

The impact of certain obstacles is evident in the problem situation of this client. Mr. J.'s substance abuse history complicates the custody issues. If he relapses, the child may be at risk for further neglect. The extent of Mr. J.'s marijuana use appears to have created a negative impression of him among some of the staff in the child protection system. Another potential obstacle is the recent revelation that the foster mother may wish to adopt Mr. J.'s daughter. This has put a strain on the visits (she brings Mr. J.'s daughter to the visits), and it seems that she has the support of the CYS worker assigned to the case.

Mr. J.'s use of marijuana on an almost daily basis since he was 11 years old may have had serious implications for his developmental life stages. It is not surprising that he appears immature in certain life domains. Addressing this issue will be important if Mr. J. is to gain insight into the source of some of his difficulties, especially with interpersonal relationships.

Mr. J.'s strengths include his decision to discontinue his substance use, the recent establishment of a healthier support system, weekly drug and alcohol and mental health counseling, having an AA/NA sponsor, PACT staff who are helping to increase the quality and number of visits with his daughter, and his supportive parents, who assist with these visits. In addition, Mr. J.'s expressed commitment to be reunited with his daughter is a real strength. He has been very cooperative with the demands that CYS has made on him in the interest of this goal.

Discussion Questions

1. Identify the various system levels associated with Mr. J.'s case. How does each system affect his attempts to obtain custody of his daughter?
2. What additional services or interventions might be appropriate for Mr. J.? To what extent has Dan been an advocate for Mr. J. in gaining custody of his daughter? How might Dan have strengthened his advocacy services? (For more information on social work advocacy, see Schneider and Lester, 2001).
3. Apply the six principles of strengths-based practice to Mr. J.'s case. How does viewing the case from a strengths perspective differ from the child protective worker's perspective?
4. What factors in Mr. J.'s background potentially influence his relationship with the PACT social worker? How might the social worker strengthen the helping relationship?
5. What additional information would you want to obtain if you were the social worker assigned to this case? What unanswered questions do you have about the case?

References

Allen, J. A. (1993). The constructivist paradigm: Values and ethics. In Joan Laird (Ed.), *Revisioning social work education: A social constructionist approach* (pp. 31–54). New York: Haworth.

Ainsworth, M., Belhar, M., Waters, E., and Wall, S. (1978). *Patterns of attachment: A psychological study of the strange situation.* Oxford, England: Lawrence Erlbaum.

Ainsworth, M. (1989). Attachments beyond infancy. *American Psychologist, 44,* 709–716.

Baker, R. L. (1995). The social work dictionary (3rd ed.). Washington, DC: NASW Press.

Bennett, S. (2008). Attachment-informed supervision for social work field education. *Clinical Social Work Journal, 36,* 97–107.

Bennett, S., Mohr, J., BrintzenhofeSzoc, K., and Saks, L. (2008). General and supervision-specific attachment styles: Relations to student perceptions of field supervisors. *Journal of Social Work Education, 44,* 75–94.

Bowlby, J. (1982). *Attachment and loss: Vol. 1. Attachment* (2nd ed.). New York: Basic Books.

Bowlby, J. (1988). *A secure base.* New York: Basic Books.

Cassidy, J., and Shaver, P. (1999). *Handbook of attachment: Theory, research, and clinical applications.* New York: The Guilford Press.

Chambon, A., and Irving, A. (Eds.) (1994). *Essays on postmodernism and social work.* Toronto: Canadian Scholars' Press.

Dean, R. G. (1992). Constructivism: An approach to clinical practice. *Smith College Studies in Social Work, 63,* 405–414.

Dean, R. G. (1993). Teaching a constructivist approach to clinical practice. In Joan Laird (Ed.), *Revisioning social work education: A social constructionist approach* (pp. 55–75). New York: Haworth.

Dozier, M., Cue, K., and Barnett, L. (1994). Clinicians as caregivers: Role of attachment organization in treatment. *Journal of Counseling & Clinical Psychology, 62,* 793–800.

Fischer, J. (1981). The social work revolution. *Social Work, 26,* 199–207.

Gambrill, E. (2003). Evidence-based practice: Sea change or the emperor's new clothes? *Journal of Social Work Education, 39,* 3–24.

George, C., and West, M. (2001). The development and preliminary validation of a new measure of adult attachment: The Adult Attachment Projective. *Attachment and Human Development, 3,* 55–86.

Germain, C. B., and Gitterman, A. (1980). *The life model of social work practice.* New York: Columbia University Press.

Gibbons, J., and Gray, M. (2004). Critical thinking as integral to social work practice. *Journal of Teaching in Social Work, 24,* 19–38.

Gibbs, L., and Gambrill, E. (2002). Evidence-based practice: Counterarguments to objections. *Research on Social Work Practice, 12,* 452–476.

Gitterman, A. (1996). Ecological perspective: Response to Professor Jerry Wakefield. *Social Service Review, 70,* 472–476.

Gordon, W. E. (1981). A natural classification system for social work literature and knowledge. *Social Work, 26,* 134–136.

Gossett, M., and Weinman, M. (2007). Evidence-based practice and social work: An illustration of the steps involved. *Health & Social Work, 32,* 147–150.

Greene, G. J., Jensen, C., and Jones, D. H. (1996). A constructivist perspective on clinical social work practice with ethnically diverse clients. *Social Work, 41,* 172–180.

Greene, R. R., and Blundo, R. (1999). Postmodern critique of systems theory in social work with the aged and their families. *Journal of Gerontological Social Work, 31,* 87–100.

Hepworth, D., Rooney, R., and Larsen, J. (2002). *Direct social work practice: Theory and skills* (6th ed.). Pacific Grove, CA: Brooks/Cole.

Heron, G. (2006). Critical thinking in social care and social work: Searching student assignments for the evidence. *Social Work Education, 25,* 209–224.

Hudson, W. (1982). Scientific imperatives in social work research and practice. *Social Service Review, 56,* 246–258.

Irving, A., and Young, T. (2002). Paradigm for pluralism: Mikhail Bakhtin and social work practice. *Social Work, 47,* 19–29.

Johnson, L., Ketring, S., Rohacs, J., and Brewer, A. (2006). Attachment and the therapeutic alliance in family therapy. *The American Journal of Family Therapy, 34,* 205–218.

Jordan, C., and Franklin, C. (1995). *Clinical assessment for social workers: Quantitative and qualitative methods.* Chicago: Lyceum.

Maluccio, A. (1979). Perspectives of social workers and clients on treatment outcome. *Social Casework*, 60, 394–401.

Marvin, R., Cooper, G., Hoffman, K., and Powell, B. (2002). The circle of security project: Attachment-based interventions with care-giver-pre-school child dyads. *Attachment & Human Development*, 4, 107–124.

Meyer, C. H. (1988). The ecosystems perspective. In R. A. Dorfman (Ed.), *Paradigms of clinical social work* (pp. 275–294). New York: Brunner/Mazel.

Mumm, A., and Kersting, R. (1997). Teaching critical thinking in social work practice. *Journal of Social Work Education*, 33, 75–84.

Murphy, J. W. (1989). Clinical intervention in the postmodern world. *International Journal of Adolescence and Youth*, 2, 61–69.

Murphy, J., and Pardeck, J. (1998). Renewing social work practice through a postmodern perspective. *Social Thought: Journal of Religion in the Social Services*, 18, 5–19.

Petr, C. (1988). The worker–client relationship: A general systems perspective. *Social Casework*, 69, 620–626.

Pottharst, K. (1990). The search for methods and measures. In K. Pottharst (Ed.), *Explorations in adult attachment* (pp. 9–37). New York: Peter Lang.

Reamer, F. G. (1983). Ethical dilemmas in social work practice. *Social Work*, 32, 31–35.

Reid, W. (1994). The empirical practice movement. *Social Service Review*, 68, 165–184.

Richmond, M. (1917). *Social diagnosis*. New York: Russell Sage.

Rholes, S., and Simpson, J. (Eds.). (2004). Attachment theory: Basic concepts and contemporary questions. In S. Rholes and J. Simpson (Eds.), *Adult attachment: Theory, research and clinical implications* (pp. 3–14). New York: Guilford Press.

Rubin, A., and Parrish, D. (2007). Challenges to the future of evidence-based practice in social work. *Journal of Social Work Education*, 43, 405–428.

Saleebey, D. (2002). *The strengths perspective in social work practice* (3rd ed.). Boston: Allyn and Bacon.

Schneider, R. L., and Lester, L. (2001). *Social work advocacy: A new framework for action*. Pacific Grove, CA: Wadsworth.

Schore, J., and Schore, A. (2008). Modern attachment theory: The central role of affect regulation in development and treatment. *Clinical Social Work Journal*, 36, 9–20.

Shulman, L. (1991). *Interactional social work practice: Toward an empirical theory*. Itasca, IL: F. E. Peacock Publishers, Inc.

Stone, D. (2000). Why we need a care movement. *The Nation*, 270, 13–15.

Sullivan, W. P. (1992). Reconsidering the environment as a helping resource. In D. Saleebey (Ed.), *The strengths perspective in social work practice* (pp. 148–157). New York: Longman.

van Ecke, Y., Chope, R., and Emmelkamp, P. (2006). Bowlby and Bowen: Attachment theory and family therapy. *Counseling and Clinical Psychology Journal*, 3, 81–108.

von Sydow, K. (2002). Systemic attachment theory and therapeutic practice: A proposal. *Clinical psychology and psychotherapy*, 9, 77–90.

Wakefield, J. C. (1996). Does social work need the ecosystems perspective? Part 1. Is the perspective clinically useful? *Social Service Review*, 70, 1–32.

Walker, J., Briggs, H., Koroloff, N., and Friesen, B. (2007). Implementing and sustaining evidence-based practice in social work. *Journal of Social Work Education*, 43, 361–375.

Weick, A. (1987). Beyond empiricism: Toward a holistic conception of social work. *Social Thought*, 13, 36–46.

Weick, A. (1993). Reconstructing social work education. In Joan Laird (Ed.), *Revisioning social work education: A social constructionist approach* (pp. 11–30). New York: Haworth.

Weick, A., and Chamberlain, R. (1997). Putting problems in their place: Further explorations in the strengths perspective. In D. Saleebey (Ed.), *The strengths perspective in social work practice* (2nd ed., pp. 39–48). New York: Longman.

Weick, A., and Saleebey, D. (1995). A post modern approach to social work practice. The 1995 Richard Lodge Memorial Lecture, Adelphi University School of Social Work, Garden City, NY, October 20.

Weick, A., and Saleebey, D. (1998). Postmodern perspectives for social work. *Social Thought: Journal of Religion in the Social Services*, 18, 21–40.

West, M., and Sheldon-Keller, A. (1992). The assessment of dimensions relevant to adult reciprocal attachment. *Canadian Journal of Psychiatry*, 37, 600–606.

Wolin, S. J., and Wolin, S. (1993). *The resilient self: How survivors of troubled families rise above adversity*. New York: Villard.

THE COLLABORATIVE MODEL PRINCIPLES AND CONCEPTS

CHAPTER **3**

Mark Richards/PhotoEdit

Julie V. was a first-year MSW student placed in a unit of a drug and alcohol rehabilitation center. Her unit provided discharge planning for patients who were leaving the facility. Typically, Julie had one or two contacts with her clients before they were discharged.

Before she entered the MSW program, Julie worked for two years in a foster care agency that served children who were in long-term placement. She spent a lot of time with her clients, and she felt that she got to know them and developed strong helping relationships with them. In contrast, her work at the rehabilitation center was fast paced and short-term. She had to complete the assessment and discharge plans after one or two brief client contacts.

By the end of her first week of placement, Julie was concerned about the effectiveness of her work. She felt that her approach was too task focused and that she was not making any connection with her clients. Instead, she was getting information as quickly as possible, filling out a form, and telling the clients about the plan. It felt rote and dehumanizing to her. She wondered what she could do to make the experience more positive for her clients and for herself. Was it possible, desirable, and important for her to engage her clients in the discharge planning process? Was it realistic to expect a positive helping relationship to develop in one or two brief contacts? How would the helping relationship in a short-term setting differ from one that developed over a longer period of time?

It is through the helping relationship and associated practice principles that social workers provide help and facilitate the change process. The helping relationship is the mechanism through which the client and the worker address the client's identified concerns. The helping relationship supports and structures clients' efforts to change. This chapter presents a model of generalist practice that focuses on the helping relationship. It begins with a review of the assumption of the collaborative model and its practice principles. The chapter concludes with a presentation of the phases, tasks, inputs, skills, and outputs of the model, followed by a review of the Helping Relationship Inventory, a rapid assessment instrument that measures the strength of the helping relationship.

By the end of this chapter, you should be able to help Julie

1. Conceptualize the helping relationship
2. Understand the importance of the helping relationship in the helping process
3. Describe the principles of a strengths-based assessment
4. Describe what is entailed in a collaborative approach to generalist practice
5. Identify ways to empower clients
6. Develop a rationale for using the Helping Relationship in work with clients

THEORETICAL PROPOSITIONS

The collaborative model of social work practice presented here is built upon three theoretical propositions and three practice principles. The propositions are:

1. Disadvantaged and oppressed clients often mistrust helping professionals
2. Client change occurs through a collaborative helping relationship
3. Relationships are built upon trust

Proposition 1: Disadvantaged and oppressed (reluctant) clients often mistrust helping professionals.   Alienation theory (Guillaumin, 1995; LaFromboise, Coleman, and Gerton, 1993) provides an explanation for the reluctance of oppressed and disadvantaged clients to fully engage in a helping relationship with social work professionals. People that are stigmatized and discriminated against on a continuous and systematic basis feel devalued by people who have power and occupy positions of authority in society (Fordham, 1996; LaFromboise and Dixon, 1981). A natural response to feelings of powerlessness, oppression, and devaluation is to distance oneself physically and emotionally from the oppressors. This sense of separateness or alienation can be viewed as a normal response or as a coping mechanism that helps protect the oppressed. Therefore, people who have experienced racism, discrimination, and other forms of oppression are unlikely to be willing to engage in an open and trusting relationship with a helping professional who, by virtue of her authority, has power and influence over their lives and well-being.

Most social work clients from disadvantaged communities have a long history of negative experiences with helping professionals and people in authority. They have learned to cope with "the system" by adopting a complying but noninvested style of interacting with it. At best, they become reluctant clients. Their experiences have conditioned them to be guarded with social work professionals and to approach them with mistrust. Marginalized people have no reason to trust social workers and other helping professionals. Overcoming mistrust is the primary obstacle faced by social workers working with marginalized client populations.

Proposition 2: Client change occurs through a collaborative helping relationship.   The helping relationship is the heart of the helping process. Several studies have examined the correlation between the client's ratings of the relationship and the outcome of therapy. In a meta-analysis of 24 of these studies, Horvath and Symonds (1991) found that client ratings were positively associated with positive therapeutic outcomes. Others have verified that this correlation occurs with at least three types of therapy: behavioral, cognitive-behavioral, and interpersonal (Dore and Alexander, 1996; Marziali and Alexander, 1991). A large study funded by the National Institute of Mental Health found strong correlations between relationship and outcome, regardless of the type of treatment provided (Krupnick et al., 1996). Thus, social work and psychology research consistently and convincingly support the association between development of a positive helping relationship and successful treatment outcomes.

Historically, the profession of social work has recognized that the success of the helping process is dependent on the quality of the worker–client relationship (Biestek, 1957; Hollis, 1970; Perlman, 1979; Richmond, 1917). Biestek (1954) characterized the helping relationship as the "soul" of the helping process, a dynamic interaction of feelings and attitudes between the worker and the client. Perlman (1979) defined the professional helping relationship as a supportive, compassionate working alliance between the worker and client. Drawing on Rogers' (1957) work, Perlman named five worker attributes necessary for the development of a therapeutic relationship: warmth, acceptance, empathy, caring-concern, and genuineness. Clients who experience their interactions with social workers as caring, empathic, nonjudgmental, and genuine are more likely to engage in the helping process and to develop a sense of trust than those who do not. Perlman's worker attributes have been widely accepted by the social work profession, and the importance of the worker–client relationship is a common assumption of social work practice. As with all assumptions, the importance of the helping relationship has been seen as a given rather than critically examined (Perlman, 1979). As early as 1979, Perlman noted that less and less attention was being paid to the helping relationship in social work research and practice literature. More recently, Coady observed "the continued neglect of relationship factors" in social work research (1993, p. 292). Although social work theory has consistently accorded the relationship between worker and client a central role in treatment, "the precise nature of this relationship and the manner in which it contributes to treatment has not been spelled out" (Proctor, 1982, p. 430).

Instead, social work research has for the most part focused on developing and testing models of intervention and on measuring outcomes (Reid, 1994). Much of the research conducted between 1970 and 1988 attempted to establish a scientific basis for clinical social work interventions (Russell, 1990). Social work practice research has consisted of outcome-oriented investigations that test the efficacy of structured interventions. There have been few direct studies of the helping relationship.

Most conceptual work and research on the helping relationship during the past 20 years has been done in the field of psychology (Dore and Alexander, 1996). It has been stimulated by the seminal ideas of Bordin (1979), who defined the construct of a therapeutic or working alliance. In social work, the focus has tended to be on the feeling dimension and on worker characteristics that promote positive feelings. In clinical psychology, on the other hand, the concept of the helping relationship has been expanded to include treatment goals and tasks (Hartley and Strupp, 1983; Horvath and Greenberg, 1986; Luborsky et al., 1983). These investigators view "the working alliance as a collaboration between the client and the therapist on the work of therapy" (Tichenor and Hill, 1989, p. 196). The relationship between therapist and client includes the specification of goals and agreed-on tasks for both the therapist and client, as well as the emotional bond between them.

In the collaborative model of generalist practice, the helping process has two components, which influence each other: a structural component and an interpersonal component (Poulin and Young, 1997). The **structural component** encompasses the purposeful activities or tasks undertaken to address the target concern or problem. The **interpersonal component** is the bond or mutual attraction that develops between the worker and the client. Both the structural and interpersonal need to develop for the helping relationship to be effective. The two components tend to develop concurrently. The process of collaborating on the structural activities builds and strengthens the interpersonal connection or psychological bond between the worker and the client. It takes time and the sharing of experiences to develop a strong interpersonal connection. The structural activities provide the interactions on which the interpersonal relationship is built. Through verbal and nonverbal interactions and collaborative efforts, the client experiences the worker as motivating and supportive.

As workers carry out structural activities, they should engage clients in an empowering collaborative process that is client centered. For example, during the initial sessions, the primary structural task is identifying concerns and strengths. The way the worker interacts with the client during this process profoundly influences

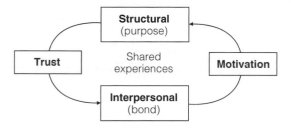

FIGURE 3.1   THE HELPING RELATIONSHIP PROCESS

the development of their interpersonal relationship. The worker should strive to motivate and support clients as they tell their stories. If the worker communicates understanding of the client's concerns and difficulties, provides comfort and calming strength, and pays attention to the client as a whole person, the client will probably experience the worker as supportive. This will in turn strengthen the client's interpersonal connection with the worker. Similarly, if the worker helps the client expand his or her self-understanding, strengthen his or her self-belief, and find hope and inspiration, the client will probably experience the worker as motivating. These experiences will also strengthen the psychological bond between the worker and the client.

Proposition 3: Relationships are built on trust.   As noted above, developing a strong positive helping relationship is a process. Relationships are built over time. A key factor in developing a strong helping relationship is having shared experiences. In a professional relationship this occurs by undertaking the activities or tasks of the helping process, such as identifying client strengths and concerns and developing goals and a plan of action. Engaging in these purposeful activities helps build trust. Trust, in turn, helps strengthen the interpersonal connection or worker–client bond, which strengthens the client's motivation to engage in the structural activities. Figure 3.1 illustrates the interrelationships between the structural and interpersonal components and the effects that positive interactions have on client trust and motivation.

A key to developing a strong positive collaborative relationship is establishing some level of trust. The client must be able to trust the social worker. Relationships cannot be built in the absence of trust. A certain degree of trust must be established between the client and the social worker for the client to engage in a collaborative helping process.

Trust is essential for relationships to develop and grow between social workers and their clients. To build strong collaborative relationships, the social worker must reduce the client's fear, suspicion, and mistrust at the same time as the worker promotes feelings of acceptance, support, and affirmation.

Building trust with reluctant clients is an interactional process. Trust cannot be built in the absence of interpersonal interactions between the client and the social worker. It is built upon a sequence of trusting and trustworthy interactions. The client must act in a trusting manner and the social worker must respond with trustworthy actions.

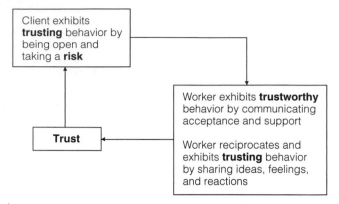

FIGURE 3.2 | TRUST-BUILDING INTERACTIONS

Within each interaction three conditions are required for trust to develop in a helping relationship. First, the client must **take a risk** (make a choice) where the potential harmful consequences outweigh the potential benefits associated with the risk. Second, the client must realize that the beneficial or harmful consequences associated with the risk **depend upon the worker's actions** (response) as the helping professional. Third, the client must **experience the worker's actions as beneficial** (Fong and Cox, 1983). All three conditions must be present for the interaction to contribute to the trust-building process. Figure 3.2 illustrates a trust-building interaction.

The bond of trust is built over time, through a series of trusting actions (risks) and trustworthy responses (confirmations). Although it takes time for trust to be established with reluctant clients, it can be destroyed through a single client risk and worker disconfirmation (nontrustworthy) response (Fong and Cox, 1983).

The critical element in developing trust is **risk**. Collaborative social work requires the client to actively participate in the helping process. The client is an active partner in the search for understanding and solutions. This cannot happen if the client is unable to take a risk by being open and honest with the social worker. Clients have to be willing to share their wants, desires, dreams, goals, skills, abilities, talents, and competencies as well as fears and concerns with a social worker. Reluctant clients usually have no reason whatsoever to be open with helping professionals. Why take a risk with someone in authority? Why risk exposing the real me to someone who can cause me harm or make my life difficult? The primary task for the social worker in working with reluctant clients is to facilitate risk taking. Trust cannot be built in the absence of risk.

Clients vary in their willingness to take risks with a helping professional. Figure 3.3 shows five levels of the worker–client risk continuum. At risk level I, the client is completely closed and unwilling to share even factual information. This type of client is often described as hostile or resistant. For people who have experienced a lifetime of oppression, prejudice, and discrimination, being unwilling to expose oneself to a stranger and authority figure is a normal and healthy coping mechanism. As one moves up the risk continuum, the client's willingness to share feeling and thoughts increases. At risk level V, the client is willing to be open about

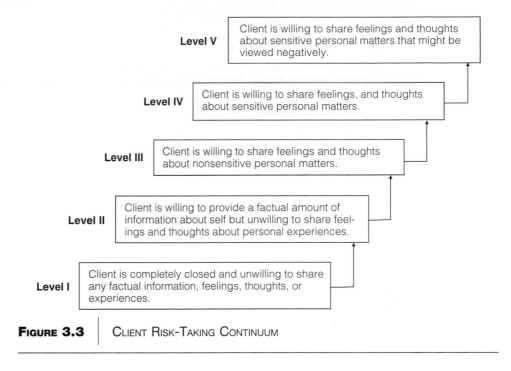

Level V — Client is willing to share feelings and thoughts about sensitive personal matters that might be viewed negatively.

Level IV — Client is willing to share feelings, and thoughts about sensitive personal matters.

Level III — Client is willing to share feelings and thoughts about nonsensitive personal matters.

Level II — Client is willing to provide a factual amount of information about self but unwilling to share feelings and thoughts about personal experiences.

Level I — Client is completely closed and unwilling to share any factual information, feelings, thoughts, or experiences.

FIGURE 3.3 | CLIENT RISK-TAKING CONTINUUM

sensitive personal matters that place him or her in a potentially negative light. This level of risk requires a high level of trust and is usually reached over time through a series of lower-level risk-taking and confirming interactions with the social worker. The three theoretical propositions discussed above are the underlying assumptions of the collaborative model of social work practice. These assumptions guide practice expectations. The following three practice principles provide additional guidance in using the collaborative model of practice.

PRACTICE PRINCIPLES

The basic assumptions of the collaborative model of practice are (1) disadvantaged and oppressed clients often mistrust helping professionals, (2) client change occurs through a collaborative helping relationship, and (3) helping relationships are built upon trust. In light of these assumptions, the collaborative model is designed to build trust with clients whose life experiences have given them very little reason to trust social workers and people in authority. This is accomplished by adopting a strengths perspective, by maximizing client collaboration and empowerment, and by adopting a system of ongoing feedback and evaluation.

Practice Principle 1: Focus on client strengths.   The basic principles of the strengths perspective are discussed in Chapter 2. The focus here will be on reviewing the application of the strengths perspective in social work practice with disadvantaged clients. The strengths perspective focuses on inherent client strengths, resources, and coping abilities (Saleebey, 2002). Clients are viewed as capable of change and as active participants in the change process. Rather than the social worker being the problem solver, the client becomes the problem solver. The social worker's primary function is to help the client recognize, strengthen, and marshal his or her inherent strengths and abilities (Weick et al., 1989).

This "requires helpers to be open to negotiation, to appreciate the authenticity of the views and aspirations of those with whom they collaborate, and to be willing to subdue their own voices in the interest of bespeaking those of their clients" (Saleebey, 1992, p. 12). The worker and the client form a partnership to help the client resolve his or her own problems or concerns. Social workers cannot promote collaboration or foster client self-determination if they see their role as reforming or changing clients. Similarly, collaboration and client self-determination are not achieved if the social worker tries to fix the problem for the client. Social work is based on the premise that clients must ultimately help themselves. Self-determination requires workers and clients to collaborate in all decisions and aspects of their work together.

Strengths-based generalist practice places the client in the role of expert regarding his or her life situation. The worker's role is to help clients identify what is best for them. In this paradigm, the emphasis is on the collaborative process between the worker and the client. Engaging clients in a collaborative helping relationship, a relationship that recognizes the client as "expert," actually increases clients' ownership of their decisions and ultimately their level of self-determination. In a collaborative partnership, the worker helps the client expand his or her repertoire of choices and behaviors. Ideally, this involves helping the client identify the range of alternatives and the pros and cons associated with each possible choice. With this approach, the worker finds it easier to balance the offering of expert help with respect for the client's autonomy.

Collaboration—a partnership between the client and the worker—has been a pivotal practice ideal since the beginning of the social work profession (Richmond, 1917). Collaboration is closely tied to self-determination (Weick et al., 1989). The NASW Code of Ethics states that "the social worker should make every effort to foster maximum self-determination on the part of clients" (NASW, 1997, p. 3). Self-determination is achieved when "the client is fully involved and participating in all of the decisions and the social worker is working with the client rather than doing things to the client" (Compton and Galaway, 1994, p. 11). Self-determination is fostered by client participation in the decision-making process.

Self-determination is, for the most part, a "grand illusion" in actual practice (Perlman, 1965, p. 410). Achieving it is difficult at best. "The challenge for every practicing social worker is that of balancing the act of offering expert help while respecting the client's autonomy" (Bisman, 1994, p. 49). Problems arise when a client makes choices that are self-destructive or inconsistent with prevailing societal norms. In these situations, the dilemma for the social worker is how to resolve the conflict between his or her values and the value choices of the client while continuing to honor client self-determination. Levy (1972) suggests that the worker and the client openly discuss the value conflicts. Differences in value positions should be aired and the right to have different views respected.

Strengths-based generalist practice is based on the belief that clients are the experts and that they ultimately know what is best for themselves. The emphasis is on the collaborative process between the worker and the client. Engaging clients in a collaborative helping relationship increases clients' ownership of their decisions and ultimately their level of self-determination.

Practice Principle 2: Put clients in charge of the helping process.   Collaboration requires the social worker to relinquish power, expertise, and control to the client. This does not mean that the worker has no expertise or role in the helping process. It does mean, however, that the balance of power and authority is distributed more equitably between the social worker and the client.

The use of empowerment in social work has grown out of the work of Solomon (1976), Rappaport (1981), and Pinderhughes (1983) and from feminist theory (Donovan, 1990; Ferree and Hess, 1985). "Feminism, like the civil rights, black power, and self-help movements, rapidly expanded the conceptual, methodological, and relational universe of empowerment-based social work of the 1970s and 1980s" (Simon, 1994). It has evolved as a method for working with women, people of color, and other oppressed groups (Gutiérrez and Nurius, 1994). **Empowerment** is defined as the "process of increasing personal, interpersonal or political power so that individuals can take action to improve their life situations" (Gutiérrez, 1990, p. 149). The process of empowerment emphasizes the acquisition of power, which is "the capacity to influence the forces which affect one's life space for one's own benefit" (Pinderhughes, 1983, p. 332).

The focus of social work practice with individuals should be on the "reduction of the power imbalance between workers and clients—specifically on increasing the client's power resources" (Hasenfeld, 1987, p. 478). The balance of power between the social worker and the client is inherently unequal. Theories of social work practice do not adequately address this power differential and tend to understate the effect of power on the helping relationship (Hasenfeld, 1987).

Social workers have three types of power: **expertise power** derived from their access to and command of specialized knowledge; **referent power** or persuasion, derived from their interpersonal skills; and **legitimate power** derived from their sanctioned position. In other words, social workers derive power from their expertise, their interpersonal skills, and the fact that they control resources needed by the client (Hasenfeld, 1987). Strengths-based generalist practice requires social workers to recognize the power they bring to the helping relationship and to engage clients in an open discussion of the various sources of power in their relationship. Acknowledging the inherent power differential is the first step in shifting the balance of power to the client. Although they rarely mention it, clients are acutely aware of the power differential between themselves and their social workers. Opening up the topic for discussion is in itself empowering (Gutiérrez, 1990). It gives the social worker and the client an opportunity to evaluate the resources available to address the client's areas of concern. The client is given a voice in defining the resources and determining how they will be used. As Hasenfeld states: "If we view social work practice as an exchange of resources, social work effectiveness, then, is predicated on the reduction of the power imbalance between workers and clients—specifically on increasing the client's power resources" (1987, p. 478).

Although strengths-based generalist practice acknowledges the client's expertise regarding his or her life situation, the social worker does not ignore his or her access to and command of specialized knowledge. This knowledge can help the client.

But the social worker's view of the situation is not imposed on the client. The client is empowered by increasing his or her feelings of self-efficacy (Evans, 1992).

The helping relationship is the basis of empowerment (Gutiérrez, 1990; Weick and Pope, 1988). The helping relationship begins with an open discussion of each participant's interpersonal styles, preferences, and abilities. Giving clients a voice in determining what works for them is empowering. The social worker communicates a willingness to be responsive to the client's interpersonal preferences. Involving the client in the definition and evaluation of the relationship empowers the client and shifts the balance of power toward the client. The social worker's referent power becomes a resource that the client controls to some extent. Empowerment also entails an analysis of the agency resources controlled by the social worker and an analysis of the client's resources (Hasenfeld, 1987). In discussing agency resources, the worker needs to describe the options available and the steps for obtaining them. The worker and client explore the possibilities and costs associated with each option. The client is empowered by being involved in the analysis and by being an active participant in the decision-making process. The worker and client should also analyze the client's potential resources. Gutiérrez suggests that part of assessing the client's potential resources or strengths "involves analyzing how conditions of powerlessness are affecting the client's situation" (1990, p. 152). After exploring the factors that might contribute to the client's perception of powerlessness, the worker and client can examine the client's potential sources of power: "Clients and workers should be encouraged to think creatively about sources of potential power, such as forgotten skills, personal qualities that could increase social influence, members of past social support networks, and organizations in their communities" (Gutiérrez, 1990, p. 152).

The worker has to adopt an empowering mind-set, which involves giving up control and essentially abandoning the role of expert diagnostician and provider of expert advice. The worker has to become a team member with the client. The client must be willing to take responsibility for all aspects of the work together. The social worker can help the client take responsibility by believing in the client's right to self-determination, by expecting the client to assume responsibility for himself or herself and the planned interventions, and by giving up the need to be in control of the helping process. The social worker can also empower the client by listening. Being listened to and heard validates the client's perceptions of his or her life experiences (Irving and Young, 2002).

The client is unlikely to immediately move from a position of powerlessness to one of power. Individual empowerment is a process and should be viewed as a long-term goal of the helping relationship. Strengths-based generalist practice recognizes the shared responsibilities of the worker and the client. Ultimately, the success of the helping process depends on the client's ability to assume responsibility. "Clients who do not feel responsible for their problems may not invest their efforts in developing solutions unless they assume some personal responsibility for future change" (Gutiérrez, 1990, p. 150).

Practice Principle 3: Continually evaluate your work and the client's progress. In strengths-based generalist social work practice, evaluation means ongoing assessment throughout the helping relationship. This involves specifying problems   and   goals   in   measurable   terms,   developing   solution-focused interventions, and using "evaluation methods in practice" (Reid, 1994, p. 176). Evaluation involves informal feedback from the client as well as the use of standardized measures and rating scales. It is a joint and collaborative effort. Both the worker and the client are involved in all aspects of evaluation.

Informal evaluation is one way of assessing the worker–client process. In keeping with the principles of collaboration and empowerment, in which the client is the expert about his or her progress, subjective assessments play a prominent role in strengths-based generalist practice. Clients' subjective assessments of their situations are the primary basis for evaluating the effectiveness of the helping process. The critical factor is whether the issues or concerns for which they are seeking help have improved.

Informal evaluation is an ongoing process. The client and worker begin by exploring the client's person-in-environment system and life experiences in order to identify concerns and factors that potentially affect them. During this and later stages, the social worker makes sure that his or her interpretations of the client's experiences are consistent with the client's perceptions. Strengths-based generalist practice emphasizes listening to the client's story and understanding the client's perceptions of experiences. The worker needs to continually evaluate the extent to which his or her understanding of the client's experiences is consistent with the client's.

As work continues, informal evaluation techniques identical to the process described above play a role. The social worker has to make a conscious effort to ensure that there is agreement about the identified goals and specifics of the helping contract. The worker and client need to evaluate the client's commitment to the plan. Is it genuine? How strong is it? What can the social worker do to help the client maintain or strengthen his or her commitment to change? Strengths-based generalist practice assumes client commitment to the helping process and stresses client responsibility. Unfortunately, clients are not always committed to addressing their concerns. A client's commitment should not be taken for granted or assumed. To address this, strengths-based generalist practice emphasizes an open dialogue between the worker and the client about commitment and responsibility.

Formal evaluation refers to the development of measurable goals and objectives and the use of standardized measures and single-item rating scales to evaluate progress on the goals. In recent years, the number of rapid assessment instruments appropriate for social work practice has increased. Such instruments are readily available and easily accessible (Fischer and Corcoran, 1994), and the range of problem areas covered is extensive. Thus, it is often possible to find a standardized scale that measures the problem area being addressed.

Standardized measures are an excellent way in which to evaluate progress. They are easily incorporated into generalist practice. Reviewing the results of standardized measures provides opportunities for the worker and client to discuss the identified area of concern. The standardized measures are first administered as part of the goal and contracting process and are readministered periodically as the helping relationship continues. They provide the worker and client with evaluative information on client progress and open the door for a discussion of why progress is or is not being made.

Individual rating scales are the second type of formal evaluation measures used in strengths-based generalist practice. The worker and client easily construct these scales. Their purpose is to assess the worker's and client's perception of progress on the identified areas of concern. Incorporating rating scales into the helping process is a way to evaluate progress and to obtain information on the client's perceptions of the effectiveness of the work. The primary value of this type of evaluation is that it provides a basis for a discussion of progress or the lack of it. It helps keep the work focused on the identified goals and opens up an opportunity to reevaluate priorities.

STRENGTHS-BASED ASSESSMENT

ASSESSMENT VERSUS DIAGNOSIS

A strengths-based assessment is more than diagnosing the client's presenting symptoms and coming up with a diagnostic label. Indeed, the diagnosis often required for insurance purposes, which is based on the Diagnostic and Statistical Manual of Mental Disorders (DSM-IV-TR) (American Psychiatric Association, 2000), is antithetical to the principles and concepts of collaborative social work. The DSM-IV-TR is useful in eliciting descriptions of symptoms from the client and talking about symptoms with others on the treatment team. The diagnostic labels themselves do not tell you everything about the unique circumstances of your clients. They may tell you something about how prescribed medications are working or not working, what type of medication is needed, or whether the client needs to be referred to a physician.

Diagnostic labeling can have negative consequences (Gambrill, 1997; Kinney, Haapala, and Booth, 1991; Kirk and Kutchins, 1992; Levy, 1972). Psychiatric labels tend to create negative expectations. They focus attention on deficits and away from the potential for change. "Labeling makes it harder for us to be warm and supportive, if we're thinking about coping with the negative traits we've assigned to our clients" (Kinney, Haapala, and Booth, 1991, p. 84).

Another negative consequence of labeling is that it reduces feelings of hopefulness. Labeling is all inclusive (e.g., a client is psychotic or has a personality disorder). Labels imply that what clients are is what they will always be (Kinney, Haapala, and Booth, 1991). These negative expectations discourage a sense of hopefulness, reduce client motivation, and minimize possibilities for change (Rapp, 1998).

Many beginning social workers like to use the DSM-IV-TR. Referring to clients by diagnostic labels makes a new social worker feel and sound professional and gives him or her the illusion of being understanding and having expertise. Avoid the temptation and the trap. Most labels create negative expectations for both you and the client, focus on a condition or trait rather than the context in which a problem occurs, and offer little help in understanding the unique circumstances of the client. They do not provide any information about how to resolve a problem.

ASSESSING CLIENT STRENGTHS

Focusing on pathologic labels promotes homogenization (Rapp, 1998). Clients are viewed as a collection of generalized problems that are finite and shared by many other clients. This results in a generic case plan that sees all clients as exhibiting the same groups of symptoms. Clients are not seen as unique individuals with unique circumstances and problem situations.

Strengths-based assessments enhance the individualization of clients. The focus is on what is unique about each client in terms of interests, abilities, and how they have coped with their problem situation. "The work should focus on what the client has achieved so far, what resources have been or are currently available to the client, what the client knows and talents possessed, and what aspirations and dreams the client may hold" (Rapp, 1998, p. 45). Cowger created these guidelines for a strengths assessment:

1. Give preeminence to the client's understanding of the facts.
2. Believe the client.
3. Discover what the client wants.
4. Move the assessment toward personal and environmental strengths.
5. Make the assessment of strengths multidimensional.
6. Use the assessment to discover uniqueness.
7. Use language the client can understand.
8. Make the assessment a joint activity between worker and client.
9. Reach a mutual agreement on the assessment.
10. Avoid blame and blaming.
11. Assess, do not diagnose. (1997, pp. 63–66)

Adherence to these guidelines will ensure that your assessment interviews are collaborative and that the process will identify client strengths. The tendency to focus on pathologic symptoms and dysfunction will be minimized.

Identifying client strengths is not always easy. Clients are often unable to name specific strengths they have used in coping with a problem situation. They often indicate that they do not have any strengths, or they respond in very general terms, such as "I am a nice person" (McQuaide and Ehrenreich, 1997). The challenge is to help clients recognize how they have "taken steps, summoned up resources, and coped" (Saleebey, 1997, p. 239). However, "whether a given client's characteristic represents a strength or a weakness depends on subtleties of personal history, the immediate social environment, the larger societal matrix, the mix of client characteristics, challenges, and the meanings the client ascribes to his or her experience and situation" (McQuaide and Ehrenreich, 1997, p. 211).

Using a strengths perspective does not negate the very real problems clients face. The problems that cause clients to seek professional help cannot be disregarded or ignored. The assessment process must attend to both the obstacles and the strengths that potentially affect the resolution of the problem and the helping process. Much of the assessment that takes place in social work is focused on client problems and deficits (Saleebey, 2002). The strengths approach seeks to provide a balance between client obstacles and strengths.

Cowger (1997) proposed an assessment axis to help attain this balance (Figure 3.4). It has two coordinates: an environmental–personal continuum and a strengths–obstacles continuum. There are four quadrants: environmental strengths, personal strengths, environmental obstacles, and personal obstacles. The quadrants for personal strengths and obstacles include both psychological and physiological

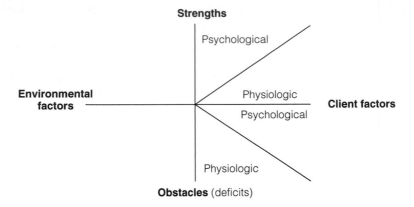

FIGURE 3.4 | ASSESSMENT AXIS

C. Cowger. In Saleebey, Dennis (Ed.). "Assessing client strengths," in *Strengths perspective in social work practice,* 3rd ed. Published by Allyn and Bacon, Boston MA. Copyright © 2002 by Pearson Education, Inc. Reproduced by permission of Pearson Education, Inc.

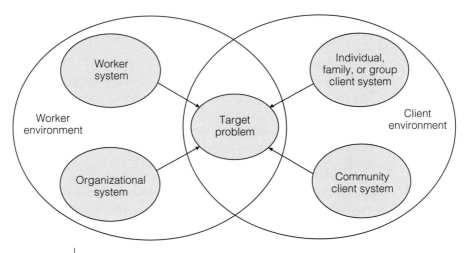

FIGURE 3.5 | PERSON-IN-ENVIRONMENT ASSESSMENT

components. Attention to all four quadrants helps ensure a comprehensive assessment that is balanced in terms of individual and environmental strengths and obstacles.

IDENTIFYING AND ANALYZING PERSON-IN-ENVIRONMENT FACTORS

A major component of a strengths-based assessment is exploring and assessing the four quadrants in the assessment axis. Figure 3.5 shows the potential effect the worker, organization, community, and client systems have on a target problem. It also shows the influence the worker has on the client's environmental system.

Worker–client transactions are viewed as a component of the client's ecological system (Germain and Gitterman, 1980). Interactions between the worker and the client and between the worker and the client's social environment become part of the client's dynamic person-in-environment system. In this respect, mutuality and reciprocity characterize the worker–client relationship. The conceptualization recognizes the mutual effect that worker and client have on one another and on the helping relationship (Petr, 1988).

The interrelationships of the systems shown in Figure 3.5 differ from the traditional ecological systems model, in which the worker is seen as a mediator operating between the individual and his or her environment. In the conceptualization presented here, the social worker is a major component of the client's person-in-environment system—a component that affects the system and is affected by the other system components.

This model also emphasizes the worker's role as a partner in the helping process. The critical issue for social workers and their clients is how the various systems in the client's person-in-environment system affect the concerns the client is attempting to resolve. Factors that affect the client system but do not affect the helping relationship system are not relevant to their work together.

Social workers need to understand clients by "tapping into their unique perspective and personal realities" (Jordan and Franklin, 1995, p. 98). In exploring the client's reality, it is important for social workers to be aware of their own biases and beliefs, which may influence their clinical perceptions. Social workers need to be able to differentiate between their interpretations and those of the client (Gilgun, Daly, and Handel, 1992). They also need to recognize that by exploring a client's subjective reality, they become part of that reality. On entering into a helping relationship, the worker becomes part of the client's person-in-environment system. Thus, the worker can influence a client's subjective perceptions of self and of experiences. Care must be taken to allow the client's subjective reality to emerge. The social worker's job is to understand the client's experiences and perceptions and to engage the client in a discussion of how those experiences influence their work together. The worker needs to incorporate his or her understanding of the client's experiences into the helping process.

Conducting a person-in-environment assessment is immensely complex and difficult. It is, however, critical to the success of the work. Assessment is an ongoing task in the helping process and should not be limited to the beginning assessment phase. It requires mutual exploration and evaluation of the client's person-in-environment system throughout the helping relationship.

THE COLLABORATIVE MODEL

As noted earlier, the basic assumption of the collaborative model is that because of prior negative life experiences and experiences with helping professionals, disadvantaged and oppressed clients are often mistrustful of helping professionals. Consequently, they are often reluctant to engage in a collaborative helping relationship. Each component of the model has been designed to build trust and promote the development of a strong helping relationship. Table 3.1 summarizes the model's phases, tasks, inputs, skills, and outputs. The collaborative model presented below

TABLE 3.1 | THE COLLABORATIVE MODEL[1]

Phase	Task	Input	Skills	Output
Pre-Engagement Sessions 1–3	**Studying** Population Culture Values & Beliefs Experiences Life Styles Environment Resources Community Organizations	Understanding Sensitivity	Information Retrieval Skills Database Searches Internet Searches Resource Identification Skills Networking	Increased Knowledge Competence
	Asking Obtain Client's Story Experiences Beliefs Expectations Strengths Coping Abilities	Respect Acceptance	Elaboration Skills Open-Ended Questions Minimal Prompts Seeking Concreteness Summarizing Containment Exploring Silences Reframing	Identifying Needs Concerns Strengths Coping Skills
	Listening Tune-in to Client's Meaning Feelings Clues	Understanding Empathy	Empathy Skills Focused Listening Reflective Empathy Additive Empathy	Identifying Feeling Content Validation
	Clarifying Explore roles, expectations and the helping process	Cooperative Intentions	Elaboration Skills Empathy Skills	Mutual Understanding Collaboration
Engagement Sessions 4-8	**Articulating** Develop an Action Plan	Hopefulness Partnership	Contracting Skills Partializing Identifying Options Seeking Consensus Sharing Data	Change Goals Action Plan Evaluation Plan
	Persevering Persistent Follow Through	Support Commitment	Intervention Skills Challenging Maintaining Focus Checking for Ambivalence Rehearsal	Client Change
Disengagement Sessions 9-10	**Solidifying** Gains made	Confidence	Ending Skills Generalizing ID Next Steps	Evaluation Generalization Aftercare Plan

[1] The model's first six tasks were identified and named by Sarah Kulp, Aurelius Cousar, Laurie Bluhm, Christiana Drescher, Louann Kenefick, and Pat Mullen as part of a class exercise in their first-year MSW practice course.

can be used with individual, family, small group, organizational, and community client systems. The model is defined as time limited. However, some client systems will need more contact and others less. The length of the helping relationship is determined by the problem situation being addressed and a host of interpersonal, environmental, and organizational factors.

PHASES

The beginning phase of the collaborative model is the **pre-engagement phase**. At this point, the client is in either the precontemplation or contemplation stages (Prochaska, DiClemente, and Norcross, 1992). The client has not yet made a decision to engage in a helping relationship. This is a critical period in the helping process. It is the time at which clients are most likely to drop out by simply not returning for the next session. The pre-engagement phase usually takes place during sessions one to three.

The **engagement phase** is the period in which clients are in preparation or action stage (Prochaska, DiClemente, and Norcross, 1992). Clients at this phase have acknowledged their commitment to make changes and are taking the necessary steps to achieve their identified goals. The engagement phase typically takes place during sessions four through eight.

The **disengagement phase** is the final phase of the collaborative model. This is comparable to the maintenance stage described by Prochaska, DiClemente, and Norcross (1992). The focus is on preventing relapse and consolidating the gains achieved. In a 10-session intervention, the last two or three weeks are devoted to the disengagement phase.

Tasks The heart of the collaborative model is its seven tasks: study, ask, listen, clarify, articulate, persevere, and solidify. These tasks are interrelated and overlapping. Although there is a logical way to implement the model, it should not be approached in a linear or step-wise fashion. All of the components overlap, and the process, more often than not, is cyclical rather than linear.

The **study task** begins before the initial contact with the client and lasts throughout the helping process. The **ask, listen,** and **clarify tasks** are begun during the pre-engagement phase and continue throughout the helping relationship. The **articulate** and **persevere tasks** take place during the engagement phase. The **solidify task** takes place during the disengagement phase.

INPUTS

Input, as used here, refers to what the social worker communicates both directly and indirectly to the client during their interactions together. Worker input is often not directly observable. It may be an attitude or expectation. For example, respect is an input. A social worker can communicate respect to clients in a number of different ways. Often, it is communicated indirectly through tone of voice, choice of words, and general attitude toward a person. Inputs are delivered through the worker's use of self in his or her interactions with the client. The various inputs identified in Table 3.1 are critical to the development of strong, positive helping relationships. For example, workers who are perceived as understanding, empathetic, comforting, and respectful tend to develop stronger relationships with their clients than those who are not (Poulin and Young, 1997). Effectively communicating the model's inputs helps strengthen the psychological bond between workers and clients, which in turn helps motivate both to engage in a helping relationship.

SKILLS

The practice skills listed in Table 3.1 are those that are compatible with the strengths perspective and are client empowering. Although the various skills are linked to the different phases and components of the model, they are used throughout the helping process. The identified practice skills are important components of the social worker's use of self. They are the primary tools used to build trust, develop the helping relationship, and help clients negotiate the seven components of the model.

OUTPUTS

Outputs refer to the expected outcomes or results obtained from the worker inputs. At each stage of the model there are identified outcomes. These outcomes specify what the social worker should strive for during each component of the model. They help the social worker and client evaluate their process on a session-by-session basis.

ASSESSING THE HELPING RELATIONSHIP

The Helping Relationship Inventory (HRI) is a rapid assessment instrument designed to assess the strength of the structural and interpersonal components of the helping relationship (Poulin and Young, 1997). There are client (HRI:C) and worker (HRI:W) versions that are sensitive to important differences in client and worker concerns (Poulin and Young, 1997). Both are reliable and valid measures of the helping relationship.

The client version, HRI:C, measures the strength of the helping relationship in social work practice from the perspective of the client (Table 3.2). It is composed of ten structural and ten interpersonal items that capture those aspects of the helping relationship that are most important to clients. The worker version, HRI:W, measures the relationship from the perspective of the worker (Table 3.3). It is composed of ten structural and ten interpersonal items that capture those aspects of the helping relationship that are most important to workers providing help.

The worker and client versions of the HRI complement and strengthen social work practice with a variety of client populations. They evolved from a conception of social work practice that focuses on a collaborative process of assessment, goal specification, intervention, and evaluation within which the social worker motivates and supports the client's efforts to achieve his or her goals. Thus, the HRI:C and HRI:W are compatible with the collaborative model and are useful tools that support the model's practice principles.

SCORING THE HRI

The worker and client versions of the HRI both contain ten structural and ten interpersonal items. Each is rated on a five-point Likert-type scale. Scores for the structural component are calculated by summing items 1 through 10, and for the

| **TABLE 3.2** | HELPING RELATIONSHIP INVENTORY: CLIENT HRI:C[1] |

1. How much input have *you* had in determining how the two of you will work together?
2. How much have you and your social worker discussed the specific problem(s) with which you want help?
3. How much input have you had in determining the specific problem(s) you are addressing in your work together?
4. To what extent have you and your social worker discussed the specific goal(s) you hope to accomplish in your work together?
5. How much input have you had in determining the goals you are working on?
6. To what extent have you and your social worker discussed the specific actions *you* will take to address your difficulties?
7. To what extent have you and your social worker discussed the specific actions *your* social worker will take to address your difficulties?
8. How much have you and your social worker discussed how your progress is going to be assessed?
9. How much input do you have in determining how you and your social worker will assess your progress?
10. To what extent have you and your social worker discussed your progress?
11. Do you feel your social worker pays attention to you?
12. Is your social worker's understanding of your difficulties similar to your own?
13. Does talking with your social worker help you get more organized about resolving your difficulties?
14. Does talking with your social worker have a calming, soothing effect on you?
15. Does talking with your social worker give you hope?
16. Does your social worker help you think more clearly about your difficulties?
17. Does talking with your social worker help you to believe more in yourself?
18. In general, do you feel you and your social worker see things in similar ways?
19. Does your social worker help you think more clearly about yourself?
20. Do you feel that you and your social worker are alike in some ways?

[1]All of the items are measured with Likert-type scales ranging from (1) not at all to (5) a great deal. The HRI:C structural index has a reliability coefficient of .91, and the interpersonal index has a reliability coefficient of .96. Overall, the HRI:C has a reliability coefficient of .96. It demonstrates concurrent and discriminant validity. Originally published in "Development of a Helping Relationship for Social Work Practice," by J. Poulin and T. Young, 1997, *Research on Social Work Practice, 7*, pp. 463–489. Reprinted by permission of Sage Publications, Inc.

interpersonal component by summing items 11 through 20. The total HRI score is the sum of the structural and interpersonal scores.

Because the reliability and validity estimates of the structural and interpersonal subscales of the HRI are strong, social workers and their clients should calculate scores from both subscales as well as the total score. Although scoring norms have not been developed for the HRI, a score of 30 or lower on either component indicates a problematic relationship. If either the worker or client rates the structural or interpersonal component of their work together at or below this level, there is a strong likelihood that a satisfactory relationship is not developing or that there has been a rupture in the relationship. Workers and clients should compare both sets of scores to identify the areas of difficulty or disagreement and discuss ways to strengthen the relationship.

The scores are rough benchmarks the worker can use to assess the need to address relationship issues with the client. There are no clinically established cutoff scores. For example, a combined score of 61 should not automatically be viewed as problem free or a score of 59 as problematic. Worker and client scores on the

TABLE 3.3 | Helping Relationship Inventory: Worker HRI:W[1]

1. How much input does your client have in determining how your work together will be approached?
2. How much have you and your client discussed the specific problem(s) with which he/she wants help?
3. How clear are you about the specific problem(s) that you and your client are addressing?
4. To what extent have you and your client discussed the specific goal(s) you hope to accomplish in your work together?
5. How much input does your client have in determining the goals he/she is working on?
6. How clear are you about your client's goals?
7. To what extent have you and your client discussed the specific actions *he/she* will take to address his/her difficulties?
8. How clear are you about the actions you are taking?
9. How much input does your client have in determining how you and your client will assess his/her progress?
10. How clear are you about how you and your client are assessing his/her progress?
11. Do you explain to your client your understanding of his/her difficulties?
12. Is your client's understanding of his/her difficulties similar to your own?
13. Is your client more organized about resolving his/her difficulties as a result of talking to you?
14. Does talking with you have a calming, soothing effect on your client?
15. Does talking with you give your client hope?
16. Are you able to handle the emotional aspects of your client's difficulties?
17. Do you enjoy meeting and talking with your client?
18. In general, do you feel you and your client see things in similar ways?
19. Do you help your client think more clearly about himself/herself?
20. Do you feel that you and your client are alike in some ways?

[1]All of the items are measured with Likert-type scales ranging from (1) not at all to (5) a great deal. The HRI:W structural index has a reliability coefficient of .86, and the interpersonal index has a reliability coefficient of .91. Overall, the HRI:W has a reliability coefficient of .93. It demonstrates concurrent and discriminant validity. Originally published in "Development of a Helping Relationship for Social Work Practice," by J. Poulin and T. Young, 1997, *Research on Social Work Practice, 7,* pp. 463–489. Reprinted by permission of Sage Publications, Inc.

HRI have to be viewed within the context of the helping relationship and the unique circumstances of the case.

APPLICATIONS OF THE **HRI** FOR SOCIAL WORK PRACTICE

The HRI is designed to help social workers and clients examine their perceptions of the helping relationship. Early in the helping process—no later than after the third session—the worker and client should complete the HRI and compare and discuss the results. Comparing the worker and client ratings of the individual items can lead to fruitful discussions about working together and what does and does not work in the helping relationship (Young and Poulin, 1998). Comparing the worker and client versions of the HRI facilitates the important process of collaboration and empowerment of the client early in the helping process.

Using the HRI:C and HRI:W as part of the helping process can provide both worker and client with important information on key elements of their work together. Clients and workers often have significantly different perceptions of the helping relationship (Horvath and Greenberg, 1994). For social workers to assume that clients share their view of their work together is risky and could impede progress.

The relationship between the worker and the client is the strongest predictor of both client change and client satisfaction (Horvath and Symonds, 1991). A solid helping relationship is a prerequisite for successful outcomes. Given the demonstrated differences in perceptions of shared experiences and the importance of the helping relationship in the change process, early and ongoing examinations of the client's and worker's perceptions of the relationship are critical.

If the client and worker do not develop a strong collaborative relationship that the client perceives as helpful, the client most likely will stop seeing the worker. Failure to develop a helping relationship is a common reason for termination (Levine and Herron, 1990). Using the HRI early in the helping process might increase client collaboration and reduce the likelihood that the client will discontinue treatment prematurely. Administering the HRI and discussing the adequacy of the relationship will in itself strengthen the helping relationship.

The HRI should be administered periodically throughout the helping process to obtain feedback on the strength of the relationship as the work evolves. This is particularly critical if clients or workers become discouraged about the possibilities of meaningful change or frustrated over what needs to be done to bring about change. Administering the HRI during the middle phase of treatment can provide the worker and client with important information on the strength of the relationship and open discussion about what they are working on and how they are doing so together.

Finally, the HRI should be administered as part of the planned termination of work. An important aspect of termination is reviewing the helping relationship. This review helps clients become better consumers of social work services. It helps them articulate what has and has not worked for them, how they have changed themselves or their situation, and how they brought about change. Reviewing the structural and interpersonal components of the HRI draws attention to specific aspects of the helping relationship. It can enhance the worker's and client's review of how they worked together. Completing the HRI during termination also allows the worker and client to compare their ratings with ratings made earlier in the process. This provides a basis for a review of progress and experiences.

SUMMARY

The collaborative model of generalist social work practice assumes that most disadvantaged and oppressed clients are at best reluctant to engage in a helping relationship and that the development of a helping relationship is the key to client change. The importance of the helping relationship cannot be overemphasized. The helping relationship is composed of a structural and an interpersonal dimension, and its development is contingent upon the development of trust between the worker and the client. The structural component of the helping relationship focuses on tasks or purposeful activities, while the interpersonal component focuses on the psychological bond between the client and the worker. For the work to proceed, both dimensions of the helping relationship must be developed.

Three practice principles contribute to the effective implementation of the collaborative model. The first emphasizes client strengths. Clients are viewed as experts about their situations; they ultimately know what is best for them and they have the strengths needed to overcome the challenges in their lives.

The second practice principle focuses on client empowerment. Empowerment is the process of increasing personal, interpersonal, or political power, so that individuals can take action to improve their life situations. In the collaborative model, social workers do not control the helping process. Workers actively shift control and power to their clients. Clients are encouraged to take an active role in defining resources and in determining how they will use the helping relationship. Ultimately, the success of the helping process depends on how well the client assumes responsibility and control.

The third practice principle focuses on evaluation and feedback. Evaluation means ongoing assessment throughout the helping relationship. It involves informal feedback from clients as well as the use of formal standardized measures and rating scales. Evaluation is a joint and collaborative effort. The worker and the client take active roles in evaluating progress and the helping process.

Diagnosis is only a small part of the assessment process. It is useful in communicating symptom types. However, diagnostic labels do not tell you anything about the unique circumstances of clients or how to approach your work together. Psychiatric labels tend to create negative expectations and focus attention on client deficits. They focus on the condition or trait rather than on the context in which difficulties occur. They also offer little in the way of understanding the unique circumstances of the client, and they do not provide any information about how to resolve the problem.

Strengths-based assessments enhance the individualization of clients. They focus on what is unique about each client in terms of interests, abilities, and coping strategies they have used with their problem situation. Clients often need help in identifying their strengths. The challenge is to help them recognize how they have taken steps to resolve problem situations and how they have managed to cope with difficult circumstances.

The assessment process must take into account the challenges and the strengths that will affect the resolution of problems and the development of the helping process. A strengths-based approach tries to balance client obstacles and clients strengths. Cowger's assessment axis can help you maintain a balanced assessment by identifying personal and environmental strengths and obstacles. The collaborative model is composed of phases, tasks, inputs, skills, and outputs. All aspects of the model are interrelated and support the three theoretical propositions and practice principles. The model has been designed to maximize client engagement and promote client strengths and empowerment.

The HRI is a tool for both the worker and the client to assess progress in the development of the helping relationship. The HRI measures the strength of the structural and interpersonal components of the helping relationship from the client's and worker's perspectives. Because the helping relationship is vital to the helping process, social workers should make a conscious effort to evaluate its development. Doing so can provide important information on differences between worker and client perceptions of how things are progressing as well as validation of what is working well. In addition to providing important feedback on the helping relationship, use of the HRI helps promote client empowerment and the development of a collaborative approach to the helping process.

CASE EXAMPLE

Heather Witt wrote the final case example in this chapter when she was a first-year MSW student. It is based on her work with a client at her field placement in a welfare-to-work program. The case illustrates the importance of developing both the structural and interpersonal aspects of the helping relationship. It also is an excellent example of how listening to clients empowers them and promotes the development of the helping relationship.

CASE 3.1	NADINE "THE DIFFICULT CLIENT"
	by Heather Witt

Practice Setting

Circle for Change is a welfare-to-work program designed to address the barriers that participants may have to obtaining and maintaining employment. To do this, Circle for Change provides individual counseling; group counseling; computer, career, and life skills training; and GED test preparation classes for participants without a GED or high school diploma. Clients are referred through the County Office of Employment and Training. Women referred to the program are considered the "Difficult Clients" who have been on public assistance for many years and who have been unsuccessful in becoming gainfully employed after participating in numerous training programs.

Problem Situation

Nadine is a 33-year-old African American woman who is currently is unemployed, although she does participate in different programs through the Delaware County Office of Employment and Training (OET) as a condition of her welfare assistance. This requires her to attend a job-training program for 12 hours a week and do community service at an approved site or do job searching at OET for 18 hours a week. Nadine was referred to our program, Circle for Change, from OET and is required to attend weekly counseling sessions as a part of the program. According to Nadine, her main problem is that she does not have a job, which stems from the fact that she does not have a high school diploma or a GED. After some time, the client went on to indicate that she has "trust issues" and has a "fear of good things." The client has coped with her financial situation by having a string of short-term positions and receiving assistance from welfare. The client also stated that she "does not get too close to nobody" because it takes her a long to time trust people.

Nadine and her caseworker at OET do not have a great relationship. The caseworker views Nadine as a "difficult client" and feels that Nadine's real issue is that she lacks motivation. The strained relationship is a problem because Nadine does not tell her caseworker anything personal about her life. Nadine has disclosed that she has witnessed her caseworker discussing other clients' personal business in front of other employees and clients. This has caused severe trust issues with Nadine and her caseworker. Nadine does not feel comfortable telling her caseworker when things come up in her life that impede her from fulfilling her requirements for her assistance, thus causing the caseworker to view her as lazy.

This was not Nadine's first welfare-to-work program. Nadine has been on public assistance for some time and continually fails to retain employment. Nadine indicated that, while she enjoyed her last position of employment, she was forced to quit when she found out she was pregnant with her youngest child. Nadine has also stated that OET is part of the problem. They continually try to convince her to train to become a Certified Nurse's Assistant, although Nadine has no interest in doing such work. Nadine has said that she wants to find a job she really likes so she does not end up leaving it again.

Nadine has stated that her life is extremely stressful. Nadine has five children and does not receive any form of child support. Her two oldest children are not currently attending school, and Nadine has stated that one of her main goals is to get them reenrolled as soon as she can. Nadine has not attempted to fight for financial support from either of her children's fathers and continues to struggle to support five children on an income of public assistance.

Nadine, over time, indicated five distinct goals she wished to accomplish as part of her case management/individual counseling sessions at CFC:

- Work on trust issues
- Obtain GED
- Get an enjoyable job
- Get two oldest children in school
- Take time out for self-care

Current Situation

Nadine was an active participant and successfully completed the Circle for Change program. She chose to continue individual counseling sessions after the program ended. She began working in an unpaid receptionist position as part of her 30-hour weekly requirement for assistance. Additionally, she successfully completed a GED preparation course. Nadine was offered a full-time receptionist position with benefits where she is currently volunteering, contingent on her successful completion of the

(Continued)

CASE 3.1 | *Continued*

GED test. She recently registered for the test and will be testing in less than a month. Nadine has also arranged for her two oldest children to relocate to another state to live with a family member and enroll in school there.

Nadine made great strides in both of her more personal goals of taking time for herself and working on her trust issues. Nadine stated that her relationship with her counselor and other members of the Circle for Change program helped her to begin to trust people again. Nadine also began scheduling alone time for herself and has done an excellent job of setting aside at least 1 hour per week to focus on self-care.

Client System Obstacles and Strengths

As previously stated, Nadine has extraordinary economic difficulties. Currently her only income is that of public assistance through cash, food stamps, and medical assistance. Many times while in counseling, she had issues paying her utility bills because of her very low income. Nadine has stated that while her housing situation is comfortable, she does not like the area she lives and wants to move when she is financially capable. Her displeasure with the area and the school district is what prompted her to make the difficult choice of allowing her children to live with an aunt to ensure that they are safe while attending school. However, the children's father is unwilling to assist her with the expense of relocating the children because he does not want them to move away.

Nadine continually stated that she felt her biggest obstacle is her lack of education, which she is currently striving to change. Although Nadine is not highly educated, she is intelligent and eager to learn. Nadine picks skills up quickly and is also very good with computers. Nadine continually assisted other Circle for Change group members with their computer assignments and is also an excellent typist.

According to Nadine's caseworker, Nadine's main problem was that of motivation. However, Nadine consistently stated throughout her individual counseling sessions that she was motivated to change her life circumstances. Nevertheless, Nadine did not always take the necessary steps she needed to take to make that change happen. Through her work in her counseling sessions and her volunteer placement in a supportive environment, Nadine's motivation strengthened. As she was given opportunities to progress, she also made great advancements on some of her other goals, including one that was difficult for her to achieve: getting her children back into school. Although she has made great progress, Nadine does seem to have the tendency to put things off, especially things that cause her anxiety or are exceptionally difficult for her. She has indicated that she in confident in her ability to pass the GED exam, and time will tell if she is able to follow through on taking the test and beginning the full-time position that is waiting for her.

Discussion Questions

1. What contributed to the development of a helping relationship between Heather and Nadine?
2. The case example focused on Nadine and the services she received in the CFC program. What other services or interventions might have been helpful for Nadine?
3. Discuss the interrelationship between the structural and interpersonal components of the helping relationship. How is the process of developing a helping relationship with a client different than and similar to that of developing a relationship with a peer?
4. Contrast the collaborative approach to social work practice with the traditional diagnostic model of practice. Describe the approach used in your field placement agency. How might you adopt a more collaborative approach in a setting that adheres to the diagnostic model?

5. Brainstorm about all the possible ways a social worker could promote client empowerment. Examine a specific case from an empowerment perspective. What needs to happen in the helping relationship for client empowerment to occur? What do social workers need to do to empower clients?

6. Discuss the use of the HRI in your practice. How might it enhance or inhibit the helping process? How would your clients react to being asked to evaluate the helping relationship? How would you feel about having your clients rate your relationship?

References

American Psychiatric Association (2000). *Diagnostic and statistical manual of mental disorders: DSM-IV-TR* (4th ed.). Washington, DC: American Psychiatric Association.

Biestek, F. (1954). An analysis of the casework relationship. *Social Casework, 35,* 57–61.

Biestek, F. (1957). *The casework relationship.* Chicago: Loyola University Press.

Bisman, C. (1994). *Social work practice: Cases and principles.* Pacific Grove, CA: Brooks/Cole.

Bordin, E. (1979). The generalizability of the psychoanalytic concept of the working alliance. *Psychotherapy: Theory, Research, and Practice, 16,* 252–260.

Coady, N. (1993). The worker–client relationship revisited. *Families in Society, 74,* 291–300.

Compton, B., and Galaway, B. (1994). *Social work processes* (5th ed.). Pacific Grove, CA: Brooks/Cole.

Cowger, C. (1997). Assessing client strengths: Assessment for client empowerment. In D. Saleebey (Ed.), *The strengths perspective in social work practice* (2nd ed., pp. 59–73). New York: Longman.

Donovan, J. (1990). *Feminist theory: The intellectual traditions of American feminism.* New York: Continuum.

Dore, M., and Alexander, L. (1996). Preserving families at risk of child abuse and neglect: The role of the helping alliance. *Child Abuse and Neglect, 20,* 349–361.

Evans, E. (1992). Liberation theology, empowerment theory and social work practice with the oppressed. *International Social Work, 35,* 135–147.

Ferree, M., and Hess, B. (1985). *Controversy and coalition: The new feminist movement.* Boston: Twayne.

Fischer, J., and Corcoran, K. (1994). *Measures for clinical practice: A sourcebook* (Vols. 1–2, 2nd ed.). New York: Free Press.

Flannery, M., and Glickman, M. (1996). *Fountain house: Portraits of lives reclaimed from mental illness.* Center City, MN: Health Communications, Inc.

Fong, M. L., and Cox, B. G. (1983). Trust as an underlying dynamic in a counseling process: How clients test trust. *Personal and Guidance Journal, 62,* 163–166.

Fordham, S. (1996). *Blacked out: Dilemmas of race, identity, and success at Capital High.* Chicago: University of Chicago Press.

Gambrill, E. (1997). *Social work practice: A critical thinker's guide.* New York: Oxford University Press.

Germain, C. B., and Gitterman, A. (1980). *The life model of social work practice.* New York: Columbia University Press.

Gilgun, J., Daly, D., and Handel, G. (Eds.). (1992). *Qualitative methods in family research.* Newbury Park, CA: Sage.

Guillaumin, C. (1995). *Racism, sexism, power and ideology.* London: Routledge.

Gutiérrez, L. (1990). Working with women of color: An empowerment perspective. *Social Work, 35,* 149–153.

Gutiérrez, L., and Nurius, P. (1994). Education and research for empowerment practice (Monograph No. 7). Seattle: University of Washington, School of Social Work, Center for Policy and Practice Research.

Hartley, D., and Strupp, H. (1983). The therapeutic alliance: Its relationship to outcome in brief psychotherapy. In J. Masling (Ed.), *Empirical studies of psychoanalytic theories* (Vol. 1, pp. 1–38). Hillsdale, NJ: Analytical Press.

Hasenfeld, Y. (1987). Power in social work practice. *Social Service Review, 61,* 469–483. Chicago: University of Chicago Press.

Hollis, F. (1970). The psychosocial approach to the practice of casework. In R. Roberts and R. Nee (Eds.), *Theories of social casework* (pp. 33–76). Chicago: University of Chicago Press.

Horvath, A., and Greenberg, L. (1986). The development of the working alliance inventory. In L. Greenberg and W. Pinsof (Eds.), *The psychotherapeutic process: A research handbook* (pp. 529–556). New York: Guilford.

Horvath, A., and Greenberg, L. (Eds.). (1994). *The working alliance: Theory, research, and practice.* New York: Wiley.

Horvath, A., and Symonds, B. (1991). Relation between working alliance and outcome in psychotherapy: A meta-analysis. *Journal of Counseling Psychology, 38,* 139–149.

Irving, A., and Young, T. (2002). Paradigm for pluralism: Mikhail Bakhtin and social work practice. *Social Work, 47,* 19–29.

Jordan, C., and Franklin, C. (1995). *Clinical assessment for social workers: Quantitative and qualitative methods.* Chicago: Lyceum.

Kinney, J., Haapala, D., and Booth, C. (1991). *Keeping families together: The homebuilders model.* New York: Aldine de Gruyter.

Kirk, S., and Kutchins, H. (1992). *The selling of DSM: The rhetoric of science in psychiatry.* New York: Aldine de Gruyter.

Krupnick, J., Sotsky, S., Simmens, S., Moyer, J., Elkin, I., Watkins, J., and Pilkonis, P. (1996). The role of the therapeutic alliance in psychotherapy and pharmacotherapy outcome: Findings in the National Institute of Mental Health treatment of depression collaborative research program. *Journal of Consulting and Clinical Psychology, 64,* 532–539.

LaFromboise, T., Coleman, H. L. K., and Gerton, J. (1993). Psychological impact of biculturalism: Evidence and theory. *Psychological Bulletin, 114,* 395–412.

LaFromboise, T., and Dixon, D. N. (1981). American Indian perception of trustworthiness in a counseling interview. *Journal of Counseling Psychology, 28,* 135–139.

Levine, S., and Herron, W. (1990). Changes during the course of the psychotherapeutic relationship. *Psychological Reports, 66,* 883–897.

Levy, C. (1972). Values and planned change. *Social Casework, 53*(8), 488–493.

Luborsky, L., Crits-Christoph, P., Alexander, L., Margolis, M., and Cohen, M. (1983). Two helping alliance methods for predicting outcome of psychotherapy. *Journal of Nervous and Mental Disease, 171,* 480–491.

Marziali, E., and Alexander, L. (1991). The power of the therapeutic relationship. *American Journal of Orthopsychiatry, 61,* 383–391.

McQuaide, S., and Ehrenreich, J. (1997). Assessing client strengths. *Families in Society: The Journal of Contemporary Human Services, 78,* 201–212.

National Association of Social Workers (1997). *Code of Ethics.* Washington, DC.

Perlman, H. (1965). Self-determination: Reality or illusion? Social Service Review, 39(4), 410–421.

Perlman, H. (1979). *Relationship: The heart of helping people.* Chicago: University of Chicago Press.

Petr, C. (1988). The worker–client relationship: A general systems perspective. *Social Casework, 69,* 620–626.

Pinderhughes, E. (1983). Empowerment for our clients and for ourselves. *Social Casework, 64,* 331–338.

Poulin, J., and Young, T. (1997). Development of a helping relationship for social work practice. *Research on Social Work Practice, 7,* 463–489.

Prochaska, J. O., DiClemente, C. C., and Norcross, J. C. (1992). In search of how people change: Applications to addictive behaviors. *American Psychologist, 47,* 1102–1114.

Proctor, E. (1982). Defining the worker–client relationship. *Social Work, 27,* 430–435.

Rapp, C. (1998). *The strengths model: Case management with people suffering from severe and persistent mental illness.* New York: Oxford University Press.

Rappaport, J. (1981). In praise of paradox: A social policy of empowerment over prevention. *American Journal of Community Psychology, 9,* 1–15.

Reid, W. (1994). The empirical practice movement. *Social Service Review, 68,* 165–184.

Richmond, M. (1917). *Social diagnosis.* New York: Russell Sage.

Rogers, C. (1957). The necessary and sufficient conditions of therapeutic personality change. *Journal of Consulting Psychology, 21,* 95–103.

Russell, M. (1990). *Clinical social work: Research and practice.* Newbury Park, CA: Sage.

Saleebey, D. (1992). *The strengths perspective in social work practice.* New York: Longman.

Saleebey, D. (1997). The strengths perspective: Possibilities and problems. In D. Saleebey (Ed.), *The strengths perspective in social work practice* (2nd ed., pp. 231–245). New York: Longman.

Saleebey, D. (2002). *The strengths perspective in social work practice* (3rd ed.). Boston: Allyn and Bacon.

Simon, B. L. (1994). *The empowerment tradition in American social work history*. New York: Columbia University Press.

Solomon, B. (1976). *Black empowerment*. New York: Columbia University Press.

Tichenor, V., and Hill, C. (1989). A comparison of six measures of working alliance. *Psychotherapy, 26,* 195–199.

Weick, A., and Pope, L. (1988). Knowing what's best: A new look at self-determination. *Social Casework, 69,* 10–16.

Weick, A., Rapp, C., Sullivan, W., and Kisthardt, S. (1989). A strengths perspective for social work practice. *Social Work, 34,* 350–354.

Young, T., and Poulin, J. (1998). The helping relationship inventory: A clinical appraisal. *Families in Society, 79,* 123–133.

4 | EVALUATION AND GENERALIST SOCIAL WORK PRACTICE

David Wells/The Image Works

Ron A., who is in his second year of a 3-year part-time MSW program, has a work site field placement at an Area Agency on Aging. Ron had worked at the agency for 3 years before he began his graduate studies. He is a case manager for elderly clients. In this role, he oversees the delivery and coordination of the various services being provided to the clients. As part of his field placement duties, Ron visits the elderly person in his or her home and completes a comprehensive assessment, from which he develops a case management plan.

Ron met with his first field placement client twice and completed the agency assessment form. He obtained all the necessary information. He felt that he had a beginning relationship with his client and that he had a clear understanding of his client's concerns and service needs.

In his job as a case manager, Ron had worked with clients in implementing their case management plans, but he had never been involved in systematically evaluating client progress. He was unsure how to measure progress on the goals they had set up. He also was unsure how his clients would react to filling out forms and questionnaires. By the end of this chapter, you should be able to help Ron

1. Construct self-anchored rating scales and goal attainment scales
2. Use client logs and behavioral observation in measuring client system progress
3. Locate standardized measures that are appropriate for use with social work client systems
4. Interpret the reliability and validity of standardized measures
5. Design a single-system evaluation to monitor client system progress
6. Plot single-system evaluation data on a line graph
7. Interpret the clinical, visual, and statistical significance of single-system evaluation data

This chapter focuses on the task of evaluating progress. The chapter describes measurement guidelines, types of measures, single-system evaluation designs, and analyses of evaluation data. The concepts and methods for evaluating client system progress presented in this chapter are very relevant for generalist social work practice. They are widely used for evaluating the progress of individual, family, and group client systems. They are equally applicable for evaluating progress with organizational and community client systems. Thus, regardless of the size of the client system, the concepts and methods discussed here can be used to evaluate the effectiveness of your work and client system progress.

These evaluation methods are very compatible with the collaborative model of generalist practice presented in this book. The collaborative model uses a goal-directed approach to practice. The worker and client system specify the desired outcomes of their work together. A single-system design is ideally suited to evaluating progress on goals. The key is identifying measures or indicators of target problems. The same process is used for individual, family, small group, organization, or community target problems.

The ability to evaluate client system progress has become increasingly important in recent years (Franklin and Jordan, 1992). Funding sources such as managed care companies now require social workers and other helping professionals to document client problems and the effectiveness of services provided.

Skill in measurement is needed to comply with this requirement. The practice environment in which generalist social workers currently find themselves requires a higher level of accountability than at any other time in our professional history. It is no longer acceptable to rely solely on professional judgment in determining client service needs and in evaluating client progress.

There are also compelling ethical reasons to measure client progress. Social workers have an ethical responsibility to provide the best services available to their clients. You are responsible for making sure the services you are providing are helping your clients. To assume that what you are doing is working without systematically evaluating effectiveness is unethical. If the client is not making progress, both of you need to know, so that you can address the lack of progress and, if appropriate, change the intervention (Berlin and Marsh, 1993).

Evaluation can also help motivate clients. If the client is making progress, concrete evidence of it can strengthen his or her resolve to make further gains. Conversely, evidence of lack of progress can be a wake-up call, a challenge to renew commitment to change. Measuring progress forces you and the client to take stock. Are we making progress? Are the interventions working? Do we need to try another approach?

A common concern about measurement is that clients will react negatively to it and that it will disrupt the helping relationship (Witkin, 1991). Research has determined that this is not the case. Campbell (1988, 1990) found that clients prefer to systematically evaluate the effectiveness of the services they receive instead of relying solely on practitioner opinion. Applegate (1992) also found that this concern was not justified. Indeed, Poulin and Young (1997) found that clients placed a higher value on evaluation procedures than did their social workers. Social workers tended to underestimate the importance clients placed on evaluating progress. They were much more interested in developing and implementing interventions than in evaluating effectiveness. Clients, on the other hand, were as interested in evaluating effectiveness as they were in developing and implementing interventions. A follow-up qualitative study obtained similar results (Young and Poulin, 1998), showing that clients are more concerned about evaluation than social workers. The message from these studies is clear: It is a mistake to assume that clients will resist measurement procedures and that they do not care about assessing and measuring progress. Clients of social work services, like other consumers, want to know that the services they are receiving are effective.

MEASUREMENT GUIDELINES

Jordan and Franklin state that "competence in measurement will improve social work's status, power base, and the profession's ability to function autonomously" (1995, p. 40). It will also improve the effectiveness of your practice and strengthen the helping relationship (Young and Poulin, 1998). Collaborative social work practice seeks to empower clients. Having clients involved in the development of the measurement plan and in constructing measures is empowering. For this reason, it is best to use measures that involve the client in the data collection process.

Drawing on the work of Barlow, Hayes, and Nelson (1984), Berlin and Marsh developed guidelines for collecting client data. They suggest that the data collection effort will be enhanced if you:

- Specify the client's problems and goals clearly
- Use multiple measures for each objective
- Collect information that is relevant rather than convenient
- Collect information early in the course of the work with the client
- Use good and accurate measures
- Organize the data
- Obtain the client's cooperation and consent (1993, p. 93)

Step 1: *Clearly specify problems and goals.* This guideline is fundamental to the measurement process. As noted earlier, client problems and expected outcomes must be specific and stated in clear, unambiguous terms. Measurable objectives related to each goal must be developed. Collecting client data is impossible without specific and observable indicators attached to each objective (Berlin and Marsh, 1993).

Step 2: *Use multiple measures.* The use of more than one measure to assess a single phenomenon is a basic research strategy referred to as **triangulation** (Royse and Thyer, 1996). The assumption behind this strategy is that all measures are to some extent flawed or imperfect. Because any one measure may not be accurate, it is necessary to use more than one measure to assess client progress. The logical assumption is that if two or more imperfect measures indicate change, there is more reason to be confident that change has occurred than if only one imperfect measure is used. Relying on a single measure of client progress is risky. The problems addressed by generalist social workers and their clients are too complex to be assessed with a single imperfect measure.

The inaccuracy of measurement strategies should not discourage you from using quantitative measures in your practice. Crude indicators of progress are preferable to no indicators. What is important is to be aware of the limitations of measurement tools. The data alone will not provide you and your clients with definitive answers. The data will, however, provide you and your clients with helpful information that can be incorporated into your work together. Analyzing the data with your clients will facilitate the helping process and provide a basis for ongoing assessment of your work together.

Step 3: *Collect relevant information.* Berlin and Marsh warn that "one of the most frequent mistakes that clinicians make is to track something that is not very important" (1993, p. 94). Typically, the client's problem is reconceptualized to fit an existing measure or instrument. The convenience factor is high, but the relevance factor is low. "If the clinician is to collect useful information, he or she must look beyond the enticements of easily acquired, but barely relevant, assessment indices and focus on whether the aspects of the problem targeted for change are really changing" (Berlin and Marsh, 1993, p. 95). If you cannot specify the expected changes, the problem may not have been conceptualized accurately or the terms may not be specific enough. Relevant measures should flow directly from clearly conceptualized problems and objectives.

Step 4: *Collect information early*. There are a number of reasons to begin the process of collecting data early in the helping process. The first reason is that measuring the target problem or objective prior to implementing the intervention provides baseline data, which are a basis for future comparisons. Change must be evaluated comparatively. Without some sort of comparison, it is impossible to assess the extent to which the desired changes have occurred. Collecting assessment data early in the helping process will allow you to periodically evaluate the effectiveness of the work throughout the helping relationship.

A second reason to begin collecting data early in the helping process is to communicate to clients that you are interested in understanding their situation and that you are committed to helping them successfully address their concerns or problems. Measurement is an active and concrete process. Developing measures communicates that you take their concerns seriously and that their concerns are important enough to warrant the effort required to develop measures and collect data.

A third reason to start the measurement process early is that it engages the client in a collaborative activity. You and the client define the target problem, develop the objectives, and develop the measurement plan. You and your client may even develop many of the measures used. The client becomes an active participant in the process. This communicates expectations about how you will work together as well as the idea that the client is the expert on his or her situation.

Step 5: *Use good and accurate measures*. Every effort should be made to use the best measures available. According to Berlin and Marsh (1993), four criteria are useful in judging the adequacy of different measures: relevance, sensitivity to change, reliability, and validity.

Relevance refers to the extent the measure is directly related to the targeted outcomes. Is there a good fit between the measure and the expected changes? For example, in Chapter 6 one of the objectives for the father who was having trouble controlling his temper was to count to 10 and take three deep breaths before responding to his son. In this situation, a measure of how many times the father counted to 10 and took 3 deep breaths would be directly relevant and very appropriate. Measuring how often he refrained from yelling at his son might appear to be an appropriate measure, but it would in fact be less relevant given the change objective. If the treatment objective was to increase the father's self-control, then a self-control measure would be directly relevant. The relevance of any measure is a function of the identified target problem or the specific change objectives.

Sensitivity to change is the second criterion of a good measure. Not all measures are capable of capturing change. Some are more sensitive than others. It may be possible to use measures that have shown change in previous evaluations and have thus been proved useful. A measure's track record of detecting change is one of the best indicators of its sensitivity to change (Berlin and Marsh, 1993; Bloom, Fischer, and Orme, 1995). Often, however, information on a measure's sensitivity is not available.

It is not always possible to know in advance whether a measure will be sensitive to change (Bloom, Fischer, and Orme, 1995). Berlin and Marsh (1993) suggest that global measures are usually less sensitive to change than measures directly related to specific behaviors targeted for change. Bloom, Fischer, and Orme state that measures of behaviors that occur more frequently are more likely to be more sensitive than measures of behaviors that occur less frequently. "This is because a high-frequency behavior is likely to be more responsive to small changes and can both increase or decrease, while a low-frequency behavior can only increase and may be responsive only to major changes" (1995, p. 52).

Reliability refers to the consistency of measurements. "In testing for change, at least two and preferably more measurements are required" (Gabor, Unrau, and Grinnell, 1998, p. 165). When measuring client change, you want to be reasonably confident that the differences among the first measurement and subsequent ones relate to changes in the client and not to problems with the measure. "It is therefore important that a measuring instrument gives the same result with the same unchanged client every time it is administered. An instrument that can do this is said to be reliable" (Gabor, Unrau, and Grinnell, 1998, p. 165).

"Every type of measure involves some kind of error, and the measure is reliable to the extent that the error is minimal" (Berlin and Marsh, 1993, p. 97). The two most common ways of testing the reliability of a measure are to assess its internal consistency and test–retest characteristics. **Internal consistency reliability** is the extent to which the individual items that make up a scale or index are correlated with one another. **Test–retest reliability** refers to the extent to which the same result is obtained when the same measure is administered to the same client at two different points in time. Both types of reliability are important. However, in evaluating client change, test–retest reliability is critical. To the extent possible, use at least one measure that has been tested for reliability and has reliability coefficients of .80 or higher.

Validity refers to the extent to which an instrument measures what it is supposed to measure and not anything else (Kyte and Bostwick, 1997). For example, if you are assessing a client's self-confidence, the instrument should measure self-confidence, not a related concept such as self-esteem. "An instrument is said to be valid when it closely corresponds to the concept it was designed to measure" (Royse and Thyer, 1996, p. 188). Because concepts in social work tend to be complex, no measure will be entirely valid, only more or less so (Gabor, Unrau, and Grinnell, 1998).

There are various ways to determine the validity of an instrument. The least rigorous kind of validity is face validity. Does the instrument appear to measure the concept? A measure is said to have **face validity** if knowledgeable persons agree that it measures what it is intended to measure. "Do the items on the questionnaire appear to be 'getting at' what they should?" (Bloom, Fischer, and Orme, 1995, p. 187).

Another type of validity is **content validity**. This method also relies on expert opinion. In this case, "experts are asked to review it to see if the entire range of the concept is represented in the sample of items selected for the scale" (Royse and Thyer, 1996, p. 188). For example, a scale designed to measure stress should have items that represent the different components of stress, such as feeling tense, feeling pressured, having difficulty sleeping, and being short tempered.

"Neither content nor face validity is sufficient for establishing that a scale has 'true' validity" (Royse and Thyer, 1996, p. 188). For this to occur, a measure must empirically demonstrate its validity. There are a number of methods to empirically demonstrate a measure's validity. "**Concurrent validity** is demonstrated by administering to the same subjects the new scale and another scale that has previously been determined (proven) to have validity" (Royse and Thyer, 1996, p. 188). If the two scales are highly correlated, at .80 or above, the new scale has demonstrated concurrent validity.

Predictive validity refers to the ability of a measure to predict future behavior or attitudes. "The simplest way to determine predictive validity would be to correlate results on a measure one time with the criterion information collected at a later time" (Bloom, Fischer, and Orme, 1995, p. 49). An example is correlating Scholastic Aptitude Test (SAT) scores with students' grade point averages.

Construct validity refers to the extent to which an instrument actually measures the concept in question. Construct validity is established by demonstrating convergent validity and discriminant validity. A measure is said to have **convergent validity** if it is correlated in a predicted manner with other measures with which it theoretically should correlate (**Bloom, Fischer, and Orme, 1999**). For example, a measure of the strength of a helping relationship should correlate positively with measures of trust and openness. Those who are more trusting and open are more likely to develop strong helping relationships with their social workers than those who are less trusting and open.

A measure's **discriminant validity** is demonstrated by a lack of correlation with measures with which it theoretically should not be correlated. This indicates that the measure can discriminate between concepts. For example, there is no theoretical basis for predicting how certain client problems will correlate with the development of a helping relationship with the social worker. Clients with high self-esteem are as likely to develop a strong helping relationship as those with low self-esteem. Similarly, a client's level of depression is not associated with the strength of the helping relationship.

Construct validity is demonstrated when a measure is correlated with other measures that it theoretically should be related to (convergent validity) and not correlated with measures with which it theoretically should not be correlated (discriminant validity). When selecting measures to evaluate client change, look for some evidence of the validity of the measure. At the very least, the measure should have face validity. Empirical verification of the measure's validity is preferable.

Step 6: *Organize the data.* For data to be useful, they have to be organized in some systematic way. It is difficult to interpret or draw meaning from unorganized raw data. Data need to be presented in a way that makes sense to both you and your client. Typically, data obtained to evaluate client change can be easily computed and presented in simple graphs.

The basic graphic presentation of change data is a line graph on which the client's scores are plotted over time. A visual inspection of the data points provides feedback on client progress. Time is plotted on the horizontal (x) axis, and scores measuring the target problem on the vertical (y) axis. The time dimension reflects the number of times the measure of the target problem is completed and the time period between measurements. The time unit selected depends on the nature of the target problem. Typically, measures of the target problem are completed on a daily or weekly basis. Figure 4.1 is a sample line graph on which a client's level of self-esteem is plotted over an 11-week period.

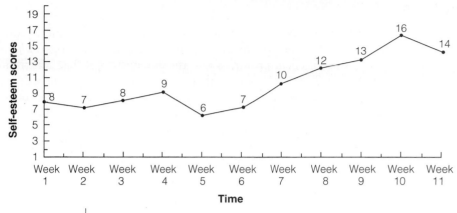

FIGURE 4.1 | CLIENT'S WEEKLY SELF-ESTEEM SCORES

An important component of the helping process is reviewing the data on the graphic displays with clients. In collaborative social work, the clients are actively involved in inspecting the organized data and interpreting the patterns and results. Most clients are interested in examining graphs of their progress and in providing interpretations of what is happening. Involving clients in this process can be a powerful tool. It keeps your work focused on the change objectives, and it provides an opportunity for you and the client to review progress, tasks, and effort as well as the appropriateness of goals and objectives. If strides are being made, it can motivate further efforts. If progress is not forthcoming, you and the client can assess the situation and make adjustments as needed.

Step 7: *Obtain client cooperation and consent.* Naturally, the process of selecting and incorporating measurement strategies into generalist practice requires the full cooperation of clients. Collaborative social work is based on the assumption that clients are full partners in the helping process. Measuring client progress without their full cooperation is a waste of time. Clients need to have ownership of the measures and willingness to engage in a process of self-assessment. Their commitment to the data collection and evaluation process reflects their commitment to achieving the changes they are seeking.

MEASUREMENT TOOLS

There are a number of measurement methods that involve clients, are easy to construct and implement, and are appropriate for generalist social work practice. The more frequently used methods are:

- Client logs
- Behavioral observations
- Rating scales
- Goal attainment scales
- Standardized measures

CLIENT LOGS

Having clients prepare narrative accounts of their activities, thoughts, and feelings is an effective method of monitoring progress. Client logs or journals help clarify the nature of client problems and the circumstances that contribute to the problem situation. Clients often find that keeping a log helps them increase their understanding and awareness of the factors that contribute to the identified problem situation. It enables them to "track the antecedents and consequences, or the feelings and thoughts, surrounding the occurrence of a specific event" (Berlin and Marsh, 1993, p. 99). Client logs allow a client to systematically take notes on the occurrence of a target problem and the events surrounding each occurrence. Doing so prevents distortions and misperceptions caused by faulty memory (Bloom, Fischer, and Orme, 1999).

Client logs also are an excellent source of baseline data on the frequency of the target problem. Baseline data obtained from logs serve as clinical measurements of client thoughts, feelings, and behaviors. "These recordings help the client and the practitioner to gain appropriate insights into the client's functioning, aid in structuring treatment tasks, facilitate client change, and monitor clinical progress during treatment" (Jordan and Franklin, 1995, p. 41).

Client logs are easy to construct. Most are divided into columns, with the types of information the client should record listed at the top of each column (Figure 4.2). "At a minimum it involves recording whether some incident occurred, when it occurred, and how the client responded to it" (Bloom, Fischer, and Orme, 1995, p. 238). Information on circumstances just prior to and just after the problem event may also be included in client logs.

Two decisions need to be made regarding the completion of logs. The first is when to record the information, and the second is what to record. Clients can record at preset time periods or immediately following the occurrence of the target event. **Recording at preset time periods** works if you have narrowed down the occurrence of a target event to a specific period, that is, if you know in advance approximately when the target problem is likely to occur. For example, a family might complain about sibling fights after school and during dinner. The client log then might cover the time period of 3:00 P.M. to 7:00 P.M. in the evening. The client keeping the log would record all the sibling fights that occurred during this time period.

Date	Time	Event	Before Problem	After Problem	Reaction

FIGURE 4.2 | CLIENT LOG

From M. Bloom, J. Fischer, and J. Orme, *Evaluating Practice: Guidelines for the Accountable Professional* (2nd ed.) Copyright © 1995, Allyn and Bacon. Reproduced by permission of Pearson Education, Inc.

The second option is to use **open time categories**. This method is sometimes referred to as **critical incident recording** (Bloom, Fischer, and Orme, 1995). With this type of log, the client decides whether to record an event. The client decides if the event is related to the problem or target and then records it as soon as possible after it occurs. This method works best when you need information about events that are likely to be spread out over the entire day.

In addition to specifying when the recording will take place, you also need to clarify in advance what will be recorded. By design, client logs give the client control over the content. Clients choose which of the many thoughts, feelings, and behaviors they experience daily to include and exclude. They employ a great deal of subjective judgment in completing logs. Information recorded on the log should be limited to what the "client perceives as significantly related to the target" (Bloom, Fischer, and Orme, 1995, p. 240). Thus, you and the client need to be clear about what constitutes a critical incident. Discuss with the client the types of events that would be appropriate for inclusion in the log. In the beginning, encourage clients to be inclusive rather than exclusive in their recordings. Review the first logs together with an eye toward the appropriateness of the entries as well as events that the client did not record but should have.

BEHAVIORAL OBSERVATIONS

"Behavioral observations represent one of the most direct and effective measures of client behavior" (Jordan and Franklin, 1995, p. 46). The frequency and duration of specific client behaviors can be observed and recorded (Bloom, Fischer, and Orme, 1995). Behavioral observation can provide detailed information on the occurrence of client behaviors and the context of those behaviors. It represents one of the most reliable and valid methods of measuring client change.

Typically, the first step in using behavioral observation is to operationally define the target behavior. An example would be specifying the types of disruptive behavior a child displays in the classroom, such as getting out of his or her seat or talking with classmates while the teacher is talking. The target problem must be clearly defined in behavioral terms and must be observable. Observation cannot be used to measure target problems that focus on feelings or thoughts. It is limited to measuring the frequency, duration, and context of behaviors.

The second step is to select the observer or observers. Often, the observers are significant others, family members, or other professionals who have access to the client's person-in-environment interactions. For example, a young child having a problem controlling his or her temper can be observed at home by a parent and at school by a teacher or teacher's aide.

Ideally, at least two people should observe the same events. This makes it possible to establish interobserver agreement and determine the reliability of the observations. "Eighty percent or higher agreement is believed to be acceptable for most clinical situations" (Jordan and Franklin, 1995, pp. 46–47). However, not all practice situations lend themselves to direct observation. If using two or more observers is impractical, you will have to settle for a single observer. "Behavioral observation using one observer lacks the scientific reliability of observation with two or more raters, but it remains an important measurement indicator in clinical assessments because it provides observations of the client's behavior in natural settings" (Jordan and Franklin, 1995, p. 47).

The third step is to train the observers. Observers must know in advance exactly what behavior to look for and how to recognize the behavior when it occurs (Jordan and Franklin, 1995). In addition, they have to be trained to conduct the observations. "Deciding how to sample the behaviors is the fundamental question in conducting a structured observation" (Berlin and Marsh, 1993, p. 107). You must decide whether to record all instances of the behavior or a sample. "Continuous recording involves recording every occurrence of a target behavior every time it occurs" (Bloom, Fischer, and Orme, 1995, p. 133). This requires the observer to be willing and available, and it works best when the target behavior does not occur with great frequency. Often, these conditions cannot be satisfied, and a sampling strategy is used. Figure 4.3 is a form for continuous recording.

Time sampling is appropriate when events occur continuously or frequently. "Time sampling requires the selection of specific units of time, either intervals or discrete points, during which the occurrence or nonoccurrence of a specific behavior is recorded" (Berlin and Marsh, 1993, p. 107). The assumption is that the sample behavior would be the same if all occurrences of it were recorded (Haynes, 1978). There are two types of time sampling: interval and discrete. **Interval sampling** involves selecting a time period and dividing it into equal blocks of time. The observer records the occurrence or nonoccurrence of the behavior during each interval. The behavior is recorded once for each interval regardless of how many times it occurs (Bloom, Fischer, and Orme, 1995). Figure 4.4 shows a form for interval recording.

Discrete time sampling involves selecting specific time periods and recording all instances of the target behavior that occur during the selected periods. The key

Client's Name _____   Recorder's Name _____
Behavior to be Observed _____
_____

Date _____   Location _____

Time	Description of Behavior and Context

FIGURE 4.3 | OBSERVATION FORM FOR CONTINUOUS RECORDING

Client's Name ———————   Recorder's Name ———————

Behavior to be Observed ————————————————————

————————————————————

Date ———— Location ———— Time Period ———— Interval Length ————

Interval	Behavioral Occurrence	Context	Comments
1.	Yes No		
2.	Yes No		
3.	Yes No		

FIGURE 4.4 | OBSERVATION FORM FOR INTERVAL TIME SAMPLING RECORDING

From M. Bloom, J. Fischer, and J. Orme, *Evaluating practice: Guidelines for the accountable professional* (2nd ed.). Published by Allyn and Bacon, Boston, MA. Copyright © 1995 by Pearson Education, Inc. Reproduced by permission of Pearson Education, Inc.

Client's Name ———————   Recorder's Name ———————

Behavior to be Observed ————————————————————

————————————————————

Time Period ———— Location ————

Date	Number of Times Behavior Occurred	Comments

FIGURE 4.5 | OBSERVATION FORM FOR DISCRETE TIME SAMPLING RECORDING

From M. Bloom, J. Fischer, and J. Orme, *Evaluating practice: Guidelines for the accountable professional* (2nd ed.). Published by Allyn and Bacon, Boston, MA. Copyright © 1995 by Pearson Education, Inc. Reproduced by permission of Pearson Education, Inc.

issue in this type of recording is to select periods that are representative in terms of the target behavior. If the behaviors occur often and regularly, you would need fewer periods to obtain a representative sample of them (Bloom, Fischer, and Orme, 1995). If the behaviors occur during certain time periods, for example, during meals, then the selected periods must correspond to the behavioral patterns of the client. Figure 4.5 shows a form for discrete time sampling recording.

Overall, direct observation is an excellent method for assessing client outcomes. It is one of the most effective tools we have for measuring behavior. When it is used with two or more observers, it can provide reliable and valid outcome data. It also has the potential to provide valuable clinical information on the context within which target problems occur. Direct observation should be seriously considered when a target problem is behavioral in nature, the situation allows for direct observation, and implementing direct observation is feasible.

RATING SCALES

Individualized rating scales are measures of client problems that are created by the client and the social worker together (Bloom, Fischer, and Orme, 1995). These types of measures are also referred to as **self-anchored rating scales** (Jordan and Franklin, 1995). The major advantage of an individualized rating scale is that it measures the specific problem or concern that you and your client have identified as the focus of intervention. Thus, a rating scale is directly linked to the feeling, thought, or event that is being addressed in the helping process.

Another advantage of individualized rating scales is that they are based on the client's unique experiences and perceptions. The anchor points of the scale are defined by the client. The low, middle, and high points of the scale are labeled with short, succinct terms. The labels (anchors) describe what the numbers represent (e.g., behaviors, thoughts, and feelings that the client would experience at various points along the scale). Having the client define the anchor points gives the measure great relevance for the client. It becomes a unique measure of the client's feelings, thoughts, or behaviors. It represents his or her perceptions and experiences.

Individualized rating scales usually have 5–10 points. Scales that have more than 10 points are difficult for clients to score and are therefore not recommended (Bloom, Fischer, and Orme, 1995). For example, if a self-esteem scale had 1–100 points, it would be very difficult to determine the difference between ratings of 70 and 75. Scales with seven points are considered ideal, allowing "for some deviations that capture the client's varying experiences, but not creating so many deviations that they lose meaning" (Jordan and Franklin, 1995, p. 43).

Individualized rating scales are easy to construct. Identify with the client the behavior, thought, or feeling that is targeted for change. A wide range of characteristics of the target can be rated: "For example, the seriousness, intensity, importance, or frequency of the target might be rated" (Bloom, Fischer, and Orme, 1995, p. 165). It is important for the target to be clearly articulated and for each rating scale to measure only one aspect or dimension of the target (Gingerich, 1979). Bloom, Fischer, and Orme warn against using different dimensions at each end of the scale, such as happy at one end and sad at the other. People often experience contradictory feelings and can feel happy and sad at the same time. It is preferable to develop two measures, a sadness scale and a happiness scale, rather than one scale on which both dimensions are rated. They also recommend that the target and its measurement be worded "in a way that emphasizes that the client is working toward something positive rather than just trying to eliminate something undesirable" (1995, p. 166). For example, if the problem is feelings of sadness, the goal might be to increase feelings of happiness, and the rating scale would measure the level of happiness.

The next step is to decide on the number of scale points and develop anchor descriptions for the two end points and possibly the middle point. Scales with seven or nine points are popular because they have a clear midpoint. The numbers on the scale represent gradations for the target problem from low to high. The higher the score, the more frequent, serious, important, or problematic the target problem. The end points of the scale are defined by the client, as are the descriptions or examples of the low, middle, and high numbers. These anchor descriptions define the meaning of the numbers on the rating scale. Begin by asking the client to describe what it would be like at one end of the scale for the given target problem. Repeat the process for the other end of the scale and for the midpoint. Anchors should describe the behaviors, thoughts, or feelings the client would experience along the continuum of the scale:

> The depressed client might characterize himself or herself as being most depressed (level 9 on the scale) when he or she can't sleep, can't work and has suicidal thoughts. Thus, when these conditions occur, the client would know to rate himself or herself at level 9. The depressed client may be least depressed, level 1, when he or she feels like going out, wants to eat a large meal, and really enjoys being with friends. (Bloom, Fischer, and Orme, 1995, p. 167)

After you and your client construct the scale, make sure that the anchors fit the client's perception of the situation and that both of you are clear about what constitutes a low or high score. This is best accomplished by practicing using the scale and asking the client to retrospectively complete a rating for different points in his or her life. This will increase the client's comfort in using the scale and provides an opportunity to determine whether the anchor points provide adequate differentiation of the target problem. Individualized rating scales are shown in Figure 4.6.

Comfort in social situations

| 1 | 2 | 3 | 4 | 5 | 6 | 7 | 8 | 9 |

Terrified, overwhelmed, completely unable to engage in conversation with strangers

Somewhat anxious, yet able to respond when spoken to

Relaxed, confident, able to initiate conversations with strangers

Ability to control temper

| 1 | 2 | 3 | 4 | 5 | 6 | 7 | 8 | 9 |

Out of control, completely unable to control temper, flying off the handle for the slightest reason

Somewhat able to control temper, only losing temper when provoked

In complete control, able to control temper even in the most trying conditions

FIGURE 4.6 | INDIVIDUALIZED RATING SCALES

Amount of anxiety

| 1 | 2 | 3 | 4 | 5 | 6 | 7 | 8 | 9 |

Little or no anxiety   Moderate anxiety   Extreme anxiety

Frequency of feeling lonely

| 1 | 2 | 3 | 4 | 5 | 6 | 7 | 8 | 9 |

Never   Sometimes   All the time

FIGURE 4.7 | GENERAL RATING SCALES

An important point to keep in mind in constructing individualized rating scales is that they must be truly *individualized*. The anchors reflect images and pictures of what the situation is like for the client. Your job is to help the client put those images into words. Make sure the words are the client's, not yours or someone else's. The strength of individualized rating scales is that they are client defined and derived directly from the identified target problem.

An alternative to individually constructed anchors is **general anchor descriptions**. Rating scales with general anchors can be used for different client situations. For example, a general rating scale measuring feelings of connectedness could be used to measure a client's relationships with each member of his or her family. The disadvantage of general anchors is that they are more ambiguous and less precise than individually tailored anchors (Coulton and Solomon, 1977). Figure 4.7 shows general rating scales.

Individualized and general rating scales are excellent tools for measuring client progress and change on identified target problems. They have a high level of face validity because they are derived directly from client problems or concerns. There is some evidence that the validity of single-item rating scales is comparable to that of standardized measures (Nugent, 1992). However, the validity and reliability of individualized rating scales cannot be readily established, because they are designed for use with individual clients (Berlin and Marsh, 1993). In this sense, "these scales are not rigorous, scientifically valid, or reliable forms of measurement" (Jordan and Franklin, 1995, p. 46). Rating scales do, however, have a high level of clinical applicability and are excellent tools for measuring client target problems and assessing progress.

GOAL ATTAINMENT SCALES

Goal attainment scaling (GAS) was developed in the field of mental health during the 1960s (Royse and Thyer, 1996). It has been used in a large number of settings and with a wide range of client populations. GAS is similar to individualized rating scales in that the client develops and defines the scale anchors or descriptors. The two methods differ, however, in that goal attainment scales are based directly on the client's goals rather than on behaviors, thoughts, or feelings. A strength of

GAS is that it can be used to monitor client progress toward the identified treatment goals (Jordan and Franklin, 1995). Thus, GAS has been effective in assessing client change related to the identified goals (Corcoran, 1992).

To use GAS, you and your client need to have specified change goals. A question that arises is which goals or how many should be measured (Seaburg and Gillespie, 1977). In general, the number of goals measured should correspond to the number of goals being addressed in the helping relationship. The number of goals being addressed at any given time should be limited. As discussed earlier in this chapter, the goals selected should be those most significant to the client that intervention is most likely to change (Royse and Thyer, 1996).

In conjunction with the client, list each goal on a 5-point scale ranging from –2 to +2. The scale categories are:

(+ 2)   Most favorable outcome expected
(+ 1)   More than expected outcome
(0)   Expected outcome
(– 1)   Less than expected outcome
(– 2)   Most unfavorable outcome

Work with the client to develop anchors for each scale point. The anchors should represent potential outcomes related to each category and should be as specific as possible. Avoid vague, general outcome statements. Figure 4.8 shows a sample goal attainment scale that was developed with an 80-year-old woman who was caring for her 55-year-old mentally retarded son. The social worker was helping the women address her anxiety and concern about her son's future.

Level	Goal 1: Increase Ability to Deal with Panic Attacks	Goal 2: Make Plans for Son's Future
Most unfavorable outcome (– 2)	Unable to calm myself down; unable to catch breath; heart racing, extreme anxiety	Unable to discuss with son his future needs and plans
Less than expected outcome (– 1)	Limited ability to calm myself down, some difficulty breathing, pacing the floor, moderate anxiety	Discussed son's future with other members of the family
Expected outcome (0)	Able to calm down using breathing/relaxation techniques, maintain composure, low anxiety	Discussed with son his future needs
More than expected outcome (+ 1)	Able to verbalize feelings, remain calm in stressful situations, almost no anxiety	Discussed with son his future needs and involved family and outside agencies in assessing son's needs
Most favorable outcome (+ 2)	Able to deal with stressful situations without experiencing panic attacks; very low anxiety; calm and relaxed	Working with son, family, and outside agencies and services to prepare son to care for himself in the future

FIGURE 4.8 | GOAL ATTAINMENT SCALE

Level	Goal 1: Increase Ability to Deal with Panic Attacks	Goal 2: Make Plans for Son's Future
No progress (0)	Unable to calm myself down; unable to catch breath; heart racing, extreme anxiety	Unable to discuss with son his future needs and plans
Some progress (1)	Limited ability to calm myself down, some difficulty breathing, pacing the floor, moderate anxiety	Discussed son's future with other members of the family
Moderate progress (2)	Able to calm down using breathing/relaxation techniques, maintain composure, low anxiety	Discussed with son his future needs
Major progress (3)	Able to verbalize feelings, remain calm in stressful situations, almost no anxiety	Discussed with son his future needs and involved family and outside agencies in assessing son's needs
Optimal progress (4)	Able to deal with stressful situations without experiencing panic attacks; very low anxiety; calm and relaxed	Working with son, family, and outside agencies and services to prepare son to care for himself in the future

FIGURE 4.9 | MODIFIED GOAL ATTAINMENT SCALE

Instead of the -2 to $+2$ scoring system, the worker is using a modified format that is more intuitive and easier to explain to clients. It uses the following scale categories:

(4)   Optimal progress
(3)   Major progress
(2)   Moderate progress
(1)   Some progress
(0)   no progress

These categories focus on desired progress to a greater extent than the traditional GAS scoring format and thus reflect a more positive orientation. Figure 4.9 contains the same examples as Figure 4.8 but in the modified scoring format.

GAS is a client-focused method of measuring progress. It is a direct extension of the goal-oriented approach to practice and is easily incorporated into generalist social work practice with a diverse range of client populations. GAS also empowers clients by placing responsibility for defining and monitoring progress with them. The client is viewed as the expert on what constitutes progress and on determining the extent to which progress is being made. In these respects, GAS is useful as a clinical measurement tool for engaging clients in the helping process.

STANDARDIZED MEASURES

Standardized measures are instruments developed following empirical scale construction techniques with uniform administration and scoring procedures (Jordan and Franklin, 1995). Their reliability is known, and their validity has usually been empirically tested.

Standardized measures are available for a wide range of client behaviors, including marital satisfaction, self-esteem, anxiety, and family relations. Some standardized measures assess global behaviors, such as generalized contentment, while others assess specific behaviors and problems, such as fear, depression, and sexual satisfaction. Standardized measures are available in rapid assessment formats with up to 25 scale items, as well as in lengthy, comprehensive formats with hundreds of scale items. Rapid assessment instruments are easy to use and to incorporate into generalist social work practice.

"Standardized measures represent the most useful quantitative clinical measurement tools that are available to practitioners" (Jordan and Franklin, 1995, p. 53). There are numerous sources of standardized measures. *Measures for Clinical Practice* by Fischer and Corcoran (1994) is an excellent two-volume collection of rapid assessment instruments. Volume 1 contains measures for use with couples, families, and children, and Volume 2 contains instruments for individual adults. The two-volume set contains more than 300 different brief assessment instruments, with supporting information on each instrument's purpose, scoring, reliability, and validity. Another excellent source of rapid assessment instruments is *Measures of Personality and Social Psychological Attitudes* (1991) by Robinson, Shaver, and Wrightsman. In this book, measures are organized by clinical topic (e.g., self-esteem, depression, anxiety).

An excellent list of commercially available measures can be found in *Clinical Assessment for Social Workers* by Jordan and Franklin (1995). The WALMYR Publishing Company is an excellent source for commercially available measurement instruments designed specifically for use in social work practice. Walter Hudson, the founder of WALMYR, pioneered the use of rapid assessment instruments in social work practice (Hudson, 1982). WALMYR sells a number of individual and family adjustment scales as well as comprehensive multidimensional assessment instruments.

Standardized measures, especially the rapid assessment variety, are well suited for use in generalist social work practice. If you can locate one that closely corresponds to identified client problems or concerns, standardized measures offer several advantages. They have known psychometric properties, that is, their reliability and validity have been established. They are also efficient, do not require extensive training, and are easy to administer and score (Fischer and Corcoran, 1994).

DESIGNING THE EVALUATION

Having established measurable goals and selected measurement strategies, the next step is to determine how you are going to implement the evaluation process. The term *evaluation design* is often used to describe how practitioners plan to evaluate progress and case outcomes (Bloom, Fischer, and Orme, 1995). One of the most widely used ways to evaluate practice effectiveness in social work is the single-system design (Miley, O'Melia, and DuBois, 1998). *Single-system designs* are sometimes referred to as single-case designs, N = 1 designs, interrupted time–series designs, and subject-replication designs. "Whatever name is used, a formal case-level evaluation is a study of one entity—a single client, a single group, a single couple, a single family, a single organization, or a single community—involving repeated measurements over time in order to measure change" (Gabor, Unrau, and Grinnell, 1998, p. 175).

Single-system designs hold great promise for generalist social workers. The requirements for using them fit well with generalist practice principles. Single-system designs require clear specification of the target problem, development of measurable goals, selection and implementation of an intervention, and continued monitoring of the client's progress on the identified target problem. All these requirements are consistent with the requirements of sound generalist social work practice.

Bloom, Fischer, and Orme (1999) provide a comprehensive and detailed description of numerous types of single-system designs (see also Tripodi, 1994). However, as Berlin and Marsh point out, "the types of designs that are likely to be used in an ongoing way in practice are more limited" (1993, p. 120). The single-system design selected depends primarily on what questions you are attempting to answer (Berlin and Marsh, 1993). Two questions appropriate for generalist social work practice evaluations are: Is the intervention working? and Is the intervention causing the change?

More complex experimental designs provide information on the causal effect of the intervention. Did the client system improve because of the intervention? What aspects of the intervention are most important in causing the change? Answers to such questions contribute to social work knowledge. They help document the effectiveness of various interventions with different types of clients and target problems. However, answering questions about causality and implementing experiential type designs are beyond the level of evaluation expected for generalist social work practitioners. They are better addressed through research than through ongoing social work practice with clients.

As social workers, we have a responsibility to promote the well-being of our clients (NASW, 1997). This entails, in part, assessing the effectiveness of our interventions. Is the client making progress? Does the intervention appear to be working? Is the target problem improving, getting worse, or staying the same? This book focuses only on designs that provide information on client progress. Such designs best fit generalist social work practice. They are easy to implement with client systems, and they provide important information on the effectiveness of the work.

COMPONENTS OF SINGLE-SYSTEM DESIGNS

There are a number of single-system evaluation designs. Some components are common to all of them. The basic components of single-subject designs are

- Specifying the target problem
- Developing quantitative measures of the target problem
- Establishing baseline measures of the target problem before intervention
- Measuring the target problem repeatedly throughout the intervention
- Displaying the data on a graph
- Making comparisons across phases

Specifying the target problem, developing measures, and displaying data on graphs discussed earlier.

Establishing Baselines. The baseline is the measure of the target problem before the worker provides service. Repeated measurements prior to the intervention are necessary to establish a baseline. The baseline allows you to compare the client's target problem before and after the intervention (Marlow, 1998).

There are two types of baselines. For the **concurrent baseline,** data are collected while other assessment activities are taking place. Repeated measures of the target problem are collected before you implement an intervention with the client system. For the **retrospective baseline,** the client reconstructs measures of the target problem from an earlier time period, using his or her memory. In many situations, delaying the intervention while a concurrent baseline is obtained is unacceptable. For example, it would be unethical to delay providing counseling services to people who experienced a traumatic event, such as a school shooting, in order to obtain baseline information on the victims' level of traumatic stress. In such cases, using a retrospective baseline is an acceptable alternative.

A common question is how many data points or measurements are needed for the baseline. The answer is that it depends. For meaningful comparisons to be made between the preintervention (baseline) and the intervention phases, the baseline has to be stable. That is, there has to be an observable pattern of measurement scores during the baseline period. "A stable baseline is one that does not contain obvious cycles or wide fluctuations in the data" (Bloom, Fischer, and Orme, 1995, p. 333). Fluctuations are acceptable only if they occur with some regularity (Marlow, 1998). Thus, ideally, the baseline phase does not end until the baseline is stable. How long this takes is influenced, in part, by the amount of variation between the data points. The greater the variation (range of scores), the more data points needed to achieve stability. Conversely, if the variation between points on the baseline is relatively small (similar scores), fewer data points are needed to achieve stability.

Using an unstable baseline is problematic. If the measures of the target problem fluctuate widely and no pattern exists, it is difficult to determine what factors are affecting changes in the target problem and whether change has occurred once the intervention starts (Bloom, Fischer, and Orme, 1995). In other words, it is unclear whether changes between the baseline and the intervention phases are due to usual fluctuations in the target problem or if change has actually taken place.

Making Comparisons. Assessing change requires making some sort of comparison. In traditional experimental evaluation designs, a treatment group is compared with a control group that does not receive treatment. In case evaluations using single-system designs, the client provides the basis for comparison. In essence, the client serves as his or her own control group. Is the client better after getting help than before? Without comparisons, it is impossible to assess change.

Work with clients can be divided into phases (Gabor, Unrau, and Grinnell, 1998). During the first few contacts, baseline data on the target problem may be collected; this is the assessment phase. The second phase is the next series of sessions, in which an intervention is implemented. If the first intervention did not achieve the desired results, a second intervention may be tried; this would be the third phrase.

Single-system evaluations use letters to label the different phases. The letter *A* is used to designate the baseline phase. "Successive interventions are represented by successive letters: B for the first, C for the second, D for the third, and so on" (Gabor, Unrau, and Grinnell, 1998, p. 180). A single-system design that consists of a baseline phase followed by an intervention is called an **AB design**. An evaluation that does not have a baseline and only one intervention is called a **B design**. An **ABA design** is one in which a baseline (*A*) phase is followed by an intervention (*B*) phase and a second baseline (*A*) period. The various phases of a single-subject design are usually labeled on the line graph and represented by dashed vertical lines. Figure 4.10 is a line graph of an AB design.

The AB design is the most frequently used single-system design in service settings (Berlin and Marsh, 1993). In this design, repeated measurements of the target problem are taken during the baseline (*A*) and intervention (*B*) phases. Measures of the target problem are taken before the intervention is implemented and throughout the intervention. As with all single-system evaluations, the findings are analyzed by plotting the data points on a chart.

The advantage of the AB design is its simplicity (Marlow, 1998). One must merely identify or develop an appropriate measurement of the target problem and then take repeated measurements during the first baseline phase and the intervention phase. This design can easily be incorporated into generalist social work practice. It is consistent with normal practice procedures in that an assessment data-gathering phase is followed by an intervention phase (Berlin and Marsh, 1993). The design usually does not compromise or hinder the development of a helping relationship and the provision of service. It fits well into a collaborative model of generalist practice, and it provides evidence of whether the intervention is working.

The one area of potential difficulty with the AB design is obtaining a baseline. This is a problem with all single-system designs used to evaluate ongoing practice with client systems. Delaying the intervention while baseline data is collected is problematic when the situation warrants immediate attention. Obtaining measures of the

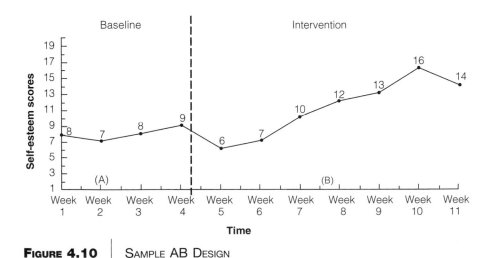

FIGURE 4.10 | SAMPLE AB DESIGN

target problem over a prolonged period of time often is not feasible or desirable. In these situations, developing a retrospective baseline is best. You and the client construct a baseline from the client's recollection of the target problem in the recent past. Although it is a compromise, a retrospective baseline provides a basis of comparison to answer the fundamental question: Is the intervention working?

The B design is the preferred option when it is necessary to intervene immediately, as in a crisis situation, without collecting baseline information or retrospective baseline information (Berlin and Marsh, 1993). The B design is often referred to as a **monitoring design** (Miley, O'Melia, and DuBois, 1998) or a **case study design** (Bloom, Fischer, and Orme, 1999). It consists solely of an intervention (*B*) phase. Repeated measures of the target problem are taken throughout the intervention. This design is weaker than the AB design because preintervention comparison data are not available. It does, however, provide information on client progress, whether the target problem is improving, and whether the goals of the intervention have been achieved.

A third design that can be used to evaluate client progress is the **ABC design**, or the **successive intervention design**. This design is an extension of the AB design. It entails the introduction of a second intervention (*C*) phase. If additional interventions are added beyond the second (*C*), they are labeled *D, E*, and so on. The ABC design is used when the first (*B*) intervention is modified or when the first intervention does not appear to be working. It does not provide information on which intervention caused change in the target problem, nor does it allow for separation of the effects of the successive interventions. It does, however, provide information on client progress.

ANALYZING SINGLE-SYSTEM DATA

Single-system design data is plotted on line graphs similar to those in Figure 4.10 and 4.11. Three types of significance can be used to judge change in the target problem: clinical, visual, and statistical.

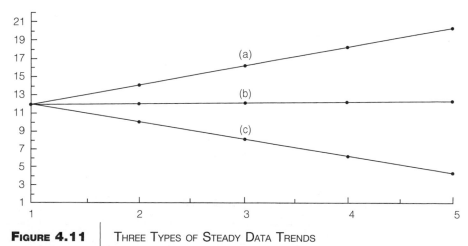

FIGURE 4.11 | THREE TYPES OF STEADY DATA TRENDS

From *Fundamental approaches to single subject design and analysis* by C. H. Krishef. Copyright © 1991 by Krieger Publishing Company. Reprinted/adapted with permission.

CLINICAL SIGNIFICANCE

Clinical significance, also known as **practical significance**, is based on the idea "that somebody—especially the client—believes that there has been meaningful change in the problem" (Bloom, Fischer, and Orme, 1999, p. 506). Clinical significance is achieved when the specified goal of the intervention has been reached (Marlow, 1998). Determining clinical significance is generally a subjective process that requires discussion and negotiation among the involved parties (Bloom, Fischer, and Orme, 1999). If everyone involved agrees that the target problem has been resolved, clinical significance has been achieved.

Determining clinical significance when a goal has not been fully achieved is more difficult: How much change is clinically meaningful? There are no criteria for establishing the clinical significance of partial change in the target problem. Client change can be considered clinically significant if those involved in the helping process agree that meaningful change has occurred.

VISUAL SIGNIFICANCE

Visual analysis is used for data that has been collected over time. It focuses on the trend and direction of the data (Krishef, 1991). A **trend** occurs when data points move directionally in a relatively steady manner. Figure 4.11 shows three basic steady trends. "The 'a' line represents a steadily increasing pattern, the 'b' line displays steadiness of the data without either positive or negative direction, and the 'c' line depicts a steadily decreasing data pattern" (Krishef, 1991, p. 43).

Visual analysis also focuses on changes in the level of the data (Berlin and Marsh, 1993; Marlow, 1998). **Level** refers to the magnitude of the data. For example, a change in level occurs when scores that were at 2 or 3 in the baseline stage jump to 8 or 9 during the intervention stage. Figure 4.12 shows a line graph in which there is a change in the level of the data.

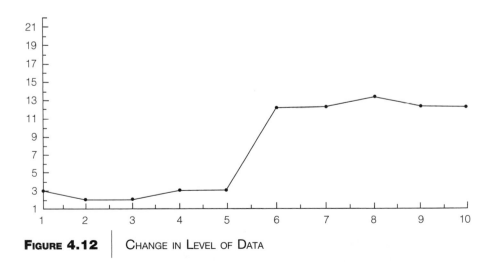

FIGURE 4.12   CHANGE IN LEVEL OF DATA

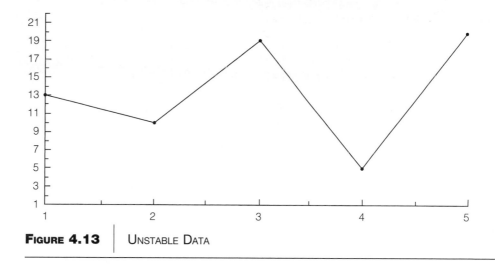

FIGURE 4.13 | UNSTABLE DATA

Data in which there are no discernible trends or patterns are considered **unstable**. Unstable data show wide fluctuations in the measurement of the target problem (Figure 4.13). The interpretation of unstable data is difficult. Little can be said beyond the fact that there is no pattern and the scores vary widely.

The visual analysis of single-system data is based primarily on a comparison of the baseline and intervention phases. For meaningful comparisons to be made, the baseline data must be stable. If they are not, interpretation of the effect of the intervention is impossible. Interpretation is also difficult if the baseline data are moving steadily in a direction that would represent improvement on the target problem. For example, if a decrease in occurrence of the target problem represents client improvement and the baseline trend shows a steady decline on the measure, it would be difficult to attribute the improved scores to the effectiveness of the intervention, because the data were already moving in the desired direction (Krishef, 1991).

Figure 4.14 shows nine configurations of change in the baseline and intervention phases. Determining change is unequivocal when the baseline is stable and the intervention has a sharply increasing or decreasing trend, as in panel a in Figure 4.14, or when the trend at the intervention phase is in the opposite direction of the trend at baseline (panels b and c). The strongest change is when there is a shift in both trend and level in the improved direction (Berlin and Marsh, 1993). Figure 4.13 shows unstable data with no trends.

Calculating a celeration line helps visually determine a trend in the data (Bloom, Fischer, and Orme, 1999). A **celeration line** connects the midpoints of the first and second halves of the baseline phase and extends into the intervention phase (Figure 4.15). The basic idea is that the trend established during the baseline phase is an estimate of what would happen if the baseline pattern were to continue and there were no intervention.

Clear evidence of change (change in direction)

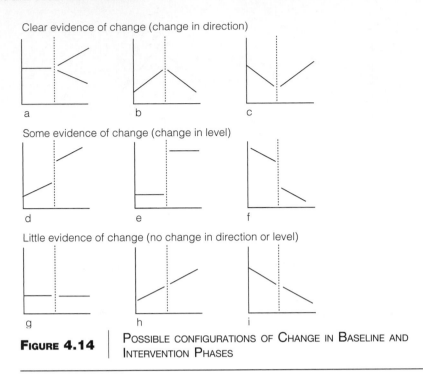

a   b   c

Some evidence of change (change in level)

d   e   f

Little evidence of change (no change in direction or level)

g   h   i

FIGURE 4.14 | POSSIBLE CONFIGURATIONS OF CHANGE IN BASELINE AND INTERVENTION PHASES

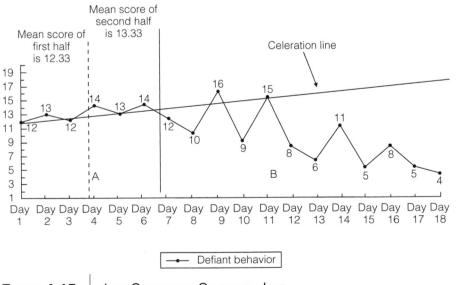

FIGURE 4.15 | LINE GRAPH WITH CELERATION LINE

The steps involved in calculating a celeration line are as follows:

1. Plot the baseline and intervention data on a line graph.
2. Divide the baseline section of the line graph in half, drawing a vertical line. If there are an even number of data points in the baseline, draw the line between the data points; if there are an odd number of points, draw the line through the midpoint number.
3. Divide each half into half by drawing dashed vertical lines on the chart.
4. Determine the mean score of the first half of the baseline by adding the scores in the half and dividing by the number of scores in the half. For baselines with an odd number of scores, omit the middle number.
5. Determine the mean score of the second half of the baseline by adding the scores in the half and dividing by the number of scores in the half. For baselines with an odd number of scores, omit the middle number.
6. Mark the dashed vertical line at the mean point for each half.
7. Draw a solid line connecting the two marks in the baseline, and extend the line through the intervention phase.

STATISTICAL SIGNIFICANCE

Statistical analysis of single-system data has become an accepted practice (Berlin and Marsh, 1993). There are a number of methods for determining statistical significance of time-series data (see Bloom, Fischer, and Orme, 1999, for a detailed discussion). One straightforward method for calculating statistical significance of single-system data is the **two standard deviation approach**. This approach, as its name suggests, is based on the **standard deviation**, which measures the dispersion of scores around the mean.

The basic idea is that $\pm$ 2 standard deviations (SD) represents about 95 percent of the scores, and the likelihood that two scores would fall outside of $\pm$ 2 SD is less than 5 times in a hundred. Thus, if two or more scores fall outside the two standard deviation band, we assume that statistically significant change has occurred. The two standard deviation approach was developed by Shewart (1931) for industrial evaluation and was first used with single-system data by Gottman and Leiblum (1974). The approach offers many advantages: "The procedure can be completed easily with a hand calculator, it can be completed even with 'short' baselines (i.e., when there are fewer than ten points in the baseline)" (Berlin and Marsh, 1993, p. 135).

The steps involved in calculating the two standard deviation approach are shown in Case 4.1.

Interpretation of the two standard deviation approach is simple. Plot the bands representing 2 SD above and below the baseline mean on a line graph that contains baseline and intervention scores. If two consecutive data points in the intervention phase go beyond the 2 SD band, the results show change that is statistically significant at the .05 level. If two or more data points go beyond the band in the desired direction, the results show improvement that is statistically significant at

CASE 4.1	STEPS FOR COMPUTING TWO STANDARD DEVIATION BAND APPROACH*

Computational steps | **Data**

1. Record baseline observations.

$$\frac{x}{\begin{array}{c}6\\6\\5\\4\\3\\4\\4\\5\\5\\4\end{array}}$$

2. Sum (Σ) these scores.

3. Calculate mean:
   divide sum by n where n is the
   number of scores in baseline phase.

   $\left(\text{Mean} = \bar{x} = \frac{\Sigma x_i}{n}\right)$

$46/10 = 4.6 = \text{mean} = \bar{x}$

4. Calculate standard deviation:
   find $(x - \bar{x})$ for all scores, then $(x - \bar{x})^2$,
   then sum and divide by $(n - 1)$.
   Find the square root.

   $\left(\text{Standard Deviation} = \sqrt{\frac{\Sigma(x - \bar{x})^2}{n - 1}}\right)$

x	$(x - \bar{x})$	$(x - \bar{x})^2$
6	1.4	1.96
6	1.4	1.96
5	.4	.16
4	−.6	.36
3	−1.6	2.56
4	−.6	.36
4	−.6	.36
5	.4	.16
5	.4	.16
4	−.6	.36
46	0	8.40/9 = .93

$\sqrt{.93} = .96$

5. Form the two standard deviation band by
   doubling the standard deviation, adding it to the
   mean for the upper band, and subtracting it from
   the mean for the lower band.

   $2 \times .96 = 1.92$
   $4.6 + 1.92 = 6.5$
   $4.6 - 1.92 = 2.7$

6. Plot the upper and lower bands around the mean.

7. If two consecutive data points during the intervention phase drift outside the standard deviation line,
   there is evidence for a statistically significant shift.

*From S. Berlin and J. Marsh, *Informing practice decisions*. Published by Allyn and Bacon, Boston, MA. Copyright © 1993 by Pearson Education, Inc. Reprinted by permission of Pearson Education, Inc.

the .05 level. If two or more data points go beyond the band in the undesired direction, the results show deterioration that is statistically significant at the .05 level (Bloom, Fischer, and Orme, 1999). Figure 4.16 is a line graph in which the two standard deviation approach is used.

Incorporating existing measures or developing your own instruments is a critical component of responsible generalist social work practice. In almost every practice setting, social workers are required to show effectiveness and to document client progress. Measurement and practice are becoming interdependent. No longer is an understanding of evaluation methods left to researchers. It is something that all social workers need to understand and master.

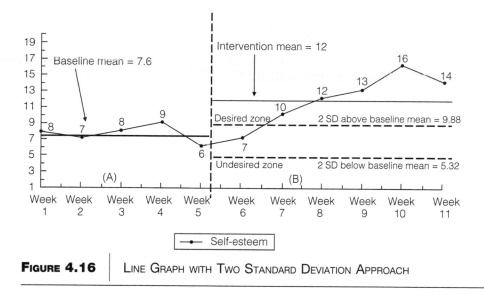

FIGURE 4.16 | LINE GRAPH WITH TWO STANDARD DEVIATION APPROACH

SUMMARY

Evaluation is not separate from social work practice; it is an integrated part of generalist social work practice. The reasons for evaluating client progress are many. Social workers have an ethical responsibility to provide the best services available to their clients and to make sure that the services are helping. To assume that what you are doing is working without systematically evaluating effectiveness is unethical. If the client is not making progress, both of you need to know.

Guidelines for collecting evaluation data stress the importance of clearly specifying problems and goals. Multiple measures should be used to assess each goal; only relevant information should be collected; and measurement should begin as early as possible in the helping process. An important consideration in selecting measures is the reliability and validity of the instrument.

Five types of measures can easily be used in evaluating practice. Client logs help clients monitor their own behaviors, thoughts, or feelings. Logs can be a powerful tool not only in documenting the occurrence of specific behaviors but also in helping clients clarify the nature of problems and problem situations.

Behavioral observation is similar to client log recording, except that someone other than the client does the recording. The other person, who may be a parent or a teacher, observes the client and records the frequency of specified behaviors. Behavioral observation can provide detailed information on the occurrence of client behaviors and the context of those behaviors.

Rating scales are easy to construct and use. Individualized rating scales incorporate the client's own descriptions of the desired changes. The scale is the client's own personal measure of progress. General rating scales are also created by the worker and client to measure desired changes. They are "general" in that the client does not describe in specific terms the lower and upper points of the scale. More general descriptors are used.

Goal attainment scales are similar to individualized rating scales in that the client develops and defines the scale anchors. They differ in that goal attainment scales are based directly on the client's goals rather than on behaviors, thoughts, or feelings. Their strength is that they can be used to directly monitor progress on the identified goals.

Standardized measures are instruments that have been developed following empirical scale construction techniques. The advantage of standardized measures is that they have established reliability and validity. There may or may not be standardized measures available that fit the identified target problem. If standardized measures are available that closely correspond to the identified client concerns, their use in evaluation is recommended.

Three single-system evaluation designs are easily incorporated into generalist social work practice. The AB design is the most frequently used single-system design in social service settings. In this design, repeated measurements of the target problem are taken during the baseline and intervention phases. Baseline data may be collected concurrently or retrospectively. This design fits well with the collaborative model of generalist practice, and it provides evidence of client progress.

The case study, or B design, is the preferred option when it is necessary to intervene immediately without collecting baseline information or even retrospective baseline information. This design is weaker than the AB design because of the lack of preintervention comparison data. Nevertheless, it does provide information on client progress.

The ABC design can be used to evaluate additional interventions. This design is used when the first intervention is modified or does not appear to be working. A second intervention is added and monitored. Additional interventions are labeled *D, E,* and so forth.

Analysis of single-system design data is derived from an examination of the data on line graphs. The data points are plotted and can be examined visually and statistically. In both methods, the baseline data points are compared with the intervention data points. Visual significance occurs when there is a distinct change in the pattern of the data points between the baseline and intervention phases. Statistical significance can be determined by the two standard deviation method.

The intervention and evaluation plan specifies what will be done by whom to achieve the identified goals as well as how progress on the goals will be evaluated. It is the contract between the worker and the client regarding the helping process. It is the plan of action that the social worker and client lay out in response to the client's problems and concerns. However, it should not be viewed as fixed once it has been developed. Priorities, goals, and plans often change and are modified as the helping process unfolds.

CASE EXAMPLE

CASE 4.2 | **THEODORE J.'S INTERVENTION AND EVALUATION PLAN**

The following case study consists of an intervention and evaluation plan for Theodore J. Denise Bubel prepared it when she was a first-year MSW student placed in an adult partial hospitalization program.

Problem Situation and Case Assessment Summary
Mr. J. is an 82-year-old Caucasian who lives with his 80-year-old wife. He attends the adult partial hospitalization program 5 days a week. He has been diagnosed with irreversible dementia. He suffers from memory loss and cognitive decline, which cause him frustration and anxiety. He also has strong feelings of shame and embarrassment about his medical condition. Mrs. J. is very stressed and is having difficulty coping with the demands of his care and his deteriorating health.

Change Goals:
Goal 1:   To have Mr. J. take more responsibility for himself.

CASE 4.2 | *Continued*

Goal 2: To reduce Mr. J.'s feelings of shame and embarrassment about his incontinence.

Goal 3: To reduce Mrs. J.'s level of stress.

Goal, Intervention, Evaluation Worksheet (1)

Goal: To have Mr. J take more responsibility for himself.

Objective: Mr. J. will review his daily "to do" list every day before each meal by December 1.

Objective: Mr. J. will take his medications every day at noon without being told to by his social worker or his wife by December 1.

Intervention Activities:

Client: Mr. J. will meet with his social worker at least once a day during the week to identify and discuss memory aid strategies.

Worker: Mr. J.'s social worker will meet with him daily to discuss memory aid strategies and to reinforce his taking responsibility for self-care.

The social worker will monitor Mr. J.'s compliance in reviewing his "to do" list before his breakfast and noon meals.

The social worker will monitor Mr. J.'s compliance in taking his medications before his noon meal.

The social worker will review with Mr. J. his progress at the end of each week.

Others: Mrs. J. will monitor Mr. J.'s compliance in reviewing his "to do" list before his meals on the weekends.

Mrs. J. will monitor Mr. J.'s compliance in taking his medications before his noon meal.

Mrs. J. will report Mr. J.'s weekend compliance to the social worker every Monday morning.

Evaluation and Measurement:

At the end of each week the social worker and Mr. J. will complete the two goal attainment scales.

Goal Attainment Scales

Level	Objective 1: Review "to do" before each meal	Objective 2: Take noon meds every day
Most unfavorable (– 2)	0 to 20% of the time	Never
Less than expected (– 1)	21% to 40% of the time	Remembers 1–2 days
Expected (0)	41% to 60% of the time	Remembers 3–4 days
More than expected (+ 1)	61% to 80% of the time	Remembers 4–5 days
Most favorable (+ 2)	81% to 100% of the time	Remembers 6–7 days

Goal, Intervention, Evaluation Worksheet (2)

Goal: To reduce Mr. J.'s feelings of shame and embarrassment about his incontinence.

Objective: Mr. J. will acknowledge his feelings of shame and embarrassment about his incontinence in his support group by October 1.

Objective: Mr. J. will feel comfortable going in public wearing undergarments designed for incontinence by November 1.

Intervention Activities:

Client: Mr. J. will attend his daily support group at the adult partial hospitalization program.

Mr. J. will meet with his social worker once a day to discuss his feelings about his incontinence.

Worker: The social worker will provide individual counseling to Mr. J. on a daily basis.

(Continued)

CASE 4.2 | *Continued*

The social worker will monitor Mr. J.'s participation in his support group.

The social worker will review with Mr. J. his progress at the end of each week.

Others: Mrs. J. will encourage Mr. J. to wear adult undergarments when they go out in public.

Evaluation and Measurement:

The social worker will monitor Mr. J.'s participation in the support group and his willingness to discuss his concerns about his incontinence.

At the end of each week the social worker and Mr. J. will complete the public comfort rating scale.

Feelings of comfort in public over incontinence issues

I am not comfortable going in public			I am somewhat comfortable going in public			I am comfortable going in public		
1	2	3	4	5	6	7	8	9

Goal, Intervention, Evaluation Worksheet (3)

Goal: To reduce Mrs. J.'s level of stress.

Objective: Mrs. J. will have a home health aide to help her care for her husband by October 1.

Objective: Mrs. J. will use relaxation techniques when she feels stressed by November 1.

Intervention Activities:

Client: Mrs. J. will apply for home health aide services.

Mrs. J. will learn and practice relaxation techniques.

Worker: The social worker will provide Mrs. J. with a referral to the home health care agency.

The social worker will teach Mrs. J. relaxation techniques.

The social worker will meet with Mrs. J. once a month to review her situation.

Others:

Evaluation and Measurement:

The social worker will monitor Mrs. J.'s referral for home health care.

Once a month the social worker and Mrs. J. will meet to discuss the effectiveness of the relaxation techniques.

Once a month Mrs. J. will complete the Index of Clinical Stress (Hudson and Abell, 1992).

Discussion Questions

1. How realistic are the stated goals and objectives for Mr. and Mrs. J. (Case 4.2)? Does the measurement and evaluation plan appear to be appropriate? How else might one assess progress on the goals? How would you proceed in evaluating progress?

2. Mrs. J. is reported to be very stressed and is having difficulty coping with the demands of her husband's care and deteriorating health. What interventions would be appropriate to help Mrs. J. cope with her situation? Would a stress management approach be warranted? For information on stress management techniques and concepts, see Greenberg 2001.

3. Discuss the use of evaluation in your field placement. How is progress evaluated? What roles do clients play in the process? How could you strengthen the evaluative component of the social work services provided by your field placement agency?

4. Discuss the strengths and limitations of the five types of measures commonly used in single-system design evaluation. Under what conditions could you incorporate their use in your generalist practice? In what ways would you have difficulty using these types of measures in your practice?

5. Discuss possible ways of introducing clients to the idea of using a single-system evaluation design. List the major points you would cover, and identify possible concerns clients might have about measurement and graphing.

References

Applegate, J. (1992). The impact of subjective measures on nonbehavioral practice research: Outcome vs. process. *Families in Society, 73,* 100–109.

Barlow, D., Hayes, S., and Nelson, R. (1984). *The scientist practitioner.* New York: Pergamon Press.

Berlin, S., and Marsh, J. (1993). *Informing practice decisions.* New York: Macmillan.

Bloom, M., Fischer, J., and Orme, J. (1995). *Evaluating practice: Guidelines for the accountable professional* (2nd ed.). Boston: Allyn and Bacon.

Bloom, M., Fischer, J., and Orme, J. (1999). *Evaluating practice: Guidelines for the accountable professional* (3rd ed.). Boston: Allyn and Bacon.

Campbell, J. (1988). Client acceptance of single-system evaluation procedures. *Social Work Research and Abstracts, 24,* 21–22.

Campbell, J. (1990). Ability of practitioners to estimate client acceptance of single-system evaluation procedures. *Social Work, 35,* 9–14.

Corcoran, K. (1992). Practice evaluation: Setting goals, measuring and assessing change. In K. Corcoran (Ed.), *Structuring change: Effective practice for common client problems* (pp. 28–47). Chicago: Lyceum.

Coulton, C. J., and Solomon, P. L. (1977). Measuring outcomes of intervention. *Social Work Research and Abstracts, 13,* 3–9.

Fischer, J., and Corcoran, K. (1994). *Measures for clinical practice: A sourcebook* (Volumes 1 and 2, 2nd ed.). New York: Free Press.

Franklin, C., and Jordan, C. (1992). Teaching students to perform assessment. *The Journal of Social Work Education, 28,* 222–241.

Gabor, P. A., Unrau, Y. A., and Grinnell, R. M. (1998). *Evaluation for social workers: A quality improvement approach for the social services.* Boston: Allyn and Bacon.

Gingerich, W. (1979). Procedure for evaluating clinical practice. *Health and Social Work, 4,* 104–130.

Gottman, J. M., and Leiblum, S. R. (1974). *How to do psychotherapy and how to evaluate it.* New York: Holt, Rinehart and Winston.

Greenberg, J. S. (2001). *Comprehensive stress management* (7th ed.). New York: McGraw-Hill.

Haynes, S. N. (1978). *Principles of behavioral assessment.* New York: Gardner.

Hudson, W. (1982). *The clinical measurement package: A field manual.* Homewood, IL: Dorsey Press.

Hudson, W., and Abell, N. (1992). *Index of clinical stress (ICS).* Tallahassee, FL: WALMYR Publishing Co.

Jordan, C., and Franklin, C. (1995). *Clinical assessment for social workers: Quantitative and qualitative methods.* Chicago: Lyceum.

Krishef, C. H. (1991). *Fundamental approaches to single subject design and analysis.* Malabar, FL: Krieger Publishing Company.

Kyte, N. S., and Bostwick, G. (1997). Measuring variables. In R. M. Grinnell, Jr. (Ed.), *Social work research and evaluation: Quantitative and qualitative approaches* (5th ed., pp. 161–183). Itasca, IL: F. E. Peacock Publishing, Inc.

Maluccio, A., and Marlow, W. (1974). The case for contract. *Social Work, 19,* 28–35.

Marlow, C. (1998). *Research methods for generalist social work* (2nd ed.). Pacific Grove, CA: Brooks/Cole.

Miley, K. K., O'Melia, M., and DuBois, B. L. (1998). *Generalist social work practice: An empowering approach* (2nd ed.). Boston: Allyn and Bacon.

National Association of Social Workers (1997). *Code of ethics.* Washington, DC: NASW Press.

Nugent, W. R. (1992). Psychometric characteristics of self-anchored scales in clinical application. *Journal of Social Service Research, 3,* 137–152.

Poulin, J., and Young, T. (1997). Development of a helping relationship inventory for social work practice. *Research on Social Work Practice, 7,* 463–489.

Robinson, J. P., Shaver, P., and Wrightsman, L. S. (1991). *Measures of personality and social psychological attitudes.* San Diego, CA: Academic Press.

Royse, D., and Thyer, B. (1996). *Program evaluation: An introduction.* Chicago: Nelson-Hall.

Seaburg, J. R., and Gillespie, D. F. (1977). Goal attainment scaling: A critique. *Social Work Research and Abstracts, 13,* 43–56.

Seabury, B. (1976). The contract uses, abuses, and limitations. *Social Work, 21,* 16–21.

Shewart, W. A. (1931). *Economic control of quality of manufactured products.* New York: Van Nostrand Reinhold.

Tripodi, T. (1994). *A primer on single-system design for clinical social workers*. Washington, DC: NASW Press.

WALMYR Publishing Co., P.O. Box 12217, Tallahassee, FL 32317-12217, (850) 383-0045. Internet: www.syspac.com/~walmyr/wpchome.htm.

Witkin, S. (1991). Empirical clinical practice: A critical analysis. *Social Work, 36,* 158–163.

Young, T., and Poulin, J. (1998). The helping relationship inventory: A clinical appraisal. *Families in Society, 79,* 123–133.

THE COLLABORATIVE MODEL TASKS, INPUTS, AND PRACTICE SKILLS

CHAPTER 5

Bill Aron/PhotoEdit

Heather is a first-year MSW student placed at Social Work Consultation Services' Circle for Change Program. Circle for Change is a welfare-to-work program designed to address the barriers that participants may have to obtaining and maintaining employment. To do this, Circle for Change provides individual counseling; group counseling; computer, career, and life skills training; and GED test preparation classes for participants without a GED or high school diploma. Clients are referred to the program from the county Office of Employment and Training, the agency responsible for providing workforce development programs for welfare recipients. All the participants in the CFC program are considered "hard to serve" clients who have been on welfare for many years. The following case example describes Heather's experience during one of the support group sessions.

CASE 5.1 | **MONDAY MORNING SUPPORT GROUP**

by Heather Witt

As part of the Circle for Change program, participants meet Monday mornings for a weekly support group. This group provides a safe space for program participants to discuss a variety of topics, such as issues with family, relationships, children, violence, etc. As a first-year MSW student, I cofacilitate the group along with another first-year MSW student and our supervisor. Our third group session was facilitated without our supervisor. Up until this point, the group would have been characterized as working in the pre-engagement phase. The facilitators and the group members were building rapport and gaining trust and comfort with one another and the process. None of the women in the program had ever been in a support group before.

Although I was not facilitating the group alone, I was quite nervous about holding the group without the assistance of our supervisor. My colleague and I met and made a plan for the session. We wanted to check in with group members, do a trust building exercise, and take time to process the experience of the exercise and the experience of being a part of the group.

However, it became apparent early in the session that these goals would have to be tabled for another time. When my cofacilitator began the check-in, the clients erupted in response. They were frustrated, annoyed, angry, sad, and upset: the full range of emotions and very intense. They discussed their children, their families, and the violence that surrounds them in their communities. For example, one client lamented

the lack of safe places for her young children to play. Another commented on the murder of her close friend and neighbor over the previous weekend. The topics were broad and serious. The other cofacilitator attempted to redirect the discussion towards community action and change, but was quickly shut down by members of the group. They needed to vent their anger and frustrations.

Our roles in the group switched quickly from our plan to listening and empathy. Our session agenda was discarded and we both attempted to employ the many skills we had discussed so thoroughly in class, such as focused listening, containment, reflective empathy, and reframing. At one point, the topic of race came up, and on three separate occasions, the clients felt compelled to apologize to me, the only Caucasian in the room, before the start of a comment. I felt uncomfortable and did not know how to respond. After the third apology, I attempted to reassure the clients that this was a safe space for them, and they did not need to apologize for expressing their feelings or concerns.

The group continued on in this fashion for quite some time, but the intensity eventually died down. My cofacilitator and I processed with the group the session and its impact on them. Much to our relief, many of the clients indicated the session left them feeling unburdened and supported. Another client stated she felt "closer" to us and the other group members.

This chapter describes in greater detail the three phases of the collaborative model: pre-engagement, engagement and disengagement introduced in Chapter 3. The tasks, inputs, practice skills, and outputs associated with each phase are also reviewed. By the end of the chapter, you should be able to help Heather

1. Understand how communicating hopefulness, support, commitment, and partnership builds trust with reluctant clients
2. Understand the power of listening to clients and responding empathically
3. Understand racial and cultural differences and their impact on the helping relationship
4. Use a wide range of practice skills in working with disadvantaged and oppressed clients

PRE-ENGAGEMENT PHASE OF COLLABORATIVE SOCIAL WORK

As noted in Chapter 3, there are four major tasks associated with the pre-engagement phase of collaborative social work: studying, asking, listening, and clarifying. Each task is described here and also how the task contributes to the development of client trust, the practice skills associated with it, and the expected outcomes.

The four pre-engagement tasks are highly interrelated. In actual practice, they would be used in conjunction with one another. They are components of a single process and are used together within the context of the helping relationship. However, for the purposes of description, each task is discussed separately.

TASK 1: STUDYING YOUR CLIENT'S CULTURE, VALUES, BELIEFS, AND ENVIRONMENT

Studying refers to educating oneself about the client population with whom one is working. The study phase begins before you have your initial contact with the client and continues throughout the helping process. Before your initial meeting, you should become familiar with the cultural traditions, values, beliefs, and lifestyles of your client's population group. You should also try to find out as much as you can about the specific life experiences of your individual client. In addition to educating yourself about the client population and your client, you should educate yourself about the community, local service network, and resources available.

Inputs: Understanding and Sensitivity. Figure 5.1 shows how the study task affects your ability to build trust with reluctant clients. Being knowledgeable about your client's culture, values and beliefs, experiences, life stage, and community increases your cultural competence and communicates (inputs) to your client **understanding** and **sensitivity**. Clients who feel understood and experience you as being aware of and sensitive to their situation, life experience, culture, traditions, and belief systems are more likely to be open and take appropriate risks than those who experience you as culturally unaware and insensitive. Cultural competence in itself does not guarantee a client's willingness to take risks. However, being culturally incompetent and insensitive does guarantee mistrust and risk aversion, especially if clients come from ethnic or racial backgrounds that differ from your own.

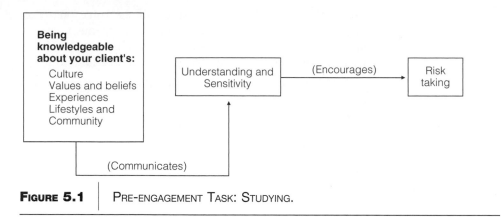

Figure 5.1 | Pre-engagement Task: Studying.

Table 5.1 | Studying: Practice Skills

Information retrieval skills
Database searches
Internet searches
Resource identification skills
Networking

Practice Skills: Information Retrieval and Resource Identification.   Table 5.1 lists the practice skills associated with the study task. These skills enable social workers to do research on client populations and become knowledgeable about their cultures, customs, values, beliefs, and person-in-environment situations as well as help them in identifying needed resources.

Information Retrieval Skills.   Computer technologies and the emergence of the Internet have changed the ways social workers do research and obtain information. Understanding how to conduct literature searches with computerized databases is now a critical social work practice skill. The amount of information available on an array of topics related to social work is enormous. The challenge is finding the information.

Currently, there are a number of searchable databases that contain summaries or abstracts of published journal articles in social work, psychology, education, social science, nursing, and other related disciplines. The major one in social work is *Social Work Abstracts,* and in psychology, *PsyLit.* Most libraries subscribe to a number of electronic databases. They can be searched using key words, authors, or titles. The search usually leads to article summaries or abstracts. The full text of articles of interest can then be reviewed in the library if available, or a copy can be requested through an interlibrary loan.

The Internet has become an excellent source of information on a variety of social work topics. There are a number of search engines that are free and easy to use. Most hosting Web sites have search functions. One of the more powerful ones is Google. Searches are conducted the same way as with electronic databases, and usually lead to a list of "hits" with links to the identified Web sites. There are also a number of social work Web sites maintained by professional organizations and schools of social work that have links pages with addresses of Web sites of particular interest to social workers.

Caution, however, must be used with information obtained from the Internet because there is no oversight or quality control. Anyone can post whatever he or she wants. Care must be taken to verify the legitimacy of the Web site, qualifications of the author, and validity of the information. Nevertheless, there is a wealth of information relevant to social workers on the Web, and the number of full text professional journals available online has increased dramatically during the past few years—a trend that will probably continue.

Resource Identification Skills.   Identifying and obtaining needed resources and services are other important generalist practice skills, especially for those working with disadvantaged and oppressed client populations. Resource mobilization and client advocacy are fundamental components of generalist social work practice. **Networking** is the key to effective resource mobilization and client advocacy. Networking is the process of developing relationships with other professionals and service providers in the community. It is the process of building relationships and of becoming informed about available resources and services. Personal contact gets things accomplished. Formal requests for services and assistance are not as effective as presenting your case to someone you know and with whom you have a reciprocal relationship. Generalist social workers need to actively develop relationships with other professionals, and, as with any other relationships, they need to actively maintain them.

Developing a network begins by identifying relevant existing programs and services in the community and region. Most communities have published resource directories of human service organizations as well as blue page listings in the telephone directory. Identify key agencies, and contact a social worker at each one to learn more about their programs and services and develop a relationship with a contact person at that organization.

Another networking strategy is to attend and join community coalitions and task forces related to your service area. Become an active member of community-wide efforts to address issues related to your professional work. Working with others builds relationships and expands your professional network. Strengthening your network increases your ability to effectively serve your clients.

Outputs: Increased Knowledge and Competence.   Knowledge and competence are the outcomes associated with the studying task. Knowledge about your client's culture, values, beliefs, experiences, and worldview as well as available resources and services is the anticipated outcome. Knowledge and competence go hand in hand. Doing research on background information of your client population, identifying existing resources, and building a strong professional network increase your competence in working with disadvantaged and oppressed clients.

TASK 2: ASKING YOUR CLIENT TO TELL HIS OR HER STORY

Asking refers to the process of asking your client to tell his or her story, including experiences, beliefs, expectations, concerns, strengths, coping abilities, and most importantly, hopes and dreams. The asking approach contrasts sharply with the telling approach that most disadvantaged clients have experienced in their prior interactions with helping professionals and other people in authority. Being asked about your hopes and concerns is empowering. Being told what your problem is and what you need to do is disempowering.

The collaborative model places a great deal of emphasis on allowing the client to be in charge of the helping process. This begins when the worker simply asks the client to tell her or his story. You should approach this task from a position of curiosity or "not knowing" (Dejong and Berg, 1998). Show an interest in hearing what your client has to say. Do not make assumptions about the client's situation and perceptions. Be open and encourage exploration. This is accomplished through the use of **elaboration skills**. Use open-ended questions and minimal prompts to encourage elaboration. Ask for specifics, explore the meaning of silences, summarize when appropriate, reframe, and, most importantly, contain yourself. Containing oneself is critical at this point in the helping relationship. The focus must be on having clients tell their story and not on the worker talking about ideas, insights, expectations, or solutions. Rushing in with solutions before clients have had a chance to tell their story has more to do with the worker feeling good about herself or himself and her or his abilities than with helping a client.

Inputs: Respect and Acceptance.   Figure 5.2 illustrates how the asking task builds trust with reluctant clients. Asking clients to tell their story communicates **respect** and **acceptance**. Collaborative social work is based on the premise that the client is the expert and the best source of information regarding his or her life situation. Proceeding from this assumption and asking clients about their experiences, beliefs, concerns, and strengths communicates respect to the client. Above all we want our clients to feel respected as people. Communicating respect is critical to building trust. Few would be willing to make themselves vulnerable and take risks in an atmosphere of disrespect.

Eliciting the client's story is the first half of the asking task. The second half is accepting the story as reality for that person. This requires receiving the message in a nonjudgmental manner. If the client perceives the worker as both respectful and accepting, the client is encouraged to take risks that will help build trust and the helping relationship. There are a number of practice skills that can be employed to

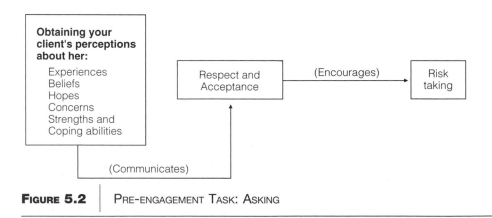

FIGURE 5.2 | PRE-ENGAGEMENT TASK: ASKING

TABLE 5.2 | ASKING: PRACTICE SKILLS

Elaboration skills
Open-ended questions
Minimal prompts
Seeking concreteness
Summarizing
Containment
Exploring silences
Reframing

help the worker communicate respect and acceptance. They are referred to as elaboration skills (Shulman, 1999) or verbal following skills (Hepworth, Rooney, and Larsen, 2002).

Elaboration Practice Skills.   Elaboration skills are micro-intervention techniques that encourage clients to tell their stories in detail. These techniques can be used with individual, family, small group, organizational, and community client systems. To understand a client's situation and perspective, we need to have their stories told in detail. The power of the story is in the specifics. Most people tend to avoid specifics and begin discussing their situation in very general terms. The social worker's job is to help the client tell a detailed story rich in facts and feelings. The seven elaboration skills, shown in Table 5.2, are using open-ended questions, using minimal prompts, seeking concreteness, summarizing, containment, exploring silences, and reframing.

Using Open-Ended Questions.   There are basically two types of questions: those with predefined responses and those without predefined responses. The former are usually referred to as closed-ended questions. They do not encourage a detailed and elaborate response, and generally should be avoided. An example of a closed-ended question is, "Do you get along well with the other kids at school?" If the client responds at all, the answer will be yes or no. This is the only answer called for. Not much information is obtained from this type of question.

Alternatively, one should ask open-ended questions that elicit more information from the client. For example, the social worker could ask, "How do you get along with the other kids at school?" This cannot be answered with just a yes or no response. The client has to formulate a more detailed or elaborate response to answer the question. Although the questions are similar, the open-ended one encourages elaboration, whereas the closed-ended one does not.

Open-ended questions are a simple and easy way to get clients to tell their stories. They give clients opportunities to tell their stories in more depth than do closed-ended questions (Kadushin and Kadushin, 1997). Limit your use of closed-ended questions. If a question is warranted, ask an open-ended one.

Using Minimal Prompts.   As the term implies, minimal prompts are brief nonverbal or verbal indications of encouragement. Nonverbal minimal prompts include "nodding the head, using facial expressions, or employing gestures that convey receptivity, interest, and commitment to understanding" (Hepworth, Rooney, and

Larsen, 2002, p. 140). These nonverbal prompts can be very effective in encouraging elaboration. They communicate in an attentive and nonintrusive way that you would like the client to tell you more and that you are interested in hearing her story.

Verbal minimal prompts are brief utterances such as "Mm-mmm" or "Ah-ha" or other short phrases such as "Tell me more" or "I see." As with the nonverbal prompts, the verbal ones encourage the client to go on without interrupting or asking a series of questions.

Another type of minimal prompt is an **accent response** in which the worker repeats a client's word or short phrase in the form of a question. The word or phrase selected should be the core component of the client's message. For example, if the client says, "I just hate all the kids at school," the social worker might say "Hate?" or "The kids?" to prompt the client to give more information about the client's feelings about the kids at school. Accent responses are easy to use, do not interrupt the flow of communication, and are very effective in getting clients to explore their feelings and concerns in depth.

Seeking Concreteness.   As noted earlier, clients tend to introduce their concerns and describe their experiences in vague, general terms. Beginning social workers often do not probe for specifics and may allow clients to keep the conversation at a general level. Hepworth, Rooney, and Larsen (2002) point out that communicating one's feelings and experiences requires specificity. They call the process of helping clients to respond in specific terms "seeking concreteness"; others refer to it as "clarification" (Cormier and Cormier, 1991) or "moving from the general to the specific" (Shulman, 1999).

Often clients begin their stories in general terms because they have never put their feelings and experiences into words. They need help in exploring their feelings and experiences. Asking for specifics helps clients articulate their stories. Thus, seeking concreteness not only deepens your understanding of clients' stories but also helps clients understand and articulate their feelings and experiences.

Seeking concreteness is easy to do. The key is to recognize and respond to vague and overly general comments. For example, a community member might say, "The neighborhood is falling apart. It is just not the same any more." This is a fairly vague statement. At this point, the social worker really does not know what is causing the frustration. The worker could seek more concrete information by asking an open-ended follow-up question, such as, "How has it changed?" or by "What do you mean by falling apart?" Both responses invite the client to elaborate on her concerns.

Asking for specific information deepens the worker's and client's understanding of the topic. The technique of seeking concreteness has the added benefit of contributing to the natural flow of the conversation. It helps the worker stay on the topic introduced by the client. Seeking clarification helps the worker avoid jumping from topic to topic, a common mistake made by beginning social workers. It also communicates to the client interest in hearing her story.

Summarizing.   Summarizing is a basic interviewing skill that is often used to highlight key points in a conversation with a client. When used this way, summarizing can help the client and worker make the transition to a different topic. Summarizing, however, can also be used as an elaboration technique. This entails making connections between relevant aspects of a client's story (Hepworth, Rooney, and Larsen, 2002). Summarizing can help clients explore in depth feelings and experiences that they might not recognize as being connected. This can be a powerful tool in helping them gain insight and understanding.

Summarizing is a more difficult skill to use than the other elaborating skills discussed above. It is a filtering and feedback process. It requires the ability to identify the key components of the story, pull them together, and repeat them back to the client in a combination statement–question form. The statement–question form prevents the social worker from taking the position of knowing or presuming to know that the different points are connected for the client.

Typically, a summary statement is concluded with a question to see if the worker's perception or summary is consistent with the client's view of the situation. Summarizing is used as an elaboration skill in this example:

COMMITTEE MEMBER: Well, I just don't know. The agency caseloads have risen to the point that we cannot provide effective services to our clients, and the paperwork is totally getting out of control. The demands on the caseworkers seem to be increasing, and the turnover problem is getting worse.

WORKER: Sounds like the working conditions here are making it hard for you to do your job, and you don't see any relief in sight. Is that right?

The worker has summarized the committee member's main points and invited her to explore the connection. In this way, summarizing is used as a practice skill to promote elaboration.

Using Containment. Shulman (1999) defines **containment** as the skill of "not acting" (p. 148). Many beginning social workers, in their desire to be helpful, rush in with solutions before the client has told his or her story. Containment is the ability to hold back on this impulse. It also is an important skill for those who have a tendency to finish a client's sentences or to focus on identified outcomes very early in the helping process. The following response by the social worker to the committee member illustrates a *lack* of containment:

WORKER: Yes, I agree. This place is falling apart, and the agency administrators really don't care about the caseworkers and the pressures they are feeling. We need to organize ourselves to put pressure on management to improve working conditions.

The worker failed to contain himself and immediately rushed in with a solution to the committee member's expressed concerns. The lack of containment shifts the focus and interrupts the exploration of the situation. The worker has single-handedly chosen the target problem and intervention. A worker skilled in containment would have continued to encourage the committee member to explore her feelings and tell her story.

Exploring Silences. Shulman (1999) calls this skill "reaching into silences" and describes it as attempting to explore the meaning of the silence. "The difficulty with silences is that it is often hard to understand exactly what the client is 'saying'" (Shulman, 1999, p. 152). The client might be processing a thought, struggling with powerful emotions, feeling bored, or any number of things. Beginning social workers are often uncomfortable with silence and rush in to fill it up. Doing so ensures that the meaning of the silence will be lost as the worker moves on to something else. The social worker needs to actively explore the silence. A clue to its meaning is the worker's own feelings (Shulman, 1999). Understanding one's own feelings at a particular moment helps one to make an educated guess about the meaning of the client's silence. Shulman's phrase "reach inside of silences" suggests that the worker should actively explore the meaning of silence.

The first strategy for dealing with silence is containment. Give the client some time, and stay with the silence. A simple probing question, such as, "You are quiet right now. What's going on?" is often sufficient to get the client to open up. You have acknowledged the silence and encouraged the client to elaborate. If your feelings suggest that the client is feeling *(hurt)* then you could ask an open-ended question, such as, "Are you struggling with the *(hurt)* you feel?" The client needs to be encouraged to let the worker know if the guess is wrong. Even if the worker is off base, there is little harm done. The client can correct the misperception. Either way, the silence has been acknowledged and its meaning explored. Rather than feeling uncomfortable during periods of silence, view them as opportunities to better understand your client and her story.

Reframing.   Reframing is a technique that is used often in family therapy (Janzen and Harris, 1997). It is sometimes referred to as relabeling. Reframing is the process of giving a positive interpretation to what the client sees as a negative or concern. It is reframing a negative into a positive. In collaborative social work, this is an important technique. It provides the worker with a way to highlight positives and help clients view their concerns from a different, more positive, perspective. It helps the identification of strengths and coping abilities. Reframing is an elaboration skill in that it invites clients to explore their stories from a different perspective. The following is an example of reframing:

GROUP MEMBER: My wife gets very upset when I have a couple of drinks and drive. It is ridiculous. Even if I only have one beer, she is on my case.

WORKER: Sounds like your wife really cares about you and your safety.

Outputs: Identification of Needs, Concerns, Strengths, and Coping Skills. The major outputs of the asking task are the identifications of client needs, concerns, strengths, and coping skills. Having the client tell her story provides the worker with the information needed to begin the assessment process. The conversation is purposeful. The client's natural focus is on needs and concerns. The worker adds to this the identification of strengths and coping skills. All four are the desired outcomes of asking the client to tell her story.

TASK 3: LISTENING FOR MEANING AND FEELINGS

Asking and listening are obviously two interrelated tasks. When a social worker asks a question, clients assume that the worker will listen to their answer. The focus here is on listening for the meaning and feeling behind the client's words. It is more about *hearing* the message than listening to the words.

What are the areas of concern? How does the client perceive the problem situation? What are the indications or manifestations of the problem? Where, when, and how often does the problem occur? How severe is the problem? How does it affect the client? What are the client's emotional reactions to the problem? What other systems within the client's environment affect the problem situation? How has the client coped with the problem? Answers to these questions provide an understanding of the problem situation from the client's perspective. The way you go about developing this understanding is as critical as the answers themselves.

Ideally the answers will emerge as the client tells his or her story. Focus on listening and on communicating your understanding of the story. Be curious. Your goal is to obtain a detailed picture of the client's concerns. The client's perception of feeling heard is going to motivate him or her to open up to you and engage in a helping process. It will set a solid foundation for the development of the helping relationship. If your client does not feel heard, your work together will probably not continue.

Asking a battery of questions without really listening to the client's responses puts the focus on you, the worker, rather than where it needs to be, on the client. A common mistake by beginning social workers is to assume that their job is to ask brilliant questions. Many are preoccupied with their own responses to the client, with saying the right thing. Rather than focusing on what you are going to say or on the questions you need to ask, you should focus on what the client is saying. Do you understand what he or she is attempting to communicate? Are you listening to the client? Are you hearing what he or she is saying? Have you communicated your understanding back to the client? If you focus on listening and ask questions that help you understand what the client is saying, the information will be forthcoming.

Inputs: Understanding and Empathy.   Figure 5.3 illustrates how the listening task builds trust with reluctant clients. Listening for the meaning behind your client's words and for feeling content and picking up on your client's indirect clues communicate **understanding** and **empathy**. Clients who perceive their social workers as being understanding and empathic are more likely to share feelings and thoughts about sensitive matters than those who perceive their social workers as not understanding them and their situation. Sharing feelings and thoughts helps build trust and strengthens the helping relationship. Communicating understanding

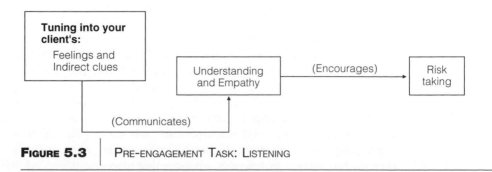

FIGURE 5.3 | PRE-ENGAGEMENT TASK: LISTENING

TABLE 5.3 | LISTENING: PRACTICE SKILLS

Empathic skills
Focused listening
Reflective empathy
Additive empathy

and empathy is critical to the development of a collaborative helping process. The key to communicating understanding and empathy is the ability to respond to the feeling content in the client's story. Practice skills that are effective in doing just that are referred to as empathic skills (Shulman, 1999). Others refer to these as skills as empathic responding (Hepworth, Rooney, and Larsen, 2002) or reflecting feelings (Sevel, Cummins, and Madrigal 1999). Table 5.3 lists three empathic skills that are related to the listening task in collaborative social work.

Empathic Skills

Focused Listening.   Focused listening (Shulman, 1999) or active listening (Chang and Scott, 1999) is the process of concentrating on a specific part of the client's message. The worker tries to identify the primary themes in the client's story and be sensitive to clues the client may give regarding the underlying feeling content of the message. The worker also tries to understand what the message means to the client (Chang and Scott, 1999). What is the client really saying, and what meaning does it have for the client?

Focused listening requires the social worker to tune in to the meaning behind the client's words. This involves listening to the client's words, nonverbal communication, and affect as well as what is not being said. Listening and understanding the client's message is the first component of empathy. The second component is communicating back to the client your understanding.

Reflective Empathy.   Conveying empathy and understanding is vital in developing a helping relationship. Clients need to feel understood. Those who feel that their social workers do not really understand them and their situations are unlikely to share personal thoughts and feelings. Why risk vulnerability with someone who does not understand you? Disadvantaged and oppressed clients' experiences of discrimination, abuse, or exploitation have left many feeling profoundly misunderstood (Cournoyer, 2000). The ability to respond empathetically is a critical social work practice skill, particularly when one has to overcome mistrust and reluctance.

In its simplest form, empathic responding is "reflecting" back to clients their message. At this level, the empathic response accurately captures the factual content and feelings expressed by the client. The response communicates an equivalent message. Reflective empathy is more effective if you paraphrase the client's words rather than just "parrot back" the same words.

The use of empathetic responding is vital to the development of trust and the building of a strong helping relationship. In practice, I do not believe that empathy can be overused. Respond empathetically whenever your client is dealing with or expressing affective content. If there is an emotional component in the message, either on the surface or below it, an empathic response is needed. The power of the relationship is in helping clients deal with and manage feelings. Understanding the facts is important, but understanding the feelings is essential. Doing so will communicate that you are listening, that you care about the client, and that you understand or, at the very least, are trying to understand.

Responding to the affective component is beneficial even if you have incorrectly described the client's feelings or their intensity. An incorrect empathetic response gives clients an opportunity to clarify their feelings. The example illustrates a reflective empathic response.

INDIVIDUAL: My parents are jerks. They are always on my back about something. I can never do anything right. My sister is the perfect one. She gets better grades, is more popular, and is always "little miss perfect." It's not fair. She isn't perfect, but my parents don't know that.

WORKER: Sounds like your parents are always on you and that they think your sister is perfect. It doesn't seem fair, and it makes you kind of angry. Is that what you are saying?

The social worker's response summarizes the facts and puts the client's surface feelings into words. Depending upon the client's tone of voice and emphasis, the surface feeling is most likely anger, but it could also be disappointment or something else. Identifying feelings underneath the surface feelings helps clients to better understand their own emotions (Hepworth, Rooney, and Larsen, 2002).

Additive Empathy. This level of empathetic responding occurs when the social worker accurately identifies **implicit underlying feelings.** "The response illuminates subtle or veiled facets of the client's message, enabling the client to get in touch with somewhat deeper feelings and unexplored meanings and purposes of behavior" (Hepworth, Rooney, and Larsen, 2002, p. 102). Not only does the social worker respond to the surface and underlying feelings, but the response connects the message to other themes of feelings expressed by the client. The use of additive empathy communicates a deeper level of understanding than the more basic reflective empathy. Both require the social worker to "risk" responding to the affective component of the client's message. Many beginning social workers shy away from dealing with clients' feelings directly. It is easier to stick to the facts and ignore the feelings. If one wants to build trust, then responding to the feeling content is necessary. This example is an additive empathetic response to the individual's statement in the example above. In this response, the worker tries to reach for the client's underlying feelings.

WORKER: Sounds like your parents are always on you and that they think your sister is perfect. I sense that this really hurts your feelings and makes you wonder if they love you as much as they love your sister. Does that capture it?

Outputs: Identification of Feeling Content and Validation. The major outputs of the listening task are (1) the identification of the client's feelings and the affective component of her story and (2) validation. These two outputs are interrelated. If you are successful in identifying clients' feelings and can demonstrate that understanding, then clients feel validated. Feeling understood is validating. Having someone recognize and acknowledge one's feelings legitimizes them. Feelings are powerful emotions and having them acknowledged is even more powerful. This is particularly important when working with clients who have experienced discrimination and oppression in their lives.

TASK 4: CLARIFY HOW YOU AND THE CLIENT WILL WORK TOGETHER

Please keep in mind the interrelated nature of the tasks associated with the pre-engagement phase. All are engaged in over the course of one to three sessions. At some point during the pre-engagement phase, you and your client need to discuss his or her expectations of the helping process as well as how you hope your work together will proceed. Clarifying expectations and agreeing on general guidelines about what will take place during the helping relationship set the framework for a collaborative process. Clients often have little understanding of the helping process, and their perceptions may differ widely from yours. Perlman (1968) found that fewer clients dropped out during intake when client expectations were clarified and worker–client discrepancies addressed. Zwick and Atkinson (1985) found similar results for clients who viewed an orientation video prior to psychological counseling.

Hepworth, Rooney, and Larsen (2002) suggest that you should determine what your client's expectations are and briefly explain the nature of the helping process when you begin working together. Unacknowledged discrepancies between your and your client's expectations about what is going to happen and how it is going to happen may jeopardize the helping process.

Clients may make it very clear what they expect you to do or what they think will happen. If they have not, ask them at an appropriate time during the pre-engagement phase. This applies to both voluntary and nonvoluntary clients. For nonvoluntary clients, review the mandated aspects of service provision, and then ask what they hope to get out of the experience. What would they like to have happen? How would they like the work to proceed?

The second component of clarifying the helping process is communicating your expectations about what you will and will not do, as well as what you expect your client to do and not do. Your job as social worker is to structure the helping process and help support and motivate the client throughout the process. The client's job is to make a commitment to engage in the helping process, to be the decision maker about choices that emerge as the process unfolds, and to follow through on those choices. Be respectful of the client's expectations, especially if they are at variance with yours. Acknowledge the client's expectations even if they are unrealistic. Be empathic regarding his or her feelings. Clients typically want help and answers to problems that they have struggled with and have been unable to resolve on their own. They are looking to you to provide expert advice and guidance. Acknowledge these feelings while emphasizing your partnership and how you will work together to address concerns. The helping relationship is a collaborative process.

It is also helpful to discuss the kind of relationship you hope to develop. A truly collaborative relationship requires openness. Your client has to be willing to share feelings, and you have to be willing to communicate openly. This requires the development of trust. Trust is built on actions and shared experiences. It is not created through words alone, and it does not happen instantaneously. You need to communicate concern, understanding, and empathy, both verbally and nonverbally, to provide opportunities for trust to develop. Share your feelings about the kind of open and collaborative relationship you hope to have with your client,

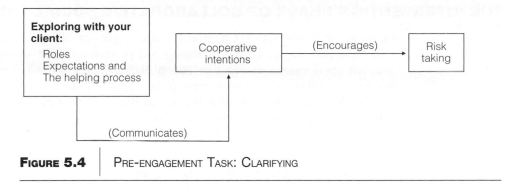

FIGURE 5.4 | PRE-ENGAGEMENT TASK: CLARIFYING

and acknowledge that you must earn his or her trust. An open discussion of your feelings will model for your client the types of interactions you hope to have and will be an example of the reciprocal nature of the helping relationship and your client's role as a partner.

Inputs: Cooperative Intentions.   Figure 5.4 illustrates how the clarification task builds trust with reluctant clients. Exploring with your client your respective roles, expectations, and how your work together will proceed communicates **co-operative intentions**. It is important for the client to have a voice in this conversation. The collaborative model emphasizes client empowerment. Telling the client "how it is going to be" is not in keeping with the philosophy of the model. Nevertheless, the approach requires client participation and involvement in all aspects of the helping process. This needs to be communicated to the client in a way that gives the client a choice in the matter. Be flexible and give the client as much say in how you work together as you can, within the framework of the model. You need to communicate your willingness to engage in a collaborative helping process and let your client know that he or she will have a strong voice in the process. This is accomplished by using the elaboration and empathy skills discussed earlier.

Outputs: Mutual Understanding and Collaboration.   The expected output of the clarifying task is mutual understanding of the helping process and how the client and social worker will work together. A related output is the establishment of a collaborative partnership. Both of these intermediate outputs are critical to the success of the helping relationship.

The clarifying task is especially important in work with disadvantaged and oppressed client populations. Typically, as noted before, their experiences with helping professionals have not been collaborative. More likely than not they have been told what their problem is and what they need to do to remedy it. Often sanctions are employed if the remedy is not achieved or followed. This is very different from the experience one would have with a social worker using the collaborative model. A successful outcome depends on clarifying roles, expectations, and the helping process.

THE INTERVENTION PHASE OF COLLABORATIVE SOCIAL WORK

As shown in Table 3.1 in Chapter 3, the engagement phase of the collaborative model has two major tasks: articulating and persevering. The **articulating** task focuses on developing a contract or action plan to address the target problem and concerns identified in the engagement phase. This chapter provides information on this process. The **persevering** task focuses on the implementation of the action plan. This is the work phase (Shulman, 1999) in the helping process.

TASK 5: ARTICULATE YOUR FOCUS AND PLAN OF ACTION

Articulation refers to the process of taking all the information you and your client gathered during the pre-engagement phase and using it to identify priorities and develop measurable goals and a plan of action. The action plan specifies a timetable and the steps that will be taken as well as how progress will be evaluated. At this point in the collaborative model you are **engaging** the client in a helping relationship. Prior to this, during the pre-engagement phase, you were setting the stage for client engagement. But it is not until your client agrees to a plan of action and makes a beginning commitment to change that he or she actually engages in a helping relationship. Prochaska, DiClemente, and Norcross (1992) refer to this as the "preparation" stage. The work that was done during the pre-engagement phase is a prerequisite to engagement. Moving to articulation without completing the tasks of pre-engagement usually results in a premature and superficial commitment to change. Most likely, the client will drop out and not return for the next session or will merely be "going through the motions" of pre-engagement. The engagement tasks must be undertaken if your client is going to truly engage in a helping relationship.

Typically, the articulation of priorities, goals, and the action plan takes place around session 3 or 4, depending on how long the pre-engagement tasks take. After the worker has a clear sense of the client's needs, concerns, strengths, and coping abilities, he or she needs to help the client move into the engagement phase. This action must be initiated by the social worker. It needs to be presented to the client as the next step in the helping process.

Many beginning social workers have trouble initiating the articulation task. They end up staying in the pre-engagement phase for a prolonged period of time. The client keeps telling his or her story, and the worker keeps listening. Although this is important, a helping relationship is purposeful. The worker and client must agree upon what it is they are going to do together. It might turn out that the agreement is to listen to the client and provide support, or a more elaborate plan of action might emerge. Either way, for the relationship to be purposeful, both parties must agree to what they want to accomplish as well as how they will accomplish it.

Inputs: Hopefulness and Partnership.   Figure 5.5 shows how the articulating task influences the trust-building process. This is a vulnerable time for clients who

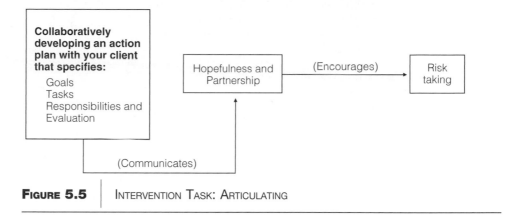

FIGURE 5.5 | INTERVENTION TASK: ARTICULATING

have not experienced a great deal of success in their lives. People from disadvantaged and oppressed backgrounds usually have a lifetime of setbacks and disappointments. Making a commitment to bring about changes in one's life, changes that are not easily made, is a difficult process. It is scary. Clients from disadvantaged and oppressed backgrounds ask: Is this possible? Will this person stick with me if I run into difficulty? Can I do this?

The worker can help the client take these risks by communicating **hopefulness**. The client needs to be assured that it *can* be done. Inputting a sense of hopefulness is very important at this stage of the helping relationship. The worker needs to clearly communicate through words, voice tone, and attitude that together the change can be made, that help is possible.

Along with communicating hopefulness, the worker needs to communicate a sense of **partnership** to the client. Stressing the collaborative aspect of their work together and the fact that both are making a commitment to the change process promotes feelings of partnership and collaboration. The challenge of making difficult changes and taking on responsibility for one's actions are substantial risks. They are major risks for people who have had to face discrimination and oppression and who in all probability continue to face discrimination and oppression in their everyday lives. The worker can help these clients take these risks by creating a sense of hopefulness and partnership. These two inputs are critical to the development of a purposeful helping relationship.

Contracting Skills.   Table 5.4 lists the practice skills associated with the articulating task. These skills help facilitate the contracting process. They are purposeful in that they all contribute to the process of specifying priorities, goals, action steps, and evaluation procedures.

Partializing.   Breaking complex problems down into component parts that can be addressed one at a time is the skill of partializing client concerns (Shulman, 1999). Often the process of telling the story results in a large number of interconnected problems. The prospect of tackling so many problems is discouraging and intimidating. Clients often feel helpless and overwhelmed about the prospect of change.

TABLE 5.4 | Articulating: Practice Skills

Contracting Skills
Partializing
Identifying Options
Sharing Data
Seeking Consensus

The worker can help the client move forward by breaking down the problems into smaller, more manageable ones that can be addressed one at a time. The following example illustrates the skill of partializing client concerns:

GROUP MEMBER: My probation officer says that I have to look for work. I can't do that because I go to "meetings" every morning and I don't have a car. It is hard for me to use public transportation because of my bad leg. I just can't walk very far or stand for any length of time. I also don't want to miss my meetings because I am really trying to stay clean. I want to reconnect with my daughter but she won't have anything to do with me unless I get my life straightened out. I'm afraid if I don't get a job my probation officer will send me back. I don't want to go back.

WORKER: That's a lot to deal with. It kind of feels overwhelming. Maybe if we look at one thing at a time we can come up with some ideas. Let's see. You need to make a good-faith effort to find a job. You want to continue attending meetings. Transportation is an issue, and reconnecting with your daughter is a concern. And you are having problems with your leg. Where should we start?

Breaking down complex and interrelated problems into more manageable parts helps the client move forward and helps set the agenda for developing a contract or action plan. Specifying the issues of concern in manageable terms helps overcome client discouragement and creates hopefulness. Change does seem possible when the focus is on small intermediate steps instead of the larger overwhelming problem.

Identifying Options.   Another skill that comes into play during the articulating task is that of helping the client identify options. Identifying options helps clients think about the various goals they might wish to address and helps them explore various solutions. A collaborative way of identifying options is to engage the client in **brainstorming**. Together create a list of all the possible options. Encourage your client to be creative and to come up with as many options as possible. In brainstorming, all ideas are correct and put down. Ultimately the client will decide upon the goals as well as the possible action steps. Brainstorming begins the process of making those decisions by exploring the full range of possibilities.

Identifying options or alternatives is a helpful way to begin the process of setting priorities. Most disadvantaged and oppressed clients have a whole host of concerns that need attention. Taking on everything at once is not generally recommended. Establishing priorities provides you and the client with guidelines about the order of the work. It helps identify a small list of issues that will be the starting point of your work together. The worker should start prioritizing by beginning with the problem that the client initially presented during the pre-engagement phase. Beginning here will make the most sense to the client (Pillari, 2002). After brainstorming and listing the options, ask the client to rank them from least to most important. Setting priorities helps establish a clear focus for the beginning work together. It is a critical step in selecting the goals (outcomes) that are sought as well as the specific actions that will be taken (Epstein, 1988).

Sharing Data. This skill refers to having the social worker share facts, ideas, values, and beliefs with the client (Shulman, 1999). The collaborative model emphasizes partnerships and relationships. Relationships are, by definition, reciprocal. They have a give and take quality. They are not unidirectional. Clients need and look for input from their social workers. Sharing information, feelings, and opinions is the input they need, and offering it has the added benefit of strengthening the helping relationship.

Shulman (1999) points out that in sharing data there are two key requirements: the data must be related to the work at hand, and it must be needed by the client for the immediate work (p. 186). Both conditions must be satisfied. They are the only two conditions under which social workers share their knowledge and beliefs with clients. Before sharing data, ask yourself: Is what I am about to share relevant to our work together, and is it immediately needed? If the answer is yes to both questions, share your observations. But make sure doing so is relevant and needed immediately. Bringing up information or ideas that might have relevance at some future date is not helpful and, in fact, is probably harmful to the helping relationship if the client does not see the connection to the work at hand.

Even if sharing information is clearly called for, caution must be taken in how the information is shared. First and foremost it must be presented as something for the client to consider and not as what should be done. It is important to give the client a clear sense that what you are offering is one perspective and not *the* perspective. Given the unequal power differential in a helping relationship, the worker has to be extra careful in sharing observations and opinions. Although the client is looking for your suggestions and thoughts, the emphasis and locus of control must remain with the client. Make it clear that you are offering your thoughts and that they are open to examination.

The skill of sharing data in a way that is open for examination means that the worker must qualify statements in order to help the client sort out the difference between reality and the worker's sense of reality. Rather than being a salesperson for an idea, the worker should present it with all its limitations (Shulman, 1999, p. 189).

The worker must encourage the client to question the ideas if they do not seem to fit his or her situation. The worker needs to explore any verbal or nonverbal signs that the client is not in agreement. It is hard for clients to disagree. Therefore, the worker needs to take the initiative in exploring the client's feelings about the information shared.

A second caution is to make sure you use brevity. Make your point, and turn the focus back to your client and his or her situation as quickly as possible. Carrying on about your thoughts and observations communicates that you are more interested in your story than your client's story. The purpose of sharing data at this point in the helping process is to help your client figure out priorities, goals, and the course of action to take. Your experiences can be helpful in this regard, but the client's experiences are most important here. Share your experiences only to the extent that you make your point and show the connection to your client's problem or concern. The following example illustrates appropriate sharing of data:

INDIVIDUAL: I am not sure how I feel. I want to reconnect with my daughter, but I am not sure how she will react if I contact her after all these years.

WORKER: I understand your reluctance. A close friend and I had a falling out. Neither one of us was willing to take the first step. As time went on, it got harder and harder. Finally, I called her on her birthday and she was glad to hear from me. I am not sure how your daughter will react, but in my situation I am glad I took the risk and called.

In the above example, the worker's sharing is related to the work at hand and deals with the immediate concern of the client. It also is fairly brief and qualified in terms of its applicability for the client.

Seeking Consensus.   The fourth contracting skill is one that is used during the final phases of the articulating task. After you and the client have partialized and set priorities, identified options, and shared data, the skill of seeking consensus brings it all together in the form of a contract. In collaborative social work, both the client and the worker have to agree on the problems that are going to be addressed, the expected outcomes, and the steps that will be taken to bring about the change. There has to be agreement. Although the client has the final say in these matters, the worker has to have input and be in agreement. It makes little sense to engage in a helping relationship in which you disagree with what the client is attempting to change and the course of action chosen.

Seeking consensus requires open communication and a purposeful search for agreement. Often beginning social workers believe they are in agreement with their clients when, in fact, there is a breakdown in communication. It is imperative that you make sure you and your client agree on both the general and specific aspects of your work together. Writing it out and reviewing it together is a good way of making sure there is agreement. A verbal agreement is more prone to misinterpretation than a written one. In reviewing the specifics, if there are areas of disagreement actively explore alternatives until a consensus is reached. Both the client and the worker own the goals and plan of action when this occurs. The work becomes collaborative.

Outputs: Change Goals, Action Plan, and Evaluation Plan.   The outputs of the articulation task are very concrete. At the conclusion of this task, the worker and client will have identified the specific goals that they will be addressing in the helping relationship, and they will have specified their intervention and evaluation plan. Once the client and worker have accomplished these intermediate outputs, they become actively engaged in a professional helping relationship. The next task in the collaborative process is to persevere through the ups and downs of the helping process.

TASK 6: PERSEVERE IN CARRYING OUT YOUR WORK TOGETHER

This phase of the helping process is called many things. Pillari (2002) refers to it as the intervention phase; Shulman (1999) calls it the work phase; Hepworth, Rooney, and Larsen (2002) call it implementation and goal attainment. No matter what it is called, this is the actual work phase of the helping relationship. During this period, usually session 4 and on, the action plan is implemented. During the articulation task, clients start to address their problems and are motivated to make the necessary changes (Prochaska, DiClemente, and Norcross, 1992). The objective is to help clients modify their behavior, experiences, or environment to overcome their problems. This is difficult for many clients. Making the needed changes is not easy. Changing long-standing behaviors or environments is extremely difficult. It is much easier to maintain the status quo than to make significant life changes.

Chapter 1 reviewed a number of system change activities (interventions) employed by generalist social workers. The action plans developed collaboratively by the worker and client specify the interventions that will be used to address the client's identified target problems and desired change goals. The specifics of the different types of interventions are not reviewed here. Rather, the focus is on the worker's use of self in helping the client follow through on the agreed-upon action plan. The approach presented here is similar to Miller and Rollnick's (2002) motivational interviewing techniques. Their work focuses on the process of helping people overcome ambivalence and resistance to change.

Inputs: Support and Commitment.   Figure 5.6 illustrates how the **persevering** task contributes to the trust-building process with reluctant clients. The key to helping clients make difficult changes is persistently and relentlessly following through on the action plan. Persistence is meeting often and regularly with your client. It is checking in with your client between meetings. It is regularly monitoring progress and exploring why or why not progress is being made. It is following up on missed appointments, and it is consistently completing your agreed-upon tasks on or before their due dates. Persevering is creating expectations for success and for making the identified changes. When this occurs the worker communicates to clients that he or she will support them in overcoming the challenge of making

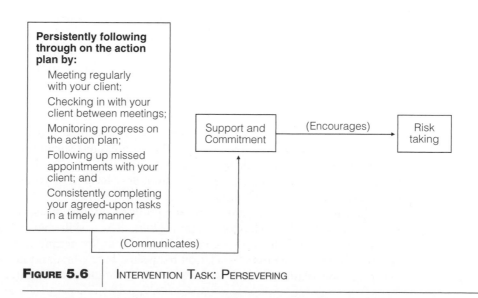

Persistently following through on the action plan by:

Meeting regularly with your client;

Checking in with your client between meetings;

Monitoring progress on the action plan;

Following up missed appointments with your client; and

Consistently completing your agreed-upon tasks in a timely manner

Support and Commitment

(Encourages)

Risk taking

(Communicates)

FIGURE 5.6 | INTERVENTION TASK: PERSEVERING

TABLE 5.5 | PERSEVERING: PRACTICE SKILLS

Intervention Skills
Challenging
Maintaining Focus
Checking for Ambivalence
Rehearsal

behavioral and environmental changes. It also communicates to clients your commitment to the change process and their success.

Inputting support and commitment encourages clients to take the risks associated with the change process. It helps solidify the trust that has developed, and it strengthens the helping relationship. These inputs are critical because the work phase requires a strong helping relationship. The relationship is tested most severely during this phase of the helping process. The focus is on client change, and this often requires confrontation and other types of intervention practice skills. Table 5.5 lists the intervention skills that are associated with the persevering task.

Intervention Skills

Challenging.   This is what Shulman (1999) refers to as "challenging the illusion of work." An illusion of work occurs when the client comes in and talks about making changes but never moves beyond the talking stage. The actual work is not being accomplished. The client gives the impression of being cooperative and engaged, but there is no action behind the words. The worker needs to challenge the lack of progress and the illusion. "For the illusion to take place, it is necessary to have two partners in the ritual" (Shulman, 1999, p. 175). Both the client and worker are "working," but in reality they are giving lip service to the situation. Goals have been written on paper, but there is no action other than lengthy social conversations. It is pure illusion.

Challenging the illusion is often difficult for beginning social workers. They want to be supportive and helpful. They are uncomfortable confronting or challenging clients. Many worry about negatively affecting their relationship when, in fact, challenging the illusion of work will probably strengthen the helping relationship.

Challenging communicates that you care, that you really want the client to be successful. This strengthens the helping relationship. It communicates to clients that you care enough to risk confronting them. It demonstrates a caring concern and a seriousness about helping them make progress in realizing their goals. Letting the illusion continue unchallenged communicates the opposite. It tells the client you are more concerned about maintaining a comfort level than you are about helping the client make difficult changes.

Challenging is a skill that draws attention to discrepant aspects of the client's verbal and nonverbal behaviors (Egan, 1999). It is a skill that helps clients focus on aspects of their behavior or communication that are getting in the way of progress. It should only be used in relation to specific behaviors, and not to some vague generalization (Patterson and Welgel, 1994). It should also be directly relevant to the work at hand. This is best assured by connecting the challenge to the agreed-upon action plan. Put the challenge in the context of your work together and progress toward goal attainment. Limit challenges to those connected to progress on the action plan. Make the challenge an invitation to examine and explore the discrepancies or illusions. Challenge in a way that encourages exploration rather than the marshalling of defenses. The purpose of the challenge is to point out the discrepancies so that the issue can be openly addressed. Blaming or attacking the client does not encourage exploration. The following example illustrates a worker's use of challenging:

WORKER: One of the goals we agreed to work on is establishing a relationship with your daughter, and for the past 2 weeks we have been talking about your contacting her and how much that means to you. I believe this is really important for you, and I'm concerned that it gets put off each week. Something is holding you back. Any ideas?

In the above example, the worker ties the challenge to the action plan and invites the client to explore the discrepancy between the client's words and behaviors in a fairly nonthreatening manner. Doing so puts the issue on the table and allows the worker and client to explore the client's reluctance. It may be that the client needs more time and that contacting the daughter at this time is premature. Or it might be something else altogether. Nevertheless, the challenge helps move the work along, whereas allowing the illusion of work to continue would have stalled progress. In this situation the worker invited the client to explore the discrepancy. In the next example the worker challenges the client while also demonstrating empathy.

WORKER: We have been talking about getting back in touch with your daughter for quite some time now. You say you want to contact her but keep finding excuses not to. I know making the first move is scary. Are you worried about being hurt or rejected? Is that what is holding you back?

In this example the worker has linked the challenge to the work, has pointed out the discrepancy, and has used additive empathy to try to help the client identify the underlying feelings. This helps the client feel understood and at the same time encourages an exploration of the discrepancy between the client's actions and words.

Maintaining Focus. The persevering task focuses on helping the client make changes and progress toward goal attainment. A critical skill in this regard is helping clients maintain their focus on the identified action plan and desired outcomes. Clients from disadvantaged backgrounds face a number of enormous challenges on a daily basis. Small obstacles, such as transportation or baby-sitting, often turn into crisis situations. It is easy for the worker to spend all his or her time with a client going from one crisis situation to another. In this respect the work becomes reactive rather than purposeful.

Some concerns need immediate attention, and others do not. The worker needs to help clients sort through the various issues as they arise and put them within the framework of their action plan. Using the action plan as the frame of reference helps the worker and client maintain the focus of their work together. The specifics of the work may shift during the helping process, but they should always be defined and articulated in a plan of action. The skill of maintaining focus is bringing the work back to the plan of action and keeping the framework of the contract in focus.

Shulman (1999) points out that sometimes "moving from concern to concern can be an evasion of work—that is, if the client won't stay with one issue, then he or she does not have to deal with the associated feelings" (p. 173). The worker maintains focus by bringing the work back to the issue the client is avoiding. This communicates a willingness to address the difficult issue and helps the client to stay focused on the issue instead of allowing the client to jump from concern to concern. The following example illustrates the skill of maintaining focus with a client who is jumping from issue to issue:

WORKER: So far today we have talked about some issues you are having with your landlord, problems with child care, and your concerns about the safety of your neighborhood. Before we get into those topics, can we spend some time on the concern that brought you here—the difficulty you are having with your teenage son?

Beginning social workers often have difficulty maintaining focus because of a desire to go "where the client wants to go." It is important to be flexible and respond to the client's immediate agenda. If the client has an issue that needs to be dealt with, then it would be inappropriate for the worker to insist on sticking to the original agenda or action plan. The key is to assess the urgency of the situation and respond accordingly. The trap is to jump from one issue to another without considering how the issues fit into the purpose of your work together.

Checking for Ambivalence.   One of the obstacles many clients face in making behavioral or environmental changes is their mixed feelings about the proposed change. Most have some degree of ambivalence. "One of the dangers in a helping situation is that the client may choose to go along with the worker, expressing an artificial consensus or agreement, while really feeling very ambivalent about a point of view or decision to take the next step" (Shulman, 1999, p. 174). Ambivalence is manifested most often during the engagement phase of the helping process. It is during this period that work involves making decisions and following through on action steps.

Social workers should assume that the client has some degree of ambivalence and incorporate checking out this ambivalence into their practice repertoire. Ambivalence is a normal reaction to change and the change process. Exploring your client's ambivalence gives him or her the opportunity to work through mixed feelings. Talking about the feelings "diminishes the power of the negative feelings" (Shulman, 1999, p. 174). The following example illustrates the skill of checking for ambivalence:

WORKER: I think we have made excellent progress in deciding on our plan of action. Before we move forward, I just want to make sure you are comfortable and ready to begin. I'm not sure, but I have a hunch that you have some second thoughts or concerns about family therapy.

Some beginning social workers are reluctant to explore their client's mixed feelings. They are worried about questioning their agreed-upon decisions for fear that the client might change his or her mind. If ambivalence is not explored, however, it often results in an "illusion of work" or the client dropping out. Expect your clients to be ambivalent, look for it, and help them express it.

Rehearsal.   A theme of this chapter is that making changes is generally not easy. Indeed, if making changes were easy, clients would not need the help of social workers. Rehearsing ahead of time what they will say or do is an effective way to support clients' change efforts. Role-play what your clients will say and do in carrying out the activities identified in their action plan. Role-playing helps clients find the words they need to sum up the real situation. The worker plays the role of the other person and gives the client feedback on their interaction. The client plays himself or herself and practices what he or she will say until feeling comfortable enough to proceed.

Another benefit of rehearsal is that it helps the worker and client identify ambivalence and other obstacles holding the client back from moving forward on the action plan. The role-play provides the client with an experience similar to what he or she would have in real life. The client experiences his or her reactions to the interaction or exchange. The role-play's affective component helps the client identify underlying feelings. It helps bring feelings out into the open so that they can be addressed.

Output: Client Change.   The major output of the persevering task is **client change.** This is the phase of the helping process where the attention is focused on helping clients make the identified changes in their lives. Keeping clients engaged in the helping process during this difficult period is the key to realizing the desired output of client change. Communicating support and strong commitment to the change process helps strengthen the helping relationship. Use of the intervention skills of challenging, maintaining focus, checking for ambivalence, and rehearsal helps clients achieve their identified goals.

THE DISENGAGEMENT PHASE OF COLLABORATIVE SOCIAL WORK

As shown in Table 3.1 in Chapter 3, the disengagement phase of the collaborative model has one major tasks: solidifying gains made. The **solidifying** task focuses on evaluation and review of the goals and objectives developed in the intervention phases and addressed through the helping process.

TASK 7: SOLIDIFYING THE CHANGES ACHIEVED

Solidifying or maintaining the gains made through the helping relationship is another task that needs to be addressed during the disengagement phase. "Workers cannot assume that beneficial changes the clients have attained will continue" (Garvin and Seabury, 1997, p. 428). One common reason is that the client's environment may not be supportive of the changes. The client may not have a support network that will bolster his or her new ways of coping. The kind of support the client received in the helping relationship may not be available. In fact, the client's environment may undermine the gains made.

Some researchers view ending as an intervention (Fortune, 1995), and others view it as a component of the helping process or as the final stage of the helping relationship (Hess and Hess, 1994). According to Fortune (1995), the ending process should

- Assess client progress and treatment process
- Generalize gains to other settings and situations

- Develop skills and strategies to maintain gains
- Assist in the transition to no service or to another service
- Deal with emotional reactions to ending treatment

Others have developed similar conceptualizations of the tasks that need to be completed during the disengagement phase (Garvin and Seabury, 1997; Miley, O'Melia, and DuBois, 1998). Regardless of the conceptualization of the specific activities, the primary objective is to solidify the client changes that have been achieved. Solidification entails maintaining the gains achieved and preventing relapse.

Input: Confidence.   Figure 5.7 illustrates how the solidifying task builds trust. Reviewing progress with your clients during the disengagement phase is a critical step in the termination process. It is important for clients to hear about and acknowledge accomplishments as well as setbacks. This review sets the stage for helping the client examine ways in which your work together can be used outside of the helping relationship. It also sets the stage for identifying the next steps and an aftercare plan following the termination of the helping relationship. Engaging the client in this process helps create an expectation for success and communicates to the client confidence in her ability to maintain the gains made and continue creating positive life changes.

Ending Skills.   The two primary practice skills, shown in Table 5.6, that are somewhat unique to the ending process are generalizing and identifying the next steps. Both of these skills help clients prepare for the termination of the helping relationship.

Generalizing   This skill entails helping clients generalize the learning from one experience to other similar experiences. "This is a key skill of living, since it equips

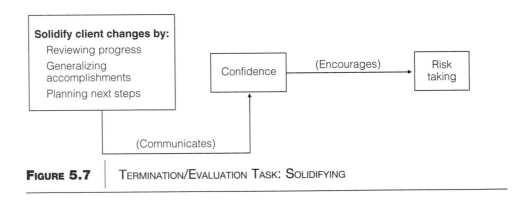

FIGURE 5.7 | TERMINATION/EVALUATION TASK: SOLIDIFYING

TABLE 5.6 | SOLIDIFYING: PRACTICE SKILLS

Ending Skills
Generalizing
ID Next Steps

the client to continue without the worker and to use the newfound skills to deal with novel and unexpected experiences" (Shulman, 1999, p. 193). The first step in helping clients generalize is to evaluate progress related to the identified concerns and challenges. Evaluation is a process that continues throughout the disengagement phase. Deciding to terminate the helping relationship is an evaluative act. In planned terminations, you and the client have agreed to end the helping relationship. A comprehensive review of progress during the termination phase is needed.

A comprehensive review can confirm or disconfirm the decision to terminate (Fortune, 1995). Is termination appropriate? Is the helping relationship no longer needed? Is the client ready to move on without service or move to a new service? Based on the outcome criteria you and your client established earlier, has sufficient progress been made? What issues have been resolved? What still needs to be done?

Reviewing progress during termination provides the opportunity to acknowledge the client's work, effort, and strengths. Termination brings mixed feelings. The client usually feels some degree of apprehension. Emphasizing client strengths and achievement is especially important when the client is feeling anxious and vulnerable. At this stage, one of your key tasks is to support the client and foster belief in himself or herself. Helping clients see how much they have accomplished and how they have successfully coped with their problems and challenges is critical.

Reviewing the helping relationship can also help in generalizing gains. The helping relationship is the heart of collaborative generalist social work practice. It is through the helping relationship that clients address their concerns and challenges. During termination, it is critical for you and the client to explore each others' experiences and perceptions about your work together. This helps clients articulate what they liked and disliked in the helping relationship. Being aware of their feelings will make them better consumers of future relationships with helping professionals. In a concrete sense, an open and candid discussion of your helping relationship will begin preparing clients for possible future service episodes.

Reviewing your helping relationship will also give you and the client an opportunity to share feelings about working together. It is critical in a collaborative relationship for both you and the client to share what the relationship has meant to you and the joys and frustrations of working together. This is not a one-way street; both you and the client are expected to be open about the relationship.

In addition, the review provides an opportunity to explore the client's feelings about ending. Clients will have mixed feelings about terminating the helping relationship. There will be feelings of joy, excitement, and pride about accomplishments as well as feelings of anticipation, sadness, and loss. The intensity of clients' reactions to ending is influenced in part by their prior experiences with separation and ending relationships and in part by the type of termination and the progress they have made. Acknowledging the mixed feelings helps make them acceptable, validates the client's experiences, and allows a discussion to occur (Fortune, 1995). Clients with strong negative reactions will need more time to process their feelings about ending. They may be experiencing intense mourning and grief reactions and should have an opportunity to work through the grieving process as they would with any other significant loss.

At the other extreme are clients who deny having any feelings about ending. One possibility is that the client is responding as if there will be no ending (Garvin and Seabury, 1997). This may occur even if the client has agreed to termination. The client may have cognitively accepted the appropriateness of ending the helping relationship but has not accepted it emotionally. In this situation, sharing your feelings about ending may help the client become aware of his or her own feelings and confront and accept the impending separation (Hess and Hess, 1994).

Use the Helping Relationship Inventory (HRI) presented in Chapter 3 as a starting point for your review of your work together. It covers the major components of the helping relationship. Comparing your responses with the client's responses is instructive. It will help you ensure that you engage in a comprehensive review of the structural and interpersonal aspects of the helping relationship.

Identifying the Next Steps.   The second ending skill is helping your clients plan for the future. Making future plans helps the client make the transition to no service or to another service and solidify the gains made during the helping relationship. Fortune (1995) suggests that increasing the sense of mastery through realistic praise and highlighting the client's role in creating and maintaining change will help ensure gains after service ends.

Whether the client is ending the process or being transferred to another service, the social worker needs to ease the transition by making the new situation real (Fortune, 1995). Events that are distant, unspecified, and abstract are less real than events that are close at hand, specific, and concrete. Your task is to make the pending change in circumstances as concrete as possible. Be specific about the future. Have the client visualize what his or her life will be like outside the helping relationship or what will need to be done to begin a new helping relationship. If the client is being transferred elsewhere, link the client with the new service, visit the new agency, and engage in other activities that promote the connection so as to help smooth the transition. If service is ending, link the client to a support network and engage in activities that will support the transition to nonservice. In both situations, explore the client's feelings and expectations and make plans for following up and checking back.

During termination, the client and worker must develop a plan that specifies how change will be maintained. This aftercare plan should lay out strategies that the client can use to avoid future difficulties and respond to challenging situations as well as proactive strategies and activities aimed at preventing the reccurrence of problems. Strategies that can be used for these purposes are overlearning, problem solving, and network interventions (Garvin and Seabury, 1997).

Overlearning focuses on helping clients practice new ways of coping after the initial learning. The key is to have the client practice the new skill or coping strategy in as many different situations as possible. Through role-playing and discussion, the client prepares to respond appropriately to a variety of anticipated challenging situations.

The second strategy is to help the client strengthen his or her **problem-solving skills**. Help your client predict problems that might be encountered in his or her environment, and brainstorm ways to effectively respond to each problem situation. Role-play with the client different strategies and approaches. The goal is to have the client develop problem-solving skills directly related to potential environmental challenges following termination.

The third strategy is **network intervention**. This entails strengthening the client's support network. The plan is to intervene in the client's environment, based on the premise that others in the environment may also require professional help (Garvin and Seabury, 1997). Network intervention requires the participation of members of the client's social support system and environment. They have to agree to support the client and to become involved in the change effort. Involvement of the support network should begin prior to the termination phase and increase as the client moves closer to ending.

Outputs: Evaluation, Generalization, and Aftercare.   The major outputs associated with the solidifying task and disengagement are (1) completing a thorough evaluation of client progress, (2) helping your client generalize your experiences together to other experiences outside the helping relationship, and (3) developing an aftercare plan. These three outputs are critical to the maintenance of the gains made and the prevention of relapse.

SUMMARY

The engagement phase of the collaborative process usually lasts through sessions 1 to 3. During this phase, the worker engages in four primary tasks: studying, asking, listening, and clarifying. The successful completion of these tasks communicates to the client understanding, sensitivity, respect, acceptance, empathy, and cooperative intentions.

The major practice skills employed during the engagement phase are information retrieval, resource identification, elaboration, and empathy. These skills facilitate the collaborative helping process and intermediate session outputs. The outputs associated with the engagement phase are increased knowledge; increased competence; identification of needs, concerns, strengths, and coping skills; identification of feeling content; validation; mutual understanding; and establishment of a collaborative partnership.

The intervention phase of the helping process focuses on developing a contract or plan of action and implementing the plan. The two major tasks are articulating and persevering. Contracting skills are used to help clients articulate their action plan. The skills of partializing, identifying options, seeking consensus, and sharing data all help facilitate the development of the change goals and the action and evaluation plans. Intervention skills are used to help the client follow through in implementing the action and evaluation plans. The skills of challenging, maintaining focus, checking for ambivalence, and rehearsal help the client persevere in implementing the action plan and achieving the desired changes.

In the disengagement phase, the gains made during the intervention phase are solidified, and future plans for maintaining the gains are developed. The worker helps solidify these changes by communicating confidence and an expectation that the changes will be maintained. The ending skills of generalizing and identifying next steps help clients complete an evaluation of their progress, generalize their experiences, and develop an aftercare plan. To simply end without attention to the outputs of disengagement is a disservice to clients.

CASE EXAMPLES

The case examples that will be used for this chapter are the three interviews on the companion DVD. The first interview represents an initial (pre-engagement session), the second a session during the engagement phase, and the third an ending (disengagement phase) session.

DVD Exercises

1. Review and critique Interview 1 in terms of the worker's use of elaboration and empathy skills. Discuss the worker's use of elaboration and empathy and the client's response to the worker's practice skills. Identify at least three examples of the use of elaboration and at least three examples of the use of empathy. Identify at three instances in which the worker did not respond to the client's feeling. Provide examples of how the social worker could have responded more empathically.

2. Review and critique Interview 2 in terms of the worker's use of contracting and intervention skills. Discuss the worker's use of contracting and intervention and the client's response to the worker's practice skills. Identify at least three examples of the use of contracting skills and at least three examples of the use of intervention skills. Identify at least three instances in which the worker did not respond to the client's feeling. Provide examples of how the social worker could have responded more empathically.

3. Review and critique Interview 3 in terms of the worker's use of ending skills. Discuss the worker's use of ending skills and the client's response to the worker's practice skills. Identify at least three examples of the use of ending skills. Identify at least three instances in which the worker did not respond to the client's feeling. Provide examples of how the social worker could have responded more empathically.

References

Chang, V. N., and Scott, S. T. (1999). *Basic interviewing skills: A workbook for practitioners.* Chicago: Nelson-Hall.

Cormier, W., and Cormier, S. (1991). *Interviewing strategies for helpers* (3rd ed.). Pacific Grove, CA: Brooks/Cole.

Cournoyer, B. (2000). *The social work skills workbook.* Pacific Grove, CA: Brooks/Cole.

Dejong, P., and Berg, I. K. (1998). *Interviewing for solutions.* Pacific Grove, CA: Brooks/Cole.

Egan, G. (1999). *The skilled helper* (4th ed.). Pacific Grove: CA: Brooks/Cole.

Epstein, L. (1988). *The task-centered approach.* Columbus, OH: Merrill.

Fortune, A. E. (1995). Termination in direct practice. In R. Edwards (Ed.), *Encyclopedia of social work* (19th ed.). Silver Spring, MD: NASW Press.

Garvin, C. D., and Seabury, B. A. (1997). *Interpersonal practice in social work: Promoting competence and social justice* (2nd ed.). Boston: Allyn and Bacon.

Hepworth, D., Rooney, R., and Larsen, J. (1997). *Direct social work practice: Theory and skills* (5th ed.). Pacific Grove, CA: Brooks/Cole.

Hepworth, D., Rooney, R., and Larsen, J. (2002). *Direct social work practice: Theory and skills* (6th ed.). Pacific Grove, CA: Brooks/Cole.

Hess, H., and Hess, P. M. (1994). Termination in context. In B. R. Compton and B. Galaway, *Social work processes* (2nd. ed., pp. 529–539). Pacific Grove, CA: Brooks/Cole.

Janzen, C., and Harris, O. (1997). *Family treatment in social work practice* (3rd ed.). Itasca, IL: F. E. Peacock Publishing, Inc.

Kadushin, A., and Kadushin, G. (1997). *The social work interview* (4th ed.). New York: Columbia University Press.

Miley, K., O'Melia, M., and DuBois, B. L. (1998). *Generalist social work practice: An empowering approach* (2nd ed.). Boston: Allyn and Bacon.

Miller, W. R., and Rollnick, S. (2002). *Motivational interviewing: Preparing people for change* (2nd ed.). New York: Guilford Press.

Patterson, L. E., and Welgel, E. R. (1994). *The counseling process* (4th ed.). Pacific Grove, CA: Brooks/Cole.

Perlman, H. (1968). *Persona: Social role and responsibility.* Chicago: University of Chicago Press.

Pillari, V. (2002). *Social work practice: Theories and skills.* Boston: Allyn and Bacon.

Prochaska, J. O., DiClemente, C. C., and Norcross, J. C. (1992). In search of how people change: Applications to addictive behaviors. *American Psychologist, 47,* 1102–1114.

Sevel, J., Cummins, L., and Madrigal, C. (1999). *Social work skills demonstrated: Beginning direct practice demonstration CD-ROM.* Boston: Allyn and Bacon.

Shulman, L. (1999). *The skills of helping: Individuals, families, groups, and communities* (4th ed.). Itasca, IL: F. E. Peacock Publishing, Inc.

Zwick, R., and Atkinson, C. (1985). Effectiveness of a client pretherapy orientation videotape. *Journal of Counseling Psychology, 32,* 514–524.

GENERALIST PRACTICE WITH INDIVIDUALS

CHAPTER 6

Spencer Grant/PhotoEdit

Norma D. is a senior BSW student with a second-year placement in a family service agency in an urban community. Norma provides case management and supportive services to a primarily minority elderly client population. She enjoys working with the elderly and hearing their stories.

During her second month of placement, rains from a hurricane that hit North Carolina flooded the river that runs through the community. The rains were unusually heavy, and the river flooded for the first time in recent memory.

The flood damage was limited to the streets relatively close to the river. Nevertheless, for those affected, the damage was extensive. Homes were flooded, cars floated down the street, and approximately 2000 people were displaced from their homes.

All agency personnel were dispatched to help the people affected by the flood. Norma was not prepared for the effect that the physical destruction of people's homes and their distress would have on her. By natural disaster standards the flood was a relatively small scale event, but Norma was overwhelmed by the magnitude of the damage and the suffering. She felt a sense of powerlessness in much the same way her clients did. Norma couldn't understand why her agency sent her out so completely unprepared.

The purpose of this chapter is to provide more detailed information on generalist social work practice with individual clients. By the end of this chapter, you should be able to help Norma

1. Conduct a strengths-based assessment
2. Plot personal and environmental client strengths and obstacles
3. Construct an ecomap
4. Write measurable goals and objectives
5. Identify a number of micro-level interventions that she can undertake with her clients
6. Describe the role of termination in the helping process

PRE-ENGAGEMENT

As described in Chapter 3, the major output of the pre-engagement phase is a collaborative assessment of the client situation, strengths and obstacles. Assessment is a process in which you and your client articulate the target problem and analyze the relevant factors in the client's person-in-environment system that may affect it. Assessment tools can help you and the client identify and organize information.

Obtaining the necessary information to complete assessment instruments requires sensitivity, compassion, caring—concern, and curiosity. Keep the focus on listening and understanding rather than on obtaining answers to the questions on the assessment tools. Attention to the interpersonal aspects of the helping relationship is extremely critical during the initial assessment phase.

Let the information flow from the interview; focus on the client's story and concerns. If the client does not feel heard or understood, he or she will probably not return to complete the assessment, or in the case of a nonvoluntary client, he or she will not engage in a collaborative helping relationship.

In recent years, a number of instruments have been developed to measure client problems and assess client functioning (Fischer and Corcoran, 1994; Nurius and Hudson, 1993; Reid, 1994). Most of the work in this area has focused on developing measurements of specific client problems, such as self-esteem, anxiety, and marital satisfaction. These types of measurements are important in the evaluation process. Quantitative measurement tools designed to assess client outcomes are not presented here. The tools presented in this chapter aid in the collection and organization of assessment data, incorporate the ecosystems perspective, are relevant to generalist social work practice, and are easy to use.

A number of instruments can be used to collect and organize assessment data. Tools can help assess individual, family, group, organizational, and community client systems. This chapter presents strengths-based and traditional assessment forms and four graphic-type assessment tools.

ASSESSING INDIVIDUAL CLIENT SYSTEMS

An individual client system consists of four major subsystems: demographic characteristics, ethnicity and culture, personal characteristics, and life experiences. These four subsystems and the specific characteristics associated with each of them are shown in Table 6.1.

DEMOGRAPHIC CHARACTERISTICS

Demographic characteristics, such as gender, race, age, and socioeconomic status, potentially affect the helping relationship and the identified target problem. Although demographic characteristics might directly influence the helping relationship, their primary influence is through transactions with the worker system. Workers and clients need to explore the effects of clients' demographic characteristics on their work

TABLE 6.1	INDIVIDUAL CLIENT SYSTEMS: SUBSYSTEMS FOR ASSESSMENT
Demographics	**Personal Characteristics**
Gender	Responsibility
Race	Commitment
Age	Motivation
Socioeconomic status	Coping skills
	Resourcefulness
Ethnicity and Culture	**Life Experiences**
Values and beliefs	Relationships
Spirituality and religion	Support networks
	Life cycle stage
	Mental health status
	Health status

together. For example, there are often significant age discrepancies between workers and their clients. Social workers who are significantly younger than their clients should raise the issue of age for discussion. If it is not a concern for the client, no harm has been done, and it opens the door for a discussion of other factors. If it is a concern, it can be addressed.

Another sensitive demographic factor is race. In the United States, race is a highly charged issue for most people. Race may be an issue when there are racial differences between workers and clients. It may also be an issue when the worker and client both have minority status. Being willing to explore the potential effect of race on the helping relationship communicates sensitivity and a willingness to enter into a partnership.

ETHNICITY AND CULTURE

The second category of client characteristics that affects the helping relationship is ethnicity and culture. This broad category includes personal ideologies and cultural values and beliefs. Assessment of this group of factors requires introspection. You have to understand your value system and how values influence your perceptions of yourself and others. Only after developing an awareness of your own value system can you explore value differences with clients.

You need to be sensitive to areas of disagreement and agreement when exploring personal beliefs, cultural traditions, and value positions with clients. It is important to explicitly recognize both. Identifying differences in values and beliefs allows recognition and acceptance of the differences and development of strategies for dealing with them. Identifying areas of agreement strengthens the connection between you and the client. It is important to limit mutual exploration of values and beliefs to areas that potentially affect the helping relationship and your work together. It is not possible or appropriate to explore all aspects of the belief systems of you and your client. However, the more that each understands what the other holds dear, the more likely it is that a strong helping relationship will develop.

PERSONAL CHARACTERISTICS

Three primary characteristics influence a client's ability to benefit from a helping relationship: responsibility, commitment, and motivation. A number of factors influence a person's ability or willingness to make a commitment and assume responsibility for creating change. Responsibility and commitment profoundly affect the helping relationship and are critical to the success of the helping process. Social workers help clients help themselves. Success requires a commitment to the change process.

It is unrealistic to expect all clients to assume responsibility for change and to be committed to the helping process at the outset. Clients need to develop commitment to the helping process and self-help through the ongoing helping relationship.

Many clients seeking social work services have difficulty taking responsibility for their actions and sustaining their commitment to improve their life situations. Thus, the interaction between you and the client is critical. You must use your interpersonal qualities and clinical skills to address the client's level of commitment and responsibility. You and the client need to explore experiences and feelings related to taking responsibility and making a commitment to change. You have to motivate clients to take responsibility for their actions and support their commitment to the process.

Two additional personal characteristics that should be assessed are the client's coping skills and resourcefulness. Identifying past ways of coping with problem situations is an important aspect of the assessment. The strengths perspective emphasizes client capacity and previous success in coping with the target problem. Clients often are unaware of their resourcefulness and past successes. Exploring past experiences and providing ideas about additional ways of coping empowers the client and enhances the helping relationship.

LIFE EXPERIENCES

The broad category of life experiences refers to the client's history, including experiences with family and interpersonal relationships, support networks, developmental life stages, and mental health and health status. These are the traditional topics of biopsychosocial assessment. You need to explore the client's life story. You need to understand the client's self-perceptions, worldview, and prior experiences, and the way these experiences may potentially influence the helping relationship.

ASSESSMENT FORMS

Generalist social workers practice in a multitude of settings. The types of assessment tools they use are as varied as the settings. Agencies adopt or develop assessment procedures based on the kinds of information they need and the types of services they provide. Most assessment tools are variations of the generic biopsychosocial assessment that has been taught in schools of social work for many years. Typically, these instruments are used to collect information on client problems and past behaviors and experiences. Little or no attention is given to client strengths. Tools that focus on client strengths are now emerging, and strengths-based assessments are beginning to be incorporated into agency-based practice.

STRENGTHS-BASED ASSESSMENT WORKSHEETS

Strengths-based worksheets were developed to help social workers and clients identify clients' strengths as well as the obstacles they face in resolving problem situations. The strengths and obstacles worksheet helps social workers and clients

- Summarize areas of concern and priorities
- Identify client strengths and obstacles
- Analyze the effects of the obstacles and strengths on the target problem

The strengths and obstacles worksheet is Form 6.1 at the end of this chapter.

You should try to complete as much of the worksheet as possible between your first and second meetings with the client. During the second meeting, review your initial assessment findings and then, with the client, revise and finish the worksheet.

Not all content areas will be related to the target problem. Explore only those areas that appear to have a major effect on the client's concerns. At this point in the helping relationship, your primary objectives are to

- Help your client select a priority area on which to focus
- Identify strengths that can be employed to help the client resolve the target problem
- Identify obstacles that will impede progress

BIOPSYCHOSOCIAL ASSESSMENT FORM

Strengths-based worksheets integrate ecosystems and strengths perspectives. They focus on the present, on the here and now. To complete the picture, some understanding of past experiences is also needed (Sheafor, Horejsi, and Horejsi, 1997). Biopsychosocial assessments incorporate an ecosystems perspective and are widely used in agency settings (Jordan and Franklin, 1995). Typically, these assessments focus on the biologic, psychological, and social functioning and the histories of individual clients. They often include a psychiatric diagnosis from the *Diagnostic and Statistical Manual of Mental Disorders*, fourth edition, text revision (*DSM-IV-TR*). A comprehensive assessment requires an examination of these factors as well as the strengths and obstacles outlined on strengths-based worksheets. Form 6.2 is a generic biopsychosocial assessment form.

Denise Bubel wrote the biopsychosocial assessment in Case 6.1 when she was a first-year MSW student placed in an adult partial hospitalization program.

CASE 6.1 | **BIOPSYCHOSOCIAL ASSESSMENT**
by Denise Bubel

Identifying Information
Theodore J. is an 82-year-old Caucasian. He is married and lives with his 80-year-old wife in their own home in a suburban community.

Problem Situation
Mr. J. has been diagnosed with irreversible dementia. He suffers from memory loss and cognitive decline, and he feels a great deal of frustration and anxiety.

Mr. J. has become depressed over his continuing physical decline and agreed to come to the partial hospitalization program for help with his depression and memory loss. He also stated that he wanted to work on issues of shame and embarrassment that result from his medical condition. Mr. J. indicated that his wife has become "stressed out" from having to care for him and that he is worried about her ability to cope with his condition.

Background
In early January, Mr. J. was admitted to the hospital because he was severely dehydrated and was not complying with his medication regimen. Apparently he was being treated for dementia and major depression with psychosis prior to being admitted to this hospital. Because Mr. J.'s original psychiatrist left his practice abruptly, previous mental health records are unavailable and only the diagnosis could be obtained. Therefore, the psychosis could not be further defined. The admitting psychiatrist reported that Mr. J.'s psychiatric history was limited to his wife's recollections, and she could not account for the "psychosis." However, the admitting psychiatrist stated that medical records revealed that Mr. J. was originally referred to a psychiatrist because of "vegetative symptoms of depression." Those symptoms were not described, nor were their duration or intensity.

CASE 6.1 | *Continued*

The admitting psychiatrist reported a "complete remission of psychotic symptoms." He reported that Mr. J. denied any suicidal or homicidal ideation. The admitting psychiatrist noted that Mr. J.'s "thought process was impoverished with mild thought blocking" and that "there are definite problems with his memory." The admitting psychiatrist's report on Mr. J.'s initial assessment and evaluation was brief and limited:

Initial Diagnosis:

Axis I   Major depression with psychosis
Axis II   Deferred
Axis III   Dementia not otherwise specified and
            coronary artery disease
Axis IV   None reported
Axis V   None reported

Medical and Psychiatric History

Approximately three years ago, Mr. J.'s prostate gland was removed, and he still experiences incontinence. Approximately two years ago, he had coronary artery bypass surgery. He suffers from exhaustion at times. Approximately 1 year ago, he had a bowel resection and suffers from continuing intermittent constipation and diarrhea as well as fear of embarrassment.

Apparently, while Mr. J. was hospitalized for the bowel resection, he threw a fire extinguisher at a window in the hallway. His wife reported that he was hollering at the nurses and going "mad" and that he needed to be restrained and medicated. Mr. J. was put on the antidepressant drug Venlafaxine, and the antipsychotic drug Risperidone while in the hospital. After discharge from the hospital, he began follow-up treatment with a psychiatrist. Mr. J. remained on the medication for 6 months. His wife reported, "Within a month after he came home from the hospital, he began to decay and would just sit around the house like a zombie."

Six months ago, Mr. J. had to give up his license as a pilot because of the decline in his memory and eyesight. At that point, he abruptly stopped taking the Effexor and Risperdol. He said, "I know the medicine was making me like a zombie and making me forget things. I couldn't get an appointment with the psychiatrist, he only saw me once after the surgery, so I just stopped taking it." Following this, Mr. J. began to become severely depressed and stated,

"I just couldn't drink anything, I stopped drinking, I just stopped drinking fluids." This resulted in his admission to the hospital 2 months ago for dehydration. This was the only change noted in his appetite and nutrition history. Prior to hospitalization in January, his weight had not fluctuated in many years.

Additional History

Mr. J. denied any past or present substance abuse and any past psychiatric problems other than those mentioned. He said he noticed that his memory has been declining for the past 3 years, and his wife reported the same. He denied any family history of psychiatric or physical problems, any past or present physical, sexual, or emotional abuse, and any suicidal or homicidal ideation. No paranoid ideation was reported. He denied allergies to any medications or foods and denied any weight loss or gain other than a "few pounds" prior to admission to the hospital for dehydration. He denied any problems with sleep, any problems growing up, and any history of trauma.

Family Situation and History

Mr. J. lives with his wife of 62 years in a large house in an upper-class suburban neighborhood. The couple is financially well off. The couple has two daughters, 39 and 45 years of age, who both live in a different part of the country. Both daughters sell real estate, and Mr. J. said that they are "very successful." He stated that the family is "very close." Before his medical problems began, he and his wife would visit their daughters four times a year for 2 weeks at a time. He has been avoiding social functions and travel because of the shame and embarrassment of having to wear adult incontinence protection. Also, he fears losing bladder and bowel control and not being able to "find a bathroom in time."

Mr. J.'s only brother passed away 11 years ago. Mr. J. stated that since his medical problems began, all his "friends have disappeared." He has no nieces or nephews, and the only support comes from his wife.

Mr. J. depends on his wife for everything, and this is how it has been for all 62 years of their marriage. She handles all the finances, shopping, and appointments and remembers all the birthdays and important dates. She picks out all his clothes, dispenses his medication, and takes care of all his "physical and

(Continued)

CASE 6.1 | *Continued*

emotional needs." He stated that he is concerned for his wife, and he feels all his problems have become an "enormous stressful burden" to her.

Education History
Mr. J. stated that he stopped attending school at the end of ninth grade.

Employment History
Mr. J. owned and operated his own printing business for "50 very successful years." He said he was a typesetter, which required great precision and detail. He stated that he was very "eye-hand coordinated" and was proud of his work. He began working in a print shop after he dropped out of high school. "I would go to the corner print shop and help out with odd jobs. In a short time, I learned the business, and when the owner retired, he helped me get started with my own business."

Current Diagnosis
After reviewing the intake assessment, the consulting psychiatrist evaluated Mr. J. Copies of lab work and other tests from admission were reviewed. Reversible causes for dementia were ruled out. The follow-up diagnosis was:

- Axis I 290.43 vascular dementia with depressed mood
- Axis II Deferred
- Axis III Cerebrovascular disease, prostate cancer s/p resection of prostate, bowel symptoms of unclear cause
- Axis IV Moderate stress of chronic illness
- Axis V Global Assessment of Functioning Scale: 37 with difficulties with memory and confusion at times

The psychiatrist planned and recommended retrieval of all medical records, a discussion with the admitting psychiatrist, strict medication monitoring, consideration of an anti-Alzheimer agent, a family meeting, a discussion with the primary physician, and 5 days of group therapy to help Mr. J. cope with memory loss.

Summary
After reviewing the initial assessment with the psychiatrist, it is clear that Mr. J.'s dementia is irreversible. It is organic, resulting in symptoms of memory loss, depression, and cognitive decline. The psychosis was isolated to a one-time occurrence in the hospital, a superimposed delirium. The medication prescribed in the hospital was the origin of the vegetative symptoms of depression.

MENTAL STATUS EVALUATION

Another type of assessment frequently used in mental health and family service agencies is a mental status evaluation (Lukas, 1993). This examination is designed to be used with individual clients. "The purpose of the mental status examination is to assess the quality and range of perception, thinking, feeling, and psychomotor activity so that the practitioner can understand how behavior is or is not symptomatic of mental disorders" (Jordan and Franklin, 1995, p. 180). The examination is usually organized around different categories of client functioning, including appearance, attitude, speech, emotions, thought process, sensory perceptions, and mental capacities (see Form 6.3).

APPEARANCE

The individual's physical appearance includes dress, posture, body movements, and attitude. What is the overall impression of the client's appearance? Are there any unusual aspects of the client's appearance, posture, movements, or demeanor? Is the "client overly flamboyant, meticulous, bizarre, exceedingly sloppy and dirty?" (Jordan and Franklin, 1995, p. 180).

Speech

Is there anything unusual about individual's speech? Does he or she speak unusually fast or slowly? Is the volume appropriate? How is the tone and pattern of the client's speech? Are there any noticeable speech problems?

Emotions

Emotions or feelings encompass two dimensions: affect and mood. **Affect** "refers to the way the client shows his emotions while he is with you, and it may or may not coincide with the internal state the client describes himself as feeling over time" (Lukas, 1993, p. 19). Is the client's affect flat or blunted, expressing little emotion? Does the client experience rapid shift in affect? Is the affect appropriate given the subject matter?

Mood refers to how the client is feeling most of the time (Lukas, 1993, p.8). Is the client happy, sad, or angry? Do the client's feelings appear to be appropriate given his or her situation? Are they understandable given the topic and the context?

Thought Process

This refers to the client's judgment about the content of speech and thought (Jordan and Franklin, 1995). **Process** concerns how the client thinks. Is there a logical flow? Are the client's thoughts all jumbled together? Is there a coherent flow of ideas? Does the client have difficulty getting to the point in responding to your questions? Does the client keep repeating certain words or phases? Does the client have difficulty connecting ideas?

Content refers to what the client says. Do the client's thoughts appear to be delusional? Does the client have thoughts that he or she believes to be true that you know absolutely to be untrue? Does the client have reoccurring thoughts that have an obsessive or compulsive quality?

Sensory Perceptions

Sensory perceptions concern indications of illusions or hallucinations. "**Illusions** refer to normal sensory events that are misperceived" (Lukas, 1993, p. 25). **Hallucinations** are sensory experiences unrelated to external stimuli (Lukas, 1993). Are there clear distortions in the client's view of reality? If so, when and under what conditions do they occur?

Mental Capacities

Mental capacity refers to orientation, intelligence, concentration, and memory. **Orientation** concerns time, place, and person. Does the client know the approximate time of day, day of the week, and year? Does the client know where he or she is and what his or her name is?

What is the client's overall level of intelligence? Does the client appear to possess average, above average, or below average intelligence? (Lukas, 1993)? Can the client concentrate and focus on what you are discussing? Is the client easily distracted? Is the client able to remember recent events? How is the client's long-term memory? Can the client remember events from his or her past?

ATTITUDE

What kind of attitude does the client project toward his or her problem, the interview, and you? Is the client cooperative and forthcoming or uncooperative and withholding? Is the client overly aggressive or submissive? "If disturbed, how aware is the individual of his or her disturbance?" (Jordan and Franklin, 1995, p. 181).

Denise Bubel wrote the mental status evaluation of Mr. J. in Case 6.2 at the same time she wrote the biopsychosocial assessment presented earlier in this chapter.

INPUT AND OUTPUT CHECKLIST

An input and output checklist is completed by the social worker following each client session and is reviewed before each session (Form 6.4). Its purpose is to provide an easy-to-use way to note worker inputs and client outputs of the collaborative

---

CASE 6.2 | **MENTAL STATUS EVALUATION**
by Denise Bubel

Theodore J. is an 82-year-old Caucasian male. He was well groomed and very well dressed in appropriate, immaculate, casual attire that had been carefully coordinated. He sat in a slouched position, legs crossed, leaning to the left of his chair. He had swollen eyes and a washed-out complexion. His attitude was one of concern, and he appeared to be worried as exhibited by his facial expression and verbal presentation.

The volume of Mr. J.'s speech was low. His pace of speech was slow, and he presented slight psychomotor retardation. Mr. J. had difficulty recalling words to finish his thoughts and sentences but was able to formulate complete sentences.

Mr. J. was engaging but appeared to lack a positive self-image. His mood and affect were depressed. His perception of his problem, content of thought, and associations were appropriate.

The patient denied any hearing deficits, and none were noted. He denied having visual or auditory hallucinations. His eyesight had significantly declined over the last 2 years, and this appeared to be of major concern to him. He wore glasses.

Mr. J. was oriented to person but could not recall the name of the program he was in, the floor he was on, or the date. There were apparent deficits in his immediate memory. He appeared to be of average intelligence and had the ability to concentrate on the subject being discussed. However, he was not able to count backward by threes. Mr. J.'s short-term memory appeared somewhat intact in relation to recent events. He was able to recall facts from his past, but he was not able to recall or trace a timeline. He remembered that he had had surgery, but he could not remember if it was 2 or 3 years ago. His insight and judgment did not appear to be impaired.

Although depressed, Mr. J. was polite and cooperative. He was easy to relate to and appeared capable of developing a helping relationship. Mr. J. appeared motivated to participate in the partial hospitalization program and to get help with his depression and memory loss.

model. Following each session the worker subjectively assesses progress in communicating the various inputs as well as client progress in achieving expected outputs. The checklist is then reviewed just before the next session as a reminder of what has been accomplished and what still needs to be accomplished.

GRAPHIC DISPLAYS

Graphic tools display information in a picture or graphic format. They condense what would be a long verbal description into a single image. Graphic displays are an effective way to summarize assessment information and present it so it is readily understandable to a wide range of clients. The two graphic displays presented here are plot forms and ecomaps.

STRENGTHS AND OBSTACLES PLOT FORM

The strengths and obstacles plot form shown in Figure 6.1 is a modified version of the assessment axis developed by Cowger (1994). It is used in conjunction with the strengths and obstacles worksheet. Brief descriptions of the strengths and obstacles identified on the worksheets are written in the appropriate quadrants of the plot form. The completed form graphically summarizes the strengths and obstacles associated with the target problem. The value of this tool is that it succinctly summarizes all the identified strengths and obstacles on a single sheet of paper. It highlights in a concrete manner client strengths as well as obstacles that need to be overcome to resolve the identified target problem.

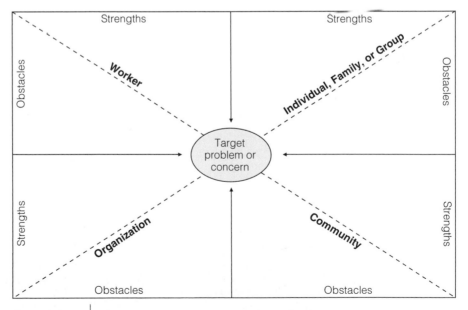

FIGURE 6.1 | STRENGTHS AND OBSTACLES PLOT FORM

ECOMAPS

Ecomaps graphically display the person-in-environment perspective. They show the ecologic context of the client system (Hartman, 1995; Mattaini, 1993). Ecomaps focus on the relationships between the client and the major systems in the client's environment. The major systems vary by client. Typically, they include kin and friendship relationships; work, school, community, and neighborhood organizations; and the social worker, agency, and other social service and health care organizations. An ecomap shows the relevant systems, whether the relationships are positive or negative and strong or weak, and the direction or flow of energy and resources between the client and the systems (Hartman, 1995). As shown in Figure 6.2, a dashed arrow indicates a weak relationship, a solid arrow indicates a strong relationship, and a dashed line indicates the absence of a relationship between the client and the subsystem. A plus sign (+) or minus sign (−) indicates whether the relationship is positive or negative. The direction of the arrowhead indicates the direction of the energy or resource flow.

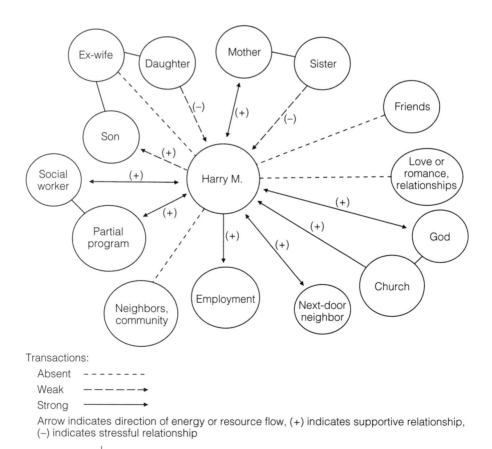

Transactions:

Absent   – – – – – – – –

Weak   – – – – – ➤

Strong   ——————➤

Arrow indicates direction of energy or resource flow, (+) indicates supportive relationship, (−) indicates stressful relationship

FIGURE 6.2 | ECOMAP OF AN INDIVIDUAL CLIENT SYSTEM

Ecomaps are constructed in collaboration with the client. The worker begins by placing the client in the middle of the ecomap, and then identifies the various personal and environmental systems with which the client interacts. The social worker reviews the relationships with the client using open-ended questions and elaboration techniques. Together, the worker and client complete the ecomap. The worker and client review and analyze the completed ecomap. This process encourages collaboration in the worker—client relationship (Hartman and Laird, 1983). Ecomaps can be very useful tools in helping clients understand their person-in-environment systems and the effects the various relationships or absence of relationships have on the presenting problem. They also help the worker and client identify areas of strength and resources.

Figure 6.2 is a completed ecomap for one client. The client is a 55-year-old African-American male named Harry M. He is divorced, has two adult children, lives alone, and is currently unemployed. He attends a partial hospitalization program for adults with mental health problems.

The ecomap indicates that Mr. M. has strong, mutually supportive relationships with the partial program, the social worker, his mother, and his next-door neighbor. He also receives support from his church and his belief in God, and from his job. Mr. M. has a weak but supportive relationship with his son and weak stressful relationships with his sister and daughter. His relationship with his ex-wife is completely dissolved. He does not have any romantic or friendship relationships or other connections with neighbors or the community.

Overall, Mr. M.'s person-in-environment assessment reveals a number of strengths and sources of support. He receives a great deal of support from formal associations, such as the partial program, his social worker, and his church. His informal support network appears to be limited to his mother and a next-door neighbor. His relationship with his ex-wife, children, sister, friends, and lovers are either weak or nonexistent.

ENGAGEMENT

As described in Chapter 3, one of the major outputs of the engagement phase is the development of an action plan that specifies the agreed-upon goals, action steps, and evaluation plan and the implementation of the interventions specified in the plan.

DETERMINING GOALS

Client goals are derived directly from client problems and concerns. The assessment process focuses on identifying the areas of concern that clients want to address in the helping process. It also identifies client system strengths and resources. The contracting process follows this up by focusing on what the client system hopes to accomplish. Problems are negative statements about the client's current situation, whereas goals are positive statements about what the client's situation will be after the identified problem has been resolved or ameliorated (Bloom, Fischer, and Orme, 1995, p. 74).

PURPOSE OF GOALS

Goals serve multiple purposes. Reid (1970) found that social workers who set overly general goals were less effective than those who set clear and specific goals. When goals were vague and very general, work was characterized by frequent shifts in direction and focus. Thus, one of the major purposes of goals is to set the direction for the work. Specifying goals ensures that the client and the worker are in agreement about what is expected. Without specific goals, the client and worker may have different expectations about what needs to be accomplished.

Goals help facilitate the development of the intervention and evaluation plan. They help determine appropriate tasks and activities that will be undertaken to address the identified target problems and concerns. Goals provide benchmarks for monitoring client progress and criteria for assessing outcomes. Without clear and specific goals, it is impossible for the worker or the client to determine whether progress is being made and whether a desired end has been attained. Without goals, you do not know where you are going, and consequently you cannot tell when or whether you have gotten there. "Goals provide the standard or frame of reference for evaluating whether or not the client is moving, and whether or not the destination is met" (Bloom, Fischer, and Orme, 1995, p. 74). In summary, goals

- Provide direction for the helping process
- Ensure agreement between the client and the worker about the desired end state of the helping process
- Facilitate the development of the intervention and evaluation plan
- Provide benchmarks for judging progress
- Provide outcome criteria for evaluating the effectiveness of the intervention and the helping process

GOALS AND OBJECTIVES

Goals are positive statements about desired ends. In fairly broad terms they describe the hoped-for end result of the helping process. They represent the client system's ultimate outcome for the resolution of the identified target problem. Goals have also been called "ultimate goals" (Rosen, 1993) and "long-term goals" (Goldstein, 1973; Jongsma and Peterson, 1995).

Goal statements do not need to be measurable (Jongsma and Peterson, 1995) but can be global statements of a desired positive outcome. Table 6.2 provides examples of target problems and related goal statements for various client systems.

TABLE 6.2 | SAMPLE GOAL STATEMENTS

Target Problem	Goal
I lose my temper with my teenage son	To be able to control my temper when dealing with my teenage son
When I try to talk with my son I always end up lecturing him	To improve my ability to listen to what my son is saying

It is usually not possible to go directly from a problem to its solution when the solution, or goal, is broadly worded (Bloom, Fischer, and Orme, 1995). Instead, clients often must move through a series of measurable steps in order to reach the goal (Sheafor, Horejsi, and Horejsi, 1994). These intermediate steps are commonly referred to as objectives (Kirst-Ashman and Hull, 1993). **Objectives** are subgoals that lead to the achievement of the long-term goal. They are the steps the client must take to arrive at the desired outcome or problem resolution. Well-written objectives answer the following questions:

1. Who?
2. Will do what?
3. To what extent?
4. Under what conditions?
5. By when? (From B. W. Sheafor, C. R. Horejsi, and G. A. Horejsi, *Techniques and guidelines for social work practice*, 3rd ed. Published by Allyn and Bacon, MA. Copyright © 1994 by Pearson Education. Reprinted by permission of the publisher.)

Objectives are specific and measurable. They describe in very concrete terms exactly what will be accomplished. Table 6.3 presents examples of objectives that answer the above five questions. The examples illustrate the relationship between goals and objectives as well as their differences. The relationship between target problems, goals, and objectives is illustrated in Figure 6.3.

Selecting and Defining Objectives

Several factors should be kept in mind when selecting and formulating objectives (Hepworth, Rooney, and Larsen, 2002; Siporin, 1975). First and foremost, objectives should be steps toward goals, and progress should be incremental. Objectives are the intermediate steps that clients need to accomplish to ultimately reach their goals.

Objectives also need to be feasible. Try to help clients set objectives that are realistic given the available resources and abilities. Make sure the objectives are obtainable. Whenever possible, write objectives in positive language. State what will be accomplished rather than what will be eliminated (Bloom, Fischer, and Orme, 1995). Use words that describe specific behaviors. Describe what the client will actually do (or think or feel) to achieve the objective.

The activities should be measurable and, if possible, observable. In Table 6.3, all the objectives describe behaviors that are measurable and observable. For

TABLE 6.3 | SAMPLE OBJECTIVES

Individual Client System Goal: *To be able to control my temper when dealing with my teenage son.*

Objective 1: I (who) will wait ten seconds and take three deep breaths (what) 80% of the time (to what extent) that I have a conversation with my son that I find upsetting (under what conditions) by August 30 (by when).

Objective 2: I (who) will express my feelings to my son (what) 80% of the time (to what extent) that I find our conversation upsetting (under what conditions) by August 30 (by when).

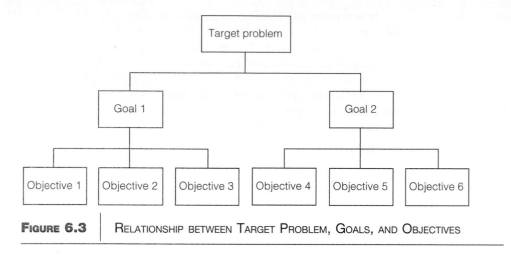

FIGURE 6.3 | RELATIONSHIP BETWEEN TARGET PROBLEM, GOALS, AND OBJECTIVES

example, in objective 1 for the individual client system, the father will wait 10 seconds and take three deep breaths before responding to his son. This behavior is both observable and measurable. It would be relatively easy to measure the extent to which the father has been successful in achieving this objective.

Another consideration in constructing objectives is to avoid confusing input with outcome (Sheafor, Horejsi, and Horejsi, 1994). A common mistake is to state objectives, especially direct service objectives, in terms of what the client will be receiving rather than a desired outcome. For example, stating that "the father will obtain counseling to help him deal with his temper problem" is both observable and measurable. However, the objective is not stated in performance terms and says nothing about the desired outcome. It is possible that the father could attend counseling and show no improvement in his temper problem. Or, on the other hand, he may make tremendous progress. However, the objective would not provide any basis for evaluating his progress. In this situation, obtaining counseling is a means to an end. It is not the desired end in itself. A desired outcome of the counseling needs to be specified for the objective to be used to help evaluate the father's progress in controlling his temper.

Another important consideration is for the objectives to be in accordance with your knowledge and skill level. "Certain problems and goals require higher levels of expertise that you may not yet have attained, and it is your responsibility to clients, the profession, and yourself not to undertake interventions for which you lack competence" (Hepworth, Rooney, and Larsen, 1997, pp. 348–349). Recognize your limitations, and when appropriate help your clients obtain the specialized services needed to address the identified target problems or concerns.

The final consideration concerns the mission and function of your agency. The objectives you and your clients develop should be consistent with the functions of your agency. Are the client's service needs beyond the scope of activities and services provided by the agency? If so, referral to another agency or service provider for those services is the appropriate course of action.

In summary, effective objectives should be

1. Steps toward goals
2. Realistic and attainable
3. Observable and measurable
4. Stated in positive terms that emphasize outcomes
5. Acceptable to both clients and workers
6. In accordance with the knowledge and skill of the practitioner
7. Consistent with the functions of the agency

GOALS, OBJECTIVES, AND THE HELPING RELATIONSHIP

Developing goals and objectives is a collaborative process. It is an extension of the assessment process. The first step is to help your client identify areas of concern that need to be addressed. A comprehensive assessment will identify a number of potential target problems. Review the list of concerns that you developed earlier with your client, and set priorities according to which concerns are most pressing and most important to the client. Together determine which concern or problem has the highest priority. Bloom, Fischer, and Orme suggest negotiating with the client so as to work first on the problem that meets as many of the following criteria as possible. The problem is one that:

• The client prefers to start with
• The client has the greatest concern about
• Has the greatest likelihood of being changed
• Is relatively concrete and specific
• Can be readily worked on given the available resources
• Has the greatest chance of producing the most negative consequences if not handled
• Has to be handled before other problems can be tackled
• Will result in tangible, observable changes for those involved, thereby perhaps increasing the participant's motivation to work on other problems (1995, p. 68)

It is critical to select only one or two problems on which to work. Failure to limit the focus of the work to one or two manageable areas is a common mistake (Bloom, Fischer, and Orme, 1995). The client needs to divide problems into component sections and to begin addressing the concerns one step at a time. It can be frustrating, discouraging, and disheartening to take on a number of problems at once or one vaguely defined large problem. Either situation can make the client feel that the task is unmanageable.

Once the priority target problem has been selected, the next step is to write down at least one goal for each problem. Use the client's words, no matter how vague they are (Mager, 1972). It is important for the client to have ownership of the goals. The goal statements should reflect the client's expectations about the desired changes in the client's own words.

After one or two goals have been developed for each target problem, specific objectives should be constructed for each goal. Every effort should be made to construct objectives that satisfy the seven criteria presented earlier. Mager (1972) suggests brainstorming with the client and writing down all the things that the client could say or do to attain the goal. This process allows the client to contribute to the identification of possible solutions. Ideally, the client will identify the activities. Encourage your clients to put forth ideas. Give them the opportunity to express their opinions. Your job is to help them identify solutions; you should not provide the solutions. At the very least, finding solutions should be a joint activity. At this point, you are focusing on the "what" component of the objective. Review all the possibilities. Is the potential solution realistic and obtainable? Is it observable and measurable? Is it a step toward the broader goal? Select the two or three activities that seem most promising and satisfy the criteria.

The next task is to determine a level of performance for each activity. This is the "to what extent" component of the objective. The client should determine the level of performance. What does the client consider a reasonable level of success? What level of progress is satisfactory? Do not set the performance standards so high that achieving them seems unrealistic and improbable. It is better to have modest successes and take small steps toward the desired result than to aim too high and fail.

After determining the performance level for each activity, discuss the timetable (by when) and the situations in which the changes are expected to occur (under what conditions). Make sure conditions are clear and specific.

Are you and your client in agreement about the conditions under which the changes will take place? Are the specified conditions related to the target problem or concern? Is the timetable realistic?

You are now ready to craft specific objectives. Under each goal, write the objectives related to that goal. Use the client's words as much as possible. Make sure each objective states who will do what, to what extent, under what conditions, and by when. Review each objective. Revise as needed until both you and the client are comfortable with the objective and in complete agreement about what is expected.

DEVELOPING THE INTERVENTION AND EVALUATION PLAN

The intervention and evaluation plan specifies what will be done by whom to achieve the identified goals as well as how progress on the goals will be evaluated. Both the social worker and the client will work on the objectives of each goal as well as how each will be measured. It is the plan of action for the helping relationship. This action plan is essentially a contract between you and the client about how you will collaboratively work toward the identified goals. The contract is connected with the "goal-setting process because goals without commitment and action plans are more difficult to realize" (Locke, Garrison, and Winship, 1998, p. 169).

Several considerations are involved in developing the intervention and evaluation plan. The contract is an evolving entity (Miley, O'Melia, and DuBois, 1998). "Contracting continues throughout the entire course of the helping venture" (Hepworth, Rooney, and Larsen, 1997, p. 360). The intervention and evaluation plan should not be viewed as fixed once it is developed. The nature of social work practice is such that priorities, goals, and plans change and are modified as the helping process unfolds. Consequently, the contract evolves and is modified to reflect the changing nature of the work.

The social worker and the client decide whether the contract will be verbal or written (Locke, Garrison, and Winship, 1998). The disadvantage of verbal contracts is that they rely on memory. It becomes increasingly difficult to keep the specifics of the contract clear and in focus as time passes. Another disadvantage of a verbal contract is that there is a greater chance of miscommunication and misunderstanding between you and the client. Because of these potential problems, a written contract should be used whenever possible. The act of putting words on paper forces you and the client to come to terms with the specifics of the contract. A written contract helps ensure agreement, and it can be easily retrieved and reviewed at a later time.

The contracting process should also clarify the roles of the participants involved in the helping relationship. At a minimum, you and the client should review your respective roles, expectations, and preferences. Clearing up possible misperceptions about the nature of the work and the way you will work together is critical to the development of a strong collaborative helping relationship and positive change of the identified target problem.

The intervention and evaluation plan developed by the social worker and the client is the integrated plan of action. Development is a collaborative undertaking. Your task as the social worker is to provide guidance and technical support. Your client's task is to create the substance of the plan. Obviously, some clients can do this more easily than others. Regardless of the client's level of functioning, it is imperative that the client participate in creating the action plan. The plan should belong to the client, not to the worker or anyone else.

The intervention and evaluation plan should specify who will do what within what time frame to achieve each of the identified goals. For each goal, specify the tasks and activities that will be undertaken. This includes intervention as well as evaluation activities. The time frame for accomplishing each task also should be specified in the plan.

Form 6.5, a sample action plan and outcome evaluation form, can be found at the end of this chapter. The form contains space for listing the desired outcomes and the action steps needed to reach the desired change goals. There is also space for rating the progress on each stated change goal and to summarize the case disposition.

GENERALIST PRACTICE INTERVENTIONS WITH INDIVIDUAL CLIENTS

Most interventions are usually done in collaboration with the client system, or the social worker does them on behalf of the client system. Interventions represent the work phase of the action plan. The two micro interventions usually undertaken by generalist social workers are counseling and case management. Within each of these broad categories, there are a number of more specific intervention tasks and activities. The following describes a number of micro interventions used by generalist social workers in their work with individual clients. The ones selected for inclusion here represent the more common generalist interventions. They do not represent the full range of intervention strategies and approaches.

COUNSELING

Supportive counseling and education and training are two traditional direct service interventions (Pinderhughes, 1995) that are frequently employed by generalist social workers.

Supportive Counseling. In supportive counseling, the social worker takes the enabler role in the helping relationship (Hepworth, Rooney, and Larsen, 2002). The social worker and client agree to meet for a specified time period and engage in a collaborative therapeutic or counseling process. The purpose of the intervention is to help the client resolve concerns and challenges, enhance coping, and improve functioning.

The example in Case 6.3 illustrates a supportive counseling intervention. In this case example, supportive counseling was one of the agreed-upon interventions. Jim recognized his difficulties with peer and family relationships, and he wanted to do something to improve the situation. Jim and the school social worker met once a week to help him improve his relationships. The social worker provided supportive counseling to help Jim gain insight into the problem and to help him develop coping strategies that would increase his effectiveness with peers and family members. Jim also used the counseling sessions to deal with his feelings of low self-worth and the hurt and anger he felt toward his classmates.

Within the supportive counseling framework the worker and client can engage in a variety of specific therapeutic modalities. The choice of a specific modality is determined, in part, by the focus of the work and the identified concerns. Two intervention modalities often used in conjunction with supportive counseling are cognitive restructuring (CR) and problem-solving therapy (PST).

CASE 6.3 | **SUPPORTIVE COUNSELING INTERVENTION**

Jim L. is a 15-year-old sophomore previously diagnosed as having a moderate learning disability. He takes regular college preparation courses and has managed to maintain a "B" average. He receives tutoring in math and science and uses the writing center at the school to help him write all of his papers. Although he struggles academically, he has been relatively successful in school.

Jim has no close friends and very few friendly acquaintances. His peers view him as odd and as a "loser." His attempts to fit in and make friends have met with rejection and ridicule, and he has withdrawn socially and makes no attempt to interact with classmates. Jim spends all of his free time at home watching television and playing computer games.

While at home, Jim appears to take out his frustration on his family. He is very demanding of his parents and causes many disturbances within the family. He gets angry quickly and lashes out at his parents over little things. He constantly picks on his younger sister, puts her down in front of her friends, criticizes her looks and abilities, and treats her with general disrespect. When Jim gets into "one of his moods" or is "on the warpath," the tension in the family gets very high. During these times, everyone seems to be mad at everyone else. His parents start fighting, and the general mood in the family is tense and hostile.

Jim's parents are concerned about his lack of peer relationships and his behavior at home. They contacted the school social worker to inquire about help for their son. To his family's surprise, Jim agreed to meet regularly with the school social worker, and together they developed an intervention plan.

Cognitive Restructuring.   Cognitive restructuring (CR) is a technique of cognitive therapy that enables one to identify negative, irrational beliefs and replace them with truthful, rational statements. For example, the statement "I am a worthless, unlovable person. No one likes me." would be replaced with "I am a worthy and lovable person." Cognitive restructuring revises the way clients think about the problems by rewriting their "internal script." The focus is on changing a negative perception to a neutral or positive one, making it less stressful. The approach is based on the belief that cognition affects one's mood and behavior (Beck, 1976; Ellis, 1962, 1977). A basic assumption of all cognitive approaches "is that a person's thoughts and beliefs can contribute to maladaptive behavior. Another is that maladaptive behaviors can be altered by dealing directly with a person's beliefs, attitudes, or thoughts" (Cormier and Nurius, 2003, p. 391).

Cognitive restructuring is the primary method of Beck's (1976) **cognitive therapy** (CT) and Ellis's (1962) **rational emotive therapy** (RET) (Cormier and Nurius, 2003; Maguire, 2002). Over the years it has been adopted as a major treatment modality in social work (Hepworth, Rooney, and Larsen, 2002) and has been used extensively to help resolve a wide variety of problems, such as depression (Beck, 1996; Beck et al., 1979; Dulmus and Wodarski, 1998), anger management (Whiteman, Fanshel, and Grundy, 1987), spouse abuse (Eisikovits and Edleson, 1989), anxiety (Carter, Marin, and Murrell, 1999), self-esteem (Horan, 1996), and career indecision (Mitchel and Krumboltz, 1987). Hepworth, Rooney, and Larsen (2002) point out that "cognitive restructuring techniques are particularly relevant for problems associated with low self-esteem, distorted perceptions in interpersonal relationships; unrealistic expectations of self, others, and life in general; irrational fears, anxiety, and depression; inadequate control of anger and other impulses; and lack of assertiveness" (p. 388).

The process of cognitive restructuring can be divided into four phases: awareness, reappraisal of the situation, adoption and substitution, and assessment and reinforcement. **Awareness** entails having your client identify feelings and emotions, the triggering situations and stimuli, the client's unproductive behaviors, and the negative thoughts that precede the behaviors. **Reappraisal** entails having your client question the rationality and productiveness of her feelings, behaviors, and thoughts and identifying new, more constructive beliefs and thoughts. **Adoption and substitution** is the process of replacing the negative thoughts with neutral or positive ones. **Assessment** is the process of reviewing with your client the effectiveness of her cognitive restructuring efforts in terms of feelings and behaviors.

Hepworth, Rooney, and Larsen (2002) have identified four practice guidelines for implementing cognitive restructuring with clients (pp. 389–397). The four guidelines outline the process of helping clients make changes in their cognitions, moods, and behavior.

Guideline 1: *Assist clients in accepting that their self-statements, assumptions, and beliefs largely mediate (i.e., determine or govern) their emotional reactions to life* (p. 389). One of the crucial first steps in using cognitive restructuring with your clients is to educate them about the connections between cognitions, moods, and behaviors. Clients must understand and accept the underlying assumptions of the model, and they must commit themselves to the process if the intervention is to be effective.

Give the client examples of how cognitive restructuring works. The more relevant the examples are to the client's situation and life experiences, the better. Before introducing the idea of using cognitive restructuring in your work together, reflect upon your client's life experiences, problem situation, culture, and values and beliefs in order to come up with examples of the approach that will have meaning for your client. Prepare the example ahead of time and plan how you will present the idea to your client. Make sure your client understands and is genuinely willing to work with you and the process.

Guideline 2: *Assist clients in identifying dysfunctional beliefs and patterns of thought that underlie their problems* (p. 390). After your client accepts the premises of cognitive restructuring, the next step is to examine the link between her thoughts, moods, and behaviors. Hepworth, Rooney, and Larsen (2002) suggest that "you begin the process of exploration by focusing on problematic events that occurred during the preceding week or events surrounding a problem the client has targeted for change" (p. 390). The key is to seek concreteness and help the client be specific about her behaviors, the situation, and her feelings. Your objective is to help your client identify the cognitive sets (thoughts) that are associated with the negative feelings and behaviors that created the problematic event. Have your client verbalize the self-statements that were going through her mind before, during, and after the event. Collaboratively review the rationality of the self-statements and the validity of your client's thoughts. "Clients, however, may not acknowledge the irrationality of certain beliefs …" (Hepworth, Rooney, and Larsen, 2002, p. 392). If this occurs, you must "be prepared to challenge or dispute such irrational beliefs and to persist in assisting clients to recognize the costs or disadvantages associated with not relinquishing these beliefs" (Hepworth, Rooney, and Larsen, 2002, p. 392). Asking the following questions can help you challenge a client's irrational thoughts:

1. What is the evidence against the belief?
2. What are alternative interpretations of the situation?
3. What are the real implications if the belief is correct?

Guideline 3: *Assist clients in identifying situations that engender dysfunctional cognitions* (p. 394). This guideline focuses on helping your client to identify the situations that trigger the negative thoughts, feelings, and behaviors. As you review the specifics of the negative cognitions, also look for patterns in terms of where the stressful situations take place and if there are any key persons or types of persons associated with the events.

Guideline 4: *Assist clients in substituting functional self-statements in place of self-defeating cognitions* (p. 394). As clients become aware of their negative thoughts, feelings, and behaviors, they need help in creating alternative thoughts and beliefs. The social worker helps her clients create realistic, affirming self-statements. Self-statements are internal thoughts that the client thinks to herself when trigger situations arise. The new positive self-statements need to be realistic and recognize the difficulty of the situation or the struggle involved. For example, a client dealing with anxiety might say, "These meetings always make me anxious. That is to be expected. I will go anyway and listen to what the others have to say." In this example, the client recognizes the struggle and sets a realistic expectation.

It is important to fully explain self-statements to your clients and to demonstrate how they would be used. It is also helpful to role-play different scenarios with your client to help her practice their use. Role-playing also helps the client increase her awareness of trigger situations and coping strategies. The process of "substituting coping self-statements for self-defeating thoughts or misconceptions is the heart of cognitive restructuring" (Hepworth, Rooney, and Larsen, 2002, p. 396).

Problem-Solving Therapy.   Problem-solving therapy (PST) is a cognitive/behavioral approach used to help clients identify effective coping strategies to deal with problems encountered in daily living (D'Zurilla and Nezu, 1999). It is structured, actively involves the client, and focuses on the present, by addressing current problems and generating solutions. The PST process entails analyzing problems, discovering new approaches, implementing the new strategies, and assessing their effectiveness in real world situations (Rose and LeCory, 1991). Cormier and Nurius (2003) report that PST has been effective with a wide range of client populations and problem situations.

Stages of Problem-Solving Therapy.   A number of conceptualizations of the stages of PST have been proposed (Cormier and Nurius, 2003; D'Zurilla, 1986; Jacobson and Margolin, 1979; Janis and Mann, 1977). The basic elements of the various models are very similar. Hepworth, Rooney, and Larsen's (2002) steps for problem solving are presented here because of their simplicity and applicability for strengths-based generalist practice.

- Acknowledge the problem
- Analyze the problem and identify the needs of the participants
- Employ brainstorming to generate possible solutions
- Evaluate each option, considering the needs of the participants
- Implement the option selected
- Evaluate the outcome of problem-solving efforts (p. 409).

The first step in PST is to help your client recognize that a problem exists and that it needs to be addressed. Often people have difficulty in accepting the reality of their situation and rationalize their problems away. At this stage, you also need to focus on strengthening your client's belief that problem solving can help her cope with the problem and improve her functioning. Thus, as the worker you need to explore with your client the specifics of the problem situation and help her acknowledge that the problem has negative consequences and that PST has the potential to help.

The next step is to help your client analyze the problem situation and her needs that are not being met. Do not seek to identify the root causes of problems or solutions. Instead help your client discover factors that produce the difficulties and identify the needs that must be met in order to solve the problem (Hepworth, Rooney, and Larsen, 2002). The focus should be on what needs to change versus how one brings the change about. The social worker uses elaboration skills to help the client tell her story and containment to focus on listening to the client's story. The goal is to have an agreed-upon description of the problem situation as well as a mutual understanding of client needs that are not being met.

After the problem and unmet needs are clearly defined, the next step is to brainstorm for possible solutions. Remember that the client is the expert and the best source of ideas for possible solutions. Remind the client that all her ideas are important and that the purpose of the brainstorming is to generate as many solutions as possible.

After writing down the ideas generated, collaboratively evaluate each option to try to identify the best possible solution. Explore the pros and cons as well as the feasibility and consequences of each proposed solution. The goal is to empower your client by having her make the decision as to which solution to select. The client must make the choice. It has to be her decision and not a decision you make for her. Your job is to help your client think through the options. You can provide input, challenge distortions, and share your feelings, but do so in a way that gives your client the power to disagree. The client must have ownership of the solution selected.

Hepworth, Rooney, and Larsen (2002) suggest that after the option has been selected, the next step is to "implement it with enthusiasm and confidence" (p. 414). Your task is to help build your client's confidence in her ability to try out the problem-solving alternative she has selected. Role-play different scenarios and practice until your client is comfortable in using the selected solution. At the same time that you are helping to build your client's confidence, you also need to help inspire hope and optimism about the possibility of change.

The final step in the PST process is to collaboratively evaluate the effectiveness of the chosen solution. Engage your client in an open discussion about how it went. Help her honestly assess her effort in implementing the solution, her feelings at the time, and her reactions to the alternative approach. The evaluation needs to assess the process and the effort as well as the outcome. This ongoing conversation is critical in helping your client sustain her change effort and in maintaining her motivation and enthusiasm. If the solution has not achieved the desired results, then you and your client need to revisit your identified options and begin the process of selecting another possible solution.

Guidelines for Using Problem-Solving Therapy.   Hepworth, Rooney, and Larsen (2002) and Cormier and Nuris (2003) provide guidelines for implementing problem-solving therapy. The first authors' guidelines are generic, and the second authors' focus on diversity. Hepworth, Rooney, and Larsen (2002) suggest that social workers using PST:

- Be specific in relating problems
- Focus on the present problem rather than on past difficulties
- Focus on only one problem at a time
- Suspend judgment about the validity of the client's concerns
- Be nonjudgmental and avoid blaming the client

Cormier and Nuris (2003) focus on guidelines for applying PST with diverse client populations. They recommend that PST "be adapted for client characteristics such as age, gender, race, and ethnic affiliation to make problem solving both developmentally appropriate and culturally relevant" (p. 412). They also recommend that PST for clients from diverse backgrounds be conducted in a culturally sensitive manner. The rituals and traditions of the client's culture must be respected. PST

CASE 6.4	EDUCATIONAL INTERVENTION

Time Out for Tots is a parenting program for teenage mothers. There are 15 two-hour sessions. The young mothers attend a weekly mother-only group session, during which information on child development and parenting is presented by the social worker. Group members also share their personal experiences and challenges. The second component of the program involves both the mothers and the children in a weekly group play session. During these sessions, the social worker models appropriate parent–child interactions and supports the mothers' use of the concepts and techniques covered in the group sessions.

must also be sensitive to the client's cultural and socioeconomic stat us, and to other issues that may affect oppressed and disenfranchised populations.

Education and Training. Education and training is a micro intervention used frequently by generalist social workers (DuBois and Miley, 1999). It involves helping individuals, families, and groups learn new concepts and skills. Many clients do not have the skills needed to meet the demands and expectations of their environment (Garvin and Seabury, 1997). Generalist social workers empower their clients through an exchange of information. This occurs as a normal part of most social work interventions. However, when it is a primary goal of the interaction, it becomes an intervention.

When functioning as an educator or trainer with any client, especially with a disadvantaged and oppressed client, it is important to be mindful of the discrepancy in power between you and your client. You have the knowledge and power, and it is easy to assume the role of expert. Minimize the power differential by taking an empowering strengths-based approach, and begin with the capacities of your clients (Freud, 1987). Have them share their knowledge of the topic. Create a learning partnership in which you and the client are colearners (DuBois and Miley, 1999). Engage in an educational dialogue as opposed to a one-way conveying of information (Freire, 1990).

An educational intervention may involve helping clients learn new skills, such as parenting, disciplining children, life care, budgeting, time management, and shopping. Skills training can take place with individual clients and families or in group settings. Groups that have an educational function are common in social work (Middleman and Wood, 1990). The example in Case 6.4 illustrates an educational intervention.

CASE MANAGEMENT

There are a number of micro generalist interventions that fall within the broad category of case management. Typically, a social worker provides one or more of the following case management interventions: service linkage, service coordination, service negotiation, resource mobilization, and advocacy.

Service Linkage. Service linkage is another traditional direct service function performed by social workers (Garvin and Seabury, 1997). The social worker takes the broker role in the helping relationship (Hepworth, Rooney, and Larsen, 2002), referring a client to another agency for service. The process is more than just making a referral; service linkage creates a new link between the client system and an existing service. This is a major function of generalist social workers, especially because many clients who are referred to agencies for service do not follow through on the referral or, if they do, are not accepted for service (Lantz and Lenahan, 1976).

"One important aspect of successful referrals is the worker's ability to develop contacts and cultivate relationships with other workers and professionals in community resources" (Garvin and Seabury, 1997, p. 318). Having relationships with key contact people throughout the professional community will help you get your client accepted for service. Often, the client does not exactly fit the eligibility criteria, or there may be a limited number of service slots available. In these situations, your relationship with the agency contact person can help smooth the way so that the client is accepted for service (Garvin and Seabury, 1997). The importance of knowing someone in the system cannot be overstated. Becoming familiar with existing services within the community as well as developing relationships with professional colleagues is an important aspect of the broker role in generalist social work practice.

You also need to make an effort to support and strengthen the linkage. Weissman (1976) identified five strategies to help ensure a successful referral: checkback, haunting, sandwiching, alternating, and individualizing. Collectively, they are referred to as **cementing strategies**. The first four strategies involve following up with the client. The **checkback** strategy requires the client to call the worker to report on how the referral went. In **haunting**, the worker assumes responsibility for the follow-up contact. **Sandwiching** is scheduling a follow-up interview with the client to review the referral process and develop other linkage strategies as needed. **Alternating** involves planning a series of interviews following each contact with the referral source. The fifth strategy, **individualizing**, refers to the worker's efforts to improve the match between client needs and agency requirements (Garvin and Seabury, 1997). Thus, service linkage involves a concentrated and sustained collaborative effort to help the client make a successful connection with a needed resource.

In the case example of Jim L. (Case 6.3), service linkage was one of the agreed-upon interventions. Jim and his social worker, in consultation with Jim's parents, decided that a referral to an agency that provides family treatment was appropriate. The school social worker acknowledged that she had limited training and experience in family therapy and that family relationship problems could be more effectively addressed by a social worker that specialized in family treatment. The social worker also referred Jim to the social worker at the neighborhood teen center in an effort to get him involved in after-school activities with other teenagers. Both referrals and her follow-up efforts were part of a service linkage intervention.

Service Coordination.   Service coordination is the **coordinator role** in the helping relationship (Woodside and McClam, 1998). Clients have multiple problems and often need more than one service. In service coordination, the social worker coordinates the various services and professionals to ensure that they are integrated and working toward common goals. This involves monitoring the current status of the client, the services delivered, and the client's progress (Woodside and McClam, 1998).

Service coordination is sometimes referred to as case management (Dorfman, 1996). However, case management generally involves a broader set of roles and responsibilities than service coordination (Moxley, 1997; Rothman and Sager, 1998; Woodside and McClam, 1998).

In the case of Jim L. (Case 6.3), a service coordination intervention was not employed. Although the social worker stayed in contact with the social worker providing family therapy and the worker at the teen center, she did not coordinate the unrelated services. No effort was made to ensure that the services were integrated. If Jim's social worker and the family therapist had developed an integrated treatment plan for Jim and the family, and if Jim's social worker had assumed responsibility for coordinating their efforts, a service coordination type of intervention would have taken place.

Service Negotiation.   Service negotiation involves helping individuals and families overcome difficulties they have encountered with service delivery systems. This function is also referred to as **mediation** (Garvin and Seabury, 1997) and the **expediter role** (Woodside and McClam, 1998). Service negotiation focuses on helping the client resolve problems and difficulties with existing service linkages. The social worker takes a position between the client and the service provider to improve linkage and resolve conflicts. The worker helps the client negotiate with system providers to address duplication of service, ineligibility, and poor service quality (Woodside and McClam, 1998). The worker's primary task is to facilitate communication between the client and service representatives so that they can reach an agreement (Garvin and Seabury, 1997). The social worker does not advocate for the client directly: instead, he or she helps mediate conflicts.

Service negotiation was not used in Jim L.'s case (Case 6.3). However, later in her work with Jim, the social worker helped the family negotiate with the school system. Jim's parents asked the school to run a full battery of psychological and diagnostic tests to assess Jim's learning difficulties. The school system's first response was that he could not be tested until the start of the following school year, a delay of more than 9 months. Jim's parents asked the school social worker to intervene. She helped the family negotiate a much earlier testing date by assisting them in presenting relevant information on Jim's functioning at home and his social isolation at school at a meeting she set up with the school psychologist. Thus, the school social worker provided a service negotiation intervention for the family by facilitating better communication between the school psychologist and the family.

Case 6.5, written by Kathleen McCabe when she was a first-year MSW student, illustrates the use of service negotiation in working with a dialysis patient.

Resource Mobilization.   Resource mobilization involves helping the client obtain needed resources, such as housing, clothing, food, furniture, financial support, or health care (Hepworth, Rooney, and Larsen, 2002). The distinction between resource mobilization and service linkage is minimal. Resource mobilization is the acquisition of needed services, while service linkage is helping clients obtain such services. Both are concerned with helping the client system gain access to needed services; both

CASE 6.5　│　My Doctors Are Not Talking to Each Other

Jerome E. is a 45-year-old African-American male diagnosed with end-stage renal disease. He has been coming to the dialysis unit for hemodialysis for less than a year. Both of his kidneys were removed due to the onset of cancer, which makes him ineligible to be evaluated for a kidney transplant for 2 years. Mr. E. also has hypertension that is kept under control with medication.

Mr. E.'s medical condition has challenged him to adjust to a different lifestyle. He can no longer perform the physical activities he performed prior to his operation for cancer. Personal relationships with the opposite sex are no longer a priority for him at this time. Mr. E. pays child support to two former wives for three children with the Social Security disability income he receives. He has frequent contact with two daughters from his first marriage, and has a good relationship with them and with his first wife. He has not seen much of his third child, a son from his second marriage, because his second wife, with whom he has a strained relationship, will not allow him to visit. She feels he is not paying enough child support. Mr. E. would like to develop a relationship with his son. He is not sure how to approach the issue, and he is concerned about having to go to court because of his financial situation.

As a result of his medical condition, Mr. E. lost his last job as a corrections officer at a prison and has been unable to seek alternative employment. He can no longer perform physical activities that he could prior to his diagnosis. His blood pressure fluctuates, which leaves him feeling weak and lightheaded at times. The doctors have not found the right combination of blood pressure medication and fluid removal during dialysis. Mr. E. is concerned that his renal doctor and the doctor who is treating his blood pressure seem to be unable to coordinate treatments or even to communicate with each other. They seem to dislike each other and have some sort of personal conflict. Mr. E. feels that his well-being is at risk because of his doctors' inability to communicate.

When Mr. E.'s treatments are correctly adjusted, he would like to find a part-time job. His treatment schedule complicates this. Dialysis treatments take up about 6 hours three times a week, and they leave him feeling tired and weak. The challenge is to find a part-time job with flexible hours in a work environment that is not physically demanding.

Mr. E. is also troubled and concerned about not being able to see his young son. He feels he is missing out on the quality time that is important to have with a child. He very much wants to resume visiting his son. Mr. E. realizes that for this to happen, he must reconcile his differences with his ex-wife.

Goals

Mr. E. agreed to the following goals:

1. To have his renal and blood pressure doctors coordinate his medical care
2. To have regular visits with his son
3. To find flexible part-time job that is not too physically demanding

Intervention

With Mr. E.'s permission and in consultation with my supervisor, I spoke to each of his doctors about the possible communication problem. I felt that it was my ethical responsibility to try to make sure my client received the best medical care possible. Neither doctor appeared receptive to what I had to say, and each indicated that it was not a problem. Mr. E. and I also role-played his speaking to the doctors about their apparent lack of communication and coordination. He did not need to confront the doctors; their communication problem disappeared before he had a chance to put his role-play into action.

Mr. E. and I also discussed possible ways to pursue the second goal, that of regular visits with his son. Mr. E. was tired of contacting his ex-wife, and he felt that their history of disagreements would interfere with their ability to communicate. I offered to meet with his ex-wife and explain the current situation to her. He agreed, and I set up an appointment. Mr. E.'s ex-wife was somewhat sympathetic and agreed to a trial visitation period of 3 weeks.

To help Mr. E. find an appropriate part-time job, I met with him to discuss his options and identify the type of work he would like to pursue. I helped Mr. E. decide that he was not ready to take on part-time work. We agreed to put the job goal on hold until Mr. E.'s treatments were better coordinated and he felt better physically.

| CASE 6.6 | RESOURCE MOBILIZATION INTERVENTION |

Joanne R. is a first-year MSW student with a field placement at Catholic Social Services (CSS), where she is assigned to a case management unit that works primarily with low-income mothers who receive public assistance. One of her clients is a 20-year-old mother, Nicole B., who was referred to CSS by her welfare caseworker. Nicole had been evicted from her apartment and had no food for her two children, no money, and very few clothes for herself and her children suitable for the approaching winter. Joanne met with her client to assess her needs. Together they developed a list of Nicole's short-term and long-term resource needs.

Joanne helped her client locate an emergency shelter in which she could live until she found an apartment, obtained clothing from the Salvation Army, and secured a one-time emergency cash payment of $100 from her own agency. Joanne continued to work with Nicole during her stay in the shelter. Together they found a one-bedroom apartment, modestly furnished it, and filled the pantry with nonperishable food. After Nicole moved into the apartment, Joanne helped her learn to budget, learn more about child development and parenting, and enroll in a GED program.

require knowledge of service networks; and both involve a referral process. The difference lies in the type of service. Resource mobilization focuses on helping clients obtain resources needed to meet basic human needs. Service linkage, on the other hand, focuses on obtaining social, psychological, and health care services. The case in Case 6.6 illustrates a resource mobilization type of intervention by a generalist social worker.

Client Advocacy. "Advocacy is speaking on behalf of clients when they are unable to do so, or when they speak and no one listens" (Woodside and McClam, 1998, p. 63). There are two types of client advocacy: case advocacy and class advocacy. In **case advocacy**, the client system is an individual, family, or group (Garvin and Seabury, 1997; Rothman and Sager, 1998). In **class advocacy**, the client system is a large collective or group of people defined by some demographic characteristic (Barber, 1995). Class advocacy is also referred to as **cause advocacy** (Miley, O'Melia, and DuBois, 1998).

Advocacy has a long tradition in social work and is defined as a professional responsibility of social workers (NASW, 1996). Ezell (1994) found that 90% of the social workers surveyed did case advocacy on a regular basis. Unlike the interventions described earlier, client advocacy requires the social worker to take a strong position on behalf of the client system (Garvin and Seabury, 1997).

Empowering practice involves the client system in the advocacy process. It is generally better to work with clients to advocate for rights, services, or resources than to advocate on their behalf without their participation in the process. Client advocacy involves educating clients about their rights, teaching advocacy skills to clients, and applying pressure to make agencies and resources respond to client needs. Case 6.5 illustrates the use of client advocacy.

DISENGAGEMENT

The disengagement phase of the collaborative model usually takes place during sessions 9 and 10. The major task to be accomplished, at this point, is solidifying the changes that have been accomplished during the engagement phase. Before reviewing the inputs, skills, and outputs of disengagement, we will review in more general terms the termination process.

In many respects, how you end with your clients is as important as how you begin. During the disengagement phase, you and your client review, evaluate, and consolidate the work; process feelings and experiences; and plan ways to maintain the beneficial changes that have occurred (Fortune, 1987; Fortune, 1995; Fortune, Pearlingi, and Rochelle, 1992; Garvin and Seabury, 1997).

TYPES OF TERMINATION

There are six common reasons for ending the helping relationship: planned ending, time-limited service, ending open-ended service by mutual agreement, ending open-ended service for unanticipated reasons, transfer to another social worker, and dropping out (Fortune, 1995). Regardless of the reason, appropriate termination helps clients solidify the gains made and prepares them for the ending of the helping relationship.

Planned Endings.   There are two types of planned endings. The first is the ending that was planned from the beginning of the service and that takes place after a specified amount of time. Managed-care companies typically require fixed time limits on social work services. As managed care becomes the norm, the occurrence of planned endings with time-limited services will increase. Because the ending is determined at the beginning of the service, the process is usually easier than in open-ended service (Fortune, 1995).

The second type of planned ending occurs when the service contract is open ended (i.e., there are no fixed time limits) and the social worker and client agree that the helping relationship does not need to continue. This usually occurs when the client has achieved the identified goals or has made sufficient progress on them and feels that other areas of concern can be handled outside the helping relationship.

In collaborative generalist practice, the client determines when to terminate the helping relationship. If the client feels ready to proceed without the help of a social worker, he or she should be given the opportunity to do so even if the social worker believes otherwise. Support the client's judgment and desire to function independently, but provide the option of returning if the need arises.

The ultimate goal of collaborative generalist social work practice is to empower clients and encourage their independent functioning. Long-term reliance on a helping relationship fosters dependency. If a client does not want to end a relationship that you believe should end, you need to communicate this to the client. One possible way of handling the situation is to revise the intervention and evaluation plan to set time limits and to identify goals related to termination. This way, the client is given a voice in the termination process and a set time frame for a successful, mutually agreed-upon ending.

Another important reason to end the helping relationship is lack of success (Fortune, Pearlingi, and Rochelle, 1992). If progress is not being made, or if you agree that the chances of making progress are minimal, it is in your client's best interest to terminate service. Of course, this should be done only after an open and honest evaluation of your relationship and the reasons for the lack of success. If you have continually monitored progress and have adjusted the interventions in response to the lack of progress, a consideration of termination is warranted.

Unanticipated Endings.   There are a multitude of reasons for unplanned endings.

A common type of unanticipated ending is transfer to another social worker. The social worker must terminate the helping relationship because he or she is leaving the agency, or the client has been reassigned to another worker or to another service agency. Termination under these conditions is difficult because the client has a continuing need for service and has to establish a relationship with the new worker. The primary tasks associated with this type of ending are to process the client's feelings about the change of workers and help the client prepare to transfer to the new worker or agency.

Another form of unanticipated ending, one that unfortunately is all too common in the human service field, is dropping out. The client simply does not return and does not inform the social worker. The primary drawback is that clients who drop out do not have opportunities to access the helping process, make plans to maintain gains achieved, or plan for continued growth.

Between 40 and 60% of cases end because of situational factors (DeBerry and Baskin, 1989; Fortune, 1995; Hynan, 1990). Thus, for approximately half of all clients, service ends without achieving the desired goals or without mutual agreement. The probability of achieving positive outcomes in these situations is small. Additionally, clients might experience disappointment, frustration, or anger over the disruption of service.

CLIENTS' REACTIONS TO TERMINATION

Separation is inherent in ending a helping relationship. It is common to have mixed feelings about any type of separation. The intensity of feelings about termination vary depending on the amount of success achieved, the strength of the relationship, the type of termination, and the client's previous experiences with terminating professional and personal relationships.

Several factors influence clients' reactions to termination. The most important is the reason for termination. Planned, agreed-upon terminations tend to be viewed as positive experiences. Unexpected terminations are more likely to result in negative feelings. Feelings of anger, disappointment, and a sense of unfinished business are common reactions to an unplanned termination (Fortune, 1995).

Not long ago, research on termination characterized the process in primarily negative terms. The emphasis was on sadness, loss, denial, depression, and other negative reactions (Fortune, 1995; Hepworth, Rooney, and Larsen, 2002). Recent research findings indicate that most clients react to termination in a more positive than negative way (Fortune, 1987; Fortune, Pearlingi, and Rochelle, 1992). The benefits gained from a positive helping relationship outweigh the loss associated with ending (Hepworth, Rooney, and Larsen, 2002). Positive feelings of accomplishment, positive feelings about the helping relationship, and increased self-worth are usually associated with planned terminations (Gutheil, 1993).

Although positive reactions appear to outweigh negative reactions, mixed feelings are the norm. Most clients experience some negative feelings about ending. Fortune (1987) found that negative reactions to termination occur more frequently in open-ended, psychosocial treatment. A common negative reaction to termination is to cling to therapy and the practitioner (Hepworth, Rooney, and Larsen, 2002). Some clients use the helping process as a substitute for interpersonal relationships. In these situations, giving up a long and meaningful relationship with the social worker is especially hard. In a sense, the client has become dependent on the relationship with the social worker. Hepworth, Rooney, and Larsen (2002) point out that it is important to stress the goal of independence within the shortest possible time frame throughout the helping relationship. If most of your clients have great difficulty ending the relationship, it is important to examine the extent to which you are fostering dependency by emphasizing weaknesses, deficiencies, and pathologic factors rather than strengths and opportunities for growth (Hepworth, Rooney, and Larsen, 2002).

Another common negative reaction to termination is reporting the recurrence of old problems (Hepworth, Rooney, and Larsen, 2002). This is sometimes referred to as regression. The client feels anxious about ending the relationship and wants to keep it going, so old problems reappear as areas of concern. A variation of regression is when the client shows deterioration in terms of current problems or concerns. Instead of getting better and maintaining improvement, the client appears to be getting worse. Hepworth, Rooney, and Larsen (2002) suggest that when this occurs, it is important to focus on the client's fears about termination and the ending process rather than on the problems that have reappeared.

Sometimes new problems are introduced as the termination date draws near. This is often a ploy to continue the relationship. Although you have to be sensitive to the possibility of real problems that require attention, it is important to explore the client's feelings about termination before turning to these new issues (Hepworth, Rooney, and Larsen, 2002). Often, the new issues disappear once an open discussion about the fears and uncertainty of termination has taken place.

SUMMARY

This chapter discussed the components of conducting a strengths-based client assessment. It also presented a number of assessment tools that can be used with individual clients. Whereas traditional assessment tools focus on deficits and past history, most of the assessment tools presented here incorporate a strengths perspective. They are designed to help you and your clients organize relevant information in a way that promotes its integration and understanding. They are not designed as interview schedules in which the social worker asks structured questions. They complement the interview and data-gathering process. The focus must remain on the client's telling of his or her story, with the worker listening. Filling out the forms should never be the focus of the assessment process.

The tools allow for a comprehensive assessment. The strengths-based assessment worksheets can be used to assess the strengths and obstacles of individual, family, group, organizational, and community client systems. The traditional biopsychosocial assessment form and mental status examination can be used for individual clients. Using a strengths-based approach in combination with a traditional biopsychosocial assessment provides a comprehensive picture of an individual client.

The graphic tools can enhance the assessment process. Ecomaps are useful in obtaining information as well as in conveying the information back to clients in a form that is readily understandable. The plot form is an excellent tool for summarizing client system strengths and challenges from an ecosystems perspective.

Generalist social workers must be skilled in the delivery of a wide range of micro interventions. Generalist social workers engage in supportive counseling, service linkage, service coordination, resource mobilization, client advocacy, and education and training activities. More specialized counseling-type interventions often used by generalist social workers include cognitive restructuring and problem-solving therapy.

Developing goals and objectives flow out of the client assessment. Goals are positive statements about what the client hopes to achieve. Objectives are measurable indicators of the identified goals. Together they specify the purpose of the helping relationship. All generalist social work practice should be purposeful, with clearly articulated goals and objectives. Strengths-based practice is client centered and client directed. Consequently, goals and objectives are based on the client's perceptions of need, not the social worker's.

Developing goals and objectives is a collaborative process. A comprehensive assessment will identify a number of potential target problems. Together you and the client determine one or two concerns that have the highest priority. The identified problem areas are then converted into statements that reflect the client's broad expectations about desired changes.

Objectives are steps towards goals. They are the intermediate steps that clients need to accomplish to reach their goals. Well-written objectives are specific and measurable. They specify who will do what, to what extent, under what conditions, and by when.

Development of the action plan follows the articulation of goals and objectives. The action specifies what the client and social worker will do to address the identified goals. Action plans should include project completion dates and an evaluation plan. During disengagement phase of the helping process, the gains made during the intervention phase are solidified, and future plans for maintaining the gains are developed.

CASE EXAMPLE

The final case example in this chapter illustrates the application of strengths-based generalist social work practice with survivors of a natural disaster (Case 6.7). It is an excellent example of how supportive counseling and case management interventions go hand in hand in the delivery of social work services to people in crisis.

CASE 6.7   # WE LOST EVERYTHING

by Hussein Soliman

The W. family was on the FEMA list of people to visit, and when my supervisor asked me to visit Gloria W., I drove to the community and discovered that the W. home was surrounded by water. A community resident took me there in his boat.

Gloria W. told me that she and her husband had not evacuated because her husband would not leave the home. He was staying in his room and refused to go to the city. In the 4 days since the flood began, Gloria had gone to the city two times with her son-in-law. She bought food and registered with FEMA. She told me that the water covered their small motel next door and that most of the furniture was destroyed.

The couple owns 10 acres of land, and Henry W. plants crops. He rents motel rooms to people who come during hunting seasons every year. Gloria mentioned that Henry had just finished renovating the eight-room motel 3 weeks before. She indicated that her greatest concern was that they would not receive compensation from FEMA because they did not have flood insurance.

Gloria told me that she wanted to leave the house and move to the city camp like everybody else, but she didn't want to leave her husband alone. Since the flood, she had not seen her only sister, who lived nearby and had moved to live with her son in Georgia after the water ruined her small house. Her only daughter moved with her husband and two children to an apartment complex, and FEMA paid their rent. Her only son called some friends who were able to get his message to her. Gloria stated, "I know that my son will leave everything and come to see me." She worried because her son just started a new job in New York, and she didn't want him to risk losing it.

Gloria was extremely worried about her husband. He wasn't sleeping or eating. She thought he might be suicidal. "I sometimes want to go and apply for loans or emergency assistance like everybody else, but I'm also afraid that if I leave him he would hurt himself. I told him that we can't stay here by ourselves because we don't have a boat, and it does not seem that the water will go away soon." When I asked about her immediate need, she said, "I know we need food and stuff, but the most important thing is to leave and go where everybody is."

She felt that her husband was traumatized by the experience. He had fought in Vietnam and still had dreams about the war. Since the flood, he had refused to take his blood pressure medicine, and she saw him crying the other day. She added, "We had a similar experience in the sixties, but the water didn't destroy everything. We helped each other, and the water receded 3 days after the flood." When I asked her what she thought would help her this time, she said, "I know we live in a floodplain area. We didn't buy insurance because the county decided to withdraw from the plan, but we have our will and many people are helping us. The thing that is difficult to accept is the flood and I try to work with the difficult circumstances, but my husband has a difficult time accepting that."

Assessment

Mr. and Mrs. W. had different perceptions of the situation. Henry was traumatized by the loss. Water covered their house, farm, and business. Henry felt isolated from his neighbors and immediate family. Gloria understood that living in a floodplain meant a high probability of flooding. She accepted the fact that the flood happened. Although she did not accept victimization, she struggled with their losses.

When I asked Gloria to assess the family's needs, she indicated that the most important thing was to move to temporary housing with the other survivors. She wanted to apply for assistance, communicate with people, and find out what resources were available. She also wanted to establish contact with her daughter, her son, and her sister. She asked for help in convincing her husband to leave and in getting him medical and professional assistance to help him deal with his feelings of loss and depression. By the end of the first interview, Gloria and I agreed on the following needs:

- Help Gloria convince her husband to move to a new place (she suggested asking Tom J., an old friend of her husband, to help convince Henry)
- Obtain information on possible places to move
- Obtain copies of and review the application procedures of emergency relief programs and loans
- Arrange for Henry to visit their family doctor

CASE 6.7 | *Continued*

*   Make arrangements with someone who has a boat to take Gloria grocery shopping

Gloria seemed highly motivated and willing to pursue solutions.

Intervention and Service Provision
I visited the W. family the next day. Prior to the visit, I had contacted Tom J., who agreed to go with me to see Henry. Tom said, "I know that Henry W. loves his place so much, but I think I will be able to talk with him and convince him to move. We have three apartments in this building, and it is only 15 miles away from our community." I also spoke with two families who agreed to visit the W. family once a day to help them.

Gloria was pleased when she saw Tom. Tom went straight to Henry's room, and in 15 minutes, Tom and Henry came out and joined the discussion.

I gave Gloria the application forms for compensation and emergency funds. Tom mentioned the difficulty that the survivors from this community are having with FEMA. Because the community had withdrawn from the flood insurance plan, residents were not eligible to receive compensation for their damaged homes. I told them that I would be meeting with a FEMA representative in 3 days and would share the results with them. Gloria was happy when I told her I had arranged a doctor's appointment for Henry and that Bob P., her old neighbor, would take them to the appointment in his boat.

I talked about applications for emergency assistance and loans. Tom thought that some of the assistance applied to their situation, but that the compensation from FEMA wouldn't apply because of the insurance problem. By the end of the visit, Henry stated that he would like to move to where Tom lived. He also agreed to meet me in the emergency center to fill out the forms and applications.

When I met the couple at the center the next day, Henry looked better and engaged in conversation.

I helped them fill out applications for small loans. I drove them to look at the apartment and visit with their daughter. Henry's spirit got a boost from visiting his daughter and seeing his grandchildren. The process of moving to the new place was easier than they thought it would be. Gloria was glad that the temporary apartment was close to her daughter's apartment.

Four days later, Gloria called me from their new apartment. She asked me to refer Henry to the community mental health center for help with his depression. I did so, and Henry had his first counseling session with a mental health therapist the following week. The W.'s support network began to take shape. Their son came from New York and spent 4 days with his parents. Neighbors and friends surrounded the family. They began to attend church services.

I worked with FEMA, the county administrator, state emergency officials, and a state representative to set up a community meeting at which residents expressed their anger and frustration with the local community leaders who had withdrawn from the National Flood Insurance Program 3 years before. Following a heated discussion, a FEMA representative announced that FEMA would meet with survivors to discuss their requests for assistance.

Some of the needs were for food and furniture. I contacted the local church and helped open a food pantry there. I also found a way to transport food and supplies that were donated by people in other states.

Follow-Up
After 6 months in the temporary apartment, Henry and Gloria W. were able to move back to their house. The loan from FEMA helped them refurnish their small motel. Local volunteer groups painted their house and did construction work. Like other families, they experienced difficulty preparing their land for farming. The flood left more than 3 feet of sand on the land. The state provided a public assistance fund to remove the sand and prepare for planting.

Discussion Questions

1. Discuss the use of ecomaps and genograms in the assessment process. In what ways can graphic tools facilitate the process? How might they hinder the process? How do assessment forms and graphic tools complement each other?
2. Critique the sample biopsychosocial assessment of Mr. J. (Case 6.1). What are its strengths? Does it provide an adequate picture of the case situation? Is it comprehensive? Is there enough detail What areas need to be strengthened? Is there any critical information missing? What are the relevant client systems in this case? If you were assigned the case, what would you focus on? How would you proceed with the case?
3. Discuss the appropriateness of using cognitive restructuring or problem-solving therapy with the W. family. Which would you choose and why? How would you implement the intervention?
4. How does social work practice in disaster relief differ from generalist practice with other client populations? How is it the same?

References

Barber, J. G. (1995). Politically progressive casework. *Families in Society, 76*, 30–37.

Beck, A. T. (1976). *Cognitive therapy and the emotional disorders*. New York: International University Press.

Beck, A. T. (1996). *Depression: Causes and treatments*. Philadelphia: University of Pennsylvania Press.

Beck, A., Rush, A., Shaw, B., and Emery, G. (1979). *Cognitive therapy of depression*. New York: Guilfoil Press.

Bloom, M., Fischer, J., and Orme, J. (1995). *Evaluating practice: Guidelines for the accountable professional* (2nd ed.). Boston: Allyn and Bacon.

Carter, M. M., Marin, N. W., and Murrell, K. L. (1999). The efficacy of habitation in decreasing subjective distress among high anxiety–sensitivity college students. *Journal of Anxiety Disorders, 13*, 575–589.

Cormier, S., and Nurius, P. S. (2003). *Interviewing and change strategies for helpers: Fundamental skills and cognitive behavioral interventions* (5th ed.). Pacific Grove, CA: Brooks/Cole.

Cowger, C. (1994). Assessing client strengths: Clinical assessment for client empowerment. *Social Work, 39*, 262–267.

D'Zurilla, T. J. (1986). *Problem–solving therapy: A social competence approach to clinical intervention*. New York: Springer.

D'Zurilla, T. J., and Nezu, A. M. (1999). *Problem-solving therapy: A social competence approach to clinical intervention* (2nd ed.). New York: Springer.

DeBerry, S., and Baskin, D. (1989). Termination criteria in psychotherapy: A comparison of private and public practice. *American Journal of Psychotherapy, 43*, 43–53.

Dorfman, R. (1996). *Clinical social work: Definition, practice, and vision*. New York: Brunner/Mazel.

DuBois, B., and Miley, K. K. (1999). *Social work: An empowering profession* (3rd ed.). Boston: Allyn and Bacon.

Dulmus, C. N., and Wodarski, J. S. (1998). Major depressive disorder and dysthymic disorder. In B. A. Thyer and J. S. Wodarski (Eds.), *Handbook of empirical social work practice: Vol. 1: Mental disorders* (pp. 273–285). New York: John Wiley and Sons.

Eisikovits, Z. C., and Edleson, J. L. (1989). Intervening with men who batter: A critical review of the literature. *Social Services Review, 63*(3), 384–414.

Ellis, A. (1962). *Reason and emotion in psychotherapy*. New York: Lyle Stuart.

Ellis, A. (1977). The basic clinical theory of rational-emotive therapy. In A. Ellis and R. Grieger (Eds.), *Handbook of rational–emotive therapy*. New York: Springer.

Ezell, M. (1994). Advocacy practice of social workers. *Families in Society, 75*, 36–46.

Fischer, J., and Corcoran, K. (1994). *Measures for clinical practice: A sourcebook* (Vols. 1–2, 2nd ed.). New York: Free Press.

Fortune, A. E. (1987). Grief only? Client and social work reactions to termination. *Clinical Social Work Journal, 15*, 159–171.

Fortune, A. E. (1995). Termination in direct practice. In R. Edwards (Ed.), *Encyclopedia of social work* (19th ed.). Silver Spring, MD: NASW Press.

Fortune, A. E., Pearlingi, B., and Rochelle, C. (1992). Reactions to termination of individual treatment. *Social Work, 37,* 171–178.

Freire, P. (1990). *Pedagogy of the oppressed.* New York: Continuum.

Freud, S. (1987). Social workers as community educators: A new identity for the profession. *Journal of Teaching in Social Work, 1,* 111–126.

Garvin, C. D., and Seabury, B. A. (1997). *Interpersonal practice in social work: Promoting competence and social justice* (2nd ed.). Boston: Allyn and Bacon.

Goldstein, H. (1973). *Social work practice: A unitary approach.*Columbia, SC: University of South Carolina Press.

Gutheil, I. A. (1993). Rituals and termination procedures. *Smith College Studies in Social Work, 63,* 163–176.

Hartman, A. (1995). Diagrammatic assessment of family relationships. *Families in Society, 76,* 111–112.

Hartman, A., and Laird, J. (1983). *Family-centered social work practice.* New York: Free Press.

Hepworth, D. H., Rooney, R. H., and Larsen, J. A. (2002). *Direct social work practice: Theory and skills* (6th ed.). Pacific Grove, CA: Brooks/Cole.

Hepworth, D., Rooney, R., and Larsen, J. (1997). *Direct social work practice: Theory and skills* (5th ed.). Pacific Grove, CA: Brooks/Cole.

Horan, J. (1996). Effects of computer-based cognitive restructuring on rationally mediated self-esteem. *Journal of Counseling Psychology, 43,* 371–375.

Hynan, D. J. (1990). Client reasons and experiences in treatment that influence termination of psychotherapy. *Journal of Clinical Psychology, 46,* 891–895.

Jacobson, N., and Margolin, G. (1979). *Marital therapy.* New York: Brunner/Mazel.

Janis, I., and Mann, L. (1977). *Decision making: A psychosocial analysis of conflict, choice, and commitment.* New York: Free Press.

Jongsma, A., and Peterson, L. M. (1995). *The complete psychotherapy treatment planner.* New York: Wiley.

Jordan, C., and Franklin, C. (1995). *Clinical assessment for social workers: Quantitative and qualitative methods.* Chicago: Lyceum.

Kirst-Ashman, K., and Hull, G. (1993). *Understanding generalist practice.* Chicago: Nelson Hall.

Lantz, J., and Lenahan, B. (1976). Referral fatigue therapy. *Social Work, 12,* 239–240.

Locke, B., Garrison, R., and Winship, J. (1998). *Generalist social work practice: Context, story, and partnerships.* Pacific Grove, CA: Brooks/Cole.

Lukas, S. (1993). *Where to start and what to ask: An assessment handbook.* New York: Norton.

Mager, R. (1972). *Goal analysis.*Belmont, CA: Fearon.

Maguire, L. (2002). *Clinical social work: Beyond generalist practice with individuals, groups, and families.* Pacific Grove, CA: Brooks/Cole.

Mattaini, M. (1993). *More than a thousand words: Graphics for clinical practice.* Washington, DC: NASW Press.

Middleman, R., and Wood, G. (1990). From social group work to social work with groups. *Social Work with Groups, 13,* 3–20.

Miley, K., O'Melia, M., and DuBois, B. L. (1998). *Generalist social work practice: An empowering approach* (2nd ed.). Boston: Allyn and Bacon.

Mitchel, L. K., and Krumboltz, J. D. (1987). The effects of cognitive restructuring and decision–making training on career indecision. *Journal of Counseling and Development, 66,* 171–174.

Moxley, D. P. (1997). *Case management by design: Reflections on principles and practices.* Chicago: Nelson-Hall.

National Association of Social Workers (1996). *NASW code of ethics.* Silver Spring, MD: NASW Press.

Nurius, P., and Hudson, W. (1993). *Human service practice, evaluation, and computers.* Pacific Grove, CA: Brooks/Cole.

Pinderhughes, E. (1995). Direct practice overview. In R. Edwards (Ed.), *Encyclopedia of social work* (19th ed.). Silver Spring, MD: NASW Press.

Reid, W. (1970). Implications of research for the goals of casework. *Smith College Studies in Social Work, 40,* 140–154.

Reid, W. (1994). The empirical practice movement. *Social Service Review, 68,* 165–184.

Rose, S. D., and LeCroy, C. W. (1991). Group methods. In F. H. Kanfer and A. P. Goldstein (Eds.), *Helping people change* (pp. 422–453). New York: Pergamon.

Rosen, A. (1993). Systematic planned practice. *Social Service Review, 67,* 84–100.

Rothman, J., and Sager, J. S. (1998). *Case management: Integrating individual and community practice* (2nd ed.). Boston: Allyn and Bacon.

Sheafor, B., Horejsi, C., and Horejsi, G. (1997). *Techniques and guidelines for social work practice* (4th ed.). Boston: Allyn and Bacon.

Siporin, M. (1975). *Introduction to social work practice*. New York: Macmillan. Washington, DC: NASW Press.

Weissman, A. (1976). Industrial social service: Linkage technology. *Social Casework, 57,* 50–54.

Whiteman, M., Fanshel, D., and Grundy, J. (1987). Cognitive-behavioral interventions aimed at anger of parents at risk of child abuse. *Social Work, 32*(6), 469–474.

Woodside, M., and McClam, T. (1998). *Generalist case management: A method of human service delivery*. Pacific Grove, CA: Brooks/Cole.

Client: _____ Worker: _____ Date: _____

**Individual/Family Client Systems – Strengths Based
Assessment Worksheet**

Instructions: Briefly describe to the best of your knowledge as many items on the worksheet as possible. Base your assessment on information you have obtained directly from your client, indirectly by your observations, case records, contacts with collaterals, and any other sources of information. The first page focuses on a description of the clients' concerns/problem situation. The remaining pages comprise an assessment of personal, family and environmental factors. For each relevant factor describe potential obstacles, strengths and its impact on the problem situation.

Concerns/Problem Situation

Briefly summarize client concerns and/or problems that the client wants to address.

List concerns/problems in order of priority from highest to lowest.

Individual Factors

Sub-system	Obstacles	Strengths	Impact problem situation
Motivation and commitment			
Coping and resourcefulness			
Values and beliefs			
Developmental life stage			
Mental health status			
Health status			
Employment/ economic status			
Interpersonal relationships			

Family Factors

Sub-system	Obstacles	Strengths	Impact problem situation
Structure & subsystems			
Power & authority			
Family life cycle stage			
Family values & beliefs			
Family rules & myths			
Emotional climate			
Communication patterns			
Boundaries			

Family Factors

Sub-system	Obstacles	Strengths	Impact problem situation
Work/school			
Clubs, churches & associations			
Community/ neighborhood			
Service organization			
Other formal services and programs			
Other factors and considerations			

Biopsychosocial Assessment

Client: _____ Worker: _____   Date:_____ / _____ / _____

(Indicate NA if problem does not exist or apply)

Problem situation (Client's perception of the problem situation)

History of problem situation (Duration, intensity, stressors, coping methods, change)

Mental health history (Sequence and description of past symptoms and treatment)

Substance abuse history (Age of onset, specific drugs, extent of abuse, family history, treatment)

Physical health and developmental history (Current and prior medical problems, family history)

Current medications (List medications, dosage, schedule, reason, and length of time)

Nutrition/appetite (Weight gain or loss, appetite, changes)

Current or prior history of physical, sexual and/or emotional abuse

Family situation and history (Current living situation, family relationships)

Employment history

Education history (Level completed, academic and behavioral functioning)

Diagnosis

Mental Status Form

Client: _____ Worker: _____   Date:____/____/____

(Be specific; if no problem exists in an area, indicate NA)

Appearance (Dress, posture, body movement, attitude)

Speech (Speed, volume, pattern, tone)

Emotions (Affect, mood)

Thought process (Content, perception, associations)

Sensory perceptions (Hearing, sight, hallucinations)

Orientation (Person, place, time)

Intellectual functioning (Intelligence, concentration, insight, judgment, memory)

Phase	Input	Output
Pre-Engagement (Sessions 1-3) Studying Asking Listening Clarifying	Understanding ____ Sensitivity ____ Respect ____ Acceptance ____ Empathy ____ Cooperation ____	Knowledge ____ Competence ____ Needs ____ Concerns ____ Strengths ____ Coping skills ____ Feeling content ____ Validation ____ Understanding ____ Collaboration ____
Engagement (Sessions 4-8) Articulating Persevering	Hopefulness ____ Support ____ Agreement ____ Commitment ____	Change goals ____ Evaluation plan ____ Action plan ____ Client change ____
Disengagement (Sessions 9-10) Solidifying	Partnership ____ Confidence ____	Evaluation ____ Generalization ____

Action Plan

Client:_____   Worker: _____   Date: ___/___/___

Case Assessment Summary

Client Situation (Provide a brief summary of the problem situation being addressed and describe client system strengths and obstacles related to the problem situation)

Change Goals (State each goal in terms of desired outcomes)

Goal 1 _____

Goal 2 _____

Goal 3 _____

Goal - Intervention - Evaluation Worksheet

Complete one worksheet for each goal identified on the Case Assessment Summary Form. For each goal: (1) state the goal; (2) list the objectives related to the goal; (3) specify the intervention activities to be completed by the client, by the social worker, and by any other persons involved in the intervention; and (4) describe how progress on the goal is going to be evaluated, including any measures that will be used.

Goal _____

    Objective_____ _____

    Objective_____

    Objective_____

Intervention Activities

Client:

1._____ To be completed by _____

2._____ To be completed by _____

3._____ To be completed by _____

Worker:

1._____ To be completed by _____

2._____ To be completed by _____

3._____ To be completed by _____

Others (Specify _____):

1._____ To be completed by _____

2._____ To be completed by _____

3._____ To be completed by _____

Goal Evaluation and Measurement Plan

_____

_____

CHAPTER 7

GENERALIST PRACTICE WITH FAMILIES

Betsy Crane

Michael Newman/PhotoEdit

Norman Gonzalez and his family face multiple challenges that bring them into frequent contact with human service systems. His 3-year-old daughter Isabel has a developmental disability. A caseworker at a program where she goes during the day has just completed an assessment of her needs and wants to meet with him to make a family plan. His 14-year-old son John who lives with his ex-wife Maria has to meet weekly with a probation officer after having been arrested for smoking marijuana with friends in a park. His partner Anna, Isabel's mother, is in her second week at an alcohol rehab program. On top of all this, he spends quite a bit of time helping his aging parents, who rely on him for nearly everything.

Mr. Gonzalez and his family also have many strengths and resources. His next-door neighbors are very supportive. They sometimes watch Isabel when he is stuck for childcare. He and Maria are members of a caring church community that stood by them when she admitted to having an alcohol problem. Members of the church's outreach ministry bring meals for him and Isabel a few times a week. As a salesman he has a flexible work schedule. He can even work from home some of the time. He worked hard to get his associate's degree in business, going to classes at night, and persisting over several years until he made it. What he learned about sales actually made a difference, and his income is even a little more than just adequate, most of the time. His cheerful and resilient personality makes him a welcome member of a support group for parents of children with disabilities. And he has been pleased to see how he and ex-wife Maria have shared the responsibility for getting John to his appointments at Probation.

Even with these supports, he frequently feels overwhelmed by what it takes to manage his life and stay on top of all the demands for his time. He knows his younger brother could help out with their parents, but as the eldest son, his siblings are used to relying on him to take care of things, and it is hard for him to ask for help.

So when Norman he got a call from Briana McNeal, the disability program caseworker, he worried that this might mean just one more person to try to satisfy. She said she was a social work intern newly assigned to work with him around planning for Isabel's needs. Might she judge him as inadequate, a single father trying to cope without Anna at home? Will she be one more worker who creates a plan *for* them, expecting them to reach goals she sets?

Norman feels relief when Briana suggests meeting with him at a coffee shop near his office, so he does not have to make a 30-minute trip to her agency. He begins to relax when she seems truly interested in what is going well in their lives, not just their challenges. He shows her photos of Isabel he took the night before on his cell phone and she laughs at the cute little funny faces his sweet daughter makes. She asks about Anna and his other children and listens attentively when he talks about his struggles taking care of his parents. Briana comments on how much progress Isabel is making at their child development center. His family must have a lot of strengths and resources, she tells him, to be doing as well as they are, given the challenges they face as a family. Being 25 years old, she says, she still sees her parents as being part of her support system. So she can imagine that it must be difficult to be at a life stage when it goes the other way, when they are the ones needing help. She listens well when he talks about how connected he feels to their church community. Norman thinks to himself, maybe Briana will be OK. Maybe she can help them.

Being able to work respectfully and in a culturally competent manner with families is a key competency for social workers. Helping whole families develop their ability to care for each other means that you not only assist one or two individuals who may be your identified client(s). Rather, it can be about moving a whole generation, or multiple levels of generations, toward a greater sense of healthy self-reliance and interdependence (Forest, 2003). Ultimately it is about empowering families and communities so they can foster the optimal development of children, youth, and adult family members.

In this chapter you will learn how to use the collaborative model of social work practice presented in chapter 3 when working with families. When asked what they most want from someone who is assisting them, families often say they want someone who will *listen* to them. When workers approach families with clipboard in hand and intake forms at the ready, it sends a message that they are only interested in talking with them about eligibility for their agency's services, rather than really wanting to get to know them—their strengths as well as their needs. By the end of this chapter, you will be able to help Briana to work with the family to:

1. Engage in a helping partnership, based on mutually trusting and respectful relationships
2. Assess their needs as well as their strengths and resources
3. Identify goals to address their needs, building on their strengths
4. Develop their own plans for reaching those goals
5. Identify and use informal and formal helping systems, building a healthy interdependence with their communities
6. Regularly assess progress and revise the plan as needed.
7. Feel more empowered and capable of handling future life challenges

WHAT IS A FAMILY?

Given the diversity of ways that people form relationships in our multicultural world, social workers need to be comfortable working with a wide range of family types. One cannot assume that the family forms you are familiar with are the same as those experienced by others. It helps to ask about whom people consider to be part of their family. Then listen respectfully. If their family type is marginalized for some reason, such as a lesbian or gay family, they will take cues from you as to what they feel safe to share. Here is a list of just some of the many family types you will encounter. Most likely you can add to this list based on your own experience or that of friends or colleagues.

FAMILY DIVERSITY: TYPES OF FAMILIES

1. Couple—Two people, same or other-sex, who share resources; may be in civil union, married, or living together
2. Nuclear family—Married woman and man with child(ren)

3. Gay or lesbian family—Same-sex couple with child(ren); may be in civil union, married, or living together
4. Single parent family—Single, divorced, or widowed woman or man with child(ren); may have child full-time or part-time
5. Joint custody family—Children live for varying times in two households, with parents who are separated or divorced
6. "Bicoastal couple or family"—Intact relationship with spouses/parents who live at a distance from each other due to employment
7. Stepfamily—Single person or couple with child(ren) from more than one partner living together full-time or on a shared parenting schedule
8. Foster family—Family caring for child(ren) on a temporary basis
9. Adoptive family—Family with one or more adoptive children
10. Family with absent parent(s)—Children living with one parent, a grandparent, or family friend because a parent is absent due to immigration difficulties, military service, prison, or employment
11. Multigenerational family—Grandparents and aunts/uncles very involved
12. Grandparents raising children, either as single adults or with a partner
13. Group home/Coop—Friends living together and sharing resources
14. Group home—Teens or adults living in residence owned by agency, often based on a particular life challenge
15. Circle of friends who consider themselves family
16. Friends treated like relatives—Friends who are so close they are treated like relatives, that is, Aunt Tanya; sometimes referred to as "fictive kin"

Being aware that the families you work with will take many forms is an important first step toward being effective in generalist practice with families. It is also important to reflect on one's own attitudes about working with families. All too often families have been seen as the source of the problem, rather than the solution. In the next section we will explore the history of helping systems, including how families were once considered the front line of caring systems, how that changed, and how they are again seen as key to building healthy communities.

FROM INTERDEPENDENCE TO INDIVIDUALISM

People reaching out to help each other—families helping families—has a long tradition. Alexis de Tocqueville, a Frenchman studying democracy in the young America of 1831, wrote about the ethic of concern and voluntary support that he saw people providing for each other. Extended families, churches, and communities provided care for the sick and the elderly. This mutual aid is still true to some extent, in some communities. However, as social work as a profession evolved in the early 19th century, immigration and the industrial revolution were splitting up extended families and disrupting community life. Social workers in the settlement house movement of the early 20th century provided an urban respite for families. They drew on and bolstered the self-help tradition, with families again helping families, often blurring the lines between helpers and those being helped. Since then an ethic of individualism and competition has often overshadowed that of communitarianism and mutual assistance.

Being able to see families as part of the solution rather than the problem is also affected by judgmental attitudes about people living in poverty and the effects of poverty. This judgment has a long history. British Poor Laws discriminated on the basis of whether someone was considered to be poor because of idleness or lack of effort, as opposed to being an innocent victim of circumstances, such as being disabled in a way that would keep one from working. Social Darwinists judged the poor on the basis of *survival of the fittest*, as if those who struggle are somehow less evolved. Calvinist theologians saw wealth as an indication of who was saved and would go to heaven, with obvious implications. The effects of such traditions of judgment, or prejudice, continue to be reflected in social policy and personal attitudes today. Consider the difference in how people on medical leave are viewed, compared to those on public assistance.

Americans have a strong ethic of individualism that implies we should all be able to *pull ourselves up by our bootstraps*. The problem, of course, is that this denies the differences in access to resources related to factors like class, ethnicity, education, and immigration status. Not everyone has the same bootstraps. And considering the debilitating differences in ability due to factors such as age, health, and disabilities, sometimes the boots aren't even there to be pulled up.

Yet even with such challenges, individuals and families often feel that they are supposed to be able to do it alone, to be *self-sufficient*. Yet in reality, both the rich and the poor are interdependent with friends and extended families, as well as with schools, businesses, healthcare providers, and oftentimes with religious communities as well. Social workers know how important it is to look at individuals within their social context. And how social situations can make it very difficult for many people to survive and compete in the global marketplace. Communities that have lost manufacturing jobs with good salaries and benefits not only have families losing their homes and middle-class lifestyle, but they may also face a deteriorating social structure. Schools without a sufficient tax base cannot meet the needs of students. Businesses without customers close or move to more affluent communities.

Human service programs funded by government and nonprofit charities fill in the gaps and help out where they can. However, these programs are often stigmatized, and those who use services may face prejudice and disrespect. Typically programs are underfunded and staff members overstressed.

To make matters worse, the way services are offered can foster a learned helplessness (Diener and Dweck, 2001) on the part of those seeking help, leading to frustration on the part of recipients and workers alike. The helplessness comes from participation in a client role in which one's problems are diagnosed, and one is given a treatment plan, rather than being encouraged to set goals and being stimulated to create solutions for oneself (Darling, 2000). This mode of practice is sometimes called the *deficit model* as compared to *strengths model*. Frontline workers face pressure to figure out what people's problems are, and try to fix them, with limited resources and a helping system that sometimes seems to be working at cross-purposes with itself. The worker who earns the trust of a formerly abusive mother who finally decides to go for drug treatment may confront a judge who pushes for a permanency plan involving relinquishment of her children instead of supporting her plan for drug rehabilitation, and giving her a little more time. Workers may respond by rationing services and providing services to those who are more cooperative (Goodsell, 1981; Lipsky, 1980; Pesso, 1978). This can lead to feelings of shame and/or a reactive attitude of passivity and dependency in those who use helping services, and a judgmental attitude on the part of many who provide health, education, and human services.

The helping practice most commonly used in human service programs grew historically out of a drive toward professionalism that attempted to imitate a traditional doctor–patient relationship. In the early 20th century, social workers began calling for a more *professional* approach to helping (Leiby, 1978). The empirical methods being used in the natural sciences were adopted by the social sciences and emerging professions who advocated a logical, evidence-based method for helping (Goldstein, 1943; Leiby, 1978; Rapp, 1998). This was seen as an advance from a moralistic tone and allowed for the development of a strategy of *intervention* that became the treatment plan. In the 1930s an increasing interest in psychoanalytic theory as a structure for understanding people's weakness lead to a language of pathology (Rapp, 1998), from which today's *Diagnostic and Statistical Manual of Mental Disorders* (DSM IV) was born. The often unspoken assumptions of the resulting problem-based or "deficit" model of helping services can be characterized as:

- If families can't manage on their own, there is something wrong with them
- The job of the worker is to figure out what is wrong with them and tell them what they need to do to fix it
- We need professionals to assess what is wrong—diagnose the problem—and prescribe services, often in the form of a treatment plan or services plan that the worker creates for the family
- If a family doesn't follow the professional's advice or plan, or if the plan doesn't work, it must be the family's fault. They are then labeled "noncompliant" or unmotivated
- The appropriate professional action is to withdraw services or, in the child welfare system, take custody of the child (Dean, 1996, p. 29)

Parents who seek help for their children, especially mothers, face prejudices fostered by treatment theories and beliefs that explicitly refer to parents as causing child behavioral and emotional problems (Collins and Collins, 1990). The "mother blaming" which attributes psychological problems to either too much "smothering" by moms, or too little affection, has added to the rift between providers of care and parents (Cohen and Latach, 1995). In fact, while stress related to family functioning has an effect on children, especially those with lower resiliency, recent research reveals multiple causes of childhood disturbances including genetics, environmental toxins such as lead, and trauma related to community violence.

Families of children with serious emotional or behavioral disturbances can face the problem of having assistance that is either too restrictive—long-term, out of community placements—or not intensive enough to meet the children's needs. Such families may face a host of challenges and be met by a service system that is fragmented and discontinuous. The categorical funding of human services according to *problem area* means that families may have service providers from several agencies and systems all making plans *for them* and their children, without knowledge of the other providers who are involved. Finally, families seeking assistance may be met with hostile, judgmental, and rejecting attitudes on the part of those who are, ostensibly, there to help (Cohen, Singh, Hosick, and Tremaine, 1992).

The genesis of strengths-based practice came in part from recognition that the conventional approach, of seeing families as the problem and telling them what to do, has not worked. What does?

WORKING WITH FAMILY STRENGTHS

Those who use strengths-based practice believe that people and families can create their own plans based on an assessment of their needs and strengths. The focus is on what's strong in this family, not what's wrong. This is a core belief of the family support movement (Weissbourd, 1994). The model of helping is one of partnership, whereby the family member(s) work with a family supportive worker who has knowledge of community resources and can help them develop and put a plan into effect. This change to a *partnership* model is part of a larger shift in human services away from what Darling (2000) describes as a *status inequality model* that values the practitioner's perspective more than the client's perspective.

Four primary elements characterize helping practices that are based on family support and empowerment principles: (1) strengths-based/assets-based approach, (2) developing and working on plans *with* individuals and families, (3) family involvement, and (4) cultural competence. Let's look at each.

Strengths-Based/Assets-Based Approach.   Refers to helping family members identify their inherent strengths, resiliency, resources, talents, cultural values, desires, and aspirations, and using these to create a plan to reach their goals (Dejoug and Miller, 1995; Rapp, 1998; Saleebey, 1992, 1996; Thrasher and Mowbray, 1995; Weick, Rapp, Sullivan, and Kisthardt, 1989). For example, a single mother may benefit from recognizing that her resources include both extended family members who want to help, and her own strength and courage, demonstrated when she left an abusive partner. Seeing these strengths may help her draw on that courage to leave a neighborhood that does not feel safe and move to live closer to a sister who wants to support her.

Developing and Working on Plans with Families.   All too often, the job of the family worker has been to plan *for* families, creating a treatment plan based on a problem-oriented assessment process. A list of what the worker sees as the family's problems or needs, and a plan for rectifying them, is presented to the family with the presumption that they will follow the worker's plan. If they don't they may be labeled as unmotivated or noncompliant. In contrast, the family support worker forms a partnership with the family, and they work together to create an individualized plan (Benett, Lingerfelt, and Nelson, 1990) based on the goal(s) the family decides to work on. The family member may hold the pencil (given language ability), write the plan, and keep the original copy. It is their plan, for their family. A focus on goal setting and taking steps toward reaching goals is related to the solutions-focused mode of practice in social work. University of Kansas social work professor Charles Rapp (1998) has found in his work with people with severe mental illness that a solutions-focused, partnership model of practice is effective even when what would be characterized as severe pathology is present.

A key point to remember is that a collaborative model of practice implies *power with*; it does not replace *power over* with *anything goes*. Frontline workers retain their power to provide or withdraw resources and are not required, for example, to approve a family's plan if it appears to present potential danger to an individual or children.

Family Involvement. in human service systems is about creating partnerships between those on the inside looking out—agencies and workers—and those on the outside looking in—the families. It means including family members as full partners in all aspects of service planning, implementation and evaluation, negotiating meeting times and sites, providing stipends to compensate them for their time, and reimbursement for transportation and child or elder care. School social workers know that parental involvement is key to their children's educational success. They work to assure that the school is welcoming to all parents, aware that work schedules and care for other children can make it difficult to volunteer during the school day.

Cultural Competence. involves learning from and relating respectfully with people who come from groups and backgrounds that are different from ours. It means recognizing that one's cultural background (defined broadly to include class, ethnicity, gender, geography, religion, sexual orientation, mental and physical ability) influences what we think about everyday life. This includes assumptions about family life, food, housing, time, space, eye contact, and other parts of life that we may just take for granted. It means honoring our own culture, and understanding what makes us view things the way we do, while we learn about and honor the culture of others. It means acknowledging where we ourselves have privilege and where we face oppression, and working to be allies to those who come from groups that are not treated fairly and respectfully. It also means adapting the way services are offered to meet cultural needs.

In the following section, we will look at situations in which you would want to take a family-focused approach, to see how these characteristics of effective helping practices of are being applied.

WHEN TO FOCUS ON THE FAMILY

Social workers broaden their focus from work with individuals to working with families in many situations. These include: (1) when families have multiple challenges, (2) participating in a family group conference, (3) working in a family-centered program, and (4) using a family systems approach in counseling. We will look at each, keeping in mind the principles of working with family strengths addressed above.

WHEN FAMILIES HAVE MULTIPLE CHALLENGES

Families who face multiples challenges can benefit from your assistance in recognizing and meeting needs for specialized services and helping them foster collaboration among their service providers. The human service system is based on categorical *silos of care*, meaning that funding and regulation is problem specific, that is, mental health, child welfare, or senior services. Each silo of care is associated with particular agencies and programs at the federal, state, and local level.

As a result one family may have five caseworkers, each from different agencies, separately assessing and making treatment plans for various family members, for various issues. For example, while one parent is meeting with you, the other parent may be attending a substance abuse treatment group, hoping to get home in time for the home visit from the early intervention worker. Later that day she or he might need to work on finding documents needed for a review of their food stamps eligibility, while the first parent attends mandated parenting education classes. You might help this family organize a family conference with all those involved, family members and agency workers, to enhance awareness of their strengths and needs, and create a coordinated service plan.

Sometimes when working with one family member you may become aware of other family challenges that are not being named or addressed. You have several options. If it does not involve child abuse or neglect, or danger to self or others, you may decide to wait or let it go. Seeking consultation from a supervisor makes sense in such a situation. You can decide to talk with the individual who is your client about what you are noticing. Together you can address the topic, then assess an openness or willingness to work together to bring attention to a situation, and to help his/her family seek appropriate help. This can range from noticing a possible developmental delay in a toddler when seeing a mother for food stamps assessment, to a more difficult situation such as possible mental health problems in a spouse, or a drug or alcohol problem. Being able to address what might be *hot button* issues is a skill. First, the person you have the relationship with will need to adjust/react to hearing your concern, and if the decision is made to move forward, then you move into the role of coach as she or he decides on the steps to take. You can also be helpful as an information provider and system-connector, but checking out possible resources for the family and sharing that information with them. If they do decide to pursue help, following up on how it is going is also part of your role, ethically. It it's going well, you can go back to your role in working with an individual. If it is not, you can again work with family to find another resource. This is the way referrals are made using strengths-based practice. You do not diagnose and refer without engaging the family in the process. It just makes sense that families are more likely to be successful using resources that they have been involved in choosing and negotiating. By taking this empowering approach, you leave the family with a greater capacity to recognize a need for help and seek assistance in the future.

FAMILY GROUP CONFERENCES

Social workers may also be working with families when they take part in a family group conference. This process, also called family group decision-making (American Humane, 2008), is increasingly being used in the child welfare and juvenile justice systems in the United States and around the world to enhance the control and responsibility exercised by family members over decisions affecting their children. The idea of convening a meeting of a whole extended family to create a plan for children's safety and well-being originated in New Zealand in the 1980s. A recognition of problems associated with large numbers of indigenous Maori children being removed from their homes due to abuse and neglect, and placed outside of their communities, led to passage of a law called the Children, Young People, and Their Families Act of 1989 (Hudson, Morris, Maxwell, and Galaway, 1996). The law required that if a child was at risk of placement outside the home, the whole family had the right and the responsibility to gather, hear the concerns, and without any professionals present, to create a plan.

This plan is negotiated with the child welfare authorities, and when agreements are reached, an ongoing partnership between the caseworkers and family may include needed resources to make the plan work. For example, if the family decides that the child will live with an aunt while the parent is in a drug rehabilitation program, the aunt may receive funds to buy an extra bed and cover increased grocery costs.

Family group conferences have also been legally mandated in New Zealand since 1989 in situations related to youth offences. In such instances the victims of a crime or offense and their families participate in the conference, along with the offenders and their families, and are involved in agreements about consequences and restitution. This process has taken many forms as it spread around the world. Known primarily by the term restorative justice or restorative practice, it involves families and community members in coming together when a crime or an offense has occurred, to share and discuss how the offense has affected them and what they see as needed by way of restitution, in order for healing to proceed. These practices are used in settings as varied as the criminal justice system, schools, whole communities, indigenous tribes, and countries, that is, truth and reconciliation commissions. Restorative justice aims at healing for the victim, the community and the offender. The U.S. Department of Justice (2007) describes restorative justice as "a compilation of principles and practices that come together to form an approach that involves all parties—the offender, victim, and community—to achieve justice (para 1).

If you work with a parent or a youth that is involved in a family group conference or restorative circle, you may be asked to attend the first part of the meeting, when the family members hear the perspectives of workers involved with the family. You would share your concerns as well as what you see as the strengths of the individual or family. You would also identify resources your agency may be able to offer the family and any *bottom lines* that their plan needs to address. For example, if you are a school social worker you might mention aspects of a child's individualized education plan (IEP) that should be kept in mind, and any resources associated with that plan.

Then, you and all the other professionals will leave the family alone while the family takes whatever time they need to decide what to do. If you are the child welfare or juvenile justice worker responsible for the case, you be available to go back in the room and answer any questions that arise. When the family has settled on a plan, they will share it with you. You will then negotiate any details you see as needed to achieve what you, and the Family Court judge who might have to approve the plan, see as needed to protect the children, or administer justice in the case of an offense.

This type of interaction with families is radically different than what occurs when workers see families as *clients* and they see workers as *the people in charge*. All too often that model leads to workers' frustration with people who do not follow the plans they make for them. As Wachtel and McCold (2004) state, "human beings are happier, more cooperative and productive, and more likely to make positive changes in their behavior when those in positions of authority do things with them, rather than to them or for them" (p. 1).

FAMILY-CENTERED PROGRAMS

Social workers also focus on the whole family when working in a family-centered intervention program. See Figure 7.1 for examples of such programs. Such programs are typically strengths based in their approach and aligned with the principles of family support (Weissbord, 1994), a movement that began in the late 1960s. This approach is similar to core social work commitments, believing that family members/individuals can work with each other and those in helping roles to meet their own needs and that families, neighborhoods, and communities can come together to create conditions of greater social and economic justice. Family support recognizes and values informal kinds of helping that friends, neighbors, grandparents, civic and fraternal organizations, faith communities, and youth groups have often provided. The family resource centers and/or family support programs of the late 1960s and early 1970s sought to mobilize these formal and informal helping systems. For example, grassroots parent support groups such as drop-in day care centers began to work with and receive support from the Community Action neighborhood programs of the War on Poverty. The federal Head Start program, founded at this time, took an early lead among human service programs in acknowledging cultural democracy as it shared power with consumers of services, families, and neighborhood and community residents through Parent Councils.

Over the last 30 years, family-centered programs have taken root across service systems, as awareness grows that partnerships with families produce positive outcomes.

Social workers who do not work as part of a family-centered program may still choose to focus on a whole family as the best way to help an individual client. At such times, having knowledge of family systems theory is extremely valuable. Since the family is the primary social unit for most people, assessment of an individual's person-in-environment system often results in seeing the family as the focus for the helping process.

Program area:	Examples:
Early childhood; child and family development	- Family-Centered Services - Early Head Start and Head Start - Home Instruction Program for Preschool Youngsters (HIPPY) - Healthy Families America - Parents as Teachers (PAT)
Child welfare	- Family Preservation and Support Program - Intensive home based services, e.g. Home builders[1] - Kinship care - Family group conferences: Family group decision-making
Community building; Economic development	- Community Action Programs - Neighborhood Transformation/ Family Development - Bartering-based currency, e.g. Ithaca Hours
Developmental disabilities	- Individualized service plans - Person-centered planning
Education	- School-community collaboration - Parent involvement
Family literacy	- Even Start - Parents as Teachers (PAT)
Health care	- Patient and family-centered health care
Mental health	- System of Care Communities[2] - Family involvement
Public health	- Community Health Worker Program - Healthy Start - Home visiting for pregnant and new moms, including teens
Youth development	- Assets-based youth development (e.g. Search Institute) - Family Support and Youth Development Services

FIGURE 7.1 | EXAMPLES OF STRENGTHS-BASED FAMILY-CENTERED PROGRAMS

[1]See http://www.institutefamily.org/
[2]see http://mentalhealth.samhsa.gov/publications/allpubs/Ca-0013/default.asp

FAMILY SYSTEMS APPROACH[3]

Imagine that you are counseling Sharon, a 13-year-old female who has been referred to you by her school due to frequent truancy. In sessions she seems to be
pleasant and has clear strengths as an athlete, but she is distant and vague when
asked about her goals and needs related to school success. Thinking that the challenges she faces as an individual may more better addressed by taking a family systems approach, you discuss this with her, and then invite her mother and
grandmother, with whom she lives, and her two older sisters, one for whom she
frequently baby-sits, to come to the next session.

Social work has a long tradition of viewing individual functioning within the
context of families. Janzen and Harris (1997) point out that even though "family
treatment as a mode of practice was formally introduced in the 1950s, some of the
underlying ideas and observations that support this process appeared in the social
work literature as early as the first quarter of the century" (p. 4). An individual's
problems and concerns usually include difficulties with transactions with others.

At its most simple level, family systems theory is about seeing members of a
family as an interactive and interdependent system. This means that changes in
one part of the system affect other parts of the system. Systems theory was first introduced in the 1940s as applied to biological systems. The human body, for example, consists of interrelated parts that are connected to a whole, and that interact
with the environment. Today systems theory is used as a conceptual framework
across many disciplines to identify, analyze, and optimize many types of systems.

A major goal in counseling with families is helping the families view their challenges as being about what is occurring within the family system, rather than as
problems with individual members of the family. Often a family seeks professional
assistance to help resolve problems created by one person that makes life in the
family difficult. The *identified patient* (Shulman, 1999) is seen as the problem, and
the family comes in wanting to have the identified patient *fixed*. The worker can
encourage the family to adopt a different way of viewing the situation (Watzlawick, Weakland, and Fisch, 1974). For example, a *difficult child* may be the identified patient, and the family seeks help in controlling the child. The worker will
encourage the family to redefine the situation as a family system problem, not one
caused simply by the child's difficult behavior. The task is to delabel the identified
patient and help family members assume ownership for the roles they play in the
problem (Hepworth, Rooney, and Larsen, 2002). Sharon's school truancy, for example, may be related to her being relied on for babysitting her nephews. Sitting
together, the family can address this as a systems issue, working together to
develop options for care of the children so Sharon can be in school.

Hepworth, Rooney, and Larsen (1997) outline two strategies for delabeling the
identified patient. One strategy is to "explore relationships between family members in lieu of focusing on the behavior of individual members" (p. 485). For example, with a two-parent family, you might first focus on the interactions between

---

[3] This section draws on and is adapted from Chapter 5: Families, Small Groups, Organizations and
Communities by John Poulin, in the second edition of this text.

the mother and the difficult child, then the father and the child, then the mother and the father, and finally the interactions among all three together. Your goal is to help family members see that the difficulties with the child do not take place in isolation and that the problems are in the functioning of the family system. This takes the blame off the identified patient and allows the problem to be viewed as belonging to the family.

The second strategy is to "focus initially on the role of blamers (or plaintiffs) in the difficulties about which they complain" (Hepworth, Rooney, and Larsen, 1997, p. 485). Instead of focusing on the child who is seen as difficult, focus on the mother's and/or father's role in the problem behaviors exhibited by the child. Doing so shifts the family away from blaming to focusing on interactions between the parents and the child. It also helps family members take responsibility for changing their own behavior to improve family functioning. This is an key concept you can help families learn. As Hepworth, Rooney, and Larsen (1997) point out, "it is critical to emphasize that members cannot change each other and that each individual can alleviate problems only by concentrating on changing his or her own behavior" (p. 486).

Helping families change the way they view problems is not easy. They may resist taking responsibility for a difficult and painful situation, being more comfortable seeing the problem as belonging to the identified patient and the solution being about *fixing* that person. The idea that one can only change oneself, not other people, may be very new, and by adopting it, you are asking them to give up long-held beliefs.

Be sensitive about how difficult it is for family members to change their view of the problem. Avoid blaming as you explore the interactions among family members. Instead, *reframe* problematic interactions. For example, if a mother is controlling and the child rebels, you might reframe the mother's controlling behavior as a positive expression of concern for the child's well-being that is well intended but is not achieving the desired result. Empathize with the mother about how difficult the problem situation has been for her and the whole family. She is more likely to be receptive to this message than if she sees you as blaming her for being too controlling.

Despite your efforts, some family members may persist in blaming the identified patient. Focus your work on helping the family view itself as a system in which all members influence one another and all interactions are reciprocal. You can do this by asking family members to identify ways they might be contributing to the problem situation. What could they do to improve? How do their reactions affect the situation? What would they like to change to help cope with the problem situation? Using a strengths-based approach, ask them to think of a time when things were going well related to the problem situation, and to identify what was happening. What was each of them doing that contributed to a positive outcome? How might they use these responses more often? This line of questioning is similar to that used in appreciative inquiry (Cooperrider and Whitney, 2005), a practice that began in the field of organizational development and is now being used in human development.

In the following section you will learn about approaches to helping families assess their needs and strengths, and develop goals. One approach, called Family Subsystems Assessment, is a framework that helps families take a close look at their family system and how it helps or hinders their ability to function well together.

As seen in this first part of the chapter, social workers may work with a family for a wide variety of reasons. Whatever the reason that you are working with a family as a unit, you will want to know about and use assessment as a tool that can help the family address their concerns and reach their goals. Using strength-based, collaborative values in the way you approach assessment is essential to building and maintaining an effective partnership with the family.

DOING ASSESSMENT WITH FAMILIES

Creating an empowering assessment process with families is similar to doing strengths-based assessment with individuals. The main difference, and the biggest challenge, is to focus your attention and efforts on the family as a whole as well as on each individual member. Assessment must be a collaborative process in which concerns are heard, strengths are recognized, and understanding, empathy, and hope are communicated. Together you will explore the family members' perceptions of their situation and work to create goals. Think of doing assessment *with* a family, rather than *of* a family. In this way the assessment process is also educative, in that the family comes to understand itself better as a functioning unit.

Assessment emphasizes the identification of family strengths as well as strengths of each individual family member. "Social workers should help families build on their strengths, gain access to resources, learn how to negotiate the many systems their members contact (school, neighborhood, social services), and overcome problems that affect healthy family development" (Hodges, Burwell, and Ortega, 1998, p. 146). Families have power from within to bring about positive change. The strengths perspective, however, may have to come from you. Although all families have strengths, family members may not always recognize or be aware of them. By adopting the attitude that strengths exist and that they can be used to help the family resolve the problem situation, you can help the family recognize their individual and collective strengths. Focus on strengths. Look for the ways the family and its members have coped with problem situations and concerns. Help them recognize past successes as well as resources and abilities they can draw on in the helping process.

A collaborative approach to family assessment empowers families by allowing their expertise in functioning and their concerns to emerge. Strive to empower the family as well as each individual member. Begin by asking the family and its members about their perceptions of their needs and their goals. Do not force your analysis and assessment of their problems, interpersonal relationships, or individual dysfunction on them, even if you believe that numerous problems exist. Engage in a collaborative exchange, sharing your insights and perceptions and exploring those of family members. "To engage in a truly collaborative relationship, each party must stay open to discussing and resolving differences in an honest and respectful manner" (Hodges, Burwell, and Ortega, 1998, p. 150). Become a partner with the family by sharing responsibility and decision-making.

Assessment is the key to the helping process. To be able to effectively help families, you need to develop a shared understanding of their concerns, their strengths, potential resources, and the challenges they face. The assessment process provides an opportunity for families to tell their stories. It is more about listening than asking questions. Strengths-based assessments focus on clients' perceptions of their situation and their goals, rather than on diagnostic labels. Ideally, the process should lead to increased family empowerment and create a sense of hopefulness. Focusing on strengths rather than deficits helps create expectations about the possibilities of change.

FAMILY DEVELOPMENT PLAN

The Family Development Plan (Forest, 2003) is a simple yet effective tool for families to use to assess their needs and strengths, and create action plans to reach their goals. Developed for an interagency, strengths-based training program called the Family Development Credential (Cornell University, 2008a), this tool puts the assessment and planning process in the hands of the family, with the worker playing the role of facilitator and coach.

If able, a family member actually fills out the plan, which is reviewed and updated each time they meet with the worker. The original copy of the plan is kept by the family and is often prominently placed on their refrigerator! The worker keeps a copy. This is more than symbolic. Who holds the pencil controls the plan. While workers may feel naked without a clipboard, forms, and a pen, if workers write, it is all too easy to record what makes the most sense to them. Then, when the family does not do what the worker thought they should do, they may be called *noncompliant*, and labeled as passive aggressive. In reality the action may not have been something the family was comfortable with, fit their cultural norms, or work given their resources. If a family member is the one filling in the form, she is more apt to record what makes sense to them. The form is deceptively simple yet powerful. According to those who use it, the plan becomes a contract between the family and the worker about what steps each will take, thus providing accountability (Crane, 2000).

The elements of the Family Development Plan are:

- Major goal (in family member's words)
- Steps leading to this goal (note date each will take place)
- Steps family will take and when
- Steps worker will take and when
- Family strengths and resources (in family member's words)
- Family strengths and resources (in worker's words)
- Concerns about the plan (in family member's words)
- Concerns about the plan (in worker's words)
- Services available (include details such as names, addresses, phone numbers, hours)
- Notes (place to write other information the family needs to know)
- Family member's signature and date
- Worker's signature and date
- Next meeting date, time, place
- Worker's name and phone number to call if a change of date is needed

Helping a family member or family group set a goal that will be the focus of your work together is a very important step. Assure them that the goal can change, but that it will help to identify at least an initial goal. It should be big enough to make a difference in their lives, but practical enough that success in reaching that

HOW TO USE THE FAMILY DEVELOPMENT PLAN: Family worker, please ask the family if they want to fill out the form or want you to write. If you write, be sure to use their words. If the family member wants you to do the writing, read out loud what you have written. Ask the family member for any corrections, and make the corrections they request on all the sections except "in the worker's words." Give a copy to the family member, and keep a copy in your file. Each of you should review the form before your next meeting, to make sure you've each taken the steps you agreed on. Begin your next meeting by reviewing the last Plan.

• **Family member's name**
_____

(Note what s/he likes to be called: Mr., Mrs., Miss, Ms., etc.)

• **Address**
_____

• **Phone(s)** (note if home, work, or friends' phone)
_____

• **Other family members involved in family development process** (Let family define who they consider family members.) Note ages and male or female.

_____
_____
_____
_____

• **Today's date**_____ • **Worker's name -** _____

• **Major goal** (in family member's words)

_____
_____
_____
_____

• **Help family brainstorm possible steps leading to their goals (**Use separate sheet)**.**

Help family choose steps to take. (Note date each will take place.)

Steps family will take & when   Progress/ Obstacle

_____

_____

Steps family will take & when   Progress/ Obstacle

FIGURE 7.2 | FAMILY DEVELOPMENT PLAN

_____

_____

_____

(At your next meeting, note progress or obstacles to each step.)

- **Family strengths and resources** (in family member's words)

- **Family strengths and resources** (in worker's words)

- **Concerns** (in family member's words)

- **Concerns** (in worker's words)

- **Services available** (include details such as names, addresses, phone numbers, hours, etc.)

- Notes

- **Family member's signature & date**

_____

- **Worker's signature & date**

_____

- **Next meeting date, time, place**

_____

IF YOU CAN'T KEEP THIS APPOINTMENT, PLEASE CALL _____

AT _____ BY. _____ THANK YOU FOR YOUR COURTESY.

Source: Forest, C. (2003), *Empowerment Skills for Family Workers*. © 2003 by Claire Forest.
Used by permission. Order info: www.human.cornell.edu/HD/FDC.

FIGURE 7.2 | CONTINUED

goal is possible during the time you are working together. If no goal is immediately clear, try using a visioning exercise such as one used in brief solutions-focused therapy called The Miracle Question (Berg, 1994; De Jong and Berg, 2002). Imagine that you wake up tomorrow and a miracle had occurred. How would you know? What would be different? Is this is too abstract, try a more concrete question such as: Let's imagine that in a month, or a year, things are going much better. Imagine yourself feeling really good about your life. What has happened? What's different or better? Then work together to list some realistic goals that can lead to this imagined better life. Let the family member choose which one to start with for your work using the Family Development Plan.

Once you have a specific goal that is clear and measurable so it will be clear when it is reached, use a brainstorming process to create a list of possible steps to reach that goal. This works well with a group but can be used with just an individual. Teach the rules of brainstorming: (1) let the ideas come without judging them, (2) write down as many ideas as possible, (3) include wild and crazy ideas, (4) build on ideas of others or previously suggested ideas, (5) laughter helps. If possible, have the family *hold the pencil* and create the list; you can facilitate and cheer them on. Once you have a brainstormed list, encourage them to go back and circle the ones that might be most useful, keeping the goal in mind. Then prioritize, creating a shorter list of action steps, listed sequentially. Make a copy of this list for yourself and give the original to the family.

Ask a family member to be the one who writes on the Family Development Plan, if literacy and functionality make this possible. Write the large goal, and the steps that the family and you will take before the next time you meet. Review these at your next session, noting what went well and what did not, so you all can reassess before deciding on the next steps. At first you may do more of the work if it means using contacts and resources you can readily mobilize. As the family gains confidence and skill, which is the most important outcome of this process, more of the steps on the plan will be theirs rather than yours.

The next section of the plan asks for family strengths and resources (in family member's words) and family strengths and resources (in worker's words). Facilitate their thinking about and recording what they see as strengths and resources that can help them reach their goal. Then, take the plan and record what you see as their strengths and resources, again as associated with their capacity to reach their goal. For example, even though their level of belief in change may be small, you may see a spark of hope, and a resiliency based on stories they have told you about past successes. If you were working with Norman's family, who we met at the beginning of this chapter, you might write in the section *family strengths and resources (in worker's words)*, "Norman clearly loves and believes in his children's abilities. Family members demonstrate flexibility needed to respond to changing life circumstances."

Sometimes people do not feel comfortable creating a plan because they are concerned that things may not go as planned, and they will feel like a failure. The next section of the Family Development Plan exists for this reason. It helps to note such concerns as possibilities, which normalizes the idea that it is OK. As the saying goes, "the best laid plans of mice and men often go awry" (Steinbeck, 1937). The family can write their concerns about the plan on the lines labeled Concerns (in family member's words). Write any concerns you may have about the plan under Concerns (in worker's words). For example, if the goal that Norman might set is to engage his siblings to a greater extent in the care of their parents, he might write that "my brother might say he will help, but then not show up." You might write, "Response of siblings is unpredictable." This may help Norman feel that it is OK to try, even if it is unknown whether the first steps toward change will make a difference.

The final sections of the plan provide a place to record important information that the family will want to write down about services, resources, or even information such as a website with useful information about their situation. Then, the family member(s) sign the plan, as do you. This commitment is important as a motivational dynamic. The date, time, and place of your next session is also recorded along with contact information for the family to use if they need to reschedule. Then, the family keeps the original and you make a copy. Some agencies using this plan have it printed on paper, such as 3M paper, that automatically makes a second copy. At your next session you review this plan with the family, assessing and noting progress on the steps. Then have them start a new plan, keeping the goal or changing it to adapt to new circumstances or directions. Look again at the brainstormed steps, or brainstorm new steps. And proceed with the plan as before.

The Family Development Plan has been shown to be a helpful strengths-based tool for the family to use as a focus for organizing their response to a life challenge. In the process of working on their goals, additional strengths and needs may emerge related to how they function together as a family and how they relate to their social environment. At such a time, consider introducing family systems concepts to help them understand what is going on. Becoming aware of patterns can help families recognize why they are stuck, why things are not getting better. They can then choose to set new goals for strengthening their family interactions.

FAMILY SYSTEMS ASSESSMENT

If a family is struggling as they work to reach their goals, it may be worthwhile to look with them at what is going on in the family system. A comprehensive assessment takes into consideration the effect of the families' internal functioning and their relationship with their environment. The strengths and challenges associated with all relevant systems are reviewed. While still keeping the focus on the present and their desired future state, you can help the family look at various aspects of family norms, culture, and behavior, based on an analysis of subsystems.

FAMILY SUBSYSTEMS ASSESSMENT

Assessment of a family system can include review of six major family subsystems: (a) structure, (b) life-cycle stage, (c) ethnicity and culture, (d) communication patterns, (e) emotional climate, and (f) boundaries. These subsystems, as shown in Figure 7.3, are highly interrelated, interdependent entities. Taken as a whole, they provide a comprehensive idea of the internal structure and functioning of a family system, an overall picture of how the family relates and functions as a unit. Figure 7.3 provides a summary of the six subsystems. We will next discuss how to translate these topics in ways that families can use to assess how their family functions, and how they can be more effective as a family.

There is no one right way to walk through this type of assessment with a family because the subsystems are so interrelated. You might briefly explain each area and then encourage the family to choose which topic they want to talk about first. Then, facilitate the discussion as an exercise in self-understanding. Any one of these areas, or looking at them in combination, may turn out to have major explanatory

Structure	Ethnicity and Culture	Life Cycle Stage
Number & ages of family members	Values and beliefs	Developmental Stage
Informal rules for interaction	Rules	Transitions
Relationship subsystems	Myths	

Emotional Climate	Communication Patterns	Boundaries
Affective tone	Verbal	Open/Closed
Involvement	Non-verbal	Ridged/Diffuse
	Contextual	Enmeshed/Detached

FIGURE 7.3 | FAMILY CLIENT SYSTEM: ASSESSMENT SUBSYSTEMS

value for the family, that "Aha" moment when they might say, "Oh, that's what's going on with us." For example, let's imagine that an elderly grandparent has recently moved into a daughter's home. Looking at how this life cycle transition is affecting their family structure and the way they communicate may help them understand why there is less closeness and more conflict, and why some family members may be more detached.

We will now take a close look at each of the subsystems, and how aspects of each may serve as a strength and/or a barrier to the family's ability to reach their goals.

STRUCTURE

Family structure includes the number and ages of family members and the way family members organize themselves into interactional patterns (Minuchin and Fishman, 1982). As Minuchin (1974) explains, "Repeated transactions establish patterns of how, when, and to whom to relate, and these patterns underpin the system" (p. 51).

A simple way to have a family look at its structure is to use sticky pads and a plain piece of paper. Ask them to put the name and age of each person in the family on a sticky note and then place the notes on the paper. Check to see if there is agreement on who is included, or excluded. Assure them that this is their family and the purpose of the activity is just to identify their family structure. Let them move the notes around on the paper to represent interaction patterns, letting individuals move the notes until there is consensus in the group. Lead a discussion, asking for various family members' perspectives on what they see and what it means.

Authority.   Closely associated with the interaction patterns are the authority systems that govern them (Janzen and Harris, 1997). Families develop informal rules for family behavior and interactions that are often not named or spoken about directly. Issues of authority and power as well as other areas of family life are defined by those informal rules. Assessment of family systems requires an exploration and understanding of the unique rules, and actual or perceived consequences, that govern family interactions.

Relationship Subsystems.   Another structural aspect of families is the relationship subsystems into which they are organized (Aponte and Van Duesen, 1981). Most families have couple, parental, sibling, and parent–child subsystems (Janzen and Harris, 1997). Understanding how the various subsystems interact and the roles they play is critical to understanding the overall functioning of the family and the effect of family structure on their strengths and challenges. Figure 7.4 displays these four primary subsystems and some of the important roles they fulfill (Jordan and Franklin, 1995).

ETHNICITY AND CULTURE

Families possess sets of beliefs that are drawn from their ethnic and cultural heritage. A family's cultural beliefs affect all aspects of family functioning and need to be taken into consideration when assessing structure, life-cycle stages, emotional climate, communication patterns, and boundaries.

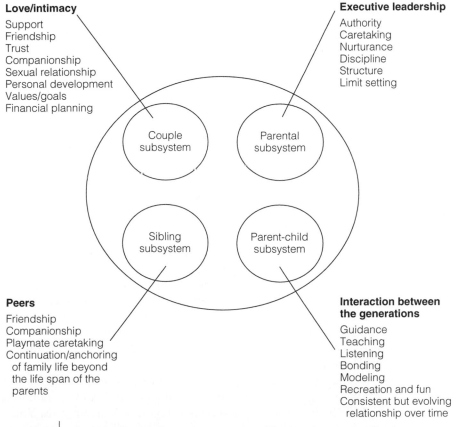

FIGURE 7.4 | FAMILY SUBSYSTEMS AND NORMATIVE ROLES

Source: From *Clinical assessment for social workers: Quantitative and qualitative methods* by C. Jordan, and C. Franklin. Copyright © 1995, Lyceum Books. Reprinted with permission.

Culture-Based Rules.   Assessment of the family's rules of behavior also needs to be culturally based. "Families have rules about who can do what to whom and what may or may not be discussed by whom in what context" (Gambrill, 1997, p. 574). Some rules are explicit and clearly stated (children don't talk back to parents), and others are implicit and not openly verbalized (be careful not to hurt mother's feelings). Implicit rules must be inferred from the interactions of family members; they are unwritten and unspoken and may be beyond family members' conscious level of awareness. Explicit and implicit family rules govern family members' behavior toward one another. The rules that emerge in families are influenced by the family's values and beliefs. "Although rules govern the processes of families from any cultural origin, they differ drastically from one culture to another" (Hepworth, Rooney, and Larsen, 1997, p. 279).

In considering family rules, you need to understand and respect the values and beliefs of the family. Understanding the cultural basis of the norms governing family members' behavior provides the context for assessing the effect of family rules on the identified target problem. Family rules can potentially have positive or negative effects on family functioning. The cultural context of a rule determines whether it enhances functioning or contributes to dysfunction. Assessment of ethnicity and culture takes into consideration values and beliefs and how they affect the functioning of the family system.

LIFE-CYCLE STAGE

Families pass through developmental life-cycle stages much the same way as individuals. Carter and McGoldrick (1989) developed a conceptual life-cycle framework with the developmental stages of the traditional two-parent family with children (see Figure 7.5). Each stage has tasks that need to be accomplished for the family to make a successful transition to the next developmental stage (Jordan and Franklin, 1995). Although Carter and McGoldrick's family life-cycle stages have been widely accepted, they are based on a middle-class, American, nuclear family model. As such it "has important weaknesses, especially when the family is not a *traditional* family, has no children, or is in some other way different from the view of the family as composed of a married couple and their children" (Garvin and Seabury, 1997, p. 218). Thus, it is important to be sensitive to diversity of family form and culture as you think about the life-cycle stages of particular families.

Family life-cycle stages all involve additions or losses to family membership (Janzen and Harris, 1997). They require adapting to change, and they necessitate changes in family roles and rules. The transitions between stages often cause family difficulties and are the points at which families are most likely to be in need of help (Janzen and Harris, 1997; Jordan and Franklin, 1995). For this reason, families can benefit from your asking them to look at important life-cycle transitions and the family's adjustment to them.

The first step is to identify the family's life-cycle stage and related developmental tasks. Carter and McGoldrick's model is based on a traditional two-parent family, so the life-cycle stages shown in Figure 7.5 may not fit. You can start by asking the family to identify any transitions the family may be experiencing. Are there additions or losses to family membership? Be sure to ask about whether there are

Leaving home: single young adults
Differentiating self in relation to family of origin
Developing intimate peer relationships
Establishing self through work and financial independence

The joining of families through marriage: the new couple
Forming marital system
Realigning relationships with extended families and friends to include spouse

Families with young children
Adjusting marital system to make space for child(ren)
Joining in child-rearing, financial, and household tasks
Realigning relationships with extended family to include parenting and grandparenting
roles

Families with adolescents
Shifting parent–child relationships to permit adolescent to move in and out of system
Refocusing on mid-life marital and career issues
Beginning shift toward joint caring for older generation

Launching children and moving on
Renegotiating marital system as a dyad
Developing adult-to-adult relationships between grown children and their parents
Realigning relationships to include in-laws and grandchildren
Dealing with disabilities and death of great-grandparents

Families in later life
Maintaining own and couple functioning and interests in face of psychological decline
Supporting a more central role of middle generation
Making room in the system for the wisdom and experience of the elderly, supporting the older
generation without overfunctioning for them
Dealing with loss of spouse, siblings, and peers, and preparation for own death; life review and
integration

FIGURE 7.5 | FAMILY LIFE CYCLE STAGES AND ASSOCIATED DEVELOPMENTAL TASKS

Source: From B. Carter and M. McGoldrick (Eds.) The changing family life cycle: A framework for family therapy (2nd ed.). Published by Allyn and Bacon, Boston, MA. Copyright © 1989 by Pearson Education, Inc. Reprinted by permission of Pearson Education, Inc.

family members who come and go, depending on factors such as custody agreements, economic challenges, or out-of-town employment.

The second step is to assess family members' adaptation to the transition from one stage to another. Are there specific tasks that are more problematic than others? How are the various family members adjusting to changing roles and responsibilities? Are family members mourning the loss of people or tasks associated with the prior life-cycle stage?

EMOTIONAL CLIMATE

Like individuals, families have emotional patterns. "When people are in close interaction (as in families or groups), the emotions of some individuals tend to be *contagious* and others begin to express similar feelings" (Garvin and Seabury, 1997, p. 218). Although the expression of individual affect within the family may vary, family patterns of emotions develop (Lewis, Beavers, Gossett, and Phillips, 1976).

A family's emotional climate can be seen as having an *affect dimension* and an *involvement dimension*, as depicted in Figure 7.6, Family Emotional Climate Matrix.

The affect dimension is the emotional tone of the family system. Some family environments are *hostile, tense, and conflicted*, shown on the left in the matrix above, while others are more relaxed and peaceful, characterized by *love, warmth, and harmony*, on the right side of the matrix.

The second dimension of the family emotional climate is the extent to which family members are involved with one another. This dimension ranges in this matrix from *disengagement*, shown in the top half of the matrix, to *enmeshment*, shown in the bottom half of the matrix (Minuchin, 1974). In families that are disengaged, members have little emotional involvement with each other. In enmeshed families, on the other hand, members may be overly involved with one another. There is "excessive closeness in which family members think and feel alike; there is little opportunity for independent functioning and what happens to one family member immediately affects others" (Gambrill, 1997, p. 575).

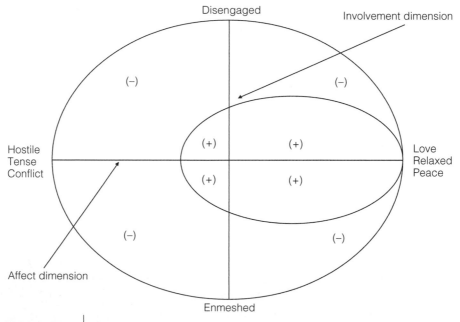

FIGURE 7.6 | FAMILY EMOTIONAL CLIMATE MATRIX

The disengagement–enmeshment dimension has also been referred to as family cohesion (Olson, Sprenkle, and Russel, 1979). Families that fall at the extremes of this continuum are at risk of dysfunction. Those that fall between the extremes are considered to have a more balanced emotional climate and less risk of family dysfunction (Thomas and Olson, 1993). Members in more balanced families are supportive, help one another, and are committed to each other, but not to the extent that the individuality of the members is lost or subsumed by the family system.

It is important to note that these ideas are based, in part, on Western ways of thinking and Western patterns of relatedness. Rothbaum, Rosen, Tatsuo, and Nobuko (2002) report that in Japan, parents are not expected to have romantic feelings for each other or open communication to resolve conflicts, and infants and children have very close ties with their mothers, all without the adverse effects on family functioning associated with these patterns in Western cultures. Given the very diverse populations with which you will be working, this represents a note of caution about the importance of cultural awareness. It appears that expectations have a great deal to do with outcomes. In other words, if a child in a close mother–son relationship lives primarily in a cultural context where this is considered normal and desirable, it will have a different effect than if he is in a family or neighborhood where he might be labeled and picked on for being a *sissy* or *mommy's boy*. Be cautious about your assumptions. Carefully observe the family's reactions as you discuss with them the various dimensions. This can help you understand whether their family patterns are in accord with cultural expectations. If there are generational differences, as can occur with immigrant families, you can help the family address conflicts related to greater acculturation of younger family members.

The interaction between the affect and involvement dimensions of family emotional climate is shown in Figure 7.6. Families with healthy emotional climates (+) are those in which the family mode tone is rated more toward the positive side of the affect dimension (love, relaxed, peace) and in the middle of the involvement dimension. Families with dysfunctional emotional climates (−) are those rated on the negative side of the affect dimension (hostile, tense, conflict) and at the top or bottom of the involvement dimension (disengaged, enmeshed).

The inner circle of Figure 7.6 represents a healthy or acceptable range of the affective and involvement dimensions within families. It is assumed that within normal families there will be some conflict, tension, and hostility and that a normal family will fall approximately in the middle of the disengagement–enmeshment continuum. It is also assumed that there cannot be too much love within a family as long as the family is centered on the involvement dimension. Problems may occur for families that are characterized by the extremes of the two dimensions.

COMMUNICATION PATTERNS

Helping a family improve its ability to communicate well and to deal with problems in communication can enhance their relationship and problem-solving ability (Satir, 1983). You can help families assess the kind of communication that occurs between family members. Is it open, direct, and clear? Is the tone and the content of the message congruent (Jordan and Franklin, 1995)? Or it a mixed message, where the words and the body language are saying two different things?

Communication problems are common when family members are having difficulty getting along and in families that show other signs of dysfunction (Satir, 1983). Janzen and Harris (1997) point out that communication modes and problems are intertwined with family structure and role divisions: "Family rules and structure are evident in the freedom or lack of it in expressing doubt or difference, and in who can say what to whom and when. Communication conveys how much each family member is valued and who has power in the system" (p. 15).

Cultural beliefs and norms can influence family communication style and the degree of openness. Many cultures discourage the open expression of feelings (Ho, 1987). In assessing family communication patterns, be aware of possible cultural differences and respect the communication styles practiced within the family's cultural system. If open, direct, and honest communication is not considered desirable by a family given their cultural beliefs, then that can be a topic for discussion. Help them think about how to best approach a family challenge given their beliefs.

The three basic types of communication are: verbal, nonverbal, and contextual (Satir, 1983). Verbal communication refers to the words and the content of the message. Nonverbal communication refers to the body language that accompanies the verbal message, including gestures, facial expressions, posture, and eye contact. Contextual communication refers to context or situation in which the message is delivered, the timing of the message, and the circumstances in which the message is delivered. Some parents, for example, find it easiest to have relaxed conversations with their teenager in the car, rather than trying to interest him in talking while he is watching television or playing a video game. Nonverbal and contextual levels of communication can reinforce or contradict the verbal message.

Effective communication requires congruency among the three levels of communication, and in dysfunctional families congruency is often lacking. Thus, an important aspect in assessing family communication patterns is to determine "the extent to which there is congruence between the verbal, nonverbal, and contextual levels of messages on the part of individuals in a family system" (Hepworth, Rooney, and Larsen, 1997, p. 311). Is the verbal message supported by nonverbal messages and the situation in which the messages are delivered?

In addition to problems related to the congruence of messages, problems may be related to the skills of the person sending the message, such as expressing and owning feelings, and/or to receiver skills, such as openness to hearing feelings, listening, and validating (Gambrill, 1997). Hepworth, Rooney, and Larsen (1997) point out that when comparing processes of optimally functioning families with those of troubled families, it becomes evident that the former possess several types of verbal and nonverbal communication skills that are noticeably absent in the latter. Included in these responses are messages that convey understanding, demonstrate respect for the uniqueness of the sender's experience, and invite further expression and exploration (p. 313). The knowledge of communication skills you gain in your professional training can be passed on to the families you serve. This includes active listening skills such as paraphrasing and nonverbal attending skills, as well as making direct statements using I messages.

To help families assess the sending and receiving skills of family members, ask how receptive or open they appear to be to the thoughts and feelings of other family members. Do they listen to each other? Do they acknowledge the sender's message? Do they encourage the sharing of feelings and the expression of thoughts? How open are the individual members to sharing their thoughts and feelings? Do they express how they are feeling or what they think? Do they take responsibility for their own feelings and thoughts? Are the messages expressed as *I* statements or as *You* statements?

In an *I* statement we share or *own* what we are feeling or thinking, such as "I'd like to replace the old car, but I'm feeling anxious about taking on another loan" rather than "What are you thinking? How do you think we can pay for a new car?" Consider the differences in the tone of the communication in the following scenarios.

I statements:

FATHER: "When I come home from work and the kitchen is a mess, I feel discouraged and angry, because now I have to clean up before I can start cooking dinner."

SON: "Sorry Dad. You're right. I got distracted and forgot."

FATHER: "I don't care if you make yourself a snack after school, as long as it's cleaned up by when I get home at 6 o'clock."

SON: "OK, Dad, sure. I'll go get the rest of the groceries from the car."

You statements:

FATHER: "You left the kitchen a mess again! How do you think I am going to cook dinner in a kitchen that looks like this?"

SON: "You're always on my back! I'm out of here."

FATHER: "That's it. Hold it right there. You're grounded."

When working with a family to assess their patterns of communication, you might ask them to think of two situations: one that is pretty easy to talk about and one that is difficult. Then, help them role-play talking with each other about these issues. First, do the easy topic, using *You* statements, and then *I* statements. Then asking how that was for them. Perhaps they will laugh as it seems silly at first. That's fine. Initially people may resist using I statements because it is not familiar. Next have them do the same role-play using the more difficult topic. It may become clearer to them that *how* they talk with each other makes a big difference.

BOUNDARIES

Family system boundaries are the invisible borders or fences that define the subsystems within a family (internal) and its interactions with larger systems (external). Nichols (1984) defined boundaries as invisible barriers between individual family members, family subsystems, and larger systems that regulate interactions. "The function of boundaries is to safeguard the differentiation and autonomy of the family and its subsystems" (Janzen and Harris, 1997, p. 37). Boundaries can be rigid or diffuse (Minuchin, 1974). Rigid boundaries allow little interaction between systems, while diffuse boundaries are loose and blurred, providing little differentiation among the family subsystems, or the family and other systems.

Internal family boundaries relate to the transactions among the various subsystems within the family. Families with rigid internal boundaries have a disengaged emotional climate. Couples who, for example, never discuss with their children the challenges the family faces can be seen as having a rigid boundary between the couple and parent/child subsystems. Families with loose or diffuse boundaries have an enmeshed climate, as discussed earlier in this chapter. An example would be a situation where the wife frequently talks about her complaints about her husband with her daughter and the daughter echoes the criticism, even though it really does not have anything to do with the father–daughter relationship.

At various times in family life, disengagement or enmeshment among subsystems can be functional. "According to Minuchin, every family experiences some enmeshment or disengagement in its subsystems as a family goes through developmental phases" (Hepworth, Rooney, and Larsen, 1997, p. 294). Most families fall somewhere between the extremes. Assessment of internal boundaries requires an understanding of the developmental phase of the family, a description of the various interaction styles among the family's subsystems, and identification of the benefits as well as liabilities of the internal boundary patterns in relation to the identified target problem. It is also important to keep in mind cultural variations in family relationships. Family interactions and boundaries should be assessed from the perspective of the family's ethnic and cultural background.

Families are also part of larger systems, such as neighborhoods and communities. They interact with these other systems on a daily basis. "They differ widely, however, in the degree to which they are open to transactions with other systems and in the flexibility of their outer boundaries" (Hepworth, Rooney, and Larsen, 1997, p. 291). The extent to which people who are not family members are allowed to interact with the family varies. Kantor and Lehr (1975) identified three family boundary types: open, closed, and random.

- *Open family systems* are those in which the family has a great deal of interaction with people outside the family. Members of open families have friends over frequently, are active in the community, and participate in outside activities.
- *Closed family systems*, on the other hand, are characterized by a lack of interaction with the external environment. The family restricts and limits involvement with others. Guests are not welcomed, family members are not involved in outside activities, and transactions with others are guarded.
- *Random family systems* have no boundary patterns. Each member of the family develops his or her own type of interaction pattern with the external environment.

Knowledge of the three boundary patterns can help families assess how they interact within their family subsystems and with their external environment. The patterns are prototypes, or typical examples, and any family's boundary pattern will probably include characteristics of all three. There are benefits and liabilities associated with each boundary type. Your task is to assist family members to identify the boundary patterns of the family and assess how these transactions affect the family's ability to reach their goals. This includes an assessment of strengths as well as obstacles associated with the family's internal and external boundaries.

Differential issues of power and authority can be important to look at within the context of this topic. For example, isolation is a key pattern in the battered spouse syndrome. If it seems that the family has frequent interactions with the friends and relatives of one spouse, but the friends and family of the other spouse are uniformly scorned and dismissed from family life, this could be important to explore.

SUMMARY: ENGAGING IN A HELPING PARTNERSHIP WITH FAMILIES

The focus of strengths-based generalist practice with families is one of empowerment—the goal is that families you work with will be more able to take positive actions on their own behalf and reach their goals than they were before they met you. As Rapp (2007) states, helping clients take charge of their plans is a core principle of strengths-based practice. Keeping families in mind also means that even when working with individuals, one is aware that each person is a part of friendship and family systems that affect their hopes and dreams, their options and choices, and their ability to reach their goals. By working in partnership with individuals and whatever members of their family/friendship circles they chose to involve, you can help them strengthen their belief in their own abilities and possibilities.

Let us look again at the Norman Gonzalez family that we met at the beginning of this chapter. As you read this story about their work with the social work intern Briana, think about and

note what they did and learned in the process. Look for these goals for the outcomes of strengths-based family-focused practice for the families. Families will:

1. Engage in a helping partnership with you and other helpers, based on mutually trusting and respectful relationships
2. Assess their needs as well as their strengths and resources
3. Identify goals to address their needs, building on their strengths
4. Develop their own plans for reaching those goals
5. Identify and use informal and formal helping systems, including having a family meeting or conference with other agencies to develop a coordinated action plan
6. Regularly assess progress and revise the plan as needed
7. Feel more empowered and capable of handling future life challenges

CASE EXAMPLE

The following case example illustrates the use of the Family Development Plan with a family. It also demonstrates how the process of completing the plan empowered the family and helped build the relationship between the social worker and the family.

CASE 7.1 | NORMAN'S STORY

Norman Gonzalez left his meeting with Briana, the caseworker at the child development center where his daughter Isabel goes feeling encouraged. He had worried that with so much going on in his life, working with her on a plan to meet Isabel's needs would create one more huge stress. While making sure that Isabel had the right start in life was important to him, he was also burdened with worries about his wife Anna's recovery, his son John's recent arrest, his aging parent's illness, and his own ability to keep his job and earn enough money to support his parents. A little rest and fun now and then might be nice, too!

Little did he know how much help Briana would provide for him and his family beyond her help with Isabel's needs. She seemed to be interested in his whole family, even with its many layers and extensions. She said she respected how he and his ex-wife Maria were cooperating to make sure their son John got to his weekly meeting with his probation officer. She called that a *strength*, and said that instead of just focusing on their *needs*, it helps to identify their strengths and resources. He saw that while some people might look at their family and just see a big mess, Briana really seemed to *respect* what they were doing well. No matter how many of their challenges he told her about, she never seemed judgmental, or like she was better than they are. It made a big difference is what he was willing to say and do, as his trust in her grew.

Briana suggested that when there is a lot going on, it helps to make a plan based on setting goals. She said he could then share this plan with the other people involved with their family, so that everyone would know what they are working on, and how they might be able to help. Norman wasn't sure, but Briana's positive energy about this idea affected his spirits, and he started feeling a little more hopeful. Perhaps making a plan could bring some order to his chaotic life!

She asked Norman if it might be possible for them to meet weekly for a little while, to work on a plan together. Perhaps he could come to the center just 30 minutes early to pick up Isabel, or stay 30 minutes after he dropped her off in the morning. She knew how many demands he had on his time, so she said that if they could do that just three times in the next

few weeks, after that he could decide when and if it would help to meet again. Norman said yes, he could do that. She also asked if he would like to bring anyone along to work on the plan with them. Normally he would have assumed that Anna and he would do it together. But she was doing her alcohol recovery program, and he did not want to put it off until she was through, so he said he thought they could start off doing it with just the two of them. Briana assured him that he could bring other family members, friends, or other support people with him anytime he wanted.

When they met to start the plan, Briana said that she sometimes starts by creating a list of the family's needs, especially if there is a crisis and some things need to be done right away. But, she said, Norman's family was really functioning well given the challenges they faced. How about starting instead with a focus on their future? She asked Norman to sit back, relax, and think about his vision for how he would really like things to be in their family. What? It felt hard for him to think beyond tomorrow! So she suggested that he imagine that it was 5 years from now, and he saw an old friend who asked how everything was going. Since this is just a fantasy, he could imagine what it would be like if everything were going really well. She left the room just to give him some space to think, jot a few notes or even a picture. Images flashed through his mind, of him and Anna, who was no longer drinking, just laughing like kids. Isabel was doing well in school, with an individualized education plan in place, and Anna was working part-time at their church. And John was 19 already! Fortunately his brush with the law had really woken him up, and the family counseling they had received together at Anna's alcohol treatment program had made him a lot more mature about using alcohol and drugs. He was still living at home, working part-time and doing well in his first year at college. He pictured John at 19 and Isabel at 8, playing silly computer games, and arguing about who would do the dishes, like any brother and sister.

When Briana came back into the room, Norman was excited about sharing some of these visions of their future, and said he wanted to ask Anna to do this exercise with him sometime. Briana said that was

CASE 7.1 | *Continued*

a great idea, and maybe he and John could start talk-ing together about the next step in creating a plan, which is to think of every possible idea about what could make those dreams come true. She taught him about brainstorming, which means that every idea gets written down, no ideas are citied or judged too impossible, and you include wild and crazy ideas, even those that seem just a little different from one already listed. She said it helps to keep it light, even silly, just to add to the creative flow. Little Isabel might have some ideas too! If he wanted, Briana said, they could then look at the brainstormed list and circle the items that seemed like important goals, the ones that made them happiest to envision. She said this would be the start of a process to focus on short-term and longer-term goals that would move them toward that ideal future. As he walked out of the center, Norman thought about how fast their 30-minute meeting had gone. He noticed that he felt a little lighter in his shoes than when he went in. Maybe dreams can come true!

At their next meeting he brought the list they had started at home. He said it had become quite the family project. John worked on it with him, as did Anna when they visited her at the recovery program, and even their next-door neighbor chimed in with some ideas. He had seen John and Norman sitting on their front porch laughing and said he wanted in on the fun! As Briana and Norman reviewed the list, they came up with even more ideas. Then, they focused in on creating three lists on three separate pieces of paper. One had the longer-term goals that had begun, amazingly enough to Nor-man, to seem possible. They settled on six goals. The second sheet became a list of actions that would help them reach those goals. And the final sheet listed some steps that he and his family could take in the next 6 months to start moving on those goals.

Then, Briana asked Norman to choose one of those steps as a goal that they would work on together as the focus of his first Family Development Plan. He chose a step on their short-term list related to his parents. He had to admit that his stress about trying to respond to their every need caused problems with his taking care of Isabel and had frankly been affecting his relation-ship with his wife Anna. She had sometimes angrily told him that she could never count on when he would be home because if one of his parents called his cell

phone, he was gone. Briana affirmed this choice and helped him turn it into a goal. On the form she gave him called the Family Development Plan, what he wrote in the line for a goal was to develop a plan with his siblings for how to share the care of their par-ents. She said they could finish the rest of the plan when they met next. When Norman left the center that day, he felt a little more sober, because he did not look forward to what he might have to do to make this change, but he knew deep inside that it was needed. He had avoided dealing with his feelings about his siblings not helping out and knew that he liked being the family hero, the big brother who makes everything all right. That needed to change if he was going to be responsible to Anna, John, and Isabel.

At their fourth meeting, Briana asked Norman if he still wanted to work on the identified goal, and he said yes and shared some of his ambivalent feelings. She acknowledged it is hard to change deeply en-grained family patterns, and that he would not be alone. She would be there along the way. She also said in her recent social work class that they had talked about services for seniors to help them stay in their homes, so maybe Norman wouldn't have to rely just on his brothers and sisters. Maybe his par-ents could get other kinds of help as well.

The next step on the plan, she said, was to list the steps needed to start work on his goal. She asked him to think what he might want or need to do first, maybe over the next month. She helped him focus his thoughts, and he wrote down in his own words the three actions that he said he would take. He would: (1) call his sister Joan, with whom he felt the most comfortable, to set up a time to have coffee and talk about their parents' needs; (2) make a list of what he did regularly for their parents, such as buy groceries, and the things that happened sometimes as a crisis, like when his mother fell in the bathroom and his father could not get her up; and (3) think about which items on this list his brothers and sisters might help with.

There was also a place on the plan for actions that Briana could do to help with the plan. She said that while she was not totally familiar with the resources for seniors in their community, being an intern, she would like to learn more about that and would be willing to find out what help was available for him and his parents. He wrote that on the plan, as well as

(Continued)

CASE 7.1   *Continued*

an action that Briana said might help in his meetings with his siblings. Because her primary responsibility related to his daughter Isabel, and she had just completed an evaluation of her needs, she knew that Isabel did better when she had a predictable, regular schedule. Briana and Norman had talked about how his having to run out and leave Isabel with the neighbors when his parents needed help was sometimes upsetting to Isabel. Perhaps a clear one-page description of Isabel's developmental needs would help as he thought about meeting with his siblings. Norman agreed and wrote that on the plan.

Normally Norman keep to the 30-minute meeting time, but today he really wanted to finish the plan, so he and Briana agreed to work for a full hour. The next section of the plan was about what he and his family saw as their strengths and resources that would help them reach this goal. Another section was for Briana to write down what she saw as their strengths and resources. After some discussion, Norman wrote, "My brothers and sisters love our parents and live close enough to be able to help out more." Briana wrote, "Norman takes a lot of responsibility for his family, and is now working on interdependence with his siblings." Norman smiled when she wrote that because he had started feeling guilty about thinking he should do everything. But when Briana reframed his sense of responsibility as a strength, he saw that taking responsibility to coordinate his parents' care was even better than doing it all himself, as it would leave him time to take good care of himself and his daughter.

He saw that the plan was almost complete, but there was a section for concerns that he or Briana had about the plan. So he wrote, "Maybe my sister will say she is too busy to help out." Briana wrote, "I don't know if Norman's parents' income would make them ineligible for senior services, but I will find out." Then, they both signed the plan and decided that they would meet again in 2 weeks, at which time they would share how their first steps had gone. Briana gave Norman her email at work and phone number and said that he should get in touch sooner if he had any questions or wanted to talk.

It is now 6 months later. The relationship that Norman formed with Briana during her one-semester internship was life changing not only because things are different with his parents, but also because he learned a process that he and his family have since used to address other needs and goals. He has he cut way back on how often he needs to be at his parents' house now that helping them is much more shared with his informal and formal helping systems, that is, his siblings and the county senior services center.

Anna is staying sober and has gotten more involved with their church. She now volunteers during the day in the church office while Isabel is at the child development center. This was an idea of Briana's when they worked together on their second family goal: how Anna might reintegrate into the community when she left the treatment center. Anna likes being out of the house during the day and is forming relationships with all the people who came in and out of the church office during the day. She feels connected with a community outside of just her family, and while she might always be a little more shy than her outgoing husband Norman, she notices that she is not so bothered when he does have to be away from home for work or helping his parents. Her minister recently said that the church would be willing to help pay for a course in bookkeeping if she would consider taking a part-time job there when their bookkeeper retired. While this was a bit scary, Anna and Norman saw that it was a step toward what they had envisioned as their ideal future! This was a particularly important blessing because she saw that being in a spiritual community was important for her long-term sobriety.

Is everything perfect now? No. While Norman's siblings are more involved with their parents, old family issues and patterns have re-emerged. He decided to contact Briana at her new placement to ask if she knew someone they could work with to help him, his siblings, and their parents communicate better. She recommended Michael Johnson, a social work colleague she knows to have strengths dealing with family system issues. She also suggested having the caseworker from the senior center be involved in at least the first session. She said that what they were experiencing was a normal reaction during times of family transitions, especially because unresolved feelings about loss often occur when parents become more frail. While he is not sure everyone would be wiling to work with Mr. Johnson, he knows he will!

Discussion Questions

1. Critique Briana's work with Norman and his family. What were some pivotal moments in their work together that strengthened the family's ability to set and reach their own goals?
2. What did Briana do to help the family assess their needs and strengths?
3. What difference did it make that Norman filled out the Family Development Plan rather than Briana?
4. One goal of strengths-based family practice is to help families have a healthy interdependence with their environment, including formal and informal systems.
   a. Where do you see this in Norman's story?
   b. What does this mean in your own life?
   c. How did you learn to be able to take good care of yourself, in a way that is interdependent with those in your formal and informal networks?
5. Looking at the family systems assessment frameworks in this chapter, and knowing Norman's family as you do, what areas do you think you might encourage them to look at if you were Mr. Johnson?
6. Can strengths-based practice help workers be more culturally responsive or aware when working with families? Why? How? What does this have to do with helping families assess their own needs and strengths?
7. What other concepts you have learned in the earlier chapters that can be applied to work with families?

References

American Humane (2008). *Family group decision making in child welfare.* Retrieved August 14, 2008 from http://www.americanhumane.org/site/DocServer/FGDM_Statements.pdf?docID=6781

Bennett, T., Lingerfelt, B., and Nelson, D. (1990). Developing individualized family support plans: A training manual. Cambridge, MA: Brookline Books.

Berg, I. K. (1994). Family based services: *A solution-focused approach.* New York: Norton.

Bronfenbrenner, U. (1979). *The ecology of human development.* Cambridge, MA: Harvard University Press.

Cohen, R., Singh, N. N., Hosick, J., and Tremaine, L. (1992). Implementing a responsive system of mental health services for children. *Clinical Psychology Review, 12*(8), 819–828.

Collins, B., and Collins, T. (1990). Parent-professional relationships in the treatment of seriously emotionally disturbed children and adolescents. Social Work, 35, 524–527.

Cooperrider, D. L., and Whitney, D. K. (2005). *Appreciative inquiry: A positive revolution in change.* San Francisco, CA: Berrett-Koehler.

Cowger, C. D. (1994). Assessing client strengths: Clinical assessment for client empowerment. *Social Work, 39*(3), 262–268.

Crane, B. (2000). *Building a theory of change and a logic model for an empowerment-based family support training and credentialing program.* Unpublished doctoral dissertation, Cornell University.

Crane, B., Wainui, A, and Dean, C. (1998). *Helping families plan for their children's safety and well-being: Practice manual for N.Y.S. Family Resolutions Project.* Ithaca, NY: Cornell Empowering Families Project.

Darling, R. B. (2000). *The partnership model in human services: Sociological foundations and practices.* New York: Plenum Publishing Corporation.

Dean, C. (1996). *Empowerment skills for family workers: Worker handbook, The comprehensive curriculum of the NYS Family Development Credential Program.* Ithaca, NY: Cornell Media Services.

De Jong, P., and Berg, I. K. (2002). *Interviewing for solutions* (2nd ed.). Brooks Cole Publishers.

Dejoug, P., and Miller, S. D. (1995). How to interview for client strengths. *Social Work, 40,* 729–736.

Diener, C. I., and Dweck, C. S. (2001). An analysis of learned helplessness. In P. K. Smith and A. D. Pellegrini (Eds.), *Psychology of education: Major themes* (pp. 383–399). New York: Taylor & Francis.

Forest, C. (2003). *Empowerment skills for family workers:* A worker handbook. Ithaca, NY: Cornell Family Development Press.

Freire, P. (1970). *Pedagogy of the oppressed,* New York: Continuum.

Goldstein, H. (1943). *Social practice. A unitary approach.* Columbia, SC: University of South Carolina.

Goodsell, C. T. (1981). Looking once again at human service bureaucracy. *Journal of Politics 43,* 761–778.

Hepworth, D., Rooney, R., and Larsen, J. (1997). *Direct social work practice: Theory and skills* (5th ed.). Pacific Grove, CA: Brooks/Cole.

Hodges, V., Burwell, Y., and Ortega, D. (1998). Empowering families. In L. Gutierrez, R. Parsons, and E. Cox (Eds.), *Empowerment in social work practice* (pp. 146–162). Pacific Grove, CA: Brooks/Cole.

Hudson, J., Morris, A., Maxwell, G., and Galaway, B. (1996). *Family group conferences: Perspectives on Policy and practice.* Monsey, NY: Criminal Justice Press.

Janzen, C., and Harris, O. (1997). *Family treatment in social work practice* (3rd ed.). Itasca, IL: Peacock.

Leiby, J. (1978). *A history of social welfare and social work in the United States.* New York: Columbia University Press.

Lipsky, M. (1980). *Street-level bureaucracy: Dilemmas of the individual in public services.* New York: Russell Sage Foundation.

Lupton, C., and Nixon, P. (1999). Empowering practice? A critical appraisal of the family group conference approach. University of Bristol, UK: The Policy Press.

Minuchin, S. (1974). *Families and family therapy.* Cambridge: Harvard University Press.

Minuchin, S., and Fishman, H. (1982). *Family therapy techniques.* Cambridge: Harvard University Press.

O'Callaghan (2005). *The MacKillop model of restorative practice.* Paper presented at "Building a Global Alliance for Restorative Practices and Family Empowerment, Part 3," the IIRP's Sixth International Conference on Conferencing, Circles and other Restorative Practices, Penrith, New South Wales, Australia. Retrieved August 27, 2008 from http://www.iirp.org/pdf/au05_ocallaghan.pdf

Pesso, T. (1978). Local welfare offices: Managing the intake process. *Public Policy, 26*(2), 305–330.

Rapp, C. A. (1998). *The strengths model: Case management with people suffering from severe and persistent mental illness.* New York: Oxford University Press.

Rapp, R. C. (2007). The strengths perspective: Proving "my strengths" and "it works." *Social Work, 52* (2), 185–186.

Rothbaum, F., Rosen, K., Tatsuo, U., and Nobuko, U. (2002). Family systems theory, attachment theory, and culture, *Family Process, 41*(3), 328–350.

Saleebey, D. (Ed.). (1992). *The strengths perspective in social work practice.* New York: Longman.

Saleebey, D. (1996). The strengths perspective in social work practice: Extensions and cautions. *Social Work, 41*(3), 296–305.

Shulman, L. (1999). *The skills of helping: Individuals, families, groups, and communities* (4th ed.). Itasca, IL: Peacock.

Simon, B (1994). *The empowerment tradition in American social work.* New York: Columbia University Press.

Stone, D., Patton, B., Heen, S., and Fisher, R. (2000). *Difficult conversations: How to discuss what matters most.* New York: Penguin

Thrasher, S., and Mowbray, C. (1995). A strengths perspective: An ethnographic study of homeless women with children. *Health and Social Work, 20*(2), 93–101.

U.S. Department of Justice (2007). *Perspectives on restorative justice.* Retrieved August 27, 2008 from http://www.ojp.usdoj.gov/nij/topics/courts/restorative-justice/perspectives/welcome.htm

Wachtel, T., and McCold, P. (2004). *From restorative justice to restorative practices: Expanding the paradigm.* Presented at Fifth International Conference on Conferences and Circles. Retrieved August 27, 2008 from http://fp.enter.net/restorativepractices/bc04_wachtel.pdf

Watzlawick, P., Weakland, J., and Fisch, R. (1974). *Change: Principles of problem formulation and problem resolution.* New York: Norton.

Weick, A., Rapp, C., Sullivan, W., and Kisthardt, S. (1989). A strengths perspective for social work practice. *Social Work, 34,* 350–354.

Weissbourd, B. (1994). The evolution of the family resource movement. In S.L. Kagan, and B. Weissbourd (Eds.), *Putting families first: America's family support movement and the challenge of change.* San Francisco: Jossey-Bass.

GENERALIST SOCIAL WORK PRACTICE WITH GROUPS

CHAPTER 8

Beth Barol

Michael Newman/PhotoEdit

Kristina K. is a BSW student intern in a first-year field placement with a community service agency in an urban community. Initially Kristina provided services including registering people for the "Adopt-A-Family" and "Adopt-A-Senior" Christmas programs. As Kristina helped people register for services, she noticed that many people requesting social services were grandparents who were the primary caregivers for their grandchildren. She noticed how worried, pressured, and socially isolated so many of the grandparents seemed to be. Rather than limit her interaction to the intake forms the agency provided in order to arrange the requested services, Kristina engaged each person in conversation about their experiences and concerns about their families. She discussed her conversations and observations with her supervisor, and they decided that she would start a grandparents' group. This was the first time this agency ever offered such a group in this community, and Kristina, herself inexperienced with leading groups, was both excited and "terrified." She had not even had a course on group work yet, and here she was trying to set up a group on her own. She was particularly concerned by the fact that she would be leading a group of people who might be much older than she was, and she was afraid that they would think that she had nothing important or wise to say to them.

This chapter provides information on generalist social work practice with a wide array of groups. By the end of this chapter, you should be able to help Kristina:

1. Broaden her understanding of the range of groups with which social workers interface on a regular basis
2. Understand the purpose and benefits of group work
3. Become familiar with the underlying issues driving the developmental progression of groups
4. Assess the functioning of a group and develop an appropriate intervention
5. Plan and implement group interventions to support the work of the group
6. Carry a consciousness of empowerment, strengths-based, and mutual support as an overarching paradigm for group work

GENERALIST PRACTICE WITH GROUPS

The primary mission of the social work profession is to enhance human well-being and help meet the basic human needs of all people, with particular attention to the needs and empowerment of people who are vulnerable, oppressed, and living in poverty. (NASW code of Ethics, Preamble, 1999)

The scope of social work's inspiring mission can feel overwhelming to many members of the profession. Societal transformation is one of the key agenda items for social workers. So many of the individual issues we face in our practice stem from social ills such as stigma, discrimination, marginalization, poverty, industrial wastes, poor allocation of resources for people in need, and so on. As social workers we understand that in order to help the individuals we serve, we have to help change the social world in which they live. While the expression "we can change the world one person at a time" is well taken, the effect is raised exponentially when we work successfully with groups.

TYPES AND PURPOSES OF GROUPS

When we think of groups, we need to first consider the groups we encounter most often such as staff groups, team meetings, organizations, families, treatment groups, classrooms, and social groups. Principles of group work apply to each of these types of groups under the framework "a group is a group." Once we understand the basic dynamics of working with groups encountered every day, we can choose to pursue the additional complexities, knowledge, and skill sets for working with groups with a therapeutic orientation.

We often think about groups only in reference to "group therapy." However, these groups are only a small component of the scope and purposes of group work practiced by social workers. We are continuously engaging in groups as we work with teams, family systems, communities, agencies, and social change initiatives. We meet with groups as team leaders or facilitators, or as group members. We also work with "invisible groups" through email and other media-based interventions. Productive experiences in groups as group leaders and as group members often depend on our awareness of group dynamics or group processes. We can influence a group's dynamics from either vantage point, as a member or as a facilitator/leader. Whether we are bold or shy, extroverted or introverted, we can each develop our own style for effectively interacting with groups by honing our skills as outlined in this chapter.

This chapter is devoted to helping the social work practitioner gain the skills to effectively contribute to groups as a group member, facilitator, or as a group leader. We will review elements of group member roles, issues related to group leadership/facilitation, basic principles of group dynamics and development, means for assessing a group's developmental stage, strategies for moving a group forward toward achieving its goal, and leadership/facilitation tools, with a number of case examples.

GROUP MEMBERSHIP

GROUP RESISTANCE

"I am not comfortable working with groups."
"Team meetings are a waste of time."
"Planning meetings are boring."
"I prefer meeting one-to-one."
"I don't speak up in groups."
"I don't consider myself to be a leader."
"I am an introvert."

The comments listed above are frequently made by social workers. They are heartfelt responses often resulting from difficult experiences with groups and indicate a lack of successful training and support in working with group dynamics. These workers wish to avoid group situations and therefore do not have an opportunity to maximize their potential as social workers to effectively participate in, facilitate, or provide leadership in the outcomes of the group. Social workers are engaged with groups in every area of practice. However, many feel that if they avoid work where they have to "lead groups" they will successfully avoid working with groups as social workers.

Some social workers have had experiences that increase their reluctance to work with groups. Let us consider Gwen's experience that results in her resistance to future group work:

CASE 8.1   A GROUP THAT IS NOT FUNCTIONING WELL TOGETHER

Gwen has been involved on a team to address the quality concerns in her agency. There are 10 people on the team. They are positive and productive supervisors and administrators across the agency. Their goal is to review a policy or a procedure each time they meet. Most of the time they "wordsmith" it and set up a new deadline for project completion. Work assignments are given to group members between meetings. However, members rarely complete the assignments. The meetings are often interrupted as members step out to answer cell phone calls, come in late, or leave early. Members jump at any excuse not to attend meetings, citing work obligations that Gwen knows are not so urgent that they could not be addressed after the meeting time. In addition, no matter how far in advance the meetings are scheduled, members plan their compensatory day and vacations days for the days the meetings are scheduled. Gwen is under the impression that members of the team would rather be anywhere else than in this group. She feels that trying to manage the team is like "herding cats." It has become a waste of time for everyone, including Gwen.

Gwen dislikes attending these meetings. They ruin her day. She feels like a failure with respect to this project. She is worried that her reputation as a competent worker is at stake. She has tried being more strict and authoritative around attendance and compliance with assignments, but the harder she works, the less the group members cooperate. It seems that they expect her to do all of the work so that they can just criticize and shoot-down her efforts.

Gwen's group experience is an example of the type of experience that turns social workers off to the power of group work as a transformational tool for change. Other participants are also turned off; they feel that there is no meaning in the exercise of teamwork. Eventually Gwen might give up and do the work all by herself. Group members will continue to complain about the product of her efforts, saying that their needs and viewpoints were not represented in the finished product and refuse to comply with any decisions stemming from the work.

SUCCESSFUL GROUP WORK

Let's imagine a counterexample of when it goes well:

CASE 8.2   A GROUP THAT IS WORKING WELL TOGETHER

Andrea is responsible for a team in her agency whose mission is to address quality within the agency. She is excited by the assignment. She enjoys working with this group of focused, productive, and positive supervisors from across the agency. The time that they meet together seems to fly by. They are usually on the same wavelength with what they are doing, and they have healthy discussions and occasional friendly arguments when they work on issues that represent their different vantage points. However, even when there is a disagreement with some tension attached to it, they are issue focused rather than person focused. After working through the tension and issues, they always seem

CASE 8.2 | *Continued*

to find common ground. Members know and respect each other and are not worried that a disagreement within the meeting will have a negative effect on their relationships on the team and their reputation outside of the meeting time. Team members are creative and excited in this work and strive to include all members of the agency in parallel processes. In fact, people think that it is an honor to be on this team and are excited when they are chosen to participate.

The creativity and energy generated through these meetings carry members through their everyday work challenges. They are able to maintain an ethic of hopefulness and enthusiasm—even in the face of significant disappointments and challenges on the job. They continue to work through problems outside of the meeting. This team has evolved into a strong work *community*.

"You can't change a group—it is all a matter of happenstance and personality"

—Common practice myth

Many people have spent their entire careers working with groups and deepening their understanding of group dynamics. Some social workers are put off by the complexity, perhaps feeling that they do not have the skills of an expert and so give up on considering themselves as effective group leaders/facilitators or even of being effective group members. While we can decide to delegate some models of practice to "experts" beyond our skill base, we cannot abdicate our work with groups for the reasons discussed above. Groups are an intrinsic part of our lives. We can have a positive effect upon groups that we are working with whether we are in the designated role of the leader/facilitator or in the role of a group member.

THE NEED TO BE SEEN, HEARD, AND KNOWN

Before we launch into our discussion, later in this chapter, on the stages of group development, it would be wise to remember something that we know about human beings in general: we all want to be seen, heard, and known. These are core needs. Meeting these core needs builds trust and creates feelings of safety. When these core needs are not met, then feelings of anxiety builds in the members of the group as well as the facilitator. While there are exceptions to every rule, most of us want to feel that we are *seen* in our fullness, *heard* in that when we speak we are listened to and people respond to what we say, and *known* as a person with helpful intent who can make valuable contributions to the group.

For example, in my work as a group leader/facilitator, I have learned that if I plunge into the opening session without first asking the group, "Who has experience or training in group work?" Then the members of the group with previous experience are often compelled to challenge me on fine points of group practice throughout the day, or to try to take over the leadership or "show off" when giving responses. If instead, as I have learned to do, I ask the group after the initial introductions "who has had experience or training in group work?" and invite them to raise their hands,

I then say, "these are your local folks with experience, I encourage you to engage with them during breaks, mealtimes, and other opportunities to hear their perspectives as well." These experienced participants then have had an opportunity to feel "seen, heard, and known" and tend to be very supportive of me in my work as a leader/facilitator as a result. We are established as colleagues rather than competitors through that simple proactive action.

When we do not offer or create opportunities for group members to be seen, heard, and known right away in a group, they will become preoccupied with finding means to establish and protect their identity with the group. They will be sure, on a conscious or on an unconscious level, that they are heard either verbally or behaviorally. As a result, group exercises and group experiences such as how we handle the introduction of new members at the start of a group meeting can have a powerful, positive effect on the group even when the approach we use is very straightforward and simple.

There are many ways this issue plays out in groups. A person might have life experience or expertise in a topic that might be overlooked or undervalued by the group. A member feeling uninvited or unwelcomed to participate may seem like a small social oversight, however it can derail the ability of the group to meet its goals if it continues without resolution. This seemingly small social oversight can derail the ability of the group to meet its goals. For example:

CASE 8.3	THE UNWELCOMING INTERDISCIPLINARY TEAM

Terry has been a friend to Jane for 10 years. When Jane has had troubles, Terry has been there for her. Terry knows what issues cause Jane pain and stress. She also knows that when Jane is involved socially and has time to enjoy her hobbies, she is much less stressed. Jane has been having a hard time lately. She went to her local mental health agency for supports. Terry was invited to an interdisciplinary team meeting by Jane to be her supporter and advocate.

When the interdisciplinary team meeting started, the group facilitator plunged right in to the usual content of the meeting. The team members all knew each other, but Terry didn't know anyone. The leader of the group had everyone state their names, in an attempt to follow group etiquette; however, it resulted in a rapid firing of first names as they went around the table. They did not tell the group about what they did as part of the team. To make matters worse, they seemed to think that the introductions were a silly routine. They rolled their eyes as if bored and smirked at each other when it was time to tell their names. Terry could not hear many of their names but was afraid that she would look foolish if she asked them to repeat them. She knew some of the members were "doctors" because they introduced themselves as Dr. Joe, or Dr. Black, but that was all she knew about the team members. By the end of the introductions Terry felt intimidated and belittled.

Once the meeting started, people started discussing Jane as a "case." Jane's input was not requested. They talked about her rather than to her—in front of Jane. Terry was becoming angry for her friend.

When the staff started talking about the types of programming Jane needed to help control her temper and contain her emotions, Terry finally spoke up and said, "I don't think those ideas will help. Jane needs to be able to relax, do her hobbies, and talk with friends when she is upset. More tasks in isolation and counseling while she is upset are the last things that she needs."

The staff ignored her comments. They acted as if Terry did not understand what they were trying to do. When Terry persisted, they said that clearly she

CASE 8.3 | *Continued*

did not understand what they were there for, and that it doesn't help Jane to be "anti therapy."

Terry became enraged. She was insulted. She radiated anger and hostility, but she kept quiet. She felt embarrassed and demeaned. She also felt that she had failed Jane. She didn't know what to do.

After the meeting, when Terry and Jane were gone, the team members reflected that this was a good example of why advocates should not be invited to meetings.

They shared the opinion that they do not have anything valid to contribute; are just hostile, negative role models for the client; and make people feel uncomfortable.

This was a very unfortunate end point for this interaction. Terry had very valuable treatment and support information and ideas to contribute on Jane's behalf. Jane, feeling disregarded, did not comply with her therapy and left treatment shortly thereafter.

What happened here? What could the facilitator of the meeting have done to remedy the situation? What could the other group members have done differently to help Terry and Jane feel more included?

First, all members of the team had a need to be *seen*. The introductions were inadequate to help the group members, including Terry and Jane, see each other in their individuality and their contributions to the group. Second, when Terry tried to contribute, no one responded to her observations and suggestions or asked for elaboration. She was not *heard*. Third, each group member assumed things about the others because they were not *known* to each other. The group members made a judgment that Terry was just "anti therapy." They did not know how long or in what capacity Terry had known Jane. They did not recognize the wealth of knowledge and firsthand experience Terry had about Jane. Further, Terry did not know anything about the members of the group. She assumed that they did not really know Jane or care about Jane. Not knowing about the level of involvement each team member had with regard to Jane invited her to assume the worst. So, within the first 10 minutes of the meeting, a variety of negative thoughts by members about members emerged, ruining the chance for the group to work cohesively on Jane's behalf.

REDUCING GROUP ANXIETY

The facilitator must address a situation like this proactively. She could have started off by welcoming Jane and Terry to the meeting. Talking about the purpose of the meeting and expressing an openness and eagerness to hear both Jane and her longtime friend's perspectives would have set a model for the other team members to welcome Terry to help guide their work. She could then have asked each group member to take the time to introduce himself or herself by name, briefly identifying the role they play on the team and in Jane's life, and how long and how well they know Jane. The facilitator could then identify and show appreciation for the time that they are taking to work together on Jane's behalf, recognizing their experiences with Jane and the valuable role each member will be playing in the work of the team. The leader, then, would be modeling a welcoming and respectful stance toward all group members for the group, setting a tone for the subsequent interactions. By allowing each person a chance to be seen and heard in the context of this meeting and known by the team would have helped the group move on to accomplish it goal of supporting Jane.

DEFENSE MECHANISMS FUNCTION IN THE GROUP

As we can see from the aforementioned scenario, the unknowing and unwelcoming dynamic sets up the group members to be wary and uncomfortable, causing them to resort unconsciously to *"projection,"* one of the key defense mechanisms at play in groups.

Hall and Lindsey explain defense mechanisms as follows:

> Under pressure of excessive anxiety the ego is sometimes forced to take extreme measures to relieve the pressure. These measures are called defense mechanisms. The principal defenses are repression, projection, reaction formation, fixation, and regression. All defense mechanisms have two characteristics in common, 1) they deny, falsify, or distort reality and 2) they operate unconsciously so that the person is not aware of what is taking place. (Hall and Lindzey, 1978, p. 52)

Projection is the defense mechanism most often brought to light and rectified through the work of the group (Barol, 1998, p. 14). In the words of Fritz Perls:

> A projection is a trait, attitude of behavior which actually belongs to your own personality but is not experienced as such, instead, it is attributed to objects or persons in the person's environment and experienced as being directed toward you by them instead of the other way around. The projector, unaware for instance, that he is rejecting others believes that they are rejecting him. It reduces anxiety by substituting a lesser danger for a greater one and it enables the projecting person to express his impulses under the guise of defending himself against his enemies. (Perls, Hefferline, and Goodman, 1980, p. 249)

Introjection is the defense mechanism closely related to projection whereby a person takes in to him or herself the identities and projections of others and accepts those characteristics or roles as part of the self.

As we witnessed in the scenario above, when we do not attend to the core needs of group members to be seen, heard, and known, the anxiety among groups members increases, and projections run rampant among group members, unintentionally undermining the purpose of the group. The remedy to this situation would be to stop the action to give group members a chance to be seen, heard, and known. While this would be the role of the group leader or facilitator to address this need, it could also be the role of any group member who identifies the problem.

How many times have we been in groups, as a stranger perhaps, where people take the worse spin on (misinterpret) what we are saying? They are quick to judge us and seem to look for ways to find us guilty of a lack of compassion or the "politically correct" response. We find that we have to build considerable context around ourselves to be understood. We yearn for a group context where we can speak what is on our mind without having to check every word before we dare to utter it. After all, as Roland Johnson (personal communication, n.d.) would remark, "I don't know what I think, until I hear what I say." We benefit so greatly when we can explore unshaped ideas with each other and further develop our thinking in dialogue with others. We need then to develop our groups in order that rich dialogue and exchange of meaning can freely take place.

PRE-ENGAGEMENT, ENGAGEMENT, AND DISENGAGEMENT

Chapter 3 described the three overarching phases of intervention for the social worker: *pre-engagement, engagement, and disengagement.* Our work with groups falls under the same pattern. The work of pre-engagement varies greatly according to the purpose of the group and the role of the social worker in the group. Often, the worker will find herself walking into a group with no opportunity for preplanning, or for individual preparation of the members. This is a common occurrence with respect to team meetings and other impromptu group meetings. Groups that have a community-building, counseling, or psychoeducational purpose often give the worker more of an opportunity to prepare in advance. This preparation might start with identifying group members and working with them to assess the needs of the group and the direction the group would like to go to address these needs. It might also start with the worker researching or being trained in a specific type of group work and enlisting or advertising for group members interested in doing group work through this process. Throughout this chapter we are reviewing vignettes that illustrate a variety of group styles demonstrating the array of uses that group work has for the social worker in generalist practice. Notice the possible relationship between the amount of pre-engagement work that goes on for each group and the type of group intervention that is involved.

While, as social workers, we think of our interventions in terms of the stages mentioned above, as group workers, we concurrently think of groups in terms of additional stage models; these are the stages of group development. The stages mentioned above will be interwoven with the stages of group development in a section following a discussion of group leaders/facilitators.

GROUP LEADERS/FACILITATORS

As a group leader, we must constantly keep an eye on the health of the group process. In the next section we will explore means of assessing a group's process issues, where they are in their development, and means to help the groups progress. Perhaps looking at a metaphor might help understand the need to develop our basic group skills.

CASE 8.4 | **THE COOK**

There are great chefs, good cooks, and downright poor cooks. How do they differ?

Poor cooks do not seem to have a clue about how to prepare and present food. They mean well; however, everything that occurs in the kitchen seems a matter of luck. Sometimes it goes well, sometimes it does not. They do not focus on the food, take lessons from their mistakes, or even from their successes. They have no understanding of the mechanics of making food taste good enough or look inviting, or

how to maximize the nutrition. Without an increase of awareness, the poor cook will never improve. They will relinquish the good meal to the good and great practitioners of the culinary arts.

A good cook understands core elements of cooking: using fresh ingredients, working with moisture and heat, knowing which cooking techniques enhance flavors, and so forth. They might have a small repertoire of recipes, but their food is consistently good and nourishing, and people come back for more.

(Continued)

CASE 8.4 | *Continued*

These cooks take lessons, talk about cooking with others to get ideas, and try new recipes.

Great chefs continue to develop from their base as good cooks. They study the fine points of taste. They can generalize between cuisines, understand the complex elements of tastes, and can make unusual food combinations work. They know how to handle the food, and after long periods of skill refinement, practice, observation of their results and frankly talent, they become experts. Cooking is their art, their joy, and their craft.

Becoming a great chef might seem daunting; however, it is easy to help a poor cook become a good cook by focusing on the mechanics, the foundations of cooking. When a poor cook learns about the ingredients, how to prepare them for cooking, and the effects of different types of cooking, such as dry or wet heat and high or low temperatures, and learns to focus on these effects, he or she can become a good cook in a few lessons.

This metaphor presents ideas that are also true of group work. As long as we go through life thinking that groups are just there, part of the environment, and that we have no influence over them, we are not going to focus on how groups work and how to help them change, and we will not learn to be a productive member, facilitator, or leader. There are fundamental principles, the "underbelly" of groups, that apply to all groups. Understanding and practicing these principles equips us to be able to do good quality group work. Further experience, study, research, and practice bring us to the realm of great group workers.

Additionally, social workers in every area of practice need to exercise self-care. Working with groups is no exception. Partaking in supervision on a regular basis with someone with experience with whom you feel comfortable is vital. Groups can be tiring and stressful, especially when they are involving people, issues, or situations that we are uncomfortable with or that might trigger our own latent or current issues. Having clarity about our feelings in the group and being clear about the process are vital elements of getting the most out of supervision. Ideally there will be someone in the agency who is available for supervision. If not, then it is important to find a trusted friend or coworker who has significant group experience to share experiences and idea with.

Tomalsulo, Keller, and Pfadt (1995) have offered a helpful list of tips for group facilitators, in Table 8.1.

TABLE 8.1 | TEN THINGS TO DO IF YOU ARE PLANNING TO RUN A GROUP

1. Learn as much as you can about running a group. Look at the process, content, and techniques when you are learning. Read, review training tapes, and attend demonstrations whenever you can.

2. Join as a participant in a group. Even a 1-day workshop where you are a member will be more helpful than trying to do something you have had no experience in encountering.

3. Attend conferences where demonstrations on group work are being shown. Talk to the people doing the work in this area. A conference is a great way to connect with new ideas and concrete suggestions.

4. Connect with professional groups who run conferences and publish articles on group work with the type of people you work with.

5. Get supervision when you are beginning to run a group. Be sure the supervision is with someone who has more experience than you in these matters. Videotape your sessions to review in supervision.

TABLE 8.1 | CONTINUED

6. Form a peer supervision group. If there are a number of people you know who are doing group work, this is an opportunity for you to share your problems and solutions with one another. It may also provide a group for supporting the work you are doing.

7. Gain experience by cofacilitating a group with a more experienced person. If this is not possible you might want to begin your group with a peer cofacilitator. This would allow the two of you to help one another in developing your skills.

8. Plan your first group with success in mind. Choose members for your group you feel rapport with, whose problems are not so severe, and whom you feel would find the experience enjoyable. The first group you run is really for you to develop your skills and become familiar with its' workings.

9. Time limit your first group to no more than 12 sessions. This will ensure that you will stop (even if it is briefly) to examine how well you are doing and what corrections need to be made before continuing.

10. Be gentle with yourself. Group work is difficult yet very rewarding. Take time to develop your skills. Both you and the people you serve will profit from this approach. (Tomasulo et al., 1995, p. 44).

By Daniel Tomasulo, Ellen Keller, and Al Pfadt.

Next we will focus on ways to become a good, solid group worker, facilitating from the leadership role or supporting the group's development from the role of group member, and set you on the way to deepen your practice if you so desire.

GROUP DYNAMICS

AN INTRODUCTION TO GROUP DYNAMICS

Many authors have studied and written about group development or group dynamics. (We will be using the two terms interchangeably in this discussion.) As a result there are many phase or stage models, each of which can be seen as complimentary and which deepen our understanding of groups. Table 8.2 depicts some of the models in common use among group workers. This table is also intended to illustrate the interface between the three stages of social work intervention (the top row in italics and the stages of group development). It is important to remember that these are not necessarily fixed phases or stages. Groups can pendulum back and forth, returning to deal with new issues as they progress in their development or to respond to changes within the group (Bion, 1961; Berman-Rossi, 1993).

As we see from Table 8.2, there are commonalities between the various stage models. Each model refers to an initial phase where the group members are being polite and getting to know each other and feeling their way, and a struggle stage where member are grappling with issues around power, control, and influence. While the need to be seen, heard, and known is important in each of these two stages, it is during the struggle stage where the need comes more dramatically to the forefront. Members are seeking to develop trust, not feeling completely safe, and are using projection to reduce their anxiety. Next comes a time of resolution, where the group members realize that they can know each other and become known. They learn that it is safe to disagree. This all leads up to the working phase, where the interpersonal dynamics take a back seat to the work that needs to be done, be it the tasks assigned to a work group or treatment team, or the therapeutic work of a group that has come together for

TABLE 8.2 | STAGE MODELS OF GROUP DYNAMICS

Social Work Intervention Stages (Poulin, 2008)	Pre-engagement/ Engagement	Engagement	Engagement	Engagement	Disengagement
Group Model/Author	Initial stage	Struggle stage	Resolution stage	Working stage	Ending stage
Garland, Jones, and Kolodny (1973)	Pre-affiliation	Power and control	Intimacy	Differentiation	Separation
Tuckman (1965)	Forming	Storming	Norming	Performing	Termination
Yalom (1985)	Initial stage: orientation, hesitant participation, search for meaning, dependency	Second stage: conflict, dominance, rebellion	Third stage: development of cohesion	Fourth stage: cohesive group work	
Peck (1987)	Pseudocommunity	Chaos	Emptying	Community	
Berman-Rossi (1993)	Pre-affiliation	Power-control	Intimacy	Differentiation	Separation
Corey and Corey (2006)	Initial stage	Transition stage	Transition stage (con't)	Working stage	Final stage

psychotherapy. The termination phase is seen as a stand-alone phase by some authors (Corey and Corey, 2006; Tuckman, 1965) and is included as part of the working stage by others (Peck, 1987; Yalom, 1985). Psychotherapeutic groups tend to focus more conscientiously on the termination phase than do job-related work groups.

For the purposes of this chapter, we will draw most heavily from the stage model put forth by Peck (1987). He has named his stages "pseudocommunity, chaos, emptying, and community." The inherent quest to build community is closely aligned with our work as social workers.

GROUP INFLUENCES

The purpose of the group and the cultures that influence us has a lot to do with how we take in the other. For example, do we look right at the person or do we keep our eyes downcast? Whenever people come together they begin by sizing each other up. Will this be a friend? A troublemaker? Am I interested in this person? Are they like me or different from me? Regardless of our mode of exploration, we are searching for cues to tell us if we are safe and welcomed. Since we are usually checking out the cues nonverbally, we often react in unconscious ways, responding to "gut reactions," that are our nonverbal social radar system.

While this is true of a short-term informal encounter, say in a grocery store line, or an elevator, the intensity of the interaction increases when we are in a formal group context, such as a work or therapeutic group. After all, we can get away from the others in a few minutes in formal contexts, but formal group membership generally means that we will be with the others for longer periods of time, with no easy avenue of escape.

PSEUDOCOMMUNITY/INITIATION STAGE

This first experience of a group starts us off in pseudocommunity (Peck, 1987). In this stage of group development, members do not really know each other yet. They mainly wish to coexist in the presence of the other group members without experiencing emotional or physical harm (Barol, 1998). Group members are seeking a feeling of comfort, and when canvassed at the close of a meeting, members deemed "successful" will reflect at this stage, "it worked, I was comfortable." While comfort is an initial desire of group members, it is the underlying group anxiety that causes the group members to feel the need so strongly.

According to Peck's (1987) theory, in this stage, most group members, feeling anxious, have been conditioned to turn to the leader for reassurance, guidance, and structure. Their conditioning has led them to believe that the leader has the answers and can protect them from the anxiety-producing potential of hostility from the other, still unknown group members.

> The reliance upon the leader is a dynamic that must be undone so that the group can develop a meaningful dialogue. A group structure that supports a free exchange of meaning and ideas will emerge from the group when the group's attention is turned to all of its members as a source of shared vision and input (Yalom, 1985, p. 30).

CHAOS/STRUGGLE STAGE

As the group experience intensifies, the anxiety level of the group mounts. The relative importance of one's perception in the group intensifies struggles generated in relationship to the purpose of the group, members' passion about the topic, as well as the size of the group. These elements play a role in how quickly the anxiety of group members increases. The group, as a result of the increased anxiety and members' heightened need to establish themselves, moves into the next stage of development. Chaos, or the struggle stage, emerges, as members feel driven to assert themselves and establish their own individuality in the group. The need to be known, to be powerful, and to be right comes to the forefront. Some members self-righteously try to convince other group members of "higher truths." Other members assert their power through withholding agreement and support, agreeing verbally when in fact they do not agree inwardly, or by being silent.

In general the feeling in the group is tense. Members often project upon the leader that he/she is weak and inadequately taking care of the problem people in the group. They instigate arguments and disagreements among themselves (Yalom, 1985, p. 47). Behavioral symptoms such as venting, showing anger and frustration, and harping on what group members might perceive as "small" or relatively inconsequential issues are aspects of the group's experience during this stage. In some groups, members withdraw their attention: they say that they are bored and don't connect. They have trouble finding meaning in their experience (Barol, 1998, pp. 21–22).

This is a high-pressure time for the group and for the group leader. If we realize that the group leader is a member of the group, with a special role, to be sure but subject to the anxiety shifts and defensive responses that other group members experience as well, then we can understand why this phase of the group is so difficult for the leader, as well as the group members. This is, of course, particularly so for the inexperienced leader, who doesn't understand these emotions in their dynamic context and is hit broadside by them. The leader then too starts to "project" and to "introject," feeling a tremendous pressure to fix things. While there is indeed a role for the leader in moving the group toward resolution, the means is not readily available to the inexperienced leader who is in a reactive mode. They will more often "escape into organization" (Peck, 1987, p. 93) by handing out assignments and ending the meeting without the resolution needed for the group to advance to the next stage. The result is that the group members continue to feel unsafe and untrusting toward each other, and are dependent and simultaneously resistant toward the group leader; this is a double bind for the group leader. The group is needing and desiring two opposing responses from the leader: to behave as a Mommy or Daddy to make the "kids behave" so that they can feel safe, and conversely, allowing the members to be self-actualized and free to think and participate autonomously.

Does this contradictory set of expectations feel familiar? Does this conjure up experiences with working with adolescents? The chaos stage of group development in many ways parallels the adolescent stage in individual development. In both individual adolescence and group chaos, conflicting needs and desires can evoke many defensive responses in caregivers, social workers, and group leaders. We must be continuously mindful of what is being evoked in us (countertransference) so that we can pick and choose our interventions mindfully. Our ability to remain "present and aware" despite the anxiety the group might evoke in us helps the group members get a handle on their anxiety. We will address tools later in this chapter that the facilitator can choose to employ to further assist the group in resolving these important issues.

EMPTYING/RESOLUTION STAGE

Emptying is the third stage of group development; it is the stage when group members progress from the tension and hostility of the chaos stage by emptying themselves of their projections in a productive manner with others, "by daring to speak from their hearts and by being open to other group members' heartfelt responses" (Barol, 1998, p. 23). Understanding what each member means when speaking becomes more important than remaining safely silent (Bohm, 1992).

Disagreement comes to be viewed as a form of difference, and diversity becomes interesting rather than threatening. There may be an air of fragility in the room as group members explore this relatively unknown territory of truly seeing, hearing, and knowing every other member of the group (Barol, 1998). Once the group has reached the emptying stage, and has worked through their projections, they flow seamlessly into the community stage of group development. The group leader then can begin to recede more into the background of the group as the group enters the community/working stage and takes on elements of self-governance.

COMMUNITY/WORKING STAGE

Now the group is a working group. Members have entered community. Each member is respected and each member's opinion is elicited. Individual members can take risks to speak openly and honestly within the group. They can talk about their needs and their feelings without feeling negatively judged on a personal basis. Members can become more witty and fun loving in part because they now feel "known." They are assured that the other group members know them in their full richness and won't hold a stray or misspoken remark against them but will instead ask them what was meant by their remark. The group then turns its attention to its agenda, replicating their experience of community through the work at hand. Natural leaders emerge from the group to carry out specific roles and tasks for the group. Members feel free to contribute to the level of their own interests, comfort level, and skills. Some members continue to heighten the awareness of the process of the group; others take responsibility for the content, each supporting the others through meaningful and productive disagreement. The group leader/facilitator role at this point varies with the purpose of the group and, at the very least, is ideally focused on shared power and encouraging the strengths of the group members toward the fulfillment of their purpose.

The behavioral symptoms presented in the section above give cues to the stage the group is in. Table 8.3 illustrates some of the tools and techniques at the disposal of the group leader/facilitator in response to behavioral symptoms portrayed by the group.

TABLE 8.3 | SYMPTOM-BASED INTERVENTIONS TO ADVANCE THE STAGES OF THE GROUP

Group Symptoms	Stage of Group Development	Interventions
Shyness, silence, lack of eye contact and attention between members	Pseudocommunity	Introductions, personal story telling on topics of common interest or experience. *"Talking Paper*,[1]*"* Warm–up exercises
Group says they get along well, but they share an external common enemy who they spend much of their time discussing.	Pseudocommunity	Challenge them to talk honestly about a serious issue. Facilitate with talking papers if necessary to find out what people's real experience of the group might be. Use of group rules?
Group members are very happy with the group, and say that they never disagree and that they have just clicked from the start. They are also unproductive and uncreative in their output.	Pseudocommunity	Leader helps group see inconsistency in statements and actions.
Conflict between individual members and/or sub-groups.	Chaos	Exercises and experiences to increase people's knowledge of the personhood of the other. Common ground exercises, "Talking Paper," biographical timelines[2], strategic planning processes. Focus on clarity or communication among members.

(Continued)

TABLE 8.3 | CONTINUED

Group Symptoms	Stage of Group Development	Interventions
Hostility toward leader, vying for leadership with the leader	Chaos	Open conversation with leader taking the vulnerable self-reflection stance first. "I feel uncomfortable and I am wondering…" Use of silence and waiting for a response.
Scapegoating: blaming, joking, or making snide remarks about another member of the group	Chaos	Leader identifies problematic group behavior and exploring with the group their style of engagement and their ability to give honest feedback in a nonaggressive manner.
A sense of thoughtful stillness, group members expressing and validating emotions, listening fully to others	Emptying	Encourage the slower pacing of the conversation; assure that each group member has an opportunity to be heard. Encourage group members to respond directly to each other, validating each other's communication attempts.
Working well together, context-rich humor, friendly disagreements, a sense of mutual respect	Community	Highlight and celebrate the gains and successes of the group. Draw attention to the group's process when struggle inevitably arises, to help them garner their best resources in addressing the conflict. Work with the group to keep motivation and creativity at a high level—keeping an eye out for slippage back into a patterned, nonengaged response

[1] See "Facilitation Tool 8.1" in this chapter for more information on *Talking Paper*.
[2] Barol, (2001) describes the use of biographical timelines to support team development and cohesion on the behalf of the individual they seek to support.

RESIST THE URGE TO CONTROL THE GROUP

Most new group facilitators are concerned that they will not be able to control the group. They wonder what they will do if someone says something unexpected or causes other group members to be upset or angry. In a work group, the facilitator is often concerned that the required end result will not be obtained. As a result, their inclination is to be very directive and to follow a prescribed script. As we saw in the discussion earlier, this maneuver will cause the group to remain in pseudocommunity or chaos or to vacillate between the two stages. The facilitator will end up feeling quite powerless indeed.

It is important for each of us to know that controlling a group is a self-defeating task in the long run. It is also a counterproductive endeavor if we take our social work values to heart. Empowerment and a strengths-based perspective are part of the underpinnings of our work with groups. Controlling the group would necessitate stifling the very essence of the group process that we are trying to enhance, which are the exploration of the self in relationship with others, the generation of free-flowing ideas, expanding our knowledge and experience base exponentially through the here-and-now experiences in the group, and the vicarious experiences of others. When a group is working in freedom and shared power with itself, group members get the opportunity to redefine their experience of the social world and contribute to a new social construction of their reality. Enthusiasm and inspiration to achieve ends that were previously thought of as impossible are made possible through the energy of the group functioning at its best.

All group members brings with them their own biography, meaning, and their own life experiences. These experiences influence how the person relates to each member of the group as well as how they each respond to each other, to things that are said, and to the leader/facilitator. In other words the behavior of each of the group members is constantly varying in response to internal and external influences. The effect is not just a linear one but also an exponential one, with each member reacting to each and every member individually and as a group. How could a group leader hope to control these interactions without squelching the very aspect of the group that she is there to enhance and support?

The answer is in supporting and engaging with the group in the "here-and-now" (Yalom, 1985). The leader, giving up responsibility to "control," engages with the group in a mindful manner around processes that present themselves, using, among others, some of the techniques we have discussed above, and finds himself or herself actually gaining a sense of power as he or she is freed up to move with the group. The social worker helps the group identify what is going on in a group and to come up with constructive ways to deal with the issues at hand, by opening opportunities for reflection, sharing, and planning in an environment that feels honest and safe to the group. As the group members rework their experiences of groups through the work of this group, they can emerge from the experience strengthened, recognized, and empowered, and with a solid work product if that is the function of the group.

PROCESS VERSUS CONTENT

As we can see from the discussion above, we must develop the capacity to tend to the process of the group through its development, style, and methods of interacting in order for the group to perform in the most meaningful way. The product of the group is exponentially greater when the group has made it to the working phase. Once we are in the working phase, we can focus most of our attention to the content, or the intended outcome.

TERMINATION

As noted in Table 8.1 earlier in this chapter, some theorists include ending or termination stages to their models. Whether there is a formal stage or not, it is important that we pay attention to how we end our group. People have a need to recognize and celebrate their successes. Too often in our busy worlds we move without pause or reflection from one assignment to the next. Small wonder that people struggle for a feeling of accomplishment and purpose. Taking the time, even after a one-time group meeting, to reflect on accomplishments is a "gift" to the participants and an investment in the future. A group that is imbued with meaning will be easier to mobilize in the future. It helps to create a culture of celebrating our works together, including where appropriate a reflection on the successful resolution of the struggles encountered.

Termination is also vital in both work and therapeutic groups in that our feelings about endings and loss are often evoked in even the most casual of group meetings. Taking the necessary time to help members gain healthy closure at the end of their time together can be very empowering and enlivening for the group members. Experiencing a successful closing can be a very meaningful gift indeed.

TOOLS FOR GROUP LEADERS/FACILITATORS

As a group leader, we must constantly keep an eye on the health of the group process. In the next section we will explore means of assessing a group's process issues: where they are in their development, and means to help the group's progress.

SETTING THE STAGE

When the group first comes together, it is natural for members to be in pseudocommunity. Since part of the issue here is the need to be seen, heard, and known, then exercises and processes that increase the group members' sense of being seen would be the first line of approach. One goal for the group leader would be to have each member of the group experience saying something, anything, aloud in the group. This starts to lay down the template of hearing one's voice in the group, and having that response respected by members of the group, thereby increasing feelings of safety and trust.

Introductions are a vital first step. This author has found it effective to ask people to give their name and to tell the group anything they would like the group to know about themselves. I also ask members to talk about what they are hoping to get from the group. This enables members to hear their voices in the group, and they have the comfort to speak about something that they know better than anyone else, their own thoughts. If the group is going to be a long-term work group, or a therapy group, I usually go for an additional talking round, where all members are asked to talk about their name and what it means to them, or the most important or enjoyable aspect of their work. I find the latter question particularly important when I am working with an in-house work group (a group that works together on a regular basis), strategic planning group, or training retreat. So many of the tensions within existing groups again arise from the sense of not knowing each other.

PROCESS VERSUS CONTENT

As we can see from the discussion above, we must develop the capacity to tend to the process of the group through its development, style, and methods of interacting in order for the group to perform in the most meaningful way. The product of the group is exponentially greater when the group has made it to the working phase. Once we are in the working phase, we can focus most of our attention to the content, or the intended outcome.

CASE 8.5	AGENCY CONFLICT RESOLUTION RETREAT

I was invited to facilitate team building in a residential services agency that was strife ridden. There had been a recent change in leadership, and the new CEO was concerned that he could not move ahead with urgent changes with an organizational team that was in a constant state of conflict, or "chaos." There was a particularly charged relationship between the head of the business office and the residential staff. Each was convinced that the others did not care about the people they were supporting. The business manager felt that the residential caregivers would misspend money and were careless about the agency's property. The residential caregivers felt that the business director did not know anything about the work they did or care about the people they supported. They felt that he was a constant obstacle to every creative endeavor they undertook.

I requested that the whole group come together for a 2-day retreat. There were more than 40 people present. The business director and the residential staff were all in attendance.

After the opening introductions, I asked all group members to talk about what brought them into the field or about what they are most moved by in their work. I told them to take their time, that we wanted to use this opportunity to know each other better. I started out with a story of my own in order to model how to tell such as story, to take an opportunity to become more known to the group myself, and to give the group members time to think and prepare for telling their own story. I then asked who would be willing to go first. I waited in silence for about 15 seconds before someone volunteered. After that person told her story, we continued to move around the

circle, with each person taking a turn to talk about him or herself.

When it came time for the business manager to speak, he talked about working as an orderly in a nursing home when he was working his way through college. He spoke with great emotion in his voice about his compassion for the people he was working with and how he tried to help people use the bedpans without feeling humiliated. He said that it was that experience that moved him to become a business manager in a residential services agency. He wanted to use his business skills to better the lives of people who were dependent on others. The other group members were shocked! They had no idea that this man had had such an experience or that his motivation was so closely akin to theirs. They remarked about how surprised and excited they were to learn this. He flushed with excitement when he realized how the other staff were responding to him. He was so used to being marginalized by them that he was expecting to be rejected once again by this group. From that point on, the stories became richer. Each member of the group was eager to share a story about what brought them to the field or a story about what meaning they had in their work. This process took close to 2 hours, as each person moved closer to being seen, heard, and known by the group. Once the group started to empty themselves of their presuppositions about each other, they were able to take on tasks to further the advancement of the agency. Using a mixture of small-group idea-generating activities and large-group consensus-building activities, they were able to define the mission that they would all eagerly work under, the roles of the various departments, as well as guidelines for working together collaboratively in the future.

EXAMPLES OF USEFUL TOOLS

There are many effective methods and tools for aiding a group in its development through each of its stages. Some of these have already been discussed and include setting the stage by being clear about the group's purpose, and through the use of in-depth introductions. In this section two tools will be presented. The first is "Talking Paper," a technique for putting dialogue onto papers on the wall to ensure that each group member has a voice, and yet contribution can be anonymous and private (Wolfson and Fowlkes, 2007). This tool is particularly useful for surfacing hidden or threatening issues in a group. A second tool is a "common ground" process where several members take up issues by dividing into groups that explore issues in considerable depth with the aid of the facilitator. The goal of the exercise is to fully understand the other person's point of view and why they are emotionally invested in their stance. Generally, once the members fully understand the other's rationale and feelings, and make that understanding known to each other, the tension dissipates, and the members who were in deep conflict can find common ground on which to problem-solve.

These types of group experiences, among others, support a group to move through the pseudocommunity and chaos stage into the emptying and community stages.

TALKING PAPER

Wolfson and Fowkes (2007) describe Talking Paper as a "resource for enhancing consensual dialogue and participative learning in groups" (p. 1). She reminds us of the principle by Brazilian educator and advocate for the oppressed, Paulo Freire: "Only dialogue which requires critical thinking is also capable of generating critical thinking. Without dialogue there is no communication, and without communication there is no true education" (Freire, 1984, p. 81).

FACILITATION TOOL 8.1 | **FACILITATING GROUP DISCUSSION USING TALKING PAPER: AN OVERVIEW**
by Julia Wolfson and Sandra Fowkes

Background

The Talking Paper process is one of many approaches available for facilitating group meetings and communication. It is also referred to as Facilitated Visual Gathering. It evolved from the pioneering work of Metaplan (Ltd.), a German consultancy group, and the cross-cultural and environmental work of Sandra and John Fowkes in South Africa.. The process seeks to achieve:

• Participation of all present
• Freedom of expression for participants
• Making visual the development of the discussion
• Accuracy of the record of discussions held
• Consensual solutions

The approach recognizes that in any discussion there are three key components:

• **Content** – what it is that is being talked about
• **Process** – the way in which the discussion is held
• **Feeling atmosphere** – individual and group reactions to the discussion and the issues.

A facilitator handles the way in which the discussion is held–the process. The facilitator's task is to assist participants to concentrate on the content of the discussion. The facilitator also assists participants to acknowledge their issues while managing the emotional aspects of the discussion in a constructive and appropriate way.

As with most facilitation techniques, there are distinct stages to the approach. The underlying reason for having different stages is to optimize the thinking of group members. There are distinct types of thinking, none of which can exist at the same time.

Silent generation of ideas

A question is posed and participants write their responses on separate cards. This is the visual element of the facilitation method. Generating the ideas on cards is done without any discussion. This is to encourage proactive thinking and to avoid the reactive responses typical of many interactive meetings. These cards are the participant's guarantee of an equal opportunity for participation.

Collation and clarification of ideas

The facilitator, effectively separating the idea from the person who generated it, gathers the cards. The cards are placed on large adhesive posters in full view of all participants, making the discussion visible. Cards

FACILITATION TOOL 8.1 | *Continued*

carrying similar meanings are clustered together. In this way a total picture of the discussion emerges. Any queries or clarification of the cards are also recorded and displayed with the relevant cluster.

The adhesive, repositionable glue used on the posters allows the cards to be moved and grouped. This is its special feature. This flexibility liberates the process from any "linear tyranny" of recording ideas as on a flip chart. Participants can arrange and rearrange cards to show the relationships that they see between ideas. This way of working visually with ideas comes to more closely resemble our patterned way of thinking and so makes the exploration of ideas more effective.

Stages 1 and 2 encourage "divergent" thinking in order to generate a diversity of ideas.

Evaluation of ideas

In this stage, the nature of the thinking changes to "convergent" thinking. Using any form of ranking or rating (for instance: dot voting, histograms), the diverse range of ideas is narrowed down. Because of the visual display, the ideas can be evaluated without at the same time "evaluating" the person who generated the idea.

Selection

Now the third type of thinking, "emergent" thinking, is applied to select the priority ideas. These can then be used as input to action plans. The posters produced during the session can be photographed using

a digital camera and form a part of the record of the discussions. This permits participants to revisit the posters and check the accuracy of any formal record of the discussion.

The total Talking Paper brainstorming process

- Encourages active participation by all
- Promotes proactive thinking
- Optimizes use of the different types of thinking
- Gives a clear record of the discussion and of key points
- Prevents cyclical discussion by keeping the focus of attention on the issue, and
- Ensures that the emotional energy generated is used creatively and not destructively.

In summary, the Talking Paper method:

- Manages the process of communication so that resources, especially people's time, expertise, emotions, and energy, are used effectively and efficiently
- Can be used as a conflict management tool because it separates people from their ideas, explores ideas in a "neutral" space, makes it less possible for people to dominate and play out hidden agendas
- Is flexible, and so its applications are varied, depending on the creativity and skill of the facilitators (Wolfson and Fowkes, 2007, pp. 1–3).

COMMON GROUND PROCESS

Common ground processing is utilized when group members have reached an impasse over a particular issue, or interaction. It is an experience that members of the group undergo with the guidance of the leader/facilitator to ensure that each member feels heard. The technique is based on the understanding that most conflict is really less about the surface issues at hand than about co-occurring negative assumptions and projections group members make about the motives and ideological stance of others in the group. This inability to see the other person as a caring human being who is deserving of compassion and an open exchange of ideas is the hallmark of the chaos stage of development. The common ground exercise offers a pathway for the group to successfully resolve this conflicted stage of the group process, empty itself of self-righteousness, of the "us against them" stance, and move into the community stage.

FACILITATION TOOL 8.2   STEPS IN THE COMMON GROUND PROCESS

Members of the group are asked to choose a side of the issue to represent. The group is asked for four volunteers, divided in half to take up opposite sides of an issue. The remaining group members are requested to sit in an outer circle and watch quietly as the inner circle of volunteers engages in the exercise.

The four volunteers are then divided up into two sets of partners. Each pair of partners will represent both sides of the issue or conflict at hand. The facilitator reminds the partners of the ground rules, assuring that each person will have a full opportunity to speak about his or her perspective on the issue. However, each person will be expected to follow the rules:

- Confidentiality—whatever is said in the room stays in the room
- Listen fully to the other person without interrupting,
- Paraphrase content and reflect upon the feelings about what is said
- Use respectful language
- This is an effort to understand the other person. It is not a debate. (Adapted from Common Ground presentation by the Quad Cities: Pedagogy of the Oppressed Conference, 1997)

The facilitator then describes their role as one of enforcing the rules and will interrupt only if the rules are broken to ensure that the process is followed. The facilitator never takes sides or offers an opinion at this juncture in the process.

One set of partners goes first. One partner talks to the other about the issue at hand, as fully as possible, talking from an "I" stance. In other words, she talks about what that issue means personally. The person's partner (with the opposing point of view) is instructed to listen carefully, and then, when the first person is finished talking, to repeat as closely as possibly what they heard the person say, and how they think the speaker feels about the subject. For example, "I heard you say ... and I see that you are passionate about this and it effects you deeply," or "I can see that this was a very sad experience for you," or "I think you are very angry

about this treatment and feel that you were treated unjustly."

The facilitator then asks the first speaker if she felt that her partner heard what she was saying and if she was right when she labeled how she was feeling. If the speaker says, "not really, she left out this part....", then the facilitator asks the second partner to try again to paraphrase the points that thefirst speaker was trying to express. This process continues until the first speaker feels that the second partner really heard her and at least understands, if not agrees with, what she was trying to convey.

Depending upon the listening skills of the members, this might move quickly or it might take several tries. This is particularly difficult the first time around for a group, since people often acknowledge that they are used to only listening to the first words a person says because they are then framing their response in their heads and shut out the rest of what their partner is trying to convey. This exercise forces the partners to stop their internal responding and focus on what is being said by the other because they will be expected to paraphrase what is being said to them before being allowed the time to speak on their own behalf. Once it is certain that the first speaker has been heard and has indicated that she felt heard, the second partner is invited to talk about the issue under the same conditions with her partner.

The second pair of partners has been listening to the interaction between the first pair. When it becomes their turn to participate, they have the advantage of building their statements upon the work of the previous pair, thereby potentially enriching the information shared. After they have experienced the process in the same manner as the first couple, the two sets of partners are now invited to respond to statements made during the session, using the same ground rules as stated above. The outside group, the silent observers, is also given an opportunity to reflect on the process as they witnessed it. Finally the process is meant to clarify individual meaning, to seek understanding rather than convincing others, to use respectful language in the delivery of information, to hear the person completely, and to paraphrase their comments before responding with their own.

Very often, at this juncture, the group members find that with an increased understanding of the other, they are able to view their fellow group members with more compassion and openness. Rather than seeing the other as an "opponent," they see each other as people who have legitimate concerns and honest feelings about their issues.

Working from this stance, the group is often able to come to some common ground about the issue and brainstorm freely about possible solutions that would meet the needs of both partners.

AN EXAMPLE OF INTEGRATION OF GROUP PROCESS AND COMMON GROUND PROCESS

CASE 8.6	USING ASPECTS OF THE COMMON GROUND PROCESS

Team meetings involving staff and family members can often be tense and even openly hostile situations. In the following case example, we see the dynamics described above played out through a variation of the common ground process.

Harriett Smith was a young woman in her late twenties. She had lived in Springview, a congregate living facility for people with intellectual and developmental disabilities, for 20 years. Springview was situated miles away from the general community. More than 80 people lived in the facility at the time. The program director and the staff were eager to offer people living in the residential center an opportunity to live more typical lives in the community. Harriet was one of the first people selected by staff to move into a community group home also run by Springview and supported by Springview staff.

The staff was very excited for Harriet, feeling confident that Harriet would blossom with the new opportunity. Much to their chagrin and dismay, however, they quickly discovered that Harriet's mother, Mrs. Smith, was highly opposed to the move and was threatening legal action to keep her daughter in the institution. There had been many hostile exchanges of words between the direct support staff, supervisory staff, and the parent. Each had accused the other of being uncaring. Mrs. Smith accused the staff of only being in the work "for the money" and said that they did not care about what happened to Harriet. The staff responded to the mother, "if you really cared for Harriet, you would have never placed her in this facility in the first place, you would not have deserted your daughter." The

Mrs. Smith was incensed by their rejoinder. There was so much rage and contempt on both sides that legal action did indeed appear pending.

The social worker decided that there was an urgent need to repair the relationships between Mrs. Smith and the other members of Harriet's team. She invited Mrs. Smith and the staff to a meeting, asking everyone to set aside an entire morning to "get to the bottom of this problem."

When everyone came together, the tension was palpable. The social worker began by welcoming Harriet's mother and talking about how grateful she was that she was willing to come and share her knowledge about Harriet with the team. She then welcomed the other members of the team and asked each member of the group to introduce themselves and to describe the way they knew Harriet and how long they knew her. Many of the staff, as it turned out, had worked closely with Harriet on a daily basis for 5–10 years. Some of the staff mentioned that they had even taken Harriet home with them on their weekends off in order to spend time with Harriet and their families.

The social worker then told that team that she had become aware that there was a serious issue about where Harriet was to live, and that the issue had caused some hard feelings among the people present. She said this concerned her because she knew that everyone in the room cared deeply for Harriet and wanted her life to be the best it could be. She told the group that they were going to have a special kind of conversation, where they make sure that they really get to know each other and their concerns

(Continued)

CASE 8.6 | *Continued*

and hopes regarding Harriet. She went on to say that everyone at the table would have the opportunity to talk about their concerns and feelings, and that she was going to facilitate the conversation so that each person had an opportunity to be heard fully. She then went over the common ground rules (confidentiality, listen to understand, paraphrase content and feelings, no interruptions, respectful language) and emphasized that it was not a debate.

The social worker then asked Mrs. Smith to describe her feelings about the issues as fully as she wanted to so that the staff could understand her perspective. Mrs. Smith talked about how sweet and cute her daughter was as a little girl. She was cheerful and liked people. Even though she was slower developing than other children in the family and she had been labeled with "mental retardation," all was well at home. Then, when Harriet started school, the other children would pick on her. They would call her names, like "retard," and they would make fun of how she walked and talked.

Harriet responded by losing her cheerfulness. She wouldn't talk as much and she would walk hunched over. Mrs. Smith started to cry when she talked about how much it hurt her to see Harriet suffer so at the hands of the children in the community. She said that the grown-ups weren't much better, and it broke her heart to see how people wouldn't accept Harriet. The staff was visibly moved when they heard Mrs. Smith's narration. They sat in absolute silence, some with eyes brimming with tears.

Mrs. Smith went on to explain that she had spoken with their family doctor who advised that they seek a residential school program so Harriet could be "with her own kind." She felt that then she would feel accepted by her peers. She said that this was before the Right To Education Law was in effect and that there weren't as many opportunities as there are now. She and her husband, now deceased, had driven up and down the east coast looking for a good place for their daughter. They were delighted when they found Springview, in their own state. Harriet was accepted to the facility, and the parents had been told that they would never have to worry again. Their daughter could live in Springview for the rest of her life.

Mrs. Smith said that she wanted the facility to keep its promise to her and to Harriet. She thought Harriet was much better off there, among people with similar disabilities and trained staff, than she had been in the community, living at home 22 years prior. She was afraid of the emotional pain to Harriet if she moved out of Springview's large campus.

After Mrs. Smith finished, the staff sat quietly for a while. The social worker asked a direct support staff person who had previously been at odds with Mrs. Smith to paraphrase what Mrs. Smith had said and tell what she thought Mrs. Smith was feeling. The staff person did a good job of relating the story back to Mrs. Smith. She then said, "You have seen your daughter broken and hurt by her experiences in the community. It must have broken your heart. You love Harriet very much and you did the best you could for her at the time. You must be sad and afraid at this time when we are talking about her possibly moving into our community home." Mrs. Smith nodded her head with tears flowing down her cheeks. Mrs. Smith added, "It has been so hard not having Harriet close to home. I visit as often as I can, but it is a long trip, I miss her very much."

The social worker then, seeing the solemn looks in the other staff person's eyes, asked if anyone else want to respond to Mrs. Smith. Several staff persons did. They expressed great sorrow for her experience and recognized that there were not nearly the numbers of community resources then as there are now. Several people said that they would have made the same choice if they were in Mrs. Smith's shoes at that time. They also said that understanding this story helped them understand why Harriet seemed to have such low self-esteem.

The social worker asked the staff person, Lynn, who had first responded to Mrs. Smith to tell her "story." Lynn talked about the fact that she had been working in the cottage on grounds with Harriet for 5 years. She talked about how much she enjoyed being with Harriet, how they hung out together during the day, and when Lynn had weekends off, she would often take Harriet to visit her own family. She said that she had noticed that it was always hard to get Harriet to look her best and take care of herself when she was on grounds; staff thought that Harriet was depressed. She required coaxing to take her shower. She walked around with her head down. She was such a sweet person but seemed so "down"

CASE 8.6 | *Continued*

much of the time. The only times Harriet seemed really happy was when her mother would come for a visit and when Lynn or the other staff would take Harriet out to the nearby towns for shopping, walks, or a meal out. She said that when Harriet knew that she was going to town, her face would light up, she would eagerly take a shower, and she would do her best to dress nicely. When they would walk in town, Harriet would smile, talk more, and look at herself in the reflection of the store windows with a happy smile. Other people would smile at Harriet when she passed them in town. Lynn had never seen the negative responses in the nearby community that Harriet had experienced in her hometown in the past. She went on to say that Harriet went to work with people who lived in the community home and that some of the people there were her friends. She had visited them with staff on several occasions and liked the house very much. Lynn said that she would miss working with Harriet but felt that Harriet would be much happier living in the community home.

Mrs. Smith then, with the social worker's support, paraphrased what Lynn had said. She then said that she could see that Lynn cared very much for her daughter, too, and wanted the best for her. She said that Lynn was passionate about the opportunity she saw for Harriet. She added that she hadn't known about Harriet's successful experiences in the community. She quickly added that she wasn't convinced that Harriet should move but that she realized that the staff was acting out of the best intentions for her daughter.

The social worker then asked the other staff if they had anything to add. Several of them shared briefly their experiences with Harriet in the community and their reason for hoping that she would be able to move there one day.

The social worker summed up the conversation by saying that it is clear that each person had Harriet's best interest at heart and had made decisions based on what they knew and what was available at the time. She then asked Mrs. Smith: if she could design a community program for her daughter, what safeguards would she need to see in place? Mrs. Smith was willing to pursue this line of thinking because she felt valued by the staff now and because she trusted their intentions. She was willing to work with them as a team. Mrs. Smith listed several safeguards that she thought were important: that Harriet would be accompanied when she went out from the house, since Harriet tended to wander, that there would be a chime on all of the exits, and that there be an awake staff person in the house all night. She also requested that house staff help Harriet stay in touch with her mother and help drive her home for home visits.

The staff readily agreed and said those were the same safeguards that they were insisting upon; in fact, most of the requests were already in place; and they would add the door chimes. Mrs. Smith said that while she still had misgivings, she was willing to give it a try, as long as they could agree that if Harriet didn't like living in the new house, or wasn't doing well there, that she could come back to Springview. Again there was an agreement.

The social worker asked the staff to work closely with Mrs. Smith to plan the transition for Harriet. They promised to work together and give regular updates on their progress to the social worker.

Before ending the meeting, the social worker asked each team member to say a few words about the meeting. Mrs. Smith expressed her gratitude to the staff for meeting with her and apologized for saying in the past that "they were only in it for the money." The staff also expressed their newfound appreciation for Mrs. Smith and all that she had gone through. They, too, apologized for angry comments to her. They said that they could see that Mrs. Smith really did love her daughter and made the best decisions she could at the time.

Postscript: Harriet did move out with her mother's support. She has enjoyed many happy years in her new home in the community. Her mother is so pleased with the new home and finds it so welcoming to her as well that she visits her daughter in her home frequently.

GROUP INTERVENTION MODELS

Now that the generalist social worker understands some of the basic tools she can use to help develop the group, she can utilize her skills as a facilitator/leader for many types of groups.

There is a growing evidence base for the effectiveness of group work in helping participants restructure their relationships with peers, family members, and others. Each of these models has its own curricula or protocols ranging from simple guidelines to complex, highly resourced and structured sequencing that details how the facilitator is to work with the group and lists the content to be shared with the group members in a more or less scripted manner. Group interventions address the range of social and personal concerns and have a wide range of applicability to various client populations and psychosocial issues including: interpersonal violence (Cranwell et al., 2007; Taft, Murphy, Musser, and Remington, 2004); victimization (McWhirter, 2006; Thun, Sims, Adams, and Webb, 2002); grief and loss (Hopmeyer and Werk, 1994; Mappin and Hanlon, 2005; Morrison and Lambert, 1996); isolation and abandonment, and drug and alcohol use (Little, 2006; Powell, 2006; Washington and Moxley, 2003); mental illness (Garrick and Ewahen, 2001; Sigman and Hassan, 2006); developmental disabilities (Focht-New, 2004; Tomasulo, 2000); physical illness, anger management, parenting, sexuality, and intimate relationship concerns, among many others. Modes of group intervention include socialization (Calhoun et al., 2005), psychoeducation (Brennan, 1995), skills training (Bellack, 2004); conflict resolution, community action, psychotherapy (Bouis, et.al., 2007; Scheidlinger, 2004) and counseling (Steen and Kaffenberger, 2007). Group work spans the life cycle with groups dedicated to meet the needs of individuals at each juncture of our personal evolution (Wasowk, 1986).

Psychotherapeutic approaches employed by practitioners also provide a wide range of options including Cognitive Behaviors Therapy (Waldron and Kaminer, 2004), Solution-Focused Counseling (LaFountain, Gardner, and Eliason, 1996), reality therapy (Fatout, 1992), and many more. Explorations of a variety of creative forms of engagement in group work from Rap and Hip Hop music (DeCarlo and Hockman, 2003; McFerran, 2004), to poetry (Bordelon, 2006) and artwork are also being added to the group work research base.

Groups such as these can be powerful vehicles for social change. Illustrative of these types of group interventions are empirically based programs such as the Incredible Years (IYS) (Webster-Stratton, 2000), the *SEE* (Support, Empowerment & Education) groups (Ruffalo, Kuhn, and Evans, 2006), and the Second Step Program (Committee for Children, 2008). Each of these comprehensive programs is meant to promote social competence and to prevent and treat behavioral and emotional problems in children of different ages (Webster et al., 2001; Ruffalo et al., 2006). The SEE group model sees the parents and professionals as a partnership, with the parents as experts in living with their children with behavioral problems and professionals as experts in the knowledge base regarding mental illness and behavioral problems (Ruffalo et al., 2006). Parents in each of these child-focused models are educated and empowered to take a leadership role as cofacilitators, partners in the healthy development of their children.

The Second Step Program has curricula for teachers and group leaders to use for preschool-, elementary-school-, and middle-school-aged children. Goals of the program are to help children to develop the proactive skills necessary to be able to manage their emotions, control their anger, prevent bullying, develop problem-solving skills, and handle conflict nonviolently (Committee for Children, 2008; Frey, Nolen, Edstrom, and Hirchstein, 2005; Grossman et al., 1997).

CASE 8.7 | AN APPLICATION OF THE SECOND STEP PROGRAM
by Pat Mullen, MSW, LSW

The Second Step Program is an evidence-based violence prevention curriculum created by the Committee for Children. Participants learn and practice social skills, such as empathy, identifying emotions, problem solving, and managing anger and stress.

The program has been implemented in a very small elementary school in one of the poorest school districts in the state. Two social work student interns and a social worker met with three groups of 17 kindergarten students for half an hour, once a week. Each of the 51 kindergartners received the program for the entire academic year.

The initial session is the most essential in laying the foundation for how the group will proceed. This is where the group's expectations are created and the beginnings of trusting relationships are formed. The children created their set of guidelines for themselves as well as for the facilitators. This critical step takes time and uses the entire session and, sometimes, part of the next one. Everyone has the choice to participate. Once their generation of new suggestions is completed, the group agrees to consolidate the list to five "guidelines to live by," which is more manageable for 4- and 5-year-olds. It is possible that some children did not contribute to the list, but it is crucial that they all "develop a sense of ownership of it, so each child is asked directly, 'Do you agree or disagree to follow these guidelines? Disagreeing is a choice that you have.'"

Children do not always have options from authority figures, especially when it comes to saying "no," so this is an empowering experience, giving them a voice. They are learning to respectfully disagree. Many, as they are asked individually, will disagree.

They are then asked, "Why? Do you think it will be hard for you to....?" If they respond yes, we talk more about it, and as a group we provide ways that can be helpful to him/her. The children are then asked, "What if we help him/her but he/she still can't ...? What do we do?" Children can be quite creative in providing consequences that work, and they are encouraged to do so. They tend to listen to their peers' suggestions. We add these to our list, and the guidelines are reviewed at the beginning of every session thereafter.

Throughout the instructional time, one social worker provides the lesson plan while the other is watching the group. Children are "caught" doing something "good" such as treating another person or thing with respect. The group has defined respect during the creation of the guidelines. Everyone has an opportunity to be "caught," and the workers distribute as many stickers, food treats, and other rewards as possible.

From time to time the social workers will deliberately make a mistake so they can model new behavior by taking responsibility for their actions and presenting alternative ways to apologize for their behavior. It is imperative that the leaders are consistent with the guidelines, rewarding and following through with consequences. This is how trust is developed among members.

The Second Step curriculum introduces a new concept with each lesson, and it is followed throughout the week; the social workers are reinforcing what was learned in that particular lesson and building on previous lessons. The program also incorporates the various learning styles: visual, a large picture of the concept is displayed for all to see and, some lessons are on DVD for viewing for those who need visual assistance; auditory, the facilitator has a dialogue with the audience and is asking questions throughout to help those whose auditory sense is great; and kinesthetic, role playing for those who learn best experientially.

Communicating clearly is the keystone to a successful group experience; know your audience, set an agenda, spends time so that there is agreement among members to the expectations, know the information and admit when you don't know something. People, especially children, can be so forgiving!

John Poulin designed a curriculum, Computer Literacy and After School Services (CLASS), to assist families of older children to develop computer literacy skills while working simultaneously to strengthen the family dynamic and community capacity in terms of mutual aid and support. Patricia Mullen describes the work of the program in the following vignette:

CASE 8.8   THE CLASS PROGRAM

Pat Mullen, MSW, LSW

The CLASS (Computer Literacy and After School Services) Program was created to assist children and adults in gaining computer skills as well as offering a safe haven for children after school hours, 2 days a week. However, there were many other benefits built into the curriculum. Homework assistance, transportation, lunch, snacks, incentives, psychoeducational groups focusing on stress management, self-esteem issues, parenting skills, self-care, conflict resolution/bullying, problem-solving strategies, and communication (as identified by the group) were all facilitated by a team of four: three social work student interns and a licensed social worker. The educational portion of the course was taught by an IT (Information Technology) professional in a state-of-the-art computer lab. Case management and counseling services were also offered during nonprogram hours, which were taken advantage of by many of the families.

This 8-week program focused on a particular population from a new public housing development in a low-income urban community. Most of the participants had previously resided on that site before its reconstruction.

Families consisted of parents, guardians, grandparents, older siblings, aunts, and uncles and their children ranging in ages from 4 to 14 years. Most were single-female-headed households, although several males participated.

Four consecutive 10-week sessions were offered over a 2-year period in which 25 families received new computers after fulfilling all of the program's requirements, of which attendance was primary.

The adults met as a group one afternoon a week, and while eating lunch together, they discussed their many concerns including parenting their children in an unsafe and sometimes violent environment. Many of them were previously acquainted but were getting to know each other intimately through the group, and because they now all lived in the same

neighborhood, they were "joining" together and coming up with their own solutions. They later talked about how this created a stronger sense of community in their newly developed housing environment.

Once the psychoeducational group concluded, they had received instruction in the computer lab beginning with "how do you turn this stupid computer on?" to resume writing, exploring career possibilities, and how to use the Internet. Once their children completed their school day and joined the parent/child group, they met in the computer classroom. This was a very empowering experience, especially for the children since most were more educated in using the computer than their parents. Together they explored the computer, and along with other activities, they created a yearly calendar incorporating pictures of their family and friends that they distributed as gifts. The children met with the Social Workers without their parents the following afternoon. They explored the topics mentioned above while having lots of fun.

At the conclusion of the program, the CLASS participants met with a focus group. Overall, the group was pleased with the program; however, one mother stated, "At first I came here because my family needed a computer. But, after a while I came because it made me feel good to be here. The social workers were kind and I was treated with respect. This doesn't happen often in my life. I still want the computer, though."

At our end-of-program celebration, the adults, clad in cap and gown, preceded to the podium to receive their certificate and computer. This was a very proud moment since most had not graduated from high school.

It is rare that we get the opportunity to see the long-term benefits and changes that our clients make as a result of working with us. But, sometimes if we are fortunate enough, we do. An example is: one of our graduate fathers from the first CLASS

CASE 8.8 | *Continued*

group volunteered his time to work with us in subsequent sessions. While doing a home visit a year after graduation, the social worker viewed the proudly displayed certificate of completion on the television set in the family's living room; years later the social worker received a telephone call from one of the younger members (he had also participated in two summer programs facilitated by the social work team) thanking him for his support. He had graduated from high school, with honors, and would be attending college the following semester.

Fulfilling goals, hope for the future, creating a sense of community, respecting each other, taking ownership, and authentic kindness is what good social work practice is made of. Oh, we need computers, too.

SUMMARY

This chapter discusses the relevance of group work as an aspect of every social worker's practice. Group work pertains to teams and communities working together as well as groups that come together for educational and psychodynamic purposes.

Working with groups is an exciting and dynamic process. When effective, groups can move and affect many people at once, building new social relationships and offering opportunities to change the context of how they see, hear, and know each other.

Understanding the developmental stages that each group undergoes is relevant to the social worker in the roles of group member as well as leader/facilitator. Guiding the group toward attaining its highest developmental level is the primary role of the group leader/facilitator, a goal that is consistent with the strengths-based paradigm of the social work profession.

Knowledge of the stages of the group and the signs that indicate these stages allows the group leader/facilitator to assess the functioning of the group and to choose interventions accordingly. Once the group is working productively, the group leader has a variety of models to choose from, many of them with a growing base of evidence, to enable the group to meet its desired outcomes.

CASE EXAMPLE

Recalling our student Kristina at the beginning of this chapter, the following case illustrates how she employed her social work group skills with thoughtfulness and creativity. Note as you read the vignette how Kirstina integrates the social work practice stage model, addressing the phases of pre-engagement, engagement, and disengagement, with the group dynamics stage model in her group practice.

CASE 8.9 | **GROUP PRACTICE WITH KINSHIP CAREGIVERS**
by Kristina Kennedy, MSW Student

During my spring internship with the agency, I developed and facilitated a support group for kinship caregivers. When it became clear that the group wished to continue beyond the 6-week time frame for the group that I had established to coincide with my internship, I collaborated with another local agency to provide a facilitator and funding for the group so that it could continue.

(Continued)

CASE 8.9 | *Continued*

Pre-Engagement, Assessment of Needs and Agency Fit:

During the fall/winter semester, when I ran the agency's Adopt-A-Family and Adopt-A-Senior Christmas programs, I had identified a significant population of older kin caring for children of relatives. These women provided the rationale leading to the support group and were the first recruits. Most of the caregivers were single women with a median age in their late fifties. These caregivers were all low-income, motivated, compassionate women struggling to meet their own financial, emotional, and health needs as well as the multiple needs of the young children now in their care. By the end of my 6-week tenure, the group consisted of a strong and consistent membership of nine African American women; five grandmothers, two great-grandmothers, one great-aunt, and one aunt. Some of the women had custody of their children, others had informal custody, and one woman had just adopted her three great-nieces and nephew. All together the nine women cared for 22 minor children. I recruited five of the women through three of the agency's Christmas gifts programs and two through the Community Center (an after-school program for children aged 5–15), and two were friends recruited by the members themselves. The women named their group "Arms Wide Open."

Prior to developing the group, I spoke with 15 identified kinship caregivers—all women, mostly African American—on the phone to get a better idea of where these women were coming from and what kind of group might best meet their needs. I invited one of them, "Ann," who had always been very forthcoming in our telephone conversations related to the Adopt-A-Family program, to the agency's office where we spent several hours talking. I used an ethnographic interview approach, asking only enough questions to encourage her to speak about her life, and particularly her life since she took on the responsibility of caring for her niece's three emotionally, physically, and sexually abused young children. After listening to "Ann," I followed up on the phone with the other 14 women already identified through the Christmas programs and the Community Center. Almost all the women spoke of feeling very alone in their caregiving responsibilities—many were older, and some needed to work and/or had health issues. Only a handful of the women were married; one husband was terminally ill, and the other two husbands were unwilling to attend a group with mostly women. Most of the women expressed excitement about a group. Interestingly, they all asked that prayer be an integral part of the group's purpose. Based on these discussions I formulated a list of the women's seven most important criteria for a group: (1) the best time of day for the meeting, (2) gathering and sharing of resources, (3) prayer, (4) providing an opportunity to share with others "in the same boat," (5) getting speakers, (6) child care, and (7) other interests/thoughts. I wanted the group purpose to reflect what these courageous but somewhat isolated and overwhelmed women needed to help them cope with a myriad of practical and emotional problems.

The agency's downtown branch was looking to revitalize its presence in the community, and the kinship caregivers group fit in nicely with its mission of serving the physical, spiritual, and emotional needs of families in need. It also addressed a nationwide trend in which 6 million American children are living in households headed by grandparents or other relatives, 200,000 of them in Pennsylvania.

At the time the group started, the greater community did not have a single functioning kinship group, and the outlying counties had only two very small groups. Before I decided on what group model to use for the kinship support group, I spent many hours on the phone and on the Internet following leads on current and previous grandparent/kinship programs in the area, in Pennsylvania, and elsewhere in the US, focusing primarily on the East Coast. I also considered the option of starting a group that would move toward being peer led. However, according to a professional I interviewed from Washington DC, peer-led kinship groups are difficult to sustain.

Because I had no training with groups or with a particular curriculum, I chose a traditional leader-facilitated support group model focusing on the needs of the clients. I believed that if the clients were given the opportunity to speak, to hear themselves, to feel heard, and to feel supported, they would discover the solutions within themselves.

CASE 8.9 | *Continued*

I believe the early strength of this group stemmed in part from the relationships I had built with many of the members over months of phone conversations. The members recognized my respect for them even before our first group meeting. I also believe that they had developed a high degree of trust in my commitment to honoring them just as they were. I had no agenda to change the women's attitudes or perceptions of their lives as they parented their relatives' children. I was, therefore, careful how I led the group. I saw my leadership role as vital in establishing member rapport, providing a safe environment for honest unpunished disclosure, setting an agenda based on expressed member needs, researching and distributing resource materials, providing babysitting and lunch, but otherwise stepping back and allowing the group members to recognize their own strengths and build a mutual support system.

Engagement/Intervention:
We met once a week on Wednesdays for 2 hours: 1 hour for the meeting and 1 hour for a cooked lunch provided by the agency. From 11 am to 12 noon, we met for the formal portion, conducted in a circle in a cozy corner of the chapel. The meeting covered greetings, prayer, rules (confidentiality, listening/sharing, expectations…), purpose of the group, roles (the members', mine, and that of my coleader and internship supervisor), around-the-circle introductions, personal sharing and responding to sharing, and finally a discussion of resources, before we closed with prayer. Flexibility was the key. If the tone of the meeting indicated a need to focus on personal sharing and support, then we skipped the resource discussion for the day. By the second meeting the group members were taking over responsibility for the prayers and bringing luncheon side dishes. I always looked to the members for their expertise regarding resources before I offered any myself. The lunch time conversation was very free flowing as the women followed up on information shared in group, disclosing some of their difficult situations, asking for resources, offering advice and resources to each other, and generally thoroughly enjoying each other's company.

One or two home-schooled teenaged girls babysat the two to seven preschoolers who attended with their "moms" every week. Although we always checked on the children before we ate lunch ourselves, the babysitters and children ate separately from the adult group members. Lunch was also an opportunity for drop-in visitors to speak to the group informally. After Easter I arranged for the agency's part-time pastor to speak to the group about a mother's/grandmother's special role in a child's life. The director, the Community Center program director, and other agency staff also dropped in briefly to meet and greet the group members. In my 6 weeks with the group, we also used the lunch hour to celebrate three birthdays and a baby shower. The members organized most of what went into the celebrations, again stressing their ownership of the group.

The group was enthusiastic about any kinship-related events that I could offer them through the generosity of the agency, even though it was always last minute because the group was new and unknown. Two of the members were able to attend an all-day out-of-town kinship conference thanks to the agency providing transportation. Four or five members of the group offered to speak at a kinship legislative lobby forum.

In our first meeting I explained that since I was neither African American nor a grandparent caregiver, I could not know their lived experience, but I had learned from others in their situations and I had read a great deal about it. As such I was no expert, but I was committed to listening to them. I also stressed that they, the group members, were the experts on kinship caregiving and that the group belonged to them. My role was to support not direct their process. I appreciated the nods and audible agreement from the members after I stated my position. It helped establish a safe environment for honest disclosure and, importantly, empowered them to find their own meaning for the group.

Once we completed the introductions, I used Talking Paper, as we learned in our practice class, to help the group feel safe in generating responses to two questions: "What is the most rewarding thing about being a grandparent or grandaunt etc.?" and "What is it that I want from a group?"

(Continued)

CASE 8.9 | *Continued*

The responses to the questions were gleaned from their individual response cards. They are summarized as follows:

The Most Rewarding Things about Being a Grandparent/Great Aunt, etc.

Love
They make me laugh
The love she gives me
Being loved
Being happy
When everyone tries to help me with chores at the same time
Just loving them for myself
When they fight to get the seat next to me at church
When the children come and say they love me for no reason
When they give me "the look" if I can make it to their programs at school

Safety
To know she is safe with me
Being safe

Sharing
Sharing their lives
Being with them and their friends
Teaching them about God and they remember it from day to day
They enjoy nice clothes, and when they came to me they didn't have any
Talking to then when they need time out from their parents.

Other wonderful things
Watching them grow
Good English
The break I get on the weekends

What We Want from A Group

Family fun
How to take bus trips
Free things to do with them (kids)

General resources
How to get information (how to use H/burg tele phone book...)
Resources of any kind that will help me
Help with utilities
Financial on-track program or resources
Health care
Knowing my resources

Support and friendship
Maybe someone needs a friend
Support
Love and sharing
Understanding each others' problems
People my age to be friends
Support of grown-ups

Legal issues
Legal rights
Help with legal issues
Custody
After school issues
Doctor's appointments
My rights for children with drug habits—to get help for them
Anything to help for them and me

The group reviewed and approved these summaries during our second meeting. I later hung up the original Talking Paper responses for my final meeting as facilitator for the group. They loved seeing them again and "oohed" and "ahhed," saying "we did that, we did that," as they pointed to their completed goals for the group. It was such a simple but effective tool.

CASE 8.9 | *Continued*

Disengagement/Handing over the group:

When the group decided to continue beyond the original 6 weeks, I contacted a second local agency with whom I had spoken early on in my research process. They agreed to provide a contract facilitator, babysitting, future recruitment, and funding for all those services while my home agency agreed to continue providing the meeting venue and lunch. The second agency already had privately solicited funding to run local support groups for grandparents, and money to provide ancillary support services to these families, but it had been unable to create any support groups of its own. Before I formalized our agreement with the second agency, I invited their contract facilitator, "Belle," to sit in on the last three meetings. She connected quickly with the women and was also committed to the group process continuing as before. Because of her funded contract, "Belle" could also provide the group members with individual support services—assessment of needs, social service connections, medical and psychological referrals, parenting help, individual counseling, etc., all free of charge. Another one of our speakers, an educator, appealed to the "Arms Wide Open" members, and I arranged for her to conduct a 6–12 week Parenting A Second Time Around program (PASTA) (Cornell University, n.d.) in the fall to coordinate with "Belle's" work as support group facilitator.

Support and nurturance for the intern social worker:

Initially I had a lot of doubts about my ability to pull off this project. But I found that by expressing my personal insecurities about leading a group and then getting appropriate feedback and support from my field supervisor, my MSW classmates, and my supervising professor, I benefited from the kind of support I hoped my group would also provide for its members. Because spirituality was a vital piece of this group (a stated need of all group members and part of the agency's mission statement), I spent time in personal prayer, and every Wednesday, prior to our meeting, I asked the agency's part-time pastor to pray with me for the group. Every member of the small agency, including the Board of Directors, knew about the project. I met with some to brainstorm ideas others showed their interest by asking for updates and offering encouragement and praise, and still others assisted in some way with the logistical aspects of the group (cooking, meeting set-up, providing small gifts for the birthdays, etc.). My field supervisor kept me focused and always showed confidence in my ability to carry off the project, cheerleading my efforts and serving as my honest compassionate sounding board.

Discussion Questions

1. What is the relevance of group work to the mission of social work as stated at the start of this chapter?
2. What are the main stages of group development? What are the underlying issues of each stage?
3. What methods and tools could you employ to help the group move through the stages successfully?
4. How would you decide which models and approaches you would use when you start a group?
5. What parallels can you identify between group work and individual work with clients?
6. Why is it so important that the group worker pays particular attention to her or his own process in the group?

References

Barol, B. (1998). *Developing "power-with" leadership through a guided group process: A case study of the Leadership Development Institute*. Ph.D. dissertation, Bryn Mawr College, Graduate School of Social Work and Social Research, United States—Pennsylvania. Retrieved July 16, 2008, from Dissertations & Theses: A&I database (Publication No. AAT 9833078).

Barol, B. (2001). Learning from a person's biography: An introduction to the Biographical Timeline process. *The Pennsylvania Journal on Positive Approaches*, 3(4), 20–30.

Bellack, A. S., (2004). Skills training for people with severe mental illness. *Psychiatric Rehabilitation Journal*, 27, 375–391.

Berman-Rossi, T. (1993). The tasks and skills of the social worker across states of group development. *Social Work with Groups: Expanding Horizons*, 69–81.

Bion, W. R. (1961). Experiences in groups. New York: Basic Books.

Bohm, D. (1992). *Thought as a system*. London: Routledge.

Bordelon, T. D. (2006). A poem to memorialize an experiential focal group. *Clinical Social Work Journal*, 34, 373–385.

Bouis, S., Reif, S., Whetten, K., Scovil, J., Murray, A., and Schwartz, M. (2007). An integrated, multidimensional treatment model for individuals living with HIV, mental illness, and substance abuse. *Health & Social Work*, 32, 268–278.

Brennan, J. (1995). A short-term psycho-educational multiple-family group for bipolar patients and their families. *Social work*, 40, 737–743.

Calhoun, G. B., Bartolomucci, C. L., and McLean, B. A. (2005). Building connections: Relational group work with female adolescent offenders. *Women & Therapy*, 28, 17–29.

Committee for Children, Second Step Program. Retrieved August 4, 2008, from http:www.cfchildren.org/

Corey, M. S. and Corey, G. (2006). *Groups: Process and practice*. (7th ed.). Belmont, CA: Thompson, Brooks/Cole.

Cornell University College of Human Ecology (n.d.) *Parenting in context: New York parenting programs*. Retrieved August 30, 2008 from Cornell University Web site: http://www.parenting.cit.cornell.edu/pp_pasta.html

Cranwell, M., Kolodinsky, J. M., Carsten, G., Schmidt, F. E., Larson, M., and MacLachlan, C. (2007). Short term change in attitude and motivating factors to change abusive behavior of male batterers after participating in a group intervention program based on the pro-feminist and cognitive-behavioral approach. *Journal of Family Violence*, 22, 91–100.

DeCarlo, A., and Hockman, E. (2003). RAP therapy: A group work intervention method for urban adolescents. *Social Work with Groups*, 26(3), 45–59.

Fatout, M. (1992). *Models for Change in Social Group Work*. Edison, NJ: Aldine Transaction.

Focht-New, V. (2004). Expanding our expectations: individual and group counseling as effective therapy with people who have disabilities. In *Positive Approaches* (2004), 6:2, 1–10.

Freire, P. (1984). *Pedagogy of the oppressed*. New York: Continuum.

Frey, K. S., Nolen, S. B., Edstrom, L. V., and Hirchstein, M. K. (2005). Effects of a school-based social-emotional competency program: Linking children's goals, attributions, and behavior. *Journal of Applied Developmental Psychology*, 26, 171–200.

Garland, J., Jones, H., and Kolodnym, R. (1973). A model for stages of development in social work groups. In S. Bernstein (Ed.), *Explorations in group work* (pp. 12–53). Boston: Milford House.

Garrick, D., and Ewashen, C. (2001). An integrated model for adolescent inpatient group therapy. *Journal of Psychiatric & Mental Health Nursing*, 8, 165–171.

Grossman, D. C., Neckerman, H. J., Koepsell, T. D., Liu, P. Y., Asher, K. N., Beland, K., Frey, K., and Rivara, F. P. (1997). Effectiveness of a violence prevention curriculum among children in elementary school: A randomized controlled trial. *Journal of the American Medical Association*, 277, 1605–1611.

Hall, C. S., and Lindsey, G. (1978). *Theories of personality* (3rd ed.). New York: John Wiley & Sons.

Hopmeyer, E., and Werk, A. (1994). A comparative study of family bereavement groups. *Death Studies*, 18, 243–256.

LaFountain, R. M., Garner, N. E., and Eliason, G. T. (1996). Solution-focused counseling groups: A key for school counselors. *School Counselor*, 43(4), 256–267.

Little, J. (2006). Harm reduction therapy groups: Engaging drinkers and drug users in the process of change. *Journal of Groups in Addiction and Recovery*, 1, 69–93.

Mappin, R., and Hanlon, D. (2005). Description and evaluation of a bereavement group for people with learning disabilities. *British Journal of Learning Disabilities*. 33, 106–112.

McFerran, S. K. (2004). Using songs with groups of teenagers: How does it work? *Social Work with Groups*, 27, 143–157.

McWhirter, P. T. (2006). Community therapeutic intervention for women healing from trauma. *The Journal for Specialists in Group Work, 31*(4), 339–351.

Morrison, S. A., and Lambert, M. (1996). A treatment outcome study of bereavement groups for children. *Child and Adolescent Social Work Journal, 13*(1), 3–21.

NASW (1996, revised 1999) Code of ethics of the National Association of Social Workers. Retrieved July 27, 2008 from http://www.socialworkers.org/pubs/Code/code.asp

Peck, S. M. (1987). *A different drum.* New York: Simon & Schuster.

Perls, F., Hefferline, R., and Goodman, P. (1980). *Gestalt therapy.* Toronto, Canada: Bantam Books.

Powell, D. J. (2006). Men in groups: Insights and interventions. *Journal of Groups in Addiction & Recovery, 1,* 95–116.

Ruffolo, M. C., Kuhn, M. T., and Evans, M. E. (2006). Developing a parent-professional team leadership model in group work: Work with families and children experiencing behavioral and emotional problems. *Social Work, 51*(1), 39–47.

Scheidlinger, S. (2004). Group psychotherapy and related helping groups today: An overview. *American Journal of Psychotherapy, 58,* 265–280.

Sigman, M., and Hassan, S. (2006). Benefits of long-term group therapy to individuals suffering schizophrenia: A prospective 7 year study. *Bulletin of the Menninger Clinic, 70,* 273–282.

Steen, S., Kaffenberger, C. J. (2007). Integrating academic interventions into small group counseling in elementary school. *Professional School Counseling, 10,* 516–519.

Taft, C. T., Murphy, C. M., Musser, P. H., and Remington, N. A. (2004). Personality, interpersonal, and motivational predictors of the working alliance in group cognitive-behavioral therapy for partner violence. *Journal of Counseling and Clinical Psychology, 72,* 329–354.

Thun, D., Sims, P. L., Adams, M. A., and Webb, T. (2002). Effects of group therapy on female adolescent survivors of sexual abuse: A pilot study. *Journal of Child Sexual Abuse, 11*(4), 1–16.

Tomasulo, D. (2000). Group therapy for people with mental retardation. In R. Fletcher (Ed.), *Therapy approaches for persons with mental retardation* (pp. 65–85). New York: NADD Press.

Tomalsulo, D., Keller, E., and Pfadt, A. (1995). The healing crowd: Process, content and technique issues in group counseling for people with mental retardation. *The Habilitative Mental Healthcare Newsletter, 12,* 43–50.

Tuckman, B. (1965). Developmental sequence in small groups. *Psychological Bulletin, 63,* 384–399.

Waldron, H. B., and Kaminer, Y. (2004). On the learning curve: the emerging evidence supporting cognitive-behavioral therapies for adolescent substance abuse. *Addiction, 99,* 93–105.

Wasowk, M. (1986). Support groups for family caregivers of patients with Alzheimer's disease. *Social Work, 31,* 93–97.

Washington, O. G. M., and Moxley, D. P. (2003). Group interventions with low-income African American women recovering from chemical dependency. *Health & Social Work, 28,* 146–156.

Webster Stratton, C. (2000). The Incredible Years training series. *Juvenile Justice Bulletin.* U.S. Department of Justice Office of Juvenile Justice and Delinquency Programs. NCJ 173422. pp.1–23. Retrieved August 28, 2008, from http://www.ncjrs.gov.pdffiles1/ojjdp/173422.pdf

Wolfson, J., and Fowkes, S. (2007). *Talking paper: An overview.* Unpublished manuscript. Canberra, Australia.

Yalom, I. D. (1985). *The theory and practice of group psychotherapy.* New York: Basic.

9

GENERALIST PRACTICE WITH ORGANIZATIONS

Stephen Kauffman

Spencer Grant/PhotoEdit

Lucy P. couldn't have been happier about her first job as a social worker. Not only had she found her "dream job" just a few weeks after completing her MSW, but the location, type of clients, salary, and benefits were all exactly what she was looking for. And perhaps most importantly, the agency had an outstanding reputation in its field of practice.

But from the very first week at the agency, things seemed strained. Case files for her new caseload were incomplete or missing, and no one seemed to have any idea where they might be. Further, many of her coworkers, although quite kind and helpful to her, often appeared distracted or "edgy." And to top things off, her direct supervisor, whom Lucy had looked forward to working with and learning from, quit on Lucy's third day.

Over the next 2 weeks, things only got more difficult. Staff increasingly stayed in their offices with their doors closed, making it very hard for Lucy to ask for guidance... And her new supervisor, a long-term employee of the agency, also quit only 4 days after her promotion. Even the clients seemed to be more and more stressed out, with angry outbursts in the halls and increasing numbers of missed appointments.

Increasingly, Lucy began to question whether this was really her dream job after all. As a new employee, she didn't feel she had the power to bring these issues to the attention of the administration—after all, she was still on probation. And reflecting back on one of her social work classes, she worried that maybe the whole problem was with the administration. If it was, what could she do? What questions, and whom, could she ask? And then finding out the answers, what could she do?

A strong argument can be made, with little exaggeration, that humanity's current condition—for good and ill—is due to the actions and power of organizations. It is in and through organizations that most of the work we do is accomplished. Even when we can identify a single person as important or powerful enough to impact our world, it is still organizations that do much of the actual work that accomplishes the vision of that person. Think about our progress in civil rights. How much longer, for example, would it have taken minorities and women to achieve the hopes and desires of a person like Dr. Martin Luther King without the support of organizations like the National Association for the Advancement of Colored People (NACCP), the Southern Christian Leadership Conference (SCLC), or even the Supreme Court of the United States? Or more problematically, would the insights of people like Albert Einstein be translated into working nuclear weapons without a "Manhattan Project" to do the work? In these, and thousands of other cases, it is the power of organizations that make dreams real.

It is therefore not a long leap to understanding why organizations are of such concern to social workers. Most simply, organizations are where we do the work that we do. But what are organizations? How do they operate? Are there differences between social service agencies and other types of organizations? And how do they fit into our model of strengths-based social work practice?

Some of the answers are easy. An organization is most basically defined as "a group of people intentionally organized to accomplish an overall, common goal or set of goals" (McNamara, n.d., p. 1). In other words, they are a collection of people who work together to achieve a purpose that all of the members share. And the types of purposes are as vast as there are human dreams. Indeed, there are virtually no limits to what the goals of an organization may be, including the whole range of possibilities from simply "getting-together," to directing the actions of nations. The concern of most social work practitioners, however, is usually a bit narrower. The goals and purposes of social workers are most often with organizations that are designed to meet or help people meet some need, or perhaps to develop some skill so that the person him/herself may meet a need.

Another way of looking at this is to think of organizations as the mediating systems between a person and fulfillment of a need. We will examine this problem of needs in greater detail later, but for now it is most important to understand that organizations do not automatically function perfectly in that role. Organizations, like any other systems, sometimes work well, and sometimes they do not. Thus, the social worker may have a range of tasks in their contact with organizations. As a worker within the organization, simply helping the organization to meet its goals may be sufficient. But when the organization is weakened, the role of the social worker may be to intervene with the organization as a client. Therefore, it is essential that generalist social workers develop a range of skills that will allow them to both effectively work *within* an organizational context and work *with* an organization as the client system.

Further, it is essential—almost critical—that all of the ethical principles and micro-practice skills that are infused in this book and much of what you have learned about social work practice be employed in your work with organizations. It should be clear by now that organizations are comprised of people, and in the case of the social service agency, the consumers are most often people. As such, the problems and opportunities that we face in any practice context apply here. Issues of communication, power and empowerment, emotions, conflict, cognitions, and use of self all apply at various times. Building trust (Homan, 2008) is always essential in macro-practice efforts. Do not fall into the trap that occasionally affects the unenlightened macro-practitioner that goes something like this. "I'm concerned with *issues*. I can't waste my effort on *people*!"

Similarly, the strengths-based principles that frame this book and the strengths-based model of generalist practice apply here as well as with any other client system. A focus on strengths, collaboration, resources, and opportunities underlie all of the skills and assumptions presented here. As Irving and Young (2002) stress, social work practice includes our attitude and stance—not just our skills.

So now, when you consider Lucy P's problem, you may begin to see why the organization may be so very important. If agency staff are stressed, or if staff turnover increases, among a large number of other problems, a real concern has to be raised about how well the agency is able to help meet client needs.

This chapter will focus primarily on seeing the organization as a client system, and helping the social worker, one just like Lucy P., develop the skills necessary to do so. Yet even with this perspective of "organization as client" will come a number of insights that are useful in the process of using an organization to achieve a desired outcome or intervention. To help you work with organizations as clients, the chapter will begin with a review of various theories of organizations—including some indicators of a well-functioning organization. Then, the chapter will follow the basic practice model outlined in previous chapters. Thus, by the end of this chapter, you should be able to help Lucy:

1. Understand the importance, purposes, and types of organizations
2. Understand the components, structures, and processes of organizations
3. Use the above knowledge to develop and apply appropriate and effective assessment methods and tools
4. Develop and apply an appropriate organizational intervention plan, including goals
5. Monitor and assess the intervention, and
6. Successfully terminate the relationship

PRE-ENGAGEMENT

The pre-engagement phase of working with an organization shares many of the components of the generalist practice model with any other client system. The tasks of studying, asking, listening and clarifying all work together to assist in meeting the goals of this phase of a thorough assessment of the current condition of the organization, as well understanding of the organization's strengths and issues of concern. Through a collaborative process of assessment and analysis, the target problem and its causes are examined and determined. And often, as is found with other client systems, the use of structured assessment tools may greatly assist in this process.

Though most components of the pre-engagement phase are near perfect reflections of what happens with other client systems, there are, however, two characteristics to the pre-engagement phase that may be somewhat different from other client systems. As such, they may require careful consideration by the social worker. First of all, an organization is a true system. It is comprised of many—and perhaps very many—different individuals, or even groups of individuals. Each of these individuals (or groups), as important interrelated components of the system (Brill and Levine, 2005), may see and react to the same phenomena somewhat differently. To the degree that the members of these different groups see things the same way, we may be able to organize them by interests, hence the term "interest groups." Each of these interest groups may be thought of as a *constituency*. And while it may not be necessary to consider every unique *individual's* perspective in an organizational assessment or treatment plan, it is often critical that each of the different constituencies' perspectives be included. Figure 9.1 lists the different constituencies typically involved in an organization and shows some of the concerns of each.

Indeed, it may be useful to think of the organization in terms of these multiple constituencies as being a characteristic of its very existence. For example, in recent years, the problems that schools face have suggested the need and value of reframing schools as "learning organizations," that embrace the collaborative team work of faculty and staff (Senge et al., 2000). Perhaps even students could have a role in the mix.

A second aspect of organizations that could differentiate them from other types of client systems is the social worker/client boundary. In the example of

Organizational Constituencies	Typical Organizational Tasks and Concerns	
Staff	Organizational Tasks	Organizational Concerns
• Administration	Policy development, planning, personnel, resource development and acquisition, compliance with external (and legal) requirements, setting organizational tone, and leadership.	• Organizational functioning • Quality of services • Resource adequacy • Legal compliance • External perceptions
• Supervisors	Translate policies from the administration to the *front line*, communicate information both up and down the chain of command, oversee job function, and provide guidance to the front line worker.	• Administrative support • Quality of services • Resource adequacy • Front line compliance
• Direct care staff	Varies by organization—carrying out the primary work of the organization	• Administrative and supervisory support • Workload • Clarity of job tasks • Resource and equipment adequacy • Client compliance
• Support staff	Varies by position—support front line by reducing distractions to agency tasks	• Administrative and supervisory support • Workload • Resource and equipment adequacy
Clients	Targets of agency efforts	• Quality of services • Cost/ability to pay • Sufficient numbers
Community members (including client family members)	Support for organizational needs	• Resource support • Concerns about negative effects of clients • Quality of service outcomes

FIGURE 9.1 | COMMON ORGANIZATIONAL CONSTITUENCIES

Lucy described previously, it would seem that some ambiguity exists between Lucy as potential practitioner and Lucy as a client vis-à-vis her position as an employee. So, it is a very important question to ask at a very early point in the process, "should an employee of the organization also be the practitioner/intervener?" Or should an effort be made to bring in someone from the outside? As a new employee, would Lucy be able to work to improve the agency, even if she were well trained, and would the organizations constituencies take her seriously?

Unfortunately, there is no easy answer here, in part because of resources. There are very few social work agencies that provide free or low-cost services to work with *organizational client systems*. At the same time, many organizations, particularly those in the human services, have few extra disposable dollars necessary for organizational care. Thus, it might fall on someone like Lucy to actually provide the services for the benefit of the organization.

ASSESSMENT

As organizations so readily serve as the intermediary between citizens and need fulfillment, concern with organizational function becomes all the more important. The key to a good assessment is knowing what represents optimal functioning of the organization. Yet, at the same time, there is no "one best way" to construct an organization to meet all desired ends. Organizations may be structured in any one of a number of ways, each of which may be effective at achieving the goals of the organization under some conditions but at the same time may be problematic at other times. This is certainly one reason for learning as much as possible about *organizational theory*. But this is also another argument supporting the collaborative involvement of the various groups or "constituencies" that make up the organization. These may variously include line staff, supervisors, support staff, administration, clients, and external collaborators. Each typically has their own set of needs and perceptions about the organization, and thus each will have something valuable to contribute to the assessment.

It may be helpful to think of your own work experience—or even your experience as a social work student. Are your needs and concerns as an entry-level employee the same as your supervisor's? Or as the Director's? Or as the supplier's? Or as the customer's? Probably not. Each of these positions sees the organization a little differently, and in those differences are valuable clues about the truth. As the strengths-based practice model strongly suggests, assessment methods need to be collaborative, based in dialogue, and *inclusive*. There may be four, five, or even more distinct constituencies. Each one may have something important to contribute, and as such, inclusiveness is vital.

THE STARTING POINT—SOMETHING'S WRONG

Assessment doesn't exist in a vacuum. Organizations, like any system, may be dysfunctional for years before there is a call for help. Sometimes, the problems are serious, even life-threatening for the organization, but if no one has the vision, or the courage (or power) to bring the threat to the surface, little or nothing can be done.

Indeed, some models of organizational change suggest that there must be an acknowledgement that a problem exists—at least among the constituencies that have the "power" to effect change—as the starting point. Horwath and Morrison (2000) have built a 10-step model of change. These are:

1. Acknowledge the need for change
2. Establish agency and interagency ownership of the change agenda

3. Assess current strengths and weaknesses
4. Identify what changes are needed
5. Identify how best to make the changes
6. Formulate a critical pathway for change
7. Establish organizational infrastructure for improved practice
8. Consolidate, maintain, and integrate changes
9. Monitor and review changes
10. Evaluate organizational and interagency learning from the changes for future use

Again, in these models, the first step is acknowledging that a problem exists. But what are indicators that problems exist? And when does a problem become serious enough to warrant attention and intervention? At least a partial answer to these questions rests in understanding what an organization is, what it does, and how it does whatever it does.

WHAT TO ASSESS

Because organizational systems are different from individual and family systems, a very important first step is learning the components of these systems. One simple model classifies these components into three domains. These are (1) organizational identity, (2) internal characteristics, and (3) environmental characteristics. From each of these groupings are found many elements that strengthen and support the organization, or act as stressors or obstacles to optimal functioning.

If the assessment is done well, stresses on the organization may be identified and addressed quickly and effectively, and the strengths of the organization may be channeled to assist in the organizational intervention. Such problems and strengths may have their source internally with the identity, or structure and processes that guide the organization, or externally and associated with some component of the environment. Examples of internal concerns may include supervisor support (Glisson and Durick, 1988; Poulin and Walter, 1992; Poulin and Walter, 1993; Silver, Poulin, and Manning, 1997). Similarly, examples of external stressors that have occurred in recent years may include changes in funding, client demographics (Schmid, 2004), and the need to be more multicultural in perspective (Hyde, 2004). Figure 9.2 shows the elements that commonly are found in each of these domains.

ORGANIZATIONAL IDENTITY

Organizational Identity refers to all of the elements of organizations that are commonly used to classify or describe organizations. Some of these are straightforward and easy to understand. Among these are: (1) *size*, meaning the number of staff, customers, or transactions; (2) *age*, or how long the organization has been in operation; (3) *location*; (4) auspice as *governmental vs. nongovernmental*—commonly referred to as an N.G.O., a nongovernmental organization, or (5) religious affiliation.

Other identity variables, however, require some explanation. For example, one common distinction in organizations is between *formal* and *informal* types. The

Organizational Identity	Internal Organizational Considerations			Environmental Considerations
	Foundation Policies	*Internal Structure*	*Internal Processes*	
Size of organization	Vision	Administration	Power authority	Client characteristics
Age	Mission	Boards of trustees	Leadership	Community support
Location	Goals	Executive directors	Information communication	Legal/policy environment
Auspice- Governmental vs. nongovernmental	Objectives	Supervision (Middle line)	Technology	Cultural environment
Religious affiliation Faith-based	Constitutions and by-laws	Front line	Skills	
For-profit vs. nonprofit	Strategic plans		Norms	
			Policies	
			Programs	
			Conflict	

FIGURE 9.2 | COMMON ASSESSMENT VARIABLES

difference here is reasonably straightforward. Formal organizations have a defined, typically legally recognized basis, and a fabricated and articulated structure and process of authority and decision making. In other words, they are legally recognized, and many of their components and procedures are written down and guided by rules.

Informal organizations, on the other hand, often evolve organically, without the legally recognized structure and process or articulated rules. Informal organizations often evolve when no formal organization is present, or if the formal organization is seen as slow and unresponsive. Thus, both are important, and informal characteristics are often found even within formal organizations. In fact, some types of informal activity, such as communication outside of formal structures, may in some cases be the source, or solution, of some types of problems.

Another common distinction is between *nonprofit* and *for-profit* organizations. This distinction is based upon a United States' Internal Revenue Service (IRS) classification of the organization, typically between the nonprofit groups (identified as 501(c) groups by the United States' code), and for-profit corporations, partnerships, and sole-proprietorships. Although there many similarities between the two types, and many nonprofits often act like for-profits (which sometimes leads to confusion as to which is which), there are some very important differences that are at the root of the distinction.

For example, although both types may actually make profits (meaning they can make money on transactions or investments), what happens to those earnings differs. For-profit organizations may distribute their earnings in any way, or to anyone, the owners choose. On the other hand, nonprofit organizations may only use their earnings to support their mission or to support the organization. Profits may be used to pay salaries, but any monies left after all the bills are paid remain with the organization—they are not distributed.

The key to this difference is ownership. For-profit organizations have legally identifiable owners or shareholders, and the organization exists to make money for the benefit of the owners. But there is a trade-off. As a consequence of distributed gains, profits and assets are taxable to federal, state, and local governments. Nonprofit organizations, however, do not have owners in the same way. Instead, the nonprofit has "stewards" or caretakers, and the organization is in existence for the benefit of society. In exchange for this social benefit, almost all taxes are waived.

Considering all types of nonprofits—both nongovernmental organizations (NGOs) such as schools, foundations, social service agencies, churches, hospitals, and governmental entities—the numbers are staggering. In 2004, over 300,000 501(c) 3 and 4 organizations filed informational returns with the IRS, with combined total revenue of 1.2 *trillion* dollars (Arnsberger, 2007). And these were of the *formal* type with incomes greater than $25,000 only—small and *informal* community groups are not included. Ignoring income and counting just the formal alone, the number in 2006 jumped to 1,478,194 nonprofit organizations of all types (charities, foundations, and similar groups) (Urban Institute, 2008).

Traditionally, in the US, most social service organizations (with some very important exceptions, such as many physicians' or social workers' practice partnerships) have been nonprofit. Most still are. But an increasing number in a variety of areas have transitioned to the for-profit arena in recent years, largely because of a belief that money can be made in these areas. Hospitals, for example, experienced a trend in the movement during the 1980s and 90s, with some areas of the US, such as the south and west, at the forefront (Collins, Gray, and Hadley, 2001). At the same time, other systems saw transitions from the nonprofit to for-profit arena, including education and criminal justice. And most recently, opportunities to make money have been found in services to the poor as the result of the so-called "welfare reform" legislation, as highlighted by Mulroy and Tamburo (2004) in a comprehensive review of the literature of the Personal Responsibility and Work Opportunity Reconciliation Act of 1996 (PRWORA).

While a full debate about the advantages and disadvantages of this movement isn't appropriate here, the central argument used in favor of the transition is one of efficiency and competition. Many people believe that the drive for profit will keep costs and waste down, and quality will improve as providers compete for consumers. On the other hand, many people mistrust profit-making services, believing that quality will suffer, and that those persons least able to pay will receive the fewest services.

Other trends have had an impact on social service organizations. For example, in recent years, one particular type of nonprofit NGO, the *faith-based organization* (FBO), has received a significant amount of attention. These are organizations that are rooted in one religious tradition or another. Although NGOs with a religious linkage are almost as old in the United States as European colonization itself, generally (and historically) these organizations have had difficulty in accessing some types of government funding due to constitutional church–state restrictions. With the rise to power of the so-called "religious right" over the past two decades, some of the restrictions have been removed through legislative and administrative efforts, although the legality of governmental funding for these organizations is still an open question.

Any or all of these identity variables are important to an organizational assessment. Consider for a moment the opportunities and obstacles that are provided when, as is increasingly common, control of an organization transitions from a nonprofit to a for-profit identity.

INTERNAL ORGANIZATIONAL CONSIDERATIONS

Beyond the issues of identity, a large number of elements are associated with the *internal* characteristics of the organization that need to be included in the assessment. These characteristics can be placed into three groupings—**foundation policies, internal structure**, and **internal processes**. Elements from each grouping must be examined for their possible usefulness as strengths to the organization or their possibility as serving as an obstacle or stressor to the organization.

Foundation Policies.   Foundation policies refer to the documents and guidelines (generally written) that give meaning and guidance to the agency. Organizations exist for a purpose, and these policies express both this purpose, as well as a description of the overarching structure and processes of the organization. At the same time, simply because something is written does not mean it is followed, and it may be that this disconnect between what is written and what is real may cause some of the organizations' difficulties. The most important types of foundation policies are the **constitution and by-laws, vision, mission, goals, and strategic plans.**

The constitution *and* by-*laws* lay out the "fundamental principles which govern an organization, and the bylaws establish the specific rules of guidance by which the group is to function. All but the most informal groups should have their basic structure and methods of operation in writing" (Holden Leadership Center, n.d., p. 1). In other words, these documents provide the "big picture," and through them the agency has firm guidance about what it is, why it is, and how it is supposed to do it.

Of course, in truth, most staff, and even many administrators, often will know little (if anything) of the minutiae contained within these documents. Such documents tend to be legalistic, and much of the content is concerned with legal issues. But these are nevertheless the ultimate guides for action, and the further the agency strays from the rules and procedures established in them, the more likely problems will evolve.

What staff and administrators may be more familiar with, as they are generally less legalistic—but are at the same time statements that further articulate the "why" of the organization, are the **Vision** and the **Mission** of the organization.

A *Vision* is a statement of the future that the organization seeks to create. The *Mission*, on the other hand, "describes the overall purpose of the organization or program, and tells what makes your program unique. It distinguishes the mission of the organization/program from other organizations/programs" (New Jersey Commission on Higher Education Educational Opportunity Fund, 2006, p. 4?).

These two statements, along with the **goals**, or statements of your agency's targets or desired accomplishments, and the **objectives**, which are specific and measurable aims of the organization, serve a critical function. Ideally, they point everyone in the same direction. They provide both the value basis for the organization, as well as tangible targets for the organization. And in so doing, they give meaning to the work. Without them, however, or without concurrence and/or shared beliefs in these powerful statements, the agency may tend to drift. This, for workers, may result in a lack of meaning and/or direction. In either case, staff may cease to care.

A further possible scenario returns us to the necessity of collaborative focus. When the organizational vision or other aspects of definition are not shared, but rather imposed in what may be viewed as an illegitimate way, employees may experience anger and frustration. This is not to say that *visions* may not change over time; they do. But when a new *vision* is created, the organization will greatly benefit when the creation is the result of a common, collective process instead of a single individual. This collective visioning will help build ownership and enhance the sense of meaning that comes from participation.

The last of these foundational documents are what are known as **strategic plans**. Strategic plans are rooted in all of the policies discussed above, but the document converts these into plans of action. "That is, a strategic plan is a road map to lead an organization from where it is now to where it would like to be in five or ten years" (Special Libraries Association, 1997, p. 1). As such, it operationalizes the ideas from the vision, mission and goals, while adding an environmental context—it interprets the ideas and provides thoughts and guideposts through the organization's world. As such, the strategic plan is a critically valuable component of organizations, and one that aids in both the maximization of opportunity and the minimization of risk for nonprofit organizations (Steen and Smith, 2007). How to develop a strategic plan will be discussed later in the chapter.

Internal Structure.   The structure of an organization varies dramatically by the purposes of the organization, but there are some commonalities that cross-cut most types. Simply stated, these are the **administration, front line workers**, as well as a large variety of **support staff**. In a somewhat more complex vein, Mintzburg (1983) classifies each structural element by its relationship to the primary task of the organization. Those whose work is directly associated with the primary function (which he calls the **operating core**) include the **strategic apex** (administration), the middle line (supervisors), and the front line (workers). He then breaks supportive employees into two clusters, support staff and the technostructure.

The central questions that an assessment should focus on here relate to the qualifications and skill of each of the positions in these structural components, as well as how staff are supported and/or how the work responsibilities create burdens for the staff. A short description of each of these components and their responsibilities is provided below.

**Vision, Mission, Goals and Objectives of Seven Arrows,
a Community Substance Abuse Treatment Agency**

Vision

The community we see is one in which all persons are free and empowered to make their own life choices, supported by caring families, neighbors, institutions, and government. All people are able to make these choices in part because they are free from the pain of addiction or unhealthy forms of dependence, but able to receive the care and treatment they need, without fear of punishment, stigma, or discrimination should life's pathways lead them in other directions.

Mission

It is the mission of Seven Arrows to provide effective, compassionate, ethically sound, and stigma-free substance abuse treatment to all persons who suffer from the pain of addiction or unhealthy forms of dependence. We seek to provide our services to all persons in need, without regard to age, gender, race/ethnicity, sexual orientation, or past experience. We will also seek a variety of funding sources so that no person will be turned away from treatment due to inability to pay.

Goals and Objectives

Goal 1: Seven Arrows will provide a variety of effective, evidence-based substance abuse treatment services, both inpatient and outpatient, to all persons in need in the North Hills region.

> *Objective 1.1*: To provide inpatient, residential treatment services to a minimum of 250 clients per year.
> *Objective 1.2*: To provide methadone maintenance services for a maximum of 500 clients per year.
> *Objective 1.3*: To provide outpatient counseling services for a maximum of 1000 clients per year.

Goal 2: Seven Arrows will achieve the highest standards of quality through support of staff, nondiscriminatory practices, and community involvement.

> *Objective 2.1*: Seven Arrows will provide a minimum of 100 hours of advanced training to each staff member each year.
> *Objective 2.2*: Staff satisfaction will be maximized by establishing a benefits package, customized for each employee, that will include health and dental care, retirement plans, and rotating sabbaticals for all full-time employees.
> *Objective 2.3*: To establish a Community Advisory Board to assist the agency in developing policies that help the agency better meet community needs.

FIGURE 9.3 | EXAMPLES OF THE VISION, MISSION, GOALS, AND OBJECTIVES OF A COMMUNITY SUBSTANCE ABUSE TREATMENT AGENCY

The support staff are employees who perform duties that directly support the operating core and/or help to maintain the organization. This includes such staff as secretaries, maintenance staff, lunchroom workers, accountants, lawyers, and bookkeepers. Again, their task is to do everything possible to free up the front line workers so that they may do the primary work of the organization without being distracted by cleaning, ordering supplies, and complying with legal organizational paperwork. Of course, most social service agencies have at least a few of these types of employees—often a secretary and a maintenance worker or two.

The other type of supportive employees is what is known as the technostructure. This class of employees is concerned with ensuring the highest quality of work. As such, they may include quality assurance and research and development staff. In most social service agencies, especially smaller ones, the actual number of these are quite small. At best, an agency may hire a part-time person or consultants to provide services such as program evaluation or IT support. Otherwise, these duties are often absorbed by other staff, usually by an administrator.

Thus, most social workers are in the administration, middle line, or front line positions. These are the workers who are most concerned with the primary tasks of the organization, whatever they may be. Generally, administrators are concerned with the overall functioning of the organization. This often includes policy development, planning, personnel, resource development and acquisition, compliance with external (and legal) requirements, as well as leadership and setting the tone of the organization. We will discuss much of this later when we address leadership in greater detail, but for now, it is critical to understand that each of those tasks are critical to not only the survival of the organization, but how they are done and the spirit of the administrator is a powerful determinant in the tone or feel of the organization. In other words, the administration sets the informal climate of the organization. A climate where workers feel supported can do a long way to overcoming the stress that is created by clients or the environment that the organization rests. On the other hand, a climate that feels oppressive, uncaring may make even pleasant work tasks feel stressful.

Supervisors (the middle line), on the other hand, serve as intermediaries between the administration and the front line. Their task in the human service organization is to translate policies from the administration to the *front line*, communicate information both up and down the chain of command, oversee job function, and provide guidance to the front line worker. The quality by which these functions are carried out may be a source of either serious problems for the organization, and/or its greatest successes. The assumption is that the supervisor understands both the needs and problems of the front line worker, while also understanding the work requirements of the administration.

Finally, the front line represents the employee who is most responsible for carrying out the primary tasks of the organization. In social service agency settings, this usually applies to working with people in some form. The tasks of the front line are vastly different depending upon the agency's function, so it is somewhat difficult to provide any generalities. It is, however, critical to consider their training, education, preparedness, and support. The quality of their work is a function of their ability, resources, and workload.

Internal Processes.   How the staff and structure operate represent the final element of the internal organizational considerations. These are what are called the **processes,** or what Mintzburg (1976) calls a "system of flows" between the structural components. And the importance of these flows cannot be overstated, for it is how these function that very often proves to be the most problematic concerns for an organization. Among these, the most well known are **power** (and its manifestations as authority and leadership, and the skill of management) and **information** (and its manifestation as communication).

Power.   Every organization demonstrates some degree of applied power. It is this applied power that ensures that the right work is done in the right amount at the right time. This form of power is what people refer to as *authority*, or the degree and type of control exerted within the organization. This control may be formal, legitimate (meaning "legal" or "rightful"), and identifiable, or it may be less obvious and/or informal (meaning distinct from the structure) organizational control. Over the years, many thinkers and researchers have examined *authority*, and as such different types have been identified. Allen (1998, 2002) has included the following types:

- **Line authority**, which is the hierarchical control from administrator to supervisor to worker. Sometimes this is thought of as the *chain of command*. How many employees a supervisor has authority over is known as the *span of control*.
- **Staff authority** is more advisory. Here, employees are permitted greater autonomy to make decisions, and supervisors serve as advisors and/or educators or providers of technical assistance.
- **Team authority** is authority that is granted to groups of employees who are empowered to make many decisions.

How this authority is applied, in what settings, and to what degree need to be considered. Authority that is used correctly and judiciously will be a positive for the organization, while incorrectly applied may damage or hurt the organization. Most particularly, authority is necessary to motivate staff to move the organization in the desired direction. This is a function of **leadership**. Staff may work to achieve organizational goals without some form of external authority, but the odds of success are greatly improved in the presence of a good leader. The problem is that after literally hundreds, perhaps thousands, of studies on leadership, differences still exist on what comprises a good or a poor leader. This is, however, no arcane concern. Organizational assessments very often find that the problems that exist in the social service agency are closely connected to the quality of the leadership provided, and how well the leader manages the agency. Thus, a good assessment will spend time examining the quality of leadership.

So what comprises a good leader? Lamb and McKee (2004) identified 75 different but critical characteristics to a good leader! But among these, trust in the leader was the highest predictor of employee satisfaction, and the ability to communicate important information engendered the highest levels of trust. Focusing more directly on human service organizations, Brody (2005) identified a number of variables that may contribute to effective management. These include a future orientation, social entrepreneurship, treating staff with dignity, effective communication, engendering trust, and inspiration. Brody (2005) also identified a number of flawed leadership styles, which include micromanagement, obliviousness, arrogance, and the loner. Consider the different case examples in Figure 9.4.

Each of these three examples represents a potential leadership problem. What, in your opinion, was the problem? What do you think could be done about it?

Interestingly, for any problems in administration and leadership in social service agencies, there may be a degree of "fault" associated with the profession of

---

Example 1: Jonna consistently sees clients who would benefit from weekend hours, when the agency is closed. Looking at her personal schedule over time, she sees that if her director would allow her to take Mondays off, she would be able to come into the agency on Saturdays. She has brought this to the attention of her director at least five times over the last 3 months. Each time, her director has told her, "We will talk about it." To date, they have not.

Example 2: Mark C. has found that clients are increasingly using computers to access information about services and coming to him knowing a great deal more than even a year or two ago. Mark wrote a well-reasoned memo to his director about expanding the agency's web presence. A week later he received a written response, which in its entirety said, "No. And remember, I make the policy decisions around here."

Example 3: It seemed like everything that Paula wrote and placed in her clients' files had comments from her new director attached to them. Most of these comments were suggestions on how to rewrite what had been written. Paula never worried about useful supervision, but since the new director had started at the agency, it seemed that everything, even confidential memos, were being examined and commented on.

FIGURE 9.4 | EXAMPLES OF LEADERSHIP

---

social work and in social work education. As writers like Wuenschel (2006) and Patti (2000) have pointed out, many more social workers have some administrative responsibility as compared to graduation with an administrative concentration in their education. This might therefore result in some limitation in administrative and leadership skills, while at the same time large percentages of administrators come from outside the profession, with very limited social work experience (Wuenschel, 2006).

In summary, all of the characteristics of a great leader may have been identified almost 1500 years ago. In the words of Lao Tzu,

> A leader is best
> When people barely know that he exists,
> Not so good when people obey and acclaim him,
> Worst when they despise him.
> "Fail to honor people, they fail to honor you"
> But of a good leader, who talks little,
> When his work is done, his aim fulfilled,
> They will say, "We did this ourselves." (Lao Tzu, p. 34)

Information.   Along with authority, a second internal process is **information**, and how this information is communicated. An organization cannot function without the free flow of information both up and down the structure. At a minimum, information about what to be done, when, and to what specifications must be clearly communicated to employees, while problems, opportunities, and needs must flow to supervisors and administrators.

But a number of obstacles can affect the flow of communication, and as with leadership, a major focus of an organizational assessment should be on communication. To begin with, as with authority, the differences between formal and informal communication require attention. In a perfectly operating agency, the right information needs to flow from the legitimate source to the legitimate recipient in an unencumbered way. Yet think about how often we hear things through the "grapevine" or at the "water-cooler." Generally, no harm derives from these alternatives. But what about situations where a person's job is in jeopardy and the consequences of people knowing this before the employee him/herself? Or what about the termination of a program? Or even knowing the salary of a person at the same job rating as you? Any of these situations can result in difficulties.

As with leadership, a large number of studies have examined communication, and a large number of potential barriers exist. As an example, Hopkins (n.d.) has identified six primary barriers to effective organizational communication. These are:

- Poor structure to the communication
- A weak delivery
- The use of the wrong medium to deliver the communication
- A mixed message
- The message is delivered to the wrong audience
- A distracting environment

Each of these should be examined within the assessment, but do so within the context of the organization. None of these exist without a meaning in a given organization, and as such a degree of understanding about the organization and its programs and activities.

Conflict.   Finally, an important process—perhaps inevitable and perhaps controllable, depending on the theorist—is conflict. Seen sometimes as positive, and sometimes as destructive, eroding commitment (Homan, 2008), conflict is a fact of life in organizations. As such, an assessment must be sensitive to conflict and its costs or benefits.

What is conflict? There are many definitions of conflict, but a commonly accepted one (Blalock, 1989), is "the intentional mutual exchange of negative sanctions, or punitive behaviors, by two or more parties, which may be individuals, corporate actors, or more loosely knit quasi-groups" (p. 7). A bit wordy, but accurate. The problem is that those negative sanctions can, again, be destructive in the wrong context.

So why is conflict seen as inevitable? In part, it is because there are so many possible causes for it. For example, one model (Fisher, 1990) suggests four dimensions to conflict, with different issues associated with the different dimensions. These dimensions are antecedents, orientations, processes, and outcomes. These are, in detail:

1.   The antecedents of conflict are (a) self-esteem; (b) authoritarianism; (c) Cohesion; (d) identity; (e) cultural differences; (f) history of antagonism; and (g) conflict of interest, values, needs, power (Fisher, 1990, p. 102).

2. The orientations which affect conflict are (a) achievement, affiliation, dominance; (b) mistrust; (c) ethnocentrism, including in-group solidarity, out-group derogation; (d) perceived threat; and (e) competitive orientations (Fisher, 1990, p. 102).

3. The processes for conflict are affected by personal style, leadership style, perceptual/cognitive biases, problem-solving competence, constituent pressure, communication, interaction, and dispute resolution.

4. Outcomes from conflict affect and include self-esteem; cohesion, satisfaction group leader; outcome satisfaction; joint payoff; and resolution effects. (Fisher, 1990, p. 102)

The model, as useful as it is, confronts a serious issue. Conflict is so ubiquitous that many ways of viewing it exist. Blalock (1989), on the other hand, has identified literally hundreds of causes from research over the years. To organize this complex theory, Blalock synthesized four general categories of conflict. These are:

1. Goals, resources, and dependence
2. Rules, constraints, fatigue, and vulnerability
3. Trust, forgiveness, and sensitivity
4. Motivation, constraints, and actual punitive behavior (p. 107)

But using these two models, a series of questions can be developed to guide the assessment. These are:

- What are the causes of conflict?
  - Is there a history, or is this a new event?
  - Are the causes concrete or are they ideological?
  - Are there motivations that support the conflict?
  - What forces sustain/reduce the conflict?
- Who are the participants?
  - Is it between individuals or groups?
  - What are the power differences between participants?
- What possible solutions exist?
  - Are there common points of agreement among the participants?
  - Are there individuals or groups that both sides trust, and who may be called upon to help reduce the conflict?

Organization Environmental Considerations

Models.   The assessment may also focus on the relationship between the organization and the environment. Schmid (2004), for example, looked at three sets of theories that are useful for understanding the relations that organizations have with their environments. These theories, which Schmid identifies as **ecological** theories, **institutional** theories, and **organizational adaptation** theories, each bring a useful frame for understanding the problems that affect organizational functioning, although he believes that the adaptation theories may be the best for analyzing the organization–environment relationship.

Ecological theories suggest that organizations have a life-cycle, and that those that are best able to find their appropriate environmental niche in times of stress, either one of "holding their own" or of expansion and change, survive and grow. The challenge for the administrator, therefore, is to be aware of changes in the environment, and to find the proper balance between the steady state and movement into new opportunities that the environment may offer.

Institutional theories, however, suggest that there are commonly accepted norms of organizational behavior and structure that give an agency "legitimacy." Organizations will best be able to grow and survive if they adopt the "symbols, myths, and rituals that facilitate the adaptation process" (p. 106), meaning that the larger institutional environment sets the rules, and organizations that follow them will better survive.

Organizational adaptation theories focus on the capacity of the organization to adapt and change. The most important implication from this theory is that executives must work to maximize organizational competence and then the structural, physical, technological, and human infrastructure that will enable the organization to survive in a competitive environment. This may be done by such things as diversifying funding streams and/or by attracting diverse client populations (pp. 107–108).

Resources.   From the standpoint of assessment, there are a number of direct variables that might be included. For example, a major potential barrier to any organization is access to **resources**. Resources for different organizations may mean different things—people, technology, information as examples. But few, if any, social service organizations can continue to exist for very long without one critically important resource—money. There are a few well-tested "truisms" that define the problem of money, and these are definitely worth remembering. First, no matter what anyone says—on paper, in person, anywhere—if you want to know what a person's (or organization's) priorities really are, look at how they allocate and spend the money they have. For example, from time to time a "dark" side is discovered in some even well-respected human service organizations that can really only be understood when salaries are examined. While a small grouping of administrators may receive very high salaries, even six figures, the workers who actually provide the care for clients may receive only a small amount over minimum wage. The author has personally experienced three such organizations in his career, and in two of the cases, the organizations were among the best known and most respected in their respective areas. In these cases, their priorities did not include a comfortable staff with low turnover.

It is also a truism that money does not grow on trees, and in the case of the human services, a substantial amount of time has to be spent acquiring funding. The methods and degree of success by which the agency is able to fund its services affects almost all aspects of the agency, from the quality of services provided to levels of employee satisfaction.

The key questions relating to resources are simple enough—is funding adequate, has there been a change in the funding source, and/or is the method effective? In any case, funding shortages or even the possibility of changes in funding can be enough to cause significant fear and disruption to the agency. But there is also an additional element to the problem of resources. Money almost never comes without some kinds of strings attached. This is the entanglement discussed in policy below.

Closely connected to the issue of resources is the increasingly important problem of sustainability. Sustainability means the long-term viability and life of an organization or programs within the organization. Such viability requires, among other organizational qualities, the nurturance of relationships with important external constituencies and the ongoing availability of resources (Wolff, 2001). A thorough literature review (Julian and Kombarakaran, 2006) has found that sustainability is linked to a variety of elements, including a clear mission statement (Bart, 1998), a results orientation, and community support (Wolff, 2001).

Technology. Technology has and continues to change at impressive rates. In brief, technology is how the organization does what it does. It may be counseling, or methadone maintenance, or community organization, or use of computers. Indeed, another technological revolution that has affected organizations in recent years is the Internet. For example, the rise of "Astroturf," or web-based organizing, will continue to affect how nonprofits do their work (McNutt and Boland, 2007).

The big issue associated with technology that any assessment should consider is its effectiveness. Technologies are being increasingly tested, and demands increase for demonstrated efficacy.

LEGAL/POLICY ENVIRONMENT

By now it should be very clear that no organization exists within a vacuum, and one area where this is most clear is related to the policy and legal environment that the organization exists within. Policies, for example, provide both opportunities and constraints for organizations. Many of the funding streams that allow organizations to survive are the results of policies. Yet there are some important truisms here. First, policies change. The priorities of a society, often embodied in its governmental policies, are strongly affected by the attention of policy-makers and the general public. And as these policies change, funding streams may dry up, change focus, and/or provide new opportunities to agencies.

Secondly, policies place a large number of constraints on an agency. For example, to be eligible for many funds, organizations may have to demonstrate compliance with a number of rules or regulations. Methadone clinics serve as a case in point. To legally be able to dispense methadone, the only truly effective treatment for narcotic addiction, the clinic must be licensed by federal agencies (the Drug Enforcement Agency or DEA), various state agencies, and in some states, by local government and/or quasi-independent groups. These are in addition to the literally dozens of laws that affect how almost any organization operates, such as the tax laws, anti-discrimination laws, workplace safety laws, environmental protection, consumer protections, and so on! Any of these laws can play a role in organizational functioning at some point.

It is also worth noting one final element of the legal/policy environment, and that is the impact of certification, licensure, and accreditation. Some or all of these may be needed by individuals and organizations if they are to operate legally. Generally, licensure is a mandatory authorization to operate a type of service, as provided by a governmental source. Accreditation, on the other hand, is voluntary, and the service may be provided without the accreditation. Certification, the least restrictive, is a demonstration of some minimal set of standards that rarely set the difference between providing/not proving (Supan, 2008).

OTHER ENVIRONMENTAL CONSIDERATIONS

In addition to the issues of resources and the legal environment, there are a number of other environmental elements that might affect the organization, and should be examined. Clients, of course, are the focus of the organizations efforts, but client needs, attitudes, and even numbers are not consistent over time. The need for many services go up and down depending on any one of a large number of socio-economic issues. Sometimes, the agency may begin a new service but no one is aware of it. This suggests the need for a marketing plan and other types of out-reach activities, yet these are processes that not many social workers have been trained to do. And there will almost certainly always be a lag between an increase in client numbers and adequate numbers of social workers to serve them.

Finally, social norms and values, the social context that agencies exist in, changes from time to time—sometimes dramatically, and sometimes imperceptibly. Yet in either case, the consequences may be dramatic. Social assumptions about clients, services, and even social workers themselves all are at the mercy of larger social forces. And any or all of these can have dramatic consequences on not only what services are provided, but also on how clients and social workers see themselves.

One of the most dramatic examples here has to do with social perceptions of "the poor." At times, the poor are viewed as innocent victims of social or economic forces outside of their control, and social workers are seen as public champions of those in need. At other times, however, the poor are seen as little more that leaches on society, while social workers are perceived as naïve "do-gooders." Neither perspective is true, but both may strongly affect the climate of the agency.

ORGANIZATIONAL ASSESSMENT: HOW TO ASSESS AND WHAT TOOLS TO USE

Awareness of the variables that affect the agency, its workers, services, and climate, is only part of the process of assessment. Determining how to assess and what tools to use is also very important. Fortunately, this need not be addressed as if from a blank page. Organizational assessment is a form of research, and like any form of research, despite the specific purpose, many of the basic tools of research may apply.

The first consideration is often the methodology, and almost any research methodology can be used. The selection of a method (or methods) for the assessment is usually dependent on many of the same factors that will affect your choice of a method in almost any situation. These factors, focusing on the assessment, include:

- Degree of ambiguity: Are the organizational components or problems to be examined "known" in advance, or is there a high degree of ambiguity?
- Degree of immediacy: Are the problems severe or are results needed immediately, or is time of little concern?
- Degree of researcher competence: Is the researcher adequately skilled in a number of methods, or are there limitations?

- Degree of support: Is the project supported financially and/or by the participants, or are these components lacking?
- Degree of subject's researchability: Are the subjects literate and available?

With these questions in mind, the assessment, as discussed above, will very likely require the input of many different constituencies. And it may be that different methods are needed for the different constituencies. Below are a few that time has shown to be very useful for the process of assessment.

FOCUS GROUPS

Focus groups are a wonderfully flexible method that may be used to gain a large amount of data quickly under almost any set of conditions—with the exception of a constituency that is unable to carry on a conversation. At its most general, a focus group is a group of 6–15 (usually) similar persons that are led through a series of directed, yet flexible questions with the purpose of finding consensus answers. The participants are often randomly selected from a population (in this case, a constituency), although constructing the sample may have benefits on occasion.

As with all of the methods to be discussed here, much more complete descriptions are found elsewhere (see, for example Center for Urban Transportation Studies, n.d.; Eliot and Associates, 2005), but a few main points for organizational assessment are provided.

- Focus groups are best used with a single constituency. As such, in organizations you may want to hold separate focus groups for clients, line staff, administration, the Board of Trustees, and collaborative agencies.
- Participants will be much more likely to be honest if they feel empowered and protected. It is essential that confidentiality and anonymity be maintained, and administrators must guarantee that no retribution will fall on participants.

In Figure 9.5 are shown the questions that were used to guide a series of focus groups with students in an after-school program. The purpose was to determine the student's perceptions of the programs.

OBSERVATIONAL PERFORMANCE RATINGS

A second approach toward assessment involves observation of the functioning of the organization, and then rating what is seen. There are a large number of assessment tools that can be used, which include a range of possible variables, from small subsets of what is included Figure 9.5 (such as only the functioning of the Board of Directors), to very comprehensive and complete variable lists from across the organization. In general, there are four questions that may guide the use of an observational performance ratings approach. These are:

1. What elements of structure and process are to be assessed?
2. What type of scale is most appropriate, and what do the ratings mean?
3. Who is doing the rating?
4. How long will the assessment continue?

Focus Group Questions for Youth Groups

1. How did you hear about the program?

2. How are you enjoying the program?

3. How do you like the tutors and staff of the program? Are they friendly and helpful?

4. Has the program helped you to improve your grades in math or reading?

5. Have your teachers or parents noticed a change in your school work? What have they said?

6. Do you feel safe in the program?

7. Do you get food in the after-school program? What kind of food is served? Is it to your liking? Is it enough food?

8. How do you get to the after-school program?

9. Are you able to get to and from the program conveniently? Is the program in a location that is convenient to you (easy to get to)?

10. Do you feel safe traveling to and from the program?

11. Is the transportation staff friendly and helpful?

12. Are there enough opportunities for you to engage in other nonacademic activities such as cultural or recreational activities?

13. Are the hours of the program convenient and sufficient (either not enough or too long)?

14. What is the most important thing that you learned from participating in the after-school program this year?

15. What can we do to improve the program? What changes would you make in the program and how?

16. Are you going to participate in this program next year?

17. Would you recommend this program to one of your friends? Why or why not?

FIGURE 9.5 | EXAMPLE OF FOCUS GROUP QUESTIONS FOR AN AFTER-SCHOOL PROGRAM

Fortunately questions 1 and 2 may be quickly addressed by the selection of an existing rating instrument. As with so many elements of organizational research, a large number of assessment tools have already been developed, and many of them are either in the public domain, or may be used with the permission of the persons who hold the copyright.

Some useful examples of these types of tools include the Checklist of Nonprofit Organizational Indicators (Greater Twin Cities United Way, 1995) developed by

Minneapolis United Way to help clarify organizational strengths and weaknesses. The rating is a very simple "Needs Work," "Met," or "Not met" in several areas, including performance indicators in legal issues, governance, human resources, planning, financial, and fundraising (Greater Twin Cities United Way, 1995). The form can even be conducted online for free at http://www.surveymonkey.com/ s.asp?u=3754722401

Kluger (2006) offers another useful tool for looking at individual programs within the organization that takes a strengths-based approach. This short tool examines five dimensions, and has each of the five areas are rated as a strong/positive influence (+2, +1), neutral (0), or a weak/negative influence (–1, –2). The five factors are strategic value, effectiveness/quality, and financial value, importance to key stakeholders, and marketing value.

A third example of a performance rating scale is provided at the end of the chapter. In this example, the questions focus most directly on the issues identified in this section. As above, the rating considers each element as a strength (strong or weak) or a challenge (strong or weak), or neutral/irrelevant. The model also allows comments from the different constituencies. Figure 9.6 shows a section of this model, with the complete example provided at the end of the chapter.

The final step in the assessment process is taking the information you have gathered and developing an implementation plan. Traditionally, a distinction is made between strategy and tactics. Strategy refers to the overall (and often long-term) approach selected for change, while tactics refer to steps or tasks in the change process.

As with the assessment process itself, collaborative action is often the key. This means involving the relevant participants and building on their strengths and knowledge of the organization. The social worker, either outsider or employee, rarely has all of the knowledge, connections, relationships, and skills necessary to make the change "stick." Moreover, involvement of more voices, particularly if empowered to speak, will help the social worker avoid some of the common traps that affect decision-making. Among these are holding on to familiar ideas, selectively allowing only supportive or confirmatory information, improperly framing

Internal Organizational Considerations	Strong Strength	Weak Strength	Neutral	Weak Challenge	Strong Challenge
Foundation Policies					
Vision					
Mission					
Goals					
Objectives					
Constitutions and by-laws					
Strategic plans					

FIGURE 9.6 | SECTION OF A PERFORMANCE RATING FROM AN ORGANIZATIONAL ASSESSMENT

the problem, and overjustifying past decisions, even if wrong (Hammond, Keeney, and Raiffa, 1998).

There are several ways that information from the assessment can be made useful for fully understanding the organization. One such approach is known as a SWOT analysis, which stands for Strengths, Weaknesses, Opportunites, and Threats, where the results of the data are organized into a four-componet framework. This perspective is shown on Figure 9.7.

What you are hoping to identify here is a framework that answers the following questions and concerns.

1. **STRENGTHS** Describe and list. Then brainstorm options for keeping/building
2. **WEAKNESSES** Describe and list. Then brainstorm options for minimizing/overcoming
3. **OPPORTUNITIES** Describe and list. Then brainstorm options to take advantage
4. **THREATS** Describe and list. Then brainstorm options for minimizing/overcoming

And as with the process of assessment, analyzing the data from the above systems may be best done collaboratively. In part this is necessary as a component of assessing the agencies' readiness for change. Horwath and Morrison (2000) suggest the need to examine three areas of the organization for its readiness to change. These are

- Practitioners' needs – the needs of front line workers who are responsible for assessment and implementation of the change
- Agency capacity – the capacity of the organization to support practitioners
- Collaborative arrangements – external relationships with other agencies needed by practitioners

STRENGTHS	WEAKNESSES
OPPORTUNITIES	THREATS

FIGURE 9.7 | SWOT ANALYSIS

Establish a committee to help you process the information and clarify its meaning. Just who should sit on this committee is another component of the negotiation process, but if possible, having a representative from each constituency (administration, staff, clients, and the social worker) will greatly help to establish needs and priorities with the insight provided from multiple viewpoints. Further, a well-functioning committee may help to cut through the misunderstandings that often create different frames through which the different constituencies see—and to "get to the heart" of—the problems at hand. The point here is that information alone is probably inadequate for coming to a decision. Often, that information is filtered through the different constituents' frames, and as such, the true state of affairs may be missed. The task here is to insure that what is believed corresponds with "what is." Organizational decision-making is rarely, if ever, truly "rational" (Shapira, 2002).

Finally, participation in the decision-making process can result in a long list of benefits. These include trust and transparency (Bartle 2008), better outcomes fromdecision-making (Landsdowne, 2003), more innovative solutions (Wilson, Wartburton, and Anderson, 2005), helping reduce or avoid conflict (Kauffman, 1995; Irvin and Stansbury, 2004), new resources (Countryside Agency, 2004), improved staff morale (Office of the Deputy Prime Minister, 2005), and increasing legitimacy/support for decisions (Countryside Agency, 2004).

The most common justification, however, for participation is that it is a tool to empower individuals. Empowerment is "a process by which individuals gain mastery or control over their own lives and democratic participation in the life of their community" (Zimmerman and Rappaport, 1988, p. 726).

ENGAGEMENT

After the assessment is completed, problems and indicators identified, and priorities determined, the engagement phase comes. In this phase, the most important activities include developing the action plan, with goals, action steps, and an evaluation plan. This is followed by the implementation of the intervention.

SETTING GOALS

Goals serve a variety of critical tasks in the overall intervention. As well as serving as positive outcomes to the intervention activity, they also help provide meaning and definition to the agency, as well as giving direction and helping to keep everyone focused (Leadership Resource Office, n.d.). Goals may also serve as an internal source of motivation and commitment (Barton, 2000). Commonly, goals are viewed as the desired end states of the activity or intervention. As such, it is essential that the goal is linked to a problem, or more specifically, to the "resolution" of the problem. Note the examples in Figure 9.8.

But, importantly, there is an issue that requires our attention here. Very often, end states have different "dimensions" or qualities, and as such it may be a bit difficult for us to really be certain that we have achieved that end state. For example, common organizational problems like "staff morale," "high-quality services," or even "client satisfaction" may each have two, three, or even more

Problem	Goal Response
Low Staff Morale	*Goal 1.* The agency will achieve a high level of employee morale.
Financial Difficulties	*Goal 2.* The agency will achieve complete financial solvency.
Poor Client Satisfaction	*Goal 3.* The agency will achieve a high level of customer satisfaction
Communication Problems	*Goal 4.* The agency will achieve a high level of quality of communication, both inside and outside of the organization.

FIGURE 9.8   EXAMPLES OF AGENCY GOALS

Low Staff Morale	Agency Financial Difficulties	Poor Client Satisfaction	Communication Problems
Staff retention	Number of authorized client admissions	Client retention	Number of missed meetings by staff due to failure to inform
Worker satisfaction ratings	Supplies available to staff	Client satisfaction ratings	Worker level of reported satisfaction with communication ratings
Level of conflicts between workers	Travel reimbursements disbursement time	Treatment compliance	Number of conflicts between workers with communication identified as cause
Worker absenteeism	Number of successful grant applications	Client absenteeism	

FIGURE 9.9   EXAMPLES OF PROBLEM DIMENSIONS OF GOALS THAT MAY BE USED AS GOAL ATTAINMENT INDICATORS

aspects, each of which must be addressed if we are to be certain that we have achieved the goal.

Building on the goal examples above, Figure 9.9 presents some of the different dimensions associated with some common organizational goals. To think about this issue in a slightly different way, it may be useful to think of the various dimensions of the problem/goal as possible indicators of the problem, and on the flip side, as indicators of goal attainment. As such, each of the indicators on Figure 9.9 may be used for an indicator of goal attainment.

So if goals have multiple dimensions, and each of these dimensions may serve as an indicator of goal attainment, how do we organize the information for planning purposes? The answer is to break the goals down into three stages—*goals, objectives,* and **tasks** (or action steps, or activities), with each stage presenting an increasingly specific level of information. The goals, again, are the first level, and are the desired end states, again often with different dimensions. The objective, or the next level, now becomes an indicator of goal attainment, and it contains a single dimension of the goal. Indeed, for complex goals, we may choose to select two, three, or even more indicators, each of which focuses on one of the dimensions of the goal. The final level, the task or activity, speaks to the specific responsibilities of the staff or client in carrying out the intervention. More on tasks/action steps will be provided later on as we conceptualize the interventions a bit more thoroughly.

In the meantime, using the problem indicators in Figure 9.9, the following examples of objectives may be developed from the goals above. Notice the difference between the measurability and specificity of the goals in Figure 9.8, "Examples of Agency Goals," with those on Figure 9.10, "Examples of Measurable Agency Objectives."

The next level, the objectives, as defined earlier, are the indicators of goal attainment, and these indicators are the measurable dimensions of the problem (and goal) at hand. Unlike goals, therefore, objectives must be highly specific in every way. Any ambiguity may potentially misconstrue the meaning of the objective. But by enhancing the measurability of the objective, demonstration of objective attainment becomes easier.

Surprisingly, there is no mystery in writing good objectives—a few guidelines will greatly assist you in creating sharp and useful objectives. Indeed, the acronym "SMART" will help. SMART stands for statements that are:

- Specific
- Measurable
- Attainable
- Relevant
- Time-bound

The characteristics of each of these terms have been nicely described (Cothran and Wysocki, 2005).

- "Specific" means that the statement has fully addressed four questions
  - Who is to be involved?
  - What is to be accomplished?
  - Where is it to be done?
  - When is it to be done?
- "Measurable" means that the statement has fully addressed three questions
  - How much?
  - How will you know when it is accomplished?
  - How many?
- "Attainable" means that the statement has a real chance of success
- "Relevant" means the statement is consistent with the mission of the organization
- "Time-bound" means the statement has a beginning and ending point.

Problem	Goal and Objective Response
Low Staff Morale	**Goal 1.** The agency will achieve a high level of employee morale.
Objective 1.1	The agency will improve staff retention, as measured by employees with more than 2 years service, by 50% by March 2011.
Objective 1.2	Employee's satisfaction with employment, as measured by quarterly satisfaction surveys, will increase by 80% from current levels by March 2010.
Objective 1.3	The rate of employees' daily absenteeism will fall by 75%, from current levels, by March 2010.
Financial Difficulties	**Goal 2.** The agency will achieve complete financial solvency.
Objective 2.1	The number of authorized client admissions will increase by 30% from current levels by March 2010.
Objective 2.2	The time between submission and payment of staff travel reimbursements for all employees will reduce from 90 days to 14 days by December 2009.
Objective 2.3	The number of successful grant applications written by the agency will increase by 100%, from current levels, by March 2010.
Poor Client Satisfaction	**Goal 3.** The agency will achieve a high level of customer satisfaction
Objective 3.1	The agency will improve client retention, as measured by clients completing treatment, by 50% by March 2010.
Objective 3.2	The agency will improve client treatment compliance, as measured by the percentage of clients who meet monthly task assignments, by 75% by December 2009.
Objective 3.3	The rate of client's daily absenteeism will fall by 75%, from current levels, by March 2010.
Communication Problems	**Goal 4.** The agency will achieve a high level of quality of communication, both inside and outside of the organization.
Objective 4.1	The number of missed meetings by staff due to failure to inform will fall by 75%, from current levels, by March 2010.
Objective 4.2	Worker level of reported satisfaction with communication, as measured by quarterly satisfaction surveys, will increase by 80% from current levels by March 2010.
Objective 4.3	The number of conflicts between workers with communication identified as cause will fall by 75%, from current levels, by March 2010.

FIGURE 9.10 | EXAMPLES OF MEASURABLE AGENCY OBJECTIVES

Now, following our examples, using the same problem indicators and goals, the following objectives may be written. Look at the examples in Figure 9.10, and notice how measurable and specific each one is.

As with analysis and the setting of priorities, a group effort that includes several different constituencies is very likely to yield the best results. And the process for setting the goals may be the same. One model has been developed by the Haas Center for Public Service at Stanford University (n.d.). This model is presented below.

Steps for Setting Goals and Objectives:

1. Brainstorm a list of potential goals as a group
2. Choose from the brainstorm list those you want to work on
3. Prioritize
4. Determine objectives for each goal and plans of action for each objective (Remember there can be several objectives for each goal)
5. Move into action, follow through (Many groups fail to evaluate and revise; thus, their goals are never achieved)
6. Include a closing statement

One final question remains as far as goals and objectives are concerned, and that is: How many goals and objectives are necessary in a plan? The short answer is as many as necessary. But a somewhat better answer is to at least *consider* adding a new goal each time (1) your problem area changes, (2) the target group changes, or (3) the major thrust of the intervention changes. Then, consider adding a new objective for each problem indicator you select. An example of a goal planning form ("Example: Organizational Goal Planning Form") is presented for your review at the end of the chapter.

INTERVENTIONS

With assessment completed, and agency goals and objectives firmly in place, the time for the actual intervention is at hand. As with any system, from single individuals to families, all the way to communities, a number of interventions are always available. The first guiding principle with an organizational intervention, and most similar to any other system, is to keep your eyes on the literature. Evidence-based practice is increasingly the norm and the expectation. Therefore, watching the changes in empirical and theoretical knowledge will only help you select the tools that will best serve you and your client.

As a starting point, however, a number of possibilities are available that have a proven track record of effectiveness. These include **productivity improvements, staff development and training, program planning**, and **resource development**. But for any of these, a plan is essential.

DEVELOPING THE INTERVENTION AND EVALUATION PLAN

The intervention plan lays out the tasks/action steps and responsibilities for all parties in the change process. Essentially, this is an action plan and a contract that provides a great amount of detail for the successful implementation of the intervention. In other words, it again presents the tasks/action steps for the project.

Tasks/action steps, as initially discussed, come from your goals and objectives, but they also are closely connected to the intervention. They are, very simply, the specific activities that each person involved in the intervention must carry out if the intervention is to be successful. They are statements of the "who, what, when, and where" of the plan.

So what then goes into the plan? Think of it as a road map and a contract that summarizes:

- What is to be done?
- How will it be accomplished?
- What are your resources in terms of people, money, and materials?
- Who is responsible for completing each task (action steps)?
- What is the deadline?
- How will you know when it is accomplished? How will you measure the results? (Haas Center for Public Service at Stanford University, n.d.).

Generally, the more detail and specificity within the plan, the more successful it will be. The specifics, however, are again linked to the objectives and the interventions. Following are some examples of interventions. An example of an intervention planning form is presented ("Example: Organizational Intervention Planning Form") at the end of the chapter.

Productivity Improvements

Productivity refers to the output of work relative to the effort involved. Often, the organization has all or most of what it needs, and as such many of the problems of organization may be improved simply by enhancing or correcting the procedures already in place (Brody, 2005). In other words, improve the productivity through building on the strengths of the organization. Rarely are organizations so lost that everything must be changed. Commonly, it only requires some element of reform or enhancement.

Technology, for example, is a common tool for enhancing productivity. Yet technology may be available at the organization but underused because of a lack of familiarity with what it may do. Further, the selection of the proper computer or software program may greatly enhance the productivity of staff. Consider for a moment the difficulties associated with agency paperwork. With the development and application of some simple programs and perhaps an intranet, many routine tasks such as case notes, internal communication, and even diagnosis may be improved.

The problem of internal communication processes serves as a case in point. It is not that difficult to greatly enhance communication through very simple processes. These may include better selecting the method of communication through matching the needs and purposes of the communication with the technique (Brody, 2005). Meetings, important as they are, do not need to be held if information can be more effectively passed on through individual contacts or electronic means.

More generally, the idea here is that any method that can improve productivity will benefit everyone. It may make more time available to staff, while reducing some complexity for administrators and clients.

STAFF DEVELOPMENT: EDUCATION AND TRAINING

Training for staff may be appropriate for some types of problems. Often, an agency's problems are related to the skills and knowledge of staff or administration. Many of us, for example, have benefited from trainings to address issues as broad as diversity and culture, or more narrow topics like the application of a particular counseling technique. The question to address in planning for this intervention is whether the need may be corrected in a single event, or if the need is for a multi-event, long-term set of trainings.

Case 9.1 illustrates the beginning steps in developing a staff workshop. This example illustrates the importance of getting input from members of the target group before implementing a training program. The probation officers' perceptions of what they were interested in were very different from their director's perceptions. The workshop turned out to be a success and was well received by the probation officers, even though it was not exactly what the director originally envisioned. If the training team had proceeded without any input from the participants, it would most likely have been less well received. The workshop would have been a trying experience for both the training team and the participants.

Leadership development is another critical component in many organizational interventions. As discussed earlier, many individuals in leadership positions lack adequate leadership abilities. As such, training to enhance such abilities are of great benefit in a variety of areas. It has been found, for example, to be a component of

---

| CASE 9.1 | EARLY STEPS IN STAFF WORKSHOP DEVELOPMENT |

Christiana D., Laurie B., and Pat M. all were graduate social work students doing their second-year field placements at Social Work Consultation Services (SWCS). SWCS provided generalist social work learning experiences for student interns and social work and capacity-building services for residents and organizations of an economically disadvantaged community. The Director of Adult Probation in the county contacted SWCS about conducting a staff development workshop for her probation officers.

Christiana, Laurie, and Pat took on the project under the supervision of a school faculty member.

The training team scheduled a meeting with the Director of Adult Probation to get a better understanding of the agency's needs and her expectations about the purpose and objectives of the workshop.

The director felt that her staff could benefit from a workshop on relationship-building skills and on how to engage reluctant, resistant, or hostile clients in a collaborative working relationship. She felt that many of the probation officers were showing signs of burnout and a lot of frustration with their clients and the legal system. Many seemed to have given up trying to make a difference in their clients' lives and were not making any efforts to connect with them. The team left the meeting with a clear understanding of what the director wanted. They felt it was something that they would be able to put together and deliver effectively.

With the approval of the director, the training team scheduled a preworkshop meeting with the probation officers who would be attending the workshop. The

CASE 9.1 | *Continued*

purpose of the meeting was to get an understanding of their training needs and interests. The meeting did not go as expected. The probation officers had absolutely no interest in learning "soft" relationship skills and were totally against the idea of having to attend a workshop on how to connect with reluctant or hostile clients. They felt that such training would be a total waste of time. They used the meeting to vent their feelings about the system and working with clients who lied and were manipulative.

The team struggled to find some common ground between the director's and staff's perceived needs. Because the probation officers were so clear about the frustrations of their job, Pat asked if they would be interested in a workshop that focused on coping strategies and burnout prevention. This, too, was rejected as a waste of time. Most of the group members claimed not to have any problems in that area and said they could take care of themselves just fine.

Having struck out making suggestions to this group, Christiana asked them what would be helpful. After quite a bit of back and forth discussion among the probation officers, it was decided that a workshop on the link between mental health and substance abuse would be helpful. All of their clients were substance abusers, and the workers felt that for many, mental health issues compounded their difficulties with substance abuse and the law. The team agreed to the proposed focus, pending approval by the probation officers' director.

many effective multicultural development programs (Hyde, 2004), where the goal is to enhance staff sensitivity to issues of diversity, or in areas of emotional intelligence. Consisting of such attributes as self-awareness, self-regulation, empathy, and solid social skills (Goleman, 1998), the idea is that a leader who understands people will help improve many workplace conditions. Emotional intelligence can be improved through training.

PROGRAM PLANNING AND DEVELOPMENT: STRATEGIC PLANNING

As discussed earlier, one of the critical documents in an organization is the strategic plan. While it makes total sense that having a plan is a critical element in any endeavor, it is often the case that plans are old, out of date, and no longer relevant to the realities in which an organization may find itself.

In some ways, the strategic plan should be a priority concern for an organization. Within it is a review of both the foundation policies, because it establishes priorities that are based in perceptions of real needs, opportunities, or challenges to the organization. As such it can become not just a guide, but a real review of what is relevant, or what is not. Brody (2005) presents a series of steps and questions that can guide the strategic planning process. These include:

1. Carefully examine the purposes for the plan. Ask what it is you hope to get out of the document
2. Determine the level of commitment of major constituencies
3. Establish a committee to oversee the effort
4. Assess the problems, opportunities, and strengths of the organization
5. Analyze and/or re-create the organizational vision
6. Examine/revise and/or draft a mission statement

7. Prioritize the challenges to the organization
8. Develop mid- and long-term goals
9. Submit a draft of the plan for multiple reviews by different constituencies
10. Implement the plan
11. Update annually (p. 35).

RESOURCE DEVELOPMENT

As discussed above, money is often the source of an agency's problems. Figure 9.11 presents these methods and some of the issues that may be experienced by dependence upon that approach. Each method brings something to the organization, but it is here that a third "truism" about money is identified. Money *always* has strings attached, meaning that money always has conditions that affect either how it may be spent or how the organization is able to operate. Sometimes, these strings are inconsequential and unimportant. But in other cases, the strings may be overwhelming. A description of each type of funding is provided on Figure 9.11, with **fee for service**, **direct solicitation**, and **grants** discussed in greater detail in the following narrative.

GRANT WRITING

Many organizations supplement or expand their resources through grant writing. And it is easy to see why. Americans have a long history of giving, and between federal, state, and local governmental sources, and the vast number of grant-making foundations, there are literally thousands of sources with billions of dollars. Indeed, over 60 foundations have assets of greater than one billion dollars, and nearly 50 more are close (Foundation Center, 2008). Looking at this a slightly different way, almost 50 organizations each gave away 100 million dollars or more in 2006/7 (Foundation Center, 2008).

The process of writing a grant can range from an endeavor that is very short and simple—typically for small, community grants—to complex and exhaustive. But in general, the general process of applying for and organizing most grant proposals is more or less done the same way. The general steps are:

1. Develop a clear project or problem
2. Select the grant source
3. Write the proposal

Step 1: Develop a clear project or problem. This part of the process is not really very different from the brainstorming that should take place while planning any intervention, with perhaps two important differences. First, in many cases the focus of the project now may expand beyond the needs of the agency itself to possibly include client needs as well. In other words, the focus of this chapter has generally been on intervention with the organization. And while you might consider seeking funding for what is known as "capacity-building," enhancement of skills or agency infrastructure, you might also consider writing a grant to address an unmet client need as well. In so doing, the funding may be of value in addressing the organizations needs at the same time as it is helping the clients.

Funding Method	Description	Issues
Fee for service	Client pays for service provided	Requires enough clients who have disposable income to support agency. Client numbers change, making planning difficult.
Third party payments, insurance reimbursements	Payments made by insurer for services	Limited types of services covered. Requires certification/licensure. Services may require preauthorization by insurance company.
Loans - commercial source	Loans provided at market rates	Market rates fluctuate—rates based on agency credit rating.
Loans - government or noncommercial source	Loans provided at nonmarket rates, often by government agencies	Eligibility often linked to specific policy/problem areas.
Contract with governmental source	Governmental source (federal, State, county) pre-selects types of services/clients, and chooses and contracts with agency to provide services	Dependent on political and legislative action. Agency must meet eligibility criteria. Contracts are competitive. Time limited. Applies only to limited types of services or clients.
Grants - governmental source	Agency writes grant proposal for funds to underwrite program. Government source evaluates and chooses among submitting agencies.	Dependent on political and legislative action. Requires grant-writing expertise. Long application period with no guarantee of funding. Time-limited funding Many limits on use of funds.
Grants - foundation source	Agency writes grant proposal for funds to underwrite program. Foundation source evaluates and chooses among submitting agencies.	Dependent on foundation attention to problem area. Requires grant-writing expertise. Long application period with no guarantee of funding. Time-limited funding. Most funding sources are small. Many limits on use of funds.
Grants - general source (United Way, Walmart)	Agency writes grant proposal for funds to underwrite program. Foundation source evaluates and chooses among submitting agencies.	Dependent on foundation attention to problem area. Requires grant-writing expertise. Long application period with no guarantee of funding. Time-limited funding. Many limits on use of funds.
Direct solicitation fundraising	Bake sales, direct mail requests, employee contributions	Unless the organization is well known or "in the public spotlight," contributions tend to be small. Usually very undependable.

FIGURE 9.11   METHODS OF ORGANIZATIONAL FUNDING

A second difference that may apply here is that most successful grants depend on a grounding in the literature. An empirical basis for any project, as drawn from the literature of social work, sociology, psychology, or similar fields, will have a much greater chance of success than one that is based on anecdotes or practice wisdom alone.

Overall, you can think about the types of projects as one of six types. They include:

- Research or planning projects – projects designed to help the agency examine a problem and/or plan for new services.
- Demonstration projects – projects designed to implement new or untested services
- Operating expenses and services support – projects designed to raise funds for existing services
- Endowment development – projects designed to help build the endowment and long-term assets of the agency
- Construction projects – projects designed to help the agency build a new or renovate the physical plant
- Capacity-building – projects designed to enhance the skills or knowledge of the staff, or to improve the agency's infrastructure

While there are grants available for all of these types of projects, some are more available than others. In general, funding will be somewhat more available for research or planning, demonstration projects, or capacity-building than for construction or endowment development. Operating expenses and services support are fairly easy to projects to fund, but rarely in the amounts necessary to do anything more than partially support an organization. To put this another way, funding is an ongoing activity, and grant writing, while of unquestionable value, is also an ongoing process.

Step 2: Select the grant source. To begin, you must find out who (what organization) is providing funding. This is actually fairly easy, as organizations that give away money must notify the public that funds are available. This is done via a document variously known as an RFP (Request for Proposals), NOFAs (Notice of Funding Availability), FOAs (Funding Opportunity Announcements), or SUPER NOFAs (groups of NOFAs). RFPs typically describe

- Name of program
- Name of organization and auspice
- What WILL be funded. This could involve

  – Discipline(s)

  – Problem area(s)

  – Client characteristics

  – Geography

  – Intervention approach, methods, or activities

- What WILL NOT be funded

  – Limitations on overhead (indirect costs), administration, travel etc.

  – Construction, lobbying, endowments

- Funding amounts and time frames

  - Min., max., and average grant size
  - 1 to 3 years, sometimes renewable
  - Expected match amount/%

- Application process

  - Due dates
  - Contact information
  - Where to get application forms (if necessary)
  - Grant/technical assistance advisor

Make sure you review these carefully. Many grant sources receive hundreds of applications, so you must prepare the RIGHT proposal for the RIGHT source.

A word is also useful about the sources of grants. Although individuals may provide grant funds, most conceptualizations of grant funding sources focus on government (federal, state, local), or a foundation. There are advantages and disadvantages to the different grant sources. Government sources are often considered to be more prestigious and high-dollar, but very competitive, restrictive, and extremely complex to write. Foundations, on he other hand, are more varied. With literally thousands of different sources, it is possible to find everything from large, high-dollar, complex grants to small, essentially noncompetitive micro-grants.

Where does one find an RFP, or out about out about grant sources? From the federal government, the *Catalog of Domestic Federal Assistance* was the standard until the opportunities provided by the Internet. Now, almost every government agency provides information about sources at their websites. And even easier is www.grants.gov, which collects information across agencies.

For foundations, comprehensive information is harder to find simply because of the number of foundations that exist. Yet again, several websites exist which can help, although they are often fee or subscription based. Among the respected sites are

- www.foundationcenter.org
- www.pafoundations.net
- www.dvg.org

Step 3: Write the proposal. Writing the proposal may seem complex, but in many ways it really only involves drawing together information that may already exist, albeit it must be put together in a clear, concise, and logical way. While every proposal MUST be specific to the RFP, and MUST follow all of the directions perfectly, it is also the case that the components of most proposals are similar. These components typically include:

- Title or cover page
- Introduction or summary
- Statement of need (problem)

- Goals
  - Outcome objectives
  - Process objectives
- Methods
  - Conceptual framework (Literature)
  - Organizational description (mission, history, staff, etc.)
  - Client issues (recruitment, etc.)
  - Tasks (activities or action steps)
- Evaluation plan
  - Outcome evaluation
  - Process evaluation
  - Deliverables
- Budget and budget narrative
  - Plan for future funding
- Appendices
  - References
  - Certifications
  - IRS notices
  - Organization budget
  - Letters of support

In addition to these sections, the strongest and most successful proposals will

- Follow directions
- Use technical assistance
- Keep the flow logical
- Avoid jargon

The problem of logical flow bears special attention. Every section of the proposal builds on what has gone before. While this might seem evident and obvious, the lack of logical connection is a common flaw. One way to avoid this is to remember that that the STRONGEST proposals will have a clear 1:1:1 relationship between indicators of need, your outcome objectives, and the degree of change in outcomes you seek to demonstrate in your evaluation. Don't identify and measure a need one way, while focusing your objectives and evaluation criteria somewhere else.

EVALUATION AND TERMINATION

TERMINATION

Termination of the relationship and the intervention with an organizational client system has some unique characteristics. Although at least six types of termination have been identified (Fortune, Pearlingi, and Rochelle, 1995), some issues apply to most, and effective strategizing will improve the long-term success of the intervention and relationship.

First, planning for the termination, including conducting ongoing conversations with your client and the various constituencies should begin soon after engagement.

The reason for this is that any one of a number of barriers or problems may arise at the point of, or soon after, the ending of the relationship, and the more that these problems may be identified, the better the client will be able to deal with them—ideally independently. As with all forms of strengths-based practice, the more the client is empowered to address potential problems, the greater the likelihood of long-term success.

Secondly, helping the organization to establish an ongoing review and monitoring process, both of the intervention and of larger organizational issues, will help the organization better prepare for difficulties over the long run. One strategy is to hold an annual review of the strategic plan—not for the purposes of major revision, but rather for its relevance over time and for the organization's commitment to its principles. It may even benefit the organization to appoint and/or hire a staff person or consultant to serve in some formal review role (Boyles and Theunissen, 2003; Poulin, Silver, and Kauffman, 2007), although the expense of such a task may make too large of a time commitment infeasible.

In some sense, this speaks to the problem of sustainability, or the long-term viability of the organization. Issues of funding are rarely one-shot concerns. Over the long term, the issue of sustainability must be addressed. Sustainability means the organization is on a firm footing, and that its long-term needs are adequately addressed. Julian and Kombarakaran (2006) list seven strategies that support sustainability:

1. Explicit statement of mission
2. Adoption of a results orientation
3. Utilization of entrepreneurial skills
4. Well-developed management practices
5. Strong community support
6. Integration of new activities into existing structures
7. Ongoing planning and program improvement activities (p. 176)

Further, there are barriers to organizational change that must be acknowledged. The intervention itself, even though it qualifies as "evidence-based practice," may experience problems, if untested. Any movement from the "laboratory" to the field is a complicated process (Simpson, 2002). Moreover, Luongo (2007) has reviewed the literature and identified a number of barriers. These include (1) differences between the lab and work in the real world, (2) the value workers place on their own clinical judgment, (3) the importance of organizational culture, (4) readiness or resistance to change, (5) leadership, (6) organizational fit, (7) motivation, and (8) effectiveness vs. efficiency.

EVALUATION

A well-designed intervention plan should have the procedures for evaluating the effectiveness of the intervention, as well as long-term monitoring, built right into the plan. Indeed, if the model of planning, goals, and objectives outlined here is followed, in most cases no additional evaluative tools need be developed. The reason for this is that the methods used to evaluate the obtainment of the objectives, as well as, perhaps, the objectives themselves, will be the same. And just to add some "icing to the cake," the very indicators used in the objectives, if all is properly designed, are the same indicators of the problem level.

The point here, once again, is that evaluation of your intervention should be built directly into the intervention plan. The same measures you use for your problem indicators, your objectives, and your indicators of goal attainment *are your evaluation*, or at least one type—what is called an "outcome evaluation."

An outcome evaluation is nothing more than determining the degree to which your objectives have been met. Evaluation is a form of applied research. All research seeks to answer some type of question, and an outcome evaluation seeks to answer the question "Did our intervention do what we said it would do?" Using our examples from above, we could look at each of our objectives and ask this question. For example, did our efforts actually improve employee retention as we intended in Objective 1.1?

Low Staff Morale	*Goal 1*. The agency will achieve a high level of employee morale.
Objective 1.1	The agency will improve staff retention, as measured by employees with more than 2 years service, by 50% by March 2011.

Or was employee satisfaction actually improved, as stated in Objective 1.2?

Objective 1.2	Employees' satisfaction with employment, as measured by quarterly satisfaction surveys, will increase by 80% from current levels by March 2010.

To answer these questions, we must confront the same types of questions that any researcher must confront. Just as with our assessment at beginning of the chapter, this requires a measure, a method, and an analytical process. Fortunately, one of the three is presented in all of the objectives themselves, and the other two are at least suggested or partially presented. The measure is nothing more than the indicator or target of change. All of the objectives should present that characteristic. The method, or how data are to be collected, may or may not be included. Above, the method is included in Objective 1.2—it is the quarterly satisfaction survey, but it is not in Objective 1.1. In this case, the determination must be made as to the best method for measuring staff retention.

As in all research, a variety of methods exist. It is up to you to choose the one that is most appropriate. Figure 9.12 presents a variety of methods that might be useful in setting up an evaluation plan.

The final attribute, the analytical process, is partially provided by the objective itself, in that each objective should provide a numeric outcome or target. Further,

Existing Data	Agency Records	Surveys
• Existing research and documents • National trends • State/County/City statistics • Research studies • Governmental documents • Census data	• Utilization data • Waiting lists • Employee data • Characteristics of consumers	• Consumer surveys • Community surveys • Key informants • Staff surveys

FIGURE 9.12 | POTENTIAL DATA SOURCES FOR OUTCOME EVALUATIONS

all objectives provide an implicit comparison between two points in time. Looking at Objective 1.1, the model works like this.

Objective 1.1	The agency will improve staff retention, as measured by employees with more than 2 years service, by 50% by March 2011.		
Measures	Measure 1 – staff retention (number of staff who have more than 2 yrs service at present)	Time passage (now to March 2011)	Measure 2 – staff retention (number of staff who have more than 2 yrs service in March 2011)
Method	Employee records		Employee records
Comparison	NOW>>> March 2011		

This method can be applied to all objectives, and is a very effective method. You can also modify the information provided to create a form for tracking the evaluation. An example of such a form that may be useful for tracking the evaluation of each objective is shown on Appendix E at the end of the chapter.

CASE EXAMPLE

The following case example illustrates generalist social work practice with an organizational client system. It describes the issues a community-based arts agency went through in the process of stabilizing and moving towards long-term sustainability.

CASE 9.2   THE PRESTON ARTISTIC HISTORY

Preston, Pennsylvania, has a long history of participation in the arts, and although neither its size nor its wealth would suggest it, many famous musicians and artists lived or worked in Preston throughout the 20th century. Examples of artists as important as Bill Haley, John Coltrane, and many others had connections to, or lived in, Preston in earlier times. Many visual artists and dancers also lived and performed in Preston in the years immediately preceding and closely following WWII.

Sadly, however, major economic changes affected the city from the 1960s onwards. Indeed, Preston lost its tax base and virtually all of its manufacturing jobs, as well as a vibrant commercial community. These events, as well as a period of political corruption, decimated the artistic community. All of the organizations and institutions that supported the arts (except for two small community groups) were forced to close. And to make matters even worse, the arts and music programs in the local school district were dramatically cut back, and even eliminated for many grades. By the early 1990s, no art galleries existed in Preston, no clubs of any type supported music, (again) except for a small school program, and small programs offered by the YWCA and one other group.

At the same time, a core of artists and musicians continued to exist in the city. And thanks to one very dedicated city resident who was able to form a 501c (3) nonprofit organization, a small art gallery was established in 1993 for the first time since the 1960s. The agency, called the Irving Fine Arts Center, grew quite fast under the direction of its founder, Elise Irving. Within just a few years, the agency had established a number of programs, including a gallery, several children's art programs, a Visiting-Artist-in-Residence program, a Friday night local music series, and an annual children's art show at the local university social work program.

Assessment

Over time, however, the director and the organization began to experience tensions. The director had a staff of three to five all-volunteer employees. Materials for the children's programs were chronically short, and after 3 very successful years, funding to support the visiting artist program ran short. One of the visiting artists, a long-time friend of the director, left in the middle of the season, with no reason given. Further, the volunteers seemed to be staying for shorter times.

To make matters more complicated still, many of the funding sources used to establish the programs were no longer available, either for reasons of state art program cutbacks or changes in foundation priorities. Some additional grants were available, but accessing them in the time available required information that the art center did not have. This information included a full description of the numbers served through the various programs, ages and other characteristics of their students, and benefits that the programs were providing for their students and the larger community.

Intervention

Due to the relationship that already existed between the art center and the local university social work program, the art center director contacted the dean and asked for help. As luck would have it, the social work program had recently redesigned a course in Social Work Practice with Organizations and Communities, and the primary assignment for that course was working with an organization. The course instructor asked the class to complete the following tasks: (1) to conduct a thorough collaborative assessment of the strengths and challenges facing the organization, (2) to collaboratively develop goals and objectives for the organization, and (3) to develop an intervention plan. Due to the semester time frame, the actual intervention and its assessment would have to be implemented by others, but this did not appear to be a problem for any of those involved.

The assessment the students developed and carried out was quite extensive. Using a combination of focus groups and surveys to examine the perspectives of the various constituencies (staff/volunteers, students, advisory board, and community residents), and an examination of the records the organization maintained, the assessment determined that the primary strengths of the organization were Elise (her energy and love of the project), community need and interest, and the relationship with the social work program. Challenges, on the other hand, included Elise (excessive micromanagement and fear of delegation of tasks), finances and lack of a financial/strategic plan, and no system for tracking services and clients.

CASE 9.2 | *Continued*

The students then followed up this assessment with goal-planning conversations with Elise and members of the advisory board. They came up with two goals for the organization, as subsequently objectives and the intervention plan. The two goals, and objectives were:

Goal I: To strengthen the long and short term financial health of the Irving Fine Arts Center.

Objective 1.1: To develop a comprehensive, 5-year strategic plan by July 2004.

Objective 1.2: To identify and apply for a minimum of five grant proposals each year between 2003 and 2008.

Objective 1.3: To establish a fundraising committee, comprised of members of the advisory board and community volunteers who will develop and implement fundraising activities on an ongoing basis.

Goal II: To establish a flexible and user-friendly data management system for the Irving Fine Arts Center.

Objective 2.1: To develop and implement a computer information management system for data tracking by December 2004.

Objective 2.2: To identify develop goals, objectives, and an evaluation plan for each program of the Irving Fine Arts Center by November 2004.

Objective 2.3: To select and train an evaluation committee, comprised of members of the advisory board and community volunteers who will oversee evaluation activities on an ongoing basis.

Beyond these goals and objectives, the action steps and responsibilities in the intervention plan were laid out in a way that *reduced* the workload on Ms. Irving. Her micro-management style, it seemed to all, was more of a response to a small organization that grew faster than the number of employees, rather than any intrinsic issues with the director. As such, it was hoped that time, along with the removal of many fundraising duties from Ms. Irving, would correct the problem of micro-management.

Further, several students and faculty of the social work program took it upon themselves *after* the end of the semester to work, as volunteers to assist with some of the objectives. Two of the students, for example, wrote the software program for the data management objective, and then taught volunteers how to use it. In addition, one of the members of the faculty developed evaluation tools, and then analyzed data as it was needed. These results were used for assistance in writing several grants over the next 2 years.

Finally, programs were developed over time that enlisted social work students to provide case management services to families and individuals associated with the programs.

Evaluation

While the center continues to face many problems, and Preston itself is undergoing changes that have unclear results, it appears that the center is making progress in overcoming its difficulties. Several grant proposals have been successfully funded, volunteers are staying longer, and Ms. Irving now has a funded, part-time assistant. In addition, two venues for music performance have opened in the city, and two charter schools have implemented arts programs. There is hope that all of these efforts will reawaken the artist spirit that once permeated the community, but only time will tell.

Discussion Questions

1. What kinds of problems do you think are commonplace for social service agencies? Are these types of problems different than might be faced by other types of organizations?

2. What do you think are the benefits and problems of for-profit versus nonprofit agencies for providing social services? Or education? Or health care?

3. What abilities, skills, or knowledge do you think you will need in order to be a good leader of an organization? Are these things something you can learn, or are you born with the tools?

4. What makes a good work environment for you? What characteristics of a job make that job comfortable or uncomfortable?

5. What are some ways you can think of that might help your field placement improve its services?

References

Allen, G. (1998, 2002). Supervision. Retrieved August 8, 2008 from http://telecollege.dcccd.edu/ mgmt1374/book_contents/3organizing/pwr_auth/ power.htm

Arnsberger, P. (2007). Charities, social welfare, and other tax-exempt organizations, 2004. *Statistics of Income Bulletin*, Fall 2007, Retrieved June 11, 2008 from http://www.irs.gov/pub/irs-soi/ 04eochar.pdf

Bart, C. (1998). Mission matters. *The CPA Journal*, 68, 56–57.

Bartle, P. (2008). Participatory management, Retrieved August 12, 2008 from http://www.scn.org/cmp/ modules/pm-pm.htm

Barton, R. (2000). Chapter 7, Organizational Goal Setting and Planning. Murray State University, Murray, KY. Retrieved August 12, 2008 from http://campus.murraystate.edu/academic/faculty/ rb.barton/40mgmt07.ppt#256,1,chapter7

Blalock, H. (1989). *Power and conflict: Toward a general theory*. Newbury Park, CA: Sage.

Boyles, R., and Theunissen, A. (2003). Barriers in Implementation of an HIV Curriculum in Three Different Community Settings. Paper presented at the National HIV Prevention Conference, July 27–30, 2003, Hyatt Regency Atlanta Hotel, Atlanta, GA.

Brill, N., and Levine, J. (2005). *Working with people; The helping process* (8th ed). Boston, MA: Allyn & Bacon.

Brody, R., (2005). *Effectively Managing Human Service Organizations* (3rd ed.). Thousand Oaks, CA: Sage.

Center for Urban Transportation Studies (n.d.). Guidelines for conducting a focus group, University of Wisconsin–Milwaukee, Retrieved June 19, 2008 from http://www.uwm.edu/Dept/CUTS/ focus.htm

Collin, S., Gray, B., and Hadley, J. (2001). The for-profit conversion of nonprofit hospitals in the U.S. health care system: Eight case studies. The Commonwealth Fund, Retrieved June 11, 2008 from http://www.commonwealthfund.org/publications/ publications_show.htm?doc_id=221349

Cothran, H., and Wysocki, A. (2005). Developing SMART goals for your organization. Gainesville, FL: University of Florida, Institute of Food and Agricultural Sciences.

Countryside Agency (2004), *Newlands community involvement research; Final report*. London: Countryside Agency.

Eliot and Associates (2005). Guidelines for conducting a focus group. Group Wisdom, Retrieved June 19, 2008 from http://cp0.ipnshosting.com/~focusgro/ documents/How_to_Conduct_a_Focus_Group.pdf

Fisher, R. J. (1990). Needs theory, social identity and an eclectic model of conflict. In Burton, John (Ed), *Conflict: Human needs theory* (pp. 89–112). New York: St. Martin's Press.

Foundation Center (2008a). Top funders: Top 100 U.S. foundations by asset size. Retrieved August 14 2008 from http://foundationcenter.org/findfun ders/topfunders/top100assets.html

Foundation Center (2008b). Top funders: Top 100 U.S. foundations by total giving. Retrieved August 14 2008 from http://foundationcenter.org/ findfunders/topfunders/top100giving.html

Glisson, C., and Durick, M. (1988). Predictors of job satisfaction and organizational commitment in human service organizations. *Administrative Science Quarterly*, 33, 61–81.

Goleman, D. (1998).What makes a leader? *Harvard Business Review*, 76, 93–102.

Greater Twin Cities United Way, 1995, Retrieved August 14 2008 from http://www.managementhelp. org/org_eval/uw_list.htm#anchor149020

Haas Center for Public Service, Stanford University (n.d.). Retrieved August 12, 2008 from Setting Organizational Goals http://haas.stanford.edu/ pdfs/Setting%20Organizational%20Goal.pdf

Hammond, J., Keeney, R., and Raiffa, H. (1998). The hidden traps in decision-making, *Harvard Business Review*, 76, 47–58.

Holden Leadership Center, University of Oregon (n.d.). Constitution and bylaws. Retrieved August

7, 2008 from http://uoleadership.uoregon.edu/tip_sheets/org_structure/constitution

Homan, S. (2008). *Promoting community change* (4th ed.). Belmont, CA: Thompson.

Hopkins, L. (n.d.). Better communication results. Retrieved August 8, 2008 from http://bettercommunicationresults.com.au/organizational-communication-barriers.html

Horwath, J., and Morrison, T. (2000). Identifying and implementing pathways for organizational change – using the Framework for the Assessment of Children in Need and their Families as a case example. *Child and Family Social Work, 5,* 245–254.

Hyde, C. (2004). Multicultural development in human service agencies: Challenges and solutions. *Social Work, 49*(1), 7–16.

Irvin, R., and Stansbury, J. (2004). Citizen participation in decision making: Is it worth the effort? *Public Administration Review, 64*(1), 55–65.

Irvine, A., and Young, T. (2002). Paradigm for pluralism: Mikail Bakhtin and social work practice. *Social Work, 47,* 19–29.

Julian, D., and Kombarakaran, F., (2006). Assessment of quality of outcomes within a local United Way organization: Implications for sustaining system level change. *American Journal of Community Psychology, 38,* 175–181.

Kauffman, S. (1995). Conflict management in citizen participation programs: The Lipari landfill Superfund site. *Journal of Community Practice, 2*(2), 33–54.

Kluger, M. (2006). The program evaluation grid: A planning and assessment tool for non-profit organizations. *Administration in Social Work, 30*(1), 33–44.

Lao Tzu (trans 1944). *The way of life according to Lao Tzu.* (W. Bynner, Trans.) New York: Capricorn.

Leadership Resource Office, University of Oregon (n.d.). Setting goals for your organization. Retrieved August 12, 2008, from http://www.smallfoundations.org/atf/cf/%7BC787FF7B-7EF1-45BB-A4C5-0AAD614C9B5F%7D/BOB%20Handout%20-%20Setting%20Goals.pdf

Luongo, G. (2007). Re-thinking child welfare training models to achieve evidence based practices. *Administration in Social Work, 31*(2), 87–96.

McNamara, C. (n.d.). Basic definition of organization. *Internet, Free Management Library,* Retrieved June 10, 2008, from http://www.managementhelp.org/org_thry/org_defn.htm

McNutt, J., and Boland, K. (2007). Astroturf, technology and the future of community mobilization: Implications for nonprofit theory. *Journal of Sociology & Social Welfare, 34*(3), 165–178.

Mintzberg, H. (1983). *Power in and around organizations.* Englewood Cliffs, NJ: Prentice-Hall.

New Jersey Commission on Higher Education Educational Opportunity Fund, 2006. Retrieved August 7, 2008 from http://nj.gov/highereducation/PPTs/mission_and_goal_setting.ppt

Office of the Deputy Prime Minister (2005). *Improving delivery of mainstream services in deprived areas - The role of community involvement.* London: Office of the Deputy Prime Minister.

Patti, R. (2000). The landscape of social welfare management. In R.J. Patti (Ed.), *The handbook of social welfare management,* (pp. 3–25). Thousand Oaks, CA: Sage Publications, Inc.

Poulin, J., Silver, P., and Kauffman, S. (2007). An integrated approach to program conceptualization, curriculum analyses, outcome assessment. *Journal of Baccalaureate Social Work, 13*(1), 81–99.

Poulin, J., and Walter, C. (1992). Retention plans and job satisfaction of gerontological social workers. *Journal of Gerontological Social Work, 19,* 99–114.

Poulin, J., and Walter, C. (1993). Burnout in gerontological social work. *Social Work, 38,* 305–316.

Senge, P., Cambron-McCabe, N., Lucas, T., Smith, B., Dutton, J., and Kleiner, A. (2000). *Schools that learn: A fifth discipline fieldbook for educators, parents, and everyone who cares about education.* New York: Doubleday.

Shapira, Z. (2002). *Organizational decision-making.* Cambridge Cambridge University Press.

Schmid, H. (2004). Organizational-environment relationships: Theory for management practice in human service organizations. *Administration in Social Work, 28*(1), 97–113.

Silver, P., Poulin, J., and Manning, R. (1997). Surviving the bureaucracy: Predictors of job satisfaction of direct service supervisors in public human services. *The Clinical Supervisor, 15,* 1–20.

Simpson, D. (2002). A conceptual framework for transferring research to practice. *Journal of Substance Abuse Treatment, 22*(4), 171–182.

Steen, J., and Smith, T. (2007). An assessment of the minimization of risk and the maximization of opportunity among private nonprofit agencies in Florida. *Administration in Social Work, 31*(3), 29–39.

Special Libraries Association (1997). Strategic planning handbook. Retrieved August 7, 2008 from http://www.sla.org/pdfs/sphand.pdf

Supan, T. (2008). Licensure vs. certification: How it can affect you! Amputee Coalition of America. Retrieved August 11, 2008 from https://www.amputee-coalition.org/absolutenm/anmviewer.asp?a=19&z=9

Urban Institute (2008). Number of nonprofit organizations in the United States, 1996–2006, Retrieved June 11, 2008 from http://nccsdataweb.urban.org/PubApps/profile1.php?state=US

Wilson, R., Wartburton, D., and Anderson, E. (2005). *People and Participation. Putting citizens at the heart of decision-making.* London: Involve.

Wolff, T. (2001). Introduction to community coalition building: Contemporary practice and research. *American Journal of Community Psychology, 29,* 165–172.

Wuenschel, P. (2006). The diminishing role of social work administrators in social service agencies: Issues for consideration. *Administration in Social Work, 30*(4), 518.

Zimmerman, M., and Rappaport, J. (1988). Citizen participation, perceived control, and psychological empowerment. *American Journal of Community Psychology, 16*(5), 725–750.

APPENDIX A

Example:
Organizational Capacity Assessment

Agency Name _____ **Assessor:** _____

Location of Agency	Address 1		Address 2	
	State	Zip		Phone
	E-mail	Fax		
	Contact person			

Is the agency for-profit or nonprofit?	For profit	Nonprofit		
Is the agency governmental or nongovernmental?	Governmental	Nongovernmental	Level of government	
Is the agency faith-based?	Faith-based	Non faith-based	Religious affiliation (Type or denomination)	

Programs (Name of program)	Description	Number of Staff	Number of Clients	Year Service Started	Annual Budget
1.					
2.					
3.					

Groups Interviewed for Assessment	Number of Persons Interviewed	Primary Expressed Concerns
Administration		
Supervisors		
Direct care staff, type I		
Direct care staff, type II		
Support Staff		
Clients		
Community members		
Other (describe)		
Other (describe)		

APPENDIX A *continued*

Part I: *Record in the Score column as Strong Strength, Weak Strength, Neutral, Weak Challenge, or Strong Challenge. Provide comments where relevant. The grade (C= 1, B=2, B+ =3, A–= 4, A= 5) that best describes the paper's coverage of each component (1–7)*

Internal Organizational Considerations	Strong Strength	Weak Strength	Neutral	Weak Challenge	Strong Challenge
Foundation Policies					
Vision					
Mission					
Goals					
Objectives					
Constitutions and by-laws					
Strategic plans					

Internal Organizational Considerations	Strong Strength	Weak Strength	Neutral	Weak Challenge	Strong Challenge
Internal Structure and Processes					
Administration—Board of trustees					
Quality of policy development, planning tasks					
Quality of resource development and acquisition tasks					
Quality of compliance with external (and legal) requirements tasks					
Quality of networking tasks					
Attention to long-term sustainability					
Administration—Executive Director					
Quality of policy development, planning tasks					
Quality of resource development and acquisition tasks					
Quality of compliance with external (and legal) requirements tasks					
Quality of networking tasks					
Quality of support for subordinate staff					

APPENDIX A *continued*

Appropriateness of use of authority					
Quality of leadership tasks					

Internal Structure and Processes (Cont.)	Strong Strength	Weak Strength	Neutral	Weak Challenge	Strong Challenge
Supervisors					
Quality of policy translation tasks					
Quality of communication tasks					
Quality of support for front line					
Quality of guidance/education to the front line worker					
Front Line Staff					
Perception of workload size					
Level of training and skills					
Perception of work-task clarity					
Quality of primary work-task outcomes					
Level of conflict					
Adequacy of resources to complete work tasks					
External Organizational Considerations	**Strong Strength**	**Weak Strength**	**Neutral**	**Weak Challenge**	**Strong Challenge**
Level of support from community, community groups					
Perception of legal and policy environment					

APPENDIX A *continued*

Comments on areas of concern. Identification of source of
problem _____
_____
_____
_____
_____
_____
_____
_____
_____
_____
_____
_____
_____

Comments on conflict (if relevant)

- What are the causes of conflict?
  - Is there a history, or is this a new
    event? _____
  - Are the causes concrete or are they
    ideological? _____
  - Are their motivations that support the
    conflict? _____
  - What forces sustain/reduce the
    conflict? _____
- Who are the participants?
  - Is it between individuals or
    groups? _____
  - What are the power differences between
    participants? _____
- What possible solutions exist?
  - Are there common points of agreement among the
    participants? _____
  - Are there individuals or groups that both sides trust,
    and who may be called upon to help reduce the
    conflict? _____

APPENDIX B

ALTERNATE EXAMPLE: AGENCY ASSESSMENT TOOL

COMMUNITY-BASED ABSTINENCE EDUCATION PROGRAM
MONITORING and SELF-ASSESMENT TOOL
COHORT 1
2007–2008

Grant Agreement #: _____ Date(s): _____

Program Name: _____ County: _____

Lead Agency Administrator: _____

Business Administrator/Fiscal Manager: _____

Project/Program Director: _____

Date(s) of Visitation: _____ Location: _____

PDE Program Officer _____

STATE REVIEWER

Lead: _____ Team Member: _____

LEAD STAFF INTERVIEWED

Name: _____   Position: _____

Name: _____   Position: _____

Name: _____   Position: _____

Name: _____   Position: _____

Name: _____   Position: _____

CONSORTIUM PARTNER/COLLABORATING AGENCY STAFF INTERVIEWED

Name: _____   Position: _____

Name: _____   Position: _____

Name: _____   Position: _____

Name: _____   Position: _____

PROGRAM PARTICIPANTS INTERVIEWED

Name: _____   Name: _____

Name: _____   Name: _____

APPENDIX B *continued*

I. Contract Management, Goal Setting, Sustainability		
A. Requirements	**Documentation**	**Status**
1. The community, parents, and students were given notice of the applicant's intent to submit an application and were invited to give input.	- Copy of the advertisement - Copy of other notification - Input documentation	❑ Exceptional ❑ Sufficient progress ❑ Needs improvement
2. The contract and any waiver, program, and budget revision requests are available for public review.	- Copy of notification/procedure - Procedure is prominently displayed	❑ Exceptional ❑ Sufficient progress ❑ Needs improvement
3. The grantee communicates the program goals/objectives to staff, participants, and the families of the participants.	- Student, parent, staff handbook - Meeting minutes and/or agendas - Program handouts/advertising	❑ Exceptional ❑ Sufficient progress ❑ Needs improvement
4. The project is being implemented as described in the contract and all activities are on schedule.	- Quarterly reports - Data - Program report - Other, please explain:	❑ Exceptional ❑ Sufficient progress ❑ Needs improvement
5. The program has implemented academic enrichment activities that are evidence based.	- Program materials - Rationale for choosing specific activities - Research documentation - Other, please explain:	❑ Exceptional ❑ Sufficient progress ❑ Needs improvement
6. The program has developed a detailed sustainability plan and has made efforts to gain other sources of funding or in-kind resources to continue after grant funding ends.	- Detailed sustainability plan - Description of any grants or resources program has attempted to secure - Other, please explain:	❑ Exceptional ❑ Sufficient progress ❑ Needs improvement

Comments:

APPENDIX B *continued*

I. Management, Staffing, and Professional Development		
A. Requirements	**Documentation**	**Status**
1. The organizational structure is sound and the program management is effective.	- Staff organizational chart - Program management materials - Written policies/procedures - Other, please explain:	❑ Exceptional ❑ Sufficient progress ❑ Needs improvement
2. The project director and staff are highly qualified, well experienced and have good morale. They all have had appropriate background checks and Act 33 & 34 clearances.	- Resumes **and** job descriptions - Act 33 and 34 documentation - Time sheets - Staff rosters	❑ Exceptional ❑ Sufficient progress ❑ Needs improvement
3. Staff receives ongoing professional development and all have been trained on program policies and procedures. Staff attend regular staff meetings	- Description of training/trainers - Which staff/volunteers enrolled? - Staff/volunteer handbook - Staff meeting schedule and minutes - Other, please explain:	❑ Exceptional ❑ Sufficient progress ❑ Needs improvement
4. The project director and relevant staff meet with school day staff on a regular basis.	- Meeting schedules, minutes - Correspondence - Other, please explain:	❑ Exceptional ❑ Sufficient progress ❑ Needs improvement
5. At least two staff have attended two national CBAE training each year.	- Training registrations - Training materials	❑ Exceptional ❑ Sufficient progress ❑ Needs improvement

Comments:

APPENDIX B *continued*

II. Management, Staffing, and Professional Development		
B. Quality Program Components	**Documentation**	**Status**
1. The student/staff ratio is low and sufficient to meet student needs. Indicate the ratio for academic activities _____ and for recreational/cultural activities _____.	- Staff rosters - Student enrollment data - Staff/Student attendance sheets	❑ Exceptional ❑ Sufficient progress ❑ Needs improvement
2. The majority of staff members represent and are able to address the diverse needs of the target student population.	- Description of staff - Staff interviews - Other, please explain:	❑ Exceptional ❑ Sufficient progress ❑ Needs improvement
3. Staff are recruited and retained through a rigorous process that results in well-qualified candidates and low staff turnover.	- Description of recruiting process - Job postings/advertisements - Staff work/retention records - Staff turnover data	❑ Exceptional ❑ Sufficient progress ❑ Needs improvement
4. Program volunteers are recruited and trained effectively and play an important role in program operation and/or student service provision.	- Volunteer job descriptions/postings - Volunteer training materials - Volunteer handbook/policies - Other, please explain:	❑ Exceptional ❑ Sufficient progress ❑ Needs improvement
5. Staff and volunteers are evaluated on a regular basis and given clear feedback for continuous performance improvement.	- Staff performance appraisals - Volunteer rating criteria/format - Other, please explain:	❑ Exceptional ❑ Sufficient progress ❑ Needs improvement

Comments:

APPENDIX B *continued*

III. Partnerships and Collaborations		
A. Requirements	**Documentation**	**Status**
1. There are formal written agreements between the grantee, the target school district(s), and collaborating partners.	- Letters of Agreement/ MOU/MOA - Contracts/subcontracts - Documentation of services/ activities - Other: please specify:	❑ Exceptional ❑ Sufficient progress ❑ Needs improvement
2. Collaborators have provided programs and services in accordance with the grant contract narrative.	- List and/or description of services provided - Written agreements - Interviews - Other, please explain:	❑ Exceptional ❑ Sufficient progress ❑ Needs improvement
3. The program has made efforts to establish and maintain partners and collaborators to ensure long-term commitments of resources and fiscal and human capital.	- Interviews - Meeting minutes/notes - Written agreements	❑ Exceptional ❑ Sufficient progress ❑ Needs improvement
III. Partnerships and Collaborations		
B. Quality Program Components	**Documentation**	**Status**
1. Challenges in working with collaborators have been handled effectively with positive results.	- Description of relationships - Correspondence - Meeting agendas, notes - Other, please explain:	❑ Exceptional ❑ Sufficient progress ❑ Needs improvement
2. The program seeks additional collaborators to address unmet needs and/or to expand/enhance services.	- Correspondence - Other, please explain:	❑ Exceptional ❑ Sufficient progress ❑ Needs improvement
3. The program has established linkages with other state, federal, and local agencies that currently provide services to the target population.	- Correspondence - Meeting minutes/notes - Other, please explain:	❑ Exceptional ❑ Sufficient progress ❑ Needs improvement
4. The program integrates CBAE activities with state funded tutoring initiatives (Educational Assistance Program, Classroom plus, SES, Accountability block Grant tutoring grants).	- Program schedules - Student rosters - Other, please explain:	❑ Exceptional ❑ Sufficient progress ❑ Needs improvement

APPENDIX B *continued*

5. If applicable, the program works effectively with the existing Student Assistance Program (SAP) and nearest DPW-funded Family Center.	- Meeting minutes/notes - Student referrals	❏ Exceptional ❏ Sufficient progress ❏ Needs improvement

Additional Comments:

APPENDIX B *continued*

IV. Participant Involvement and Center Operation		
A. Requirements	**Documentation**	**Status**
1. The program has identified and is servicing eligible students and their families consistent with the approved contract.	- Participant list - Registration form - Academic and low income data - Other, please explain:	❑ Exceptional ❑ Sufficient progress ❑ Needs improvement
2. The grantee has advertised its program and services.	- Newspaper, radio, TV ads - School postings, announcements - Outreach activities - Other, please explain:	❑ Exceptional ❑ Sufficient progress ❑ Needs improvement
3. The hours, activity schedules, and locations are available, accessible, and meet the needs of the target population.	- School postings, announcements - Registration information - Activity logs - Other, please explain:	❑ Exceptional ❑ Sufficient progress ❑ Needs improvement
4. Academic enrichment activities are provided on a daily basis, involve innovative teaching strategies and are individualized to meet students' needs.	- Curricular materials - Activity logs/descriptions - Registration information - Other, please explain:	❑ Exceptional ❑ Sufficient progress ❑ Needs improvement
5. The program integrates the school day curricula into its activities, and the educational activities offered support regular school-day learning.	- Description of activities - Curricula materials - Course outlines - Other, please explain:	❑ Exceptional ❑ Sufficient progress ❑ Needs improvement
6. Transportation is provided for activities and to insure that all children have safe passage home.	- Transportation logs - Other, explain:	❑ Exceptional ❑ Sufficient progress ❑ Needs improvement
7. The program has accommodated children with special needs.	- Documentation of accommodations provided, e.g., assistive devices, aides, special transportation	❑ Exceptional ❑ Sufficient progress ❑ Needs improvement
8. The program maintains an open-door policy for parents and holds quarterly open house meetings for children's families.	- Open door policy information - Open house announcements - Activity logs - Other, please explain:	❑ Exceptional ❑ Sufficient progress ❑ Needs improvement

APPENDIX B *continued*

9. The program has established a CBAE Advisory Board that meets quarterly and is comprised of private, public, and community representatives AND at least two parents and two students.	- Meeting notices, agendas, minutes - Sign-in sheets - Activity logs - Other, please explain:	❏ Exceptional ❏ Sufficient progress ❏ Needs improvement

Additional Comments:

APPENDIX B *continued*

IV. Participant Involvement and Center Operation		
B. Quality Program Components	Documentation	Status
1. There is an aggressive attendance policy to reduce program and to insure children participate in the program on a regular, consistent basis.	- Written policy/procedure - Home visit report/phone log - School and program attendance records	❑ Exceptional ❑ Sufficient progress ❑ Needs improvement
2. The program operates for at least 12 hours.	- Program schedules - Activity logs - Student activity rosters - Student sign-in sheets	❑ Exceptional ❑ Sufficient progress ❑ Needs improvement
3. Parental involvement is encouraged, and a variety of activities are provided to address family needs.	- Parent meeting minutes - Correspondence - Surveys - Activity logs - Other, please explain:	❑ Exceptional ❑ Sufficient progress ❑ Needs improvement
4. Communication with parents is frequent and includes information on students' experiences, behavior, and achievements in the program. Information is transmitted to Limited English Proficient and special needs families in language/methods/modes that are appropriate and easily understood.	- Correspondence - Parent meetings - Translation/assistive materials - Other, please explain:	❑ Exceptional ❑ Sufficient progress ❑ Needs improvement

Comments:

APPENDIX B *continued*

V. Evaluation of Program Progress and Effectiveness		
Requirement	**Documentation**	**Status**
1. A local level evaluation process has been established.	- Evaluation plan, instruments, data - Vendor contract - Reports - Other, please explain:	❏ Exceptional ❏ Sufficient progress ❏ Needs improvement
2. The program has evaluated its progress towards meeting program goals and objectives and is using information collected for continuous improvement.	- Program indicator data/ measurements - Interviews/surveys - Reports - Changes made to program based on feedback - Other, please explain:	❏ Exceptional ❏ Sufficient progress ❏ Needs improvement
3. If applicable, is there a written release form to secure parental permission to get performance data from the child's school?	- Written policy - Signed release forms - Correspondence - Other, please explain:	❏ Exceptional ❏ Sufficient progress ❏ Needs improvement

Additional Information:

APPENDIX B *continued*

V. Evaluation of Program Progress and Effectiveness		
B. Quality Program Components	**Documentation**	**Status**
1. Qualitative and quantitative program information and data on participation, performance, and outcomes have been collected, analyzed and reported to the US Department of Education and other relevant agencies/parties.	- Statistics - Reports - Attendance logs - Student grades - Annual performance report data - Other, please explain:	❏ Exceptional ❏ Sufficient progress ❏ Needs improvement
2. Evaluation findings have been communicated to staff, collaborators, parents, students, and other stakeholders.	- Correspondence - Announcements - Meeting minutes - Other, please explain:	❏ Exceptional ❏ Sufficient progress ❏ Needs improvement
3. In addition to evaluation data, the program has collected anecdotal stories about program impacts on the students/their families.	- Student/parent reports, comments - Letters, testimonies - Other, please explain:	❏ Exceptional ❏ Sufficient progress ❏ Needs improvement

Additional Information:

APPENDIX B *continued*

VI. Safety, Health, Nutrition		
Requirements	**Documentation**	**Status**
1. The vehicles used for transportation have been inspected for safety.	- Inspection information - Contracts - Other, please explain	❏ Exceptional ❏ Sufficient progress ❏ Needs improvement
2. The program provides daily nutritional snacks and files for USDA reimbursement for those snacks.	- List/description of snacks - USDA reimbursement materials	❏ Exceptional ❏ Sufficient progress ❏ Needs improvement
3. The program addresses participants' unique health needs that have been identified by the parents and/or the school.	- Student records - Other, please explain	❏ Exceptional ❏ Sufficient progress ❏ Needs improvement
4. Emergency contact information for students and staff is maintained in an easily accessible, but secure central location.	- Staff and student emergency contact information - Other, please explain:	❏ Exceptional ❏ Sufficient progress ❏ Needs improvement
5. The program has established procedures for authorized student pick-ups and has provided these procedures to staff and families.	- Parental release forms - Sign-in/sign-out forms - Other, please explain:	❏ Exceptional ❏ Sufficient progress ❏ Needs improvement
6. Adequate security and appropriate equipment are in place at every program site.	- Site information - Security personnel logs - Equipment inventories by site - Other, please explain:	❏ Exceptional ❏ Sufficient progress ❏ Needs improvement

Additional Comments:

APPENDIX B *continued*

VI. Safety, Health, Nutrition		
B. Quality Program Components	Documentation	Status
1. The spaces used for all program sites are adequate, appropriate, and safe.	- Activity location descriptions - Facilities use criteria and policies - Other, please explain:	❑ Exceptional ❑ Sufficient progress ❑ Needs improvement
2. Do you have an emergency readiness plan? If so, what is it, where is it located, and how have staff and parents been informed of it?	- Emergency exit plan - Snow closing plan (inclement weather) - Staff meeting minutes, correspondence, handouts - Other, please explain:	❑ Exceptional ❑ Sufficient progress ❑ Needs improvement
Additional Comments:		

APPENDIX B *continued*

VII. Summary				
Evaluation of Records and Procedures	**Completed**	**Sufficient Progress**	**Noncompliant**	**Comments**
Contract management, goal setting, and sustainability				
Management, staffing, and professional development				
Partnerships and collaborations				
Participant involvement and center operation				
Evaluation of program progress and effectiveness				
Safety, health, and nutrition				

As the representative of the above-mentioned program, I hereby confirm and verify the validity of the information reported.

Signed   Title

PLEASE PRINT YOUR NAME CLEARLY   DATE

Signed by Reviewer   Title

PLEASE PRINT OR TYPE   DATE

Witness Signature   Title

PLEASE PRINT OR TYPE

APPENDIX B *continued*

Example: Organizational Goal Planning Form

Agency Name: _____ Social Worker: _____

Problem Area 1:	
	Define problem here from assessment. Include specific indicators in the description.

	Goal and Objective Response: In space below, write a goal to address problem area 1. Follow the goal with objectives as needed. For each objective, be sure to include problem indicator, amount of desired change in the indicator, and time for completion of objective. Use additional pages if more than five objectives per goal.
	Goal 1:
Objective 1.1	
Objective 1.2	
Objective 1.3	
Objective 1.4	
Objective 1.5	

Problem Area 2:	
	Define problem here from assessment. Include specific indicators in the description.

APPENDIX B *continued*

Goal and Objective Response: In space below, write a goal to address problem area 1. Follow the goal with objectives as needed. For each objective, be sure to include problem indicator, amount of desired change in the indicator, and time for completion of objective. Use additional pages if more than five objectives per goal.	
Goal 2:	
Objective 2.1	
Objective 2.2	
Objective 2.3	
Objective 2.4	
Objective 2.5	

Problem Area 3:	
	Define problem here from assessment. Include specific indicators in the description.
Goal and Objective Response: In space below, write a goal to address problem area 1. Follow the goal with objectives as needed. For each objective, be sure to include problem indicator, amount of desired change in the indicator, and time for completion of objective. Use additional pages if more than five objectives per goal.	
Goal 3:	
Objective 3.1	
Objective 3.2	
Objective 3.3	
Objective 3.4	
Objective 3.5	

APPENDIX B *continued*

Problem Area 4:	
	Define problem here from assessment. Include specific indicators in the description.
	Goal and Objective Response: In space below, write a goal to address problem area 1. Follow the goal with objectives as needed. For each objective, be sure to include problem indicator, amount of desired change in the indicator, and time for completion of objective. Use additional pages if more than five objectives per goal.
	Goal 4:
	Objective 4.1
	Objective 4.2
	Objective 4.3
	Objective 4.4
	Objective 4.5

APPENDIX C

Example: Organizational Intervention Planning Form

Agency Name: _____   **Social Worker:** _____

Goal 1:				
Objective 1.1				
Task/Action	Responsibility	Completion Date	Comments	Completed?

Goal 1:				
Objective 1.2				
Task/Action	Responsibility	Completion Date	Comments	Completed?

Goal 1:				
Objective 1.3				
Task/Action	Responsibility	Completion Date	Comments	Completed?

APPENDIX D

Organizational Evaluation/Objective Attainment Tracking Form

Agency Name: ———————————— Social Worker ————————————

Goal 1:			
	Objective 1.1		
Measures (Identify measure/ indicator)	Measure	**Time frame (Identify baseline date and completion date)**	Time frame Baseline— Completion—
Method (Identify data source	Method	**Responsibility**	Responsibility
Outcome (Circle final outcome)	Objective met	Objective partially met	Objective not met

Goal 1:			
	Objective 1.2		
Measures (Identify measure/ indicator)	Measure	**Time frame (Identify baseline date and completion date)**	Time frame Baseline— Completion—
Method (Identify data source	Method	**Responsibility**	Responsibility
Outcome (Circle final outcome)	Objective met	Objective partially met	Objective not met

Goal 1:			
	Objective 1.3		
Measures (Identify measure/ indicator)	Measure	**Time frame (Identify baseline date and completion date)**	Time frame Baseline— Completion—
Method (Identify data source)	Method	**Responsibility**	Responsibility
Outcome (Circle final outcome)	Objective met	Objective partially met	Objective not met

10 | GENERALIST PRACTICE WITH COMMUNITIES

Marina Barnett

Trina is a senior BSW student. She has an interest in working with youth in an educational setting and has been placed in an inner city school district. She has been working with Adia, a fifth grade girl who has been skipping school. Sessions with the Adia reveal that she doesn't like coming to school because she is being teased by other students in the class. Trina schedules a home visit with Adia's parents to discuss the truancy issue. Adia's parents both work at the local university. Adia's mother is an administrative assistant, and her father is a security guard.

"I don't know what to do with that girl." Adia's mother states dispiritedly. "I take her to school every day and drop her off myself. She won't stay. Those kids down there are so mean to her. We've tried to help her lose the weight, her doctor says that she is 25 pounds overweight now and it seems to be getting worse. She has gained 10 pounds in the past 3 months since this mess all started." "We try to keep the junk out of the house," said Adia's father, "but she sneaks it. And that cafeteria is the worst! Hot dogs, hamburgers, pizza, hot wings! Soda machines in the cafeteria and candy galore in the school store. The homemade lunches we send with her every day can't compete with that. Not to mention that they just got rid of another gym period at the school in order to give more time to preparing for the achievement tests. We can't keep up."

Trina asks the parents if they are members of the Home and School Association. Both parents indicate that their schedules are hectic and that they don't have time to attend the meetings. Trina lets them know that there is a meeting scheduled every third Wednesday at 7:30 p.m. The meetings only last an hour and Trina encourages them to come to the meeting to discuss their concerns about the nutrition and exercise at the school. Adia's mother attends the meeting and brings up the issues. At the meeting she meets several parents who have the same concerns. They form a committee to investigate the issue further.

The next day, Trina receives a call from Adia's mother. Several of the parents are getting together to discuss a strategy for addressing obesity among their children and she invites Trina to attend. Trina asks if it is OK to invite her supervisor and the school nurse to the meeting. At the meeting the school nurse indicates that their last round of health screenings indicate that as many as 20% of the youth in the district are overweight.

Trina has just had her first experience engaging the community in which she was placed. Her willingness to be led by the clients rather than to identify the issues for them allows for the clients to define their own direction and to have more control in the outcomes. By the end of the chapter, you will be able to help Trina:

1. Conduct a community assessment
2. Develop a community-based intervention
3. Evaluate the impact of your intervention

SOCIAL WORK PRACTICE WITH COMMUNITIES

Many social workers find that the problems their clients face fall outside of the traditional office work place. Often our work takes us out of the office and into the community to work with our clients. Simply stated, a community is a group of people who share a common place, experience, or interest. **Communities** may include people who live within a particular physical geography (West Philadelphians, Texans), or may include people who have shared interests (Star Trek enthusiasts, runners, cyclists), or share certain characteristics (ethnic and or cultural backgrounds, language, race).

Community practice is the application of generalist social work skills to alter the behavioral patterns of community groups, organizations, and institutions, or people's relationships and interactions with these entities (Hardcastle, Powers, and Wencour, 2004). Community practice includes community organization and development, social planning, social action, and social administration (Hardcastle, Powers, and Wencour, 2004). Within communities there are three major subsystems: ethnicity and culture, community conditions, and community resources. These subsystems are highly interrelated and affect your community work as a generalist social worker.

ETHNICITY AND CULTURE

All communities vary in terms of ethnicity and culture. This subsystem is composed of the community's values and beliefs. Cultural beliefs shape a community's value system the same way they shape an individual's value system. Community values play a major role in the helping relationship. They influence the client's and worker's values and beliefs. They also affect the agency's organizational policies and procedures. In assessing the client's concerns, you and your clients need to take prevailing community values and beliefs into account. If there is a value clash between the client and the community values, the implications of the clash need to be explored from the worker's, the client's, the agency's, and the community's perspectives. Often, value positions are taken for granted and not directly addressed in the assessment process.

COMMUNITY CONDITIONS

Community conditions can also have a significant effect on clients and on the helping relationship. Employment opportunities, housing quality and availability, accessibility and affordability of transportation, quality of the educational system, availability of leisure activities, and other conditions can profoundly affect clients, their life situations, and the helping relationship. You and your clients need to assess all the potential environmental factors that might influence the client's ability to resolve the identified target problem. Many interpersonal or social functioning problems have environmental components. The helping relationship might focus on environmental change or on overcoming the difficulties associated with the environmental problem (Young, 1994). In other instances, simply increasing awareness of environmental conditions helps you and the client understand the client's subjective reality.

COMMUNITY SERVICES AND RESOURCES

Community services and resources can also affect the helping relationship system. Community resources include social service organizations, community groups, and religious organizations. You and your client need to review the client's past and current history with social service and community groups. This review can identify important sources of assistance in the client's life as well as the client's nonuse of available community services. It is also important to understand clients' perceptions of their experiences with other helping professionals and community groups. Helping clients think through and articulate what they like and disliked about their previous interactions with helping professionals provides important clues about how to productively work together. The process also helps the client put this helping relationship into a perspective that differentiates it from previous experiences. If the client has not used other social or community services, you and the client need to explore the reasons the client did not use these available resources.

PERSPECTIVES IN WORKING WITH COMMUNITIES

Generalist social workers engaged in community practice tend to work with professional task forces, community coalitions, and neighborhood or community citizen's groups. Often the purpose of community practice is to improve community or neighborhood conditions, empower residents, develop resources, increase community awareness of social and economic problems, and mobilize the community to advocate for needed resources and changes.

Our professional code of ethics calls upon us to work not just with individuals, but also the surrounding environment in which they live and interact. How we view the community influences the manner in which we interact with them and the type of services we provide. The perspective of the social worker is key in determining the type of intervention that they will engage in with the community.

DEFICIT APPROACH TO ADDRESSING COMMUNITY PROBLEMS

Traditional social work has utilized a deficit approach to organizing. This approach derives from the medical model and seeks to identify community dysfunction. The focus of this approach is for social workers to identify social issues that exist in the community and to develop programs to address those problems. The explicit assumption is that the solutions to the community's problems are to be addressed by outside intervention. The responsibility for defining the issues lies with the social worker or the professional. This approach often focuses solely on the identification of community pathology and deficits. Often social workers rely on secondary data (e.g., census data and reports) to ascertain community issues and to assess the adequacy of services. The questions for the analysis are designed by the professional. Interviews, if conducted, generally focus on the perceptions of other professionals and do not include the voices of the community members themselves. This information, once compiled, can often present a dismal picture of the analysis or target area. Efforts are then focused on how we as social workers can meet these needs rather than seeking the expertise of the indigenous population to address its concerns.

Although the problem-solving approach allows the social worker to ascertain the knowledge of the community in assessing the problems, the tools to address the problems are often seen as external to the community itself. The message that is transmitted to the community is that when they (the community) have problems, it is we (the professionals) who are most capable of defining and implementing the solutions. This messianic approach negates the capacity of the client to identify potential solutions and perpetuates negative stereotypes of the community itself.

EMPOWERMENT APPROACH TO ASSESSING COMMUNITY NEEDS

The empowerment perspective is useful to conceptualize the manner in which social workers approach the work that they do in communities. As stated earlier, "Empowerment is the process of increasing personal, interpersonal or political power so that individuals can take action to improve their life situations" (Gutierrez, 1990, p. 149). The empowerment perspective focuses on the dialogues and building relationships with community members. The community is seen as capable of identifying and addressing their own issues. The social worker acts not as an expert, but as a partner in the helping process.

The empowerment perspective recognizes that everyone is endowed with qualities and strengths that allow them to solve their own problems. This strengths approach allows for increased investment and participation of the clients and views them not merely as passive recipients of services, but as partners in the process of solving their own problems.

THE COLLABORATIVE MODEL AND COMMUNITY PRACTICE

Community practice is an "intervention process used by social workers and other professionals to help individuals, groups, and collectives of people with common interests or from the same geographic areas to deal with social problems and enhance social well-being through planned collective action" (Barker, 2003, p. 84). Social work practice with communities involves formulating plans, developing strategies, mobilizing necessary resources, identifying and recruiting community leaders, and encouraging interrelationships between them to facilitate their efforts.

In order to carry out these tasks, social workers use a variety of analytic, political, and interactional skills. Social workers engaged in community practice use analytic skills to identify intervention alternatives, compare their relative merits, and develop recommendations for implementation. Social workers use political skills to help assess the feasibility of an action agenda, identify power resources, and develop and implement political strategy. Social workers use interactional skills to help community members make contacts, develop networks, build personal relationships, identify political and economic power in a community, and facilitate coalitions and committees. Finally, social workers use value clarification skills to consider the morality of certain program or action proposals and strategies to obtain support for them (Rivera, 1998).

In order to create change in a community, organizers are involved in a wide array of activities. These include identifying problem areas, analyzing causes, formulating plans, developing strategies, mobilizing necessary resources, identifying and recruiting community leaders, and encouraging interrelationships among them to facilitate their efforts. Figure 10.1 outlines the application of the collaborative model to community practice.

Collaborative Model	Traditional Problem-Solving Model	Input	Skills	Output	Activities
Pre-Engagement	• Recognition of a problem and establishing a need for change • Information gathering • Assessment and development of a theory for change	• Staff time • Meeting space • Community and staff knowledge • Financial resources	• Analytical • Interactional • Research • Values clarification • Commitment to working with the community-driven process and basic respect of people. • High energy, strong motivation • Flexibility and patience, ability to live with ambivalence • Analytical thinking • Sense of humor, perspective and vision • Persistence, focus and follow through	• Community meetings • Needs analysis • Assets analysis • Power analysis	• Identifying problem areas, • Prioritizing problem areas • Analyzing causes (Framing a social/community problem)
Engagement	• Intervention and the change effort	• Intervention models • Expertise in grant writing and program development • Financial resources	• Planning • Management • Supervision • Political • Advocacy • Values clarification • Negotiation • Conflict management • Fundraising • Communications	• Intervention strategy • Programs • Asset map • Resource directory	• Formulating plans, • Developing strategies, • Mobilizing necessary resources, • Identifying and recruiting community leaders, • Encouraging interrelationships among them to facilitate their efforts
Disengagement	• Evaluation and termination of the change effort	• Evaluation expertise • Financial resources	• Critical analysis • Values clarification • Communications • Commitment to social justice • Research	• Evaluation Report	• Evaluation of impact

FIGURE 10.1 | THE COLLABORATIVE MODEL AND COMMUNITY PRACTICE

PRE-ENGAGEMENT

The pre-engagement phase of the collaborative model as it applies to community practice includes the recognition by the community that a problem exists. In this stage, community members may seek out a social worker to help them to solve the problem. The initiator, or the person or persons who "first recognize the existence of the problem and bring attention to the need for change" (Hardcastle, Powers, and Wencour, 2004, p. 13), can be a community member, client, professional in the community, politician, or community group. This phase also includes assessment of the community problem or issue.

Rubin and Rubin (2001) state that "Organizing is about people gaining power to undertake collective actions successfully. The purpose of these actions is to overcome shared problems that are systemic and structural and that have been ignored or incorrectly handled by the government, businesses or charities" (p. 25). Social problems are concerns that have been identified by a large number of community members about a condition that negatively affects their quality of life. Examples of social problems include unemployment, racism, social inequality, poverty, and homelessness. Social problems do not exist on their own; they are socially constructed (Rubin and Rubin, 2001). They are determined by the power and status of those that identify them and the numbers of people that have identified them. In trying to identify social problems, it is helpful to consider the various definitions of the problem. Definitions of the problem may vary depending on who initiates the discussion and are influenced by their values and cultural beliefs.

The relationship between the social worker and the community residents is key to the success of any change effort. Community problems can be identified by residents, professionals, or clients. Community organizers "believe in people, in the ability of regular folks to guide their lives, to speak for themselves, to learn the world, and how to make it better" (Beckwith and Stoecker, 2001, p. 1). In using our interpersonal skills and ethnically sensitive practice, we are able to engage the community members in discussions that allow us to identify the nature of the social problem or issues they would like to address, examine the cultural context of the community, and set goals for addressing those issues.

Social workers act in partnership with community members to address social problems that have been identified by community members. The social work problem-solving strategy is a useful framework for identifying and addressing social problems in a community. The process begins with the identification of a problem or issue that someone in the community wants to change. The social worker engages in working with the community to gather information, conducts an assessment, sets goals and objectives, develops an intervention, and evaluates their efforts (Compton and Galaway, 1979; Epstein, 1980; Lippitt, Watson, and Westley, 1958; Netting, Kettner, and McMurtry, 2008; Pincus and Minahan, 1973).

Generalist social workers need to be skilled in community assessment. Understanding community functioning is vital to the provision of services to individuals, families, and groups as well as to the development of interventions aimed at community change. The ethnicity and culture, social and economic conditions, and the services and resources of communities vary widely. Ignoring the effect of these factors on client systems can result in an unbalanced assessment. Environmental conditions and concerns have a tremendous effect on everyday lives, especially the lives of those living in impoverished and disadvantaged communities. As members of a profession committed to social and economic justice, generalist social workers must make efforts to strengthen and empower disadvantaged communities and their residents. There are three basic types of assessment in community practice: needs assessment, assets assessment, and power assessment. This next section will describe and give examples of these methods of identifying both strengths and deficits in a community.

NEEDS ASSESSMENTS

"Community assessments help to empower community residents to create services and programs that respond to their challenges, concerns and opportunities. It is a systematic way to identify the resources and needs of residents by gathering data, soliciting the perspectives of residents and leaders, and surveying service providers and other community resources" (Samuels, Ahsan, and Garcia, 1995, p. 8).

The social worker and the community partners develop a community profile that incorporates the use of quantitative statistics, demographic indicators, focus groups, and key informant interviews that provide information on political and sociocultural factors. Needs assessments focus on identifying social problems as well as specify direction for action (Haglund, Weisbrod, and Bracht, 1990, p. 91; Marlow, 2005). Royse et al. (2005) state that needs assessments can be used to:

1. Determine if an intervention exists in a community
2. Determine if there are enough clients with a particular problem to justify creating a new program
3. Determine if existing interventions are known or recognized by potential clients
4. Determine what barriers prevent clients from accessing existing services
5. Document the existence of an ongoing or exacerbating social problem (Royse et al., 2005, p. 53).

Regardless of how the needs assessment will be used, the process entails the identification and documentation of issues identified by the community that represent an issue, problem, or gap in services that needs to be addressed.

Steps in the Needs Assessment Process. This section will describe 10 steps in the needs assessment process, these include: defining the goal, defining the community, identifying and collecting existing data, analyzing data, identifying additional data needs, collecting and analyzing additional data, identifying community needs/problems, inventorying existing resources, identifying gaps in services, and planning programs (Philadelphia Health Management Corporation, 1997). Figure 10.2 outlines the steps to completing a needs assessment and the activities associated with each stage.

Step 1: *Define the Goal.* When conducting a needs assessment, it is important to understand how you want to use it. Generalist social workers utilize needs assessments to provide information to mobilize for social action, identify potential partners, and to develop "buy-in" for the community. The key to conducting an assessment from the empowerment perspective is to define the needs by the community, not the social worker.

Step 2: *Define the Community.* As stated earlier, communities encompass various geographic localities, interests, and a diversity of people. It is necessary to define the

Stage	Activities
Define the goal	• Defined by the community • Interviews with key decision makers
Define the community	• Geographic and political boudaries • Service areas
Identify and collect existing data	• Population based-U.S. census, demographic and descriptive data • Resource based-government and agency reports
Analyze data	• Population-socioeconomic, demographic, health, crime • Environment-economic, physical, social
Identify additional data needs	• Identify gaps in information • Collect additional data
Collect and analyze additional data	• Observation • Surveys • Focus groups
Identify community needs/problems	• Needs and issues in the commuity-home, school, neighborhood/streets, psychosocial
Inventory existing resources	• Asset assessment, individual capacity assessment, organizatioal capacity assessment, resource mappiing
Identify gaps in services	• Compare problems and needs to existing resources. • Prioritize needs and predict chances of success.
Plan programs	• Modify existing programs • Develop new programs • Best practices

FIGURE 10.2 | STAGES AND ACTIVITIES IN CONDUCTING NEEDS ASSESSMENTS

Source: Philadelphia Health Management Corporation (1997) Assessing Community Needs

boundaries of the community in which you are working. Examples of community definitions may include physical boundaries (counties, zip codes, neighborhoods where the agency provides services) or may include a specific population (immigrants from Vietnam, Spanish-speaking residents). It is important to involve the community members in the needs assessment process. Often indigenous residents are able to uncover issues that may not be known to the professional community.

Step 3: *Identify and Collect Existing Data.* In documenting the needs of a community, multiple sources of information and a variety of research methodologies are available to you. A mixed methods approach to analyzing needs will allow for a balanced presentation of the information that not only describes phenomena in a community, but also may provide information on the history of the phenomena and potential explanations for causes or contributing factors. You can find information about a social problem in a variety of places. A good place to start is with your clients and professionals in the field who may know something about the existence of the problem that you are trying to address. You will also need to obtain data from the research literature as well as from existing sources of secondary data.

RESEARCH LITERATURE

Effective needs assessments must be grounded in the research literature. In conducting analyses of the literature, we want to consider the following questions: What do we know about the causes and consequences of the problem? What is the magnitude and scope of the problem? What has worked? What has not worked? How does the target community or population vary from those reported in the literature?

Answers to these and other questions place your needs assessment within a context and provide a basis for comparing the significance of the problem being studied and the relevance of the proposed solution with the problem in general and in other communities. The information and retrieval skills discussed in Chapter 5 will help facilitate your literature search and the identification of existing research studies on your topic.

POPULATION AND RESOURCE DATA

The use of multiple population-based and resource-based information is needed to provide a demographic assessment of the community. Population-based information includes the use of census data, public health vital statistics data, and community surveys conducted by either professionals or community residents. These data are generally available from government agencies at the federal, state, and local levels. Census data are available online at *www.census.gov* and can be analyzed by state, county, municipality, and census track. A wealth of population and neighborhood data are contained within the census data. In addition to federal data, "every state maintains a wealth of useful data for planners and evaluators" (Royse et al., 2005, p. 59). Most states have databases of crime and arrest statistics, health indicators, teen pregnancy rates, educational statistics, and many other kinds of information that can be helpful in conducting needs assessments. Other types of government data from over 70 federal government agencies can be accessed on the World Wide Web at *www.fedstats.gov*.

Resource data are government reports that are available on a specific topic. Data from published reports and from private foundations can also be used to document need. Secondary data sources are excellent resources for needs assessments. These reports are available from service providers or private vendors, if available, are relatively cheap to access, and provide a wealth of quantitative and qualitative data on many social and community problems. An example of resource data is the National Survey of Children's Health (http://www.nschdata.org/Content/States.aspx) or the Philadelphia Safe and Sound Community Report Card, 2006 (http://www.phila.gov/pdfs/reportcard2006.pdf).

Figure 10.3 provides a sample listing of Internet sites where you can access demographic data and reports. "Research Navigator Guide: The Helping Professions" is an excellent reference for social workers (Kjosness, Barr, and Rettman, 2004). You might also check with the reference librarian at your university. Often academic departments have designated library liaisons that create specialized reference listings of resources on the Internet that are discipline specific. The categories are usually listed on the library website.

Conducting an assessment of the population and resource data will provide you with information regarding age, race, ethnicity, educational attainment, population size, marital status, morbidity and mortality, income inequality and socioeconomic status, wages, population mobility, employment trends, and community and academic definitions of social problems and previous attempts to address them.

Step 4: *Analyze Data.* Once you have collected the appropriate data, you can now prepare a profile of the community that describes the population (socioeconomic, demographic, health, crime, etc.). You have conducted an assessment of who lives in the community, what it looks like, and what some of the health or economic issues that may need to be addressed are.

Step 5: *Identify Data Needs.* The quantitative analyses tell us what the conditions are, but not necessarily what caused the conditions or why they continue to exist. The analysis may also not give us an accurate picture of the composition of the community. In many communities disenfranchised populations do not necessarily show up in census data. Many minorities go undercounted and unnoticed. Accurate measures of, say, the number of gay or lesbian Spanish-speaking residents in a community are not likely to be documented in a report or on the web. This information can often only be discovered through discussion with community partners. In Step 5 it is necessary to determine what information you still need to collect in order to accomplish your needs assessment goals.

Step 6: *Collect New Data.* There are many ways to collect the data that you need for your community assessment. Observation, surveys, and focus groups provide three options.

OBSERVATION

This type of data collection focuses on documenting behavior as it occurs. The observation may be conducted independently from the group being observed or as a participant. Observation includes going out into the community, walking the streets, interacting with community members, or attending meetings. This allows you to get to know the people and the environment.

- Child Trends (http://www.childtrends.org)
- Children's Defense Fund 2007 Annual Report
  (http://www.childrensdefense.org/site/DocServer/CDF_annual_report_07.pdf?
  docID=8421)
- Children Now (http://www.childrennow.org/)
- ChildStats.gov (http://www.childstats.gov)
- CSU Long Beach Social Work Statistics by Topic
  (http://www.csulb.edu/library/subj/swork/sworkejournals.html)
- FedStats (http://www.fedstats.gov/)
- Institute for Research on Poverty (http://www.ssc.wisc.edu/irp/)
- KIDS COUNT Data Center (http://www.kidscount.org/datacenter/)
- National Clearinghouse on Child Abuse and Neglect Information - Statistics and Research
  (http://nccanch.acf.hhs.gov/general/stats/index.cfm)
- National Data Archive on Child Abuse and Neglect
  (http://www.ndacan.cornell.edu/)
- National Sexual Violence Resource Center (http://www.nsvrc.org/)
- Neighborhoods Online (http://www.neighborhoodsonline.net/)
- Social Statistics Briefing Room
  (http://www.whitehouse.gov/fsbr/ssbr.html)
- State and Local Government on the Net
  (http://www.statelocalgov.net/index.cfm)
- State of the World's Children
  (http://www.unicef.org/sowc05/english/sowc05.pdf)
- Statistics Sites
  (http://www.pc.maricopa.edu/departments/library/internet/webliographies/statistics.html)
- University of Louisiana Statistics Sources for Social Work
  (http://www.lib.lsu.edu/soc/socwork/resources.html#Statistics)
- University of Michigan Statistical Resources on the Web/Sociology
  (http://www.lib.umich.edu/govdocs/stsoc.html)
- World Health Organization Project Atlas: Resources for Mental Health and Neurological Disorders
  (http://www.who.int/globalatlas/default.asp)

FIGURE 10.3 | SAMPLE DATA RESOURCES INTERNET SITES

SURVEYS

Using questionnaires and/or interview schedules are excellent ways of "checking the pulse of the community and getting specific and current information from a cross section of residents in a timely manner" (Andranovich and Howell, 1995, p.1). When developing a community survey, it is important to consult with community partners to understand the purpose for conducting the survey. Reaffirm the need or problem that they seek to address. What information do they want to know in the end? How will the information be used? Who are the best people to interview? How can interviewing these people help the community to achieve its goals? What is your timeframe for completing the analysis? The three most common types of community assessment surveys are key informant surveys, community surveys, and client satisfaction surveys.

Key Informant Surveys. "Key informants are those persons who are informed about a given problem because of training or work experience— usually because they are involved in some sort of service with that population" (Royse et al., 2005, p. 62). Typically, they are the community residents, block captains, organizational leaders, local politicians, ward leaders, local business owners, law enforcement officers, school officials, and human services professionals who work with the client population whose need is being assessed.

"Snowball" sampling techniques are often used to generate a list of key informants. One begins with a few key informants and asks them to identify other persons knowledgeable about the problem or population being studied. Depending on the size of the key informant list, the key informants can be interviewed by telephone, in person, or by a mailed questionnaire. The interview or questionnaire obtains their perceptions of the community issue being studied as well as information about possible solutions. Survey research methods are used to construct the questionnaire and to conduct the data analysis. Key informant surveys are a relatively inexpensive and convenient way to obtain subjective (expert opinion) needs assessment data.

Community Surveys. A survey of households or community residents is another approach for assessing needs. Typically these types of surveys are more expensive and require a high level of survey research expertise to carry out. Community surveys can provide information on residents' perceptions of their needs and community conditions as well as empirical data that can be extrapolated to the community or population being investigated. The benefit of a well-executed community survey is that the findings are representative and can be generalized with a specified degree of confidence to the community or population being studied. The downside is cost and difficulties in carrying them out.

Client Satisfaction Surveys. These types of surveys are similar to community surveys except that current or past recipients of a service or program are queried instead of community residents in general. Obtaining a sample of former or current clients tends to be easier than community surveys because the study population is known, defined, and more limited. Client satisfaction studies can provide useful information for needs assessments. Clients are in a unique position to provide feedback on how well the service or program is meeting their needs, additional unmet needs, and the operation of the service or program.

FOCUS GROUPS

Another approach to documenting needs is to conduct focus groups with key informants, community members, or clients. A focus group is "a carefully planned discussion designed to obtain perceptions on a defined area of interest in a permissive, non-threatening environment" (Kreuger, 1994, p. 6). The sources of information are the same as for surveys. The difference is in the method used to collect the information. Focus groups are discussions guided by an interviewer (Ginsberg, 2001). The groups generally have a small number (6–12) of participants. The social worker facilitating the focus group uses open-ended questioning and elaboration skills to obtain in-depth information on the topic under investigation. Focus group participants are selected based on their knowledge of the problem as well as how representative they are of the population group. They are not scientifically selected. Often convenience sampling is used. People are selected based on their perceived knowledge of the subject matter and on the extent that they appear to accurately represent the target population.

Focus groups usually last 1–2 hours and are run as discussion groups. The facilitator's role is to encourage discussion and elaboration. Prior to the group meeting, the facilitator identifies broad topic areas to be covered during the meeting. Using a series of specific closed-ended questions would not be appropriate for focus groups. The goal is to help "participants build upon each other's contributions" (Ginsberg, 2001, p. 139). The benefits of using focus groups for needs assessments are convenience, ease of administration, low cost, and depth of information obtained. The biggest negative is that there is no way to assess the validity of the findings obtained from focus groups. They may or may not be representative of the target population.

DATA COLLECTION

After you have decided whom you want to interview, it is now important to sit down with your community partners to determine how you want to get the information. Do you want to send out a quantitative survey and have the participants respond to a set of predetermined choices, or do you want to have the respondents respond in their own words to open ended questions? Do you want to conduct one-on-one interviews, conduct meetings with a focus group of 7–10 members, or would a larger group in a town meeting format provide the most accurate information? Whichever format you choose, it will be necessary to be specific, understand your respondents, keep it simple, and remain neutral.

Writing a good survey requires that you be specific in the development of your questions. Your questions should be detailed. Often it is necessary to ask more than one question on the same topic to get the answer that you desire. It is also important to understand your respondents and to choose wisely to determine if they have necessary knowledge, information, or experience to answer your questions. Always use appropriate reading and language skills. Keep it simple: Ask one thing at a time, and omit jargon and double negatives. Finally, be neutral in the phrasing of your questions. Avoid loaded language and questions that might be considered leading. Figure 10.4 lists the differences between using closed-ended versus open-ended survey questions.

Sensitive Issues. It is also helpful to place sensitive questions at the end of the survey. These questions might include topics such as age, income, race/ethnicity, gender, home address. Issues of race and gender are very sensitive and often difficult to capture in a predetermined set of responses. Participants who are biracial

Closed-Ended	Open-Ended
• Respondents choose answer from a predetermined set of choices	• Respondents answer questions in their own words
• Quantitative data	• Qualitative data
• Information may be superficial in nature	• Allows for distinctions that are not possible with precoded formats.
• Guaranteed comparability of responses	• Information is subject to interviewer and coder variance
• Precoded responses are easier to analyze and summarize	• Information may be difficult to analyze in a concise manner
• Surveys, polls	• Focus groups, key informants
• Example: What do you consider to be the most important issues facing this community? (Fill in three) ❑ Litter, graffiti, or other cleanliness issues ❑ Number of abandoned or run-down buildings ❑ Poor-quality schools ❑ Unreliable public services ❑ Police nonresponsiveness or harassment	• Example: What would you consider to be the three most important issues facing this community? • _____ • _____ • _____

FIGURE 10.4 | CLOSED-ENDED VERSUS OPEN-ENDED QUESTIONS

are often unwilling to check the traditional Black, White, Asian, or Hispanic boxes and are disappointed that often their only option is to check "other." Beginning in the year 2000, the United Census Bureau permitted participants to check more than one box in the race category. For transgendered respondents, "the question of gender with seemingly simple "female" and "male" options can pose a challenge for transgendered people, particularly those that are in the process of or are considering transitioning genders. Some may be concerned about how that data may be used or compared to personal records, or they may feel limited by the "female" or "male" options" (UNESCO, 1999). The Human Rights Campaign (HRC, 2008) suggests instead that either a box for "other" be added, or simply make the question and open-ended one (Gender? _____).

Confidentiality and Informed Consent. At the beginning of your survey, you need to include a statement that outlines the purpose of the survey, an explanation of how to complete the survey, and instructions about where to place the answers. You will also need to indicate how the information will be kept confidential and how the anonymity of the respondent will be protected. These two concepts are not synonymous. Confidentiality refers who will have access to the information. Anonymity ensures that the respondent will not be named or identified in any way in the study. The respondent must be assured that his or her information will be aggregated and not presented individually so that he or she can feel free to answer questions honestly and without fear of retaliation. The information once collected is usually kept in a locked file cabinet.

Informed consent refers to the "granting of permission" by the respondent to the researcher to conduct the research (Barker, 2003, p. 217). Researchers must disclose to the respondents all risks, alternatives, and benefits of participating in the study. The respondent signs and returns the consent form *before* completing the survey. An example of an informed consent form is included in the appendix.

Step 7: *Identify Needs.* The needs statement should define the issues and problems that face the community. This would include, but would not be limited to, home, school, work, services, businesses neighborhood/streets, psychosocial, and recreational activities. The needs statement should be supported by evidence gathered from your community assessment including: your own experience, quantitative data/statistics, and qualitative data from persons or organizations that are knowledgeable about the community. The statement should be clearly related to the goals articulated by the community, clear and concise, and stated in terms of those who will benefit in the community rather than the needs or problems faced by your organization.

Step 8: *Inventory Resources.* One of the functions of social work is that we often act as resource managers. In order for us to provide adequate services to our clients, we must be knowledgeable about what resources, assets, or opportunities exist in our community. Resource mapping requires us to leave our offices to look around the community to see what is out there and available to our clients. There are various sources of resource data. These include personal observation, existing resource manuals, and the Internet. Useful tools for identifying resources include the Individual Capacity Assessment and the Organizational Assessment. A more detailed explanation of these tools will follow in the next section on asset assessment.

Step 9: *Identify Gaps in Services.* This stage involves the use of critical analysis skills to compare problems and needs that have been identified to existing resources. Here it is necessary to determine whether you have the resources available in the community to actually address the social problem. Social workers engage community members in a discussion to decide which problems they would like to address first. This is not an easy process. We all have our own conceptions about which problem we think is the most important. Addressing the problems is a collaborative process that will involve all of the community partners. The challenge is to encourage buy-in and to keep partners engaged throughout.

Step 10: *Plan Interventions.* Program planning, which is also known as social planning (Kurzman, 1985; Lauffer, 1978), is the development, expansion, and coordination of social services and social policies (Lauffer, 1981). It involves activities that "address the development and coordination of community agencies and services to meet community functions and responsibilities and to provide for its members" (Hardcastle, Powers, and Wencour, 2004, p. 2). Program planning can be conducted at the individual agency level, by a consortium of human service agencies, or by regional or state human service planning agencies (Weil and Gamble, 1995). Generalist social workers typically become involved in program planning activities that seek to improve the operation of existing services and programs and to develop new services and programs at the agency and community level by working with agency task forces, professional task forces, or community coalitions.

ASSETS ASSESSMENT

"A change agent must be able to recognize and build on the resources available in the community. This requires both a belief in the presence of resources and an ability to note opportunities for their use. A change agent who sees only threats and weaknesses will invite the community to stay stuck in the belief of their dependency and powerlessness" (Homan, 2008, p. 56).

Asset assessment is the process of determining the extant social capital within the community. The solutions to community challenges are seen as residing within the community residents themselves. Community assets, as defined by Kretzman et al. (2005), refer to those strengths that exist in a community. These strengths include individual, economic, institutional, and organizational resources that are available to community residents. Additionally, a strengths-based assessment reveals the existing opportunities for residents to both access needed resources and contribute their individual "gifts" toward the betterment of the communities in which they live.

Components of an asset assessment may include:

1. Local residents—their skills, experiences, passions, capacities, and willingness to contribute to the project. Special attention is paid to residents who are sometimes "marginalized"
2. Local voluntary associations, clubs, and networks—for example, all of the athletic, cultural, social, faith-based, etc., groups powered by volunteer members—that might contribute to the project.
3. Local institutions—for example, public institutions such as schools, libraries, parks, police stations, etc., along with local businesses and nonprofits—that might contribute to the project.
4. Physical assets—for example, the land, the buildings, the infrastructure, transportation, etc., that might contribute to the project.

5. Economic assets—for example, what people produce and consume, businesses, informal economic exchanges, barter relationships, etc.

An excellent resource for organizers seeking to understand asset-based community development is the Asset-Based Community Development (ABCD) Institute at Northwestern University (http://www.sesp.northwestern.edu/abcd/). The website provides a detailed description of Asset-Based Community Development, tools and instruments for conducting assessments, and case examples of the use of ABCD.

1. Discovering the strengths in our communities
   a. Talents, skills, and knowledge of people
   b. Strengths, resources and new capacities in our community associations, institutions and businesses.
   c. More about our environment, eg waterways, open space, parks, and forests.
2. Connecting with each other and our community
   a. Connections between people
   b. Building relationships
   c. Linking people and their knowledge and skills to community projects.
   d. Creating or enhancing relationships between community projects and activities.
   e. Ideas, solutions and opportunities
3. Coming together to build on our knowledge and skills
   a. Take personal action and find shared interests for action with others.
   b. Form strong relationships and partnerships
   c. Solve problems and see new opportunities
   d. Use what we know to bring in more resources.
   e. Invite others to join in.
   f. Create opportunities for the future

FIGURE 10.5 | ABCD IN THREE SIMPLE STEPS

Source: Reprinted with permission from Central Coast Community Congress Working Party (2003). "Making Headway: Building Your Community. How to Get Started an Asset Based Community Development Tool Kit").

Asset Mapping.   A useful tool in the assessment process is the development of an asset map. Asset maps are visual representations of a community's resources. Organizers use capacity assessment instruments to determine the strengths and skills of individual residents (individual capacity assessment) and opportunities and resources available to residents through the provision of social service programs offered by agencies or organizations (organizational capacity assessment). Once information is collected regarding community resources, community social workers use GIS mapping to represent the special relationships the existing resources and the community residents.

CASE 10.1 | IDENTIFYING PARENT STRENGTHS

In an effort to increase parent participation in the local school, Jim, the social worker, and a group of concerned teachers organized a parent meeting. At the meeting, parents were asked to fill out the individual capacity assessments. After the surveys were completed, each member of the group was asked to discuss their strengths and areas they would like to improve, and to identify at least one thing that they could contribute to the school that year. Parents identified a variety of vocational and interpersonal skills. By the end of the meeting, parents organized themselves into three committees: those who couldn't volunteer at the school but could do work from home (making phone calls, stuffing letters, contacting community partners or funding sources), those who could volunteer at the school (participating in school activities, serving as teacher aides, and organizing safe passage corridors for students who walk home), and parents who could be available on a one-time basis to provide technical service (teaching computer, home economics, or crafts to students; writing grants, organizing fund raisers).

INDIVIDUAL CAPACITY ASSESSMENT

The individual capacity assessment is designed to measure the skills of individual residents in the community and to determine what resources they have available to address a particular social problem. Community members respond to questions that assess their vocational, interpersonal, and associational capacities. The goal is to ascertain not only the individual's personal assets, but also to determine the amount of interaction that person has in the community. Often community members belong to or have connections with organizations or associations that can be helpful in addressing a problem. The inventory also asks residents to identify skills they would like to learn or that they could teach.

ORGANIZATIONAL CAPACITY ASSESSMENT

Organizational capacity assessment involves bringing together the various organizations, agencies, and associations in a given area to determine who can provide what services to your client population or who can contribute to the elimination of the identified social problem. Organizations are asked to provide a description of the services they provide, the population they serve, and their level of community involvement.

RESOURCE MAPPING

Resource mapping is a visual representation of the data that is collected in the organizational assessment that allows you to see where the resources in a community are in relation to your client population. Data can be mapped using a variety of tools that are available either through purchase or by using free resources on the Internet. Ideally, information is mapped using the ArcGIS program. This is a highly technical process that requires training in the use of the software. Organizations such as New Urban Research (http://www.urban-research.info/home/) provide one-day training sessions designed to teach you how to use GIS data to create community

| CASE 10.2 | IDENTIFYING ORGANIZATIONAL STRENGTHS |

Local organizations were invited to a meeting by the Youth Collaborative, an organization that is dedicated to the development of youth leadership in the city. The Youth Collaborative identified school dropout as a major problem in their service area. In an effort to assess the resources available to youth in the city, 35 organizations were identified that indicated that they provide services to youth. The organizational representatives filled out the Organizational Capacity Assessment and were asked to identify one program that they could offer to the youth in the service area that might address the problem of school drop out. Examples of programs include tutoring and study skills services, recreation services, job skills training, mentor programs, and self-esteem workshops, Over a period of 6 months, the organizations worked together to develop a listing of the services they could provide, and develop and implement the programs and a community calendar that detailed the dates, times, and location of the programs. The organizations meet monthly to coordinate activities, identify gaps in services, and strategize for future events.

analyses and maps. Programs like Microsoft MapPoint are relatively inexpensive and are fairly easy to learn. In both cases, it is necessary to develop a database of information to categorize your resource findings.

GEOGRAPHIC INFORMATION SYSTEM (GIS)

GIS is a computer technology that uses a geographic information system (GIS) as an analytic framework for managing and integrating data; solving a problem; or understanding a past, present, or future situation (ESRI, http://www.gis.com/whatisgis/glossaries.html).

Before the data can be mapped, you must develop a database. Each data set that you want to map must contain at least one column of location information so that the GIS software knows where to place your records on the map. The more columns of location information you have, the easier it is for to accurately map your data. For example, if a worksheet contains street addresses in the U.S., it should also have a column for city, state, and ZIP code at a minimum.

Resource	Address	City	State	Zip	Asset Type	Description of Services Provided	Phone Number
The Nia Center, Inc., Freeman Cultural Arts Complex	419 Edgmont Ave	Chester	PA	19013	Organization	YSO	610-499-1026
Chester Boys and Girls Club	425 West Front St.	Chester	PA	19013	Organization	YSO	610-591-2269
CityTeam Ministries	634 Sproul Street	Chester	PA	19013	Organization		610-236-5596

CASE 10.3 | **RESOURCE MAPPING**

Weed and Seed is a federally funded program operated out of the Community Capacity Development Office in the Department of Justice. The program is a comprehensive approach to community development that focuses on law enforcement, crime prevention, and community revitalization. The program seeks to "weed" out violent offenders via intensive law enforcement and prosecution efforts and "seed" neighborhoods with prevention, intervention, treatment, and revitalization services. The Weed and Seed program is where Nicole, a second-year student, is placed is in a small urban environment. Using GIS data to map census and crime statistics for the city, the organizers determined that a neighborhood on the west side of the city represented the greatest concentration of crime, unemployment, high school attrition, and teen pregnancy. This neighborhood houses approximately 10,000 of the city's 36,000 residents.

Phase 1: Identifying and Mapping Resources

Weed and Seed organizers consulted with a local university to conduct a resource assessment of organizations in the target area. Student volunteers collected data by canvassing neighborhoods, conducting Internet searches, and contacting local agencies to identify resources. groups will walk each off the streets in the community to identify resources. This approach allows the organizers to uncover existing resources that might not be found in resource guides or phonebooks. In collaboration with the Environmental Studies Department at the university, census block maps will be developed as a template for data collection.

Each of the maps represented a four-block area. Students were divided into groups, and each group consisted of three students and a community volunteer. Community volunteers were solicited to guide the students through the neighborhoods, explain community culture, and to aid the students in making community contacts. The groups walked the streets of the neighborhoods and plotted the resources on the maps. The template included information regarding the nature of the resource (person, physical space, service, organization, business, government, school), the population it serves, target audience for the resource (children, youth, adult, seniors), its location, and contact information. After the students completed their map, they then entered the data into an Excel spreadsheet. Keeping track of the data was an onerous task. It was important to make sure that information was not duplicated and that every block of the target area was surveyed. Once the data has been entered, the census blocks were highlighted on the master map of the analysis area to signal the completion of the data collection phase in that area. The groups were then given another map to proceed to the next census block. In total, students collected data on more than 500 resources in the city.

Mapping the Data

The students created a data set that included over 500 resources in the area. They then created the map below. Ultimately, the map will be displayed on the Internet as an interactive resource for community members.

2008 Chester Asset Map

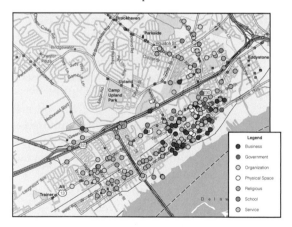

Phase 2: Community Interviews

When the maps were completed, Phase 2 began. Phase 2 involved having the groups complete a series of interviews in the analysis area with key decision makers, residents, civic and religious leaders, and members of the professional community to assess the community's strengths. With the help of community organizations, surveys are distributed to community members to assess their opinions regarding existing community resources, their current civic involvement, and their individual gifts and talents that might support agencies, associations, or businesses.

ENGAGEMENT

COMMUNITY INTERVENTIONS

The engagement phase of generalist social work practice with communities involves the development of interventions and the change efforts. The purposes of macrotype interventions at the community level is to improve community conditions, empower residents, develop community resources, increase citizen awareness of community issues, and mobilize citizens to work for change. Three macro interventions that generalist social workers often undertake with community client systems are community development, education and training, and program planning.

COMMUNITY DEVELOPMENT

Community development involves the participation of community members in developing a capacity and consensus in identifying and solving their own problems (Fellin, 1999). Social work interventions are aimed at improving community conditions and empowering residents to seek community change. Community development also has a social action component, which is activities aimed at challenging inequalities, confronting decision makers, and empowering people to change unjust conditions (Rubin and Rubin, 2001). Social action focuses on social, political, and economic justice for the disadvantaged and disenfranchised (Weil and Gamble, 1995). Thus, community practice is the "development, redistribution, and control of community statuses and resources, including social power, and the alteration of community relations and behavior patterns to promote the development or redistribution of community resources" (Hardcastle, Powers, and Wencour, 2004, p. 2).

Community development is used as an intervention strategy when disadvantaged populations have been excluded from the decision-making process and when the prevailing power structure does not appear to be responsive to the community as a whole or its representatives (Staples, 1990). Community development strategies seek to improve community conditions, empower residents, develop resources, and mobilize citizen groups. To achieve these purposes, the generalist social worker organizes constituent groups, builds community coalitions, conducts community needs assessments, lobbies political and government leaders, and advocates on behalf of constituent groups.

Social workers involved in organizing constituent groups often take responsibility for convening and facilitating meetings. They do the planning and the legwork to get participants to attend. This requires skill in managing groups and conducting meetings. An empowering approach to the process focuses on having community residents assume control and leadership of the development effort. The social worker helps get the process going, but ultimate responsibility for the effort rests with participants and indigenous leadership.

Coalition Building. Coalition-building occurs when representatives of diverse community groups join forces to influence external institutions on one or more issues affecting their constituencies (Mizrahi and Rosenthal, 1993). The goal is to

CASE 10.4	**ADVOCACY IN ACTION**

Students learning about the 2003 Medical Modernization Act in their social policy class contacted their local legislators and scheduled meetings to discuss their experiences in volunteering to help enroll beneficiaries in the program in the Part D Prescription Drug Program. In particular, as a result of their experiences students strongly recommended extending the May 15th deadline for enrollment of beneficiaries in the program. Students also advocated for increased training for providers in the county; increased outreach to disabled, low-income, and non-English speaking beneficiaries; and the development of a more accessible, "user-friendly" enrollment process.

build a power base sufficient to influence decision-making and the allocation of resources (Weil and Gamble, 1995). Often, there is inherent tension between the coalition members' interest in maintaining the autonomy and power of their constituent groups and the need to share power and resources to make the coalition successful. Social workers need well-developed mediation and negotiation skills to effectively build coalitions, as well as skills in interorganizational relations and planning (Weil and Gamble, 1995).

Advocacy.   Class advocacy involves organizing oppressed and disadvantaged groups to exercise their influence to correct inequality. This requires the active participation of citizens who are vulnerable or disenfranchised (Miley, O'Melia, and DuBois, 2007), and it provides an opportunity for whole groups of people to assume responsible participation in the social or public realm (Lewis, 1991). The social worker's role involves informing groups of disadvantaged people of their rights and entitlements, mobilizing citizen groups, and bringing pressure to bear on organizational decision makers, government officials, and political leaders.

EDUCATION AND TRAINING

Education and training at the community level tend to focus on increasing community awareness and understanding of social issues and community problems (DuBois and Miley, 2008). Generalist social workers make formal presentations at community meetings, serve as panelists at public forums, and conduct community workshops and seminars. Examples 1 and 2 in Case 10.5 illustrate how generalist social workers may use education and training as a macro-level practice intervention.

PROGRAM PLANNING

To plan an effective program, there are some questions that need to be answered: Who, What, When, Where, Why, and How?

- Who do you want to target?
- What do you want them to learn?
- When will you have the program?
- Where will it take place?

| CASE 10.5 | EDUCATION AND TRAINING INTERVENTIONS |

Example 1

Marcus W. is the social worker with the Chester Community Improvement Project, a grant-funded agency that provides community residents with information to assist them in home ownership. The project seeks to address the needs of families through its rehabilitation project, new housing construction project, mortgage counseling, and job training for youth. Marcus designed a series of workshops for the local residents that were designed to educate them about financial literacy, saving for a first home, and understanding mortgages. Marcus discussed the current condition of the local neighborhood and cited statistics showing that the neighborhood could be stabilized by increasing home ownership among the residents.

Example 2

Sharon D. is a second year student placed with the local charter school. Last year the school was in jeopardy of not making the Annual Yearly Progress benchmarks. Significant numbers of students scored below grade level in reading and math.

In consultation with parents, students, and staff, Sharon and a staff member from the school developed a homework after school project for parents. The program is designed to tutor parents in upper level math and science so that they will be able to provide assistance to their children. In addition to the classes, Sharon has developed a monthly newsletter to communicate to parents about school events and provide tips on subjects such as time management and reducing stress.

- Why is this subject important?
- How will you deliver the information?

You also need to develop a recruitment strategy for getting people to your program. Questions to consider include:

- Who is your target?
- What is your marketing strategy?

Now that you have decided who is coming to your meeting and how you are going to entice them to get there, it is necessary to set goals and objectives. Goals are the large statements of what you hope to accomplish but usually aren't very measurable. They create the setting for what you are proposing. Objectives are operational, tell specific things you will be accomplishing in your project, and are measurable (see Chapters 6 and 9). In order to define your goals and objectives, you should consider: What do you want the community to learn from the experience? Are there specific skills or competencies that they will acquire as a result of their participating?

The macro practice task of conducting staff development training or an educational workshop can be broken down into seven steps. The amount of time needed to complete the various steps depends upon the scope of the training. A single 2-hour workshop for 15 people will obviously be much quicker to plan and carry out than a training program that consists of a series of workshops for a large number of participants. The steps described below pick up the process after the social worker or training team has been asked to conduct the training or workshop. The steps are:

1. Meet with decision makers to assess needs and interests
2. Meet with participants to assess needs and interests

3. Brainstorm with the team to plan the program
4. Meet with decision makers for program approval and implementation planning
5. Do research assignments and prepare program materials
6. Rehearse and finalize program
7. Deliver workshop and obtain feedback

Step 1: *Meet with decision makers.* Organizations have various ways of selecting topics for staff development training or workshops. In some organizations the chief executive or a management team makes the decision. In others there is a management–staff committee charged with developing the staff development program. Regardless of the locus of the decision making, you need to meet with the decision makers to assess the needs of the organization and staff in terms of the proposed workshop. This assessment meeting is critical in making sure you are clear about the purpose and focus of the workshop. The meeting also provides you with an opportunity to obtain additional information and insights about the organizational climate, service needs, staff morale, and other factors that might affect the training.

Step 2: *Meet with training participants.* It is important to schedule a meeting with members of the target audience. The purpose of this meeting is to get their input about what they perceive as their training needs and interests. It also provides you with an opportunity to better understand their job pressures and the specifics of their work requirements in order to tailor the workshop to meet the staff's training needs.

After meeting with the staff, if there are discrepancies between what the decision makers envision and what the staff would like, a follow-up meeting with the decision makers is warranted. You need to find a focus for the workshop that meets the needs of both groups of stakeholders. Doing so is critical if there is a wide disparity between what management wants and what the staff feels would be helpful.

Step 3: *Brainstorm and plan the program.* After the general focus of the workshop has been agreed on, the next step is to brainstorm the structure and content of the workshop. Participants usually respond better to workshops that are well organized, participatory, draw upon their knowledge and expertise, have experiential components, summarize the content information in handouts, and provide materials they can take home. At this point, you need to outline the program and identify logistic considerations that will need to be addressed. Generally in this planning session, the trainer identifies (1) an opening groundbreaker exercise and the session introductions, (2) the structure and content of the program, (3) how the workshop will be evaluated, (4) the supplies needed, (5) refreshment needs, (6) and room and equipment needs. If a team is conducting the training, specific tasks and responsibilities are assigned.

Step 4: *Program approval and implementation planning.* In most cases, it is probably a good idea to tell the decision makers about the finalized program and get the official go-ahead for the workshop. Doing so gives you an opportunity to make any last minute changes as well as strengthen the decision makers' commitment to the training.

This meeting can also be used to plan the specifics of implementing the workshop. The details of promotion, staff attendance, room selection and availability, equipment requirements, and other details related to running the workshop need to be addressed.

Step 5: *Do research assignments and prepare program materials.* At this stage you and your team need to do research on your specific assignments to begin the process of putting together the information and content that will be delivered in the workshop. This includes preparing handouts, presentation materials, and experiential exercises. Each member of the team should also practice his or her part of the presentation and make sure it fits within the allotted time frame. A common mistake is to overestimate the amount of information that can be covered in a given amount of time. It always takes longer than you think, especially if the audience members are active participants and have been encouraged to ask questions and share their ideas and experiences.

Step 6: *Program review and finalization.* If there is more than one trainer, the team needs to have at least one additional meeting to rehearse the workshop. This gives the team an opportunity to fine tune the program and give feedback and suggestions to each other. It is also a good idea to check to make sure all the pieces of the program fit together, get a sense of the flow, and see how much time is needed.

Step 7: *Implement the program and obtain participant feedback.* The final step in this process is to deliver the training workshop and obtain feedback from the participants. If you have prepared well, it should go smoothly. However, it rarely goes exactly as planned. The participants' level of involvement, interest, and receptiveness is unknown and can vary from one workshop to the next. Expect the unexpected, and be willing to make adjustments as the need arises. Do not become overly tied to your plan. Some things might take longer than you expected, or your participants might be interested in pursuing one topic more than the others. Use your group assessment and intervention skills to engage the participants in the learning process.

Solicit feedback from the participants at the conclusion of the program. Simple self-constructed feedback questionnaires are used most often. Typically, participants are asked to comment or rate the extent to which the program met their needs, level of information, coverage of the materials, adequacy of the facilities, pace of the workshop, and other aspects of the program. They are also often asked to describe what they liked best, what needs to be changed, and what they would recommend for future workshops. Getting this feedback empowers the participants and provides the trainers with useful information for developing and delivering future workshops or trainings.

EVALUATION AND TERMINATION

In the evaluation and termination phase of the social planning process, outcomes of the interventions are assessed, and the need for future interventions is identified. A research method used in community practice is community-based participatory research (CBPR). Community- based participatory research is a research strategy that emphasizes the development of a partnership between community members, researchers, and government in a nonhierarchical relationship to conduct research on issues identified by the community (Israel et al., 2003).

CBPR involves the development of a partnership between the human service agency, university, or organization with a community-based organization or with individual community members. Typically, research issues are identified by the community. The role of the social worker is to develop training tools and to provide necessary technical support to aid the community in the design of research protocols and implementing a research study. The following example describes the development of community-based intervention that resulted in the development of an organization that seeks to address health disparities in the African American community.

Social workers also consider the extent to which communities have developed capacity, or "The increase in community groups' abilities to define, assess, analyse and act on health (or any other) concerns of importance to their members" (Laverack

---

CASE 10.6 | **THE PHILADELPHIA AREA RESEARCH COMMUNITY COALITION (PARCC) "CONNECTING SOLUTIONS FOR HEALTH"**

Purpose

The Philadelphia Area Research Community Coalition (PARCC) is a community-based participatory research partnership which comprises community-based organizations, faith-based organizations, nonprofit health organizations, and academic institutions. The mission of PARCC is to:

> Establish, facilitate, and coordinate effective long-term and sustainable health research partnerships between community organizations and institutions that have a shared vision and leadership to change and improve the health of the community in West and Southwest Philadelphia.

Ultimately, PARCC strives to encourage the development of mechanisms that will positively affect the health of the community. This outcome will be achieved by engaging in activities and piloting projects that are relevant to and focused on the social, economic, and cultural conditions that influence the health status of residents of West and Southwest Philadelphia.

Rationale

The prevalence of significant health disparities between residents of these communities and the majority population establishes the critical need to educate and include members of the community in the development and implementation of health research projects.

Ultimately, it is expected that vital disease prevention and health promotion strategies and programs can be instituted or improved in West and Southwest Philadelphia to address the needs identified by the research conducted by PARCC.

Principles

PARCC is built on the basic principles of the "community-based participatory research (CBPR)" model. CBPR is a collaborative approach to research that involves community members, organizations, and investigators in all aspects of the research process—from establishing research priorities to analyzing and disseminating results. Governed by a community action board (in formation) of partner organizations and individual leaders, partners share leadership, responsibility, and resources to ensure that each partner has an equal value and an equal voice. The community action board is charged with identifying and designing research, intervention and prevention projects, securing funding for PARCC, and evaluating and disseminating information.

PARCC encourages cohesiveness and inclusion by:

1. Setting roles, norms, and processes agreed upon by all partners
2. Respecting and applying equally the expertise and knowledge of all participants.
3. Building the capacity of community-based organizations to conduct community-based participatory research and serve the community by establishing ongoing training, resource attainment, and skill development programs.
4. Building the capacity of researchers to identify, understand, and respond to the cultural, social, and environmental dynamics within the community, while conducting community-based participatory research that will have a sustainable benefit to the community.

and Labonte, 2000). Laverack (2001) has outlined nine domains for community empowerment and capacity. These include

- *Participations*: The extent to which community members are active participants in the development of community programs
- *Leadership*: There is an organic development of indigenous leadership
- *Role of outside agents*: The community has equitable relationships with outside agents,
- *Organizational structures*: Organizations and associations that exist within the community that serve as a mechanism for members to interact and that have the capacity to address community problems
- *Problem Assessment*: The ability of the community to identify social problems and to strategically implement a plan for their resolution
- *Resource mobilization*: The extent to which the community is able to identify and leverage assets to support community members and to solve community problems
- *Links to other organizations and people*: The ability of community members and leaders to develop collaborations and partnerships with other entities within and outside of the community.
- *Stakeholder ability to "ask why"*: The ability of the community to "critically analyze the social, political, and other contextual causes that contribute to their level of disempowerment" (Laverack, 2001, p. 140)
- *Control over program management*: Community members are active decision makers in the development and implementation of programs (Laverack, 2001).

Ultimately, the key to successful community interactions is the extent to which the community members are in charge of the development of the strategies that will impact their lives. Kretzman et al. (2005) remind us to make sure that we are involving all aspects of the community. Social workers must ensure that they are including members of traditionally marginalized groups in the development of community strategies. The goal is for community members to transition from being mere recipients of services to being in control of shaping goals, strategies and community evaluations.

SUMMARY

Social workers utilize an empowerment approach to interacting with community members. Social workers engage in a partnership to work collaboratively with community members and to identify assets and resources that exist in the community. At the macro level, generalist social workers engage in education and training, program planning, and community-development-type interventions. The purposes of these macro-level interventions at the organizational level are to improve the functioning of organizations, to improve the delivery of existing services, and to develop new services. Their purposes at the community level are to improve community conditions, empower residents, develop community resources, increase citizen awareness of community issues, and mobilize citizens to work for change.

Social workers utilize a variety of assessment tools to address social problems in a community. These include needs assessment, assets assessment, and resource mapping. Needs assessment involves: defining goals and the community, identifying and collecting existing data, analyzing data, identifying community needs/problems, inventorying existing resources, and identifying gaps in services and planning programs. Asset and resource mapping involve the identification of all available individual, organizational, and operational resources in a community. Social workers use the individual and organizational capacity assessments developed by the Asset Based Community Development Institute to determine uncover resources that may exist in a community that could help in the amelioration or elimination of a social problem.

In planning interventions at the community level, social workers utilize a problem-solving strategy. Once the community has identified an issue they want to address, social workers engage with the community to conduct an assessment, set goals, develop interventions, and evaluate their efforts. Community development and education and training activities involve the participation of community members in developing capacity and consensus in identifying and solving their own problems (Fellin, 1999). Social workers activities include program development, advocacy, and coalition building.

Evaluating community practice involves determining the extent to which community members have become active participants in the assessment and implementation of community strategies. Ultimately, it is the members of the community who will identify and address their own problems. Our role as social workers is to partner with members to develop strategies that are ethnically sensitive and involve all aspects of the community.

CASE EXAMPLE

The following case example is representative of a community intervention that demonstrates the use of the problem-solving model to develop a workshop to educate case managers, caretakers, and recipients about the new provisions of the Medicare Modernization Act of 2003.

| CASE 10.7 | NAVIGATING THE MEDICARE PART D. MAZE |

On January 1, 2006, the Medicare Part D Prescription Drug program was implemented in the United States. This plan was designed to decrease the burden of prescription drug costs to Medicare beneficiaries. This was to be a watershed moment in our history, the government taking responsibility to provide for the needs of vulnerable citizens burdened with the costs of ever increasing prescription drugs. In reality what we witnessed was the outsourcing of the Medicare program to private interests. Beneficiaries and their caregivers were left in the dark as to how to negotiate the maze of enrolling in the program, understanding the drug formularies, and selecting a plan that would suit their needs. Dual eligible beneficiaries, who were passively enrolled in a plan, were horrified as they were charged expensive co-pays or were denied life-sustaining medications and treatments because they were no longer covered under the new plans. Legal Aid hotlines were jammed with calls from beneficiaries and their caregivers who desperately tried to find solutions. Those who consulted with their case managers regarding their concerns found that there was little help available.

Simone is a graduate social work student doing her second-year field placement at County Services for the Aging. COSA provides a wide range of free and low-cost services to seniors in the county. Simone was assigned to the Towers, an independent residential facility for seniors and disabled community members. Her assignment included discussing the new Medicare D program with the residents. Simone had not been introduced to the provisions of the new law before and was feeling overwhelmed at the prospect of having to discuss insurance coverage with her senior clients.

Simone's supervisor, Sandra, was the director of communication and community services at the agency. One of the tasks of the director was to conduct information sessions with seniors and assist them in signing up for the insurance plan that best met their needs.

CASE 10.7 | *Continued*

Simone's assignment was to assist Mary in developing and implementing a plan for informing residents about service modifications and to answer any questions that they had about the program changes. In conducting background research on the issue, Simone noted that the lack of information was not only a problem for recipients, but for professional caregivers as well. In her discussions with professionals in the field of aging, Simone found that she was not alone in her confusion. Many professionals and caregivers admitted that they were not well informed about the nuances of the Part D program and that they wished that a training program for them was in existence.

At the end of the week, Simone reported this information back to her supervisor. Simone and Sandra concluded that a Part D training would benefit professionals and caregivers in the county. To develop the training, Simone used the traditional problem-solving methodology. Simone focused on the accomplishment of six basic steps: problem identification, goal setting, assessment and analysis, planning, implementation, evaluation, and termination.

Problem Identification

During this phase of the project, Simone focused on identifying the concerns and problems associated with the implementation of the Medicare Modernization Act of 2003 and its impact on vulnerable client populations. In an effort to further understand the establishment of the policy and the results of its implementation, Simone reviewed the law (the Medicare Prescription Drug Improvement and Modernization Act of 2003 [Pub. L. 108-173]), conducted an Internet search to begin to understand the salient issues, and interviewed service providers and caregivers. Simone brainstormed with her supervisor to identify client and administrative concerns. The community that Simone has identified has case managers and caretakers who are responsible for educating clients about the new benefits and program changes in the prescription drug program. Lack of training for case managers was identified as a key issue during the discussion.

Problem Assessment

In the problem assessment phase of the project, Simone wanted to understand the nature of the problem through the identification of needs and the collection of relevant data.

She tracked the growing media attention on the subject to determine community responses and conducted interviews with residents and case managers. Simone's initial beliefs were corroborated regarding the lack of information available to community residents concerning the program benefit. Through all of these sources, it was generally apparent that while community members and professionals were aware of the existence of the benefit, they were unsure of how to actually conduct an analysis of the 66 available prescription drug programs in Pennsylvania in order to make an informed decision for themselves, their clients, or their loved ones.

Simone next searched the Internet to explore whether there were any initiatives for disseminating Medicare D information to professionals in the region. The search revealed that although many advocates, case managers, and professionals were conducting workshops for potential Medicare D recipients, there was not a similar forum designed to teach professionals how to access the information and resources needed to enable them to serve their client populations. In addition to the lack of information available to the professionals, Simone found that many recipients who had been automatically enrolled in the program ("dual eligibles" or beneficiaries who are eligible for both Medicare and Medicaid) were not necessarily enrolled in the specific insurance plan that most suited their individual needs.

Planning

The planning phase of the problem-solving framework involved the selection of a course of action from alternative strategies. Brainstorming with her supervisor, local residents, and case managers, Simone identified a variety of strategies designed to address the problem of the growing crisis surrounding the launching of the Medicare D program. First, they developed a forum to provide information to professionals regarding the Medicare D prescription drug benefit; second, Simone would be trained as short-term MMA (Medicare Modernization Act) advisor to assist seniors in enrolling in the new program; and third, she would advocate for the needs of the community by writing letters to local legislators regarding her experiences.

Implementation

In the implementation phase of the process, Simone carried out the activities she identified as a result of

(Continued)

CASE 10.7 | *Continued*

problem identification and planning processes. The first activity was to design a strategy for providing information for professionals serving individuals who were facing the May 15th Medicare D enrollment deadline.

Training the Professionals—The Medicare D "One-Stop-Shop" Conference

Simone and her supervisor considered various ways to organize a forum in which they could present the needed information to the professional community. It was decided to hold a full-day public conference at the local university to which a diversity of professionals, advocates, and community members would be invited. A "One-stop-shop" informational session for understanding the Medicare prescription drug benefit was used in order to minimize the often conflicting information that community members receive regarding program benefits from the various administering agencies. This format allowed all of the major players to be in one room at the same time to present a balanced view of the issues. Because of the expansive nature of the program, the planning team (students, COSA, and a faculty member) felt that it would be necessary to bring the various administrators and advocates together in one room so that participants would gain an understanding of the totality of the Medicare D prescription drug benefit.

An 8-hour training and information session was developed that included presentations from representatives from the Centers for Medicaid and Medicare, the Social Security Administration, the County Services for the Aging, Southeastern Pennsylvania Legal Aid, APPRAISE (the state insurance company), and the three largest insurance providers.

In order to publicize the event, an invitation was sent via the COSA "web blast" to providers across the county. The e-mail contained a link to "zoomerang.com," a free online survey tool that allows you to create and send online surveys, and view the results in real-time. Seventy-five providers representing long-term care, mental health, hospital, COSA case managers, nurses, and community advocates attended the program. Participants received information regarding the background and benefits of the Medicare D Prescription Drug Plan, a discussion of the terminology, how to access special programs for low-income beneficiaries, step-by-step, hands-on instruction of how to navigate the online

Medicare.gov website, and presentations from the three largest health insurance providers. All participants were provided with a "Medicare Survival Packet" that included 15 handouts of resources, contact numbers, program summaries and applications, and instruction guides for the Medicare.gov website.

Evaluation

Conference participants were asked to complete a program evaluation questionnaire at the end of the session. Analysis of the responses to the questionnaire revealed that 95% of the respondents reported that they learned material that they believed would help them to better serve their clients. In responding to the question "What did you gain from today's conference?", 88% (n = 38 out of 43 responses) of the participants indicated that they gained resource material that they could use, 86% of participants (n = 37) listed gaining new information, and 67% reported that they gained the names of people or agencies to contact. In the qualitative responses, the survival tools packet was most frequently cited as the aspect of the conference that participants found most useful.

In their evaluation of the conference, participants discussed the value of participating in the event. "When we begin to understand the complexity of the Medicare Part D benefit, collaboration among consumers, educators and the community is the key to providing a 'bridge' for organizing and accessing information." Another participant stated "The opportunity to have all of the key Medicare Part D advocates and educators in one room was an invaluable experience for providers. Conference attendees were able to direct their questions regarding both general and specific cases to high-ranking administrators from the various offices that serve the Medicare recipient population." One of the most significant comments came from the community partner herself. The COSA representative, who played such a major role in the implementation of the workshop, felt that the activity reinforced her strong conviction about the importance of the collaborative process in addressing community issues. "The partnership between the university, through the work of its faculty and students, and the County Office for Services Aging COSA representative helped to initiate broader community

CASE 10.7   *Continued*

collaboration. The partnership was able to provide a 'bridge' for the professional community to come together to share and access resources and tools to address the looming Medicare Part D enrollment crisis facing the community. By providing the forum for bringing together such a variety of community resources (hospitals, nursing homes, housing

developments, community action agencies, the Social Security Administration, health care providers, mental health agencies, and retirement communities), the conference helped to forge the beginning of a collaborative network that might continue to address the needs of providers and consumers" (COSA Representative).

Discussion Questions

1. Describe the problem-solving model and the various interventions used by the social worker to plan and implement the workshop. What skills described in Figure 10.1 did the student use to identify and implement the social work strategy?
2. Discuss an advocacy strategy that the student could develop with community members to communicate her experiences to local politicians.
3. What additional resources might have existed in the community that the student could access? How would you assess the degree to which the student involved members of traditionally

marginalized groups in the development of the program?
4. How would you assess the impact of the program on the community?
5. Conduct your own community needs and assets assessment. What resources exist in your community? Do members of the community interact with one another? How do members of the community interact with organizations, outside resources, or community leaders? What social problems would your community identify and why?

References

Andranovich, G., and Howell, R. (1995). *The community survey: A tool for participation and fact-finding*. Pullman, Washington: Western Regional Extension Publication WREP0132. Retreived September 15, 2008 from http://cru.cahe.wsu.edu/CEPublications/wrep0132/wrep0132.html

Barker, R. (2003). *The Social Work Dictionary* (5th ed.). Washington, DC: NASW Press.

Beckwith, D., and Stoecker, R. (2001). *Community organizers: Who are they*. Retrieved May 19, 2008, from Community Organizing Toolbox: http://www.nfg.org/cotb/12organizers.htm

Central Coast Community Congress Working Party (2003). "Making Headway: Building Your Community. *How to Get Started an Asset Based Community Development Tool Kit*. Retrieved May 19, 2008 from Building Your Community: an Asset Based Community Development Toolkit. http://www.communitybuilders.nsw.gov.au/download/Making_Headway_ToolKit.pdf

Compton, B., and Galaway, B. (1979). *Social work processes* (2nd ed.). Homewood, IL: Dorsey Press.

Dubois, B., and Miley, K. (2008). *Social Work: An empowering profession* (6th ed.). Boston, MA: Allyn & Bacon.

Epstein, L. (1980). *Helping people: The task-centered approach* (2nd ed.). Columbus, OH: Merrill.

Fellin, P. (1999). *The Community and the social worker* (2nd ed.). Itasca, Illinois: F. E. Peacock Publishers, Inc.

Ginsberg, L. (2001). *Social work evaluation: Principles and methods*. Boston: Allyn and Bacon.

Gutierrez, L. (1990). Working with women of color: An empowerment perspective. *Social Work, 35,* 149–153.

Haglund, B., Weisbrod, R., and Bracht, N. (1990). Assessing the community: Its services, needs, leadership, and readiness. In Bracht, N. (Ed.), *Health promotion at the community level* (pp. 59–81). Newbury Park, CA: Sage.

354 Part II Generalist Practice with Special Populations

Hardcastle, D., Powers, P., and Wencour, S. (2004). *Community practice: Theories and skills for social workers.* New York: Oxford University Press.

Homan, M. (2008). *Promoting community change: Making it happen in the real world* (4th ed.). Belmont, CA: Thompson Brooks/Cole.

Human Rights Campaign (2008). *Collecting transgender-inclusive gender data in workplace and other surveys.* Retrieved September 1, 2008 from Human Rights Campaign: http://www.hrc.org/issues/transgender/9596.htm

Israel, B., Parker, E., Rowe, Z., Salvatore, A., et al., 2003. Community-based participatory research: Lessons learned from the Centers for Children's Environmental Health and Disease Prevention Research. *Environmental Health Perspectives, 113*(10), pp. 1463–1471.

Kjosness, J., Barr, L., and Rettman, S. (2004). *Research navigator guide: The helping professions.* Boston, MA: Allyn & Bacon.

Kretzman, J., and McKnight, J. (1996). A Guide to Mapping Local Business Assets and Mobilizing Local Business Capacities. Institute for Policy Research, Northwestern University.

Kretzman, J., McKnight, J., Dobrowolski, S., and Puntenney, D. (2005). "Discovering community power: A guide to mobilizing local assets and your organization's capacity". Retrieved September 8, 2008 from www.northwestern.edu/ipr/abcd.html

Kreuger, R. A. (1994). *Focus groups: A practical guide for applied research.* London: Sage.

Kurzman, P. (1985). Program development and service coordination as components of community practice. In S. H. Taylor and Roberts W. R. (Eds.), *Theory and practice of community social work* (pp. 59–94). New York: Columbia University Press.

Lauffer, A. (1978). *Social planning at the community level.* Englewood Cliffs, NJ: Prentice Hall.

Lauffer, A. (1981). The practice of social planning. In N. Gilbert and H. Specht (Eds.), *Handbook of the social services* (pp. 583–597). Englewood Cliffs, NJ: Prentice Hall.

Laverack, G. (2001). An identification and interpretation of the organizational aspects of community empowerment. *Community Development Journal, 36*(2), 134–145.

Laverack, G., and Labonte, R. (2000). A planning framework for the accommodation of community empowerment goals within health promotion programming. *Health, Policy and Planning, 15*(3), 255–262.

Lewis, E. (1991). Social change and citizen action: A philosophical exploration for modern social group work. *Social Work with Groups, 14*, 23–34.

Lippitt, R., Watson, J., and Westley, B. (1958). *The dynamics of the planned change.* New York: Harcourt, Brace, and World.

Marlow, C. (2005). *Research methods for generalist social work* (4th ed.). Pacific Grove, CA: Brooks/Cole.

Miley, K., O'Melia, M., and DuBois, B. (2007). *Generalist social work practice: An empowering approach* (5th ed.). Boston: Allyn and Bacon.

Mizrahi, T., and Rosenthal, B. (1993). Managing dynamic tensions in social change conditions. In T. Mizrahi and J. D. Morrison (Eds.), *Community organization and social administration* (pp. 11–40). New York: Haworth.

Netting, F., Kettner, P., and McMurtry, S. (2008). *Social work macro practice.* NY: Allyn & Bacon.

Philadelphia Health Management Corporation (1997). *Doing the right thing: Community-based program planning and evaluation.* A Community Health Database Seminar for the William Penn Youth Violence Prevention Grant Program.

Philadelphia Safe and Sound (2006). *Report Card 2006. The Wellbeing of Children and Youth in Philadelphia.* Retrieved May 19, 2008 from Philadelphia Safe and Sound: http://www.phila.gov/pdfs/reportcard2006.pdf

Pincus, A., and Minahan, A. (1973). *Social work practice: Models and methods.* Itasca, IL: F. E. Peacock.

Rivera, F. E. (1998). *Community organizing in a diverse society.* Needham Heights, MA: Allyn and Bacon.

Royse, D., Thyer, B., Padgett, D., and Logan, T. (2005) *Program evaluation: An introduction* (4th ed.). Stamford, CT: Brooks Cole.

Rubin, H., and Rubin, I. (2001). *Community organizing and development* (2nd ed). New York: Macmillan.

Samuels, B., Ahsan, N., and Garcia, J. (1995). *Know your community: A step-by-step guide to community needs and resources assessment* (2nd ed.). Family Resource Coalition. Retrieved September 24, 2008 from http://eric.ed.gov/ERICDocs/data/ericdocs2sql/content_storage_01/0000019b/80/15/c3/fc.pdf

Staples, L. (1990). Powerful ideas about empowerment. *Administration in Social Work, 14*, 29–42.

Weil, M., and Gamble, D. (1995). Community practice models. In R. Edwards (Ed.-in-Chief),

Encyclopedia of Social Work (19th ed.). Silver Spring, MD: NASW Press.

Young, T. (1994). Environmental modification in clinical social work: A self-psychological perspective. *Social Service Review, 68,* 202–218.

United Nations Educational, Scientific, and Cultural Organization [UNESCO]. (1999). Retrieved September 23, 2008 from Guidelines on Gender Neutral Language: http://unesdoc.unesco.org/images/0011/001149/114950Mo.pdf

APPENDIX A

TOOLS FOR COMMUNITY ASSESSMENT AND DEVELOPMENT

© Adapted from Kretzman and McKnight (1996).

Resident Skills Inventory[1]

Dear Weed and Seed Community Resident,

Thank you for attending this community meeting. Your local Weed and Seed Coordinators are collecting information about resident skills and abilities to help us plan improvements for our neighborhood, including more local job and business opportunities.

Please place a check ✓ in the box beside each skill or ability that you've learned through your hobbies or experience at home, with your family, on the job, or in the community (e.g., church, volunteer work).

Thank you.

PART 1 – INDIVIDUAL SKILLS

Health Care

- ❑ Caring for the Elderly (e.g., parents or grandparents, working in a nursing home)
- ❑ Caring for the Mentally Ill (e.g., family member with Alzheimer's)
- ❑ Caring for the Sick
- ❑ Caring for the Physically Disabled (e.g., person in a wheelchair)
- ❑ Caring for the Developmentally Disabled (e.g., child with mental retardation)

If you checked any of these health care skills, please tell us what kind of care you've provided.

- ❑ Bathing
- ❑ Feeding
- ❑ Preparing Special Diets
- ❑ Exercising (including going on walks with someone)
- ❑ Transporting (e.g., driving someone to the grocery store)
- ❑ Accompanying the Person on Outings (e.g., medical appointments)
- ❑ Grooming
- ❑ Dressing
- ❑ Keeping the Person Company (e.g., visiting with someone)
- ❑ Housekeeping
- ❑ Going on Errands (e.g., grocery shopping for someone)

[1] This is an adapted version of the Individual Capacity Inventory © 1993 John P. Kretzmann and John L. McKnight (1993), pp. 19–25 from *Building Communities from the Inside Out: A Path Toward Finding and Mobilizing a Community's Assets.* Evanston, IL: Institute for Policy Research. http://www.northwestern.edu/ipr/abcd/abcdci.html

APPENDIX A *continued*

Construction and Repair

- ❏ Painting
- ❏ Porch/Stair Construction or Repair
- ❏ Tearing Down Buildings
- ❏ Knocking Out Walls
- ❏ Wall Papering
- ❏ Furniture Making, Repairs, or Refinishing
- ❏ Repairing Locks
- ❏ Building Garages
- ❏ Bathroom Upgrades
- ❏ Building Room Additions
- ❏ Tile Work
- ❏ Installing Drywall and Taping
- ❏ Plumbing Repairs
- ❏ Electric Repairs
- ❏ Bricklaying and Masonry
- ❏ Cabinetmaking
- ❏ Kitchen Upgrades
- ❏ Installing Insulation
- ❏ Plastering
- ❏ Soldering and Welding
- ❏ Concrete Work (e.g., sidewalks, driveways)
- ❏ Installing Floor Coverings
- ❏ Repairing Chimneys
- ❏ Cleaning Chimneys
- ❏ Heating/Cooling System Installation
- ❏ Putting on Siding
- ❏ Tuckpointing
- ❏ Installing Windows
- ❏ Building Swimming Pools
- ❏ Carpentry
- ❏ Roofing Repair or Installation

Maintenance

- ❏ Window Washing
- ❏ Floor Waxing or Mopping
- ❏ Washing and Cleaning Carpets/Rugs
- ❏ Washing and Ironing Clothes
- ❏ Routing Clogged Drains
- ❏ Using a Hand Truck
- ❏ Caulking
- ❏ General Household Cleaning
- ❏ Fixing Leaky Faucets
- ❏ Mowing Lawns
- ❏ Planting, Weeding, and Other Caring for Gardens
- ❏ Pruning Trees and Shrubs
- ❏ Cleaning/Maintaining Swimming Pools
- ❏ Washing Cars
- ❏ Shoveling Snow
- ❏ Sanding or Stripping Floors
- ❏ Wood Stripping or Refinishing

APPENDIX A *continued*

Office

- ❏ Typing
- ❏ Operating Adding Machine/Calculator
- ❏ Filing
- ❏ Greeting People and/or Taking Phone Messages
- ❏ Writing Business Letters (not typing)
- ❏ Taking Phone Orders
- ❏ Operating a Switchboard
- ❏ Keeping Track of Supplies
- ❏ Shorthand or Speedwriting
- ❏ Bookkeeping
- ❏ Computer Data Entry
- ❏ Computer Word Processing

Food

- ❏ Catering
- ❏ Serving Food to Large Groups (10 or more people)
- ❏ Preparing Meals for Large Groups (10 or more people)
- ❏ Cleaning/Setting Tables for Large Groups (10 or more people)
- ❏ Washing Dishes for Large Groups (10 or more people)
- ❏ Operating Commercial Food Preparation Equipment
- ❏ Bartending
- ❏ Meat Cutting
- ❏ Baking
- ❏ Canning (e.g., fruits, vegetables, jam)

Child Care

- ❏ Caring for Babies (under 1 year old)
- ❏ Caring for Young Children (1–6 years old)
- ❏ Caring for Older Children (7–13 years old)
- ❏ Supervising Teenagers (14–17 years old)

Transportation

- ❏ Driving a Car
- ❏ Driving a Van
- ❏ Driving a Bus
- ❏ Driving a Taxi
- ❏ Driving a Truck
- ❏ Driving a Tractor Trailer
- ❏ Driving a Delivery Vehicle
- ❏ Furniture Moving
- ❏ Hauling or Trash Removal

Operating Equipment and Repairing Machinery

- ❏ Repairing Radios, TVs, VCRs, CD/DVD Players, Tape Recorders, Camcorders
- ❏ Repairing Other Small Appliances (e.g., sewing machine, vacuum cleaner)
- ❏ Repairing Automobiles/Motorcycles/Trucks/Buses (mechanical repairs)
- ❏ Repairing Automobiles/Motorcycles/Trucks/Buses (body repairs)
- ❏ Repairing Bicycles
- ❏ Using a Forklift

APPENDIX A *continued*

❑   Repairing Washers or Dryers
❑   Repairing Other Large Household Appliances (e.g., refrigerator, stove)
❑   Repairing Heating and Air Conditioning Systems
❑   Operating a Dump Truck
❑   Repairing Elevators
❑   Operating a Crane or Other Heavy Equipment
❑   Assembling Items (e.g., bookshelves, cabinets, desks)

Supervision and Management

❑   Writing Reports
❑   Filling out Forms
❑   Planning Work for Other People
❑   Managing the Work of Other People
❑   Property Management
❑   Making a Budget
❑   Making a Time Schedule
❑   Keeping Records
❑   Interviewing and Hiring People

Sales, Interviewing, Campaigning, and Fundraising

❑   Door-to-Door Sales, Interviewing, Campaigning, or Fundraising Experience
❑   Phone Sales, Interviewing, Campaigning, or Fundraising Experience
❑   Wholesale or Retail Store Sales Experience
❑   Real Estate Sales Experience (Commercial or Residential)

Security and Emergency Services

❑   Security Guard Experience
❑   Crowd Control (e.g., concerts, bars, night clubs)
❑   Installing Alarms or Security Systems
❑   Repairing Alarms or Security Systems
❑   Firefighting
❑   Paramedic, Ambulance
❑   Military Experience
❑   Law Enforcement or Corrections Experience (e.g., police, prison guard)

Music, Dance, Art, and Theatre

❑   Singing (e.g., in your church choir)
❑   Playing an Instrument. If yes, what type(s) of instrument? _____
❑   Dancing (e.g., ballet, jazz, swing, African, tap, ballroom, etc.)
❑   Art (including drawing, painting, etc.)
❑   Theatre (including acting, building sets, making costumes, etc.)

Artisan, Crafts, and Hobbies

❑   Upholstering
❑   Sewing, Dressmaking, or Tailoring
❑   Crocheting, Knitting, or Embroidery
❑   Quilting
❑   Jewelry Making
❑   Jewelry Repair (including watch repair)
❑   Photography
❑   Wood Carving

APPENDIX A *continued*

Personal and Pet Care

- ❏ Hair Cutting, Coloring, Styling, or Braiding
- ❏ Manicures and Pedicures
- ❏ Pet Grooming, Walking, or Boarding

Second Language Skills

- ❏ Spanish
    - ❏ Speaking
    - ❏ Reading
    - ❏ Writing
    - ❏ Translating
- ❏ Other Language. If yes, which language? _____
    - ❏ Speaking
    - ❏ Reading
    - ❏ Writing
    - ❏ Translating

Have we missed any other skills that you have? If yes, please list these below.

_____

_____

_____

_____

PART 2 – PRIORITY SKILLS

What are your three best skills?

1. _____
2. _____
3. _____

Please list any skills that you have taught or would like to teach.

1. _____
2. _____
3. _____

What three skills would you most like to learn?

1. _____
2. _____
3. _____

APPENDIX A *continued*

PART 3 – COMMUNITY INVOLVEMENT

Which of the following activities have you organized or participated in, and which would you be willing to participate in?

	Willing	Organized	Participated
Boy Scouts/Girl Scouts	❏	❏	❏
Big Brothers/Big Sisters	❏	❏	❏
Other Youth Mentoring	❏	❏	❏
Fundraisers	❏	❏	❏
Toy, Food, or Clothing Drives	❏	❏	❏
Bingo	❏	❏	❏
School–Parent Associations	❏	❏	❏
Sports Teams	❏	❏	❏
Other Athletics (e.g., Karate)	❏	❏	❏
Summer Camp for Kids	❏	❏	❏
Field Trips for Kids or Elderly	❏	❏	❏
Political Campaigns	❏	❏	❏
Block Groups	❏	❏	❏
Block Parties	❏	❏	❏
Neighborhood Watch	❏	❏	❏
Yard, Garage, or Rummage Sales	❏	❏	❏
Community Garden	❏	❏	❏
Community Co-op	❏	❏	❏
Community Cleanups	❏	❏	❏
Weed and Seed TALL Team	❏	❏	❏
Weed and Seed AID Team	❏	❏	❏
Other Community Groups/Organizations	❏	❏	❏
Tutoring Math or Reading	❏	❏	❏
Other Volunteer Work	❏	❏	❏

PART 4 – WORK EXPERIENCE

Now that we have discussed your skills, we would like to get a sense of your work experience.

1. Are you currently employed? Yes _____ No _____
    Are you between jobs? Yes _____ No _____
    A. If employed, what is your job title and what skills do you use on the job?
    _____

        1. Are you employed part-time or full-time? _____
        2. If working part-time, would you like additional work?
            Yes _____ No _____

    B. If not employed, are you interested in a job? Yes _____ No _____
    1. Full-time
    2. Part-time
    3. Are there things that would prevent you from working right now?
    _____

2. What were your previous jobs?
    A. _____
    B. _____
    C. _____

3. Have you ever been self-employed? Yes _____ No _____
    If yes, describe:
    _____
    _____

APPENDIX A *continued*

4.   Have you ever operated a business from your home? Yes _____ No _____
     If yes, describe:
     _____
     _____

PART 5: EDUCATION AND TRAINING

1.   What grade in school did you complete? (Please circle)

     1   2   3   4   5   6   7   8   9   10   11   12
     (High School Diploma) (College Degree) (Technical Degree) (Advanced Degree)

2.   Do you have a GED? Yes _____ No _____

3.   Have you participated in any training programs that were not part of your regular school
     studies? Yes _____ No _____

     A. If yes, what kind of training did you participate in?
     _____
     _____
     _____

     B. What kind of work did that training prepare you for?
     _____
     _____
     _____

PART 6. ENTERPRISING ATTITUDES AND EXPERIENCE

1.   Most small businesses grow one step at a time. Have you ever considered starting a
     small business including any kind of money-making activity such as babysitting in your
     home, mowing lawns, repairing small appliances, sewing, or something else?

     ❑ Yes – Type(s) of business: _____
     ❑ No

2.   Do you currently have a business (either alone or with partners) that you operate or man-
     age from your home or another location?

     ❑ Yes - Type(s) of business: _____
     ❑ No

3.   Are you interested in starting a business (either alone or with partners)?

     ❑ Yes - Type(s) of business: _____
     ❑ No

4.   Did you plan to operate it out of your home? Yes _____ No _____

     B. Whom do you sell to?
     _____
     _____
     _____

     C. How do you do this?
     _____
     _____
     _____

APPENDIX A *continued*

5.   What types of businesses are needed in the neighborhood?

_____

_____

_____

6.   What is the biggest obstacle you face in starting a business?

_____

_____

_____

7.   Are there others?

_____

_____

_____

PART 7 – COMMUNITY STRENGTHS AND WEAKNESSES

1.   What are the three things you like best about living in this community?
     A. _____
     B. _____
     C. _____

2.   What are the three most serious problems faced by this community?
     A. _____
     B. _____
     C. _____

PART 8 – DEMOGRAPHIC INFORMATION

❑ Male   ❑ Female
❑ Under 21 Years Old   ❑ 21 Years Old or Older

PART 9 – CONTACT INFORMATION

❑ Mr.   ❑ Mrs.   ❑ Ms.   ❑ Dr.

First Name: _____ Last Name: _____

Address: _____

E-mail: _____

Phone: _____

FOR OTHER COMMENTS OR QUESTIONS, PLEASE USE THE SPACE BELOW, DROP BY THE WEED AND SEED OFFICE, OR CALL US AT:

[INSERT ADDRESS AND OFFICE HOURS]

[INSERT COORDINATOR NAMES AND CONTACT NUMBERS]

APPENDIX A *continued*

COMMENTS OR QUESTIONS:

_____

_____

_____

_____

_____

_____

_____

_____

_____

_____

_____

APPENDIX B

COMMUNITY ORGANIZATION RESOURCE INVENTORY[1]

Dear Weed and Seed Community Organization Representative,

Thank you for attending this community meeting. Your local Weed and Seed Coordinators are collecting information about all of the organizations operating in our community to help us plan and coordinate improvements for our neighborhood.

Please answer each of the following questions about your organization.

Thank you.

(a) Organization Information:

Name of Organization: _____

Local Street Address: _____

Number of Years Operating in Target Area _____ and/or Municipality _____

Brief Description of Organization: _____

_____

_____

_____

_____

_____

_____

(b) Contact Person Information:

❏ Mr.   ❏ Mrs.   ❏ Ms.   ❏ Dr.

First Name: _____ Last Name: _____

Position in Organization:

_____

Mailing Address:

_____

E-mail:

_____

Phone:

_____

---

[1] This is an adapted version of the Community Tool Box Community Capacity Inventory developed by the University of Kansas, Department of Education (2007). http://ctb.ku.edu/en/sub_section_tools1043.htm

APPENDIX B *continued*

PART 1 – GENERAL INFORMATION

Please place a check ✓ in the box or boxes that best describe your organization.

Grass Roots or Residents' Association

❑ Local Neighborhood Organization (e.g., block group)
❑ Community Center
❑ Senior Citizens' Group
❑ Local Leader, Official, or Politician
❑ Other: Please Specify

_____

Institution

❑ Public or Private School, College, or University
❑ Other Educational Institution (e.g., technical or vocational school)
❑ Municipal Agency
❑ County Agency
❑ State Agency
❑ Federal Agency
❑ Library
❑ Jail, Prison, or Juvenile Detention Center
❑ Fire Station
❑ Police Station
❑ Other Emergency Personnel (e.g., ambulance)
❑ Park or Playground
❑ Recreation Center (indoor or outdoor, e.g., skating rinks, gyms)
❑ Municipal Swimming Pool
❑ Other: Please Specify

_____

Health Care Provider

❑ Hospital
❑ Health Clinic (e.g., Well Baby Clinic, STD Testing)
❑ Substance Abuse Treatment
❑ Assisted Living Residence
❑ Assisted Living Services (e.g., nurse home visits)
❑ Hospice
❑ Medical Services
❑ Dental Services
❑ Psychological Services (includes counseling)
❑ Physical Therapy
❑ Occupational Therapy
❑ Other: Please Specify

_____

Nonprofit Community Organization

❑ Housing or Tenant Organization
❑ Food Kitchen or Pantry
❑ Domestic Violence Shelter
❑ Emergency Housing or Shelter (e.g., homeless shelter)
❑ Halfway House, Substance Abuse Group Home
❑ Place of Worship/Faith-Based Congregation (e.g., church, mosque, temple)
❑ Advocacy Group (e.g., safety, drug abuse reduction, environmental)

APPENDIX B *continued*

❏   Financial Counseling
❏   Legal Services
❏   Employment Services (including job readiness, job training)
❏   Literacy Enhancement or Remedial Education (serving youth or adults)
❏   English as a Second Language or Translation Services
❏   Community Development
❏   Other: Please Specify

_____

Private Sector

❏   Bank or Credit Union
❏   Other Check Cashing
❏   Tax Preparation
❏   Legal Services
❏   Chamber of Commerce
❏   Local Business Association
❏   Retail Business
❏   Wholesale Business
❏   Real Estate Business (residential or commercial)
❏   Rental Property Owner or Management
❏   Construction (e.g., general contracting)
❏   Vehicle Maintenance (e.g., gas station, mechanic, body shop)
❏   Restaurant
❏   Bar or Night Club
❏   Barbershop or Beauty Services (including hair, nails, facials, etc.)
❏   Child Care
❏   Elder Care
❏   Academic Tutoring
❏   Arts, Cultural, or Educational Enrichment (e.g., dance, art, or music lessons)
❏   Funeral Home
❏   Florist
❏   Other: Please Specify

_____

Please check each category that describes the people your organization serves.

❏   Local Community Residents
❏   Single Parents
❏   Young Adults
❏   Youth
❏   High-Risk Youth
❏   Young Children
❏   Infants and Toddlers
❏   Families in Need
❏   Low-Income Families or Individuals
❏   First-Time Home Buyers
❏   Renters
❏   Public Assistance Recipients
❏   Incarcerated Adults and/or Their Families
❏   Adult Ex-Offenders (released into the community) and/or Their Families
❏   Incarcerated Juveniles (Delinquents) and/or Their Families
❏   Juvenile Ex-Offenders (released into the community) and/or Their Families
❏   Homeless Families or Individuals (including runaways)

APPENDIX B *continued*

❑   Substance Abusers (drugs or alcohol)
❑   Victims of Domestic Violence
❑   Elderly Adults
❑   People with Disabilities
❑   Caregivers
❑   Minorities
❑   Immigrants
❑   Other: Please Specify

_____

How many people are involved in your organization? Please write the number or your best estimate in the brackets provided.

[   ] Number of Paid Staff in this Municipality (including part and full-time)

[   ] Number of Paid Staff from this Target Area (including professional and support)

[   ] Number of Volunteers in this Municipality (including part and full-time)

[   ] Number of Volunteers from this Target Area (including part and full-time)

[   ] Number of Board Members from this Municipality

[   ] Number of Board Members from this Target Area

[   ] Number of People Served in this Municipality per Year[2]

[   ] Number of Residents Served in this Target Area per Year

Are you interested in having your organization listed in a neighborhood directory?

❑   Yes
❑   No

Does your organization have any written material (e.g., brochures, flyers, newsletters, or other printed information) that you can provide to Weed and Seed?

❑   Yes
❑   No

PART 2 – WEED AND SEED INVOLVEMENT

Is your organization currently represented on this community's Weed and Seed AID Team?

❑   Yes
❑   No

Has your organization ever been represented on this community's Weed and Seed AID Team?

❑   Yes
❑   No

_____

[2] The general term "people" refers to patients, students, customers, clients, prisoners, victims, or any other group served by the organization.

APPENDIX B *continued*

Has your organization ever donated time, equipment, meeting space, food, or any other resource to this community's Weed and Seed activities?

❑   Yes
❑   No

Has your organization ever offered or participated in any Weed and Seed programs or activities before this meeting?

❑   Yes
❑   No

Was your organization aware of Weed and Seed's presence before this meeting?

❑   Yes
❑   No

Is your organization interested in participating in this community's Weed and Seed initiative?

❑   Yes
❑   No
❑   Not Sure

PART 3 - COMMUNITY INVOLVEMENT

Which of the following programs and activities has your organization contributed to or participated in, and which would you be willing to participate in or sponsor?

	Willing	Contributed	Participated
Boy Scouts/Girl Scouts	❑	❑	❑
Big Brothers/Big Sisters	❑	❑	❑
Other Youth Mentoring	❑	❑	❑
Other Youth Violence Prevention Programs	❑	❑	❑
Faith-Based Fundraisers	❑	❑	❑
Other Faith-Based Activities	❑	❑	❑
Other Fundraising	❑	❑	❑
Special Events (e.g., concerts, fairs)	❑	❑	❑
School–Parent Associations	❑	❑	❑
Sports Teams (e.g., Police Athletic League)	❑	❑	❑
Summer Camp for Youth	❑	❑	❑
Field Trips for Youth, Elderly, or Disabled	❑	❑	❑
Other Recreational Activities	❑	❑	❑
Political Campaigns	❑	❑	❑
Block Groups	❑	❑	❑
Neighborhood Watch	❑	❑	❑
Other Crime Prevention	❑	❑	❑
Rummage, Yard, or Garage Sales	❑	❑	❑
Community Garden	❑	❑	❑
Community Co-op	❑	❑	❑
Community Cleanups	❑	❑	❑
Community Development Planning	❑	❑	❑
Community Restoration	❑	❑	❑

APPENDIX B *continued*

Community Business Development	❑	❑	❑
Community Organizing	❑	❑	❑
Job Readiness or Training	❑	❑	❑
Offender Re-Entry Projects	❑	❑	❑
Conflict Resolution	❑	❑	❑
Summer Employment for Local Youth	❑	❑	❑
Weed and Seed TALL Team Projects	❑	❑	❑
Other Community Groups/Organizations	❑	❑	❑
Affordable Housing Projects	❑	❑	❑
Tutoring Math/Reading, Remedial Education	❑	❑	❑
Before and After-School Care	❑	❑	❑
Academic Enrichment Programs	❑	❑	❑
Arts, Music, or Cultural Activities	❑	❑	❑
Adult Education, Literacy, GED Programs	❑	❑	❑
Other Community Service	❑	❑	❑

APPENDIX C

PLANNING DOCUMENT TEMPLATE

Goal: _____

Objective: _____

Activities	Resources	Outputs	Short- & Long-term Outcomes	Impact	Responsibility	Timeline for Completion
In order to achieve our goal we will conduct the following activities:	In order to accomplish our set of activities we will need the following:	We expect that once completed or underway these activities will produce the following results:	We expect that if completed or ongoing these activities will lead to the following changes in 1–3 then 4–6 years:	We expect that if completed these activities will lead to the following changes in 7–10 years:	The following persons, auxiliaries, etc. are responsible for ensuring that this activity occurs:	This activity will occur by this date:

APPENDIX D

EVALUATING THE PARTICIPATION OF TRADITIONALLY MARGINALIZED GROUPS

	Recipients	Information Sources	Participants	In Control
Minorities				
People on Welfare				
People w/ Disabilities				
Elders				
Immigrants				
Youth				
Ex-Offenders				
Other				

Source: Kretzman, J., McKnight, J., Dobrowolski, S., Puntenney, D. (2005) Discovering community power: A guide to mobilizing local assets and your organization's capacity. Retrieved May 19, 2008 from the Asset Based Community Development Institute. http://www.sesp.northwestern.edu/images/kelloggabcd.pdf

11 | GENERALIST PRACTICE WITH ECONOMICALLY DISADVANTAGED PEOPLE AND COMMUNITIES

Stephen E. Kauffman

Rob Crandall/SCPhotos/Alamy

Martha K. is a first-year MSW student placed in a community-based program that provides consultation services to grassroots human service programs in an economically disadvantaged community with numerous social problems. The agency's mission is to increase the number of services available to community residents as well as to strengthen the capacities of the local service organizations. Kelly is developing a collaborative program with the local legal aid clinic. The clinic provides legal services to the low-income residents, many of whom also need social work and case management services. The objective is to develop a program that will provide social work and case management services to the legal aid clients.

Kelly is excited and overwhelmed about helping develop a new service for the residents that would also strengthen an existing community agency. She knows that her first step is to learn all she can about the community and the experiences of the low-income residents who will use the new program. What is it like to be a member of a disadvantaged community? What is it like to be poor? What kinds of services and assistance do the potential clients need? How is working with disadvantaged communities and citizens different than working with other client populations? In what ways is it similar? What professional and community groups need to be involved in the planning process?

Poverty is without question the most ubiquitous, complex, and intractable of all social problems. It is a worldwide issue of concern, and it affects individuals and families in rich and poor nations alike. Poverty is often associated with a wide variety of other social problems, including substance abuse, domestic violence, disease, and environmental degradation. As a result, understanding poverty and developing skills for working with the poor are critical elements of effective generalist social work practice.

Social work owes its existence to the problem of poverty. The very first social workers, the Charity Organization Society and the settlement house volunteers, were driven by a concern for the poor. From these two groups of early social workers evolved the basic micro and macro practice approaches that are the core of the profession today. Such contemporary practice methods as case management, advocacy, community organization, and policy development all are linked to the historical relationship between the profession and the problem of poverty.

Although social work practice areas today are often diverse, and the populations that social workers serve demonstrate a range of problems and economic classes, the issue of poverty is as important today as it was a hundred years ago. Many of the principles of social work practice and the values of the profession are defined by the relationship of the profession to the poor. The concept of empowerment, for example, comes in part from recognition that discrimination and oppression are among poverty's most important causes. Empowering individuals and communities is therefore a significant tool for remediating these problems. Similarly, much of the curriculum in social work education is oriented toward educating students to understand the problem of poverty and develop skills to work with the poor.

In light of the critical necessity for social workers to understand poverty, this chapter examines the issues associated with generalist practice with the poor. By the end of this chapter, you should be able to help Martha understand

1. The size and scope of poverty in the USA
2. Macro policy issues associated with poverty

3. Micro and macro practice issues, including various theories about the causes of poverty
4. Issues related to human behavior and social environment, including the consequences of poverty on individuals, families, and communities
5. Practice issues for social workers that engage in generalist practice with welfare recipients

In many ways, if there is any problem social workers should prepare for, it is the problem of poverty. Most of our clients, whether we are talking about individuals, families, organizations or communities, experience a variety of interconnecting needs and problems, and poverty is almost always connected to that variety in some way. Further, the experience of being on one or more social welfare programs is something that many clients understand. Indeed, the experience of poverty often serves as a matrix from which many other problems arise, and it may be that a client's presenting problem may not even be the most important concern over the long term, for presenting problems may be the result or symptom of this other, critical concern.

The fact is that there is a real likelihood that poverty, economic need, unemployment, or even the welfare service response is a possible cause, or at least a co-occurring event with the presenting problem. Poverty is ubiquitous, and people suffer from it, or its consequences, in a range of ways. But at the same time, responding to poverty, at any systemic level—individual, family, group, or community—is a significant, and some would argue fundamental, function of society and/or government. This response, generally lumped into a broad category we call "welfare," takes up a huge portion of our society's attention and resources. Again, almost any client with almost any problem will in some way be connected to poverty, welfare, employment, or the consequences of these subjects.

Thus, in many ways this is one of the most important subjects of study for a social worker who is learning how to conduct generalist practice. The knowledge and skills associated with this course of study will be invaluable, almost across the field of practice spectrum, and across the micro, mezzo and macro systems levels.

This chapter will help prepare you for practice across these levels. Building on the generalist practice components found in the earlier chapters, this chapter will examine the issue of poverty and services to people on welfare. The chapter will discuss the problem of poverty from the standpoint of theory, experience of the poor, and policy issues and services. Following this, it will look at some of the components of the basic practice model outlined in previous chapters as they connect with the interrelated problems of poverty, employment, and welfare services.

THE PROBLEM OF POVERTY AND THE WELFARE RESPONSE

THE PROBLEM OF POVERTY

Poverty knows no boundaries. Almost half of the world's population, about 3.2 billion people, lives on less than $2.50 per day, and almost 1.4 billion people live in extreme poverty, with incomes of less than $1.25 per day (Chen and Ravallion, 2008). While extreme poverty is rare in the United States, in 2007, over 37 million individuals—about 12.5% of the U.S. population—are poor (DeNavas-Walt, Proctor, and Smith, 2008). Depending on how poverty is measured, and considering the near-poor, the number may actually be much higher. Almost 42% of households in the United States either live in poverty or live in a household with no more than twice the income defined as "poverty" (DeNavas-Walt and Cleveland, 2002).

However we count the poor, it is clear that certain subgroups in the United States, including children (18.0%), African-Americans (24.7%), African-American children (34.5%), and Latinos (21.5%), have even higher poverty rates (DeNavas-Walt, Proctor, and Smith, 2008). Female-headed households, no husband present, have a rate of 30.7% (DeNavas-Walt, Proctor, and Smith, 2008). And again, if we consider the near poor, the numbers rise dramatically.

With so many people defined as poor, it is the case that poverty has a profound effect on the American economy. For example, public expenditures for social welfare (funds dedicated to addressing poverty or its consequences) are large. In 2006, the primary federal/state means-tested programs' expenses came to $354.3 billion. Means-tested programs are defined as services that are provided after examining a person's (or family's) need as determined by their income, assets, and/ or demographics. These include Temporary Assistance to Needy Families (TANF), Medicaid, food stamps, family support assistance, Supplemental Security Income (SSI), child nutrition programs, refundable portions of earned income tax credits (EITC and HITC) and child tax credit, welfare contingency fund, childcare entitlement to states, state children's health insurance and certain veterans pensions (U.S. Office of the President, 2008). If expenditures for education and Social Security pensions are added, the cost jumps to over $1.505 trillion, or about 20.9% of the Gross Domestic Product (GDP) in 1997 (U.S. Department of Health and Human Services, Social Security Administration , 2001). Another example is even more dramatic. Health expenditures from all public and private sources in 2001 came to a staggering $1.4 trillion, or over $5,000 for every man, woman and child in the U.S. (Centers for Medicare and Medicaid Services, n.d.)

The number of individuals receiving public assistance is large. Medicaid, the primary governmental medical assistance program for the poor, served more than 45.5 million Americans in 2006 (U.S. Department of Health and Human Services, Social Security Administration, 2008). Social Security, a collection of programs targeting the poor and designed to keep many Americans from slipping into poverty, provided benefits to 46.4 million people in 2002 (U.S. Department of Health and Human Services, Social Security Administration, 2003). The largest income support program for the poor, known as Temporary Assistance for Needy Families (TANF), served more than 5 million monthly recipients in fiscal 2002 (U.S. Department of Health and Human Services, 2003), and slightly more than 4 million monthly in fiscal 2007 (U.S. Department of Health and Human Services, 2008), with an annual program cost of more than $16 billion. Though there have been declines in state welfare caseloads in TANF in the past few years, there is uncertainty as to whether the change reflects an improvement in the poverty picture or simply a consequence of new, more restrictive rules.

In terms of indirect costs, which are costs to the economy beyond dollars spent by federal, state, and local programs, the figures are equally staggering. Looking at childhood poverty alone, it has been estimated that "the costs to the United States associated with childhood poverty total about $500 billion per year, or the equivalent of nearly 4 percent of GDP" (Holzer, 2007).

Measuring Poverty.   Poverty may even be more pervasive than the official statistics presented above suggest. Like many social indicators, the number of people classified as poor depends on the way poverty is defined. Although we might think that defining poverty is a simple task, it is in fact a complex problem. Definitions differ according to what is actually being measured.

The official U.S. definition of poverty is what is called "an absolute" measure. It is a strict dollar figure that changes only with family size, and that adjusts from year to year due to inflation. This income figure was initially computed using 1950s American family spending patterns, food costs, and corrections for family size. The original computation used an estimate of the cost of food an individual would need for short-term survival, multiplied by three to account for other living expenses (Fisher, 1995, 1992). The underlying assumption was that spending patterns for all Americans were similar. Since the average American family of the time spent about one-third of its income on food and two-thirds on everything else, the pattern was assumed to also apply to the poor. Using this measure, the poverty level is currently $20,614 for a family of four, as compared to $3,128 in 1963 (Fisher, 1992). The poverty line changes from year to year, but only with amounts equaling inflation. Certain other factors, such as age 65+ also impact the figure, but that is the limit of the calculation. Table 11.1 below presents the 2008 poverty levels for different family size.

There are benefits, but also problems with using this absolute measure. The primary value is its ease of application. Most of our social welfare programs use the figure for the determination of eligibility, and having an absolute measure for comparison is quite useful. But on the other hand, there are questions about the adequacy of this measure (Citro and Michael, 1995; Fisher, 1995). Among these, for example, is that the measure does not take into account changes in average income created by noninflationary factors such as worker productivity. Worker

TABLE 11.1 | 2008 POVERTY LEVELS BY FAMILY SIZE

Family Size	Maximum Yearly Family Income (May 2008)
One person (unrelated individual)...	10,294
Under 65	10,488
65+	9,669
2	13,167
3	16,079
4	20,614
5	24,382
6	27,560
7	31,205
8	34,774

Source: U.S. Bureau of the Census, 2008

productivity is the output of a worker per unit of work. Increased worker productivity has resulted in wage increases over the past 40 years at a pace much greater than inflation.

As an illustration of a productivity change, consider how much easier, faster, and cheaper communication has become in the past 20 years. With the advent and widespread adoption of email, the Internet, cell phones, text messaging, and the fax, people may contact literally millions of people in the time that it once took to contact a few at most. This is of course in addition to other influences on productivity, such as the use of satellites and computers, or even the increasing number of college graduates in the workforce. The consequence of this for the measurement of poverty is simply that the average poor person today is "poorer" relative to the average worker than a poor person 30 years ago. Figure 11.1 provides an illustration of this widening gap.

Nor has the official poverty measure been adjusted for changes in spending patterns over time. The cost of food is no longer as significant an expense as it was in the past. Generally, Americans now spend a lower percentage of their income on food and a higher percentage on housing and medical care than they did in the 1950s.

Adding to the problems associated with the absolute measure are all of the complex characteristics of life. Wealth, assets, power, education, and other psychological and social quality-of-life variables are not addressed by the measure. Some of these other variables might be as important as income in determining an individual's status in the larger society. For example, there is evidence that the accumulation of wealth contributes to the development of behaviors and attitudes consistent with those of the dominant culture (Sherraden, 1991), and the effect of wealth might be more important on the development of these values and behaviors than income (Yamada and Sherraden, 1997). Although this perspective has been ignored in the measurement of poverty, it has had important policy implications, with a number of governmental programs now more supportive of assets accumulation than in years past.

In 2002, the median assets owned by the poorest 20% of American households were $5,466. This compares quite unfavorably with the median for all American households of $58,905, and even more so when compared to the richest 20% of $188,712 (Gottschalck, 2008). The poor are literally "in a class by themselves,"

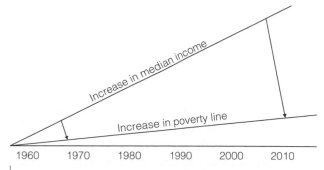

FIGURE 11.1 | DISTANCE BETWEEN MEDIAN INCOME AND POVERTY LINE, 1960–2010

and by focusing on income alone, the absolute measure of poverty misses important differences between the poor and the "typical" American.

Yet to be fair, the absolute poverty measure has value. It is a useful and consistent number and tool for setting income thresholds, and therefore for determining benefit eligibility for many government antipoverty programs. It also allows us to identify trends over time and to identify groups in the population that might require special attention. It highlights certain risk factors for poverty that are important in the assessment process.

WELFARE

The second term requiring attention is "welfare," or perhaps "social welfare." For a number of reasons, welfare is a term that is wrapped in confusion. Think about this. If you stop and ask people on the street to define welfare, you will typically get one of two very different answers. The first response, and possibly the most common in America, is usually something like, "Welfare? It means government programs for the poor." And if you press a little harder, perhaps asking the person to define a "welfare recipient," you will hear terms like "lazy," addict, cheat, leech, parasite, and perhaps some characterization of the person as a minority, uneducated, and full of children. In other words, the term is quite pejorative. And is you take this line of questioning just a bit further, a whole range of unconnected ideas may follow, including high tax rates, the "welfare state," or even socialism and communism.

The second response (or definition) to the term welfare, on the other hand, is somewhat more neutral. Welfare in this sense refers to a person's state of being, or perhaps their quality of life. And again, if you push a bit more, the welfare recipient becomes instead a person who receives some form of government benefit necessary to sustain or enhance a person's needs. Indeed, this could mean any or all of us!

Without going too deeply into the theory of need right here, a good way to conceptualize this latter definition is to link the term to a definition of "needs." Although there is no single definition of need, most definitions approximate statements like,

> "Physical, psychosocial, spiritual, intellectual, developmental, and environmental requirements necessary for the client's survival and self-actualization." (Indiana State University, 2008)

These ideas are commonly crystallized in the work of Abraham Maslow (1954). Maslow, a psychologist, argued that human motivation was linked to the degree that his/her needs were addressed. These needs, as he organized them included:

1. **Biological and physiological needs** – food, water, shelter, and sex
2. **Safety and security needs** – protection from external harm
3. **Belongingness and love needs** – satisfying relationships, etc.
4. **Esteem needs** – self-esteem, independence, status, prestige, etc.
5. **Self-actualization needs** – personal potential, personal growth and peak experiences

Using this framework, needs are the building blocks of a person's (or a society's) "quality of life," some of which are necessary to survive, while others help to enhance the way a person "feels" about, or enjoys, their life. But in either case, they are the key elements to an understanding of welfare as the "quality of life." Social welfare in this sense is then the collective response to need—or perhaps society's or a government's response. Programs and policies that attempt to meet a need are all a part of social welfare.

To complete this discussion, you may ask why are welfare or social welfare such pejorative terms? The answer is complex, but it can be partially understood by an examination of certain beliefs about identity, values, and ideology. People who believe that a person's needs should be met more or less exclusively through personal or family effort, supplemented (only under the most extreme conditions) by larger social institutions, are more likely to see social welfare (and therefore the recipient of aid) in some negative way. Indeed, this perspective is further supported by a belief that helping others by impersonal governmental structures may actually harm the recipient because it lessens the motivation to do things for one's self. It also harms the larger public because of the reduction in personal choice that results from taxation. Thus, welfare is viewed by some quite negatively.

THE CAUSES AND CONSEQUENCES OF POVERTY

The large number of people who are poor and the costs to the economy associated with poverty result in significant attention by policymakers. Thousands of federal, state, and local policies have been enacted in the last century to deal with the problem of poverty. Why does the problem remain?

There are many differing opinions about what causes poverty and, therefore, how to address the problem. Poverty is associated with almost every component of the human condition, including employment, health, values, ideology, social relations, psychological factors, and social and economic justice. Even religions have affected thinking about poverty. Thus, policymakers are confronted with an extremely complicated issue, and one that changes through time.

Of course, the importance of understanding the cause(s) of poverty is the linkage between cause and solution. Among the many approaches to the problem of poverty that have been implemented are governmental employment programs, child-care assistance, cash assistance, tax-based approaches, education and training, entrepreneurship assistance, and asset development. Some argue that none of these approaches should be used, and in fact, the central policy thrust of recent years has been to decrease policy efforts to eradicate poverty. Here, the idea has been to remove public assistance because of a belief that assistance itself may perpetuate poverty. This belief is ingrained in the current "welfare reform" approach.

THEORIES OF CAUSATION ON THE MICRO LEVEL
(INDIVIDUALS AND FAMILIES)

Perhaps the critical question affecting policy choices about poverty as well as the effectiveness of direct practice with the poor is "What causes poverty?" An important distinction has been drawn between those who are poor through no fault of their own, "the deserving poor," and those whose poverty is linked to some kind of failure of personal responsibility, "the undeserving poor" (Katz, 1989). The deserving poor usually includes children, the elderly, women with very young children, people who are sick, and people who are disabled. The capacity of these individuals to work is limited, and there is general agreement that the provision of assistance is both acceptable and necessary.

On the other hand, poverty among able-bodied men and women creates questions about the reasons for their poverty. Causality theories have been developed to explain poverty among these individuals. In general, there are three types of theories that attempt to explain poverty causation: (1) theories that focus on individual deficits, (2) theories that focus on social and structural causes, and (3) theories that link the individual with the social environment. Although each model has serious limitations, they all offer some utility for understanding poverty.

Table 11.2 below draws upon the various theories of poverty and presents the variables that have been identified as causative.

Individual Deficits.   Theories of poverty that focus on individual deficits suggest that poverty results from one or more of a variety of biological, behavioral, or psychological deficits. These models suggest that the poor are poor because of genetic tendencies, such as low intelligence levels, that limit their ability to function in a modern, competitive capitalistic economy, or because of a psychological or behavioral limitation, such as laziness (Goodwin, 1983; Handler and Hasenfeld, 1991; Katz, 1989).

There is little doubt that such personal attributes as problem-solving ability and personal efforts affect the capacity to earn a living. The principal weakness of these theoretical perspectives, however, is that they do not take into account the role of the environment. Biological, behavioral, and psychological deficits may be caused by the environment or may result from the interaction of the environment and genetic factors. Inadequate nutrition, exposure to toxic substances such as lead, instability of social relationships, poor schools, few opportunities for steady employment, and many other similar factors have all been demonstrated to affect behavior and/or brain development and learning capacity (Bower, 1994).

Social and Structural Causes.   A second set of poverty theories focuses more on the consequences of social and environmental conditions than on individual deficits as the cause of poverty. According to these models, the larger society has failed to provide the opportunities necessary for personal success or has placed roadblocks in the way of the poor. Unjust occupational and merit structures, lack of power, the inaccessibility of high-wage employment (Danziger and Gottshalk, 1995; Wilson, 1987), poor schools and limited educational opportunities, and discrimination are all seen as social conditions that cause and perpetuate poverty.

There is evidence that, at least in the past, structural factors have created or reinforced poverty. Until very recently, women, African-Americans, Latinos, and other minorities experienced legal, institutionalized discrimination that limited their opportunities to move out of poverty (Polenberg, 1980). Though almost all forms of legal discrimination have now been eliminated, the legacy continues. Unintentional discriminatory acts rooted in the value systems of the past and even intentional

TABLE 11.2 | POSSIBLE POVERTY CAUSATIVE VARIABLES

Individuals and Families		
Personal/Behavioral	**Environmental/Structural**	**Mixed (Culture of Poverty)**
Deficits models	Unemployment	Family composition
Substance abuse	• Poor job opportunities	• Values
Family structure (single parenthood—esp. female-headed households)	• Structural barriers	
	• Reserve labor force	
Personal motivation (i.e., laziness)		
Genetics	Quality of education/schools	Welfare dependency
Low intelligence	Quality of health care	Continuing discrimination
Brain development	Unfair merit structures	
Illness	Discrimination	
Race	Lack of power	
Ethnicity		
Gender		
Age		
Teenage pregnancy		
Lack of employment skills (hard and soft)		

Communities & Larger Systems
Low tax revenues
Corruption
Globalization
Public debt
"Broken windows"—community decay starts small and builds on itself
Regressive taxation

illegal discrimination still affect employment patterns and living and social conditions.

In employment, for example, the upward mobility of women and minorities is slowed by a "glass ceiling," through which few pass. As a consequence, these groups tend to remain in lower-paying jobs, earning significantly less on average than their white male colleagues. Moreover, since women are the primary care-givers for children, their special needs, such as childcare or time off work for child-birth, affect their employment patterns.

Another structuralist perspective suggests that the foundations of poverty are deeply rooted in the social and economic organization of society. There has never been a time when poverty did not exist, and it is unclear whether, under the best of circumstances, the American economy can produce enough jobs or enough in-come for welfare recipients to escape poverty (Poole, 1995, 1997). Poverty, at least in terms of relative deprivation, will probably exist as long as our economy is structured as it is now.

The argument supporting this position is based in part on the perception that poverty is useful to the affluent in American society (Gans, 1976). Further, poverty is embedded in the goals, processes, and assumptions that guide the marketplace. A primary goal of a capitalistic free-market economy is efficiency in the distribution of goods and services. Efficiency here refers to the optimal or best price, which takes into account the demand for the product or service, competition between producers, and the cost of production. One of the predominant elements of the cost of production and, in turn, the ability of a producer to compete is the price of labor. There will always be a desire on the part of producers to find the lowest possible labor cost. One way to ensure low labor cost is to have a ready pool of the unemployed who are willing to work at low wages—what Marx (1867) referred to as the "industrial reserve army."

This ready pool of the unemployed ensures low labor costs but in so doing serves another function for the economy. It helps keep inflation low. If everyone were employed, employers would have a difficult time finding employees. Prospective employees would be able to demand higher wages, and employers would have little choice but to pay more or risk losing the employee. To ensure an adequate return on their investments, the employers would then have to charge higher prices to their customers. As all employers would presumably face the same wage pressures, the aggregate increase in costs would result in society-wide inflation. As the cost of everything increased, workers would see their spending power decrease. To keep up with the increased cost of living, workers would demand higher wages, causing even more cost and wage increases. Thus, a pool of the unemployed improves the capacity of a producer to compete and serves to keep inflation low.

Other factors are also involved. Improvements in productivity can improve the ability of a producer to compete and keep inflation low. But such improvements may also serve to reduce the need for new workers. In addition, the globalization of the economy means that low labor costs and an even larger pool of the unemployed are available outside of the United States.

A second argument supports this assertion of inevitability. The central thesis is that as wealth accumulates, reasonable investments will generate new wealth. In other words, "the rich get richer." Those without a reserve supply of cash (wealth) may be forced into borrowing money for even small household emergencies such as car repair or a minor illness. Significant debt can accrue, and catching up may not be possible: "the poor get poorer." Wealth has been moving from the poor to the rich in recent decades (Center on Budget and Policy Priorities, 1997). In the years between 1980 and 2005, the percentage of income earned by the poorest one-fifth of Americans has fallen from 4.2% to 3.4%, while the wealthiest one-fifth have seen income grow from 41.1% to 50.4%, and the wealthiest 5% have seen a rise from 16.5% to 22.2% (U.S. Bureau of the Census, 2008b). This redistribution of wealth has been caused by changes in federal tax rates that have favored high-income individuals even as many benefit programs targeting the poor have been reduced or eliminated. This trend appears likely to continue (DiNitto, 1996; Murdock and Michael, 1996).

Structuralist perspectives have limitations. The primary issue is that many of the preconditions of poverty have been addressed by the implementation of a variety of social policies. Most forms of discrimination, for example, were made illegal with such laws as the Civil Rights Act and Voting Rights Act of the early 1960s. Unemployment and higher educational access also have less effect because of legislative actions such as unemployment insurance and student aid programs. Further, focusing on social conditions ignores the fact that some individuals thrive and become wealthy under deplorable environmental constraints, and a substantial number of children who attend the poorest schools are able to escape poverty through personal efforts.

Individual–Social Linkages.   A third set of theories examines the relationship between individual and social causes. Perhaps the best known of these theories are those collectively known as the "culture of poverty" (Cherry, 2007; Lewis, 1959, 1961, 1966). According to these theories, people have historically suffered from social constraints such as low wages, legal discrimination, and limited educational opportunities. Individuals have adapted their behaviors to the conditions in order to survive. Socially questionable behaviors are such adaptations, with crime, drug dealing, and gambling adopted as means of making a living. As families and communities accept these behaviors as tools for survival, individuals develop a tolerance for the behaviors. The behaviors and tolerance of the behaviors are passed from one generation to the next, representing a change in what constitutes normative behavior (Banfield, 1968, 1974).

At this point, culture of poverty models diverge into a more conservative and a more liberal perspective. The more conservative perspective argues that the social conditions initially leading to the antisocial behaviors have been remedied by such social policies as the Civil Rights Act and unemployment compensation. At the same time, other social policies, such as Aid to Families with Dependent Children (AFDC) or programs put in place during the War on Poverty in the early 1960s, created another form of antisocial behavior: welfare dependency.

The argument is that welfare dependency becomes a barrier to mainstream American life because it destroys individual initiative and creativity (Bane and Ellwood, 1994; Mead, 1986, 1992): why work or even dream of a better life when all your needs are being met? Thus, according to this perspective, the solution to poverty is to eliminate (or at least severely restrict) welfare assistance and antipoverty programs (Gilder, 1981; Murray, 1984). This perspective has recently come to prominence and fits nicely with what have been identified as historical American beliefs about hard work and individualism (Katz, 1989).

The more liberal culture of poverty perspective, on the other hand, does not agree that the barriers of discrimination and limited opportunities were removed by the policies of the last few decades (Wilson, 1987). Although legal discrimination has been dismantled and greater educational and employment opportunities have been created, say proponents, less overt forms of discrimination continue to exist. Likewise, available employment is generally limited to low-wage occupations. The social policies put in place to help the poor are often so full of restrictions and disincentives that they help only a small percentage of those who need assistance. The policy implications of this perspective are not focused toward eliminating assistance, but rather toward expanding it to address ongoing barriers to mainstream life while vigorously attacking the continuing problems of subtle discrimination and a low-wage economy.

Employment and Income.   As may be deduced from the analysis above, it is, however, that almost whatever theory or perspective one takes on poverty, the problem of employment and income is at the center. And these topics are absolutely critical for assessment and intervention as well, so an extended discussion is worthwhile here.

As a starting point, the United States, as an advanced capitalist country, allows the marketplace to make many of its decisions about the production, distribution, and consumption of goods and services. Such decisions are usually expressed by the exchange of cash or credit for goods or services. Most people do not directly trade a good or service for some other good or service, nor do most people have the skills to produce all of the products necessary for survival. Instead, our economic system requires people to exchange some skill or form of labor for cash, which is then exchanged for the items that people need or desire.

Cash is necessary in order to purchase many of the products that are necessary for simple survival. This includes almost all of the resources needed for adequate biological functioning, such as food, water, clothing, and shelter. A lack of any of these resources can cause stress and can lead to illness and death. Hence, the most immediate consequence of poverty is its potential effect on the capacity of an individual to survive, let alone thrive. We exist within a fairly narrow set of biological imperatives, and if sufficient resources are not available, the consequences may be catastrophic.

Most people, excepting the retired, children, people with a disability, or other groups, earn (or potentially earn, as in the case of the unemployed) cash as income through employment. So understanding what affects a person's employability and pay scale are critical for an assessment. So what factors improve or challenge a person's likelihood of employment?

The question is important due to the large number of people who are unemployed. In the United States, unemployment over the last 3 years (2005–2008) has ranged from a low of about 4.5% to a high of 6.1% (U.S. Department of Labor, 2008). With the size of our working population, an unemployment rate of 6.1% means that 9.4 million people are unemployed. Much higher rates exist for some categories of the population, such as teenagers (16+ %), African-Americans (9+ %) and Latinos (7+ %) (U.S. Department of Labor, 2008).

What causes unemployment? Most basically, employment depends upon finding work. There are two parts to this—the availability of employment, and the employability of the client. The issue of availability falls beyond this chapter and is within the domain of both macroeconomics, and certain classes of microeconomic theory—in other words, issues of job creation, government economic policy, and entrepreneurship. Here, the focus will instead be on the employability of the client.

Employability is complex, but it may be broken down for our purposes into two broad categories—external factors and client characteristics. Client characteristics may be further classified as individual characteristics, soft skills, and education and training. Table 11.3 presents these variables.

TABLE 11.3 | FACTORS INFLUENCING CLIENT EMPLOYABILITY

External Factors	Individual Factors				
	Nonskill Characteristics[1]			Skills	
	Innate, Physical or Psychological	*Client Environment*	*Behavioral*	Life or Soft Skills[2]	Education and Training[1]
Discrimination based on age, race, ethnicity, gender or sexual orientation	Very low self-esteem	Sick child or family member	Drug and/or alcohol abuse	Job search skills[2]	Low basic skills/no high school diploma or GED
Discrimination based on health or mental health	Chronic health problems	Housing problems	Little or no work history	Communication skills[2]	Limited English proficiency
Location of employment	Mental illness	Transportation problems	Criminal records	Interpersonal[2]	Now/low technical skills
Educational opportunities	Learning disabilities	Children		Team players[2]	
Stigma	Intelligence	Family support		Ethics[2]	
		History of domestic violence		Value diversity[2]	
				Fast and responsive[2]	
				Creative[2]	
				Problem solving and critical thinking	
				Professionalism	
				Enthusiasm	
				Networking	

[1]Ohio Department of Juvenile & Family Services (2002).
[2]Buhler (2001).

While some of these variables are more pervasive than others, all are important in some way, and indeed, a large number of families experience more than one barrier to employment. Some research has suggested that the likelihood of a recipient finding employment falls as the number of barriers experiences increases (Goldberg, 2002).

Like our previous discussion on the causes of poverty, there are different categories of the variables that influence employability. To simplify the categories, we will classify them as **external factors** or **individual factors**. And individual factors may further be broken down into a number of subcategories—nonskill characteristics and skills. Many of the variables are possibly located in multiple categories due to the fact that the impact on employment may be due to the external source of the problem and the client's individual application. An example is education. In some cases, the problem is a lack of educational opportunity, but in other cases the problem is the client's actual educational attainment.

External factors are those variables that are rooted in culture or in the dynamics of larger social systems. Perhaps the most important of these variables are associated with discrimination or stigma. Although most forms of discrimination are illegal due to laws such as the Civil Rights Act of 1965 or others (see Table 11.4 below), there is little doubt that some types still exist.

For example, people commonly talk about problems like "the glass ceiling"—limitations on upward mobility in occupational settings, or "old boy's networks"—associations of people with a high degree of familiarity, and from whom employment opportunities are distributed. Both of these are examples of ways in which discrimination still exists in, if not a legal way, at least a way that is difficult to uproot. Likewise, despite progress associated with the Americans with Disabilities Act, in a study of the visually impaired, for example, employment barriers found included transportation problems and lack of needed adaptive equipment, and accommodations (Crudden and McBroom, 1999). Further, there are types of discrimination that, if not legal, are not fully illegal either. Sexual orientation has very limited protections at the federal level, and only a handful of states provide some protection. Discrimination based on genetics, as well, may be a major issue as our ability to predict a person's potential health or behavior improves.

Another very serious external issue is the quality of education, and the opportunity to attain a high-quality education. Many American schools are failing, and many students, particularly from economically distressed areas, are trapped in poor schools. In addition, many of the jobs that are being created in America are being created in areas located at some distance from where the poor live. Higher job creation today tends to be located in the south and west, while larger numbers of the poor are still living in northern rust belt cities. Yet even in small regional contexts, job creation does not tend to be centered in inner cities, but in suburban

TABLE 11.4	FEDERAL ANTI-DISCRIMINATION LAWS

The 14th Amendment to the U.S. Constitution
The Civil Rights Act of 1965 (and Amendments)
The Americans with Disabilities Act
The Rehabilitation Act
The Workforce Investment Act
The Vietnam Era Veterans' Readjustment Assistance Act
The Civil Service Reform Act (U.S. Department of Justice, 2005)

or rural areas. Indeed, some people have suggested that moving people closer to employment, and away from inner city poverty, may be highly beneficial (Wilson 1987), but not all studies have supported the potential benefits (Turney et al., 2006).

Individual factors are those variables that are unique to the client—in some cases they are associated with the client's demographics, health, behavior, or education, and in some cases they are associated with the client's immediate environment and/or family. For example, Goldberg (2002) found that physical and mental health and low levels of education are the most common document barriers among TANF recipients.

The client's **immediate environment** also creates barriers to employment. As noted above with the focus on location, Danziger and Seefeldt (2002) found, for example, that almost one-third of women on welfare have transportation problems—a rate much higher than the general workforce. Having children, finding reliable and affordable childcare, and having children or family members who are sick also form substantial barriers to employment (Smith et al., 2002). Other prevalent barriers (Goldberg, 2002) include a past history of domestic violence.

The client's past or present behavior also has an impact. Criminal records and/or past jail time, for example, are major influences or employability (Holzer, Raphael, and Stoll, 2003). Over 600,000 criminals are released each year, and in their review of the literature, they find lower rates of employment at lower pay. And such barriers may be even more significant for women ex-offenders (O'Brian, 2002).

The last general category is associated with what a person has actually learned—their job skills and what are known as "soft skills." In terms of education, there is an increasing demand that a person have at least a high school degree or equivalent. But it is also likely that the high school degree is not enough—college or technical education is of major and ongoing importance.

At the same time, finding and holding a job is rarely simply a function of a person's education and job skills—especially a person's first job. Even if many people are able to find a first job, keeping it may be difficult. Why? The answer seems to be in a category of knowledge and skills that are beyond a specific vocational ability. Rather, the answer may be found with what are called "soft skills" or "life skills". These are the skills and attitudes that form a person's workforce readiness—and these are skills that are commonly learned either outside of the world of work, or early in the employment process.

So what are soft kills? The list varies. For example, The Vocational Information Center lists hundreds of sources for such information (http://www.khake.com/page3.html), but a few variables are found across lists. Generally, these include (1) professionalism or work ethic skills, (2) teamwork and collaboration skills, (3) critical thinking or problem-solving skills, and (4) oral and written communication skills.

While these variables may seem "old hat" to many of us, the reality is that they are learned, and some people have never had the opportunity to learn things like dressing properly for work, limiting personal socializing at work, speaking respectfully to employers, coworkers, and clients, or even calling in to work if you are sick and cannot make it to work.

The effect of some of these variables can be quite profound. For example, the difference in employment due to education in August 2008 serves as a case in point. The unemployment rate for people with less than a high school degree was 9.1%, while only 3.1% for a person with a bachelor's degree or higher (U.S. Department of Labor, 2008). Likewise, a single female household with a child experienced an unemployment rare of 9.6% versus 6.1 overall and 3.7 for women, spouse present.

Summary.   So what causes individual and family poverty? While the absence of money is the core problem, the reasons given for this deficit depend very much on the values and beliefs of the person asking the question. Clearly, poverty has both a personal and a social dimension. Individuals differ in their innate abilities, motivation, and physical capacity, all of which affect their income. But at the same time, the environment's ability to nurture and the capacity and will of the social, political, and economic systems to provide or limit opportunities also play a major role. Thus, effective social work practice with the poor requires careful attention to the attitudes, behaviors, and environmental situation of the client.

POVERTY CAUSATION ON THE MACRO LEVEL—COMMUNITIES AND LARGER SYSTEMS

The factors affecting community poverty are only slightly better understood, and but no less controversial, than those affecting individuals and families. A variety of interrelated factors limit the capacity of the environment to nurture. At the community level, poverty can often be traced to the interplay of two issues: economics and political power.

Economic Issues.   Just as individuals do, communities require an adequate supply of income to pay for the services they provide. These services usually include public safety, education, infrastructure, and governance. The quality and quantity of these services are dictated, at least in part, by the tax base: the revenues generated by personal, property, and business taxes. Other revenue sources include fees charged by the community for various services, grants from the state or federal government, and credit obtained by public debt financing (loans to the community through financial instruments such as bond sales).

In a community populated by a large percentage of middle- and upper-income wage earners and/or characterized by a vibrant business and commercial sector, the taxes and fees generated will most likely be adequate to purchase and provide the desired services. Similarly, public debt financing is easier when the community is perceived as having adequate future revenues to make loan payments.

On the other hand, when a community is populated by a large percentage of low-income wage earners and/or characterized by a weak business sector, the taxes and fees generated may be inadequate. Under these conditions, very few options exist for the community, all of which will result in the same set of problems. First, the quality and quantity of needed services may be reduced in order to keep tax rates low. Second, the community may attempt to raise taxes or fees, but increased taxes often will drive taxpayers away to live or work in communities with lower tax rates. Third, the community will attempt to borrow money, but higher interest rates will be charged because the credit worthiness of the community is in question. This last option may lead to the need to raise taxes to pay the debt, or it may strap the community with a high future debt or reduced services (Karger, 1994), which may force the community to again raise taxes in the future. All three options almost inevitably result in service cutbacks, since they all depend on having a wage-earning or commercial population that can pay the taxes necessary to pay for the services.

Many communities lack a strong wage-earning or commercial sector for several reasons. One of the most important is that the American economy has undergone sweeping changes in the last 30 years, generally due to a process known as globalization. Many of the high-wage, low- to moderate-skill manufacturing jobs that were available from the 1940s to the 1970s have moved to areas where labor costs are much lower, such as to Mexico or Central America through the 1990s, or to China, India, Vietnam, and other Asian countries in the last few years.

At the same time, job growth in this country has centered on two very different sets of skills. At one level, the high-technology and financial services sectors have expanded and have created a large number of high-paying jobs that require significant training and education. At another level, a large number of low-paying, low-skill jobs have been created in the service economy in areas such as retail commerce. Communities that have seen significant high technology or finance job creation have done well in maintaining civic services, while communities that have not experienced such growth have suffered.

Political Power. To at least some degree, a community can overcome the lack of a strong tax base if community leaders can muster the political coordination to efficiently develop new resources, such as external grants or new businesses. Such efforts may succeed, but they often result in substantial tax giveaways by the community as incentives to business development. The degree to which these tax giveaways benefit the community and the poor is an open question (Vidal, 1995).

A far more common outcome is that communities are unable to muster sufficient political strength. Instead, political fragmentation and, occasionally, political corruption are what emerges. As a community begins to spiral downward, a form of competition emerges among various interests in the community to hold onto available resources. With mounting and diverse problems facing the community, interest groups may erect barriers to prohibit other interest groups from allocating scare resources differently. In light of diminishing external resources, this trend could get worse (Bailey and Koney, 1997).

Broken Windows. To end this section, a final word may be useful as relates to the concept of "broken windows." There are researchers who believe that community poverty is closely connected to the general and reinforcing effects of a spiral of decay. In other words, if windows are broken and no one fixes them, then it is considered acceptable to have evident decline. And the more decline that is accepted by the community, the more decay will result—often in more and more serious forms. In recent decades, mayors such as Giuliani in New York used this perspective, drawing on early authors such as Wilson and Kelling (1982) to support major community efforts of zero tolerance to crime and decay (Miller, 2001; Bratton and Kelling, 2006).

Whether this perspective is correct or not is hotly debated, but it fits well within the moral decay viewpoint of the "culture of poverty." It is likely to continue to influence some policymakers for years to come.

CLIENT NEEDS: THE CONSEQUENCES OF POVERTY FOR INDIVIDUALS AND FAMILIES

There are numerous consequences of poverty for individuals and families, and the consequences should also be examined in the assessment. Many of these consequences are interrelated. Further, the consequences of poverty are often more serious, or of a higher priority to the client, to as the lack of cash itself. Thus, it often makes sense to aim interventions at the secondary problem even though the root cause, poverty itself, continues unabated. Only your conversations with the client will ultimately clarify where the attention should focus. For individuals and families, the consequences of poverty include hunger and poor nutrition, inadequate shelter, and other consequences.

Hunger and Nutrition.   The number of hungry people in the United States is open to some debate, but the number, no matter who measures it, is large. In 2006, 12.6 million households, or 10.9% of all U.S. households were judged food insecure (Nord, Andrews, and Carlson, 2007). This is a slight increase from 2001, with 10.7% of U.S. households (11.5 million) food insecure. Of these, about 3.5 million households actually experienced some degree of hunger during the year (Nord, Andrews, and Carlson, 2002). Of the 2006 numbers, about 6 million households with children (15.7% of all households with children) were food insecure, and of these 1.6 million were very food insecure during the year (Nord, Andrews, and Carlson, 2007). As many as 1 in 12 American children under the age of 12 suffer from hunger (Hunger Action Coalition, n.d.).

Another measure of the size of the hunger problem in America comes from examining the utilization of governmental food services. At the federal level, 15 food and nutrition programs administered by the U.S. Food and Nutrition Service assist 1 in 6 Americans. The largest federal food program, Food Stamps, was estimated to serve 26.7 million people in fiscal 2006, with an average benefit of about $96 per month (Nord, Andrews, and Carlson 2007). This is an increase from 19.1 million individuals in fiscal year 2002, at a cost of $20.6 billion. The federal Women, Infants, and Children (WIC) program, specifically designed to address nutritional deficits, served about 8.1 million people in 2006 (Nord, Andrews, and Carlson 2007), up from 7.5 million people in 2002 . Finally, about 30 million children received free or low-cost lunches each day through the school lunch program (Nord, Andrews, and Carlson 2007).

The consequences of hunger and inadequate nutrition are substantial and far reaching. Problems can range from inadequate physical and mental development to death. The problem is especially acute among children. The more severe the poverty a child experiences, the more likely nutritional deficits will exist (Brown and Pollitt, 1996).

Shelter. Shelter is of equal importance to food and nutrition for survival. A steady income is necessary for adequate shelter, and the two most important variables are the availability of shelter and the quality of living conditions. Both may suffer when an adequate income is not available.

For most people, housing represents the largest ongoing expense, particularly among the poor and low income. "Half of all working households with incomes between $19,000 and $37,500 spend more than 30 percent of their monthly incomes for housing, and 15 percent spend more than 50 percent" (Dreier 2007, as cited in Acs and Turner, 2008, p. 2).

Because of the cost, many people are barely able to afford housing. For example, among renters, the number of households with what are called worst case housing needs in 2005 was 5.99 million, up from 5.18 million in 2003. Households with "worst case needs" are defined as "unassisted renters with very low incomes who have one of two 'priority problems'—either paying more than half of their income for housing ('severe rent burden') or living in severely substandard housing" (U.S. Department of Housing and Urban Development, 2007a, p. 1).

Homeownership, a component of the American dream, is also too costly for many. Although about 68% of American householders own their homes (U.S. Bureau of the Census, 2008a), home affordability for many people is questionable at this point in time. The current credit crisis following the housing bubble of the early 21st century has tightened income requirements, even as the median monthly housing cost in America for homes of $1404 (U.S. Bureau of the Census, 2006) has placed a purchase beyond the grasp of many. In 2002, the last full study of the subject found that 44% of all families (even current homeowners) would not be able to buy a home in their state due to costs (Savage, 2007). More than 5.3 million American households report that housing costs consume more than half of their total income (U.S. Department of Health & Human Services, 1999). With such high costs associated with shelter, it is not surprising that an estimated 3.5 million people, 1.35 million of them children, experience homelessness each year (Urban Institute, 2000). On any given day, between 313,000 and 415,000 people are homeless (U.S. Department of Housing and Urban Development, 2007b).

The living conditions in American housing are also problematic. Over 20% of American households have significant external problems including damaged roofs, sagging walls, or broken windows. Additional problems include unsafe water supplies (8%), inadequate plumbing (2%), and a complete lack of kitchen facilities (4%) (U.S. Bureau of the Census, 2002a).

Among the more important problems facing those who live in older, substandard housing is lead poisoning. Lead was used extensively in the past in paints, plumbing fixtures, and gasoline. Thirty million homes in the United States contain lead-painted surfaces (Congressional Quarterly Weekly Reports, 1991), and more than 80% of all homes built before 1978 have lead-based paint in them (Centers for Disease Control and Prevention, n.d.a). Lead poisoning can cause learning disabilities, behavioral problems, seizures, and death, and as many as one child in six has toxic levels of lead in his or her blood. Over 310,000 children in America have elevated blood lead levels (Centers for Disease Control and Prevention (n.d.b).

While the severity of lead poisoning is recognized in the larger public health community, one study suggests that few social workers have been trained to recognize or act on the symptoms (Kauffman, Soliman, and Silver, 1999). It is highly likely that a substantial number of children have behavioral problems that might best be addressed through lead treatment interventions.

Other Consequences.   There are many other undesirable consequences associated with poverty. Forty-seven (47) million Americans, for example, lack health insurance (U.S. Bureau of the Census, 2007). Other consequences include

- Higher rates of diseases, including cancer
- Higher family stress levels (Brooks-Gunn, Klebanov, and Liaw, 1995)
- Greater childhood abuse rates
- Lower levels of educational attainment
- Higher levels of mental illness
- A greater likelihood of crime victimization
- Lower income and earnings potential (Mizell, 1999)
- Lower self-esteem, occupational status, and educational attainment levels (Mizell, 1999)
- Reduced access to legal assistance and health insurance

With such a vast array of problems, frustration and a form of learned helplessness may also appear. Most of these consequences are due to increased stresses on the individual and the family, which result from an ongoing attempt to adapt to their situation. The effect of these stresses and traumas may carry across generations (Cattell-Gordon, 1990).

THE CONSEQUENCES OF COMMUNITY POVERTY

As a community spirals downward, a variety of social problems are likely to manifest themselves. These problems include increasing crime rates; higher rates of substance abuse; deteriorating schools, transportation, and recreational infrastructure; and a decline in the accessibility of high-quality medical care. The community simply does not have the money to provide the services that may stop the spread of problems.

Moreover, as city services deteriorate and taxes increase, individuals and families who can afford to move from the community often do so. This not only reduces the tax base even further, it also removes other valuable assets from the community, including the political strengths and knowledge of those who move and their function as role models for children. It has been argued, for example, that one of the principal reasons for the development of what has been called the "underclass" was the departure of the middle class and professionals from inner-city communities (Wilson, 1987). Many of the social programs of the last four decades helped those who were most able to be helped, primarily the better-educated middle class. These individuals moved to the suburbs or other affluent communities while the poor remained in areas characterized by inadequate services, high crime rates, and high unemployment.

Another consequence of poverty in poor and powerless communities, and also one little recognized by the social work profession, is the problem of environmental justice. Because there is a desperate need for employment and because of the intentional targeting of such communities for undesirable types of business (Kauffman, 1994; Rogge, 1993, 1994), poor communities are likely to be home to prisons, factories that discharge large amounts of pollutants, and waste management companies. The concentration of such businesses may result in a variety of negative social and health effects ranging from lowered property values and disagreeable odors to increased rates of respiratory diseases and cancer. One community has even noted an increase in prostitution to serve the truckers who bring garbage into several recently built trash incinerators (Resident of Chester, PA, personal communication, May 1997)!

POLICY ISSUES

As the number of the poor and as the complexity of the problem of poverty have increased, the number of social policies to address poverty have increased. Collectively, these are what we commonly call "welfare," if we use the services definition of the term.

Before we look at the various programs and services that are available, there are a few general comments about the programs that might be useful. First of all, the U.S. might have the most complex system of social welfare of any country in the world. As you have learned in your policy classes, this complexity is due to our history and values. Unlike the social welfare democracies of Western Europe, we carve out roles for virtually every social system in the provision of welfare. We have roles for every level of government (federal, state, and local), for the private sector (nonprofit, for-profit, religious, and nonreligious institutions), and for professionals (social workers, physicians, nurses, teachers, and more) as well as for volunteers.

Secondly, our system generally has different policies and programs for different types of problems. With the exception of a few cash programs, such as the TANF program (Temporary Assistance for Needy Families), for which recipients may maximize choice about the benefit, most of our programs are problem specific—meaning that the recipient has to demonstrate a specific need in order to receive a specific benefit.

Finally, building upon the previous point, our social system is a residual system, as opposed to the universal system more often found in Western Europe. What this means is that in the U.S., virtually all of our social welfare programs are selective and means tested. To receive the benefits, the recipient must have not only the problem, but also the inability to pay for it on their own (or through their employment). Thus, most programs have a very extensive assessment process.

Unfortunately, the assessment process may be quite complex as well. As discussed earlier, we have a poverty line that determined the income level at which people are considered poor. Using this figure, even if inadequate, might be a reasonable level for setting benefits and services. But in reality, benefits are based on many different dollar figures—some above and some below the poverty level—and in many cases, these figures also differ from state to state. Knowing what benefits are available for which clients requires significant training for social workers in the U.S.

On the other hand, many programs in Western Europe (and Canada) are universal. This means that citizenship, or even presence, is enough to receive the benefit. Health care, education, family services, and childcare are common examples of programs that all residents get in such countries, as opposed to perhaps K–12 education only in the U.S. Below are descriptions of the major welfare programs in the U.S.

HEALTH POLICY

For approximately two-thirds of our population in the U.S., the quality of health care is close to the best in the world. Of these people, most will receive their health care from their employment source. About 64% of women, for example, receive health care from personal or spousal employment, while an additional 2% purchase their own (U.S. Department of Labor, n.d.a). In 2005, 19% of women 18–64 (17 million) had no health insurance (U.S. Department of Labor, n.d.a). For individuals who need assistance with health care, and who qualify, the federal government has two very large programs, Medicare and Medicaid, and a number of smaller support programs.

Medicare, a component of Social Security, is not commonly thought of as a "welfare" program, although it is not a universal program either. Medicare provides major medical insurance (Part A), physician payments (Part B), and pharmaceutical benefits (Part D) for people who qualify for Social Security Old Age pensions, as well as for certain disabilities. Anyone who is eligible for Social Security is probably eligible for Medicare. Medicare is administered by the federal government, and in the case of Part D, drug benefits are administered by approved state plans. Funding for the program is drawn from worker and employer contributions to a federally administered trust fund. Application for benefits is either automatic (as in the case of Old Age pensions), or through federal Social Security Administration branches located across the country.

The most recent development in Medicare is Part D, is a voluntary program that provides prescription drug coverage to Medicare recipients through the federal Medicare Prescription Drug, Improvement, and Modernization Act of 2003. This is the one part of Medicare that has a substantial role for the states, in helping to establish approved plans, and in providing (in many cases) assistance to low-income seniors.

Medicaid, or more properly Medical Assistance, is the health insurance program that is more commonly thought of as a welfare program. The program is again a component of Social Security, but unlike Medicare, states have a major role in policies, funding and administration. Generally, the federal government establishes service minimums and pays the bulk of costs, but then states are given the discretion to expand services and eligibility, with a responsibility to partially fund both the minimums and the expanded services.

Eligibility and application processes are somewhat different across the states, but as a means-tested program, there are income, asset, and categorical requirements. The income and asset requirements are somewhat different depending on the eligibility category. For example, income and asset levels are much more generous for the low-income elderly couples who have a spouse that requires nursing home care than for TANF recipients who apply for Medicaid benefits. In the majority of states, applications are made in state or county assistance offices, often at the same time as other program applications are made. Many states also allow applications to be made at the point of service as well—such as in a hospital or nursing home.

A few programs under Medicaid require some additional comments. For example, the large number of children whose parent(s) do not have health insurance are not eligible for insurance through programs like Pennsylvania's CHIP—the Children's Health Insurance Program. The program is funded by federal Medicaid and state dollars. CHIP families must have incomes of less than 200% of federal poverty line, and depending on the income, CHIP may be free or very low cost (CHIP, n.d.).

In addition to Medicare and Medicaid, there are a number of smaller support programs. These small programs include such things as the Newborns' and Mothers' Health Protection Act of 1996 that requires health insurance plans to pay for a minimum of a 48 hours in the hospital for childbirth (longer for a cesarean section), or the Mental Health Parity Act that requires parity in lifetime insurance limits.

CASH ASSISTANCE

In the U.S., there are a number of cash assistance programs for the poor, or for those with specific types of need. Some of these programs are jealously protected by Americans, while others might be the most controversial and reviled of all welfare services. Listed in order of increasing controversy, the programs include Social Security Old Age pensions (SSOA), Survivors benefits (SSS), Disability benefits (SSD), Unemployment benefits (UI), Supplemental Security Income (SSI), and Temporary Assistance to Needy Families (TANF). There are also some state-specific programs such as Workers Compensation and General Assistance.

Social Security Old Age, Survivors, and Disability Insurance (OASDI).   As previously indicated, OASDI is a generally noncontroversial program, although this could change quite dramatically in the future. They are generally noncontroversial because, although they are not true universal programs, they do provide benefits for almost all employed people—and almost all employed people have paid into the insurance trust fund that pays for them. The future controversy has to do with some inevitable changes in funding, benefits, or both. These changes are being forced largely because American workers are growing older and living longer, and the payments will be unsustainable in just a few years. Indeed, many changes have already taken place in order to support the program. These current changes include a gradual increase in retirement age eligibility, as well as recent increases in the tax rate and amount of a person's earnings that are eligible to be taxed. Despite these recent, and upcoming changes, at the moment, these are very popular programs.

These three programs, OASDI, are lumped together because of the similarity of funding and administration. All three are components of the Social Security Act of 1935, or later amendments. They are all funded out of a federally administered trust fund that receives dedicated tax revenues from employed people and their employers. The theory upon which the program was founded was that the program would operate on a "pay as you go" premise. In other words, current workers and employers would fund current recipients.

Old Age.   For Old Age pensioners, enrollment and eligibility were opened to (almost) all workers, simply through the provision of a federally assigned Social Security number. Once enrolled, all oversight and administration of benefits would occur through the federal Social Security Administration, and benefit payments were to begin automatically at age 65. Vested people could also apply for early benefits at age 62½, but these and all future benefit payments were reduced. The benefit amount, at either age, was to be determined by the recipient's contributions, with higher earning individuals receiving higher benefits, up to a maximum. Recipients with a spouse receive a higher benefit than do single people. As long as no problems would arise, it is not necessary for most people to ever see an SSA representative.

Survivors.   Survivors insurance does require an application, and there are some increased eligibility issues. First of all, this is not a program for survivors of people who were recipients at the time of their death. In most cases, that category of survivor would continue to receive benefits automatically. Instead, people eligible for Survivors benefits are minor children (under the age of 18), commonly, although not necessarily, with a surviving parent. Upon the death of the otherwise eligible adult, the survivor applies at an SSA office, and assuming approval, benefits will continue until the child's 18th birthday. Like pensions, benefit levels are determined by the amount of contribution.

Disability.   Disability insurance is available, again, to people who are vested in Social Security, but who then become permanently and totally disabled prior to their 65th birthday. The eligible person must apply through an SSA field office and must demonstrate through a physician's certification that they are in fact disabled.

It sounds easy enough, but if any of the OASDI programs are currently controversial, this is it. Because of concerns about expenses, Social Security has a generally standard procedure of refusal for applicants. Applicants may appeal the decision through several levels of appeal, and in fact most people with a legitimate disability will receive benefits if they appeal long enough. Many people, however, do not appeal, and as such, they do not receive benefits. Thus, if one piece of advice can be given to social workers with eligible clients, it is appeal, appeal, appeal.

Unemployment Insurance.   Also a component of the Social Security Act of 1935, though few people think of it as such, is Unemployment Insurance (UI). UI is in many ways similar to OASDI, with some important differences. The main similarity is how it is financed. UI, like OASDI, is paid for through a dedicated tax that again workers and their employers jointly pay. These funds also go into a federal trust fund for future disbursement.

The main difference with OASDI is that UI is largely administered by state unemployment offices. When an eligible worker is involuntarily unemployed, it is the worker's responsibility to apply for benefits at the state-run office. If approved, the worker will become eligible for up to 36 weeks of benefits at an xx proportion of his salary. During this time, the recipient is required to look for employment. It is this requirement that established the major differences with OASDI. First of all, the assumption is that employment is best found by those closest to the job pool. This means that the state UI office also serves as a placement agency of sorts. Secondly, UI is the first program we have looked at that places a responsibility on the recipient. To receive benefits, the beneficiary must show evidence of the job search. This element of responsibility becomes more pronounced with other programs.

Supplemental Security Income.   Supplemental Security Income, or SSI, is a component of amendments to the Social Security Act that most people would classify as a welfare program. In other words, SSI is paid for out of general governmental tax revenues, as opposed to a dedicated trust fund, and the amount of the benefit is determined by the person's family's income.

SSI is largely funded from federal dollars, but state welfare offices are responsible for application and oversight. Eligibility is slightly different across the states, but as with other means-tested programs, there are income, asset, and categorical requirements, and the category of eligibility affects the income and asset amounts. The categories of benefits include the low-income elderly and the low-income disabled. The idea behind the benefit is that people with some form of vulnerability, such as age or disability, are entitled to at least a minimum quality of life. Elderly or disabled people may even, in fact, collect a Social Security cash benefit, but at levels below what are needed to meet that minimum quality of life.

As suggested above, SSI is not without some controversy. Most of this is related to the definition of disability. Many people ask whether people with a disability brought about by an addiction, such as drugs or alcohol, deserves to be treated the same way as a physical disability, such as blindness. Many people believe that addiction is the "fault" of the client, and therefore they do not deserve the same level of attention as a person who is affected due to accident or birth. In addition, some disabilities for which a diagnosis is more subjective, such as Attention Deficit Disorder, cause concern. Such people believe that such a diagnosis may be easily falsified in order to "cheat" the system.

Temporary Assistance for Needy Families (TANF).   TANF, our largest cash assistance program, has only been in place since 1996. Replacing Aid to Families with Dependent Children (AFDC), the Personal Responsibility and Work Opportunity Reconciliation Act (PRWORA) created TANF as what many people refer to when they talk about "welfare reform" (Cherry, 2007). Whether it is reform or not is an open question, but it most certainly is very different from AFDC.

TANF is a true joint federal/state program. The federal government sets the requirements and funds most of the program, while states partially fund, administer, and may modify elements of the program. Eligibility is slightly different across the states, but as with other means-tested programs, there are income, asset (less than $1000), and categorical requirements (one or more children under the age of 18).

There are also substantial expectations and responsibilities placed on the recipient. For example, unless the recipient has a very small child, or is excused for some health or disability reason, the client must seek employment or participate in an employment and training program. The client must also work on an Agreement of Mutual Responsibility, which is a plan for permanent employment.

In exchange, the client will receive up to 5 years of cash assistance, and a variety of other services (differing by state) that may include

- Needs assessment
- Health care services
- Access to special services
- Job coaching
- Education and training
- Child care assistance
- Transportation assistance

FOOD AND NUTRITION PROGRAMS

As noted earlier, the federal government provides a number of food and nutrition programs (15), with the largest being the Food Stamp program. Other large programs include the School Lunch program, and Women, Infants, and Children (WIC).

Food Stamps.   Food Stamps were served to an estimated 26.7 million people in fiscal 2006, with an average benefit of about $96 per month (Nord, Andrews, and Carlson, 2007). Food stamps are vouchers (or increasingly debit-type swipe cards) that are used to buy food and help low-income households obtain more nutritious diets by increasing their food purchasing power.

The program is federally funded through the U.S. Department of Agriculture, but largely administered by the states. Eligibility is based on income and assets only—no categorical determinations are included. Currently, assets are limited to $2,000 per household, or $3,000 if at least one household member is 60 or over or is permanently disabled. The current income limits and benefit levels are shown on Table 11.5. In 2005 recipients, 27.7% had some form of earned income, while about 79% had some form of unearned income, including Social Security (24.1%), SSI (31.1%), or TANF (17.5%) (Pennsylvania Department of Public Welfare 2008a). PA Dept. of Public Welfare, 2008b. Retrieved from Internet August 21, 2008.

In 2005, in Pennsylvania, fairly typical of the US, 27.7% or recipients had some form of earned income, while about 79% had some form of unearned, including SS (24.1%), SSI (31.1%), and TANF (17.5%) (Pennsylvania Department of Public Welfare 2008a).

National School Lunch Program.   Of the nutrition programs, it can be argued that the National School Lunch Program is one of the broadest in scope. It is a federally assisted meal program that serves free or low cost means at over 101,000 schools and residential childcare institutions daily to over 30.5 million children each school day in 2007 (U.S. Department of Agriculture 2008).

TABLE 11.5 | FOOD STAMP INCOME LIMITS AND BENEFIT LEVELS FOR 2008

Household Size	Maximum Gross Monthly Income	Maximum Net Monthly Income	Maximum Monthly Food Stamp Benefit
1	$1,107	$851	$162
2	1,484	1,141	298
3	1,861	1,431	426
4	2,238	1,721	542
5	2,615	2,011	643
6	2,992	2,301	772
7	3,369	2,591	853
8	3,746	2,881	975
9	4,123	3,171	1,097
10	4,500	3,461	1,219
Each additional member	+377	+290	+122

Source: From the Pennsylvania Department of Public Welfare (2008), Food Stamps. Retrieved from the internet August 21, 2008. http://www.dptw.state.pa.us/SerivcesPrograms/FoodStamps/

It is a federal program, but it usually administered by state education agencies, which operate the program through agreements with school food authorities. Children whose families earn 130% of poverty level or lower receive free meals, while those with incomes up to 185% receive reduced-price meals, for which students can be charged no more than 40 cents.

HOUSING AND ENERGY

Housing and energy are increasingly areas of considerable concern for all Americans, and no less for the poor and low income. There are three substantive programs for the poor in this area—public housing, Section 8 housing, and Low Income Energy Assistance.

Public Housing & Section 8.   Although a national priority, public housing has a relatively short history. The first low-rent public housing projects in the United States were constructed during the depression of the 1930s. Subsequently, the federal Housing Acts of 1937, 1949, and 1954 created the urban renewal programs of the 1950s and established publicly owned housing, and Section 8 programs still in operation today. More recently, a series of block grants to state and local governments have been established to allow a degree of flexibility in housing approaches. All of these programs are intended to assist the poor to afford shelter. The public housing programs are generally under the control of approximately 3,350 local public housing authorities (PHAs) and Indian Housing Authorities (IHAs). Funding for the programs of the PHAs and IHAs comes largely through grants from the U.S. Department of Housing and Urban Development (HUD), a cabinet level department created in 1965.

TAX POLICY

One last area of services to the poor is benefits receive through the Earned Income Tax Credit. This federal benefit essentially returns all taxes paid by low-income workers. It is a federal program, resulting in a substantial work incentive for the low-income worker.

PRACTICE ISSUES

PRE-ENGAGEMENT

As may be seen by now, a large and complex area like poverty and welfare requires significant study on the part of the social worker. Yet, with what we have covered so far, it is hoped that some of the issues make more sense now. We will now turn to some practice issues that are likely to be addressed as you work with these clients.

As described in earlier chapters, the important goal of the pre-engagement phase is an assessment of the client's situation that is developed through a rich collaborative process. In this process, the client and the worker are mutual partners who together and seek to identify the strengths and the problems or obstacles that limit desired outcomes. During this phase, dialogue, trust, and developing the relationship are key elements to a successful process.

THE BOTTOM LINE: WHAT TO ASSESS

As may be seen from the variety of causal factors and consequences, an assessment with people and families who are poor or who are receiving some form of welfare assistance can be quite extensive. Yet even the most comprehensive assessments need not ask a client about every item we have examined so far. The key is to use the frameworks addressed in previous chapters, collaborating with the client through dialogue, and then *being prepared* to move into more specific areas with more specific questions as they arise.

The value of this flexibility is that the types of interventions and services that are available to you are largely determined by the needs you and your client identify. The large number of varying consequences and the problems of unclear or different causality also make practice with the economically disenfranchised both challenging and rewarding. Individuals, families, and communities differ in their unique circumstances. They also differ in the tools and resources available to them. Hence, a significant amount of time must be spent in assessing individual as well as community needs. Effective practice requires getting to know the community and having various members of the community articulate their concerns as well as their strengths. Only a well-developed familiarity with the community will prepare you for work with this population.

The values, cultural standards, and past history of interventions with the community also must be examined. Some poor communities have experienced a kind of roller-coaster effect. The community has often been promised the moon by social workers and others. Great expectations arise, only to be shattered as the scope of the problems overwhelms the process. Or, more likely, funding priorities change and monies available for even a promising and successful project dry up before the community is back on its feet. This roller-coaster effect, moreover, is the basis for some of the powerlessness felt by residents in the community.

On the other hand, it is a mistake to focus only on the problems the community faces. Using the strengths perspective articulated in earlier chapters avoids the tendency to focus on deficits (Saleeby, 1992). The reasons for bringing a strengths perspective to the relationship are both practical and conceptual. The resources of the individual or the community will be the available tools for change. Thus, knowing what these tools are is critical. But, in a larger sense, keeping your attention on the problems or deficits is disempowering to the client (Hepworth, Rooney, and Larson, 1997). The residents already know what the problems are. Constantly reminding them of problems may bring up feelings of powerlessness from the past. Moreover, focusing on problems or deficits can result in a "blaming the victim" perspective. Thus, you need to keep the focus on the possibilities for change and the means to achieve the desired outcomes.

ENGAGEMENT

The complex, multidimensional aspects of poverty demand flexibility from the generalist social work practitioner. Individuals and communities will almost inevitably present a range of different problems, each requiring different skills and knowledge. Because of the scope of the problem, this section will not attempt to address all of the practice issues with these client groups, but instead will focus on a set of generalist concepts as they apply to this rewarding area of practice. These concepts include (1) the range of target problems and goal setting, (2) the importance of research and planning, (3) collaboration, coalition building, and the importance of relationships, and (4) effective interventions.

THE RANGE OF TARGET PROBLEMS AND GOAL SETTING

The essential starting point in generalist social work practice with economically disadvantaged clients and communities is determining the desired outcomes of the intervention. At least three types of goals apply to this area of practice:

1. Goals that seek improvements in intangible concepts, such as the distribution of rights or psychological status
2. Goals that seek improvements in processes
3. Goals that seek specific, measurable, targeted outcomes

Table 11.6 links each goal to a partial list of potential target problems. This may serve to guide your thinking about where to focus your intervention. Specifically, after the identification of the target problem, the client, whether an individual, a family, or a community, may require assistance in determining where best to focus

TABLE 11.6 | POSSIBLE TARGET PROBLEMS AND GOAL TYPES

Goals Which Seek Improvements in Intangible Concepts		Goals Which Seek Improvements in Processes		Goals which Seek Specific, Measurable, Targeted Outcomes	
Microsystems	Macrosystems	Microsystems	Macrosystems	Microsystems	Macrosystems
Target Problems	Target Problems	Target Problems	Target Problems	Target Problems	Target Problems (Rates)
Lack of empowerment	Environmental racism	Low political participation	Low political participation	Unemployment Family violence	Unemployment Crime
Lack of self-efficacy	Social injustice Discrimination	Poor family communication	Poor community planning	Substance abuse Mental illness	Family violence
Resident apathy	Community isolation		Service availability	Literacy Hunger	Substance abuse Pollution Cost/availability of Housing

corrective efforts. Consider, for example, the problem of poor community planning. Here, the appropriate goal is improvement of the processes the city uses to make its decisions. This may then require interventions at the level of city government. On the other hand, violence within a family might be better addressed by direct practice with the family to improve its internal communication or problem-solving skills.

The process of selecting goals is as important as the goals themselves, if not more so. It is critical to work closely with the client system. You bring a level of expertise to the relationship, but it is the client who experiences the problems, and more often than not, it is the client who actually implements the intervention. This means, at the very least, that the client is ultimately responsible for the change.

The goal when addressing poverty is empowerment. It does not matter if the target of change is the individual, the family, or the community. In all cases, improvements in the quality of life will be achieved through the desire and efforts of individuals, either alone or in groups, to bring about change. You will seek to assist individuals and communities to work for and advocate on their own behalf. It is a collaborative process. Empowerment comes about by helping individuals, families, and communities "take action to improve their situation" (Gutierrez, 1994, p. 202) through the development of "organized responses to circumstances that affect their lives" (Nystrom, 1989, p. 161).

Empowerment of clients who have a long history of powerlessness is not a fast process. Education and support of the clients' own problem-solving abilities are effective empowerment strategies (DuBois and Miley, 1996). Beyond this, collaboration, use of a strengths perspectives, and adopting a perspective that shows the client the relationship between personal problems and the social and structural causes of those problems all promote empowerment (Simon, 1994). Shared responsibility, mutual trust, and a track record of small successes are also important. Strategies that use community and/or small groups are also useful as tools of empowerment (Breton, 1994; Gutierrez, 1994; Hirayama and Hirayama, 1987).

COLLABORATION, COALITION-BUILDING, AND THE IMPORTANCE OF RELATIONSHIPS

A collaborative partnership approach is effective with economically disadvantaged clients. First, as discussed above, empowerment is a central goal for this type of practice, and working collaboratively with the client is essential for meeting this desired outcome. Second, there is strength in numbers. Only in a few instances can an individual or single agency bring all of the resources and expertise necessary for correcting complex, multidimensional problems for a single client or an entire community. Developing coalitions brings together expertise from a variety of different areas, which may expand resources, better integrate existing services, and increase the likelihood of reaching the identified change goals (Alter and Hage, 1993).

A range of skills is essential for practice with poor individuals and families. The worker may be required to provide different services at different times, including advocacy, counseling, linkages with other services, information, and referrals. Further, the client will need multiple services from multiple providers, and the social worker provides a vital coordination role. In this context, the whole realm of micro practice skills outlined in Chapter 5 come into play. In fact, it would be difficult to find a social work practice domain where the range of generalist practice skills is more necessary than with this client population. Any individual client, particularly a long-term welfare recipient, is likely to have a variety of different needs for a variety of different services. As a generalist social worker with low-income clients, you will see needs for employment, training, childcare, transportation, health services, life skills, substance abuse or mental health counseling, and legal assistance, all in a single day. As such, collaborative service networks with the social worker and the client at the center are inevitable and necessary.

Collaborations and coalitions are equally necessary when working with communities. The same argument about strength in numbers applies, and you will need even more resources and technical skills. Increasingly, funding sources, such as foundations and governmental agencies, are demanding collaborative components. They recognize that single-focus community programming is not as effective in bringing about change as are multifocus coalitions and partnerships. If community development activities do not voluntarily organize, efforts to bring about coalitions will be facilitated by the demands of resource providers (Bailey and Koney, 1997).

Residents should be participants in the coalitions. Partnerships should create a meaningful role for citizens in voluntary community associations and other institutions (Florin and Wandersman, 1990). Citizen participants are likely to improve outcomes (Bendrick and Egan, 1995; Mier, 1994), and intentional efforts to involve citizens in community coalitions leads to stronger communities (Unger and Wandersman, 1983; Woodson, 1981) and increased feelings of personal and political efficacy (Cole, 1974; Cole and Caputo, 1984; Florin and Wandersman, 1984; Zimmerman and Rappaport, 1988).

There is a downside to casting a wide net. Coalitions and the involvement of citizens may slow down processes in at least two ways. First, planning is substantially more complicated as the number of participants increases. Setting priorities is more difficult. Competition for scarce resources may overwhelm the planning process. Second, as individuals move in and out of the coalition, substantial time may have to be spent educating new members about the processes and decisions already made. Skillful group facilitation can minimize these problems. Over the long term, the time spent in planning and educational efforts will pay off through a more cohesive and committed coalition membership.

In almost any social work context, relationships are critical to the helping process. When working with economically disadvantaged clients, relationships are of particular importance. Past encounters with other outsiders may have eroded trust. Poor individuals and poor communities may have a long history of problematic relationships with social workers, government officials, or other authoritative figures and agencies.

Besides collaboration, the best way to build trust and a positive relationship is to

• Move slowly
• Avoid making promises you can't keep
• Take time to educate clients about your actions
• Explain the limits of your programmatic efforts
• Avoid demanding more from clients than they can give.

In addition, don't be disappointed if your ideas and suggestions are not initially carried out or if you feel you are being tested by the community (Gutierrez, Alvarez, Nemon, and Lewis, 1997). Low-income clients face a variety of demands on their time and have scarce resources. To some degree, even with the best of intentions, social work interventions represent an imposition.

Research activities, for example, such as surveys or interviews, not only demand time but may also be perceived as a significant intrusion into the clients' personal lives. Some planning activities like public meetings, or interventions like social actions, may not be well attended, as people do not feel comfortable. The process of building trust and effective collaborative relationships take time.

Almost all generalist social work skills are potentially useful when working with economically disadvantaged clients. In a short time, you may see clients with problems as straightforward as needing assistance finding a job all the way to complex problematic familial and community relationships. It is important to be prepared for any and all eventualities.

It cannot be stressed enough that you must start where the client is. This means understanding the client's needs, strengths, and cultural perceptions. Most social workers do not work with people like themselves, and many of our assumptions are rooted in our cultural background. Avoid assuming that your client sees the world the same way you do. Assume that you are different, and find out the specifics of your differences. Keep up with the literature. The current welfare reform activities have begun to generate a large amount of research that will be useful for your practice. The more you know about current policies, practices, and your client population, the more effective you will be.

In this context, a number of strategies have demonstrated success. Welfare reform under TANF, with its work-first philosophy, may have some value. Stressing work does seem to help, but with some concerns (Cherry, 2007). Teaching effective job search skills appear critical, perhaps even more so than some types of education (Michalopolous, 2004). Similarly, programs that offer a range of characteristics, including common characteristics found among the successful programs, include the following: (1) focus on employment-related goals, (2) hands-on work experience, (3) collaboration with welfare agencies and other community organizations, (4) early intervention and personal attention in addressing problems, and (5) commitment to continuous staff development. These programs showed statistically greater successes than single-focus programs (Murphy and Johnson, 1998).

For many hard-to-serve clients, wraparound services and transitional employment to gain work experience are a critical component (Brader and Frank, 2006). These jobs still meet the standards of the work-first philosophy, but also provide valuable soft skills training for clients as well.

At the level of the community, a wide range of knowledge, skills, and activities are necessary and useful. Collaborative programs that bring together diverse services seem to be among the most effective (Monsma and Soper, 2003; Michalopolous, Schwartz, and Adams-Ciardullo 2000.). These include the knowledge and practical application of different practice modes, such as locality development, which attempts to improve cooperative problem solving; social planning, which attempts to address concrete deficiencies; and social action, which attempts to force legislative or organizational change (Rothman, 1995). It also requires multicultural sensitivity (Gutierrez, Alvarez, Nemon, and Lewis, 1997). More specifically, skills include group problem solving, group and collaborative facilitation, research and analysis (McNeely, 1996), resource development (Rubin and Rubin, 1992), planning and organizing, and skills in dealing with conflict, such as active listening and consensus-building (Gutierrez, Alvarez, Nemon, and Lewis, 1997).

As may be clear, practice work with economically disadvantaged clients and communities is complex and challenging. It demands a range of skills and knowledge perhaps greater than any other form of social work practice. The rewards are great. The opportunities to work with a large number of committed and concerned individuals presents an experience rarely felt elsewhere. By engaging in this practice domain, you are working to correct the central problem of our society—poverty. Many, perhaps most, of our social problems are either caused by or closely connected to poverty. Finding solutions will improve the quality of life for many Americans.

SUMMARY

Poverty is a worldwide problem. In the United States, more than 37 million people representing 12.5% of the population are poor (DeNavas-Walt, Proctor, and Smith, 2008). The number of people classified as poor depends on the way poverty is defined. The accuracy and adequacy of the poverty threshold has been called into question.

Poverty has been a persistent social problem with multiple theories of causation and multiple consequences. Some theories focus on individual deficits, others attribute poverty to social and structural factors. A third set of theories examines the relationship between individual and social causes.

Factors affecting community poverty are better understood and less controversial. At the community level, poverty can often be traced to the interplay of economics and political power. Poor communities lack the economic base to pay for needed community services. These services include public safety, education, infrastructure, and governance. Most poor communities also lack political power. Political fragmentation and, occasionally, political corruption characterize poor communities. There often is competition for scarce resources, which further contributes to the downward spiral of economically disadvantaged communities.

The consequences of poverty for individuals and families are profound. The most immediate is its effect on an individual's capacity to survive.

Hunger and poor nutrition are common. Inadequate housing, exposure to environmental risks, unsafe streets and neighborhoods, and increased health problems are all associated with poverty.

Generalist social work practice with this population focuses on individual and community empowerment. The goal is to empower the poor individually and collectively to improve the quality of life socially, physically, and economically. This entails developing collaborative helping relationships with individuals and families to facilitate and strengthen their capacities to cope with the challenges that come with being poor as well as building community-based coalitions that seek resources and solutions to the economic and political problems facing economically disadvantaged communities.

CASE EXAMPLES

The following two case examples illustrate generalist social work practice with a community client system, and with an individual. The first describes the process the author went through in helping a low-income community develop and implement a community-based social service center. The second describes the work Heather Witt, an MSW student intern at Social Work Consultation Services, did with one of her clients in a welfare-to-work program run by the agency.

CASE 11.1 | THE CHESTER EXPERIENCE

Chester, Pennsylvania, presents a classic case of a distressed city in the United States. The city has a population of approximately 36,000 and is located one-half hour south of Philadelphia. Chester was once a thriving manufacturing center, producing ships, steel, iron, cloth, pottery, paper, and refined oil. But between the 1950s and the 1980s, the city lost 32% of its jobs, the economy collapsed, and much of the middle class moved away. The city's problems were compounded by several decades of corrupt political leadership.

Assessment

Economic changes and political inefficacy have created a number of socioeconomic problems for the community. Needs assessments demonstrated that

unemployment, crime, housing, substance abuse, environmental pollution, truancy, and low adult educational attainment rates are all serious problems in Chester. In addition, a number of barriers made services to residents inaccessible. These included a poor transportation network, service fragmentation, and a lack of awareness of the services that were available.

Intervention

Recognizing the need for better coordination between services and the reduction of barriers to service, several agencies met in the summer of 1995 to discuss methods to overcome these problems. The meetings were called by an organization that had been contacted by the Ford Foundation about a new program initiative designed to develop collaborative

CASE 11.1 | *Continued*

relationships between service providers. I was invited to help develop the program proposal and to formulate a client assessment and program evaluation plan.

The Ford Foundation provided funds for a program in Chester, in 1996. Endless hours were spent on the telephone with organizations like the United Way and combing the telephone directory to generate an exhaustive list of agencies. Next, questions had to be resolved about which agencies should be members: Was the organization to be open to social service agencies only, or should government agencies, church groups, and informal groups be invited as well? We decided to be as inclusive as possible, even inviting unaffiliated residents.

More than a hundred social service organizations banded together in a formal network. Their organization, which they named Communities That Care (CTC), began holding regular monthly meetings and planning new service initiatives. The focus of these meetings was to improve coordination, which, it was hoped, would not only improve client functioning, but would also facilitate dialogue among service providers and strengthen the process of community advocacy.

There were questions about how to organize the meetings. Should one agency take the lead in calling and coordinating the effort, or should the meetings be less structured and controlled? If one agency served as the leader, would other agencies be jealous and refuse to participate? We decided to utilize a formal structure, with the agency that had been approached by the Ford Foundation as the lead agency. The justification was that this agency would be the grant recipient and would therefore be accountable for the funding. Fortunately, our fears were unwarranted.

CTC meetings have since become forums for the exchange of information. Newsletters and information pamphlets inform clients and other providers of services offered at the various agencies. The meetings have also generated ideas that individual agencies and small groups of agencies have formalized into proposals and/or grants for new programs. In discussions at CTC meetings, for example, it was determined that a real need existed for some form of a centralized social services facility in Chester. Centralized service provision could help ameliorate problems faced by clients in accessing services, such as transportation, lack of

awareness about available services, and excessive time expenditures.

Fortunately, a facility became available immediately. One of Chester's two hospitals was acquired by the other, much larger hospital. The larger hospital was a member of CTC, and it decided to use the smaller hospital building for its social service programs, including inpatient and outpatient substance abuse and mental health treatment. Unused space was made available to other providers at low or, in some cases, no cost. The new facility, called the One-Stop Shop (OSS), opened in mid-1998. More than 20 public and private social service agencies are now located in the facility. Services available include job training and placement, domestic and family mediation, childcare, counseling, computer skills training, and educational support. Because many clients failed to follow up on referrals from and to such public social services as Medical Assistance and Temporary Assistance for Needy Families, an onsite county assistance office was established at the OSS in the fall of 1998.

Another initiative of the CTC network has been the development and adoption of a standardized assessment and client service planning system to make practice and program evaluations easier. Prior to the implementation of this system, clients often underwent several different assessments by the different agencies helping them. At the request of several agencies, I formulated a plan to eliminate this burden on the clients, meeting frequently with the various providers to address issues of client confidentiality, agency needs, and the overall assessment process.

In addition, several initiatives focus on the development of community leadership skills. Several of the agencies using the One-Stop Shop are offering newly designed programs to strengthen client leadership skills and problem-solving capacity. These interventions not only empower clients to self-advocate, they also promote ownership of change efforts, thus avoiding the perception that change has been imposed by outsiders.

Finally, several of the agencies provide intensive case management to families and individuals. Case management enables service linkage and follow-up assistance. In two of the agencies, the case management system has undergone major expansion because of grants to enlarge their service scope.

(Continued)

CASE 11.1 | *Continued*

Evaluation

While Chester continues to face many problems, it appears that the CTC network and the One-Stop Shop are having a significant effect on the community. Several initiatives of the CTC network have been funded, although these successful initiatives have depended upon the hard work of a few extremely dedicated agency partners. It is unclear if these efforts would have been successful without these "go-getters." In addition, many agencies that would fit well with CTC either do not participate or remain on the fringe. The agencies operated by the city of Chester, for example, fall into these categories. Along this same line, there are starting to be a few "cliques" of organizations that are seeking funding to the exclusion of others. Also, only a few residents are members of CTC. As a result, the planning of activities is slowed because agencies must spend time to gather the support of the residents.

Finally, in an impoverished community like Chester, job development is critical, and the One-Stop Shop does not address this need. My hope is that reducing barriers to service will assist clients in their attempt to have their immediate needs met, and as their capacity to self-advocate improves, real change will take place with the community as the change agent. Empowering the residents is an important byproduct of several of the programs of the One-Stop Shop, and in time, I believe this will be the most beneficial outcome.

CASE 11.2 | ### THE LONG HARD ROAD OFF WELFARE
Heather Witt, MSW Student

Social Work Consultation Services (SWCS) is a nonprofit human services agency in Chester, PA. SWCS was developed by the Center for Social Work Education at Widener University in association with the Chester Education Foundation. The staff of SWCS consists predominantly of graduate interns in both Social Work and Clinical Psychology. SWCS provides a variety of services to the community of Chester, including a welfare-to-work program called Circle for Change (CFC). CFC is a program that provides career skills training (e.g., interviewing), life skills training (e.g., conflict resolution), computer training (e.g., Microsoft Office), GED courses, individual counseling, and a support group. The majority of the clients are required to fulfill 30 hours a week through the program sessions, outside "homework" assignments, and to fill out applications.

Problem Situation

Anne is an African-American woman in her late thirties who has five children. The oldest three children are grown or live with their father. Upon entering the program, Anne lived with her younger two children, a daughter, age 15, and a son, age 7, in her sister's home with her sister's family. Anne is unemployed and both of her children are enrolled in school. Anne's only source of income was from welfare. Anne's live-in boyfriend was incarcerated due to a probation violation that stemmed from a drug-related arrest.

Anne was referred to the Circle for Change program in October of 2007 due to her long history on welfare. Anne has exhausted her paid allowance and receives only a small cash allowance every 2 weeks, as well as food stamps. Anne successfully completed the CFC program in December 2007, but decided to continue on with Phase Two of the program.

Intervention Activities

During her individual sessions, she indicated that she had five main goals:

- Get a job
- Get own housing
- Learn to tell people "no"
- Think before acting
- Get driver's license

For each goal, Anne and her counselor decided upon practical action steps to help her make progress.

CASE 11.2 | *Continued*

To achieve the goal of obtaining a job, Anne decided that continuing her job skills training through the Circle for Change program would be helpful. Also, with the help of her counselor, Anne explored her options of career choices. After deciding that childcare was the field she was most interested in, Anne set aside a specific amount of time per week researching childcare positions so she could be prepared for interviews when the program ended.

Anne and her counselor worked together on her application for housing. While there was much "red tape" for Anne to work through, she secured housing rather quickly once she put her energy into the process.

In working with Anne to help her feel more comfortable telling people that she was unable to do certain things, her counselor explored with her why she felt she had an issue in this area. It became apparent that Anne had a great fear of disappointing people or "letting them down." She enjoyed being the person that people came to when in need. After some work, Anne felt more comfortable setting some boundaries with how far she was willing to go to help others. Anne took time to document instances when she was able to verbalize to her friends and family members that she could not be of assistance and also times when she was unable to say "no," even though she wanted to. She brought these examples to her individual sessions to process with her counselor. After she realized that her loved ones would continue to come to her for support even with those boundaries in place, this task became much easier for her.

Anne indicated that she had a "short temper" at times, especially with her children, and wanted to work on "thinking before reacting." Anne felt she benefited greatly from taking the time to document examples to bring into therapy with other work, so she decided to do the same. However, Anne rarely was able to give examples of this occurring. When her counselor brought this to her attention, Anne stated that she felt that simply being in individual and group therapy was curtailing this behavior because she wasn't feeling as "stressed out." Anne also stated that simply being aware of her tendency to behave in such a way has helped her take her time before reacting.

Toward the end of counseling sessions, Anne stated that she wanted to add a new goal, which was to get her driver's license. Anne planned on obtaining a study guide from her sister, applying for a permit, and deciding upon a practical amount of study time each night.

However, the counseling sessions ended before much progress was made on this goal.

Current Situation

Anne successfully completed the second phase of Circle for Change in April 2008. She decided to continue receiving individual counseling after the program concluded. Anne was placed in a volunteer position in a day care in order for her to gain experience in the field. Shortly after the ending of the program, Anne's boyfriend was released from prison and moved back in with Anne and her children.

Anne continued attending counseling sporadically and informed her counselor at her last session that her childcare placement did not work out because her "performance was not good enough." Anne hoped to be placed in another childcare facility because she stated she did enjoy her position. After this meeting, Anne did not keep another scheduled appointment and she did not return her counselor's calls. It is unclear if Anne was placed at another childcare site, obtained employment, or is currently doing another program.

Client System Obstacles and Strengths

Anne has great economic obstacles. Although the return of her boyfriend does help financially, as she stated that he already has a job, her only income is that from her welfare benefits. She does not receive assistance in the way of child support or alimony from her children's father.

Anne's youngest son has severe asthma that is regularly flared. There were occasions throughout her time in the program where he needed to be hospitalized due to his illness. His medical condition makes it difficult for Anne to consistently attend her placements. However, Anne did not miss a single day during the first phase of Circle for Change, which was a testament to her dedication to the program.

Anne is extremely resilient and hard working. Additionally, she is a high school graduate and does have a work history, often times holding down several jobs at once. Her most recent position ended in 2006 due to her inability to find transportation after her co-worker, whom she carpooled with, quit. Anne always seemed quite motivated and achieved or made great progress on most of her stated goals while in counseling. Even when obstacles presented themselves, Anne refused to let these circumstances stop her.

Discussion Questions

1. What strategies could be used to address the multiple problems in a city like Chester? What role should the residents play?
2. Why would a community like Chester be selected for the development of new, environmentally unfriendly businesses, like hazardous waste incinerators?
3. Which, if any, social problems in the United States are caused by poverty? If a problem is caused by poverty, is it better to address that problem or to address poverty?
4. What is the role of the generalist social worker when working with a poor person and his or her family? In other words, assuming no other problems, such as substance abuse or domestic violence, what strategies would you use?
5. Is poverty the fault of the poor person? Is it the responsibility of the poor person to solve the problem?

References

Acs, G., and Turner, M. (2008). *Making work pay enough*. Washington DC: Urban Institute.

Alter, C., and Hage, J. (1993). *Organizations working together*. Newbury Park, CA: Sage.

Bailey, D., and Koney, K. (1997). Interorganizational community–based collaboratives: A strategic response to shape the social work agenda. In P. Ewalt, E. Freeman, S. Kirk, and D. Poole (Eds.), *Social policy: Reform, research and practice* (pp. 72–83). Washington: NASW Press.

Bane, M. J., and Ellwood, D. T. (1994). *Welfare realities: From rhetoric to reform*. Cambridge, MA: Harvard University Press.

Banfield, E. (1968). *The unheavenly city*. Boston: Little, Brown.

Banfield, E. (1974). *The unheavenly city revisited*. Boston: Little, Brown.

Bendrick, M., and Egan, M. L. (1995). Worker ownership and participation enhances economic development in low–opportunity communities. *Journal of Community Practice, 2*, 61–85.

Bower, B. (1994). Growing up poor. *Science News, 46*, (July 9), 24–25.

Brader, A., and Frank, A. (2006). *Transitional jobs: Helping TANF recipients with barriers to employment succeed in the labor market*. Washington DC: Center for Law and Social Policy.

Bratton, W., and Kelling, G. (2006). There Are No Cracks in the Broken Windows. *National Review online*. Retrieved September 18, 2008 from http://www.nationalreview.com/comment/bratton_kelling200602281015.asp

Breton, M. (1994). On the meaning of empowerment and empowerment–oriented social work practice. *Social Work with Groups, 17*(3), 23–37.

Brooks–Gunn, J., Klebanov, P. K., and Liaw, F. (1995). The learning, physical, and emotional environment of the home in the context of poverty: The Infant Health and Development Program. *Children and Youth Services Review, 17*(1/2), 251–276.

Brown, L., and Pollitt, E. (1996). Malnutrition, poverty and intellectual development. *Scientific American, 274*(2), 38–43.

Buhler, P. (2001). The growing importance of soft skills in the workplace, *Supervision*, June 1, 2001. Retrieved September 20 2008 from http://www.allbusiness.com/management/788014–1.html

Cattell–Gordon, D. (1990). The Appalachian inheritance: A culturally transmitted traumatic stress syndrome. *Journal of Progressive Human Services, 1*(1), 41–57.

Center on Budget and Policy Priorities (1997). *Poverty rate fails to decline as income growth in 1996 favors the affluent: Child health coverage erodes as Medicaid for children contracts*. Washington, DC: Author.

Centers for Disease Control and Prevention (n.d.a). *What every parent should know about lead poisoning in children*. Atlanta: Author.

Centers for Disease Control and Prevention (n.d.b). *Lead*. Retrieved September 29, 2008 from http://www.cdc.gov/lead/

Centers for Medicare and Medicaid Services (n.d –1.). Table 112. *Gross domestic product, federal and state and local government expenditures, national health expenditures, and average annual percent change: United States, selected years 1960–2001* SOURCE: Centers for Medicare & Medicaid Services, Office of the Actuary, National Health Statistics Group, National health accounts, Retrieved

September 16, 2008, from ftp://ftp.cdc.gov/pub/
Health_Statistics/NCHS/Publications/Health_US/
hus03/Table112.xls

Chen, S., and Ravallion, M. (2008). *The Developing World Is Poorer Than We Thought, But No Less Successful in the Fight against Poverty*. New York: World Bank.

Cherry, R. (2007). *Welfare transformed*. Oxford: Oxford University Press.

CHIP (n.d.). What is CHIP. Retrieved August 21, 2008 from http://chipcoverspakids.com/interior.php?subPage=AboutExplanation

Citro, C., and Michael, R. (1995). *Measuring poverty: A new approach*. Washington, DC: National Academy Press.

Cole, R. L. (1974). *Citizen participation and the urban policy process*. Lexington, MA: D. C. Health.

Cole, R. L., and Caputo, D. A. (1984). The public hearing as an effective citizen participation mechanism: A case study of the General Revenue Sharing Program. *American Political Science Review, 78*, 404–416.

Congressional Quarterly Weekly Reports (1991). Lead exposure bill stalls in markup. *Congressional Quarterly Weekly Reports, 49*, 3206.

Crudden, A., and McBroom, L. W. (1999). Barriers to employment: A survey of employed persons who are visually impaired. *Journal of Visual Impairment & Blindness. 93*(6), 341–350.

Danziger, S., and Gottshalk, P. (1995). *America unequal*. Cambridge, MA: Russell Sage Foundation and Harvard University Press.

Danziger, S., and Seefeldt, K. (2002). Barriers to employment and the 'hard to serve': Implications for services, sanctions, and time limits. *Focus 22*(1), 76–82.

DeNavas–Walt, C., Proctor, B., and Smith, J, (2008). U.S. Census Bureau, Current Population Reports, P60–235, Income, Poverty, and Health Insurance Coverage in the United States: 2007. Washington, DC: U.S. Government Printing Office.

DeNavas–Walt, C., and Cleveland, R. (2002). Current Population Reports P60-218, *Money Income in the United States: 2001*. Washington, DC: U.S. Government Printing Office.

DiNitto, D. (1996). The future of social welfare policy. In P. Raffoul and A. McNeece (Eds.), *Future issues for social work practice* (pp. 254–265). Boston: Allyn & Bacon.

Dreier, P. 2007. 'Housing the Working Poor.' *Shelterforce*, Retrieved September 18, 2008 from http://www.nhi.org/online/issues/151/housingtheworkingpoor.html

DuBois, B., and Miley, K. K. (1996). *Social work: An empowering profession* (2nd ed.). Boston: Allyn & Bacon.

Fisher, G. (1995). Is There Such a Thing as an Absolute Poverty Line Over Time? Evidence from the United States, Britain, Canada, and Australia on the Income Elasticity of the Poverty Line. Poverty measurement working papers. Washington, DC: U.S. Census Bureau. Retrieved September 1, 2008 from http://www.census.gov/hhes/poverty/povmeas/papers/elastap4.html

Fisher, G. (1992). The development and history of the poverty thresholds. *Social Security Bulletin, 55*(4), 3–14.

Florin P. R., and Wandersman, A. (1984). Cognitive social learning and participation in community development. *American Journal of Community Psychology, 12*(6), 689–708.

Florin, P. R., and Wandersman, A. (1990). An introduction to citizen participation, voluntary organizations, and community development: Insights for empowerment through research. *American Journal of Community Psychology, 18*(1), 41–54.

Gans, H. (1976). The positive functions of poverty. *American Journal of Sociology, 78*(2), 275–289.

Gilder, G. (1981). *Wealth and poverty*. New York: Basic Books.

Goldberg, H. (2002). *Improving TANF program outcomes for families with barriers to employment*. Washington, DC: Center for Budget and Policy Priorities.

Goodwin, L. (1983). *Causes and cures of welfare: New evidence on the social psychology of the poor*. Lexington, MA: Lexington Books.

Gottschalck, A. (2008). Net Worth and Asset Ownership of Households: 2002. *Current Population Reports, P70–115*. Washington, DC: U.S. Bureau of the Census.

Gutierrez, L. (1994). Beyond coping: An empowerment perspective on stressful life events. *Journal of Sociology and Social Welfare, 21*(3), 201–219.

Gutierrez, L., Alvarez, A., Nemon, H., and Lewis, E. (1997). Multicultural community organizing: A strategy for change. In P. Ewalt, E. Freeman, S. Kirk, and D. Poole (Eds.), *Social policy: Reform, research and practice* (pp. 62–71). Washington, DC: NASW Press.

Handler, J., and Hasenfeld, Y. (1991). *The moral construction of poverty: American welfare reform.* Newbury Park, CA: Sage.

Hepworth, D., Rooney, R., and Larson, J. (1997). *Direct social work practice: Theory and skills* (5th ed.). Pacific Grove, CA: Brooks/Cole.

Hirayama, H., and Hirayama, K. (1987). Empowerment through group participation: Process and goal. *American Journal of Community Psychology, 15,* 353–371.

Holzer, H. (2007). The Economic Costs of Child Poverty, Testimony before the US House Committee on Ways and Means. *Urban Institute.* Retrieved September 16, 2008 from http://www.urban.org/url.cfm?ID=901032

Holzer, H., Raphael, S., and Stoll, M. (2003). Employment Barriers Facing Ex–Offenders. Employment Dimensions of Reentry: Understanding the Nexus between Prisoner Reentry and Work. Paper presented at Urban Institute Round Table May 19–20, 2003, New York: University Law School.

Hunger Action Coalition (n.d). Factsheet. Retrieved September 4, 2008 from http://comnet.org/hacmi/facts.htm

Indiana State University (2008). Glossary of terms. Retrieved August 21, 2008 from http://www1.indstate.edu/nursing/organization/glossary.htm

Karger, H. (1994). Toward redefining social development in the global economy: Free markets, privatization, and the development of a welfare state in Eastern Europe. *Social Development Issues, 16*(3), 32–44.

Katz, M. (1989). *The undeserving poor: From the war on poverty to the war on welfare.* New York: Pantheon.

Kauffman, S. (1994). Citizen participation in environmental decisions: Policy, reality, and considerations for community organizing. In M. D. Hoff and J. G. McNutt (Eds.), *The global environmental crisis: Implications for social welfare and social work* (pp. 219–239). Brookfield, MA: Avebury Press.

Kauffman, S., Soliman, H., and Silver, P., (1999). Environmental Hazards: Social Worker Practices and Attitudes. Paper presented at the Annual Program Meeting of the Council on Social Work Education: San Francisco CA.

Lewis, O. (1959). *Five families: Mexican case studies in the culture of poverty.* New York: Basic Books.

Lewis, O. (1961). *The children of Sanchez.* New York: Random House.

Lewis, O. (1966). *La Vida: A Puerto Rican family in the culture of poverty.* New York: Basic Books.

Marx, K. (1867). *Capital* (S. Moore and E. Averly, Trans.). Retrieved September 10, 2008 from http://www.marxists.org/archive/marx/works/1867–c1/index.htm

Maslow, Abraham (1954). *Motivation and Personality.* New York: Harper Press.

McNeely, J. B. (1996). Where have all the flowers gone? In R. Stone (Ed.), *Core issues in comprehensive community building initiatives* (pp. 86–88). Chicago: Chapin Hall for Children.

Mead, L. M. (1986). *Beyond entitlement.* New York: Free Press.

Mead, L. M. (1992). *The new politics of poverty: The working poor in America.* New York: Free Press.

Michalopolous, C. (2004). *What works best for whom: Effects of welfare and work policies by subgroup.* New York: MRDC.

Michalopoulos, C., Schwartz, C., and Adams–Ciardullo, D. (2000). *National evaluation of welfare–to–work strategies.* What works best for whom: Impacts of 20 welfare–to–work programs by subgroup. New York: Manpower Demonstration Research Corporation.

Mier, R. (1994). *Social justice and local development policy.* Newbury Park, CA: Sage.

Mizell, C. (1999). Rising above poverty: The consequences of poverty status and individual characteristics on earnings. JCPR Working Paper *106,* 09–01–1999. Chicago: Joint Center for Poverty Research, Northwestern University/University of Chicago.

Monsma, S., and Soper, J., (2003). *What works: Comparing the effectiveness of welfare–to–work programs in Los Angeles.* New York: Manhattan Institute.

Murdock, S., and Michael, M. (1996). Future demographic changes: The demand for social welfare services in the 21st century. In P. Raffoul and A. McNeece (Eds.), Future issues for social work practice (pp. 3–18). Boston: Allyn & Bacon.

Murphy, G., and Johnson, A. (1998). *Integrating basic skills training into welfare to work.* Washington, DC: National Institute for Literacy.

Murray, C. (1984). *Loosing ground: American social policy, 1950–1980.* New York: Basic Books.

Nord, M., Andrews, M., and Carlson, S. (2002). *Household food security in the U.S., 2001.* Washington, DC: United States' Department of Agriculture.

Nord, M., Andrews, M., and Carlson, S. (2007). *Household food security in the U.S., 2006.* Washington, DC: United States' Department of Agriculture.

Nystrom, J. F. (1989). Empowerment model for delivery of social work services in public schools. *Journal of Social Work Education, 11,* 160–170.

O'Brian, P. (2002). *Reducing barriers to employment for women ex–offenders: Mapping the road to reintegration.* Chicago: SAFER.

Ohio Department of Juvenile & Family Services (2002). *Addressing employment barriers.* Retrieved September 19, 2008 from http://jfs.ohio.gov/owf/prc/Guidance/prc50a.pdf

Pennsylvania Department of Public Welfare (2008a). *Characteristics report.* Retrieved August 21, 2008 from http://www.dpw.state.pa.us/Services Programs/CashAsstEmployment/003673735.htm

Pennsylvania Department of Public Welfare (2008b). *Food stamps.* Retrieved August 21, 2008 from http://www.dpw.state.pa.us/ServicesPrograms/FoodStamps/

Polenberg, R. (1980). *One nation divisible: Class, race, and ethnicity in the United States since 1938.* New York: Penguin.

Poole, D. (1995). Beyond the rhetoric: Shared responsibility versus the Contract with America. *Health and Social Work, 20,* 83–86.

Poole, D. (1997). Welfare reform: The bad, the ugly, and the maybe not too awful. In P. Ewalt, E. Freeman, S. Kirk, and D. Poole (Eds.), *Social policy: Reform, research and practice* (pp. 96–101). Washington: NASW Press.

Rogge, M. (1993). Social work, disenfranchised communities, and the natural environment: Field education opportunities. *Journal of Social Work Education, 29,* 111–120.

Rogge, M. (1994). Environmental injustice: Social welfare and toxic waste. In M. D. Hoff and J. G. McNutt (Eds.), *The global environmental crisis: Implications for social welfare and social work* (pp. 53–74). Brookfield, MA: Avebury Press.

Rothman, J. (1995). Approaches to community organization. In J. Rothman, J. Erlich, and J. Tropman (Eds.), *Strategies of community intervention* (5th ed., pp. 23–63). Itasca, IL: Peacock.

Rubin, H. J., and Rubin, L. S. (1992). *Community organizing and development* (2nd ed.). New York: Macmillan.

Saleeby, A. C. (1992). *The strengths perspective in social work practice.* New York: Longman.

Savage, H. (2007). Who could afford to buy a house in 2002? *Current Housing Reports,* July 2007, Washington, DC: U.S. Bureau of the Census.

Sherraden, M. (1991). *Assets and the poor: A new American welfare policy.* New York: M. E. Sharpe.

Silver, P., Kauffman, S., and Soliman, H. (1998). Environmental hazards: Social worker practices and attitudes. Unpublished manuscript.

Simon, B. L. (1994). *The empowerment tradition in American social work: A history.* New York: Columbia University Press.

Smith, L. Romero, D., Wood, P., Wampler, S., Chavkin, W., and Wise, P. (2002). Employment Barriers among Welfare Recipients and Applicants with Chronically Ill Children. *American Journal of Public Health, 92*(9): 1453–1457.

Turney, K., Clampet–Lundquist, S., Edin, K., Kling, J., and Duncan, G. (2006). Neighborhood effects on barriers to employment: Results from a randomized housing mobility experiment in Baltimore. *Princeton IRS working paper 511.*

Unger, D. G., and Wandersman, A. (1983). Neighboring and its role in block organizations: An exploratory report. *American Journal of Community Psychology, 11,* 291–300.

U.S. Bureau of the Census (2002). *American housing survey of the United States, 2001.* Washington, DC: Author.

U.S. Bureau of the Census (2006). *Median Monthly Housing Costs for Owner–Occupied Housing Units With a Mortgage (Dollars).* Retrieved September 18, 2008, from http://factfinder.census.gov/servlet/GRTTable?_bm=y&–geo_id=01000US&–_box_head_nbr=R2511&–ds_name=ACS_2006_EST_G00_&–format=US–30

U.S. Bureau of the Census (2007). *Income, poverty and health insurance coverage in the United States, 2006.* Washington, DC: Author.

U.S. Bureau of the Census (2008a). *Poverty Thresholds 2006.* Retrieved from Internet August 22, 2008, http://www.census.gov/hhes/www/poverty/threshld/thresh06.html

U.S. Bureau of the Census (2008b). *2008 Statistical abstract of the United States.* Washington, DC: Author. Available Internet: http://www.census.gov/prod/www/statistical–abstract.html

U.S. Bureau of the Census (2008c), *Housing Vacancies and Homeownership (CPS/HVS).* Retrieved September 18, 2008 from http://www.census.gov/hhes/www/housing/hvs/qtr208/q208ind.html

U.S. Department of Agriculture (2008). *National School Lunch Program*. Retrieved August 21, 2008 from http://www.fns.usda.gov/cnd/lunch/AboutLunch/NSLPFactSheet.pdf

U.S. Department of Health and Human Services (1999). *The state of the cities, 1999*. Washington, DC: Author.

U.S. Department of Health and Human Services, Social Security Administration (2001). *Social security bulletin: Annual statistical supplement 2001*. Washington, DC: Author.

U.S. Department of Health and Human Services (2003). *TANF: Total Number of Recipients Fiscal Year 2002*. Washington, DC: Author.

U.S. Department of Health and Human Services (2008). *Combined TANF and SSP–MOE: Fiscal and Calendar Year 2007. Total Number of Recipients*. Washington, DC. Author. Retrieved September 16, 2008 from http://www.acf.hhs.gov/programs/ofa/data–reports/caseload/2007/2007_recipient_tanssp.htm

U.S. Department of Housing and Urban Development (2007a). *Affordable housing needs 2005: Report to congress*. Washington, DC: United States' Department of Housing and Urban Development.

U.S. Department of Housing and Urban Development (2007b). *Annual homelessness assessment report to congress*. Washington, DC: United Statesí Department of Housing and Urban Development.

U.S. Department of Justice (2005). *Employment Laws: Disability & Discrimination*. Retrieved September 19, 2008 from http://www.dol.gov/odep/pubs/fact/laws.htm

U.S. Department of Justice, Bureau of Justice Statistics (n.d.). *Victim characteristics*. Retrieved September 12, 2008 from http://www.ojp.usdoj.gov/bjs/cvict_v.htm

U.S. Department of Labor (2008). *News*, Sept 5, 2008.

U.S. Department of Labor (n.d.). Soft skills: The competitive edge. Retrieved September 19, 2008 from http://www.dol.gov/odep/pubs/fact/softskills.htm

U.S. Department of Labor, Employee Benefits Security Administration (n.d.). *Fact sheet: consolidated omnibus budget reconciliation act*. Retrieved August 21, 2008 from http://www.dol.gov/ebsa/newsroom/fscobra.html

U.S. Department of Labor, Employee Benefits Security Administration (n.d.a). *Fact sheet: General facts on women and job based health*. Retrieved August 21, 2008 from http://www.dol.gov/ebsa/newsroom/fshlth5.html

U.S. Office of the President (2008). *Budget of the United States*. Washington, DC: U.S. Government Printing Office.

Urban Institute (2000). *A new look at homelessness in America*. Washington, DC: Author.

Vidal, A. (1995). Reintegrating disadvantaged communities into the fabric of urban life: The role of community development. *Housing Policy Debate, 6*, 169–230.

Wilson, J. Q., and Kelling, G. E. (1982). *Broken windows: The police and neighborhood safety*. Atlantic Monthly, *249*(3), 29–38.

Wilson, W. J. (1987). *The truly disadvantaged: The inner city, the underclass and public polity*. Chicago: University of Chicago.

Woodson, R. L. (1981). *A summons to life: Mediating structures and prevention of youth crime*. Washington, DC: American Enterprise Institute.

Yamada, G., and Sherraden, M. (1997). Effects of assets on attitudes and behaviors: Advance test of a social policy proposal. In P. Ewalt, E. Freeman, S. Kirk, and D. Poole (Eds.), *Social policy: Reform, research and practice* (pp. 193–205). Washington, DC: NASW Press.

Zimmerman, M. A., and Rappaport, J. (1988). Citizen participation, perceived control, and psychological empowerment. *American Journal of Community Psychology, 16*, 725–750.

Generalist Practice with People Affected by Addictions

John R. Giugliano

Steve Nagy/Index Stock Imagery/Photolibrary

Frank is a BSW student who is starting his senior internship at an addiction program. The program has a residential unit and an outpatient unit, and offers referral services. Frank is excited about his placement. He is an adult child of an alcoholic and understands the impact of addiction on the addict and family members.

After Frank completed the agency orientation, he spent time with his supervisor to review some of the paperwork requirements specific to his assignment. Frank will begin by performing brief intakes for service assignment, followed by a thorough biopsychosocial assessment.

After a few weeks Frank was feeling good about his new learning experience. Frank received a call for an intake from a woman named Lucille. Lucille is a 42-year-old divorced African-American who comes to the agency for assistance with depression and alcohol counseling. She was recently arrested for a DUI. It is her first-time offense. The courts did not require treatment, but Lucille, who has been extremely depressed, is requesting treatment voluntarily. She has been struggling with thoughts of suicide, although she denies any intent. When questioning Lucille, Frank finds out that Lucille rarely drinks. In fact, she only drinks at social occasions and special events. However, Lucille admits when she does drink she tends to drink to the point of extreme intoxication. As a matter of fact, the night of her DUI her blood alcohol level exceeded twice the legal limit. The night of the DUI, she was returning from a retirement party for one of her colleagues. She has very little memory of what happened that evening but does remember spending the night in jail.

Lucille states that there have never been any consequences for her drinking prior to the DUI. Lucille doesn't sound like an alcoholic, plus she claims she will never drink again. Lucille reports that her father was an alcoholic and she fears becoming one herself. She wants to help with "her drinking problem." She states that her life has been "an unhappy mess."

Frank is unsure how to help Lucille. According to the brief interview, it appears that Lucille does not drink often and she does not appear to be alcohol dependent. Indeed, she now intends to permanently give up alcohol. She has not had a drop to drink in the last 3 weeks and has not experienced any withdrawal nor feels any cravings. Lucille is clearly depressed and requesting help. But is a drug program the appropriate treatment for Lucille?

The purpose of this chapter is to provide social workers with a generalist understanding of addiction and the various resources available to assist individuals affected by drug use. Upon completion of this chapter, the reader should be able to help Frank to:

1. Understand the classification of various drugs and the potential short-term and long-term effects on a person's mind and body
2. Assess a client's drug use and the emotional, physical, and spiritual consequences that result from problematic behaviors and drug use
3. Make an assessment of the client's strengths and obstacles that may contribute to helping him or her reach their goals
4. Understand the difference between substance abuse and substance dependence
5. Understand how the addiction cycle and the brain's "reward circuit system" maintains an individual's dependence on drugs

6. Become familiar with the various interventions that are available to clients and help fit the client with the most appropriate resource available

ADDICTION OVERVIEW

According to the Substance Abuse and Mental Health Services Administration's National Survey on Drug Use and Health in 2006:

*   23.6 million persons aged 12 or older needed treatment for an illicit drug or alcohol abuse problem. Of these, only 2.5 million or 10.8% of those who needed treatment received it at a specialty facility.
*   There were nearly 1.8 million admissions for treatment of alcohol and drug abuse in 2006. Forty percent of those admissions were for alcohol treatment. Heroin and other opiate admissions were 18%, followed by 16% for marijuana.
*   Of patients entering treatment, 14.4% were 20–24 years old, followed by 14% of those 25–29 years old and, 13.9% 40–44 years old.
*   About 59% of admissions were White, 21% were African-American, and 14% were Hispanic/Latino. Another 2.3% were Alaska Native or American Indian, and 1% were Asian/Pacific Islander. The remaining 2% fell into the "Other" category (NIDA, 2008).

Most people have been affected by an addiction in one way or another. People can have addictions to substances such as alcohol, nicotine, and cocaine, or behaviors such as sex or gambling. Mental health professionals struggle to understand the nature of addiction and why some people become addicted and others will not with the same exposure to the substance or the behavior. There are many people who drink socially, or have smoked marijuana or even tried other drugs, but they do not progress to addictive usage.

Pathological gambling and out-of-control sexual behaviors are examples of addictions that do not require the ingestion of a drug (Goodman, 1990). Rarely is the addiction label given to behavioral excess that does not include taking a substance. The original research on addiction comes from alcoholism. Not surprisingly, therefore, the definition focuses on the ingestion of substances. The original definition emphasized a physiological dependence upon some foreign substance. Nevertheless, individuals can become addicted to the chemicals that our bodies produce as a result of excessive repeated behaviors (i.e., adrenaline for gambling or endorphins for sex and exercise).

The concept of addiction has changed over the years. Originally it was thought that addiction is due to a defect in moral character or lack of will power. Four decades ago as a result of extensive research, the American Medical Association acknowledged alcoholism to be a disease (American Medical Association, 1961).

In the past decade, advances in technology have allowed scientists to examine the brain in search of what causes and maintains addictions. Neurobiological explanations of addiction have become increasingly popular as newer technology permits increased information about brain activity. Many professionals agree that some people can use/abuse drugs and still exert control. However, some people cannot maintain control. Ironically the more we know about neurobiology, the more we realize that the social, psychological, and cultural factors still remain important in explaining why some individuals who are genetically predisposed to substances never become addicts and others who are not predisposed will become addicts.

It is not uncommon to see the term "alcohol and other drugs" used to in the addiction literature. This phrase is outdated and gives the impression that alcohol is something separate from drugs. The reality is that it is not different or separate; alcohol is a drug. Originally this phase was meant to distinguish alcohol from *illegal* drugs. Today when we refer to drugs, we include alcohol, illegal drugs, prescription drugs, and excessive behaviors. In this chapter the word "drug" will be used to refer to any of the aforementioned mood-altering substances or behaviors.

This chapter is to give an overview of addiction for the generalist social work practitioner. Often social workers will encounter addiction problems with their clients regardless of the setting in which they are working. Therefore, this chapter will give a broad view of various kinds of addictions. It is beyond the scope of this chapter to go into the details involved with each specific drug. The reader is asked to keep in mind that there are significant differences and effects that each drug has on the body. The research is rapidly changing, and you are encouraged to stay current to reduce the possibility that you will pass on outdated or misinformation to your clients. The following is a cursory view of the effects that different classes of drugs have on a person.

CLASSIFICATION OF DRUGS AND THEIR EFFECTS

In this section, a partial list of various drug classifications will be reviewed:

1. Depressant
2. Depressant: Sedatives/tranquilizers
3. Opioids
4. Stimulants
5. Hallucinogens
6. Inhalants

Class – Depressant

- **Substances** – Alcohol (beer, wine, hard liquor)
- **Street names** – Booze, brew, cold one, juice, sauce
- **How they are used** – Consumed as a beverage
- **Effects on the body and mind** – Euphoria, relaxation, lowered inhibitions, reduced intensity of physical sensations, body heat loss, slurred speech, clumsiness, delayed reflexes, lethargy, confusion, dehydration, blurred vision, irritability, vomiting, and/or unconsciousness
- **Effects with prolonged use** – Coronary heart disease, heart attack and stroke, dementia, hepatitis, fatty liver, cirrhosis, ulcers, chronic diarrhea, amnesia, vomiting, brain damage, internal bleeding, debilitation
- **Withdrawal symptoms** – Dry mouth; headache; nausea; shakes; sensitivity to movement, light, and noise; convulsions; hallucinations; loss of memory;

muscular spasms; psychosis (Oscar-Berman and Marinkovic, 2003; White, 2003).

Class – Depressant: Sedatives/tranquilizers

- **Substances** – Alprazolam (Xanax), barbiturates, chloral hydrate (Soma), clonazepam (Klonopin), chlordiazepoxide hydrochloride (Librium), diazepam (Valium), diphenhydramine (Benadryl, Nytol), eszopiclone, (Lunesta), ethchlorvynol (Placidyl), gamma-hydroxybutrate (Liquid X, GHB), glutethi-mide (Doriden, codeine), lorazepam (Ativan), pentobarbital sodium (Nembu-tal), methaqualone (Quaalude), nitrous-oxide (laughing gas), triazolam (Halcion), zaleplon (Sonata), (Ambien)
- **Street names** – Reds, Red Devils, RDs, Fender Benders, Yellows, Yellow Jackets, Blues, Blue Heavens, Rainbows, Christmas Trees, Pink Ladies, Mickey Finn, Knockout Drops, Ludes, Barbs, Downers, Busters, GBs, Goof Balls, Green Dragons, Peanuts
- **How they are used** – Smoked, swallowed in pill form (sometimes injected)
- **Effects on the body and mind** – Lowering of inhibitions, elevated mood, euphoria, increase in confidence, reduces heart rate, blood pressure, and breathing, irritability, paranoia, suicidal thoughts, agitation or aggression, memory problems, unsteady gait, slurred speech, eye twitching, poor judgment, vertigo, nightmares, lethargy, confusion dizziness, anxiety, nausea, vomiting, constipation, skin rashes, delirium stupor
- **Effects with prolonged use** – Respiratory depression, circulatory collapse, fee-ble rapid pulse, decreased body temperature, depressed reflexes, stupor and coma, death results from respiratory failure followed by cardiac arrest

Withdrawal symptoms – Anxiety, weakness, nausea, vomiting, muscle cramps, twitching, delirium, insomnia, tremors, mania, psychosis, seizures (Duncan, 1988; Galanter and Kleber, 2004)

Class – Depressant: Opiates

- **Substances** – Opiates: codeine, Darvon, dilaudids, heroin, methadone, morphine, opium, and Percodan
- **Street names** – Smack, Horse, Junk, "H," Hard Stuff, Shit, Mexican Brown, China White, Chiva, Goma, Gumball, Schoolboy, Downtown, Dolls, Dollies, Drug Store, Miss Emma, Morf, "M," Morpho, Black Tar, Boy, Brown Sugar, Crown Crap, Doogie, Hairy Harry, Hazel, Henry, George, Smack, Radish, Mud, Muzzle, Scag, White Lady
- **How they are used** – Swallowed in pill form, "snorted" in powder form, injected using a needle and syringe
- **Effects on the body and mind** – Euphoria, a sense of calm, dizziness, drowsi-ness, light-headedness, lethargy, headaches, mental clouding, dry mouth, heavy feeling of limbs, suppression of pain, nausea, vomiting, constipation, skin rash, slow and shallow breathing, lowered blood pressure, disruption of menstrual cycle, hallucinations, clammy skin, convulsions, coma, sluggish "rubber-like" movements, possible death

- **Effects with prolonged use** – Depressed sexual drive, lethargy, general physical debilitation, infections, hepatitis, death
- **Withdrawal symptoms** – Watery eyes, runny nose, diarrhea, sweating, muscle spasms, insomnia, aches of the muscles and joints, nausea, gooseflesh, slight tremors, loss of appetite, dilation of the pupils, weakness, depression, hot/cold flashes, muscular and abdominal cramps, fever, jerking movement of legs, repeated gagging and vomiting, possible rapid weight lose (10–15 pounds within 24 hours), and severe tremors (Glasper, Gossop, de Wet, Reed, Bearn, 2008; van Wormer and Davis, 2003)

Class – Stimulants

- **Substances** – Amphetamines, Dexedrine, diet pills, cocaine, caffeine, Methamphetamine, Methylphenidate (Ritalin), nicotine, Ecstasy
- **Street names** – Coke, Snow, Nose Candy, Flake, Blow, Lady, White, Snowbirds, Speed, Uppers, Ups, Hearts, Black Beauties, Pep Pills, Bumble Bees, Footballs, Meth, Crank, Crystal, Ice, Fire, Crypto, White Cross, Glass, Ice, Freebase, "C," Bump, Candy, Charlie, Rock, Toot, Speedball, Bennies, Truck Drivers, Chalk, Tina, Rits, Vitamin R
- **How they are used** – Orally, injected, snorted, or smoked
- **Effects on the body and mind** – Euphoria, heightened sense of well-being, increased vigor, giddiness, and sense of enhanced mental acuity and performance, increased sexual desire, alertness, agitation, restlessness, irritability, poor concentration, exaggerated self-esteem, hypervigilance, enhanced sensory awareness, fearlessness, suspiciousness, impaired judgment, poor impulse control, aggression, dilated and dried-out bronchi, insomnia, paranoia, temporary psychosis, palpitations, increase blood pressure, rapid sweating, appetite loss, teeth grinding, tremors, dilated pupils, dizziness
- **Effects with prolonged use** – Severe depression (not true for caffeine), impotence, high blood pressure, heart failure, chronic sleep problems, extreme mood swings, paranoia, anxiety, irritability, seizures (mostly for cocaine), extreme weight loss, severe dental problems, confusion, violent behavior, visual and auditory hallucinations, delusions (the sensation of insects creeping under the skin), convulsions, malnutrition, stroke
- **Withdrawal symptoms** – Fatigue, long periods of sleep, psychomotor retardation, irritability, depression, suicidal ideation, homicidality, paranoia, lethargy, insomnia, appetite loss, dangerously high body temperature, irregular heartbeat, cardiovascular failure, lethal seizures (Fisher and Harrison, 2000)

Class – Hallucinogens

- **Substances** – LSD, Peyote, Psilocybin, DMA, DOM, DMT, 2C-B, 2C-T7, and Ayahuasca, psychedelics, mescaline, PCP, marijuana
- **How they are used** – Snorted, smoked, swallowed, chewed, applied to membrane surfaces, cooked in foods, or injected into the bloodstream (mainlining), muscles, or under skin (skin popping).

- **Street names** – "A," Acid, Adams, Buttons, The Beast, Blue Cheers, Blue Mist, Brown Dot, Cube, Dot, Flat Blues, Gelatin, Green Wedge, Hawk, LSD, M and M's, Mescal, Mighty Quinn, Mind Detergent, Owsley Acid, Owsley Blue Dot, Pearly Gates, Pink Wedge, Pink Owsley, Purple Owsley, Sandoz's, Strawberries, Sugar Cube, Sunshine, Uncle, Vacation, Window Panes
- **Effects on the body and mind** – Euphoria, sense of well-being, visual and auditory hallucinations, perception distortions, panic, stupor, aggressive behavior (with PCP), catatonia, convulsions, coma, high blood pressure, blurred vision, confusion, difficulty concentrating and focusing, anxiety, agitation, paranoia, dizziness, impaired coordination, increased heart rate and breathing rate, nausea, vomiting, numbness, dilated pupils, heavy sweating, fever, loss of appetite, sleeplessness, dry mouth, tremors, rigid muscles, unpredictable flashbacks that can occur years later
- **Effects with prolonged use** – Psychosis, continued hallucinations, delusions and bizarre behavior (can occur after a single dose or after chronic use), flashbacks, organic brain damage, such as impaired memory and attention span, mental confusion, and difficulty with abstract thinking
- **Withdrawal symptoms** – No physical withdrawal symptoms reported, but heavy users may experience flashbacks, restlessness and depression (Dyck, 2005)

Class – Inhalants

- **Substances** – Glue, gasoline, hair spray, paint thinner, degreasers, dry-cleaning fluids, gasoline, lighter fluid, deodorant sprays, whipped cream, ether, chloroform, halothane, and nitrous oxide ("laughing gas"), amyl nitrites
- **Street Names** – Air Blast, Bagging, Bolt, Boppers, Bullet, Bullet Bolt, Buzz Bomb, Discorama, Hardware, Highball, Hippie Crack, Huff, Laughing Gas, Medusa, Moon Gas, Oz, Pearls, Poppers, Quicksilver, Snappers, Satan's Secret, Spray, Thrust, Whippets, Whiteout
- **How are they used** – Sniffing, snorting fumes, spraying aerosols directly into the nose or mouth, or placing an inhalant-soaked rag in the mouth ("huffing"). Users may also inhale fumes from a balloon or a plastic or paper bag that contains an inhalant
- **Effects on mind and body** – Euphoria, slurred speech, an inability to coordinate movements, dizziness, lightheadedness, hallucinations, delusions, disinhibition, hypoxia (oxygen deprivation), cell damage, irregular and rapid heart rhythms leading to heart failure
- **Effects with prolonged use** – Damage to the heart, lungs, muscle spasms and tremors, kidney abnormalities, liver damage, memory impairment, attention deficits, and diminished nonverbal intelligence
- **Withdrawal symptoms** – Weight loss, muscle weakness, disorientation, inattentiveness, lack of coordination, irritability, depression, headaches, confusion, nausea, vomiting, muscle cramps, visual disturbances, anxiety, difficulty concentrating (McNeece and DiNitto, 1998)

ASSESSMENT

Social workers are trained to make an assessment of clients from a strengths perspective. This can present challenges when assessing for drug addiction. It can be difficult getting accurate drug use information from clients because their perspective of their drug usage and the resulting consequences can be distorted and well defended. The social worker must understand that the client may not be forthcoming with information regarding their drug usage—not because the client is lying or being deceptive but because it is part of the complex nature of substance abuse and dependence. Tolerance, environmental factors, and knowledge of consequences of drug addiction are difficult dynamics for a trained professional to disentangle no less for someone who is experiencing them. For the client to observe and comprehend these factors is part of his or her recovery and healing.

Clients may have made previous attempts to stop using drugs only to be met with failure. This only increases the client's negative feelings about themselves and thus maintains their dependency. It is unempathic to expect a client to be further in the process of change than they are. This type of assessment requires the social worker's patience and acceptance that assessment is an ongoing process. The assessment is to gather information to better understand the client. Once a worker shifts into a detective role, the assessment becomes a game of "gotcha," and the relationship will be ruined.

Regardless of the amount or frequency of drug use, or type of drug being used, the social worker should conduct an assessment based on a client's strengths. As noted in Chapter 6, there are strengths-based worksheets that were developed specifically to help social workers and clients identify strengths as well as the obstacles that they face in resolving problem situations. Clients' strengths can be personal attributes that help clients cope with their life challenges, support and spirituality that they draw upon, their ability to access that support when needed, and their personal desire for good health. The obstacles can also relate to personal attributes, supports and spirituality (or lack of), or environmental circumstances and motivation.

Use, Abuse, Dependence, and Addiction

Many clients will seek help for an immediate problem without consideration of how their drug use may be impacting the issue. It is not uncommon for people to feel uncomfortable discussing these concerns with mental health professionals. For example, a person may seek support because they are feeling depressed after breaking up with their partner. The social worker may not find out until much later that the person has a drinking problem. An individual may seek help disciplining her child but neglects to tell the social worker that she has a cocaine problem. In any helping situation, the best way to identify the "real" issues is by developing trust so that the client can feel free to open up and the worker can make a thorough assessment. In Chapters 3 and 6, this book discusses in length the assessment process. This chapter is written with the assumption that the reader already has learned about empathy, positive regard, respect, and warmth necessary for establishing a working relationship. This chapter will only focus on the assessment of signs and symptoms that would indicate a possible problem with drugs or addictive behaviors. The generalist social work practitioner does not need to conduct the drug assessment or make a diagnosis but should be aware what is required and what is involved in that process. Assessment is the process of gathering information about many aspects of the client's life.

Assessment is not a single event; it is a continual process. The worker naturally would start off asking questions that are comfortable for clients to answer about their psychosocial history before asking about substance use. Remember, no single answer will let the worker know that the client has a problem. It can be difficult getting direct answers regarding substance use. Clients may minimize usage because of shame or may not realize that the amount of their drug consumption is excessive. The worker should ask about each of the class of drugs described earlier including tobacco and caffeine. Specific questions are more helpful than subjective questions. For example, if you ask a client, "How much do you drink?" you may get answers like, "Not much...less than most of my friends" or "I just drink when I'm socializing." These are subjective and vague answers. You may later find out that the individual spends most of the day hanging out with beer buddies in a bar, and most of his or her friends drink 15–20 beers a day. So the client is giving honest answers from his or her vantage point. It is more helpful to ask questions like, "When was the last time you had a drink?" "How many drinks did you have at that time?" and "What were you drinking?"

The worker should try to get a full picture of the client's usage. Besides quantity, it is also important to ask about frequency of usage, where the person uses (home alone, at friends' house), and how they are used (injected, snorted, and/or smoked). Are there times when the usage has increased or decreased? If increased, is it related to life changes? Is the increase sudden or gradual over time? At what age did the client first use this drug? Age of first usage can be predictive of future problems. It also gives some information about the client's early history.

A family history is particularly important when assessing drug problems. For either genetic or environmental reasons, having alcoholic- or drug-addicted family members is a risk factor for the client. You do not want to ask the client if he or she has alcoholic/drug-addicted family members. The client is not qualified to diagnose and may be uncomfortable applying these labels to their family members. It is advisable to ask if the client feels there were drug problems or if there were family problems (financial, communication, violence, and conflict) that may have resulted from a family member's drinking or using. This is important information even if the client does not report any drug usage. There are also many problems that are a result of being raised by addicted parents. This can give the worker insight to current relational problems that the client is reporting.

The social history may show that the client discontinued participating in activities that were once enjoyed. As addictions progress, sports, movies, and dinners are often abandoned for drug-related activities. Old friends are replaced with drug-using friends. School and occupational problems escalate as drug use increases. Clients may report: dropping out of school, jobs loss, absenteeism, tardiness, fights, or suspensions, and decline in performance. Legal problems may include: DUIs, stealing for drug money, or bartering sex for drugs.

The particular signs and symptoms of drug use and dependence vary depending on the type of drug. In each case the addiction eventually becomes the main priority in the person's life. Things that once had value become less important. The person starts to organize their life around their addiction. The addict will lie, keep secrets, and live a double life in order to maintain their substance use or continue problematic behaviors. The substance or behavior becomes the "central organizing principle" in the addict's life (Ketcham and Ashbey, 2000).

When a person senses that they have no control over their substance use or behavior, anxiety results. Defenses like denial, rationalization, and minimization help reduce or alleviate this anxiety. Although ego defenses have an adaptive value for most people, they are considered maladaptive if they are used chronically in order to deny or distort the realities of life. Rather than look at all the negative consequences that their drug use or addictive behavior causes, the addict will deny to him or herself that there is a problem so he will not have to stop using drugs. By definition addiction is the inability to stop use of a substance or behaviors despite the adverse consequences. There is a range of adverse consequences experienced by a person with an addiction:

Emotional Signs and Consequences

- Thoughts about committing suicide
- Attempted suicide
- Homicidal thoughts
- Mood swings
- Feelings of hopelessness and despair
- Depression, paranoia, or fear of going insane
- Loss of self-esteem
- Strong feelings of guilt and shame
- Strong feelings of isolation and loneliness
- Strong fears about the future
- Emotional exhaustion or weakness
- Blackouts
- Flashbacks
- Delusions

Social Signs and Consequences

- Inability to relax or have fun without drug use
- Associating with and befriending others drug users
- Talking about drugs all the time and encouraging others to use
- Estrangement from old friends and loved ones
- Talking incoherently or making inappropriate remarks
- Deterioration of physical appearance and grooming
- Physical problems (ulcers, high blood pressure)
- Unexplained injuries and infections
- Physical abuse by others

- Involvement in potentially abusive or dangerous situations
- Vehicle accidents
- Self-injury from drug usage or excessive behavior
- Sleep disturbances (not enough or too much)
- Physical exhaustion

Spiritual Signs and Consequences

- Feelings of spiritual emptiness
- Feeling disconnected from self and the world
- Feeling abandoned by God or higher power
- Anger at your higher power or God
- Loss of faith in anything spiritual

Signs and Consequences Related to Family

- Risking the loss of a partner
- Jeopardizing the well-being of your family
- Loss of family's/partner's respect
- Loss of custody of children
- Increase in problems with children
- Loss of partner
- Increase in problems with primary relationship
- Loss of family of origin
- Neglect of family responsibilities
- Keeping secrets from family and friends

Career and Educational Signs and Consequences

- Decrease in productivity at work or school
- Demotion at work
- Problems with schoolwork, such as slipping grades or absences
- Loss of coworkers' respect
- Loss of the opportunity to work in the career of your choice
- Loss of educational opportunities
- Loss of business
- Forced to change careers
- Not working to your level of capability (underemployed)
- Termination from job

Quality of Life Signs and Consequences

- Loss or severe limiting in interests, hobbies, and activities
- Risky behavior, such as driving under the influence of drugs, starting fights, or engaging in unprotected sex
- Few or no friends who do not participate/condone your using or behavior

- Loss of life goals
- Acting against one's own values and beliefs
- Living two separate lives—one public and one secret
- Evidence of money problems: frequent borrowing, selling possessions, or stealing items from employer, home, or school
- Legal problems rooted in drug use: possession of a controlled substance, disorderly conduct, embezzling, stealing
- Using drugs first thing in the morning
- Increasing doses of a drug
- Secretive or suspicious behavior: frequent trips to the restroom, basement, or other isolated areas for privacy while using drugs
- Prison
- Spending an inordinate amount of time obtaining, using, or recovering from the addictive behavior or substance

It is only when an individual stops denying that these consequences are a result of their drug use or problematic behavior that the addict can begin to take responsibility for their recovery. This is why it is believed that a person has to "hit bottom" before achieving sobriety. Some individuals will deny the consequences until they become so severe that the problems are undeniable, thus "hitting bottom."

ADOLESCENCE AND ADDICTIONS

A teenager may intend to only try a drug once. Most teens don't think that they will become addicted and simply use drugs to have a good time and be more like their friends. So what may start as innocent fun can result in drug abuse or even worse, dependence. Some drugs, such as heroin and cocaine, result in physical addiction quickly. Very few addicts recognize when they have crossed the line from casual use to addiction.

Drug abuse among teenagers is a problem for all of us, considering not only the effects that it has on the brain of the individual but also the damage it does to society. The earlier in life someone starts using drugs, the more likely that use will proceed to abuse and addiction and the tougher it will be to quit later.

TEENAGERS AT RISK

The adolescent brain functions differently than the adult brain, and that puts adolescents at a higher risk to want to experiment with drugs. In the adolescent brain, the centers for judgment and self-control are still developing, making many teens less than careful about the decisions they make and more open to risk-taking behaviors and impulsive decisions (Vega and Gill, 1998). The frontal lobe is the part of the brain that slows us down and interrupts impulsive behaviors. The front portion of the brain considers the risks and benefits of our actions. It evaluates the consequences, which will ultimately decide if we want to take action or stop (Childress, 2007). This front part of the brain is still developing connections to the rest of the brain until adulthood, so adolescents' brains lack the ability to send a message to "stop," "wait," and/or "find out more information," to the rest of the brain. Because of this teenagers' risk of becoming dependent is greater than adults, and the damage to the brain is also greater (NIDA, 2008).

Warning Signs of Teen Drug Use

- Sudden dislike of school and multiple excuses to stay home
- Truancy—attendance record does not match what you know about the individual's days absent
- A drop in performance, possibly failing courses or receiving minimally passing grades
- Increased secrecy about possessions or activities
- Withdrawal from hobbies, sport teams, and/or family life
- Marked change in behavior
- Increased aggression, hostility, or violence
- Use of incense, room freshener, or perfume to hide smoke or chemical odors
- Association with a deviant peer group or gang involvement
- New clothes that highlight drug use or suggest inappropriate conduct
- Money, prescription drugs, or valuables missing from the home (they maybe being sold to support a drug habit)
- Evidence of drug paraphernalia, such as pipes and rolling papers
- Evidence of inhaling products, such as hairspray, nail polish, correction fluid, paper bags and rags, and common household products
- Sudden requests for money without a reasonable explanation for its use
- Wearing sunglasses indoors or using eye drops to mask bloodshot eyes or dilated pupils
- Increased irritability, decreased motivation, listlessness, apathy, mood swings, depression; expressing suicidal thoughts or behaviors

Generalist social workers must assess for these signs by asking parents if they noticed any of these warning signs. The challenge is to distinguish between the normal, sometimes volatile ups and downs of adolescent development and the red flags of substance abuse. Individuals who have family members with an addiction history are at greater risk of developing an addiction. Adolescence is prime time for developing a dependence on the two deadliest drugs: alcohol and nicotine. Drug use can affect the developing brain, causing permanent damage to the brain's ability to control impulses and regulate emotions. The earlier you catch the problem, the more effective the treatment will be, and the more likely that the treatment will stick.

WHAT IS ADDICTION?

The term "addiction" is not used in the American Psychiatric Association's *Diagnostic and Statistical Manual of Mental Disorders*, the DSM. Instead, the manual uses the terms "substance dependence" and "substance abuse." When the general public uses the word "addiction," they are usually referring to what professionals call "dependence."

A person can use a substance or behavior without abusing it. A person can abuse a substance or behavior without having an addiction. For example, just because Tony got drunk a few times doesn't mean that he has an addiction. Substance abuse may lead to addiction or substance dependence. Dependence almost always implies abuse, but abuse frequently occurs without dependence, particularly when an individual first begins to abuse a substance.

This can be confusing, so professionals follow specific criteria to determine if a person abuses drugs. This criteria is also used to mark whether the substance abuse has progressed to dependence.

Substance abuse, according to the most current DSM (IV-TR), is defined as a maladaptive pattern of substance use leading to clinically significant impairment or distress, as manifested by one (or more) of the following, occurring within a 12-month period (APA, 2000):

1. Recurrent substance use resulting in a failure to fulfill major role obligations at work, school, or home (e.g., repeated absences or poor work performance related to substance use substance-related absences, suspensions or expulsions from school; neglect of children or household)
2. Recurrent substance use in situations in which it is physically hazardous (e.g., driving an automobile or operating a machine when impaired by substance use)
3. Recurrent substance-related legal problems (e.g., arrests for substance-related disorderly conduct)
4. Continued substance use despite having persistent or recurrent social or interpersonal problems caused by the effects of the substance (e.g., arguments with spouse about consequences of intoxication, physical fights)
5. The symptoms have never met the criteria for substance dependence for this class of substance (dependence is considered more severe)

Currently, abuse is seen as an early form or less hazardous form of substance dependence. Many involved recognize that the terminology has often led to confusion, both within the professional community and with the general public. In the future, it is likely that The American Psychiatric Association will change these definitions to clear up all ambiguities.

Substance dependence is characterized by impaired control over the drug, preoccupation with use, and continued use despite negative consequence. Psychological addiction happens when the cravings for a drug are psychological and/or emotional. People who are psychologically addicted feel overcome by the desire to have a drug. They may lie or steal to get it.

A person crosses the line between drug use and addiction when he or she becomes dependent on it. The addicted person's whole life centers around the need for the drug. An addicted person—whether it's a physical or psychological addiction or both—no longer has a choice in taking a substance.

According to the DSM-IV-TR, a person who is substance dependent has experienced three or more of the following signs during a 12-month period (APA, 2000).

1. Tolerance is evident when (1) a need exists for increased amounts of a substance to achieve intoxication or desired effects or (2) the effect of a substance is diminished with continued use of the same amount of the substance.

2. Withdrawal is evident when (1) characteristic and uncomfortable symptoms occur with abstinence from the particular substance or (2) taking the same (or closely related) substance relieves or avoids the withdrawal symptoms.

3. The substance is used in greater quantities or for longer periods than intended.

4. The person has a persistent desire to cut down on use of the substance, or the person's efforts to cut down on use of the substance have failed.

5. Considerable time and effort are spent obtaining or using the substance or recovering from its effects.

6. Important social, employment, and recreational activities are given up or reduced because of an intense preoccupation with substance use.

7. Substance use is continued even though some other persistent physical or psychological problem is likely to have been caused or worsened by the substance (for example, an ulcer made worse by alcohol consumption or emphysema caused by smoking).

Reprinted with permission from the "Diagnostic and Statistical Manual of Mental Disorders", Text Revision, Fourth Edition. Copyright 2000 American Psychiatric Association.

Remember, tolerance is when a person's body actually becomes dependent on a particular substance to feel normal. When a person who is physically addicted stops using a substance like drugs, alcohol, or cigarettes, he or she may experience withdrawal symptoms. However, drug abuse can occur with or without tolerance or withdrawal. As indicated above, in order for a person to be considered substance dependent, he or she only need to have *any* three symptoms out of the seven listed. Even professionals in the field of addictions often forget this point. Tolerance and withdrawal often indicate dependence but are not required for the diagnosis. The key issue in evaluating addiction is if a person is unable to stop using the harmful substance (loss of control). Often people who are addicted to a drug do not have insight to their inability to stop drug use and falsely believe they could stop if they "wanted to." This is called denial.

NEUROBIOLOGY

Current technology has given us an opportunity to observe how the brain functions. As we know, all addictions begin with a pleasurable experience. Usually, when we think of addictions, we think of substances that people ingest into their bodies. But there are also addictions to behaviors. In this case, our own body internally produces the chemicals that create the addiction. The activity may be a game, sex, gambling or being with a particular person that results in mood altering sensations. All psychoactive substances have an effect on neurons in the brain that form what is called the pleasure or reward circuit.

THE PLEASURE OR REWARD CIRCUIT

Addiction begins with the basic pleasure or reward circuits in the brain. These reward centers are designed to activate during pleasurable acts such as sex, eating, or gambling. Whenever ingesting a substance causes these reward circuits to activate, addiction/dependence is possible.

Physical addiction appears to occur when repeated use of a drug (ingested or produced) alters the reward pathways in the brain. The addicting drug/behavior causes physical changes to some neurons (nerve cells) in the brain. The neurons use chemicals (neurotransmitters) to communicate with each other. Dopamine is a "reward neurotransmitter" that is produced by pleasurable activities. The connection between dopamine and reward-seeking behaviors is an important discovery. Research discovered that rats that were engaged in gratifying activities had an increase in their dopamine levels in certain parts of the brain (Yamamoto et al., 2007).

Research demonstrates what happens when there is a decrease in dopamine levels. The relationship between dopamines and reward-seeking behaviors was observed in lab mice after removing the gene for VMAT2, an essential part of the dopamine system. With the absence of this gene, the newborn mice had a diminished supply of dopamines resulting in a failed reward system. Without pleasure (reward) the mice were not motivated to eat or drink. Even if the pups were placed on their mother's nipple, they did not nurse. Without a reward system the mice lost the desire to seek pleasure (eating or drinking) and thus could not survive (Yamamoto et al., 2007).

> The brain's main function is to help with survival, so we can stay alive and reproduce. The "desire-action-satisfaction cycle" drives the behaviors that are vital for our survival. There are three important phases in the pleasure cycle (Childress, 2007):
>
> 1. In response to stimuli, **the brain drives us to take actions** to satisfy our needs. For example, hunger makes us eat, sexual desire drives us to seek available partners, and loneliness makes us want to socialize.
> 2. Our actions **are rewarded by sensations of pleasure**. But it is important to note that it is mainly the action itself that is rewarding, not just the actual reward. For instance, receiving a nicotine patch will satisfy your craving for a cigarette, but it will never give you as much pleasure as having an actual cigarette while socializing. The action, which often takes the form of a ritual, therefore is at the very heart of the pleasure experienced.
> 3. In the third phase, **the feeling of satisfaction brings an end to the actions**. For example, when we feel full after a meal, we realize that our hunger, which drove the activity, is satisfied and we no longer need to continue eating. An orgasm is often seen as completion or an ending point when being sexual. When an action is rewarded, the behavior that was the source of this satisfaction is reinforced. (Hoffman and Froemke, 2007).

So how does this relate to addiction? Why don't we always act on pleasure? Our brain lets us know when to take action and when to stop the action. Scientists have learned which parts of the brain send these messages. Addictive substances or behaviors change the reward circuits in the brain. It is this system that keeps us from having that one drink for the road, because the brain will tell us that doing so would be both dangerous and illegal. In this case, the "stop" system sends a message that the consequences of doing the pleasurable behavior (drinking) are too negative (Childress, 2007).

According to Dr. Anna Rose Childress, researcher at the University of Pennsylvania, the reward circuitry and the "stop" circuitry really are interconnected and communicate with each other to help weigh the consequences. That means if you had one too many drinks, you will think of the consequences and choose to find a ride, call a cab, or sleep over a friend's house rather than risk the chance of being pulled over or hurting someone. "Rewards (go)" and "consequences (stop)" have communicated with each other, and "consequences (stop)" prevailed. For addicted people, these "stop" and "go" systems are impaired and become functionally disconnected (Childress, 2007). It is as though the "go" system discontinues listening to the "stop" system, and the individual is unable to slow the impulse to act. Drugs damage a person's ability to make decisions. This explains, in a general sense, why people with addictions sometimes forsake all other life activities and obligations and even their own health in pursuit of the addictive substance. This is addiction.

THE ADDICTION CYCLE

Once an addiction takes hold, it develops a life of its own. This is what maintains an addiction even when the person would like to quit. When a person starts seeking temporary relief rather than dealing with the source of their unhappiness, he begins an unnatural way of taking care of his or her emotional needs. Addicts give up the comfort of human relationships for the serenity they find through a relationship with an object or behavior. This is the beginning of the addictive cycle. Addicts seek mood alteration as illustrated in the first three phases of the addiction cycle: (1) preoccupation, (2) ritualization, and (3) compulsive behavior or drug use (Carnes, 1991). The cycle ultimately ends in despair. The despair, shame, guilt, and self-loathing act as a trigger to begin the cycle all over again. Figure 12.1 illustrates the cycle of addiction.

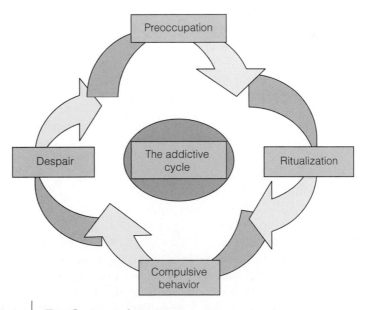

FIGURE 12.1 | THE CYCLE OF ADDICTION

1. **Preoccupation**
   a. Thoughts become focused on drugs or acting out behavior
   b. Obsessing about anticipated events and euphoric recall of past events
   c. A kaleidoscope of feelings, fantasies, memories, hopes, expectations
   d. A trance-like state that blots out the demands of life
   e. Most of the addict's time is spent in preoccupation

2. **Ritualization**
   Ritualization entails special routines that begin to alter a person's mood and reduce anxiety. Rituals can include cruising for sex or drugs, organizing the day so using or acting out can happen (leaving work early, pretending to work late, socializing with drug buddies, or even setting up a fight with our partner to give us justification for acting out).

3. **Compulsive Behavior or Drug Use**
   a. The inability to control drug use or behavior demonstrates one's powerlessness over the addiction
   b. It is not frequency or type of drug or behavior that is as important as the degree of destructiveness to the person's life
   c. The drink, drug or the compulsive "act" is the primary relationship—more important than friends, partners, work, children, or anything else that gives one meaning in their lives

4. **Shame and Despair**
   a. The emotional pain is initially transformed into pleasure
   b. Then, the hangover—the addict plummets into shame and despair
   c. The outcome is isolation, isolation, and more isolation
   d. When withdrawal begins to set in, the addict gets high again with preoccupation
   e. Addicts use or act out to escape negative feeling and avoid withdrawal

DIFFERENT THEORETICAL MODELS

There are various theoretical models that attempt to explain the phenomenon of addiction. Of course, how we view an addiction will inform our attitude and treatment for the person who is addicted. The different models also affect how the addicted person is treated by the legal system, policymakers, general public, and significant others.

THE MORAL MODEL

The moral model is based on beliefs or judgments of what is right or wrong, acceptable or unacceptable. In this case, the moral model professes that drug usage and habitual behaviors are a result of an individual's personal choice. Certainly Nancy Reagan, the former First Lady, exemplified this model in her antidrug campaign, "Just say NO!" The moral model has it roots in the prescientific era.

The belief is that drugs are deviant, and their use/abuse a sign of moral weakness. This model still persists today, but it is not as formidable as it once was. Because addiction is seen as a personal choice, the treatment is often punitive and blameful, which may include jail and repentance. An example of how the moral model can drive policy and the legal system is the Supreme Court's 1988 ruling that crimes committed under the influence of alcohol were considered willful misconduct rather than due a disease (Miller and Rollnick, 1991).

THE SOCIOCULTURAL MODEL

While the moral model looks at the internal factors such as moral character or spiritual weakness, the sociocultural model looks at the external factors that influence an individual, such as those from communities, families, schools, culture, and socioeconomics.

This model fits nicely with learning theory, which postulates that an individual's behavior is dependent on what one observes and who the individual models him or herself after. So the behavior is learned as a result of poor socialization, poor modeling, and poor coping mechanisms and skill deficits. The good news is that if an individual can learn these maladaptive behaviors, then the individual can also unlearn them.

This applies on the larger level. Society can create change by modeling and educating differently. In the United States we have seen this happen with cigarette smoking. National antismoking campaigns changed public opinion and awareness regarding the health hazards for smokers and those around them. The sophisticated and fashionable image of smokers in the 1940s to 1980s deteriorated. Eventually social attitudes shifted to stigmatize cigarette smokers. Restrictions were placed on advertisers. Cigarette companies were required to disclose the health hazards on every pack of cigarettes sold, and smoking was banned from the workplace, restaurants, airlines, bars, and most indoor facilities. As a result the number of cigarette smokers in the U.S. decreased. The degree of acceptance or disapproval from an individual's cultural or social group regarding drugs and problematic behaviors will be a strong indicator of whether or not that individual will develop problems with those drugs and/or problematic behaviors.

DISEASE MODEL/PSYCHOLOGICAL MODEL

This is currently the most popular model of addictions. Groups like the twelve-step programs are based upon the belief that drugs and problematic behaviors are a disease. The disease model supports the principle that drugs and problematic behaviors are a chronic and progressive disease. Drugs and problematic behaviors are believed to fit the definition of an illness in that it involves an abnormality of structure in or function of the brain that results in behavioral impairment. The model emphasizes that the individual is unable to reliably control his or her drugs and problematic behaviors. This theory assumes that the disease is irreversible and not curable—the goal is lifelong abstinence from mind-altering substances. In the case of behavioral addictions, the goal would be to abstain from the addictive behavior that is destructive and develop a healthier behavioral pattern. This would be the case for sex addiction or eating disorders. Once there is any return to the substance or problematic behavior, then the disease will progressively deteriorate the individual's ability to function.

If drugs and problematic behaviors are defined as a disease, it will be treated as a healthcare problem. As a result, addicted individuals will be granted the right to receive proper medical treatment. The treatment of drugs and problematic behaviors will be covered by health insurance, and ongoing biomedical research (which relates drugs and problematic behaviors to other diseases) will be funded.

INTERVENTIONS

Addiction is an illness that requires treatment because people with addictions often cannot quit on their own. Treatment may include counseling, behavioral therapies, self-help groups, or medical treatment. People often assume that those with addictions should be able to quit by simply making up their minds to do so. Self-regulation and impulse control around the person's drug of choice are difficult for people with addictions.

There is a wide range of chemical substances to which a person can become addicted. To emphasize the relationship between the addicted person and the drug or excessive behavior serves to remind us that no single set of factors adequately represents the multifactorial causes of addiction (Shaffer, 1987, 1992; Zinberg, 1984).

The ultimate goal of drug addiction treatment is to enable an individual to achieve lasting sobriety. People come to treatment hoping to reduce drug abuse, improve their ability to function, and minimize the medical and social complications of drug abuse and dependence. Like people with diabetes or heart disease, people in treatment for drug addiction will also need to change their behavior to adopt a more healthful lifestyle. Research confirms that treatment can help many people change destructive behaviors, avoid relapse, and successfully remove themselves from a life of substance abuse and dependence. Recovery from drug addiction is a long-term process and frequently requires multiple attempts at treatment. Based on this research, criteria have been established to provide guidelines for effective treatment:

Criteria for Effective Treatment

- **Treatment needs to be readily available**. It is a difficult task to ensure treatment will be available at the exact time a person who finally is ready to accept help for his or her drug addiction. If there is a delay, the addict may be rescued from or return to a state of denial believing he no longer needs treatment. The opportunity will be lost, at least for the moment.
- **One treatment doesn't fit all**. There is no such a thing as a one-size-fits-all treatment. In order for clients to be able to return to a healthy family life and become productive members of society, interventions and treatment modalities must be properly matched with the individual's unique issues. Finding the right treatment or program is important to assure successful recovery.

- **Effective treatments are often fluid and organic and not rigid.** It is critical that service providers monitor a client's needs continually to make course correction in his or her treatment approach. Often, a patient's changing needs may necessitate therapeutic interventions not previously needed, such as medication, parenting instruction, or even social and legal services. Ultimately each treatment must be customized to the patient's multifaceted variables such as gender, age, sexual orientation, culture, and religious belief, to name a few.

- **The ability to receive treatment for a time period that allows for effective changes.** Studies have consistently shown that new habits, routines, and a shift in perspective occur approximately after 90 days of initiation of a treatment program. Once a client is acclimated to a new routine, a continuation of treatment will serve to strengthen the roots and produce greater chance for permanent success. An early discontinuation of treatment will significantly reduce the chance for breaking the cycle of addition.

- **Individual and group therapies are essential components.** An effective drug treatment must be fashioned with multifaceted approaches to overcome this terrible dependency. Therapies from individual to group are all-important elements in the war. It is only through a combination of approaches that a patient can address a whole host of issues and develop the ability to decide nondrug activities instead of succumbing to drug use. Furthermore, studies have shown that once clients are exposed to the dynamics of various treatment modalities, they are able to develop better problem-solving skills, function more productively in their communities, and have an increased level of interpersonal functioning.

- **Treatment that attends to the whole person.** In order for a treatment to have any degree of success, it must be comprehensive in its approach to address not only the drug use issues. Beyond the drug problems, the treatment must address the reasons that created and maintained the addiction. As mentioned before, there is a confluence of psychological, social, and biological forces that determines addiction, and they can stem from issues in the past and/or present.

- **Combination of modalities is very effective.** There is abundant evidence that medications in combination with talk therapies increase the success of the treatment. If administered properly under medical supervision and coordinated with the treating professional, it will fortify the client's ability to stay in treatment and remain sober. For example Levo-alpha-acetylmethadol (LAAM) and methadone are extremely useful in helping heroin addicts as well as those addicted to opiates. They help stabilize the addict's out-of-control habits and reduce the physical need to use the illicit drug. In the case of smoking addiction, products such as nicotine gum or the patch can have a surprising success rate.

- **Dual-diagnosed individuals should attend to both disorders in an integrated way.** It is most common that individuals with addictions also suffer from some form of mental disorder. In cases where an individual suffers both from drug addiction and a mental disorder, the treatment plan must be designed in a way that treats both disorders in an integrated and comprehensive approach (NIDA, 2008).

MOTIVATIONAL INTERVIEWING

At one time it was assumed that if a person knew the risks associated with unhealthy behavior, it would be motivation enough for him to change. Thus, the millions of dollars invested in the "Just say NO" campaign did not show remarkable results. Regardless of efforts to educate people of the risks of drug use, people's beliefs are not based just on what they are told to believe (Turner, Perkins, and Bauerle, 2008). People must reach a personal state of readiness or eagerness to change. William Miller first developed motivational interviewing in 1983 in the treatment of problem drinkers; Bill Miller and Stephen Rollnick later elaborated on further concepts in 1991. Their technique was designed to motivate people to seek help for addiction problems. The premise is that people need to explore and resolve their ambivalence around making changes in their lives before they can commit to change (Miller and Rollnick, 1991). Prior to motivational interviewing, it was believed that addicts needed to be "scared straight" and aggressively confronted with current and possible future consequences of their addiction. The goal was to break through the addicts' "denial" so that they can see the destruction the addiction has caused in their lives and thus be motivated to make changes. Although motivational interviewing does, in one sense, seek to "confront" clients with reality, this method differs substantially from more aggressive styles of confrontation.

Motivational interviewing is a tactical approach to help individuals develop a commitment to changing problematic behavior. It addresses the client's reluctance to change and explores their ambivalence about modifying their behaviors. Motivation to change is elicited from the client, and not imposed from without. This is very consistent with social work values, "be where the client is." People come into treatment with different levels of motivation (or readiness) to change. A clinician needs to start at the client's readiness level in order to minimize resistance and gain cooperation. Motivational interviewing is designed to clarify and resolve ambivalence in a client-centered and respectful manner. Motivational interviewing relies upon identifying the client's values and goals to stimulate behavior change. Ambivalence takes the form of a conflict between two courses of action (e.g., indulgence versus restraint; "I want" to versus "I don't want to"), each of which has perceived pros and cons. Ambivalence is normal, acceptable, and an understandable state of mind. Many clients have never had the opportunity of expressing the confusion and contradictions of this conflict, for example, "If I stop drinking I will feel healthier, have more money, spend more time with my family, but I may not be able to sleep, escape from life's pressures, feel calm, or see my drinking buddies." It enables the clinician to minimize resistance to change, thereby becoming a helper in the change process (Sobell and Sobell, 2003). The counselor's task is to facilitate expression of both sides of the ambivalence. Advising or persuading the client to change generally increases the client's resistance. Client resistance is often a signal that the counselor is assuming greater readiness to change than is the case, and it is a cue for the worker to modify motivational strategies (Miller and Hester, 1995; Miller and Rollnick, 1991).

The role of the generalist social worker:

- Developing a collaborative relationship with the client
- Expressing empathy, acceptance, and affirmation

- Communicating respect for and acceptance of client's feelings
- Supporting self-efficacy, self-determination, and client's strengths—making it clear that if he or she chooses not to change that too is his or her right
- Removing obstacles to resources
- Reinforcing the client's own self-motivational statements and intention to change
- Listening rather than telling
- Examining the inconsistency between client's goals, beliefs, values, and current behavior
- Rolling with, rather than opposing, the client's resistance
- Monitoring the client's degree of readiness to change

Empathy is basic to all talk interventions. It is more than identifying with a person's experience or expressing sympathy for the client. Empathy is conveying a real understanding of the person's conflict and what maintains the ambivalence. It demands active listening and reflection so that the practitioner can offer a succinct statement that summarizes what the client has tried to express (Miller and Rollnick, 1991).

Some "DO NOTS" for the generalist social worker:

- Argue that the person has a problem and needs to change
- Offer direct advice without client's receptiveness
- Prescribe solutions
- Threaten to withhold services or resources
- Use an authoritative/expert stance leaving the client in a passive role
- Talk more than the client
- Function as an instructor
- Impose a diagnostic label
- Behave in a punitive or coercive manner

Arguments are contrary to motivational interviewing. If the social worker pushes, debates, or argues with the client, then the client will defend him or herself and present arguments for not changing. It is not helpful for the client to hear himself rehearse arguments for not changing. This is counter to what motivational interviewing tries to accomplish. The worker wants to capture and reflect the client's motivation, abilities, and obstacles (Resnicow, Dilorio, Soet, Borrelli, Hecht, and Ernst, 2002).

THE MOTIVATIONAL STAGES OF CHANGE

This model identifies a cycle of change that people rotate through before effecting permanent change. These stages include:

1. **Precontemplation** – when the individual does not see a need for or is not even considering change
2. **Contemplation** – when the individual considers change, acknowledges ambivalence, and considers obstacles but has not made a commitment to begin changing

3. **Planning** – considering concrete plans and figuring out different recovery strategies

4. **Action** – attempting to start recovery and implement the plan of action

5. **Maintenance** – Commitment to continue with the change program and monitor behaviors, thoughts and feelings. It's normal for a person to go through the process several times before achieving sobriety or stable change. Therefore, slips and relapses are considered a normal occurrence, from which the addict can gain more tools and understanding of his or her vulnerabilities. The model also differentiates between a slip (a temporary return to the previous behavior) and a relapse (a permanent return to the behavior being changed) (Prochaska and DiClemente, 1982).

Much of the evidence based for motivational interviewing comes from the addictions literature, but its usage has expanded to other fields of mental health such as eating disorders, relational problems, and phobias.

Drug treatment helps modify a client's attitude and behaviors related to drug use and abuse. A variety of scientifically based approaches to drug addiction treatment exist. Most of the programs involve individual or group drug counseling. It is important to note that there are several types of addiction treatment programs, and each addiction treatment program may vary in its treatment philosophy, services, and population it treats. The generalist social worker needs to be familiar with the different types of treatment in order to match the client with the resource that will be most helpful.

TYPES OF TREATMENT

DETOXIFICATION

Detoxification is a process whereby individuals are systematically withdrawn from drugs under the care of healthcare practitioners. Detoxification is sometimes seen as a distinct treatment modality or a precursor to treatment. Detoxification may involve gradually reducing the dose of the drug or temporarily substituting other substances, such as methadone, that have less severe side effects. For some people, it may be safe to detox on an outpatient basis; but for severe cases it is usually done in a hospital or a residential treatment center. Medications are available for detoxification from various different pharmaceutical drugs. When drug use is abruptly discontinued, the individual begins to experience the onset of withdrawal. Withdrawal symptoms may include sweats, cramping, constipation, and anxiety or can be as medically complex as seizures, convulsions, or delirium tremors. The risks associated with suddenly discontinuing use can be dangerous or even fatal without medical supervision. Detoxification is not designed to address the psychological, social, and the behavioral problems associated with addiction, but it does not typically produce lasting behavioral changes necessary for recovery. Detoxification is most useful when it incorporates formal processes of assessment and referral to subsequent drug addiction treatment.

Medications offer help in suppressing withdrawal symptoms during detoxification. However, medically assisted withdrawal is not in itself "treatment"—it is only the first step in the treatment process. Clients who go through medically assisted withdrawal but do not receive any further treatment show drug abuse patterns similar to those who were never treated (Langrod, 1977).

AGONIST MAINTENANCE TREATMENT

Agonist maintenance treatment for opiate addicts usually is conducted in out-client settings, frequently called methadone clinics. These clinics use a long-acting synthetic medication, usually methadone or LAAM, to prevent opiate withdrawal and decrease opiate craving. Clients on methadone or LAAM maintenance can function normally. Once stabilized on methadone, an individual can participate in counseling crucial to recovery. The best and most effective opiate agonist maintenance programs include individual and/or group counseling, as well as provision of, or referral to, other needed medical, psychological, and social services. Methadone mimics the action of the opiate on the central nervous system and is referred to as a full agonist medication. Other types of agonist medications are designed to give the opposite effect of the drug of choice; these are called inverse agonist medications. An example of an inverse agonist is Naltrexone, which is also used for opiate addicts. Naltrexone completely blocks all the effects of opiates, including the euphoria. Individuals must be medically detoxified and opiate-free for several days before Naltrexone can be taken. Clients can stabilize on Naltrexone and return to normal functioning. There are many other types of agonist medications that work in different ways for different drugs. Regardless of the agonist medication used, favorable treatment outcome requires effective counseling, a positive therapeutic relationship, and careful monitoring of medication compliance (Wechsberg, Kasten, Berkman, and Roussel, 2007).

COURT-MANDATED TREATMENT

The judicial system is often the first system with which the addict comes in contact. Courts can mandate drug addiction treatment programs to drug-involved offenders, actively monitor their progress in treatment, and arrange for other services. Treatment does not need to be voluntary to be effective. Research has shown that combining criminal justice sanctions with drug treatment can be effective in decreasing drug use and criminal behavior. Individuals under legal coercion tend to stay in treatment for a longer period of time and do as well as or better than others not under legal pressure (NIDA, 2008). Treatment may be delivered prior to, during, after, or in lieu of incarceration (i.e., pretrial release conditional on treatment).

RESIDENTIAL TREATMENT PROGRAMS

Residential programs can be short- or long-term depending on the client's individual circumstances. For their treatment, clients who live in the facility 24 hours a day, 7 days a week, are considered to be "residents" during their stay, thus the name, *residential treatment*. Even though other services such as detoxification, counseling, or partial hospitalization may be offered at these centers, their primary focus is to provide around-the-clock care for clients who need it. Most insurance companies provide coverage for such a service, but generally they do not exceed coverage beyond 3 weeks. On the other hand, if the facility is federally funded, the cost can be covered for up to 6 months.

The client's needs determine if the residential treatment is short-term or long-term. Short-term programs are brief but intensive treatment. They were originally designed for alcohol addiction and were based on a twelve-step approach. However, during the rise in illicit drug use of the mid 1980s, many facilities began tailoring their short-term treatment programs to treat clients with other drug addictions. Many individuals go to a residential program because they have failed at outpatient treatment. They need to be away from the environmental factors that maintain their addiction in order to improve. In the early days, prior to managed care, these programs consisted of 2–8 weeks of residency followed by regular participation in groups such as AA. Today the twelve steps are still encouraged, but the average length of stay is considerably shorter and could be as little as 1 week.

While short-term residential programs offer a solid foundation for drug addiction recovery, many clients can only succeed by participating in longer term programs. These programs have several distinguishing features. Clients typically have completed an initial course of treatment either through inpatient hospitalization or short-term care, but for many reasons must continue to receive ongoing services to get or stay sober. Client's who need long-term care are evaluated and often exhibit similar symptoms, which requires extended care. These symptoms include "drug-seeking" behavior or a repeated drug relapse after the completion of short-term care.

THERAPEUTIC COMMUNITIES

Therapeutic addiction treatment communities were popular in the early 60's. The therapeutic community is a drug-free residential setting that uses a hierarchical model with treatment stages that reflect increased levels of personal and social responsibility. It is a "community" because this approach views addiction in the full context of person's psychological, medical, socio-economical, spiritual and mental dimensions. Addiction treatment that negates one or more aspect of a person's makeup tends to be less effective. The program also incorporates its treatment with family members of the addicts. Peer influence, mediated through a variety of group processes, is used to help individuals learn and assimilate social norms and develop more effective social skills. Therapeutic communities differ from other treatment approaches principally in their use of the community, and comprise of treatment staff who has gone through the program.

In the past therapeutic communities shunned all twelve-step programs. Their approach was confrontational and highly structured. It intended for the client to examine old damaging self-concepts and develop a new sober identity. The individuals in therapeutic communities tended to have more violent and criminal elements in their history that is why structure was so critical in their approach. Today, most therapeutic communities have come to realize that recovery is more than a matter of willpower and embrace the teachings of the twelve-step programs.

The average length of stay in a therapeutic addiction treatment community is approximately 6 months to 2 years (De Leon, 1997).

OUTPATIENT TREATMENT

Most outpatient treatment involves individual, group, and/or family counseling. Outpatient treatment costs are less than the cost of residential or inpatient treatment. The ultimate goal of all addiction treatment programs is to provide the client the "tools" necessary to achieve long-term sobriety. In order for someone to achieve this goal, addiction treatment programs:

- Address medical and psychiatric needs
- Assist healing family dynamics
- Develop interpersonal skills
- Explore self-care
- Replace destructive addiction-related activities with more constructive activities
- Improve problem-solving abilities
- Improve daily living skills
- Incorporate twelve-step principles and attend meetings

Clients of outpatient addiction treatment programs generally reside at home and attend the program several evening or days during the week. While most people with substance abuse problems would rather attend outpatient addiction treatment, not everyone is appropriate for this level of care. Most clients in outpatients programs are productive, highly motivated, and most importantly, have a strong network of social support. It is this latter feature that makes a client suitable for an outpatient treatment. During the week, clients generally attend one or more support groups that are firmly established in the twelve-step model.

There are many different types of outpatient care. Some may be psychoeducational about the effects of drug use, while other outpatient programs offer what is known as "intensive-day" treatment services. Similar to residential programs, outpatient programs also encourage group counseling, family involvement and often help clients who may have co-occurring mental health issues.

COUNSELING

Behavioral therapies can help an addict develop ways to cope with drug cravings, suggest strategies to avoid drugs and prevent relapse, and offer suggestions on how to deal with a relapse if it occurs. Counseling also can involve talking about your job, legal problems and relationships with family and friends. Counseling with family members can help them to develop better communication skills and to be more supportive. Treatment usually includes educational and therapy sessions focused on establishing sobriety and preventing relapse. This may be accomplished in individual, group or family sessions. Family members, friends and coworkers can play critical roles in motivating individuals with drug problems to enter and stay in treatment. Family therapy is often important, especially for adolescents. Involvement of a family member in an individual's treatment program can strengthen and extend the benefits of the program.

SELF-HELP GROUPS

Twelve-step model of recovery is a free support program that was first developed by Alcoholics Anonymous. Hundreds of support groups are available for any kind of addiction, whether it is an addiction to drugs or to a certain behavior. The message is that addiction is a chronic disorder with a danger of relapse. Today, it is an ongoing maintenance program for relapse prevention that works in conjunction with other treatments. Participation in support groups will increase the chances of positive recovery outcomes when combined with other treatment options, including inpatient facilities, therapy or pharmaceutical treatment.

There are also twelve-step programs for family members. Al-Anon is for relatives and friends of alcoholics who have been impacted by common problems. They believe alcoholism is a family illness, and that changing family dynamics can promote recovery. Al-Anon members practice the twelve-steps and give comfort to families of alcoholics. Twelve-step programs can be an essential source of ongoing assistance for people working to maintain long-term recovery (Alcoholics Anonymous, 2008).

ONLINE SUPPORT

Historically, twelve-step meetings have always been conducted face to face in a group setting. With the phenomenal growth of the Internet in the past few years, millions of twelve-step members from various recovery groups began to find ways of gathering together for mutual online support. There are many different ways that members of support groups can gather together online from e-mail discussion groups, real-time chat rooms, blogs boards, and now voice chat.

E-mail Groups.   One of the most popular methods of holding topic discussion over the Internet is e-mail discussion groups. The main advantage to e-mail groups is that the meetings are conducted 24 hours a day, 7 days a week, but members can join in the meeting at any time that is convenient for them. Typically, members of the group send messages to a single e-mail address, which is then forwarded to all members on the list. Usually someone "leads" the meeting by introducing a topic, and then other members share their experience on that topic.

Live Chat Meetings.   These meetings take place in "real time." There is a lead or chairperson at chat meetings. Unlike e-mail meetings, however, participants do have to be at a certain website and a certain time to join the meeting, but those participants may be joining the meeting from locales across the globe.

Message Boards.   Message boards or bulletin boards are one of the oldest methods by which members of the recovery community first began to gather together on the Internet. Participants can join in any time, even weeks or months after the topic was first introduced. Anyone can begin a discussion by starting a "thread" on the board to which others can reply.

Voice Chat and Video Chat. New technology offers a "voice chat" in which participants can actually hear each other share on the meeting topics. These meetings may be the closest to the "real thing" that we have available thus far. Although "voice chat" meetings are a relatively new addition to online recovery, they have become very popular. Technology has also brought about the ability to hold video chat meetings, which allow participants to see others in the meeting via small video cameras, or web cams.

NONSTEP SUPPORT GROUPS

Although the twelve-step support groups have been around since the 1930s and are generally more widely available, the twelve-step approach does not work for everyone. The Twelve Steps that originated by Alcoholics Anonymous is based on a spiritual foundation for personal recovery. In recent years, other nonstep support groups and programs have developed for those who prefer a more secular approach to recovery. SMART Recovery, Rational Recovery, Life Ring Recovery, Women For Sobriety, Moderation Management, and SOS Recovery are a few of the non-twelve-step free support programs. These programs offer alternatives to the twelve-step principles for those people who do not believe in a higher power, want a feminist approach, or do not believe in total abstinence.

Groups. Whether it is a support group or a psychotherapy group, group treatment is the preferred treatment for addictions. Both inpatient and outpatient programs facilitate groups for many reasons. Groups are cost effective, provide a safe environment, and offer positive support. Because groups consist of peers in similar circumstances, they can break the aloneness and isolation felt by so many people who are trying to get sober. Often when a person is well defended they have difficulty looking at themselves, but in a group they are able to see themselves in others. Being among peers with similar circumstances, feedback is received more easily and with more credibility. Groups are also an opportunity to gain communication and new socialization skills.

Social workers need to assist clients to identify their special needs so that the proper referral can be made. Research shows that correctly matching a client with the right group will increase the likelihood of success. Some factors to consider are: culture, ethnicity, age, gender, sexual orientation, race, drug of choice, socioeconomic status, spirituality, and disabilities (NIAAA, 2006).

ADOLESCENT TREATMENT (TEEN PROGRAMS)

Adolescent substance abuse continues to be a major issue in our society as teen substance abuse remains at an alarmingly high rate. Adolescent drug users differ from adults in many ways. The physical differences between adolescents and adults are one reason why adolescents need treatment tailored to their age group. Teenagers' physical attributes, including their brains, have not finished developing. Their drug/alcohol use often has different causes, and they have even more trouble seeing the consequences of their drug use for the future. In treatment, adolescents must be approached differently from adults because of their unique developmental and psychiatric issues, differences in their values and belief systems, and environmental considerations (e.g., strong peer influences).

Adolescents generally are at greater risk for using drugs and at greater risk for physical and other consequences related to their use. The use of substances may also negatively affect their mental and emotional development because the use of drugs interferes with how people learn to handle situations and experiences. Adolescents are also always part of a larger family unit, so family involvement plays a critical role in an adolescent's treatment and recovery. Finally, most adolescents have entered drug or alcohol treatment involuntarily; however, treatment does not need to be voluntary to be effective, and special consideration needs to be given to these issues as part of the adolescent's treatment plan. Although relatively few treatment programs are designed specifically for adolescents, these important differences demonstrate that adolescent treatment needs to be specifically tailored to the unique needs of adolescents and not just based on adult models of treatment (Crowley and Whitmore, 2008).

Questions to Ask a Treatment Provider When Looking for Teen Programs:

1. What types of treatment do you have?
2. Have there been any research studies of this type of treatment?
3. What evidence do you have that your program is effective?
4. How do you specifically address the needs of adolescents?
5. Can you assess and treat my child's mental health problems at the same time as his/her substance problem?
6. How is the family involved in the treatment process?
7. How long will this treatment last?
8. What things do you do to help adolescents engage and stay in treatment?
9. Do you have aftercare or a continuing care program for when this treatment ends?
10. What happens if my child is not successful here?
11. What other options do we have?
12. How much does this cost and how much will I have to pay?
13. Are there any state, county, or grant funds to help pay for this treatment? (Crowley and Whitmore, 2008)

Researchers show that children who start drinking alcohol younger than 15 years old are four times more likely to have an alcohol addiction by the age of 21 years (NIDA, 2008). Talking with children early about the negative effects of alcohol and drugs may help guide them to healthier behaviors. There are also support groups specifically for teens and younger people.

SUMMARY

It is extremely likely that a generalist social worker will come into contact with clients who need assistance with drug problems. If one wishes to work specifically with individuals struggling with addictions, training beyond a generalist education is necessary. If the generalist social worker does not work specifically with addictions, he is responsible for understanding the difference between substance use and substance dependence and having a cursory knowledge of the classes of drugs and their possible effects on the human body and mind. Because the results of drug use or even stopping drug use can be so serious, relying on supervision is always wise.

A generalist social work practitioner should understand the process of assessment and diagnosis of addictions without overlooking that chemical changes produced by some behaviors can become an addiction, too. In order to make a comprehensive assessment, a level of trust and comfort must be developed with the client. Clients may not disclose any drug usage or underestimate how much it relates to other aspects of the problem they are presenting. How the worker asks the questions can determine the accuracy of the assessment.

Shame often prevents a client from giving up his or her denial. If the social worker has an understanding of the causes and consequences of addictions, it is easier to empathize with the client's experience. The number of emotional, relational, physical, financial, and spiritual consequences that the addicted individual must face can be devastating. Yet, the addiction can help someone to cope by escaping problems and medicating emotional pain. The motivation to obtain sobriety may be obstructed by the client's ambivalence.

Understanding motivational interviewing will help "to be where the client is" and to be able to meet that client at the appropriate stage of motivation. If the social worker experiences resistance, he or she should consider the possibility that they may be pushing beyond the client's readiness.

Social workers are central to helping clients negotiate their way through service systems. There are so many choices of treatment modalities that can help a client. Matching the client with an effective modality is crucial to the client's recovery. Teenagers are a population at risk who require special attention. Programs designed for adolescents understand the different developmental needs of teenagers. Advocating for the client to receive the resources in a timely manner can avoid missed opportunities. Beyond the initial referral, ensuring follow up support will increase a client's likelihood for success.

With today's technologies we understand so much more about how the brain functions. Understanding what happens to the reward circuit system helps us understand what is necessary for an addict to finally have the ability to rewire his or her brain. Future treatments may simply require a single pill. If and when that time comes, it will not eliminate the generalist social worker's role—just makes it easier. We still treat people, not disorders.

| CASE 12.1 | SOCIAL WORKER ASSESSMENT OF A CLIENT WHO MAY HAVE ONE OR MORE ADDICTION |

Philadelphia Health Center provides primary health care to the uninsured and underinsured members of the community in the Philadelphia area. The Center has a small mental heath department that provides crisis intervention and short-term (8–10 sessions) treatment. Clients who need higher level care or more extensive treatment are referred to other agencies and programs. Bill came to the health center for problems with anxiety. The nurse practitioner referred Bill for an intake evaluation.

Melissa is a first-year MSW student interning at the Philadelphia Health Center. She has been assigned

to conduct the intake with Bill to assess if he is an appropriate candidate for their agency or refer him to a suitable program that will match his or her needs.

Bill is a 28-year-old single heterosexual Latin male who is 5'11", weighing 165 pounds, and casually dressed in jeans and shirt. Bill has completed 1 year of college studies. He worked as a customer service representative for a cell phone company until 7 months ago when he was fired for inappropriate e-mails to a female coworker and for having accessed porn sites on his work computer. Bill lives in an

(Continued)

CASE 12.1 | *Continued*

apartment alone. Bill is friendly, has a pleasant smile, and appears to be of average intelligence. He is oriented times 3.

Bill reports that in the past 6 months he has been experiencing "panic attacks" during which times he feels as though he is going to die. "I become scared, feverish, light-headed, I can't catch my breath, and my heart races." He describes symptoms consistent with DSM-IV diagnosis of panic disorder, e.g., hot flashes, faintness, sweating not due to heat. Bill admits having occasional suicidal ideation but denies intent. He denies any current alcohol use and only uses "Crystal Meth" when he parties, which Bill claims, is rare.

When asked about treatment goals, Bill expressed concern for his health because of the anxiety symptoms. He also complained about his inability to sustain a relationship, although he maintains an abundance of casual sexual partners. He complains about constantly experiencing feelings of emptiness and insecurity. He is functioning with poor impulse control and a lack of anxiety tolerance. Bill seems to have low self-esteem and bases his self-worth on his appearance and sexuality.

Bill has been in therapy with three different social workers in the last 2 years for which he presented with depressive symptoms. His longest therapeutic relationship was 2 months. He reports negative experiences with all his previous social workers. Bill is being treated by his primary care practitioner with Prozac but is dissatisfied because it causes delayed ejaculation.

Bill grew up as the youngest of three children in a middle-class family. He was raised Catholic but no longer practices Catholicism and does not believe in God. He was born in Seattle, Washington, and lived there until he was 22 years old, when he moved to Philadelphia to attend college.

Bill's mother was born in Guatemala but grew up in San Francisco. Bill disdainfully depicts his mother as "a self-centered, depressed woman who is always the victim." Bill's father, also of Latin decent, was born and raised in California. About his father, a supervisor in a paper mill, Bill states, "He is a spineless jellyfish, a functional alcoholic…an impotent castrated man." Bill reports a distant relationship with his sister of whom he speaks very little. She is 6 years his senior, married without children, and lives near their parents in Seattle. Bill's brother is 5 years his senior, single, gay, and living in Manhattan. While growing up Bill reports that he and his brother didn't get along, however they have become closer in recent years. Bill has one close male friend, who lives in Seattle. He has maintained contact with his friend through weekly telephone calls.

Although a nice looking and fit man today, Bill reports adolescence was a painful and shameful time. During his teens, Bill developed acne, had glasses, and was overweight. He was harassed, humiliated, and heckled by his peers.

Bill has never sustained a romantic relationship longer than 2 or 3 months. He meets women through computer chat rooms and usually sleeps with 10–15 different women in the span of a month. Bill reports he uses sex to feel better about himself and relax. His indulgences into sexual stimulation are abounding, including his fascination with sex toys, pornographic videos, masturbation, and Internet hook-ups.

Bill disclosed all the above information during the initial intake. Bill has a charming, outgoing, and at times subtly flirtatious demeanor with the female social work intern. He appeared open and comfortable answering questions and even volunteered personal information without being asked. The intern wanted to explore some gaps in information, but Bill's lack of boundaries made her uncomfortable to probe further. After consulting with her supervisor, Melissa was granted two more sessions to complete her assessment with Bill.

Discussion Questions

1. Identify Bill's strengths and coping strategies based on the information given.
2. Bill's panic attacks started not long after he lost his job; how can Melissa discern if there is any connection between the two? Bill also reports using Crystal Meth occasionally. What kinds of questions could Melissa ask to determine if Bill is denying or minimizing the amount of Meth usage? Knowing that Crystal Meth is a stimulant, what connection may that have with Bill's reported symptoms of anxiety? What kind of questions could Melissa ask that will help her tease out if the "panic attacks" have any connection to Bill's Meth usage?
3. Bill seems to use his sexuality as a means to medicate his anxiety and cope with emptiness and possible loneliness. What are the chances that Bill is a sex addict? What kind of information would Melissa need to obtain to get more clarity of the effects of Bill's sexual behavior?
4. Bill is a Latin man born in the United States. Are there any cultural issues that may need to be taken into consideration? What other family-of-origin issues should be considered?
5. Bill seeks help for problems with anxiety, not sex or drug use. If it appears that there is a problem with drugs or sex, how does Melissa deal with referral recommendations?
6. If drug and sex are issues, how might Melissa assess for readiness to address these concerns? What might Melissa do if Bill demonstrates resistance or hostility at the suggestion that there may be a drug and/or sex issue?
7. Is it appropriate for Melissa to deal with Bill's lack of boundaries and flirtations? If so what might she say or do? Is Melissa's discomfort with the sexual content of the session countertransference? If so, how might she use that to better serve her client?
8. Have there been consequences for Bill's sexual behavior? If so what are they?
9. How is Bill's support system? What might be helpful to bolster support for Bill?
10. If Bill were a teenager, what other considerations would you address?
11. Are there physical health and/or safety concerns regarding Bill's Crystal Meth use or sexual behavior that need to be addressed?
12. If determined that Bill is a sex addict, what type of programs can Melissa recommend considering that Bill is an atheist and does not believe in a higher power?

References

Alcoholics Anonymous (Assessed August, 2008). Available online at: www.aa.org

American Bar Association (1961). *Drug addiction, crime or disease?* Interim and Final Reports of the Joint Committee of the American Bar Association and the American Medical Association on Narcotic Drugs. Indiana University Press, 1961 Library of Congress catalog card number: 61-9838.

American Psychiatric Association (2000). *Diagnostic and Statistical Manual* (4th ed.). Text Version.

Carnes, P. (1991). *Don't call it love: Recovery from sexual addiction.* New York: Bantam Books.

Childress, A. R. (2007). Imaging the brain vulnerability to disorders of desire: Opiates, brownies, sex and cocaine. *Addiction and Psychiatry*, Gainesville, FL: University of Florida.

Crowley, T., and Whitmore, E. (Accessed August, 2008). Why Adolescent Treatment is Different from Adult Treatment. Available online at www.hbo.com/addiction/treatment.html

De Leon, G., (1997). *Community as Method: Therapeutic Communities for Special Populations and Special Settings.* Westport, CT: Greenwood Publishing Group.

Duncan, J. (1988). Neuropsychiatric aspects of sedative drug withdrawal, *Human Psychopharmacology: Clinical and Experimental, 3*(3), 171–180.

Dyck, E. (2005). Flashback: Psychiatric experimentation with LSD in historical perspective. *Canadian Journal of Psychiatry, 50*, 381–387.

Fisher, G. L., and Harrison T. C. (2000). *Substance abuse: Information for school counselors, social workers, therapists, and counselors* (2nd ed.) Boston: Allyn and Bacon.

Galanter, M., and Kleber, H. D. (2004). *Textbook of substance abuse treatment* (3rd Ed.). Arlington, VA: American Psychiatric Publishing.

Glasper, A., Gossop, M., de Wet, C., Reed, L., and Bearn, J. (2008). Influence of the dose on the severity of opiate withdrawal symptoms during methadone detoxification. *International Journal of Experimental and Clinical Pharmacology, 81,* 92–96.

Goodman, A. (1990). Addiction: definition and implications. *Addiction, 85*(11), 1403–1408.

Hoffman, J., and Froemke, S. (2007). *Addiction: Why can't I just stop?* Emmaus, PA: Rodale Books.

Ketcham, K., and Ashbey, W. F., (2000). *Beyond the influence: Understanding and defeating alcoholism.* New York: Bantam Books.

Langrod, J. (1977). *Drug detoxification: A comprehensive examination.* New York: Dabor Science Publications.

McNeece, C. A., and DiNitto, D. M. (1998). *Chemical dependency: A systems approach* (2nd Ed.) Needham Heights, MA: Allyn and Bacon.

Miller W. R., and Hester R. K. (1995). Treatment for alcohol problems: Towards an informed eclecticism. In R. K. Hester and W. R. Miller (Eds.), *Handbook of alcoholism treatment approaches: Effective alternatives.* (2nd Ed.), pp. 1–11. Boston: Allyn and Bacon.

Miller, W. R., and Rollnick, S. (1991). *Motivational Interviewing.* London: Guilford Press.

National Institute on Drug Abuse (NIDA). (Accessed August, 2008). NIDA Infofax. Available online at www.nida.nih.gov/Infofax/Infofaxindex.html

Oscar-Berman, M., and Marinkovic, K. (2003). Alcoholism and the brain: An overview. Alcohol Research and Health, 27(2), 125–133.

Prochaska, J. O., and DiClemente, C. C. (1982). Transtheoretical therapy: towards a more integrative model of change. *Psychotherapy Theory, Research, Practice Journal, 19,* 276–88.

Resnicow, K., DiIorio, C., Soet, J. E., Borrelli, B., Hecht, J., and Ernst, D. (2002). Motivational interviewing in health promotion: It sounds like something is changing. *Health Psychology, 21*(5), 444–451.

Rose, S. D., and LeCroy, C. W. (1991). Group methods. In F. H. Kanfer and A. P. Goldstein (Eds.), *Helping people change* (pp. 422–453). New York: Pergamon.

Sadock, B. J., Kaplan, H. I., and Sadock, V. A. (2007). *Kaplan and Sadock's Synopsis of psychiatry: Behavioral sciences/clinical psychiatry* (10th Ed.). Philadelphia: Lippincott Williams and Wilkins.

Shaffer, H. J. (1987). The assessment and diagnosis of addictive disorders: The use of clinical reflection and hypotheses testing. *Psychiatric Clinics of North America, 4,* 103–113.

Shaffer, H. J. (1992). The psychology of stage change: the transition from addiction to recovery. In J. H. Lowinson, P. Ruiz, R. B. Millman (2nd ed.). *Comprehensive Textbook of Substance Abuse,* (pp. 100–105). Baltimore, MD: Williams and Wilkins.

Sobell, L. C., and Sobell, M. B. (2003). Using motivational interviewing techniques to talk with clients about their alcohol use. *Cognitive and Behavioral Practice, 10,* 214–221.

Turner, J., Perkins, H. W., and Bauerle, J. (2008). Declining negative consequences related to alcohol misuse among students exposed to a social norms marketing intervention on a college campus. *Journal of American College Health, 57*(1), 85–94.

Van Wormer, K., and Davis, D. R. (2003). *Addictions treatment: A strengths perspective.* Pacific Groves, CA: Brooks/Cole.

Vega, W. A., and Gill, A. G. (1998). *Drug use and ethnicity in early adolescence (Longitudinal research in the social and behavioral sciences: An interdisciplinary series).* New York, NY: Springer.

Wechsberg, W. M., Kasten, J. J., Berkman, N. D., and Roussel, A. E. (2007). *Methadone maintenance treatment in the U.S.: A practical question and answer guide.* New York: Springer Publishing Company LLC.

White, A. M. (2003). What happened? Alcohol, memory blackouts, and the brain. Alcohol Research and Health, 27(2), 186–196.

Yamamoto, H., Kamegaya, E., Hagino, Y., Imai, K., Fujikawa, A., Tamura, K., Enokiya, T., Yamamoto, T., Takeshima, T., Koga, H., Uhl, G. R., Ikeda, K., and Sora, I., (2007). Genetic deletion of vesicular monoamine transporter-2 (VMAT2) reduces dopamine transporter activity in mesencephalic neurons in primary culture. *Neurochemistry International, 51*(2-4), 237–244.

Zinberg, N. E. (1984). *Drug, set, and setting: the basis for controlled intoxicant use.* New Haven: Yale University Press.

Generalist Social Work Practice with the Elderly

Cheryl Seaman Sadeghee

Danielle, a first-year MSW student, and Ashley, a senior BSW student, were assigned to a community social work agency for their field placement. The community in which they are located is identified as oppressed and poverty stricken with many residents struggling to get by. The agency supervisor has given Danielle and Ashley the task of providing social work services to the older population who attend the local senior center. An arrangement has been made with the center to have the students provide 4 hours of social work service each week. On their first day at the center, the director, Ms. N., introduced them to the group of seniors. She told the group that they were social work students who were coming weekly to "help you." She then provided Danielle and Ashley with a table at which to work. The students dutifully sat at the table and awaited clients. After an hour with no one approaching for assistance, they decided to walk around the center and talk to individual participants. As they came to each table of seniors, they asked if anyone had any problems with which they needed help. They either received a shake of the head or were told, "No, dear, I'm just fine, thank you." After 4 hours with no requests for help, they returned to their supervisor and reported that the members of the senior center had no need for social work services and asked to be given another assignment.

This chapter will present information about generalist social work practice with elderly clients. It opens with an overview of the demographic changes and challenges occurring in our country with the population of adults over the age of 65. It continues with a discussion of policy issues related to the provision and availability of services for our aging adults. This lays the foundation for exploring the skills and knowledge required to provide effective generalist social work practice to this age group with a thorough discussion of assessment and models of intervention. At the completion of this chapter, you will be able to help Danielle and Ashley:

- Understand the changing demographics of the population over the age of 65
- Understand the history of social policies in the United States and how they continue to affect the provision of services to the elderly
- Strengthen their observation and assessment skills
- Build successful, professional relationships with older clients
- Implement interventions with their older clients

DEMOGRAPHICS IN AGING

The United States, indeed the world, is experiencing a dramatic transformation in the demographics of the population. The World Health Organization states, "Population ageing is one of humanity's greatest triumphs. It is also one of our greatest challenges. As we enter the 21st century, global aging will put increased economic and social demands on all countries. At the same time, older people are a precious, often-ignored resource that makes an important contribution to the fabric of our societies" (World Health Organization, 2002, p. 6). This transformation represents an explosion in terms of numbers of individuals over the age of 60 worldwide. In the United States, estimates foretell of doubling population numbers as we approach the second and third decade of the 21st century. In many ways, the future of social work will be defined by this tremendous increase in the geriatric population and their need for services and supports. The National Association of Social Workers recognizes this impending challenge, issuing the following statement:

> The United States is undergoing a demographic transformation. By 2030, the number of people aged 65 and older is expected to double, rising to 70 million. This growing population of older adults will create an unprecedented demand for aging related programs, policies and services. NASW has established an *Aging Initiative* to raise awareness about the breadth of geriatric social work practice, and increase the numbers of professionally trained and credentialed social workers who serve older adults and their families. (NASW, n.d.)

To adequately plan for this changing demographic, it is necessary to take a closer look at the future image of the elder population in the United States. The United States Census projected that the number of people aged 65 and over in 2007 would be approximately 37,191,004, up from 34,991,753 as determined by the 2000 census (United States Census Bureau, 2006). It is now projected that this number will increase to 40,229,000 by 2010 and to 72,092,000 by 2030 (United States Census Bureau, 2008). This means that a full 20%, or one in five citizens, of the U.S., will be over the age of 65 by 2030.

What are the factors that contribute to this massive increase in seniors? One factor is the decrease in the overall death rate in those over age 60. The medical community has done an admirable job of educating the population and, thus, decreasing mortality and morbidity due to risk factors such as smoking, high blood pressure, and high cholesterol. Another factor is the greater access to improved and more sophisticated healthcare services, thus reducing early deaths from heart disease and stroke (Butler, Lewis, and Sunderland, 1991). The overall life expectancy has increased. In 1900, the average citizen of the United States was expected to survive until the age of 47. Those born at the turn of the 21st century are given a life expectancy of 77.4, an increase of 30 years.

The age group with the highest projected growth in numbers is people over the age of 80. This elder expansion is spurred by the spike in the birth rate after World War II, which continued into the early 1960s. These babies born between the years of 1946 and 1964 are commonly referred to as "baby boomers." The first of the baby boomers are currently in their early 60s and by 2025 will be approaching their 80s. There are identifiable trends associated with the aging of the baby boom generation. It is expected that many in this group will be more active politically, be more economically capable, more independent, and more mobile than previous cohorts. By the same token, as they survive to the oldest ages, they will present increased needs and require more years of care, thus placing a strain on the medical and social service industry (Holosko and Feit, 2004). It is obvious that the sheer number of these seniors will assure that they will consume a greater share of the resources to address their declining health and increasing disability and their social service needs. We will see a predominance of women as they continue to outlive men and these women will be frailer, poorer, and sicker and many will live alone (Hooyman, 2002). A new challenge is being offered to social workers and social work educators. As this generation enters old age, they will need and use an inordinate amount of services, and their families, friends, and communities will be in need of support and guidance to navigate the service systems in order to meet these needs (Gellis, Sherman, and Lawrence as cited in Bergel, 2006).

Particular attention will need to be focused not only on gerontological competence but also cultural competence as the elderly population will be an increasingly diverse group. While Whites will double in numbers, the elderly population of African-Americans is expected to triple, and there will be a fivefold increase in Hispanic and Asian older adults (McInnis-Dittrich, 2002; Holosko and Feit, 2004). This group will also reflect diversity in areas of sexual orientation, ethnicity, mental disabilities and illnesses, single households, prison inmates, immigrants, and refugees. Overall, the picture that emerges for us is one of increasing numbers of U.S. citizens over the age of 65 who represent a wide spectrum of diversity.

How is older adulthood defined? In 1973, the U.S. government set the minimum age for accessing services under the Older American's Act at age 60. The standard retirement age for receiving social security benefits has been 62–65 years of age. In 1983, the Social Security Act was amended to adjust for the improving condition of aging adults and has expanded the age criteria for receiving social security retirement benefits to age 67. As members of the "baby boomer" or post-WWII generation arrive at this momentous point in their lives, the definition of old age requires further description. Social scientists have found it more descriptive to identify the ages of 65–74 as young old age and the ages of 75 and above as old or advanced old age. It is important to realize that these determinations are at best arbitrary and not an accurate indication of an individual's status, physically or mentally (Butler, Lewis, and Sunderland, 1991). A more decisive description of the functionality and physical changes observed is a more accurate indicator of aging than chronological age. While there are some standards of physical change expected in the aging process, many other factors affect each person. These factors include genetic makeup, lifestyle choices, education, and even personal attitudes toward aging (McInnis-Dittrich, 2002). However, for the purpose of this discussion, the terms "elderly" and "senior" will refer broadly to adults of age 65 and above. This designation of 65 and older is the most widely used definition associated with development and implementation of age-specific programs. In the original legislation establishing the Social Security program, the age 65 was used as the standard age of retirement (Holosko and Feit, 2004).

Another designation of age that helps to define the group is their unique birth cohort. An example of this is the baby boomer generation. Those born between 1946 and 1964 have a unique set of shared experiences that inform the projected needs as they enter into old age. This group has had higher divorce rates than ever before with smaller family size. This may result in their having smaller family support systems in their elder years. They, in general, have enjoyed a higher standard of living than their predecessors, but in their old age face economic uncertainty with the strains placed on social security and other pension plans and the volatility of the stock market. Boomers of color were brought up prior to the civil rights movement of the 60s and 70s and experienced legally segregated schools, as well as discrimination in the workplace, thus severely limiting their opportunity for quality job placement and social class upward mobility (Stoller and Gibson, as cited in Cummings and Galambos, 2004). Some experienced chronic poverty in substandard housing, a condition that will most likely continue in their old age.

Gay and lesbian boomers also came up through a time when being gay was considered a "pathology," an illness to be treated and cured. In truth, there is still limited recognition of the social and legal rights of lesbians and gays even now, in the 21st century. As those who "came out" in the late sixties and early seventies enter their old age, social workers will need to be sensitive to the unique experiences and circumstances that inform the needs of this population.

POLICY ISSUES

By the late 1950s, Americans were living longer, and families were struggling to address the needs of the older population. In 1961 the first Conference on Aging was held, resulting in the establishment of the Older American's Act of 1965 (OAA). The OAA directed funding to provide services for those reaching old age. The OAA's mission is broad: to help older people maintain maximum independence in their homes and communities and to promote a continuum of care for the vulnerable elderly (O'Shaughnessy, 2008). Beginning in the mid-sixties, Area Agencies on Aging (AAA) were developed in each state to coordinate the provision of services. From the time of its conception, the OAA has directed federal funding to see that older Americans are provided with suitable housing, the ability to access transportation, access to the best possible healthcare, access to efficient and affordable community services, adequate income to meet their living requirements, and freedom from discrimination due to age (Gelfand, 1993). This law has been reauthorized and expanded at various time over the years. The most recent reauthorization was in 2006. At that time, congress expanded the role of the Administration on Aging (AoA) and the states' Area Agencies on Aging (AAA) to "promote home and community-based long-term care services, authorize funds for competitive grants to states to promote comprehensive elder justice systems, and required AoA to develop demonstration programs to help older people 'age in place' (including in naturally occurring retirement communities) and systems for mental health screening and treatment services" (O'Shaughnessy, 2008). Figure 13.1 shows the aging services network in the United States.

> Our mission is to develop a comprehensive, coordinated and cost-effective system of long-term care that helps elderly individuals to maintain their dignity in their homes and communities. Our mission statement also is to help society prepare for an aging population. (Dept. of Health and Human Services Administration on Aging, n.d.)

While the intent is positive and progressive, the reality is that funding is limited, and as with so many social initiatives, these agencies are being asked to respond to demands that far outstretch their abilities to respond effectively. Historically, social policy initiatives and social service agencies are vulnerable to loss of federal funding. Given its size the older adult population wields power as a voting group, and we can expect to see this cohort responding to policy changes and service needs through the voting process. Despite this, however, policies protecting the older adults are lagging behind those protecting children and families. There are pending threats to the financial viability of Medicare and Social Security as more and more people reach the age to apply for benefits. As the numbers of older Americans grow, the needs of seniors and our ability to service those needs

Aging services network

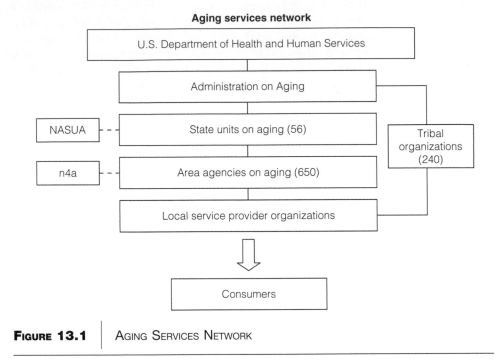

FIGURE 13.1 | AGING SERVICES NETWORK

will increase. Traditionally, it is the most vulnerable who are hit the hardest. Those who rely on public services, being unable to afford private care, are least likely to get the services they need.

What is the overall economic reality for this growing segment of the population? There is some discrepancy regarding poverty rates for people over the age of 65 in the current literature. While U.S. Census Bureau (2006) indicates that the percentage of individuals over the age of 65 who fall at or below the poverty level has declined from 10.2% in 2003 to 9.8% in 2004, other estimates reflect an increase in numbers of poor elderly (Hooyman and Kiyak, 2002). The fact is there are many older adults in the United States who experience incomes near or below the poverty level. Widowed elderly women, older adults living alone, elders in rural areas, and the oldest old are likely to have marginal incomes, leaving them at risk of poverty. There are a greater number of African-American seniors who fall into this category due to historical social challenges such as poor education and sporadic work history (Hooyman and Kiyak, 2002). The total numbers of people over 65 in poverty can be deceiving. There is also a segment of the population that is termed the "near poor": those who fall between the poverty line and 12.5% above it. In many ways, this group is actually more vulnerable than those in poverty. While they do not have enough income to meet their basic needs, their earnings place them slightly over required guidelines so that they cannot access public support programs (Holosko and Feit, 2004). This can lead to elders having to make difficult decisions, such as whether to put food on their tables or heat their homes.

While improved healthcare has contributed to the increase in the number of people living to old age, the struggle to access adequate healthcare is still an issue. Predictions for the future of this growing population include improved health for a longer period of time given access to adequate healthcare. However, with advanced aging one can expect decline in health and in function. For those who are unable to access adequate healthcare, they will experience a long and slow decline in their physical abilities as they age with chronic illnesses. What does this mean for the aging services industry? There will likely be twice the number of seniors requiring assistance with activities of daily living by 2030 and triple the number needing nursing home care (Hooyman, 2002). As healthcare costs climb, we are already seeing a shift in healthcare systems retooling to provide affordable in-home care for nursing-home-eligible clients, as well as increased supports for family caregivers. Also, more seniors are predicted to choose to age in place, eschewing institutional care (Hooyman, 2002). The American Association of Retired Persons (AARP) reported in 2005 that 31% of total Medicaid expenditures went toward long-term care. This represents an increase of 38% from 2000 to 2005 (AARP, 2006).

As people grow older and the numbers of elderly increase, we will also see an increase in the number of living generations in families. People providing care for their older relatives will be older themselves and present challenges to the social service network providing support to them. There are indications that this influx of baby boomers will likely be more open to complimentary resources in healthcare and personal growth (Hooyman, 2002). This will also have implications for the service providers over the next 20 years. The growth of alternative medical providers and the popularity in the media of personal consultants indicate a willingness to explore new avenues of wellness, both physical and emotional. Social service agencies, including social workers in the field, will need to prepare themselves by being knowledgeable about alternative approaches to health, wellness, and well-being as this cohort enters their sixties and beyond.

GENERALIST SOCIAL WORK PRACTICE WITH ELDERLY CLIENTS

Ageism, defined as stereotyping, prejudice, and discrimination based on age, has prevented a more aggressive movement toward preparing for the needs of this growing population (Bergel, 2006). There are persistent myths regarding older adults that hinder their access to appropriate resources and negatively impact their ability to fully engage in life in their older years. Some oft-heard myths about the elderly suppose that they are set in their ways, unable to learn new things, and, generally, have negative attitudes (Thomas, 2005). The elder population has actually demonstrated remarkable flexibility. Our world has changed dramatically over the past few decades, and yet older adults have managed to keep up with these changes. They have learned new technologies and incorporated their use in their daily lives. Many older adults maintain contact with distant family members through connection to the Internet and are able to manage their affairs with the use of computers and other advanced technologies. They have been adapting and adjusting to change throughout their lives. Other than as a result of a physical or psychological disorder, one's personality remains relatively stable throughout the life span.

There is still a heavy emphasis on child welfare and clinical interventions with families and younger adults in statewide social service departments, while the elderly receive basic case management services. Interventions tend to be focused on crisis management rather than prevention. Often the elderly are seen as a low-priority population. In 2004, Kane (as cited in Bergel, 2006) wrote of "therapeutic nihilism," a form of ageism in the professional community that holds that older adults will not improve, even with intervention, so providing focused resources to them is useless. This attitude has been observed in medical, as well as social service, arenas, where older adults may face challenges to their access to advanced treatments due to their age. The National Association of Social Workers (NASW) and Council for Social Work (CSWE) have emphasized the need to train competent gerontological social workers to meet the demands of this ever increasing population (see Figure 13.2). The social worker needs always to remember when working with the elderly that dignity, self-determination, and the ability to be involved in decision making are central (Holosko and Feit, 2004). Areas in which a social worker will need some knowledge and expertise are multiple and varied. They include law, economics, family dynamics, stress in family caregiving, alcoholism and addictions in the elderly, sexuality and safe sexual practices in the elderly, elder abuse and neglect, end-of-life planning and advanced directives, medical interventions and medications, spirituality and religions, and more.

Cultural competence is another arena in social work that requires increased emphasis and sensitivity in gerontological social work. In 1980, American Hispanics represented 5% of the elderly poor and American Blacks represented 20%. In comparison, they represented only 3% and 5% of the total elderly population respectively (Holosko and Feit, 2004). It is predicted that 25% of the elderly population in the United States in 2030 will fall under the description of minority populations. Currently there are a large number of immigrants who came to this country during the first half of the 20th century who are reaching older adulthood now and coming to the attention of service providers (Bonder, Martin, and Miracle, 2001). Specifically, there is an increase in the numbers of elderly immigrants from Indochina, Asia, and Latin America (Holosko and Feit, 2004). Current service providers, as well as those in the future, must educate themselves in the "ways" of these varied cultures so as to meet their needs adequately and respectfully. Being a culturally competent service provider means having "the skills to gather culturally influenced information, interpret it within the context of the individual's situation, and incorporate it into intervention planning and implementation" (Bonder, Martin, and Miracle, 2001, p. 36). This also requires the service provider to examine his own cultural values and beliefs and evaluate the impact on his work with the client. Caution against stereotyping is of high value. A modicum of cultural knowledge can be indiscriminately applied, discounting the uniqueness of the individual, family, and community. An example would be to assume that all Hispanic immigrants have the same cultural values and beliefs. In reality, Puerto Ricans differ from Mexicans who differ from Ecuadorians, and so on. Each group is unique and each individual within that group is unique. "A person is not a bundle of cultural 'facts' but rather a complex bundle of cultural influences and other factors" (Bonder, Martin, and Miracle, 2001, p. 37). Cultural information is to be sought when working with these clients, respecting their expertise in their

CSWE SAGE-SW National Competencies Study Knowledge:

- Normal physical, psychological, and social changes in later life
- The diversity of attitudes toward aging, mental illness, and family roles
- The influences of aging on family dynamics
- The diversity of elders' attitudes toward acceptance of help
- The diversity of successful adaptations to life transitions of aging
- The availability of resources and resource systems for the elderly and their families
- Theoretical models of biological and social aging
- The relation of diversity to variations in the aging process (e.g., gender, race, culture, economic status, ethnicity, and sexual orientation)

Skill:

- Use social work case management skills (such as brokering, advocacy, monitoring, and discharge planning) to link elders and their families to resources and services
- Gather information regarding social history such as: social functioning, primary and secondary social supports, social activity level, social skills, financial status, cultural background, and social involvement.
- Collaborate with other health, mental health, and allied health professionals in delivering services to older adults.
- Engage family caregivers in maintaining their own mental and physical health.
- Assist individuals and families in recognizing and dealing with issues of grief, loss and mourning.
- Assist families that are in crisis situations regarding older adult family members.
- Recognize and identify family, agency, community, and societal factors that contribute to and support the greatest possible independence of the older client.
- Enhance the coping capacities of older persons.
- Incorporate knowledge of elder abuse (physical, sexual, emotional and financial) in conducting assessments and intervention with clients and their families.

Professional Practice:

- Assess one's own values and biases regarding aging, death, and dying.
- Educate self to dispel the major myths about aging.
- Accept, respect, and recognize the right and need of older adults to make their own choices and decisions about their lives within the context of the law and safety concerns.
- Respect and address cultural, spiritual, and ethnic needs and beliefs of older adults and family members.
- Identify ethical and professional boundary issues that commonly arise in work with older adults and their caregivers, such as client self-determination, end-of-life decisions, family conflicts, and guardianship.
- Evaluate safety issues and degree of risk for self and older clients.
- Apply knowledge of outreach techniques with older adults and their families.

FIGURE 13.2 | GERONTOLOGICAL COMPETENCIES FOR ALL SOCIAL WORKERS

Source: (Tompkins and Rosen, 2006)

own cultural emersion. While the worker can seek information about a particular cultural tradition to inform their work with clients, it is the wise worker who empowers the client to teach them what their particular cultural experience is and how it impacts their particular situation. Emphasis here is on respect and validation of one's experience, beliefs and values, spiritual practices, and environment. The bottom line is that service providers who ignore or indelicately handle the cultural dimension when providing aging services to the community are inadequately prepared at best and, at worst, violating the civil rights of their multicultural clients (Geron, 2002). Needless to say, for minority groups in this birth cohort, the psychological scars of being treated as second-class citizens remain (McInnis-Dittrich, 2002). Stoller and Gibson (as cited in Cummings and Galambos, 2004, p. 13) write that "focusing upon hierarchy based on gender, race or ethnicity, and social class enables us to recognize elements of discrimination that have influenced the lives of older adults." They indicate that some in this group are facing "multiple jeopardy," meaning that they find themselves in several disadvantaged positions simultaneously. This leads to an even increased risk that they will suffer with negative outcomes in their aging process. These are all areas in which the gerontological social worker must be attuned and knowledgeable in order to provide effective and equitable service provision. Figure 13.2 list competencies for gerontological social workers.

It is often the case that elders and their families are coming into the social, medical, and health service arena for the first time when a crisis strikes. They are unaware of available services, uncertain how to access those services, and often find themselves confused, frustrated, and discouraged by the effort required to navigate the systems. They may even find that the services they seek are not available due to budgetary constraints and/or lack of appropriately trained service providers and that their expectations of services being covered by insurance do not meet their needs. Initially, the family may encounter a social worker due to the hospitalization of their family member. Medical social workers are well informed of the various available services throughout a community. These practitioners assess the estimated needs of the client and can provide vital information regarding Medicare and other insurance coverage to meet such needs. Most elder Americans have health insurance coverage via Medicare, but there are limitations in the extent of coverage. It is important for the client and the family to understand what will be covered under their insurance plan and what they can expect to pay before engaging in the search for services. A reliable resource for information regarding Medicare is the pamphlet, *Medicare and You*, published by the U.S. government. Pamphlets are available through the Department of Health and Human Services or accessible via www.medicare.gov

When looking for help in caring for an older adult, the family may well be referred to the Area Agency on Aging. AAA case workers provide a detailed assessment, determine the needs of the consumer, and begin to research, identify, and contract various local service providers to meet those needs. Well-trained generalist social workers are perfectly suited for these positions. Their training in utilizing a strengths perspective to recognize and validate the abilities and coping skills of the client and their families and their practice of engagement and collaboration with the client to synthesize personalized treatment plans render them ready to cope with the diversity of situations that arise.

Unfortunately, AAA case workers are often burdened with high caseloads and decreased options for referral as budget cuts frequently reduce services. The generalist social worker can exercise their advocacy in addressing these issues. Definitely, the presence and involvement of a skilled social worker will aid the family in getting those services that are currently available, and they will be able to advocate for these families to receive a greater level of assistance by identifying the gaps in services and seeking resources to fill those gaps.

Another focus of concern for the gerontological social worker is family caregiving. Community services are usually complementary, not exclusive, in helping the elder to continue to live independently. This means that services are not around the clock. The cost 24-hour care is prohibitive, seldom covered by insurance plans, and unattainable to the average consumer. Elders must depend on having their daily needs of personal care provided by a family member or friend. In the United States, this care falls overwhelmingly to the wives, daughters or daughters-in-law (McInnis-Dittrich, 2002). The husbands, sons, or sons-in-law become involved in nondirect, less personal ways, such as assisting with financial matters and home repair needs. It is often difficult for adult children to break out of their childhood roles when attempting to provide care for their elder parents. Thus, the process of decision making when faced with a status change in an elder parent can be complicated and emotionally draining for all involved (Naleppa, 1996). The social worker must be prepared to address not just the immediate needs of the elder client, but also the needs of the extended family involved in care.

McInnis-Dittrich (2002) points out that when adult children or spouses are required to provide care for a rapidly declining family member, there is a sudden change in reciprocity. The relationship becomes lopsided as the care receiver is unable to reciprocate the time and energy to provide equal care for their loved one. This is even more evident when the care receiver is experiencing cognitive decline and is unable even to express gratitude for the care given or affection for the care provider. The social worker can play a key role in mitigating these changes in power dynamics within the family.

There is an abundance of literature about the overload of physical and emotional demands placed on family caregivers. When the caregiver is an adult child, they are usually being pulled in many directions. They often have growing children, spouses, and jobs they must maintain. Yet, they feel the familial obligation to respond to the needs of their failing parent. They often sacrifice their social network and self-care activities to focus on the needs of their families. Caregiver burnout is a real and serious concern for the social worker when designing a care plan for an elder client. A caregiver who is depressed, exhausted, and isolated can become angry and resentful. This, if left unrecognized and untreated can result in abuse toward the care receiver or in the extended family, or in physical and mental/emotional decline of the caregiver. The care-giver is also at risk for self-destructive behaviors. The caregiver needs help and support in learning the signs and symptoms of burnout and needs to be provided with the tools necessary to balance their caregiving responsibilities with time for relaxation and emotional release. The social worker can assist the caregiver to call a family meeting to discuss the situation. By explaining the possible outcomes and inviting support and assistance in meeting the increasing needs of the declining elder, the social worker can ease the tensions and keep things on an even keel. There are also numerous caregiver resources available. Support groups are invaluable to family caregivers as they not only provide education about the role of caregiver and the subsequent challenges and risks, but they also provide a social outlet with others who intimately understand the experience of family caregiving. Figure 13.3 list caregiving tips for family members.

1. Choose to take charge of your life, and don't let your loved one's illness or disability always take center stage.
2. Take respite time. Remember to be good to yourself, love honor and value yourself. You are doing a very hard job and you deserve some quality time for you.
3. When people offer help accept the offer and suggest specific things that they can do. Hire intermittent private caregivers to help.
4. Watch out for signs of depression, and don't delay in getting professional help when you need it.
5. Educate yourself about your loved one's condition. Information is empowering.
6. There is a difference between caring and doing. Promote your loved one's independence as much as possible.
7. Trust your instincts; they will lead you in the right direction.
8. Grieve for your losses, and then allow yourself to dream new dreams.
9. Stand up for your rights as a caregiver and a citizen. Speak to your local, state, and federal constituents about your needs and wants as a caregiver.
10. And last seek support from other caregivers. There is strength in knowing you are not alone.

FIGURE 13.3 | 10 TIPS FOR FAMILY CAREGIVERS

Source: (http://www.family-caregivers.com/index.php?option=com_content&task=view&id=17&Itemid=31)

There are numerous online resources available as well, which are particularly useful for those caregivers who either cannot get out to meetings or who live in rural communities with limited access to groups.

Another intersection at which families encounter the need for specialized social work support is when facing end-of-life issues with elderly loved ones. Death and dying remains a subject that is not discussed in many families until the very end of life. Well-trained social workers are invaluable to families and their elders in helping them prepare for the death of a loved one. In order to do this, social workers need to explore their own feelings and thoughts about end-of-life planning and death and dying. They need to be able to listen compassionately and clearly to their clients' needs and desires (Holosko and Feit, 2004). Social workers educate clients about the nature and purpose of advanced directives and can assist clients in preparing the documents. Advanced directive documents, such as wills, living wills, and durable powers of attorney for healthcare decisions, are available in each state. A will provides for the distribution of one's belongings after their death. A living will provides instruction for healthcare decisions should one become incapacitated and unable to make his or her desires known.

A durable power of attorney, also known as a healthcare proxy, is a legal document which designates another person to be the decision maker when the client becomes unable to do so. In 1990, Congress passed the Patient Self-Determination Act. This act

> requires many Medicare and Medicaid providers (hospitals, nursing homes, hospice programs, home health agencies, and HMO's) to give adult individuals, at the time of inpatient admission or enrollment, certain information about their rights under state laws governing advance directives, including: (1) the right to participate in and direct their own health care decisions; (2) the right to accept or refuse medical or surgical treatment; (3) the right to prepare an advance directive; (4) information on the provider's policies that govern the utilization of these rights. The act also prohibits

institutions from discriminating against a patient who does not have an advance directive. The PSDA further requires institutions to document patient information and provide ongoing community education on advance directives (Ascension Health, Patient Self-Determination Act, n.d.).

There is some variation between states and their laws regarding the content and process of advanced directive documents (McInnis-Dittrich, 2002). It is a good idea to become familiar with the laws of your state in order to provide accurate information to your clients.

The worker can help the family deal with the emotions involved in making these delicate and difficult decisions. At times, family members will disagree with the wishes of the older client. The social worker can be effective in mediating a discussion about these areas of disagreement. This will assist in avoiding conflict at critical moments in the care of the loved one. Funeral planning, wills, advanced directives, and so forth, are fraught with challenges for families as they try to deal with the complex emotions inherent at the end of life. Ideally, such decision making can be addressed early on with the intent of being prepared for whatever outcomes. Recent media attention on controversial disagreements regarding the desires of an incapacitated person has highlighted the legal and ethical morass to be suffered if advanced directives are not in place. In several cases, the families, healthcare providers, religious leaders and even public officials became embroiled in very bitter conflicts over maintaining or discontinuing life support for the severely incapacitated individual. While impossible to predict such disasters, documenting one's desires for healthcare in extraordinary circumstances helps to prevent placing the burden of making such a difficult decision as turning off life support on loved ones. By being educated and familiar with the purpose and intent of these documents, social workers can help individuals and families prepare for any eventuality.

Figure 13.4 lists the many and varied sites in which a generalist social worker would pursue a career in the field of geriatrics. Generalist social workers are exposed to geriatrics in most agency settings due to the presence of multiple generations in the populations served. An example would be the child welfare worker who works directly with the grandparent who has stepped in to raise grandchildren due to the absence of their parents. Developing skills and understanding of the elder population is vital to good social work practice.

ASSESSMENT

Assessment is a complex undertaking and requires skills not only in interviewing the older adult, but in planning the intervention/s needed to respond to their needs. The first step in approaching assessment with seniors is taking a broad view, incorporating examination of the medical, psychological and social factors involved. Studies have indicated there is a correlation between physical challenges and decline, environmental and personal losses, and the incidence of mood disorders, primarily anxiety and depression (Horowitz, 2003). It is thus important for social workers to inquire as to their client's health history and to encourage them to have a current and complete health examination. A client may be experiencing insomnia, sadness, mild confusion, restlessness, and fatigue. These symptoms, when viewed independently, meet the criteria of major depression (American Psychiatric

- Social Service Agencies: AAAs, Social service departments in states and counties, secular social service agencies such as Catholic Social Services and Jewish Family Services.
- Home Health Care: Visiting Nurse Associations, Hospice organizations.
- Congregate Living Centers: Independent living centers for over 65, such as in public housing settings.
- Adult Day Care: Provision of care between independent living and skilled nursing care.
- Assisted Living and Continuum of Care Facilities: Providing in-home support services to maximize independent functioning.
- Hospitals: Assisting with discharge planning; collaborating with the health professionals, patient and family/friends, and community resources; putting together a discharge plan that assures the client's continued recovery.
- Nursing Homes: Long-term care and rehabilitation centers.
- Policy: Boards of social service agencies providing care to elders; city and county councils making decisions about funding for care to elders; universities educating social service workers in the field of gerontology.

FIGURE 13.4 | PRACTICE SETTINGS FOR GERONTOLOGICAL SOCIAL WORKERS

Association, 2000). However, when a thorough medical examination and history is performed, it may reveal that a combination of medications prescribed by numerous physicians is the possible cause for the incidence of this combination of symptoms. When proper adjustments are made in the medication regimen, the client may begin to feel much differently, returning to their previous level of functioning. In assessment, the social worker will find that a multidimensional approach to identify strengths and weaknesses over the range of health and social dimensions is the most effective in rating the client's functioning and/or well-being, guiding the provision of services. There are some challenges to using such an approach to assessment. The length of the assessment tool will increase, as will the time needed to complete it. The social worker may find it necessary to break up the interview into two or three sessions in order to prevent client fatigue and to get more accurate responses from the client while they are still fresh and able to participate fully.

The social worker is the detective in this process, seeking clues to an accurate determination of strengths and challenges in each client. The social worker needs to develop an accurate picture of the *whole* person to proceed with planning appropriate interventions. It is a mistake to make any judgment about the status of a client before completing a thorough and detailed assessment. For example, the presentation of confusion and memory loss does not necessarily indicate dementia as certain physical changes and/or medications can cause similar symptoms. Also, the appearance of delusions and erratic behaviors does not necessarily indicate psychiatric illness, but could be a sign of stroke, changes in sensory processing, or numerous other medical problems (McInnis-Dittrich, 2002). Unfortunately, many valuable resources have been depleted in responding to invalid needs due to a weak or nonexistent assessment.

The assessment phase must begin with engagement and trust building. While this is true of work with any one of any age, it is particularly true with older clients. Many seniors feel vulnerable in a society that emphasizes youth and vitality and devalues age and experience. They may fear exposure of physical and mental weaknesses and certainly fear the loss of their independence. The social worker must listen carefully for the underlying truths presented in interviews with the senior. Genuine empathy and validation are vital to establishing a safe place for this individual to open their life to the worker. The skills of life review and reminiscence come in handy during this phase. It is key that the worker expresses interest in the early life of the senior, relaying the genuine belief that the client is the expert of his or herself. It has been experience and knowledge that has allowed the client to survive and develop resiliency in life. Taking time during this phase of the interaction both allows the senior client to develop trust in the worker and provides valuable information.

Further, it is worth considering how the client came to be assessed. What has brought this client to your attention? Was it the family who was concerned about a recent decline in their loved one's condition? Are they concerned about his or her welfare? Did the senior herself call for services in hopes of improving her situation? Did a healthcare provider or neighbor contact your agency for assessment, perhaps suspecting some neglect or abuse? The context of the introduction to services will help guide the social worker in establishing a rapport with the client.

Patience but persistence allowed this social worker in training to engage with this client. Having just experienced the transition of her husband to nursing home care, this woman feared that she would be seen as frail and unable to live alone, losing her last chance at independence. Once she developed trust in this worker, she was able to speak openly about her fears and receive validation and support from the worker as they pursued their work together.

A vital assessment tool for the gerontological social worker is educated observation. Social workers begin their assessments as soon as they encounter the client,

---

CASE 13.1 | **PERSISTENCE PAYS OFF**

Jill, a senior BSW student, is working in a community agency that provides free services to the community. Jill visits a high-rise, subsidized, senior apartment building. In consulting the management staff, she is asked to visit an elderly resident who recently placed her husband in a nursing home. The staff states that the woman has remained isolated and alone since leaving her husband at the nursing facility. She comes downstairs only to pick up her mail and then returns immediately to her apartment. Jill knocks on the woman's door and it is opened only a crack. Jill explains that she is a social work student with the local university providing friendly visits in the building and asking if they have any needs. The woman responds that she is okay and doesn't need anything. Jill returns to her apartment a week later, the door opens again only a small amount and the student, maintaining a friendly and nonthreatening stance, says she is just checking in to see how the woman is doing. The woman states she has a cold, but is doing okay and still has no needs. Jill returns in 1 week, tells the woman through the small crack that she has been thinking about her and wondering if her cold is better. The woman opens the door slightly wider and states she is feeling a little better. The woman talks with Jill a little longer, stating she has a brother who lives near the university. Jill encourages this venture into sharing, talking about the city as it used to be. Finally, Jill asks if she can stop by again next week to check on the woman and she agrees. At the next visit, the woman opens her door and welcomes Jill into her home. Jill and the woman establish a trusting relationship and, ultimately, she is able to conduct an assessment of need and refer the woman to a variety of services that will support her living alone and independently.

whether it is an initial phone call, a home visit, or an official assessment appointment. Social workers must be attuned to every nuance of the client's initial presentation. Is his voice weak or excessively loud? Voice volume could reflect a hearing problem or a neurological processing problem. Does he hesitate in speaking as if looking for words? Or does he jump from one thought to the next? Differences occurring in cognition can indicate early onset dementia, or may be a side effect of medications. Depression and anxiety can present in the older age group as mild confusion or physical symptoms. Often, the depressed older adult initially presents in their primary care doctor's office with vague physical symptoms, such as fatigue and aches and pains (O'Neil, 2007).

When making a home visit, observe both the client and the home environment. Is the client neatly dressed and groomed? The actual clothing is less important than the appearance. Is the clothing clean or soiled? Is the client wearing them appropriately? Are they inside out? Do her or his clothes fit properly or are they too tight or loose? And notice their personal appearance. Is the client clean and neat in appearance? Is the hair combed? With females, one will notice if the face is overly made up with exaggerated amounts of lipstick or eye shadow. With males, the social worker will notice if he is clean-shaven or well-groomed. Does the client have an odor about them? The assessment of personal appearance has nothing to do with fashion or style. Each individual must be seen within their own context. A woman who has worn make-up daily all of her adult life will most likely continue to do so. Changes in the appearance of her make-up (i.e., too heavily and unevenly applied) may have more to do with changes in her eyesight rather than changes in her mental status. All of these clues are important in forming a complete picture of the client. A helpful hint is to seek out photos in the client's home with which to compare the client's current appearance to their previous appearance in family photos. While allowing the worker to observe the client's custom of dress and appearance, it also provides an opportunity to connect with the client on a more personal level. Who doesn't enjoy sharing personal photographs with another? It can stimulate some friendly reminiscence of past experiences and lead to informative stories about the client's life. This can assist the social worker in forming a more complete and accurate image of the client's current status. This author recalls a home visit with an elderly client who was consistently dressed in her robe and slippers. One might wonder if this indicated a lack of motivation to dress for the day, which might possibly be a symptom of isolation and depression. However, when viewing her photos, it became clear that she, as her mother before her, considered her robe a "housedress" and felt it was completely appropriate apparel for daytime wear around the house.

While in the home, the observant worker notes the living conditions. Is the home clean and neat? Are there excessive amounts of "stuff" in the room? Are there piles of magazines or papers, stacks of boxes, and other materials? Does the client simply have a large collection of mementos—surface areas covered with knickknacks? This can be indicative of a long life well lived as opposed to hoarding behavior. Is there an odor in the home—the smell of urine or perhaps the smell of burned food? One's home generally reflects much of one's personality. Again, it is not the design or age of the furnishings that is noted, but rather obvious changes and inconsistencies. A client who is well dressed and clean, but whose home is cluttered and dusty, raises the question of how well the client is physically able to handle the daily tasks of housekeeping.

As the worker converses with the client, other aspects of the client's demeanor will be noted. Is the client making eye contact with you? Is he or she responding appropriately to the flow of the conversation? Is she or he able to follow the gist of the conversation? All of these observations will give you hints at the total picture of the client even before the more formal assessment interview begins. However, be warned that assumptions about a client's mental status and competence based solely on observation can be misleading. You must be ever mindful to keep these observations in perspective, putting together the pieces like a puzzle until a complete and accurate picture begins to emerge. Input from family members, neighbors, medical professionals, and others with whom the client has regularly interacted will help provide a more balanced assessment. A good assessment is one in which all factors are taken into consideration (Genevay, 1997).

Ideally, the use of a formal assessment tool will begin after the worker has established a trusting relationship with the client. Pulling out a lengthy form and proceeding to ask dry and detailed questions can be off-putting to the elderly client. As in the case example, the client may perceive the worker as a friendly visitor and be looking for some shared conversation. While consideration must given to the value of the worker's time, it is suggested that spending a little time chatting and putting the client at ease will later reap many benefits in allowing the worker to pursue the needed information. Many of our elderly clients view home visitation as a social visit and view the assessment interview as a secondary goal. They were raised in a time that demanded certain social graces be observed when entertaining guests in one's home. The astute social worker will respect this and will use this social sharing as a time to make crucial observations, to tune in to the client, and to reach for the client's confidence and trust.

Assessment tools vary from agency to agency and differ in terms of what they are intended to assess. Also, the time allotted for the assessment varies similarly. In a large Area Agency on Aging (AAA), the case manager generally will be scheduled to do multiple assessments daily and will also be assigned a number of clients to be followed as services are provided. Obviously, this case manager cannot afford the luxury of establishing a relationship with each client. These assessments are meant to highlight the most pressing needs of the clients, with referrals then made to other agencies that will provide more detailed individual services. For the purpose of this chapter, we will look at an array of assessment tools available to the gerontological social worker.

In general, a thorough assessment tool will include instruments that will help to identify the strengths and weaknesses of your client and give direction to your work together (Positive Aging, 2005). Assessment of cognitive functioning is a good place to start, thus helping in determining whether the client will be able to fully participate in further individual assessment. Those who are experiencing some reduction in cognitive functioning may try to hide it and usually do so very well. They are able to read the cues during conversation and cover their confusion with reflection of affect and minimal responses. It takes a skilled interviewer to recognize this attempt at concealment. One of the effective ways of evaluating the cognitive function of a client is through conducting a mental status examination as

CASE 13.2 | TOO MUCH STUFF

The state Division of Aging is asked to send a social worker to the home of Ms. G. by her primary care physician. It is reported that her home is filled with "junk" and she needs help cleaning. Pat, a senior BSW student interning with the Division, is assigned this case. Pat calls Ms. G. to schedule a visit and is welcomed. Ms. G. states she enjoys the company. When Pat arrives, she notes the yard and exterior house look neat and well kept. When she approaches the door, Ms. G. comes out to greet her and asks her to "overlook the mess," stating she hasn't gotten around to cleaning up. Pat makes her way into the living room area with difficulty. The piles of newspapers, magazines, and junk mail allow only a small pathway through the room. Ms. G. moves several piles of papers and stuffed animals from the sofa in order to make room for Pat to sit. Ms. G. herself is dressed appropriately for the weather and the time of year; her hair is combed and she appears to be clean. Her home, while extremely cluttered, does not have any foul odor or even a hint of mustiness. Pat begins talking with Ms. G. by asking her why she thought her doctor had referred her to the agency. Ms. G. states she lost her husband one and a half years before and just hasn't been the same since. She thought the doctor recognized her loneliness and asked the agency to send someone to visit her, to provide some company. Ms. G. talked about her husband in loving terms. She stated that he had been the housekeeper in their family and things had gotten out of hand after his death. Pat gently engaged Ms. G. in a review of her life, asking specific questions about the circumstances of her current situation when appropriate. Over time, Pat notes that Ms. G. is jumping from topic to topic with little or no logical connection. She appears to remember incidents from her past with some detail, while recent occurrences are fuzzy or not remembered at all. For example, she can't remember what she has eaten for breakfast that morning or even if she has eaten, but she is able to describe in detail a Christmas visit she and her husband had made to her birthplace in Georgia some 20 years before. Ms. G. is able to answer general questions about current public events, but is unable to accurately name the date and day. Ms. G. shows Pat her kitchen, which is cluttered, but well stocked with

fresh foods and frozen meals, which, Ms. G. informs Pat, came from her daughter. Ms. G. agrees to a conversation between Pat and her daughter, although she indicates that she and her daughter are not very close. The daughter reveals that Ms. G. has always been a "collector," but that her father had indeed organized and controlled the clutter. After her father's death, the daughter has attempted to help Ms. G. declutter her home, but Ms. G. becomes angry and resentful and ultimately refuses any further help. The daughter states that she thinks her mother should give up the house and move someplace where people can take care of her, but Ms. G. adamantly refuses. The daughter has "given up" and now only comes to take care of the lawn and keep up the exterior of the home so that "the neighbors won't complain."

Pat takes the results of her initial visit and assessment back to her agency and reviews the findings with her supervisor. Together, they plan for the most effective way to work with Ms. G. and her support network. Pat begins her treatment plan with Ms. G. by scheduling regular visits with her to develop a trusting relationship with her. Pat is then able to begin to identify some areas of need with Ms. G. and, slowly, Ms. G. begins to accept some community services. Ms. G. agrees to have someone come and help with her finances and bill paying and to have meals delivered to her home by a friendly visitor who will also spend a few minutes chatting with her daily as he delivers the meals. Ms. G. begins to socialize with her neighbors again. They have been checking in on her regularly and also provide transportation for her to doctors' appointments and to the store. Now they are able to see Ms. G. more regularly and provide stimulation by visiting her more regularly. Her daughter continues to help with the yard and exterior house. With Ms. G. receiving in-home services and supports, the daughter stops talking about moving her mother, and Ms. G. once again welcomes her daughter for visits. With permission from Ms. G., Pat keeps in touch with the referring doctor, keeping her informed of any changes in Ms. G's mental status, which has been stabilized with the addition of supports. While not allowing any removal of materials, Ms. G. also agrees to the redistribution of her collection, creating a safer living environment for her. She also agrees not to

CASE 13.2 | *Continued*

add any more things to her collection. She and Pat continue the home visits. Ms. G. reports feeling less lonely, stating she is enjoying her life again.

By engaging the client through home visits and review of her life, Pat is able to increase Ms. G.'s support network and services. The results are that Ms. G. is able to remain in her own home and maintain her lifestyle. Although her "junk" is still present, it is organized in such a way as to not be a threat to her safety. She is now able to enjoy her life and at the same time receive the necessary monitoring of her situation to assure her safety and comfort.

discussed in Chapter 6. This simple method allows the interviewer to evaluate the client's thoughts, mood, and behavior through questions that elicit their orientation to time and place, their ability to hear and understand the speaker, their short- and long-term memory function, their ability to engage in higher intellectual activities, and their ability to engage in symbolic processes (Positive Aging, 2005). An effective, simple, and quick examination is available in the Mini-Mental Status Examination developed by Folstein, Folstein, and McHugh in 1975 (see Figure 13.5). The MMSE has a scoring range from 0 to 30 with the higher scores indicating higher cognitive functioning. A social worker can easily incorporate some of these questions into their initial interview with a client, thus obtaining a quick indication of the client's mental status.

If a problem is suspected, the social worker can then choose a more comprehensive exam to determine the exact nature of the client's cognitive decline. An example would be the Dementia Rating Scale (Mattis, 1989, as cited in Hill, 2005). This instrument requires a paper and pen and comprises 36 tasks. The scoring provides more detailed information regarding the areas of mental deficits. It also requires that the examiner have more skill working with older adults, particularly those with dementia or Alzheimer's disease. Once it is established that the client is able to fully participate in a more comprehensive assessment, the worker can proceed. In many agencies, a biopsychosocial assessment will be available, created with their particular service delivery in mind. Such a tool provides for gathering a broad range of information necessary to determine the types of services the client may need. The ultimate goal is to assist the client in preserving his or her lifestyle and independence as much as possible. It allows the client, the family, and the social worker to illuminate areas of concern or risk and guides them in the decision-making process of matching needs to available services. As indicated in the title, the "bio–" portion of the assessment typically asks questions about the client's physical/medical condition. These include asking about one's physical abilities; physicians involved in the client's case; medications prescribed; medical insurance information; mobility issues including transportation (ability to drive or ride public transportation); navigability of the home (are there stairs or tight corners?); activities of daily living (ADLs), such as bathing and dressing; and so on.

The assessment of the client's psychological functioning begins as soon as the worker interacts with the client and incorporates some of the observations previously described. Questions about the clients' thoughts on this process, their ability to cope with stress, how they approach problems, and how they perceive their lives

The Mini-Mental State Exam

Patient _____ Examiner _____ Date _____

Maximum   Score

Orientation

5   ( )   What is the (year) (season) (date) (day) (month)?
5   ( )   Where are we (state) (country) (town) (hospital) (floor)?

Registration

3   ( )   Name 3 objects: 1 second to say each. Then ask the patient
                  all 3 after you have said them. Give 1 point for each correct answers.
                  Then repeat them until he/she learns all 3. Count trials and record.
                  Trials _____

Attention and Calculation

5   ( )   Serial 7's. 1 point for each correct answer. Stop after 5 answers.
                  Alternatively spell "world" backward.

Recall

3   ( )   Ask for the 3 objects repeated above. Give 1 point for each correct answer.

Language

2   ( )   Name a pencil and watch.
1   ( )   Repeat the following: "No ifs, ands, or buts."
3   ( )   Follow a 3-stage command:
                  "Take a paper in your hand, fold it in half, and put it on the floor."
1   ( )   Read and obey the following: CLOSE YOUR EYES.
1   ( )   Write a sentence.
1   ( )   Copy the design shown.

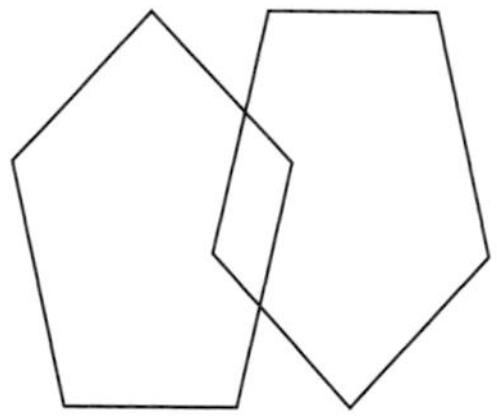

_____   Total Score
         ASSESS level of consciousness along a continuum _____

                                    Alert Drowsy Stupor Coma

"MINI-MENTAL STATE." A PRACTICAL METHOD FOR GRADING THE COGNITIVE STATE OF
PATIENTS FOR THE CLINICIAN.
Journal of Psychiatric Research, 12(3): 189-198, 1975. Used by permission.

FIGURE 13.5 | MINI-MENTAL STATE EXAM

will give the worker insight into their personality. Studies have indicated that older adults who believe that they have control over most aspects of their lives seem to adapt a stronger coping mechanism than those who don't (Neeman, 1995). Referred to as locus of control, elders who feel that they have options and some agency in determining their future (internal locus of control) seem to fare better in times of high stress. Elders who feel things just happen to them due to powerful others (external locus of control) struggle to maintain stability when faced with crises (Kemper, van Sonderen, and Ormel, as cited in Hooyman and Kiyak, 2002). The worker is looking for those qualities that have provided the client with the resilience to face and conquer the challenges in their lives and to find meaning and acceptance in their lives. This approach allows the social worker to focus on the client's strengths. The worker helps the client to review their younger years, asking them to examine the ways in which they moved forward, adapted, and healed following adverse life events. These coping skills are protective qualities that help the client to survive and become resilient older adults. The social worker must recognize that all of these competencies are culturally defined, reflecting the oppression or privilege, the social stigma or elevated status, and financial strains or stability experienced by the particular client. At times the adaptive qualities expressed by the minority client may fly in the face of the standards of the majority. The social worker must take care to view each client through a culturally competent lens and not make judgment based on his or her own values and beliefs (Greene and Cohen, 2005).

As mentioned previously, many elderly clients do present with symptoms of depression and anxiety. When these symptoms are recognized as other than related to a medical condition, a more detailed evaluation is indicated. While the MMSE gives some indication of mood, a more detailed evaluation is needed when depression and/or anxiety is suspected. These mood disorders can really sap the strength and resolve of an elderly client, making independent living and successful aging more challenging than it needs to be. The popular Beck's Depression Inventory (Beck, 1984), while a useful tool, was not designed to be particularly sensitive to the elderly client. Older clients who are experiencing loss due to changes in their circumstances, such as some health decline, may be identified as severely depressed on the Beck's scale. However, they may be reflecting their sadness while slowly exercising their ability to adapt to the changes thrust upon them (Ahmed and Takeshita, 1996–97). In the 1980s, researchers at Stanford University developed a more sensitive tool that is designed for clients in older adulthood. This instrument is the Geriatric Depression Scale (GDS) and assesses 15 areas that relate to depressive affect (see Figure 13.6) (Hill, 2005). The GDS allows the social worker to assess the client's mood in the context of his or her life situation and uses a person-in-environment perspective, thus giving a more accurate indication of the presence or absence of a diagnosable mood disorder. The complete GDS along with scoring information is in Figure 13.7.

RESOURCES

Geriatric Depression Scale web site: http://www.stanford.edu/~yesavage/GDS.html
Depression and anxiety also occur in clients with dementia, and assessing their mood levels requires a particular tool designed for those with cognitive impairment. The Cornell Scale of Depression in Dementia (Hill, 2005) allows the

- Life satisfaction
- Changes in activities
- Feelings of emptiness
- Feelings of boredom
- Mood levels
- Fears about the future
- Feelings of happiness
- Feelings of helplessness
- Community involvement
- Changes in memory
- Gratefulness in living
- Feelings of worthlessness
- Energy level
- Feelings of hopelessness
- Comparisons with other persons

FIGURE 13.6 | DIMENSIONS OF THE GERIATRIC DEPRESSION SCALE

Source: (Positive Aging, 2005)

interviewer to question the client directly or the caregiver if the client is unable to respond or a combination of both. It is relatively quick and easy to score. Using a three-point rating, this instrument evaluates whether certain symptoms of depression are absent, mild, or intermittent, or severe. It can also be used with clients who have no cognitive impairment. As mentioned before, the worker who is directly involved with services for clients with cognitive impairment may be better able to identify and refer clients with issues of depression or anxiety in the case of dementia. Anxiety is another common complaint among the older population, which will be explored in more detail later in this chapter. One must accurately assess these symptoms to be able to more adequately refer clients for effective treatment. The Schedule for Affective Disorders and Schizophrenia (Endicott and Spitzer, 1978) has been used successfully with the older population in identifying and differentiating anxiety from other disorders (Endicott and Spitzer as cited in Hill, 2005).

In addition to assessing for cognition and mood, it is often necessary to assess the older client for competencies. Competency involves not just ability to attend to one's daily needs and personal affairs. It also involves issues such as one's ability to consent to medical and psychological treatment, to be involved in research studies, to handle one's finances, and to drive safely and responsibly, to name a few. Competency is also based on many factors, not just cognition and behavior. Normal age-related changes in sight, hearing, physical agility, and response time all come into play when evaluating competency. The determination of competency may fall to the social worker who is making an assessment. It may also fall to government personnel, such as the motor vehicle department, which is responsible for evaluating the driving ability of citizens. In some cases, the state courts are included in this assessment by being asked to establish legal competency (Marson, 2002). The study of competency actually began in relation to the capacity of psychiatric patients to consent to treatment. Now, our growing aging population has presented the need for accurate, empirically based, and standardized instruments to measure

Questions: Short Form (Positive answer in parentheses)

A.   Are you basically satisfied with your life? (No)

B.   Have you dropped many of your activities and interests? (Yes)

C.   Do you feel your life is empty? (Yes)

D.   Do you often get bored? (Yes)

E.   Are you in good spirits most of the time? (No)

F.   Are you afraid something bad is going to happen to you? (Yes)

G.   Do you feel happy most of the time? (No)

H.   Do you often feel helpless? (Yes)

I.   Do you prefer to stay at home, rather than going out and doing new things? (Yes)

J.   Do you feel you have more problems with memory that most? (Yes)

K.   Do you think it is wonderful to be alive now? (No)

L.   Do you feel pretty worthless the way you are now? (Yes)

M.   Do you feel full of energy? (No)

N.   Do you feel that your situation is hopeless? (Yes)

O.   Do you think most people are better off than you? (Yes)

Interpretation

1.   Normal: 0 to 4

2.   Mild Depression: 5 to 8

3.   Moderate depression: 8 to 11

4.   Severe depression: 12 to 15

FIGURE 13.7 | GERIATRIC DEPRESSION SCALE

competency in nonpsychiatric older adults. Various instruments may be used to measure decline in ability to function independently. One such instrument is the Katz Adaptive Living Scale (Katz, Downs, and Grotz, 1970, as cited in Hill, 2005). This scale measures the older adult's performance of various activities of daily living as completed either without help, with help, or unable to perform task even with assistance (Hill, 2005). As mentioned previously in this chapter, the Dementia Rating Scale (Mattis, 1989, as cited in Hill, 2005) provides a measure of cognitive decline and helps to determine whether the client is able to participate in decision making and consent to treatment. Needless to say, competency judgments require that the people involved exercise thoughtful examinations of ethics and moral values as such judgments determine the autonomy of the individual being evaluated (Marson, 2002).

Addiction is an area that is often overlooked in the assessment process with older adults. The use of illicit drugs is rarely reported in the elderly. However, use and abuse of alcohol and prescription drugs is a documented concern (Hooyman and Kiyak, 2002). Due to the stigma associated with addiction, family and even professionals avoid labeling overuse of medications or alcohol as addiction. While alcohol may be incorporated into the social lives of many older adults, this use may slip into abuse inadvertently as individuals attempt to "self-treat" their insomnia or worry (anxiety). Social drinking may expand to include drinking prior to and following social events. It has been estimated the 10% of the population of persons over the age of 65 may qualify as problem drinkers (Adams and Cox as cited in McInnis-Dittrich, 2002). Alcohol in excess is implicated in a variety of medical complications, some leading to disability and even to death. Other threats to the elder population from the misuse of alcohol are impaired driving, poor judgment, imbalance and possible falls, poor nutrition, and so forth. It is important to note that aging affects the ability of the body to absorb alcohol and in the body's reaction to it. It requires less alcohol to raise the blood content of a 70 year old person than that of a 35 year old. Thus, someone who has commonly had a drink or two before dinner may find themselves much more impaired as they grow older (McInnis-Dittrich, 2002). While a delicate subject to broach, it is an important component of the biopsychosocial assessment.

The population over the age of 60 represents the majority of prescription drug users and over the counter drug users in this country. It is documented that older adults are more likely to use various tranquilizers and sedatives than younger adults (Hooyman and Kiyak, 2002). Becoming dependant on medication is a potential problem in this age group. At times, so many medications are prescribed by numerous different doctors that the elder becomes unable to accurately monitor their medication schedule. It is difficult for family members to be present at every scheduled dosage. Also, such clients may determine for themselves that if one pill helps moderately, maybe two will be even better. This can rapidly become a crisis situation. During the assessment phase, the social worker will record the medications prescribed and assess the ability of the client to maintain the correct schedule of dosage. The worker can also encourage the client to ask and record the purpose of each medication, its proper dosage and a description of the pill to be kept handy to refer to as needed.

Sexuality and sensuality are topics of conversation and entertainment throughout our world. Sex and the City, a contemporary television show about 30-something women in New York, broke many of our society's barriers in openly discussing topics such as women's desires and sexual response, masturbation and fetishes. However, a topic that remains taboo is sex and the senior. It is the rare assessment that even broaches this subject with elderly clients. While it is commonplace for the younger cohort to be asked about sexual activity and safe sex practices, seldom are these questions included in assessments with the elderly. In the 80's, Masters and Johnson (1981) included the senior population in their study of sexual behavior in America. They concluded that sexual behavior and desire is life-long (Hooyman and Kiyak, 2002). It is important for the gerontological social worker to include discussion about safe sex practices with their older clients. Education about HIV/AIDS and other STDs is necessary with many elderly clients as they have little information provided by healthcare providers.

As you can see, the assessment phase covers a lot of ground and can be quite lengthy. Usually, the worker will continue to assess the client and collect valuable information while addressing the most urgent of case management needs. As the worker identifies areas of need for their client, they are also researching the community for appropriate agencies and programs to meet those needs. At times, the worker will discover a gap in services; an area of need that has either not been addressed or is under funded or unavailable due to restricted eligibility criteria.

The social worker is in a position to advocate for change in these cases, using their macro-practice skills in informing the public of the gap and the increased need.

An area of concern for the social worker working with elder adults is that of social isolation. One possible explanation for the incidence of apparent social withdrawal in the older age group is social exchange theory. This theory, as described by Dowd (as cited in Hooyman and Kiyak, 2002), suggests that older adults feel out of balance in terms of reciprocal social exchanges. In all relationships, the people involved have some expectation of a return on their investment of time and energy. For example, a neighbor may collect the mail and water the flowers while their friend is away in expectation that they will be able to call on their friend for help with some project in the future. When there is no ability for the returned favor, the relationship is out of balance. Older, infirm adults may believe they no longer have the ability to reciprocate in their social relationships and they begin to withdraw from them (McInnis-Dettrich, 2002). Numerous studies have noted the detrimental effects of social isolation and loss of social ties in all ages, but particularly the elderly (Wenger, 1997). Such reduction in social networking can be linked to physical illness and decline. At the same time, participation in social activities and maintenance of social roles has been shown to decrease the incidence of psychological distress (Reich and Zautra, 1989).

Is social withdrawal an inevitable result of aging? Some aspects of aging result in loss of certain social roles and ties, such as when adult children leave the home or when a spouse dies (Sluzki, 2000). A helpful way of conceptualizing these shifts in social connections that impact the elderly population is the systems theory. Moving out of the phase of adulthood in which their primary focus was raising children and building a career and into the phase of empty-nester and retiree requires role changes and adjustments on the part of the individual. Through these changes there are necessary changes in the systems in which they function. Where the individual may have had daily interactions and long-term affiliations with their place of employment, upon retirement, they now find themselves disconnected. A parent who gave much time and energy to volunteering at the schools attended by their children is no longer involved as their children graduate and move on into adulthood. Even in places of worship change occurs. People once called upon to participate in committee work and active roles with the religious community are now seen as less fit for these roles. They may be honored for their wisdom and history within the community, but their defined roles definitely change. Changes, while often positive, still require adjustment. An ecomap is useful in allowing us to compare the person-in-environment perspective of the individual during young adulthood with that in older age. In young adulthood, the stronger connections, reflecting reciprocal energy flow, are with a spouse or partner, with our place of employment, our place of worship, our children's schools, our friends and neighbors, various clubs and/or sports activities, and so on. As one ages, this flow of energy begins to change, as do the connections with the various relationships and organizations. This change may occur gradually, allowing for incremental adjustment or it may be abrupt and bring feelings of chaos to the system until one is able to begin to adjust. Energy flow, where once reciprocal, may become other directed and weak. Significant social ties may be broken, as in the case of retirement, moving or death. A move to retirement housing or assisted-living facilities or a move out of state to be nearer one's adult children may interrupt or even disconnect relations with neighbors and friends. Health challenges may prevent the continuation of club/sport participation and represent another loss of connection within the system. In aging, new people and agencies enter the system; however, the flow of energy may be quite different overall. An example is when an older person moves into an assisted-living facility, they suddenly find themselves navigating the system of the facility, including the service staff, the management staff, and the greater community of other residents, as well as increased involvement with the healthcare network. Many of these new ties represent energy flow in, rather than reciprocal flow between the parties.

The ecomap is a useful tool also to use with one's clients. Such a map helps the social worker to identify areas in which adjustments either have been made or where they still need to be made. This map is also helpful in demonstrating for the client the ways in which we are all impacted by the changes in our lives. They are able to see that they do indeed still have a support network; the people and groups involved may have changed, but there are others taking their place. And it can also depict the areas in which the individual may want to strengthen old connections or create new ones. Having not just the individual client, but the whole family participate in completing an ecomap is also useful in helping them understand the changes that the elder is experiencing and to stimulate discussion on ways to address areas of stress and strengthen areas of positive energy flow.

These ecomaps (see Figures 13.8 and 13.9) depict the client system of Mrs. Cleaver at age 30 and, secondly, at age 78. In the first map, one sees that Mrs. C. is married with two children. While she doesn't work outside of her home, she does belong to several social and church groups with which she shares her skills and talents and receives social supports. She has a strong faith and feels intimately connected to God and her church. She is active in her children's schools, serving as Home Room mother and as secretary for the PTA. Mrs. C. and her husband socialize with their neighbors as well as share favors. Mrs. C.'s parents live in another town and they visit during holidays and for summer vacation. Her older sister lives near them and takes primary responsibility for their care. This has resulted in some tension between Mrs. C and her sister. Mrs. C. and her mother-in-law have a strained relationship and have very little contact.

In the second map, we note some significant changes. Mr. C. has died after a long illness and Mrs. C. is now living with her daughter. This arrangement has been stressful for both of them as Ms. C. misses her independence and her previous home and her daughter is trying to balance a family, a job and her mother's care. A rift has occurred between the daughter and son, with the daughter feeling unsupported in the provision of care to her mother. During her husband's illness, Mrs. C. has lost touch with various neighbors and friends, who themselves have declining health. Neither she nor they could assist one another anymore and they drifted apart. Her church involvement also stopped during that time and, now, she is living too far away to return to her church. She does not enjoy attending her daughter's church because she feels she is an outsider and has no desire or energy to start new relationships. Of course, Mrs. C. no longer has any connection with the schools after her children graduated. The relationship between Mrs. C. and her sister has improved over the years after their parents' death and their own widowhood. They speak on the phone daily and

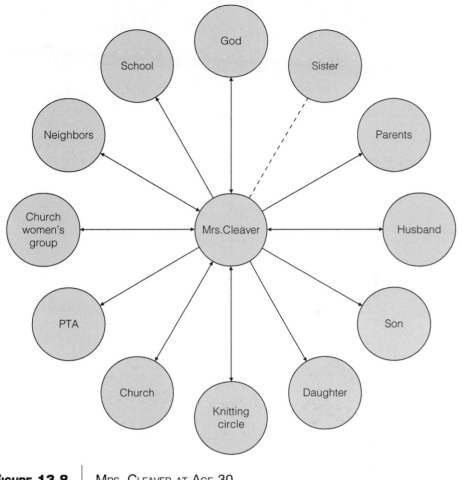

FIGURE 13.8 | MRS. CLEAVER AT AGE 30

visit as often as they can. Mrs. C. receives physical therapy following hip replacement surgery and enjoys chatting with her physical therapist while completing the exercise regimen. Mrs. C. continues to have a strong faith and enjoys watching religious programming on television, expressing that at times she feels the preacher is talking directly to her. Mrs. C. receives monthly visits from a social worker assigned by the area agency on aging. The social worker has connected Mrs. C. to Community Transit so she can get to her doctor's appointments without having her daughter take time from work. The social worker also has talked with Mrs. C. about the local senior center and she is thinking about visiting it to see if she might enjoy spending some time there. During their visits, Mrs. C. is teaching the social worker knitting, a skill she has practiced for many years.

In developing and reviewing the ecomap with Mrs. C. and her family, the social worker is able to point out the extreme changes with which Mrs. C. has had

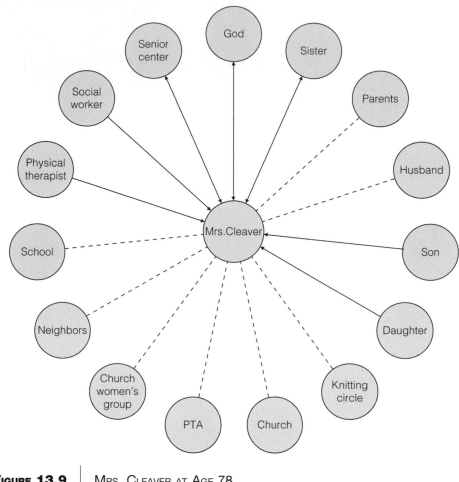

Figure 13.9 | Mrs. Cleaver at Age 78

to cope over the years. She is also able to identify her strengths and supports that remain stable. Together, the family and worker can see areas that require some attention. Mrs. C.'s daughter may decide that to return to their home church once every month to re-establish a positive connection for her mother. Mrs. C. may begin attending the senior center three days per week and volunteer to start a knitting circle, teaching knitting to the other seniors. Mrs. C.'s son may take his mother to visit her sister every other week, enjoying dinner out with them while sharing some quality time together. The worker can then revisit the ecomap in six months to re-evaluate the stability of the system and make changes as needed.

Hooyman (2002, p.194) states "depression, dementia and paranoia are the three most prevalent forms of late-life psychopathology." Most workers in the field of aging would agree that depression is the most commonly seen disorder of the three. It is estimated that depressive symptoms occur in 15% of the elderly living in community (Ahmed and Takeshita, 1996-97). This number is higher for those who have medical complications requiring ongoing treatment. It is suggested that between 5% and 7% of people over the age of 65 will develop symptoms of depression serious enough to require treatment. This estimate is higher for those over the age of 80. The rate of suicide in this age group continues to be the higher than in the general population (American Association of Suicidology, 2005). As previously mentioned, depression in this age group often presents as physical complaints and is at times overlooked by the primary healthcare providers who consider it a natural part of aging (Ahmed and Takeshita, 1996-97). While useful in recognizing the symptoms of a major depression, the DSM-IV-TR criteria do not include the usual physical symptoms with which older clients will present.

Most elderly clients with depression initially present to their general practitioner with physical complaints and tend to avoid talking about their feelings. Due to misconceptions associated with aging and with mental illness, older adults may either assume their feelings are normal aspects of the aging process or may be too ashamed to seek help. If they do seek help, they may present with vague complaints of fatigue or aches and pains (O'Neil, 2007). Rather than reporting feeling sad and hopeless, they will admit to irritability, social withdrawal, and anxiety (Moutier, Wetherell, and Zisook, 2003). By the nature of the life stage, many older adults are experiencing traumatic life events. The death of a spouse or other family member, loss of contemporaries, loss of physical abilities, relocation, revocation of driver's license, and so forth, are all occurrences that could trigger a depressive episode. Grief over numerous losses can contribute to an increased incidence of depression (Rando, 1984). If no further evaluation is pursued, these older adults may go untreated and suffer unnecessarily and, in the worst case scenario, become a suicide statistic. The rate of suicide among the elderly is alarmingly high. In 2005, the American Association of Suicidology reported that those aged 65 and older represented 16.4% of the total number of suicides reported.

Anxiety also is a commonly identified complaint in older adults. It is usually described as a co-occurring symptom with depression. Anxiety symptoms can sometimes be mistaken for early dementia. Some of the most common symptoms are as follows: poor concentration, agitation or irritation, headache, dizziness, heart palpitations, muscle aches, and a sense of restlessness (Wetherell, 1998). Because of the focus on physical complaints, anxiety has been associated with increased use of pain medications, not to mention increased alcohol abuse. Unfortunately, this can result in increasing numbers of falls and accidents. Those who do seek treatment usually do so from their primary care physician. Again, there is a denial of psychological symptoms, focusing instead on the physical, and a resistance to psychotherapeutic interventions. One study indicated that the majority of patients receiving anti-anxiety medications were over 50 years of age (Mellinger, Balter, and Uhlenhuth, as cited in Wetherell, 1984).

There has also been a tendency of this age group to resist mental health treatments due to the perceived stigma attached. Fear of no longer being in control mentally can also prevent elders from accessing mental health counseling (Neeman, 1995). Elders also may find treatments inaccessible due to physical disabilities hampering mobility or due to financial constraints. Medicare does not cover many mental health treatments. Life stressors accumulate in the later years, confronting elders with many challenges at a time in their lives when they are least able to withstand the emotional assaults. They are often at their lowest levels of emotional and financial resources. It is clear that untreated, depression and anxiety symptomatology causes a significant challenge to quality of life. The tendency to deny depression and avoid treatment is reducing and will continue to do so as the growing cohort of baby boomers are generally more receptive to counseling and nonmedical and alternative approaches to health issues. There are more elderly consumers who are familiar and more comfortable with mental health interventions than ever before. Also, when faced with making a choice between taking medications and entering counseling, many are more willing to engage in talk therapies due to fears of drug interactions, side effects, and general medical complications (O'Neil, 2007).

INTERVENTIONS

ENGAGEMENT STRATEGIES

The generalist social worker may work with elders in community-based home settings, such as senior high-rise buildings or retirement communities. In such environments, the social worker may be involved in a multidisciplinary team providing for the social and health needs of the residents. Community nurses, intensive care managers, mental health workers, and others join the social workers in monitoring the well-being of the residents, collaborating to create joint interventions in response to those needs that may arise that encompass the entire community and thus require a community-wide outreach. An example would be assisting the residents in adjusting to changes in management or addressing maintenance issues that affect the whole community. The social worker, with the team, may organize group meetings to encourage open communication with new management. By providing a comfortable, respectful, and safe space and by modeling and facilitating clear communication techniques, the social workers can help establish a functional and collaborative relationship between the community residents and the new management.

The social worker can also assist in educating the residents as to their rights and responsibilities in the community, empowering them to advocate for necessary changes and assisting them in negotiating the bureaucracy of the system. The worker can use the community environment to establish trust and build a relationship that then allows him or her to identify and address individual needs. Working with recognized leaders within the community will assist the social worker to be identified as trustworthy and as a viable resource. Residents' groups, such as tenant councils or community social organizations, provide the social worker with a forum to present general information about available resources and assistance as well as the opportunity to socialize and engage with the residents. These meetings also give the workers information regarding the outstanding concerns and needs of the community. There are a variety of ways to connect with community residents. When introducing new service providers to the community, the social work team, with their colleagues from other disciplines, could arrange for a social gathering, an open house, for example. This event can be advertised through the distribution of flyers throughout the community, inviting all to participate. With an eye toward collaboration and cooperation, the workers can give community leaders an active role in planning the event. This not only assures their support of the effort, but also allows them the opportunity to encourage the larger community to participate. Light refreshments can be served, encouraging community members to sit and converse with each other and with you. The social service teams can take turns giving short presentations describing their role in the community and answer any questions the audience may have about their work and their presence. Games can be developed with small, dollar store prizes available for those who participate. Handouts are prepared that give more information about areas of interest. For example, handouts listing various tips on staying warm in the winter or cool in the summer, recipes for healthy, affordable meals for one, or a list of area senior centers may be helpful.

During the event, the social workers must also "work the room," introducing themselves to individuals and chatting with them to establish a comfortable rapport. All service providers should not only be prepared to provide contact information to the participants, but also to gather contact information from them. *Asking permission to remain in contact is important.* It reflects the worker's respect of their individual rights and sends the message that the worker is interested in their well-being, not in being intrusive and controlling. An event such as an open house can jump-start the work of the social service providers in a community. In socializing with the residents, the providers are seen as more human and approachable.

CASE 13.3 | BUILDING BRIDGES

A team of two first-year MSW interns and one senior BSW student were assigned to a senior high-rise building to provide services as needed by the residents. The students were joined at the site by two undergraduate nursing students and a mental health counselor. This group of providers was able to access only a few of the community's residents, and those encounters were very infrequent. They came together and discussed ways in which they might reach more people who would benefit from their help. They asked to meet with the tenant council members and talked with them about the community and its members. During this discussion they were told of several deaths that had occurred in this building over the past year. The people who had died were long-time residents who succumbed to advanced age and illness. The council identified their own grief over these losses, describing the difficulty in seeing one's contemporaries die and there being no mention of them again. The social workers decided to address this sense of loss by planning and implementing a memorial service to honor those neighbors and friends who had passed in recent years. The council

members were asked to assist in the planning of the event, thus making it culturally relevant for this community. A local pastor was contacted and agreed to speak. One resident invited their church choir to sing. A local florist donated flowers, and each of the service providers donated some light refreshments. The BSW team created a beautiful poster board display of pictures and other memorabilia of the now deceased residents. Flyers were distributed and posted throughout the building. The event was held in the community room of the building and was attended by many of the residents. They were able to celebrate the lives of these former neighbors and friends, while being able to collectively grieve their loss with the respectful support of the social workers and other service providers. At the completion of the service, as refreshments were shared, the residents socialized with each other and the providers, sharing many stories of their time in the community. In the weeks that followed, the service teams found the residents much more receptive to their visits, actually seeking them out for assistance when needed.

ADVOCACY

Social workers are guided in practice by the mission statement and Code of Ethics of NASW. The preamble states that the primary mission of the social work profession is to enhance human well-being and help meet the basic human needs of all people, with particular attention to the needs and empowerment of people who are vulnerable, oppressed, and living in poverty. In addition, one of the six values and ethical principles is shown in Figure 13.10.

As stated, the NASW expects social workers to pursue social change on behalf of those most vulnerable in our society. Certainly, many of the elder population, by nature of their advanced age and increased needs, fall into the vulnerable category. Considering the ageism present in contemporary society, social workers can begin their work with this population by addressing the negative attitudes and stereotypes directed at the aging cohort. Ageism starts young. Advertisements for anti-aging products send both subtle and blatant messages in worship of youth. From wrinkle creams to plastic surgery, marketing firms hook the audience with a message that they must remain young in order to remain worthy participants in culture. Those identified as elderly have endured rejection or invisibility, and are seen to be invalid, unworthy, and irrelevant. There is an assumption that all elders display similar sensory losses, behaviors, and general decline. This reflects the myth of homogeneity of the elder population.

Social workers can join in speaking out against ageist beliefs. They can join the many people associated with organizations dedicated to improving conditions for vulnerable, older adults. Two such organizations provide a multitude of supportive initiatives for adults over the age of 50. Perhaps the best known was begun in the late 40s. A retired teacher, Dr. Ethel Percy Andrus started an organization to assist other retirees in finding much needed health insurance. At that time, older adults virtually had no health insurance available to them. She also promoted her strong belief in productive aging. This early organization was the National Retired Teachers Association. Dr. Andrus soon realized that the need for advocacy extended beyond retired teachers and the American Association for Retired Persons (AARP) was born. Dr. Andrus and her organization were instrumental in the passage of Medicare, the government senior health insurance program. Today, the organization boasts over 39 million members aged 50 and above, and it provides much more than affordable insurance coverage. The organizational mission is "to enhance quality of life for all as we age. We lead positive social change and deliver

Ethical Principle: *Social workers challenge social injustice.*

Social workers pursue social change, particularly with and on behalf of vulnerable and oppressed individuals and groups of people. Social workers' social change efforts are focused primarily on issues of poverty, unemployment, discrimination, and other forms of social injustice. These activities seek to promote sensitivity to and knowledge about oppression and cultural and ethnic diversity. Social workers strive to ensure access to needed information, services, and resources; equality of opportunity; and meaningful participation in decision making for all people.

FIGURE 13.10 | SOCIAL JUSTICE

Source: NASW Code of Ethics, 1999

value to members through information, advocacy and service" (AARP, n.d.). AARP provides goods and services for its membership, supports research and education regarding issues important to adults 50 and above, and lobbies for positive change in policies affecting older adults. Another group supporting political and social change came into being in the 1970s when several friends who were retiring from social work and religious careers gathered to create an organization to "*look at the common problems faced by retirees – loss of income, loss of contact with associates and loss of one of our society's most distinguishing social roles, one's job*" (Gray Panthers, n.d.). The organization grew and was ultimately named the Gray Panthers. Today, the Gray Panthers still actively is seeking social and economic justice and peace for all through honoring maturity, unifying generations, active engagement, and participatory involvement. Social workers can take up the charge, working locally in their communities, providing education that dispels the myths surrounding aging, and supports understanding throughout the generations. The older generations have much wisdom they have gained in surviving many challenges in the life and experiencing the world as it has grown and changed. The social worker can advocate for opportunities to have this wisdom shared and appreciated by the younger generations. Assisting in developing intergenerational programming will provide positive outcomes for all involved.

Another area in which the generalist social worker may work and advocate for change is in the field of long-term care. Traditionally, nursing homes have provided a last-choice option in the provision of care for physically disabled and debilitated older adults who could no longer be maintained in their homes. Many families have struggled with the decision of placing their loved one in long-term care once the level of need exceeded their capacity to provide the care. Given the dearth of alternatives, families have experienced the anxiety and tremendous guilt that comes with having to place a cherished family member into a nursing home. Often, they not only suffer the recriminations of their loved one who wants only to stay in their own home, but also of their community at large who are ignorant of the overwhelming demands required to keep a physically dependent adult at home. Most people do not plan to move to nursing home care. It is thrust upon them when their health severely declines and their care needs intensify and they are no longer able to be cared for at home. As the cost of institutional care has increased (to levels at times over $5000 per month), and the quality of that care has come under scrutiny, society has been forced to look to other resources to meet this need (Consumer Affairs, 2004; Silverstone, 2005). The aging cohort of baby boomers is also driving the desire to develop creative alternatives to the traditional medical-model nursing home care. Under the medical model, nursing home residents are identified as patients, and their care needs are labeled with diagnoses that require treatment. As in a hospital, their caregivers are nurses and aides who schedule treatment regiments around their shift schedule, not the convenience of the patient. Thus, patients are forced to bathe, eat, socialize, and even toilet on the staff's schedule, not their own. Such patients do not live, but merely exist in a world unfamiliar to them and out of their control.

One creative response to the challenges presented by nursing home care is the Eden Alternative. Dr. William Thomas identified the three plagues of the human spirit after working in a nursing home: loneliness, helplessness, and boredom (Eden Alternative, n.d.). He recognized that the current medical model of nursing home care was warehousing elders, not providing the loving care they deserved. He developed what he termed The Eden Alternative, proposing an approach to elder care that involves them, respects them, and while providing necessary physical care, also nurtures spiritual, social care. Some of the principles of the alternative are provision of close contact with plants, animals, and children; a daily agenda that includes spontaneity, unexpected and unpredictable interactions to fend off boredom; and inviting involvement from the elders and their loved ones in decision making at the facility (Eden Alternative, n.d.). This approach to providing humanistic care for our elderly is in line with the social work perspective of seeing the client's strengths and understanding that each client is an integral part of his or her environment, with all systems interacting and supporting each other. As the number of elderly increases over the next decade, social workers will be called upon to present choices to their clients, focusing on their individual needs, prime among them their need to thrive in their environment. In another response to the nursing home challenge, agencies are developing programs that provide affordable intensive care in the home. Also, adult day-care programs allow family caregivers options to return to work or pursue interests while their loved one attends a day program that stimulates socialization and activity outside of the home. These alternatives are helping to reduce the number of admissions to nursing facilities. Social workers are working to support this trend toward progressive care of the elderly, both in the legislature and in the field.

CASE MANAGEMENT

One of the most vital services provided in social work with geriatric clients is case management. Various agencies and service providers employ case workers or care managers and define this work in different ways. Case management is primarily an intervention in which a human service professional assesses the needs of the client, plans an optimum package of services to meet those needs, links the client to community resources, then monitors the provision of arranged services, and finally advocates for the client in a variety of ways (Morrow-Howell, 1992). Today, case management can range from basic assessment and provision of purely concrete services to a combination of assessment, consultation with families, collaboration with other treatment providers, psychoeducation and supportive counseling, and crisis interventions as needed to meet the needs of the individual client (Kanter, 1989). The latter approach is called clinical case management and is particularly efficacious in working with elderly clients who have multiple challenges and needs and have numerous health and social service providers involved. The clinical case manager is able to coordinate services and assist the elder and the family in navigating the various systems, and provide supportive counseling.

While there are agencies that use untrained workers to provide connection to concrete services and even some who use volunteers to provide such support, the social worker is uniquely trained to meet the needs of the older, more vulnerable population and apply the dual focus on person and environment. With the upcoming demands to respond to an aging population, geriatric case management services are extremely valuable and in demand, as evidenced by the increasing number of private geriatric case managers (PGCM). The National Association of Professional Geriatric

Care Managers (NAPGCM) defines the care worker as a "health and human services specialist who helps families who are caring for older relatives. The PGCM is trained and experienced in any of several fields related to long-term care, including, but not limited to nursing, gerontology, social work, or psychology, with a specialized focus on issues related to aging and elder care" (National Association of Geriatric Care Managers, n.d.). The NAGCM recognizes four certificates of competency in the field of geriatric case management. They are as follows: Care Manager Certified (CMC); Certified Case Manager (CCM); Certified Advanced Social Worker in Case Management (C-ASWCM) requiring a MSW degree; and Certified Social Work Case Manager (C-SWCM) requiring a BSW degree. The NASW provides credentialing for Social Work Case managers, recognizing the level of professionalism needed to guarantee the provision of quality services to the general population (NASW, n.d.).

This trend will likely continue, if not expand, with the increase in numbers of older adults with special needs. Social workers who provide geriatric clinical case management services combining concrete service provision with supportive counseling and psychosocial support will continue to be in demand. It is a win-win approach to work with the elderly. Many older adults only access services as a means of connecting with a particular concrete support. It is through the successful building of the relationship with their generalist social worker that they access a variety of needed services. Kantor (1989) makes the point that a client-centered approach combines individual supportive work, teaching independent living skills, reflective listening with clarifying and interpretive responses, information provision, and monitoring compliance. Without these, the linkage to various services is useless in preventing destabilization and crisis (Morrow-Howell, 1992). In order to assist the client in making real changes that will enhance their late-life experience, the social worker must see that basic needs are met and that an ongoing relationship is fostered. Through a thorough assessment, the social worker can begin to determine and prioritize those needs while building trust and engagement, and thus an ongoing relationship with the client.

LIFE REVIEW

Many theorists have informed our understanding of the psychosocial responses to aging. Erikson wrote of psychosocial stages of development throughout the life cycle. He described the tasks to be accomplished and the conflicts to be faced in each stage. Keep in mind that this model is meant to provide a theoretical overview of our growth and development. It is not intended to be used as a measure of one's success or failure. Differences are expected from individual to individual within and between each stage. Erikson described in the eighth stage of development, later adulthood, ages 60–75, that the individual is facing the psychosocial crisis of integrity versus despair, with introspection being the central process (Erikson, 1963, 1968, 1982; Erikson et al., 1986, as cited in Hooyman and Kiyak, 2002). He explained that older adults were coming to grips with their own mortality and looking to share their life lessons and personal wisdom with younger generations. Various modes of intervention have been researched for their effectiveness in working with older adults. Reminiscence or life review therapy (Butler, 1963) is particularly popular and efficacious given the life stage of the client as described by Erikson. Reviewing one's life allows for examination and introspection wherein the individual is able to appreciate and celebrate their successes as defined personally, while re-evaluating, processing, and reframing those perceived failings and regrets. This is a very useful tool for the social worker to use when working with the older client. As engagement and trust have been established, the worker can then encourage the clients to share their thoughts and knowledge about life, about their ability to survive the challenges they faced, and give them the opportunity to pass along their wisdom and advice regarding the meaning of life. When faced with clients who reflect despair in reviewing their life, finding little success to celebrate can be gently guided by the social worker to reframe their negative memories as coping strategies that allowed them to survive. In very old age, 75 and above, the individual grapples with immortality versus extinction and, again, reviewing one's life and sharing one's life story supports the desire to leave something behind. Specifically, life review encourages a look back at life events in such a way as to give meaning to one's present circumstances. This allows an older adult to find comfort and satisfaction in a life well-lived and highlights positive coping mechanisms that will help to support them as they deal with issues related to aging. Robert Butler (as cited in Weiss, n.d.) stated the goal of life review therapy to be helping the client attain and maintain a consistent view of self in the face of age-related decline. Life review also helps to build and sustain the client–worker relationship, allowing the worker to share the client's reality as he or she describes the intimacies of his or her life. Asking the clients open-ended questions about their life stimulates the telling of their unique story and provides a forum for exploring and emphasizing their strengths in overcoming the many challenges they faced during their lifetime.

SUPPORTIVE COUNSELING

A standard form of intervention used by the social worker is validation of feelings and supportive counseling. Supportive counseling puts to use active communication skills, including reflective listening and collaborative problem solving. Validation helps the client to identify and accept their feelings, while working with the social worker to find appropriate ways to express these feelings to others in their environment. Both validation and support empower the older client to be an active participant in the development and implementation of his or her care plan, whether it is to achieve a personal goal or is a more complicated combination of goals and services to address a variety of needs. In referencing the case of Mrs. Cleaver, the social worker would validate her feelings of loss and resentment at having to leave her home and move in with her daughter. Through supportive counseling, the worker would also facilitate Mrs. C.'s communication with her daughter and with others in her environment to assist her in regaining her sense of control over her life and identifying areas of strength and resilience. Such an outcome can be defined as successful adaptation (Greene and Cohen, 2005). Successful aging is a concept that recognizes the challenges and risks that are faced by individuals as they move through life. It is their ability to negotiate these risks and adapt to the implied changes that reflect a measure of resilience that contributes to successfully advancing in age. A client, made aware of his or her resilience across the life span, is given hope that positive change is possible and empowered to engage in the process of effecting that change (Greene and Cohen, 2005).

Supportive counseling is very useful in responding to grief reactions in the elderly. Given the life stage, many older adults experience the loss of one's spouse and/or contemporaries. Older adults are also experiencing the subtle losses of physical prowess and functional abilities. Widowhood can be especially stressful and may put the person at risk for declining health, mental illness, and even death and suicide (Raveis, 1999). In cases when the spouse is caring for a terminally ill loved one, the social worker can facilitate communication between them, thus helping the surviving spouse prepare for the impending change and loss. While grief is a natural response to loss, prolonged grief can put older adults at extreme risk. However, provision of supportive counseling with nonjudgmental listening, validation of feelings, and encouragement toward healing can reduce the risk of prolonged grief and health decline (Hooyman, 2002).

COGNITIVE-BEHAVIORAL THERAPY

It is important for the generalist social worker in direct service positions to have some understanding of the various therapeutic interventions available and effective with older adults in order to plan and implement appropriate referrals (Popple and Leighninger as cited in Vandsburger, Crawley-Woods, Gottlieb, and Shelek-Furbee, 2005). There are many possible approaches available when working with the older adult. In the late 19th and early 20th century, Freud declared psychodynamic psychotherapy to be contraindicated in work with older adults. He argued that the mind of adults over the age of 50 was too inflexible to effectively engage in the process of psychotherapy (Leigh and Varghese, 2001). Fortunately, age is no longer considered a barrier to effective psychotherapeutic interventions. In actuality, even older adults who have mild cognitive decline can still participate and benefit from some forms of psychotherapy (Leigh and Varghese, 2001). Cognitive-behavioral therapy (CBT) and interpersonal psychotherapy have been found to be effective models of treatment for elderly clients who present with behavioral symptoms requiring intervention. Both have been studied in relation to treatment of late-age depression and anxiety (Hillman and Stricker, 2002). In psychodynamic psychotherapy, the client explores internal conflicts and works with the therapist to discover new understanding about the ways these conflicts informed their maladaptive behaviors and thinking, creating an opening for resolution and change.

In CBT, the counselor assists the client in recognizing negative thought patterns that influence behavior and feelings. Once exposed, the client is instructed in ways to alter their thoughts with exercises such as deep breathing and relaxation, journaling, and rewards. Some of these exercises must be modified taking into account any age-related changes in the learning capacity of the client. With moderately cognitively impaired adults, the therapist can use techniques of behavior modification wherein new, positive behaviors are presented and, as learned and practiced by the client, the behaviors are rewarded and sustained (Hyer, Kramer, and Sohnie, 2004). As previously mentioned, life review therapy has been shown to have positive results in working with older adults. Using techniques from both life review and CBT helps older clients review and reevaluate their life experiences and then reframe them, thus helping the older client to find positive meaning and purpose in their life (Weiss, n.d.). Using a combined, integrative approach with older clients based on their particular biopsychosocial presentation promotes the best outcome for the client (Hillman and Stricker, 2002).

SUMMARY

Due to changes in the mortality rate, advances in medical science, and the large number of individuals born in the wake of World War II, it is predicted that by 2030, 20% of the U.S. population will be over the age of 60. Specifically, there will be more people than ever over the age of 80. This generation of elders will live longer, be more mobile, more economically self-sufficient, and more politically active than previous geriatric cohorts, and they will be more diverse in terms of race and ethnicity. There will be a majority of women, and many of them will live alone. Despite the advances in medical care, this population will be facing the physical decline of old age; as such they face vulnerability and will require an inordinate amount of services from the social work community. They will also consume a greater share of these and other services than any previous generation. Though overall this generation is wealthier than previous genera-

tions, the increase in numbers also means an increase in the number of poor or near-poor elderly.

To the social worker at the dawn of this age, it is vital to hone the skills of cultural competence, clinical case management, and working in community, as all of these skills will be amply drawn upon when working with this cohort. A working knowledge of medical symptoms and care will also be requisite in working with this population.

Support for caregivers will be in high demand, as 24-hour care is prohibitively expensive, and therefore more families and individuals will be caring for aging parents or relatives. Understanding such issues as geriatric depression, drug and alcohol addiction in the elderly, and the working of ageism in our society are all key issues for the geriatric social worker as well as the generalist social worker in the years to come.

CASE EXAMPLE

The following case example illustrates the importance of patience and persistence in working with elderly clients. It is an excellent example of an empowering approach to building the relationship between the generalist social worker and the client.

CASE 13.4 | **NO ONE CAN STAND HER**

Tiffany is a first-year MSW student assigned to the Spring Haven Nursing Home for her first field placement. Her tasks include daily interactions with residents of the home and biweekly meetings with nursing home staff to discuss issues and concerns with the long-term care residents. At her first meeting, she is told about a resident, Mrs. K., who is a "problem" on the New Castle wing. It is reported that she has been a resident for 4 years, is consistently resistant to care, and is confrontational with staff and other residents. The staff report that she often refuses care, and they must then restrain her and bathe her forcefully as it is a state requirement that she be kept clean. This was the case 2 days ago and Mrs. K. is still "acting out." Yesterday, she threw a book at her

roommate, and now the roommate and her family are insisting that she be moved. Mrs. K. has been moved four times in the past year due to such confrontations. The staff tells Tiffany that she needs to "control this woman" before she seriously injures somebody. Tiffany asks for more information regarding Mrs. K.'s history and overall condition. She is informed that Mrs. K was admitted to Spring Haven after a fall in her home left her immobilized. Physical therapy was attempted, but Mrs. K reported too much pain to continue. This resulted in the family deciding that she must stay at Spring Haven for long-term care as they could not provide such intensive care in the home. They sold her home in order to pay for the care and, once the money was gone, Mrs. K. was placed on Medicaid,

CASE 13.4 | *Continued*

which covers the cost of her care. Mrs. K is wheelchair bound, has some symptoms of early dementia, has chronic pain from her injury, and is diabetic. Tiffany asks about visits from her family and is told the family stopped visiting three and a half years ago because of Mrs. K.'s behavior. Now, they come in on holidays, but only stay a short time, usually talking more with the staff and other residents than with Mrs. K., because "no one can stand her." Tiffany decides to visit Mrs. K. in her room and begin the engagement process. Tiffany takes some time to tune in to possible feelings Mrs. K. may have about her situation. Tiffany reflects on the feelings of loss of home and independence and wonders about Mrs. K.'s previous relationships with her family and friends. Tiffany also thinks about the anger that Mrs. K. is expressing and wonders about her feelings of frustration at having others bathe and dress her.

On the day of her visit, Tiffany approaches Mrs. K. calmly and with a smile. Mrs. K. is not receptive, frowning and telling Tiffany to "get out!" Tiffany replies that she is sorry that now is not a good time for a visit and will return later, respecting Mrs. K.'s demand. Tiffany tries several more times over the next week to visit with Mrs. K. Each time she is turned away. On the fifth attempt, Mrs. K. nods and allows Tiffany to approach. Tiffany speaks softly and respectfully with Mrs. K., asking for permission to sit and spend time with her. Tiffany assures Mrs. K. that she will respect her wishes and her confidentiality. Mrs. K. responds positively to Tiffany's efforts to return some control to her life. Tiffany allows Mrs. K. to lead the conversation and validates her feelings of anger and frustration at being "disrespected" by others at the nursing home. Mrs. K. agrees to a return visit, asking that Tiffany come at a particular time between television shows that she watches. Tiffany complies with this request and they begin to meet biweekly. Tiffany uses a life review approach with Mrs. K., asking about her early life and her family. Tiffany discovers that Mrs. K. was widowed very early in her life and struggled to work and raise her son alone. Sadly, her son died of AIDS in the early 1990s, and Mrs. K. is still feeling guilty that she wasn't more accepting of his lifestyle, even though she took care of him until his death. Mrs. K. also expresses great sadness at losing her home where she and her son spent the last days of his life. She doesn't understand why her family has placed her here and what has happened to her treasured belongings. Tiffany asks for permission to talk with the family and speaks with Mrs. K.'s niece. The niece shares that the family still feels guilty about having to place Mrs. K. at Spring Haven. The doctors advised them that Mrs. K. was no longer able to walk, and they realized a nursing home was the only option. The hospital social worker helped them find Spring Haven, and they admitted Mrs. K. straight from the hospital. Although they know it has been the correct decision, it still hurts them. Tiffany asks both the niece and Mrs. K. to come together to express their feelings to each other. This meeting goes very well and, although Mrs. K. still doesn't quite understand why she can't go home, she loves her niece and asks her to visit more often, promising her a warmer reception. The niece agrees to bring in some of Mrs. K.'s belongings remaining from the sale of her home to decorate Mrs. K.'s room at Spring Haven. Among these belongings is a picture of Mrs. K. and her son, which takes a place of honor on her dresser. In future visits, the niece and Mrs. K. begin to reminisce about times spent together with her son and other family members.

Tiffany speaks to the nursing home staff about ways to include Mrs. K. in the scheduling of her daily activities. The staff insists they must maintain a rigid schedule to serve all the residents under their care. Tiffany asks them to participate in problem solving, and they decide to offer at least two options to Mrs. K., allowing her to pick between two times for bathing or eating. This helps to restore a sense of agency and control to Mrs. K. After much discussion, the staff agrees to a trial period of 1 month. While there is some difficulty at the start, by the end of the month, the staff reports that Mrs. K. is now much more compliant with care. She still has her moments, according to her nurses' aides, but she will generally settle down when given options. Staff also reports that Mrs. K. is attending facility activities with more regularity than before. They also report that she is less forgetful and more engaged with other residents. Tiffany continues to visit Mrs. K. weekly and enjoys talking with her about her life and her loves. Mrs. K. shares stories about her work at the

(Continued)

CASE 13.4 | *Continued*

munitions factory during World War II, referring to herself as a real-life "Rosie the Riveter." On Veteran's Day, Mrs. K. is asked to speak at the honorary luncheon held at the home and is delighted to share her memories with others.

Through careful and deliberate preparation, assessment, and planning, Tiffany has been able to assist Mrs. K. in improving the quality of her life at Spring Haven. Tiffany correctly identified Mrs. K.'s strengths, respecting the years of self-reliance and effort put into being a single mother and the sole breadwinner of her family. She also recognized Mrs. K.'s struggle to regain some control over her life and her frustration at being forced into total dependence. Using these strengths, Tiffany was able to involve Mrs. K., her niece and the facility staff in problem solving, collaborating, and creating a workable treatment plan.

Discussion Questions

1. How would you have responded to the nursing home staff when presented with the problems they were having with Mrs. K.? What would your plan be to control this woman? What safety issues should be considered?

2. When tuning in to this client, what feelings do you think she would have given the initial information given? What do you believe would be the best way to approach a person who may be threatening and aggressive?

3. The social worker asked the client for permission to contact the niece, although she was her legal guardian. Who would have been your initial contact and why? Given the diagnosis of early dementia, perhaps the client would be unable to participate in logical conversation. Would you want to spend valuable time engaging with this client? How would you compensate for any cognitive loss in your interactions with the client?

4. Mrs. K. mentions that she was unable to accept her son's lifestyle. How would you have handled this revelation? When faced with a situation that is counter to your values, how do you address it?

5. The staff members of the nursing home are professionals and have busy and intensive work schedules. How would you have worked with them to meet the needs of your client while respecting their intense schedule? As a student, how would you react to being responsible for approaching this professional staff and asking for change?

6. Working in a nursing home environment that functions from a problem-focused perspective can be challenging for the strengths-based social worker. What options would you explore to meet these challenges?

7. As the numbers of physically challenged older adults increase the demand for in-home services, what are some ideas for creative programming that will be able to meet these needs?

8. The increasing elderly population demands an increase in the number of trained social workers to assist the older adults and their families cope with the changes of old age. How would you suggest recruiting new social workers into this field of study?

References

AARP Public Policy Institute (2006). Across the States: Profiles in Long Term Care. Retrieved June 6, 2008 from http://assets.aarp.org/rgcenter/general/profile_2005.pdf

AARP History (n.d.). Retrieved June 6, 2008 from http://www.aarp.org/about_aarp/aarp_overview/a2003–01–13–aarphistory.html

Ahmed, I., and Takeshita, J. (1996–1997). Late-life depression. *Generations, 20,* 17–21.

American Association of Suicidology (2005). Retrieved June 6, 2008 from http://www.suicidology.org/associations/1045/files/2005 elderly.pdf

American Psychiatric Association (2000). *Diagnostic and statistical manual of mental disorders* (text revision). Washington, DC: Author.

Ascension Health (n.d.). *Patient Self-Determination Act of 1990.* Retrieved August 8, 2008 from http://www.ascensionhealth.org/ethics/public/issues/patient_self.asp

Beck, A. T, and Steer, R. A. (1984). Internal consistencies of the original and revised Beck Depression Inventory. *Journal of Clinical Psychology, 40*(6), 1365–1367.

Bergel, D. P. (2006). Baccalaureate social work education and courses on aging: The disconnect. *The Journal of Baccalaureate Social Work, 12*(1), 105–118.

Bonder, B., Martin, L., and Miracle, A. (2001). Achieving cultural competence: The challenge for clients and healthcare workers in a multicultural society. *Generations, 25*(1) 35–42.

Butler, R. (1963). The life review: An interpretation of reminiscence in the aged. *Psychiatry 26,* 65–76.

Butler, R. N., Lewis, M., and Sunderland, R. (1991). *Aging and Mental Health: Positive psychosocial and biomedical approaches* (3rd ed.) New York: Merrill/Macmillian.

Consumer Affairs (2004). Nursing home cost hits $70,000 per year. Retrieved September 20, 2008 from www.consumeraffairs.com/news04/nursing_home_costs.html

Cummings, S. M., and Galambos, C. (2004). *Diversity and aging in the social environment.* New York: Hawthorn Social Work Practice Press.

Dept. of Health and Human Services Administration on Aging Mission (n.d.). Retrieved June 6, 2008 from http://www.aoa.gov/about/over/over_mission.aspx

Eden Alternative (n.d.). Our Ten Principles. Retrieved June 6, 2008 from http://www.edenalt.org/about/our-10-principles.html

Endicott, J. and Spitzer, R. L. (1978). A diagnostic interview: The schedule for affective disorders and schizophrenia. *Archives of General Psychiatry, 35*(7), 837–844.

Gelfand, D. E. (1993). *The aging network: Programs and services* (4th ed.). New York: Springer.

Genevay, B. (1997). See me! Hear me! Know who I am! An experience of being assessed. *Generations, 21*(1), 16–18.

Geron, S. M. (2002). Cultural competency: How is it measured? Does it make a difference? *Generations 26*(3), 39–45.

Gray Panthers Age and Youth in Action (n.d.). Gray Panthers' Founding. Retrieved June 6, 2008 from http://graypanthers.org/index.php?option=com_content&task=view&id=25&Itemid=17

Greene, R. R., and Cohen, H. L. (2005). Social work with older adults and their families: Changing practice paradigms. *Families in Society, 86*(3), 367–373.

Hill, R. D. (2005). *Positive aging: A guide for mental health professionals and consumers.* New York: W. W. Norton & Company.

Hillman, J., and Stricker, G. (2002). A call for psychotherapy integration in work with older adult patients. *Journal of Psychotherapy Integration, 12*(4), 395–405.

Holosko, M. J., and Feit, M. D. (2004). *Social work practice with the elderly* (3rd ed.). Toronto, Canada: Canadian Scholars' Press.

Hooyman, N. R. (2002). The future of gerontological social work. Special lecture, School of Social Welfare, University of California-Berkeley.

Hooyman, N. R., and Kiyak, H. A. (2002). *Social gerontology: A multidisciplinary perspective* (6th ed.). Boston: Allyn & Bacon.

Horowitz, A. (2003). Depression and vision and hearing impairments in later life. *Generations, 7*(1), 32–38.

Hyer, L., Kramer, D., and Sohnie, S. (2004). CBT with older people: alterations and the value of the therapeutic alliance. *Psychotherapy: Theory, Research, Practice, Training, 41*(3), 276–291.

Kanter, J. (1989). Clinical case management: Definition, principles, components. *Hospital Community Psychiatry, 40,* 361–368.

Leigh, R., and Varghese, F. (2001). Psychodynamic psychotherapy with the elderly. *Journal of Psychiatric Practice, 7,* 229–237.

McInnis-Dittrich, K. (2002). *Social work with elders: A biopsychosocial approach to assessment and intervention.* Boston: Allyn & Bacon.

Marson, D. (2002). Competency assessment and research in an aging society. *Generations, 26*(1), 99–103.

Morrow–Howell, N. (1992). Clinical case management: The hallmark of gerontological social work. In M. J. Mellor and R. Solomon (Eds.), *Geriatric Social Work Education* (pp. 19–131), New York: Haworth Press, Inc.

Moutier, C., Wetherell, J. L., and Zisook, S. (2003). Combined psychotherapy and pharmacotherapy for late-life depression. *Geriatric Times, 4*(5), 14–15.

National Association of Geriatric Care Managers (n.d.). What is a geriatric care manager? Retrieved June 6, 2008 from http://www.caremanager.org/displaycommon.cfm?an=1&subarticlenbr=76

National Association of Social Workers (1990). Code of Ethics. Retrieved June 6, 2008 from www.socialworkers.org/pubs/Code/code.asp

National Association of Social Workers (a) (n.d.). Aging. Retrieved September 20, 2008 from http://www.socialworkers.org/aging.asp

National Association of Social Workers. (b) (n.d.). New aging specialty credentials. Retrieved June 6, 2008 from http://www.socialworkers.org/credentials/specialty/aging.asp

Neeman, L. (1995). Using the therapeutic relationship to promote an internal locus of control in elderly mental health clients. *Journal of Gerontological Social Work, 23*(3/4), 161–176.

O'Neil, M. (2007). Depression in the elderly. *The Journal of Continuing Education in Nursing 38*(1), 14–15.

O'Shaughnessy, C. V. (2008). The Basics: The Older American's Act of 1965, National Health Policy Forum, Background Paper. Retrieved June 6, 2008 from http://www.nhpf.org/pdfs_basics/Basics_OlderAmericansAct_04-21-08.pdf

Rando, T. A. (1984). *Grief, dying, and death: Clinical interventions for caregivers*. Michigan: Research Press, Inc.

Raveis, V. H. (1999). Facilitating older spouses' adjustment to widowhood: A preventive intervention program. *Social Work in Health Care, 29*, 13–32.

Reich, J. W., and Zautra, A. J. (1989). A perceived control intervention for at-risk older adults. *Psychology and Aging, 4*, 415–424.

Silverstone, B. (2005). Social work with the older people of tomorrow: Restoring the person-in-situation. *Families in Society, 8*(3), 309–319.

Sluzki, C. E. (2000). Social networks and the elderly: conceptual and clinical issues and a family consultation. *Family Process, 39*(3), 271–284.

Thomas, N. D. (2005). Generalist practice with older people. In J. E. Poulin (Ed.), *Strengths-based Generalist Practice: A Collaborative Approach* (2nd ed.) (pp. 366–397). Belmont, CA: Brooks/Cole-Thomson Learning.

United States Bureau of Census (2000). Retrieved April 28, 2008 from http://factfinder.census.gov/servlet/DTTable?_bm=y&-geo_id=01000US&-ds_name=DEC_2000_SF3_U&-mt_name=DEC_2000_SF3_U_PCT049

United States Bureau of Census. (2006). Retrieved September 20, 2008 from http://factfinder.census.gov/servlet/ACSSAFFFacts?

United States Bureau of Census (2008). Retrieved September 20, 2008 from http://census.gov/population/www/projections/summarytables.html

Vandsburger, E., Crawley– Woods, G., Gottlieb, J., and Shelek–Furbee, K. (2005). Applying a stress and resiliency framework for teaching adult development and aging throughout the social work undergraduate-level curriculum. *The Journal of Baccalaureate Social Work*, Special Issue, 67–81.

Wetherell, J. L. (1998). Treatment of anxiety in older adults. *Psychotherapy: Theory, Research, Practice, and Training, 35*(4), 444–458.

Weiss, J. C. (n.d.). Cognitive therapy and life review therapy: Theoretical and therapeutic implications for mental health counselors. *Journal of Mental Health Counseling*, 157–172.

Wenger, G. C. (1997). Social networks and the prediction of elderly people at risk. *Aging and Mental Health, 1*(4), 311–320.

World Health Organization. (2002). *Active aging: a policy framework*. Retrieved September 20, 2008, from http://whqlibdoc.who.int/hq/2002/WHO_NMH_NPH_02.8.PDF

World Health Organization. (2008). *Age-friendly cities* (Publication Ageing and Life Course, Family and Community Health). Retrieved April 28, 2008, from http://www.who.int/ageing/age_friendly_cities/en/print.html

Generalist Practice with Gay, Lesbian, Bisexual, and Transgender People

CHAPTER 14

Brent A. Satterly and Don A. Dyson

Jeff Christensen/Reuters/Landov

Shanay is an MSW student doing her foundation year field placement at a local community-based counseling center. After a few months, Shanay has numerous cases and is feeling relatively comfortable providing services to a variety of different populations. Recently, Shanay started seeing a few clients who identify themselves as sexual minorities. This was a new experience for Shanay, as she has not had much personal experience with people who are gay, lesbian, bisexual, or transgender.

As Shanay works with these new clients, she finds herself feeling some discomfort because she has never known or worked with a folks who were different from her in this way before. While Shanay has never been a religious person, her family's values have clearly sent the message that being gay is not normal. Shanay's reading of the *NASW Code of Ethics* has left her in a quandary. Is Shanay supposed to give her clients "permission" to be open about their sexuality? Is Shanay "culturally competent" if she refers these clients to another intern? What is in the best interest of her clients? Shanay is unsure what to do.

This scenario is not uncommon. Many social work students struggle with understanding human sexuality, specifically sexual orientation and gender identity. This chapter will explore sexual minority individuals and their communities. Definitions of gay, lesbian, bisexual, transgender, queer, and questioning (GLBTQQ), forces of oppression, social policies, and social work practice interventions will be examined. At the end of this chapter, you should be able to help Shanay:

1. Understand basic identities of gay, lesbian, bisexual, and transgender clients
2. Conduct a strengths-based assessment of GLBT clients
3. Assess personal and environmental client strengths and obstacles
4. Identify best practices for working with her GLBT clients
5. Use an evidence-based practice technique (cognitive-behavioral therapy) to help GLBT clients set and achieve measurable goals and objectives

CLIENT POPULATION NEEDS AND CIRCUMSTANCES

Individuals construct their identities throughout their lifetimes. Mother, social worker, Christian, Black are all identities that people develop and express in different ways. Some of these identities are a result of family roles, culture, demographic variables, faith, field of study, and so forth. The term "sexual minority" is a term used to describe a wide variety of people who identify as gay, lesbian, bisexual, transgender, queer, questioning, and intersex. This client population is varied and diverse. In this chapter, the authors will use GLBT (gay, lesbian, bisexual, and transgender) to refer to this diverse population.

In order to understand some of the needs of this unique group, one must first review the vocabulary of identities referring to sexual orientation and gender identity. To accomplish this, this chapter will first walk through sexual orientation terminology, identity development, and the forces of oppression experienced by lesbian, gay, and bisexual individuals. Then, the chapter will then explore gender identity terminology, identity development, and the forces of oppression experienced by transgender individuals. Specific populations will then be addressed. Following this, social policies that affect GLBT clients and recommended social work practice will be discussed. Finally, case studies will be utilized throughout this chapter to exemplify and highlight the information presented.

SEXUAL ORIENTATION

Sexual orientation is a complex and often misunderstood component of human sexuality. Parker (2008) describes sexual orientation as the direction of an individual's erotic, love, and interpersonal feelings toward men, women, or both genders. The terms **heterosexual, gay, lesbian,** or **bisexual** are often used to refer to sexual orientation; however, these are somewhat limiting based upon how an individual understands his or her sexuality. Generally, the term *homosexual*, while often used in historical literature, is not used. Instead, the terms gay, lesbian, or bisexual reflect the choice of the terminology the population uses (Parker, 2007).

The term "queer" emerged in the late twentieth century (Jagose, 1996). Originally used to mean "strange" or "odd," it was later employed as an epithet toward GLBT people. In the 1990s, the sexual minority community embraced the term **queer** as a self-identifier with numerous implications, including empowerment (i.e., using the oppressive term as a positive label) and fluidity of identity. This latter implication embraced individuals who did not feel they fit within the categorical strictures of the terms gay, lesbian, or bisexual.

FORCES OF OPPRESSION

Whenever discussing issues related to a sexual minority sexual orientation, it is negligent to avoid an analysis of the forces of oppression that contribute to the development of prejudicial attitudes and discriminatory behaviors.

Homophobia. Coined by Weinberg (1972), homophobia refers to the irrational fear or hatred of gay people. This definition has been reassessed multiple times to include those suspected of being gay (often predicated upon atypical gender expression) as well as to incorporate the role of internalized homophobia (i.e., self-loathing) in identity development (Weinberg, 1972).

Homophobia can manifest itself in varied ways, ranging from employment discrimination (i.e., not being hired due to the sexual orientation of an applicant) to tragic violent hate crimes (i.e., the death of Matthew Shepard, a gay man who was beaten to death for being gay) to suicide (i.e., a lesbian who kills herself because she does not want to be lesbian). Additionally, this form of oppression can be reflected in negative attitudes of society, limitation of civil rights, condemnation by religious institutions, and familial rejection.

Herek (2000) claimed that the term homophobia was based solely on an irrational fear and therefore too dismissive of the various attitudinal factors that support prejudice. Further, Herek stated that Weinberg's definition did not incorporate the entirety of oppression that sexual minorities experience. He asserted that heterosexism was a more accurate description of the realities of antigay prejudice.

Heterosexism. Like homophobia, heterosexism has similarly undergone a process whereby researchers have attempted to understand, define, and categorize this

phenomenon numerous times. Heterosexism first emerged from the feminist movement: "Audre Lord (1984) described heterosexism as a form of oppression incorporating a belief in the inherent superiority of one form of loving over all others"
(Neisen, 1990, p. 36). The Sexuality Information and Education Council of the US
(SIECUS) considered heterosexism to be "the institutional and societal reinforcement
of heterosexuality as the privileged and powerful norm" (1993, p. 1).

> Neisen (1990) included the issue of power into his definition:
> Heterosexism = Prejudice + Power. Heterosexism is the continued promotion by the major
> institutions of society of a heterosexual lifestyle while simultaneously subordinating any
> other lifestyles (i.e., gay/lesbian/bisexual)...When our institutions knowingly or unknowingly
> perpetuate these prejudices and intentionally or unintentionally act on them, heterosexism is
> at work. (p. 25)

Bi-negativity.   Bi-negativity is a distinctive oppressive force defined by Eliason
(2001) as negative attitudes about bisexuals. Bisexual people often experience bi-
negativity from both heterosexual and gay and lesbian communities (Alexander
and Yescavage, 2003; Eliason, 2001). These attitudes are exemplified in stereotypes such as "bisexuals don't exist"; "bisexual are promiscuous"; and "bisexuals
are actually gay or lesbian people in denial" (Fox, 2006).

ORIENTATION–BEHAVIOR–IDENTITY

Cook and Palowski (1991) distinguish between three separate constructs to aid in
understanding sexual orientation as a whole. Orientation (O) refers to whom a

---

CASE 14.1 | **TONY: EXAMINING SEXUAL ORIENTATION**

The interaction of O (orientation), B (behavior), and I (identity) can better be understood by thinking about one of Shanay's clients, Tony. Tony is a male sopho-more and chemistry major who grew up in a rural community. While Tony often recognized his same-sex sexual feelings growing up, he has never really ex-plored them. Tony's first year of college has introduced him to new experiences, including developing sexual feelings for one of his male friends. Tony is now ques-tioning his sexual identity and thinks he might be gay.

Remember that Tony has recognized his sexual feelings for other guys most of his life. In this case, he might describe his orientation (O) as gay. However, he has never engaged in any behavior (B) with a mem-ber of the same sex. In fact, his sexual behavior has always been with girls, mostly because that was what people in his family and community expected him to do. As a result, his behavior (B) was not consistent with his orientation (O); he was acting in ways that he did not feel were true to who he was inside.

Because Tony lived in a family and community that expected him to like girls, he has always told people that he did, in fact, like girls. He saw how people who were different were treated poorly, beat up on the playground, and harassed in the hallways. He knew that he did not want to lose his friends and family or get hurt. So Tony always identified (I) as heterosexual.

Tony, then, has a gay orientation (O), has only had heterosexual behavior (B), and identifies (I) as heterosexual. What is important to remember in this model is that someone's orientation, behavior, and identity do not always match one another. Someone can have a same-sex sexual encounter (B), but know on the inside that it was not true to how he or she feels inside (O), and therefore not call him or herself gay (I). Engaging in behavior does not "make" some-one gay, lesbian, or bisexual. "Being" gay, lesbian, or bisexual is about how one feels inside, not about what one does sexually or what one calls her or himself.

CASE 14.1 | *Continued*

Put this all together now in considering Shanay's client Tony again.

Tony grew up in a suburban region outside of Philadelphia. Like many of his peers, he received homophobic societal messages from his family, his friends, his church, and his TV shows: "Gay people are sick" or "Lesbians are sinful." Because of heterosexism, Tony's parents also assumed that he was heterosexual and expected that he would get married and have children.

Tony's orientation (O) is a Kinsey 6; he is romantically and sexually attracted exclusively to men. Because he struggled with his own internalized homophobia (i.e., recognizing his attractions and experiencing self-loathing), Tony did not share his romantic or sexual feelings with anyone. Rather, he worked hard at being an "average" straight teenage boy; he dated girls in high school and has been dating Tina for 2 years.

Tony's behavior (B) is a Kinsey 0; he has only engaged in sexual behaviors with women. Tony has significantly invested in maintaining his friends and not losing his family. He also does not want to get harassed in school and has heard what people say about gay men when they are not around. As a result, whenever he feels an attraction toward any man, he adamantly pushes these feelings deep inside himself.

Tony's identity (I) is a Kinsey 0; he calls himself *heterosexual*. Tony is displaying a classic sexual identity conflict. He has a strong internal desire to be "true" to himself and to allow himself to fall in love with another guy. Yet he has had to tell people in his life that he was straight so that he did not get ostracized or harassed. Now, he is coming to Shanay to help him work through this conflict. Should he tell his parents that he is gay? Should he tell his friend, for whom he is developing feelings? What if he gets rejected?

Shanay is trying to figure out her own feelings about sexual orientation based on the negative messages she received growing up, while at the same time trying to help Tony with his issues. She needs some help. To begin, understanding the experience of gay identity development will help.

person is attracted, romantically or sexually. Behavior (B) simply refers to sexual behaviors in which a person engages (e.g., kissing, oral sex, intercourse, etc.). Identity (I) encompasses the varied sexual identities that a person calls oneself (gay, lesbian, heterosexual, bisexual, queer, etc.). Understanding the differences between orientation, behavior, and identity (O-B-I) can simplify the often confusing interplay of these constructs.

THE KINSEY SCALE

Alfred Kinsey is a well-known sexologist who, along with his colleagues, conducted extensive research on human sexuality in the 1940s and 1950s. He published two groundbreaking works in that era: *Sexual Behavior in the Human Male* (1948) and *Sexual Behavior in the Human Female* (1952). Some of his more famous findings include that 10% of adolescent males and 6–8% of adolescent females engage in same sex sexual behavior to the point of orgasm. As a result of these findings, Kinsey developed the Kinsey Scale. This 7-point scale was originally designed to measure sexual behavior (see Figure 14.1).

0 – Exclusively heterosexual with no homosexual

1 – Predominantly heterosexual, only incidentally homosexual

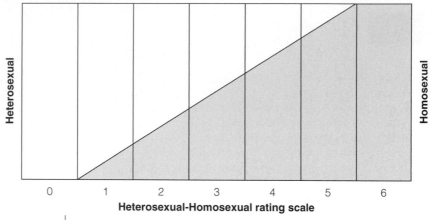

FIGURE 14.1 | KINSEY SCALE

2 – Predominantly heterosexual, but more than incidentally homosexual

3 – Equally heterosexual and homosexual

4 – Predominantly homosexual, but more than incidentally heterosexual

5 – Predominantly homosexual, only incidentally heterosexual

6 – Exclusively homosexual

A "0" on the Kinsey scale indicates that a person has exclusively engaged in sexual behavior with people of the other sex. This was categorically referred to as **exclusive heterosexual**. A "6" indicates that a person has exclusively engaged in sexual behavior with people of the same sex, referred to as **exclusive homosexual**. A "1" to "5" meant an individual had engaged in some varying sexual behavior with individuals of the other and same sex. This was referred to as **ambisexual**, now more commonly known as **bisexual**.

GLB IDENTITY DEVELOPMENT

GLBT people experience unique developmental milestones throughout childhood and adolescence. Growing up gay, lesbian, or bisexual in a homophobic, bi-negative, and heterosexist culture creates numerous psychosocial challenges for GLB youth that their heterosexual counterparts do not experience.

Gay, Lesbian, and Bisexual Identity Development and Coming Out. GLB people are identifying their sexual orientations publicly at younger ages. Herdt and Boxer (1996) report that gay and lesbian adolescents *come out,* or acknowledge their sexual orientations to themselves and others, at an average age of 16. Rust (2007) frames coming out as "a goal-oriented, stage-sequential developmental process whereby individuals who are sexually attracted to others of their own sex first questions their culturally prescribed heterosexual identity and then gradually come to adopt—and accept—a non-heterosexual identity" (p. 4). This experience is a process, not an outcome. Individuals make daily decisions to disclose sexual orientation in a variety of contexts, often based upon personal feelings of privacy, safety, and levels of perceived internalized homophobia (Morrow, 2000). It is important to note that coming out can occur throughout the lifespan. Some GLB people come out in adolescence while others may come out in mid- or later-life (see Case Studies 14.3 and 14.4).

There are numerous theoretical models documenting different aspects of GLB identity assumption (for a detailed discussion, see Cass, 1979; Coleman, 1982; Eliason, 2001; Klein, 1985; Morrow, 2007; Ossanna, 2000; Troiden, 1989). Each of these models highlights the importance of identity formation and self-acceptance as a precursor to healthy development.

One of these, Cass' (1979) six-stage identity developmental model for gay men and lesbians, is a good example of the stage models described above.

1. **Identity confusion** involves the recognition of difference in one's self and that such a difference may be coined gay or lesbian. Self-loathing may occur as the individual explores their identity.
2. **Identity comparison** reflects a greater degree of openness that one may be gay or lesbian by comparing themselves to the dominant heterosexual culture.
3. **Identity tolerance** reflects relative certainty of gay or lesbian identification. Social isolation may encourage individuals to seek out other gay or lesbian people.
4. **Identity acceptance** involves adoption of a gay or lesbian identity as a positive aspect of one's self.
5. **Identity pride** reflects recognition of difference between a positive sense of gay self and the negative stigmatization the dominant culture holds. Immersion in gay and lesbian culture and community may occur.
6. **Identity synthesis** involves acknowledgement that some heterosexuals are gay affirmative. Gay identity is not as central to everyday life.

While Rust's (2007) definition of coming out may be reflected in contemporary research from such a linear, stage-model perspective (e.g., Cass, 1979; Coleman, 1982; Troiden, 1989), adolescents often explore multiple sexual identities (see O-B-I above) throughout their teen years.

While a significant amount of literature reflects gay and lesbian identity development, there has been little research conducted on bisexual identity development. Weinberg, Williams, and Pryor (1994) developed one such model (as cited in Morrow, 2006). It is also a stage model, with four stages. The first stage, **initial uncertainty**, reflects an internal confusion about having sexual feeling for men and women to varying degrees. Some emotional conflict may occur as a result of this confusion. **Finding and applying the label**, the second stage, involves a resolution of the confusion and an adoption of the label "bisexual." A bisexual person may experience frustration here due to categorization by others as gay or lesbian rather than bisexual. **Settling into the identity** reflects self-acceptance and diminished concern about negative attitudes of society. Finally, **Continued uncertainty** involves the ongoing questioning that a bisexual person may experience as they develop relationships with men and women over time.

Gender Identity.   The term *sex* is often incorrectly used interchangeably with *gender*. Sex refers to a person's biological, anatomical, hormonal, and genetic makeup. Gender is a social construction, however. In other words, gender is a set of social norms and roles based upon culture.

Beyond the Binary.   Traditionally, many societies predominantly view gender as a binary construct; this means "two and only two" genders (i.e., male and female) (Bem, 1995). This is often based upon anatomical body parts (i.e., a boy has a penis; a girl has a vulva). Think about the fact that in every airport terminal across the world, there are bathrooms marked with signs that indicate that one is for men and the other for women.

The challenge, however, is that throughout human history there have been some people who do not "fit" neatly into either category. For many people, their sense of themselves does not match their anatomical parts. For others, the categories of "male" and "female" are too narrow and confining to help them explain who they are. To understand a little better, it is necessary to pull apart ideas about gender.

In 1976, Money and Dalery first started to identify different parts of someone's gender. This helps us think about people's sense of themselves in important ways. Money was the first person that talked about three basic pieces of someone's gender: core gender, gender role and gender identity.

- *Core gender* refers to the inner sense of gender (i.e., maleness, femaleness). Most people, when they think about themselves, have a sense inside them that says, "I am a man" or "I am a woman."
- *Gender role* means the social proscriptions of behavior based upon perceived gender. Think about the ways that society says girls are *supposed* to act and how that differs from the ways that boys are *supposed* to act. This can be as simple as the toys one is allowed to play with (trucks versus dolls) or as complex as the message women get to not be "too smart" or they will scare potential husbands away.
- *Gender identity* encompasses the various labels that refer to gender. Traditionally, these include male, female, boy, girl, men, women, and so forth. It also, however, includes other terms that reflect nonbinary gender identities and expressions such as transgender, transsexual, gender queer, drag queen and kings, crossdressers, and intersex people (see Table 14.1).

With this in mind, think about the reality of the world for people whose core gender does not match their biological body. This can be a really challenging experience for people. Then consider how much more complex it could be for someone whose core gender did not match what other people expected him or her to be: a person who feels like a boy, but who is only allowed to do "girl" things and is expected to always act like a girl, even though he does not feel that way inside.

Transgender. is an umbrella term that refers to people who do not fall into the binary constructs of gender in Western society (Embaye, 2006). Transgender people report that their inner sense of gendered experience does not correspond with the gender assigned at birth (Pauling, 1999).

Figure 14.2 shows the traditional, binary way that people experience their gender. The figure below might be named John. When he was born, the doctor looked

TABLE 14.1	TRANSGENDER IDENTITIES: BASIC DEFINITIONS
Term	**Definition**
Transgender	Umbrella Term; person who doesn't fall into the binary constructs of gender in Western society.
Male to Female Transgender (MTF)	A person whose core gender (female) doesn't match their biological sex (male).
Female to Male Transgender (FTM)	A person whose core gender (male) doesn't match their biological sex (female).
Gender Queer	Persons whose gender identity falls outside the traditional binary categories of male or female.
Drag Queen	A gay male who dresses up in costumish clothing of another gender for entertainment or lifestyle expression.
Drag King	A lesbian who dresses up in hypermasculine clothing to participate in cultural contests.
Crossdresser	A heterosexual male who dresses up in female clothing for erotic satisfaction or stress management.
Intersex	A person who is born with blended or ambiguous genitalia

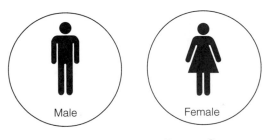

FIGURE 14.2	GENDER BUBBLES: TRADITIONAL, BINARY GENDER

at his body, saw a penis, and told his parents, "It's a boy." In John's case, he has always felt inside like he is a boy, and has always felt comfortable being called a boy and doing "boy" things.

Figure 14.3 shows one of the different ways that people experience their gender that are outside of the binary system most people experience. In this case, the doctor might look at the newborn person and declare, "It's a boy", and the boy's parents assign the name Jerry. But as Jerry grows up and learns about boys and girls, Jerry ALWAYS has felt that she is not a boy, but a girl. Many parents report that this internal sense of gender can show itself at as early an age as three or four. So, Jerry has never felt like a boy inside, but has always felt like a girl. When someone has this experience, they often call themselves transgender. In this case, Jerry was assigned a male (M) gender at birth, but feels internally like a female (F). Jerry might be referred to as an MtoF (or MTF) Transgender person. The situation can also

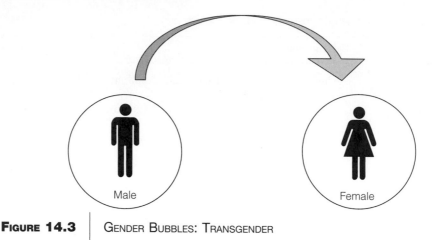

FIGURE 14.3 | GENDER BUBBLES: TRANSGENDER

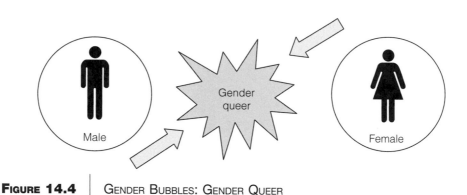

FIGURE 14.4 | GENDER BUBBLES: GENDER QUEER

occur for a person born with a vulva who feels inside like a boy. That person might be identified as a female (F) to male (M) transgender person (or an FTM) Transgender person.

In recent years, the term transgender has been shortened to "Trans", and connected to the gender that the person feels like inside. In this case, Jerry might change his name to Jenny and call herself a "transwoman." Or, in the second case above, the person might refer to himself as a "transman" or "transguy."

Finally, figure 14.4 shows the experience of being gender queer (see Table 14.1). In this experience, a person can be born into either gender category, and feel as if they do not "fit" into the category the doctor gave them at birth. However, they might also feel that the alternative category does not "fit" for them either. In those cases, people describe their internal sense of their gender as being "different" or "blended" in some way, and might adopt the gender identity label of "gender queer."

Forces of Oppression

Transphobia   Like bi-negativity, transphobia is the force of oppression that encompasses negative attitudes and discriminatory behaviors about transgender people. Also like bisexuality, transgender people experience transphobia from both heterosexual and GLB communities (Alexander and Yescavage, 2003).

TRANSGENDER IDENTITY DEVELOPMENT

Transgender individuals, similar to GLB people, have unique identity developmental experiences. Everyone develops a gender identity, but for transgender people, that experience is complicated by the cultural expectations that are contrary to a transgender individuals internal sense of gender. Lev (2006) proposes a developmental model known as Transgender Emergence. It involves six stages:

1. **Awareness.** This first stage involves recognition of gender variance accompanied by significant distress about it.
2. **Seeking information.** In this stage, transgender people seek out educational information and social support about transgender issues.
3. **Disclosure to significant others.** This coming out involves sharing transgender identity with other significant people (e.g. partner, family, co-workers, etc.).
4. **Exploration—identity and self-labeling.** This stage involves the exploration of numerous transgender identities.
5. **Exploration—transition.** This stage involves exploring options for transitioning gender presentation, body modification, and identity.
6. **Integration—acceptance and posttransitioning.** In this stage, a transgender person is attempting to integrate transgender identity within the context of the whole self.

This model is intended to assist transgender people from a stage of self-loathing to one of acceptance. Shanay has a new client who is transgender. That case will be explored a little later.

SPECIFIC POPULATIONS IN THE GLBT COMMUNITY

GLBT YOUTH

GLBT youth are faced with a number of psychosocial issues that result, not from their orientation or gender identity, but from the environment of discrimination and oppression in which they live. While many sexual minority youth grow up with positive experiences, it is doubtful that any escape the effects of prejudice and discrimination. The psychosocial issues that might occur for GLBT youth include:

- Suicide and suicide attempts. Gay, lesbian, and bisexual youth are three to four times more likely to attempt and commit suicide than their straight counterparts (D'Augelli, Hershberger, and Pilkington, 2001; Garofalo, Wolf, Kessel, Palfrey, and DuRant, 1998). Eighty-three percent of transgender youth surveyed by Sausa (2003) had thoughts of suicide while 54% of them attempted suicide.
- Family rejection. GLBT youth are often abused or ejected from their homes after coming out to their families (Lev, 2006; Savin-Williams, 1994).

- Homelessness. Whether as runaways or as a result of expulsion from their homes, some estimate the percentage of homeless youth who are GLBT to be as high as 25 to 40 percent (Ryan and Futterman, 1997).
- Verbal and physical abuse. Studies range between 74-83 percent of all GLBT youth suffer from verbal harassment and abuse while more than 21 percent of these youth report physical violence within their own schools (Kosciw and Cullen, 2001).
- Truancy and drop out rates. Harassment from peers was cited as a primary reason by the 28 percent of GLBT youth who dropped out of school (Savin-Williams, 1994).
- Substance use. As compared to their peers, GLBT youth were almost twice as likely to report heavy drug and alcohol use (Savin-Williams, 1994).
- Loneliness, social isolation, and depression. GLBT youth report much greater incidence of these negative emotional states that their heterosexual and non-trans counterparts (Cianciotto and Cahill, 2003).

It is important to note that numerous protective factors can serve to enhance the overall development and well being of GLBT youth. For example, Morrow (2006) cites Tharinger and Wells' (2000) discussion of the role of family support in coping with the daily exposure to oppression. Additionally, such factors as high self-esteem, positive peer relationships, self-confidence, and a validating faith can also provide a "psychosocial buffer" to such stress (Morrow, 2006).

GLBT PEOPLE OF COLOR

In considering the identities of GLBT people, one must acknowledge the realities of racism in GLBT communities (Signorile, 1997). While GLBT culture is varied and diverse, one of the overarching aspects of some GLBT communities is the assumption of the norms of whiteness. As a result, many GLBT people of color find that they do not fit into the norms required for GLBT culture, and they must begin, almost immediately, redefining their own sense of self within the context of their sexual orientation or gender identity and their racial and ethnic experiences.

While it is beyond the scope of this chapter to explore all the challenges that racism creates within GLBT communities, it is important to examine some of the ways in which GLBT people of color make meaning of their experiences through the adoption of sexual (GLBT or other culturally specific sexual identities) and racial/ethnic (Black, Asian, Latino, etc.) identities that make sense in the context of their experiences. In this aspect, identities for GLBT people of color might reflect cultural components that are connected to their racial and ethnic sense of self (For a more thorough discussion of some of these issues, see Brown, 2005). Yet, one of the unique challenges that some GLBT people of color face is the management of these dual identities.

For instance, many communities of color do not define masculinity and femininity in the same ways or with the same fluidity that feminism has afforded mainstream white culture. In some African-American communities, for example, the belief exists that homosexuality is a white practice and is inconsistent with manhood and black identity (Fanon, 1967; Nagel 2000). As a result, this reality of cultural norms in conflict with GLBT community norms can create significant challenges for dual identity management.

The distinction of this from the populations discussed above, however, is the reality of the privilege of whiteness (McIntosh, 1993). For many white GLBT people, the privilege exists for individuals to prioritize their sexual orientation or their gender identity as a central identity. Trebay (2000) argues that in communities of color, one often must juggle multiple identities that confound and complicate the expression of other equally important identities. In the words of one self-identified African American bisexual man, "You can walk through the projects and be gay, but you can't walk through the projects and be a faggot" (Trebay, 2000, para. 1).

CASE 14.2 | **TAMECA: MANAGING DUAL IDENTITIES FOR GLBT PEOPLE OF COLOR**

Shanay has another client who is working through dual-identity issues. Her name is Tameca, and she is both African American and a lesbian.

Tameca is 28 years old and has two children: Arthur who is 3 and Jewel who is 5. Both children were conceived while she was dating her high school sweetheart, Kevin. While she dated Kevin all through college, they broke up shortly after she graduated from the university. Kevin had proposed to her and asked her to marry him, but Tameca knew that while she loved him dearly, she was not interested in being married to a man.

Tameca has known since she was very small that she was sexually attracted to other women. She regularly had crushes on her best girlfriends, and even experimented a little with her best friend in college. After she broke up with Kevin, she started the process of coming out to her family and friends. She also started dating Ellen, a Caucasian woman she met in the city.

Tameca came in to talk with Shanay because she is having a really difficult time trying to figure out where she belongs in the world. Since she told her family that she was lesbian, they have pulled back from her, telling her that being gay is a sin, that homosexuality is something that white people do, and that they loved her, but they did not want to see any of "that behavior" when she was around her family, especially not around her nieces and nephews. They also told her that they were worried about her children being brought up "in that way."

This has been really difficult for her, since her family has always been really supportive of her being a

single mother. Her mother and sisters have also been the people she went to for support when she was dealing with the racism that she faces every day at work. Unfortunately, her family also told their church community about Tameca's "problem" with being gay, and she is no longer welcome in her faith community, either. She feels like she is losing all of her supports.

Ellen, whom she is dating, has been supportive, but since she is Caucasian, there are some things about Tameca's experience that she just does not understand. Ellen's family has always supported her identity, and Ellen has never been very religious. Ellen thinks that Tameca overreacts, and thinks that if her family and church can't accept her, then she should "leave them behind" and find new connections.

Tameca had a big fight with her mother just before she came in to talk with Shanay. Her mother told her that she needed to turn away from the people who were making her gay, come back to the church, and live her life as a "good, black woman." Tameca feels torn. She feels like she has to choose between two very important parts of herself: is she African American, or is she a lesbian? She doesn't see how she can be both, and is getting depressed and desperate.

Shanay can see that the challenge is not Tameca's sexual orientation. Instead, it appears to be the conflict between her sexual orientation and her African American identity. To help Tameca find an answer, Shanay needs to spend some time helping her understand how both identities are important to her and how she might be able to find supportive people who can help her manage the conflict.

LESBIAN AND GAY PARENTS AND THEIR CHILDREN

Lesbian- and gay-headed households with children seem to be becoming more prominent in society. Estimating the number of gay and lesbian families with children, is difficult due to the risk that disclosing one's gay or lesbian orientation may increase the likelihood of discrimination regarding custody or visitation rights (Blumenfeld and Raymond, 1988). Regardless, the National Adoption Information Clearinghouse, a service of the U.S. Administration for Children and Families, estimated that as of 1990, 6 million to 14 million children in the United States are living with a gay or lesbian parent (Children of Lesbians and Gays Everywhere, n.d.).

Lesbian and Gay Parents.   Gay and lesbian parenting is inextricably linked to marriage equity (see the section below titled "Marriage Equity" for more information) through the legal and social implications of custody decisions, foster parenting, visitation rights and adoption (Van Wormer, Wells, and Boes, 2000). Without legal recognition of gay or lesbian partners as spouses, the implication is that such families lack legal protections. As a result, gay or lesbian parents are vulnerable to a judge's subjective interpretation of their parental fitness (Payne, 1978). Much of this is generally based upon homophobic stereotypes including the assumptions that that lesbians are incapable of being maternal, gay men and lesbians are mentally ill, and that all gay men are promiscuous (Editors of the Harvard Law Review, 1990).

Research does not support these assumptions (Falk, 1989, 1994; Patterson, 1994b, 1995b, 1996). In fact, heterosexual mothers and lesbian mothers do not display any significant child-rearing styles or overall mental health differences (Kweskin and Cook, 1982; Lyons, 1983; Miller, Jacobsen, and Bigner, 1981; Mucklow and Phelan, 1979; Pagelow, 1980; Rand, Graham, and Rawlings, 1982; Thompson, McCandless, and Strickland, 1971). Further, research demonstrates that lesbian mothers who co-parent display an egalitarian division of family tasks and household labor (Patterson, 1995a). Finally, evidence suggests that gay fathers show no reasons why they would be deemed unfit to parent children (Barret and Robinson, 1990; Bigner and Bozett, 1990; Bozett, 1980, 1989).

Children of Gay and Lesbian Parents.   Besides the "fitness" of parents, one of the concerns voiced by those who oppose gay and lesbian parenting is that the environment in which children of gays and lesbians are raised will somehow negatively impact their sexual identity development or gender roles. Numerous research studies dispel these unfounded concerns by showing that children of gays and lesbians neither displayed atypical gender roles nor assumed a gay or lesbian identity (Bailey, Bobrow, Wolfe, and Mikach, 1995; Bozett, 1980, 1989; Golombok, Spencer, and Rutter, 1983; Gottman, 1990; Green, 1978; Patterson, 1994a). The evident conclusion of this research is that children raised in heterosexual households are no different from those raised in gay and lesbian households.

A final concern often voiced is that children of gay and lesbian parents will have a harder time developing positive peer relationships in social settings. Again research indicates normal development of peer friendships (Golombok, Spencer, and Rutter, 1983; Green, 1978). Indeed, the challenge that children of gays and lesbians most often encounter is the homophobia children encounter in others. Their personal development is in no way adversely affected by the sexual orientation of their parents.

GLBT OLDER ADULTS

In a society where older adults are often invisible, and the baby boomer generation ages, the experience of aging for older GLBT individuals can be particularly challenging. Jones (2001) identified three primary problems that older individuals encounter: (1) ageism; (2) loneliness; and, (3) health status. Like any older adult, GLBT older adults can encounter ageism throughout their daily life experiences. They also encounter, however, GLBT-related prejudices. For example, a 73-year-old lesbian whose partner passes away may not be afforded the same legal protections (e.g. inheritance rights, life insurance beneficiaries, etc.) as a legally married couple. Additionally, Jones (2001) points out the need for health care providers to be sensitive to the medical needs of GLBT older adult people as well as for the need to advanced planning for aging.

GLBT older adults also experience marginalization within the GLBT community. For instance, within the culture of gay male identities, an overarching prescriptive norm may include valuing youth and beauty, visiting clubs and bars, using drugs and alcohol, and working out consistently (Signorile, 1997). These cultural norms often reflect "an overriding, mostly white, youth focused, and often drug-fueled social and sexual gay male scene that is highly commercialized an ideal" (Signorile, 1997, p. xviii). Older gay men, as one might suspect, who may no longer fit into the culture of youth and beauty (Signorile, 1997) and feel excluded from a highly sexualized GLBT culture (Jones, 2001).

An additional challenge is the generational differences that exist across GLBT age cohorts. Fullmer (2006) reviews some of the differences that exist for GLBT older adults who grew up in a time period when being open about one's sexual orientation or gender identity was less common. For example, the concept of coming out in contemporary society might imply doing so in adolescence; for GLBT older adults, this process may have occurred later in life in light of the cultural differences that existed about disclosure of identities when they were younger.

It is important to note that the specific populations discussed here are not a comprehensive list. There are unique psychosocial issues, strengths, and cultural dimensions among a myriad of GLBT populations (e.g. GLBT people with cognitive, physical and emotional disabilities, GLBT people who struggle with mental illness, and GLBT people who are religious minorities).

SOCIAL POLICY ISSUES

MARRIAGE EQUITY

In the United States, the cultural controversy of marriage equity (i.e. gay marriage) has been around for many years, with lawsuits seeking legal recognition of same-sex couples dating as far back as 1971 (Johnson, 1997). Since that time, the issue of marriage equity has arisen in politics, with the signing of the Defense of

Marriage Act (DOMA) in 1996, and in the presidential campaign of 2004 as a cultural issue with which to mobilize conservative voters. Indeed, in most arguments the players take sides based on those who identifies as more conservative/traditional (and frequently religious) and those who identify as more liberal/progressive. These ideological pools of thought, however, are not limited to the United States. In fact, the controversy over legal recognition of same-sex couples has been going on for decades around the globe.

Consider the situation in the European Union (EU). In 2003, the parliament of the EU ruled that member nations must recognize the same-sex marriages of citizens from the Netherlands and Belgium (Fish, 2005). Prior to this, a couple's marriage was not recognized when they crossed borders, and the custody of their children could be in question from country to country.

In this way, the struggle in Europe mirrors current struggles in the United States. As same-sex couples marry in Massachusetts and California, their relationships are not recognized when they cross the border into another state. Similarly, the relationships of same-sex couples who are married in Canada are not recognized when they travel in the United States. This creates great concern in the case of emergency hospitalization or other serious events, when some hospitals or other emergency personnel would not recognize the rights of the same-sex spouse. Additionally, Kendell (2003) describes the more subtle aspect of discrimination in child custody cases that may be related to same-sex couples' inability to marry in most states:

> In some states, for example, courts may prohibit divorced parents from living with an unmarried partner as a condition of custody or visitation. While this rule may appear neutral with regard to sexual orientation, it is not. As the Indiana Court of Appeals recognized in striking down a restriction of this type in a recent case, the practical effect of such a rule is to prohibit lesbian and gay parents "from ever being involved in a long term relationship that is the equivalent of marriage." (Downey v. Muffley, 767 N.E.2d 1014, 1021 (Ind. Ct. App. 2002)

As some nations and states adopt policies that recognize marriage equity, the global repercussions abound. As the world becomes smaller through international travel, the Internet, and instant communications, social workers are forced to confront and manage these issues in a pluralistic and ethical manner.

NONDISCRIMINATION POLICIES

Nondiscrimination policies are pivotal in order to provide ethical social work services to GLBT clients. Currently, discrimination based upon gender identity and sexual orientation with regard to housing, employment, and public accommodations is legal in most states (Burke, 2002). In other words, a homophobic landlord could legally eject a same-sex couple from their home due to the mere fact they are gay in many areas of the country. The implications of such discrimination reveal the need for inclusive nondiscrimination policies. However, there exists no Federal Non-Discrimination Law that includes sexual orientation or gender identity.

Recently, the Employment Non-Discrimination Act (ENDA) was the center of a controversy within the GLBT community. A version of ENDA that includes sexual orientation and gender identity has been presented to Congress numerous times in the last 30 years. During the most recent attempt to pass this legislation, multiple versions of the bill arose; one of these included gender identity and one did not. The country largest gay and lesbian rights organization, the Human Rights Campaign (HRC), endorsed the noninclusive version of ENDA, with the hope of gaining more congressional votes to pass. In November of 2007, the House of Representatives voted to pass the ENDA version of the bill that did not include gender identity (Human Right Campaign, 2007). This resulted in a GLBT community split on the bill.

A Policy Example.   The NASW Code of Ethics (1999) mandates that social workers provide culturally competent social services to their clients. One of the ways that social service agencies can ensure this is to make sure their agencies have nondiscrimination policies that include sexual orientation and gender identity (Hash and Ceperich, 2006). An example on one such policy, developed by the Vancouver Board of Education (School District 39), is below:

> Vancouver Board of Education of School District No. 39 (Vancouver), Vancouver, B.C. is committed to establishing and maintaining a safe and positive learning environment for all students and employees including those who identify as lesbian, gay, bisexual, transgender, transsexual, two-spirit, or who are questioning their sexual orientation or gender identity. These students and employees, as all students and employees, have the right to learn and work in an environment free of discrimination and harassment. The letter and spirit of the Canadian Charter of Rights and Freedoms, the B. C. Human Rights Acts and the Collective Agreements shall be carefully observed, enforced, and supported, so that all members of the school community may work together in an atmosphere of respect and tolerance for individual differences. Specifically, the Board will not tolerate hate crimes, harassment or discrimination, and will vigorously enforce policy and regulations dealing with such matters.
>
> The Board will provide a safe environment, free from harassment and discrimination, while also promoting pro-active strategies and guidelines to ensure that lesbian, gay, transgender, transsexual, two-spirit, bisexual and questioning students, employees and families are welcomed and included in all aspects of education and school life and treated with respect and dignity. The purpose of this policy is to define appropriate behaviours and actions in order to prevent discrimination and harassment through greater awareness of and responsiveness to their deleterious effects. This policy is also drafted to ensure that homophobic complaints are taken seriously and dealt with expeditiously and effectively through consistently applied policy and procedures. The policy will also raise awareness and improve understanding of the lives of people who identify themselves on the basis of sexual orientation or gender identity. By valuing diversity and respecting differences, students and staff act in accordance with the Vancouver district's social responsibility initiative. (Vancouver Board of Education, 2004, para. 1-2)

As evidenced by this comprehensive nondiscrimination policy specifically addressing LGBT people, the Vancouver School Board crafted the policy to prohibit discrimination (e.g., hate crimes, harassment, etc.), but also included a separate section on providing inclusive environments for GLBT people. Such nondiscrimination policies in social work organizations would certainly help to fulfill the NASW ethical mandate of culturally competent service delivery to GLBT clients.

PRACTICE ISSUES AND BEST PRACTICE RECOMMENDATIONS

Providing effective and ethical social work services to GLBT clients is often a challenge due to the realities of prejudice and discrimination that face this population daily. The following section will address some of the ways that social workers (1) display biased, inadequate, or inappropriate attitudes and behaviors towards their GLBT clients; and (2) provide affirmative social work practice guidelines.

OPPRESSION IN PRACTICE

In counseling, the literature reveals significant amounts of data regarding the impact of oppression (homophobia, heterosexism, bi-negativity, and transphobia) on the part of the straight helping professional working with the sexual minority client. Negative attitudes and behaviors of mental health professionals, including social workers, regarding sexual minorities are well documented (Casas, Brady, and Ponterotto; 1983; DeCrescenzo, 1984; Firestein, 2007; Fort, Steiner, and Conrad, 1971; Garfinkle and Morin, 1978; Garnets, Hancock, Cochran, Goodchilds, and Peplau, 1991; Gartrell, Kramer, and Brodie, 1974; Graham, Rawlings, Halpern, and Hermes, 1984; Messing, Schoenberg, and Stephens, 1984; Morin, 1977; Morrow and Messinger, 2006; NASW National Committee on Gay, Lesbian, and Bisexual Issues, 2000; Riddle and Sang, 1978; Winsniewski and Toomey, 1987).

In many social work schools, GLBT issues are briefly addressed. As a result, much of the theory that currently guides social workers in their practices is based upon a heterosexual and gender-binary approach to growing up and living in the world. For example, few developmental theories account for a transgender child who recognizes a difference between their core gender and biological sex at age 7. Indeed, because clinical training is often provided from a heterosexist and gender-binary worldview in mental health training institutions, such an approach can generate social workers who display unexamined homophobic, heterosexist, bi-negative, and transphobic attitudes (Newman, Dannenfleser, and Benisheck, 2002; Pfohl, 2004; Phillips and Fisher, 1998).

GAY AND LESBIAN CLIENTS

According to DeCrescenzo (1984), "homophobic attitudes might well generate behavior which is counter-therapeutic, counter-productive, or renders the worker less able to be effective with [GLBT] clients" (p. 120). DeCrescenzo (1984) continued by stating that negative attitudes of homophobic social workers will be communicated to clients accompanied with negative practices possibly affecting the self-esteem of such clients.

Messing, Schoenberg, and Stephens (1984) stated that some of the homophobic reactions of social workers were varied and contextually bound, but counterproductive nonetheless. The manifestations of homophobia in straight therapists toward gay and lesbian clients included (1) indifference, (2) hostility, (3) overpathologizing (4) pity, and (5) hidden agendas. For those social workers who liked to think of themselves as liberal, indifference was expressed, as "sexual orientation does not matter at all," which flatly ignored the reality of oppression that impacts gay, lesbian, and bisexual people on a daily basis in American culture (Messing, Schoenberg, and Stephens, 1984).

Hostility was another common reaction of social workers (Messing, Schoenberg, and Stephens, 1984). Some social workers may feel threatened by a gay or lesbian client, and the worker may react by subtly or obviously putting the client down, showing less patience, getting angry or frustrated quickly, and so forth. (DeCrescenzo, 1984). In addition, social workers might simply have refused to work with gay, lesbian, or bisexual clients or attempt to alter his or her sexual orientation (Messing, Schoenberg, and Stephens, 1984; Riddle and Sang, 1978). Unfortunately, some clients may be frightened by their gay feelings, leaving them vulnerable to the suggestions of the homophobic social worker.

Another reaction was the opposite of indifference: the exaggeration of the significance of sexual orientation (Messing, Schoenberg, and Stephens, 1984). This spotlighted sexual orientation in a manner inappropriate to the presenting problem. In this situation, a social worker might see a clients' sexual orientation as the "real" problem, rather than the issue with which the client presented. Social workers also displayed the common reaction of pity. This arose because they viewed homosexuality or bisexuality as a burden or a problem deserving of help. Clients perceived such pity as offensive and demeaning (Messing, Schoenberg, and Stephens, 1984).

Some social workers may also have had a hidden agenda, either liberal or conservative (DeCrescenzo, 1984). Similar to the indifference reaction above, some social workers that felt the need to establish themselves as liberal may have continually expressed that they did not hold homophobic views when such discussions were irrelevant to the treatment (DeCrescenzo, 1984). Conversely, a social worker who believes that gay or lesbian clients are immoral or sinful may steer the client toward their own conservative religious perspective.

Heterosexist assumptions and practices also permeated counseling with gay and lesbian clients. A typical heterosexist reaction was denial. This manifested as presuppositions about specific populations (i.e., all older adults are heterosexual) or about clients generally in the form of heterosexist assessment tools (e.g., The Marriage Quiz) and heterosexist practice interventions (Elze, 2006; Messing, Schoenberg, and Stephens, 1984; Morrow, 1993).

BISEXUAL CLIENTS

Bisexual clients often faced many of the above oppressive practices, but also encountered additional ones. For example, many social workers display an assumption that heterosexual relationships are more mature and preferred. This especially becomes evident when social workers highlight the positive aspects of a bisexual client's heterosexual relationships (if they have had any) and the negative aspects of a bisexual client's homosexual relationships (if they have had any). Without focusing on a client's same-sex relationships or tendencies in a positive way, the bisexual client does not get the opportunity to develop much needed social skills in same-sex relationships (Riddle and Sang, 1978).

While not all bisexual people are involved in multiple relationships at any given time, many polyamorous bisexual people (individuals who are openly and honestly involved in multiple relationships at one time) encounter social workers who believe that all nonmonogamous relationships are psychologically unhealthy, immature, and potentially damaging (Dworkin, 2001; Elze, 2006). Additionally, bisexual clients were found to have experienced more heterosexist bias from mental health professionals than did their gay and lesbian counterparts (Lucksted, 1996; Moss, 1994).

TRANSGENDER CLIENTS

Perhaps some of the most stigmatized clients in social work are transgender individuals. Presently, the diagnosis of Gender Identity Disorder (GID) stigmatizes transgender clients by automatically framing their experiences and feelings as pathological (Israel and Tarver, 1997). As a result, if transgender clients wish to receive counseling services, they must accept a mentally ill label, regardless of their psychological health (Bornstein, 1994).

Elze (2006) also noted that mental health professionals often inappropriately encourage their transgender clients to keep their identity a secret. Such a recommendation may emerge from the professional's own transphobic reactions. In his qualitative study on transgender youth, Sausa (2003) captures the poignant experience of a trans youth seeking help from a counselor: "they would never give me [the] help I needed, like they wouldn't try to hook me up with...transgender resources and stuff like that." (pp. 145–146).

Additionally, transgender clients have experienced discrimination in residential treatment facilities, such as substance abuse centers, where such clients have been verbally and physically assaulted, and forced to room with those of their biological gender (Lombardi and van Servellen, 2000, as cited in Elze, 2006).

PRACTICE RECOMMENDATIONS: A STRENGTHS PERSPECTIVE

In light of such pervasive oppressive practices in social work, providing inclusive practice models using a basic tenet of social work is necessary. The following section will address the role of the strengths perspective in one example of a positive practice model: the affirmative practice model (Messinger, 2006). Additionally, this model will be supplemented with a macro-systemic assessment tool called the Levels of Response.

Van Wormer, Wells, and Boes (2000) propose that a strengths perspective is especially useful and adept at analyzing the experience of the sexual minority community. They identify this perspective as "a presumption of health over pathology, a focus on self-actualization and personal growth, and recognition that the personal is political and the political, personal" (p. 20). Indeed, focusing on the deficit (or pathological) approach

> ...often impairs the practitioner's best intentions of promoting client growth and
> awareness of inner strength and resources. The relationship between client and worker,
> similarly, is impaired when pathology-based assessment becomes pathology-based
> treatment, when instead of partnership and client self-determination, emphasis is on the
> profession-as-expert. (Van Wormer, Wells, and Boes, 2000, p. 21)

Assessment	Intervention	Identity	Relationships	Family	Therapist Expertise & Education
View homosexuality as psycho-pathology, developmental arrest, or disorder	Focus on orientation when it was not relevant	Lack of understanding of gay identity development	Under-estimation of the importance of relationships for gay clients	Presumption of gay client as inappropriate parent	Lack of know-ledge about gay issues; reliance on client to educate the therapist
Automatic attribution of client's homosexuality as the problem	Discourage gay identity formation; mandating renunciation of homosexuality as condition for treatment; attempts to alter a client's orientation	Minimization of the degree to which internalized homophobia impacted gay identity development	Insensitivity to the nature and diversity of relationships or utilization of heterosexuality as frame of reference	Insensitivity to the impact of prejudice and discrimination on gay parents and their children	Distribution of inaccurate or prejudicial information about gay people; active discrimination against gay students and/or colleagues
Failure to recognize symptoms as being affected by the client's self-perception of homosexuality	Expression of negative belief regarding homosexuality thereby demeaning homosexuality	Under-estimation of the potential consequences of client disclosure of orientation to others			
Assumption of heterosexuality or the discounting of client self-identification as gay	Transfer of gay client upon disclosure of orientation without appropriate referrals				

FIGURE 14.5 | BIASED, INADEQUATE OR INAPPROPRIATE PRACTICE WITH GBL CLIENTS

They present five distinct themes of the strengths perspective relevant to affirmative generalist social work practice with GLBT clients:

1. Seek the positive. Transcend assessment of pathology in order to identify coping skills, including insights, talents, and social supports.
2. Listen to the personal narrative. Spend time hearing the story of an individual from his or her perspective while reframing it in terms of unrecognized insights.

3. Validate the pain. Support strategies that attempt to ease the pain of themselves and others. Help people identify and recover from specific wounds of oppression.

4. Don't dictate, collaborate. Identify mutual and realistic solutions using families, friends, and social networks as determined by the client with their coping skills.

5. Move from self-actualization to transformation of oppressive structures. Prepare an individual for personal growth by helping others.

Each of these themes strengthens the counseling strategies for GLBT clients. One such practice model, founded in the strengths-based perspective, is the affirmative practice model.

Affirmative Practice.   Lori Messinger (2006) provides a strengths-based model of affirmative social work practice with GLBT populations. Built upon the concept of cultural competency (i.e., professional standards of socioculturally sensitive practice that enable social workers to work effectively with different populations) and empowerment practice (i.e., aiding clients to develop skill sets that help them to meet their own needs), affirmative practice consists of generalist social work practice stages of building rapport, conducting assessment, and planning interventions.

The affirmative practice model has three separate stages: (1) building rapport, (2) assessment, and (3) planning. Each of these stages is presented as a guide only. Some of the stages will be supplemented with additional information and recommendations.

Building Rapport.   According to Messinger (2006), rapport building involves numerous factors. First, social workers must be able to reflect upon their own attitudes and biases about GLBT people. Such awareness allows social workers to continuously examine their own internalized oppressive or discriminatory beliefs and attitudes, regardless of their sexual orientation or gender identity.

Second, social workers should assess their own presentation of self, including their office space, their assessment tools, and their use of language. Offices should reflect some GLBT-inclusive literature or books. Assessment forms should use terminology that is not heterosexist (i.e., "marital status" versus "relationship status") or gender-binary (e.g., check boxes of "male" or "female" for "sex"). During early conversations with clients, using inclusive GLBT language creates a sense of welcoming (e.g., partner vs. spouse). Social workers should also be prepared for some degree of mistrust with GLBT clients as many of them have often experienced negative encounters with mental health professionals in the past (Messinger, 2006).

Third, GLBT social workers need to give consideration to their own identity disclosures prior to meeting with clients (Messinger, 2006; Satterly, 2006). This may include examining (1) their own professional identity development, or how GLBT social workers frame their professional identity; (2) the organizational culture of their agencies, or the policies, procedures, and practices of their agencies toward GLBT issues; (3) their theoretical orientation, or the various schools of thought to which they as social workers practice; and (4) alternative ways of understanding self, client, and the helping relationship other than through self-ascribed theoretical orientation (e.g., transference and countertransferential reactions) (Satterly, 2006). Such forethought allows GLBT social workers to consider their own identity management before they find themselves sitting across from a client who asks an understandable, but loaded question, such as "Are you married?"

Assessment.   In addition to a comprehensive biopsychosocial assessment, Messinger's (2006) affirmative practice model also highlights a myriad of unique variables to consider when conducting assessments with GLBT clients:

1. How knowledgeable are the clients about sexual orientation and gender identity?
    Many GLBT clients have little knowledge about the unique sociocultural aspects of GLBT communities, culture, history, and so forth. Providing sensitive and culturally appropriate information for GLBT clients may empower them to explore such components of themselves in a new light. Adaptation, coping skills, and social support may emerge as outcomes.
2. Where are GLBT clients in their own sexual identity development?
    As previously discussed, the experience of coming out to one's self is a process that is constantly evolving over the lifespan. Assessing where GLBT individuals are in their own coming out processes will aid social workers to design developmentally appropriate interventions based not only on chronology, but on identity development as well.
3. How comfortable are GLBT clients with their own sexual orientation or gender identity?
    Because GLBT clients have encountered oppression throughout their lives based around sexual orientation and/or gender identity, the internalization of negative attitudes and beliefs in not uncommon (Weinberg, 1972). Assessing their comfort level in a sensitive manner may reveal some strengths or struggles.
4. Are there other aspects of their identity that are important to them?
    It is a mistake to assume that sexual orientation and gender identity are the only aspects of identity that are important to GLBT individuals. Race, ethnicity, religion, and class are just a few of the other identity markers that a GLBT person may embrace. Exploring all of these complexities is a critical aspect of assessment.

In addition to these points, conducting assessments with bisexual and transgender people requires particular sensitivity as they often are inappropriately grouped with the gay or lesbian population. For example, when conducting assessments with bisexual people, it is critical to understand how such clients cognitively and emotionally understand and experience their bisexuality (Israel, 2007). Assuming it is simply an equal attraction to men and women is too simplistic, often incorrect, and neglects to differentiate between orientation, behavior, and identity.

Regarding transgender clients, many social workers often confuse the distinction between sexual orientation and gender identity. Israel and Tarver (1997) recommend that transgender clients learn how to advocate for themselves when they encounter mental health professionals who display transphobic and/or gender-binary attitudes. While self-advocacy is certainly a skill set that social workers encourage in their clients, it is the responsibility of social workers to educate themselves about transgender culture, terminology, and history.

The answers to these questions may reveal some unique struggles, but may also allow the social worker to identify a wide variety of strengths-based skills that GLBT individuals embody as a result of managing oppressive structures throughout their lives. For example, GLBT people have often had to confront and manage their own internal feelings that make them different from their heterosexual and non-trans counterparts. Such a process requires a significant degree of introspection, emotional literacy (i.e., the ability to identify and communicate emotion as well as to benefit from their own insight), and courage in the face of oppressive messages from a variety of sources, including family, friends, faith communities, and the media.

Planning.   The third stage of Messinger's (2006) affirmative practice model is planning. It is a client-centered approach to intervention design that neither pathologizes sexual orientation and gender identity nor assumes that GLBT clients are seeking help related to their identities. According to Messinger (2006), treatment interventions should consider client self-determination regarding coming out and self-disclosure. For example, it may seem wise to counsel a bisexual 15-year-old to

---

| **CHART 14.1** | **THE LEVELS OF RESPONSE: AN ECOLOGICAL ASSESSMENT TOOL** |

Nelson (1978) identified four theological stances to represent the range of theological opinions about homosexuality in the Church. Adapting these perspectives as the *Levels of Response Model*, it can be used by social workers as a systematic analysis used to determine the response of individuals, families, groups, communities, and organizations to LGBT individuals, communities, and culture. The model includes five possible levels of response communicated through individual relationships, policies, and actions.

Rejecting Punitive
Refers to a homophobic response often found in hate groups (e.g., KKK) and antigay religious groups. They encapsulate the message "Gay people are evil and must be punished."

Rejecting Non-Punitive
Views gay people as sick and in need of help. Ex-gay groups and reparative therapies exemplify this level.

Qualified Acceptance
Refers to those who often claim to not be homophobic because they have gay friends. They think gay people are OK; they just don't want to see it. The U.S. Military's Don't Ask, Don't Tell policy, codifies this level.

Full Acceptance
Views gay people as a normal and natural part of a pluralistic community. The organization, Parents, Friends of Lesbians and Gays (PFLAG) exemplifies this response.

Advocacy
A new perspective from the original theological stance, which takes the response one step further by acknowledging the realities of oppression requiring action to safeguard civil rights. Some organizational examples are the Human Rights Campaign (HRC) and the Gay and Lesbian Alliance Against Defamation (GLAAD).

come out to her family to seek out their support; in fact, this may result in a harmful outcome, including being thrown out of her home due to her family's negative reaction to her disclosure.

Planning should also revolve around listening to the narrative of the individual. When clients tell their story, they re-create emotional and psychological experiences to a certain degree. When GLBT clients share parts of themselves and their experiences with social workers, they may begin to embrace that stigmatized part of their identities (Messinger, 2006). Finally, managing such stigma should also be considered when planning interventions. The daily experience of discrimination or oppression that GLBT people face presents unique challenges. A strengths-based approach may reveal a level of resiliency, however, that enhances coping skills. Community integration and support of GLBT individuals can empower them to develop the skill sets required for self-actualization and advocacy.

BEST PRACTICE RECOMMENDATIONS FOR WORKING WITH GLBT CLIENTS

The American Psychological Association's Division 44 (Committee of Lesbian, Gay, and Bisexual Concerns, 2000) has developed a set of guidelines for providing clinical services to GLB people. While these guidelines specifically target psychologists, such recommendations are pertinent to social workers as well. A few recommendations are provided below:

- Social workers are encouraged to recognize how their attitudes and knowledge about lesbian, gay, and bisexual issues may be relevant to assessment and treatment and seek consultation or make appropriate referrals when indicated;
- Social workers strive to understand the way in which social stigmatization (i.e., prejudice, discrimination, and violence) poses risks to the mental health and well-being of lesbian, gay, and bisexual clients;
- Social workers strive to understand how inaccurate or prejudicial views of homosexuality or bisexuality may affect the client's presentation in treatment and the therapeutic process;
- Social workers strive to be knowledgeable about and respect the importance of lesbian, gay, and bisexual relationships;
- Social workers strive to understand the particular circumstances and challenges faced by lesbian, gay, and bisexual parents;
- Social workers recognize that the families of lesbian, gay, and bisexual people may include people who are not legally or biologically related;
- Social workers are encouraged to recognize the particular life issues or challenges that are related to multiple and often conflicting cultural norms, values, and beliefs, that lesbian, gay, and bisexual members of racial and ethnic minorities face;
- Social workers consider generational differences within lesbian, gay, and bisexual populations and the particular challenges that lesbian, gay, and bisexual older adults may experience;
- Social workers are encouraged to recognize the particular challenges that lesbian, gay, and bisexual individuals experience with physical, sensory, and cognitive-emotional disabilities.

GUIDELINES FOR WORKING WITH TRANSGENDER CLIENTS

Similar to the American Psychological Association, Israel and Tarver (1997) provide a set of recommended guidelines for mental health professionals working with transgender clients. Some of these include:

- Social workers recognize that transgender identity and gender identity issues are not mentally disordered, diseased, or pathological;
- Social workers recognize that, while stereotypes and discrimination exacerbate circumstantial difficulties, transgender individuals are not known to have a higher incident of mental disorders than the general population;
- Social workers who work in residential facilities (e.g., substance abuse treatment centers, psychiatric hospitals, etc.) are encouraged to consider a transgender client's current gender presentation, the individual's placement requests, and gender history;
- Social workers should consult with a gender specialist to plan transgender-inclusive and appropriate interventions;
- Social workers should consult with a gender specialist to provide sensitivity training for staff;
- Social workers should use the terminology (e.g., gender pronouns, name, etc.) requested by the transgender client.

While Messinger's affirmative practice model (2006) highlights building rapport, assessment, and planning as the foundation for effective social work with GLBT clients, intervention design and implementation is also critical. Many interventions used often emerge from social work practice wisdom through experience, but evidence-supported interventions should also be employed.

EVIDENCE-BASED PRACTICE

Evidence-based practice (EBP) was defined in Chapter 2. In short, Rubin (2008) defines EBP as "a process for making practice decisions in which practitioners integrate the best research evidence available with *their practice expertise and with client attributes, values, preferences and circumstances*" (emphasis added, p. 7). These three factors, practitioners expertise, research evidence, and client preferences and actions, can govern a social worker in the planning phase of Messinger's (2006) aforementioned affirmative practice model.

In addition to Messinger's model, there are a number of other evidence-based interventions that can be used with GLBT populations. One of these, cognitive-behavioral therapy, is grounded in significant evidence regarding its efficacy (Gray, 2000).

COGNITIVE-BEHAVIORAL INTERVENTIONS

Cognitive-behavioral treatment (CBT) is an evidence-based psychotherapeutic school of thought that examines the relationships between and among emotions, thoughts, behaviors, and the environment (Gray, 2000). CBT pays particular attention to the distorted thoughts or beliefs that contribute to emotional distress. Such distorted thoughts develop as a result of inaccurate meanings given to early experiences through socialization processes. For example, an obese 12-year-old girl who is told she is fat by peers and family members has this message reinforced through the images of beauty she sees in magazines and television. She believes she is fat and attaches negative emotion to that belief. Even if she grows up and loses a significant amount of weight, she may still believe that she is fat. Social workers can assist clients in re-examining such beliefs to reframe them in a more positive light.

In GLBT populations, the implications for this approach are numerous. Two general areas can be addressed using CBT: (1) problems that are related to their sexual orientation or gender identity, and (2) problems where their sexual orientation or gender identity intersect with a general life issue (Gray, 2000). An example of a problem relating to their sexual orientation would be the self-loathing a gay person has as a result of growing up in a homophobic environment (e.g. ,internalized homophobia). A problem where sexual orientation or gender identity intersects with a general life issue might include the social anxiety that a person experiences when trying to romantically date.

Assessment and Interventions.   In CBT, conducting assessments and employing interventions focus upon the explicit beliefs clients have related to the presenting problem and their sexuality. The techniques employed make CBT unique. For example, keeping a *thought log* enables clients to identify specific emotional reactions and their corresponding automatic thought. Some additional assessment questions may include:

- What does it mean to be attracted to someone of the same sex?
- What does it mean to be a "good" trans man?
- What are the "truths" about bisexual people?
- How long have you held this belief?

Through this process of assessment, a social worker, in collaboration with a client, should then develop answers the following four CBT questions:

- What are the difficulties?
- When did they arise (early experiences and triggering events)?
- Why was I vulnerable to these events (belief systems)?
- What is maintaining the problem (behaviors, thought processes, etc.) (Gray, 2000)?

In addition to such assessment questions, challenging negative and distorted beliefs is an important component of CBT. Evaluating beliefs and thoughts can be accomplished by using the following questions:

- What is the evidence for and against this?
- What thought distortions are present?
- What is the effect of thinking like this?
- What is an alternative view (Gray, 2000)?

Some thought challenges may assist a social worker in adapting such beliefs. Case study 14.3 employs one such example.

CASE 14.3 | MICKEY: COMING OUT TRANS

Recently, Shanay got a new client named Mickey. Mickey is a 35-year-old FTM (female-to-male) transgender-identified client (for clarification, see the section on transgender identities). He came in to see Shanay to talk about his relationship with his partner, Tina. Tina is a biological female who fell in love with Mickey almost 2 years ago. The presenting problem revolves around Mickey's coming out as trans to Tina's family. Tina wants Mickey to sit down with her family and talk about Mickey's trans identity, but Mickey is somewhat resistant to do so. He reports significant social anxiety when he considers such a disclosure.

Throughout the joining and assessment process, the social worker discovers that Mickey holds the cognitive belief that "everyone will reject me if they knew I was trans." Shanay decides that using CBT will be the most effective way to help Mickey get through this experience. As a result, she decides to challenge Mickey's belief about his situation with a series of questions that ask Mickey to predict outcome of disclosure:

- Is it better that they know this information now or several years from now?

- Is it better to realize that you can never be friends now or later?

- Will the person still be rejecting after the initial shock has worn off?

- What is the worst that can happen if they reject you?

- How will you cope with this (Gray, 2000)?

Gray (2000) highlights a CBT approach to managing such thought challenges related to coming out:

Where beliefs are seen to have a basis in fact then a person can approach them in a problem solving way, rather than avoiding the issue. It may be necessary for the client to change aspects of their environment. There will almost certainly be some true loss to process, but being able to distinguish which are the "real" problem issues and which are the unwarranted unrealistic fears can be powerfully enlightening. (p. 32)

After engaging in this introspective thought analysis with Shanay and his partner, Mickey was able to discover that his real fear was based upon coming out to his own family of origin rather than Tina's family.

GAY–STRAIGHT ALLIANCES

A second example of an evidence-based social work intervention is group-based social support groups for GLBT youth in youth-based settings called Gay-Straight Alliances (GSA). GSAs are social support groups consisting of GLBT youth, questioning youth, and heterosexual and non-trans youth who are supportive of the their GLBT peers). These groups are often found in school-based settings, but can also be facilitated out of social service agencies and community centers. Within these youth-oriented organizations, GLBT youth have the opportunity not only to discuss some of the challenges they have faced with their GLBT and heterosexual peers and to gain support in sometimes hostile environments, but also to begin to develop self-empowering and proactive behaviors that can lead to social change within their communities (Cianciotto and Cahill, 2003).

As these young people begin to move beyond their individual experiences of coming out and managing the world, they have the opportunity to learn important advocacy skills in combating not only homophobia, transphobia, and bi-negativity, but also sexism, classism, and racism; they learn connections between oppression and the ways in which power can be used both to oppress and liberate. And herein lies the strength-based perspective: rather than continuing to focus on the negatives, the challenging and multifaceted psychosocial hurdles that many GLBT youth must overcome, these programs capitalize upon the resiliency that is built by meeting and overcoming those challenges.

As identified by Cianciotto and Cahill (2003), many of these GLBT youth have incredibly refined skills and remarkable strengths. They develop problem-solving skills and adaptive functioning beyond their years and the ability to both access and create support networks when necessary. GLBT youth learn to become role models for themselves and each other, learning from one another, supporting one another, and bringing their communities along with them in that process. This strengths-based programming allows them to develop their own sense of accomplishment within a world that at times feels hostile and threatening. This is not to wish upon any GLBT youth challenge and difficulty from which to develop this resiliency, and it is hopeful that future generations can gain these skills from life experiences other than oppression and harassment.

SUMMARY

This chapter has examined the gay, lesbian, bisexual, and transgender (GLBT) populations within the context of strengths-based social work practice. It also reviewed the various definitions of sexual orientation and gender identity. Identity development and forces of oppression were examined and discussed. These factors were explored to help social workers understand some of the unique factors that affect GLBT people in their daily lives.

Additionally, some specific populations within GLBT communities were explored. These populations include youth, older adults, people of color, gay and lesbian parents, and their children. It is important to note that when providing social work services to these populations, it is the responsibility of the social workers to spend time learning about the cultural norms of any of these groups. It is also critical to recognize that this list is by no means a comprehensive list and that other populations within the GLBT community were not explored here (e.g., GLBT people with disabilities, GLBT religious minorities, etc.).

This chapter also looked at the role of social policies that affect GLBT people, including marriage equity and nondiscrimination policies. Further, social work practice with GLBT people was also examined in some depth. The role of social worker biases and prejudices were explored as were strength-based affirmative practice models. Both of these components are particularly important for social workers to both reflect on their own biases as well as to consider GLBT-inclusive assessment and intervention design.

Finally, as part of this affirmative practice model, this chapter discussed evidence-based interventions and provided examples of two of these: cognitive-behavioral therapy with GLBT clients and the role of GSAs for GLBT youth.

CASE EXAMPLE

This final case example presents a complex family situation where one gay-identified adolescent is struggling with his decision to come out.

CASE 14.4 | A GAY YOUTH COMES OUT

Sean, a 15-year-old white male growing up in rural Pennsylvania, was brought in for counseling by his mother and father at the Family Counseling Center. Shanay, the social worker, was assigned to work with Sean.

During the initial counseling session, Sean's parents expressed great concern because they caught Sean kissing his neighbor, a 15-year-old boy named Luis. Sean's father, George, a local police officer, exclaims that he is disgusted by his son's behavior and insists that Sean is not one of those "AIDS-carrying sex maniacs." Sean's mother, Nancy, explains that she loves her son, but that she wants Shanay to make sure he is "on the straight and narrow path." She continues by saying that she is very active in the local Methodist church and is very worried about what other people with think if they find out. Sean's 17-year-old sister, Debbie, is embarrassed by her parents' behavior and tries to consistently explain that Sean is "perfectly normal" and that her best friend, Joanne, is a lesbian. Sean expressed very little during this first session. Shanay requested to meet with Sean alone the following week. He agreed.

During the second session, Shanay asked Sean his experience of the first session. He hesitantly explained that it was hard to hear his mom and dad say such things, but that he loved them and didn't want to disappoint them. Shanay asked in what ways Sean thought he would disappoint them. Sean pointedly said, "Well...I think I like guys and they don't want me to." He continued to explain how he realized something was different about him from when he was very young, but it wasn't until he was 7 years old that he connected the term "gay" with his feelings. Sean said that he sometimes was verbally assaulted at school and was worried that if he didn't "butch it up," the assaults would get physical. He never told his parents about these incidents. Sean also said that he believed that he would get AIDS if he told people he was gay, just as his father claimed. Sean also stated that over the course of the last few months, he has had difficulty sleeping for fear of getting beat up at school.

After numerous counseling sessions with Shanay, Sean began to use the term "gay" to refer to himself. He explained that while it felt right, he wasn't sure he wanted to say this to his parents. Shanay asked about what Sean thought might happen if he were to come out to his family. Sean hesitated, and quickly thought his father would disown him, except that his mother would probably try to stop George from doing anything "crazy." Shanay provided Sean with numerous gay-affirmative websites and resources for him to look at over the course of the next few weeks.

About one month later, Sean reported to be developing feelings for his neighbor, 15-year-old Luis. Luis told Sean that he liked him, but he wasn't sure about how he felt about telling anyone. As a result of this, Sean stated that he was tired of hiding and wanted to "tell the world who I am." Shanay cautioned Sean about such a decision, but also applauded his courage and confidence.

Discussion Questions

1. Using the Levels of Response Assessment Tool as discussed in Chart 14.1, where does each of the family members fall?
2. Given what you know, what is your opinion about how motivated each family member is to become involved in counseling? Should all four family members be involved in this counseling? Why or why not?
3. What do you think Nancy's (Sean's mother) "agenda" is for insisting that Sean attend counseling? What types of barriers do you think Shanay will encounter if she invites the entire family back into the counseling session? How will Shanay engage George (Sean's father) and Nancy without alienating Sean?
4. What are some of the psychosocial issues that Sean is confronting? How has his experience at school contributed to Sean's struggles with his parents?
5. What are some of the cognitive distortions that Sean holds?
6. What are some of Sean's strengths?
7. What types of resources might Shanay give to Sean?

References

Alexander, J., and Yescavage, K. (2003). Bisexuality and transgenderism: InterSEXions of the others. *Journal of Bisexuality, 3*(3/4), 1–23.

American Psychiatric Association (1968). *Diagnostic and statistical manual of mental disorders* (2nd ed.). Washington DC: Author.

American Psychological Association Division 44/ Committee on Lesbian, Gay, and Bisexual Concerns Joint Task Force (2000). Guidelines for psychotherapy with lesbian, gay, and bisexual clients. *American Psychologist, 55*(12), 1440–1451.

Bailey, J. M., Bobrow, D., Wolfe, M., and Mikach, S. (1995). Sexual orientation of adult sons of gay fathers. *Developmental Psychology, 31,* 124–129.

Barret, R. L., and Robinson, B. E. (1990). *Gay fathers.* Lexington, MA: Lexington Books.

Bem, S. L. (1995). Dismantling gender polarization and compulsory heterosexuality: Should we turn the volume up or down? *Journal of Sex Research, 32*(5), 329–334.

Besen, W. (2003). Political science. *Journal of Gay and Lesbian Psychotherapy, 7*(3), 69–82.

Bigner, J. J., and Bozett, F. W. (1990). Parenting by gay fathers. In F. W. Bozett and M. B. Sussman (Eds.), *Homosexuality and family relations* (pp. 155–176). New York: Harrington Park Press.

Blumenfeld, W. J., and Raymond, D. (1988). *Looking at gay and lesbian life.* Boston: Beacon Press.

Bornstein, K. (1994). *Gender outlaw: On men, women, and the rest of us.* New York: Vintage.

Bozett, F. W. (1980). Gay fathers: How and why they disclose their homosexuality to their children. *Family Relations, 29,* 173–179.

Bozett, F. W. (1989). Gay fathers: A review of the literature. In F. W. Bozett (Ed.), *Homosexuality and the family* (pp. 137–162). New York: Harrington Park Press.

Brown, E. (2005). We wear the mask: African American contemporary gay male identities. *Journal of African American Studies, 9*(2), 29–38.

Bull, C. (2001, June 19). Much ado about changing. *The Advocate, 840,* 30–32.

Casas, J. M., Brady, S., and Ponterotto, J. G. (1983). Sexual preference biases in counseling: An information processing approach. *Journal of Counseling Psychology, 30*(2), 139–145.

Cass, V. (1979). Homosexual identity formation: A theoretical model. *Journal of Homosexuality, 4*(3), 219–235.

Children of Lesbians and Gays Everywhere (n.d.). *Facts about kids with gay and lesbian parents.* Retrieved January 14, 2006, from http://www.colage.org/resources/facts.htm

Christianson, A. (2005, October). A re-emergence of reparative therapy. *Contemporary Sexuality, 39*(10), 8–17.

Cianciotto, J., and Cahill, S. (2003). *Educational policy: Issues affecting gay, lesbian, bisexual, and transgender youth.* New York: National Gay and Lesbian Task Policy Institute.

Coleman, E. (1982). Developmental stages of the coming out process. *Journal of Homosexual, 7*(7), 31–43.

Cook, A. T., and Pawlowski, W. (1991). *Issue paper: Youth and homosexuality,* P-FLAG, PO Box 27605, Washington, DC, 20038.

D'Augelli, A. R., Hershberger, S. L., and Pilkington, N. W. (2001). Suicidality patterns and sexual orientation-related factors among lesbian, gay, and bisexual youth. *Suicide and Life Threatening Behavior, 31,* 250–264.

DeCrescenzo, T. A. (1984). Homophobia: A study of attitudes of mental health professionals toward homosexuality. *Journal of Social Work & Human Sexuality, 2,* 115–136.

Drescher, J., and Zucker, K. J. (2006). *Ex-gay research: Analyzing the Spitzer study and its relation to science, religion, politics, and culture.* New York: Harrington Park Press.

Dworkin, S. (2001). Treating the bisexual client. *Journal of Clinical Psychology, 57*(5), 671–680.

Editors of the Harvard Law Review (1990). *Sexual orientation and the law.* Cambridge, MA: Harvard University Press.

Eliason, M. (2001). Bi-negativity: The stigma facing bisexual men. *Journal of Bisexuality, 1*(2/3), 137–154.

Elze, D. E. (2006). Oppression, prejudice and discrimination. In D. F. Morrow and L. Messinger (Eds.), *Sexual orientation & gender expression in social work practice: Working with gay, lesbian, bisexual, & transgender people.* (pp. 43–80), New York: Columbia University Press.

Embraye, N. (2006). Affirmative psychotherapy with bisexual transgender people, *Journal of Bisexuality, 6*(1/2), 51–63.

Falk, P. J. (1989). Lesbian mothers: Psychosocial assumptions in family law. *American Psychologist, 44,* 941–947.

Falk, P. J. (1994). The gap between psychosocial assumptions and empirical research in lesbian-mother child custody cases. In A. E. Gottfried and A. W. Gottfried (Eds.), *Redefining families: Implications for children's development* (pp. 131–156). New York: Plenum.

Fanon, F. (1967). *Black skin, white masks: The experiences of a black man in a white world.* New York: Grove.

Firestein, B. A. (2007). *Becoming visible: Counseling bisexuals across the lifespan.* New York: Columbia University Press.

Fish, E. (2005, Summer). The road to recognition: A global perspective on gay marriage. *Harvard International Review, 32–35.*

Fort, J., Steiner, C., and Conrad, F. (1971). Attitudes of mental health professionals toward homosexuality and its treatment. *Psychological Reports, 29,* 347–350.

Fox, R. C. (2006). Affirmative psychotherapy with bisexual women and bisexual men: An introduction. *Journal of Bisexuality, 6*(1/2), 1–11.

Fullmer, E. M. (2006). Lesbian, gay, bisexual, and transgender aging. In D. F. Morrow and L. Messinger (Eds.), *Sexual orientation & gender expression in social work practice: Working with gay, lesbian, bisexual, & transgender people.* (pp. 285–303). New York: Columbia University Press.

Garfinkle, E. M., and Morin, S. F. (1978). Psychologists' attitudes toward homosexual psychotherapy clients. *Journal of Social Issues, 34*(3), 101–112.

Garnets, L., Hancock, K. A., Cochran, S. D., Goodchilds, J., and Peplau, L. A. (1991). Issues in psychotherapy with lesbians and gay men: A survey of psychologists. *American Psychologist, 46,* 964–972.

Garofalo, R., Wolf, R. C., Kessel, S., Palfrey, J., and DuRant, R. H. (1998). The association of health-risk behaviors and sexual orientation among a school-based sample of adolescents. *Pediatrics, 101*(5), 895–902.

Gartrell, N., Kraemer, H., and Brodie, H. K. (1974). Psychiatrists' attitudes toward female homosexuality. *Journal of Nervous Disorders and Mental Diseases, 150*(2), 141–144.

Golombok, S., Spencer, A., and Rutter, M. (1983). Children in lesbian and single-parent households: Psychosexual and psychiatric appraisal. *Journal of Child Psychology and Psychiatry, 24,* 551–572.

Gottman, J. S. (1990). Children of gay and lesbian parents. In F. W. Bozett and M. B. Sussman (Eds.), *Homosexuality and family relations* (pp. 177–196). New York: Harrington Park Press.

Graham, D. L. R., Rawlings, E. I., Halpern, H. S., and Hermes, J. (1984). Therapists' need for training in counseling lesbians and gay men. *Professional Psychology: Research and Practice, 15*(4), 482–496.

Gray, J. (2000). Cognitive-behavioural therapy. In D. Davies and C. Neal (Eds.), *Therapeutic perspectives on working with lesbian, gay, and bisexual clients,* (pp. 24–38), Philadelphia, PA: Open Universtiy Press.

Green, R. (1978). Sexual identity of 37 children raised by homosexual or transsexual parents. *American Journal of Psychiatry, 135,* 692–697.

Hash, K. M., and Ceperich, S. D. (2006). Workplace issues. In D. F. Morrow and L. Messinger (Eds.), *Sexual orientation & gender expression in social work practice: Working with gay, lesbian, bisexual, & transgender people* (pp. 405–426). New York: Columbia University Press.

Herdt, G., and Boxer, A. (1996). *Children of horizons* (2nd ed.). Boston: Beacon Press.

Hudson, W. W., and Ricketts, W. A. (1980). A strategy for the measurement of homophobia. *Journal of Homosexuality, 5,* 356–371.

Human Rights Campaign (2007). *Employment Non-Discrimination Act.* Retrieved on August 14, 2008, from http://www.hrc.org/laws_and_elections/enda.asp

Israel, G. E., and Tarver, D. E. (1997). *Transgender care: Recommended guidelines, practical information & personal accounts.* Philadelphia, PA: Temple University Press.

Jagose, A. (1996). *Queer theory: An introduction.* New York: New York University Press.

Johnson, F. (1997). Reinventing marriage. In M. Lowenthal (Ed.), *Sex, spirit, community: Gay men at the millennium* (pp. 187–199). New York: Tarcher/Putnam.

Jones, K. L. (2001). Is having the luck of growing old in the gay, lesbian, bisexual, transgender community good or bad luck? *Journal of Gay and Lesbian Social Services, 13*(4), 13–14.

Kendell, K. (2003, Summer). Lesbian and gay parents in child custody and visitation disputes [Electronic version]. *Human Rights Magazine, 30*(3).

Kinsey, Alfred C., et al. (1948/1998). *Sexual Behavior in the Human Male.* Philadelphia: W.B. Saunders; Bloomington: Indiana U. Press.

Kinsey, Alfred C., et al. (1953/1998). *Sexual Behavior in the Human Female*. Philadelphia: W.B. Saunders; Bloomington: Indiana U. Press.

Kosciw, J. G., and Cullen, M. K. (2001). *The GLSEN 2001 national school climate survey: The school-related experiences of our nations lesbian, gay, bisexual, and transgendered youth*. New York: The Gay, Lesbian, and Straight Education Network.

Kweskin, S. L., and Cook, A. S. (1982). Heterosexual and homosexual mothers self-described sex-role behavior and ideal sex-role behavior in children. *Sex Roles, 8*, 967–975.

Lev, A. I. (2006). Transgender emergence within families. In D. F. Morrow and L. Messinger (Eds.), *Sexual orientation & gender expression in social work practice: Working with gay, lesbian, bisexual, & transgender people*. (pp. 263–283), New York: Columbia University Press.

Lombardi, J., and van Servellen, G. (2000). Building culturally sensitive substance use prevention and treatment programs for transgendered populations. *Journal of Substance Abuse Treatment, 19*, 291–296.

Lorde, A. (1984). *Sister Outsider*. Trumansburg, NY: The Crossing Press.

Luckstead, A. (1996, March). *Lesbian and bisexual women who are mental health care consumers: Experiences in the mental health system*. Paper presented at the Annual Conference of the Association of Women in Psychology, Portland, OR.

Lyons, T. A. (1983). Lesbian mothers' custody fears. *Women and Therapy, 2*, 231–240.

Messing, A. E., Schoenberg, R., and Stephens, R. K. (1984). Confronting homophobia in health care settings: Guidelines for social work practice. In R. Schoenberg, R. S. Goldberg, and D. A. Shore (Eds.), *Homosexuality and social work* (pp. 65–74). New York: The Haworth Press.

Messinger, L. (2006). Toward affirmative practice. In D. F. Morrow and L. Messinger (Eds.), *Sexual orientation & gender expression in social work practice: Working with gay, lesbian, bisexual, & transgender people*. (pp. 460–470). New York: Columbia University Press.

Miller, J. A., Jacobsen, R. B., and Bigner, J. J. (1981). The child's home environment for lesbian versus heterosexual mothers: A neglected area of research. *Journal of Homosexuality, 7*, 49–56.

Moats, D. (2004). *Civil wars: The battle for gay marriage*. New York: Harcourt.

Money, J., and Dalery, J. (1976). Iatrogenic homosexuality: Gender identity in seven 46XX chromosomal females with hyperadrenocortical hermaphroditism born with a penis, three reared as boys, four reared as girls. *Journal of Homosexuality, 1*(4), 357–371.

Morin, S. F. (1977). Heterosexual bias in psychological research on lesbianism and male homosexuality. *American Psychologist, 32*, 629–637.

Morrow, D. F. (2000). Coming out to families: Guidelines for interventions with gay and lesbian clients. *Journal of Family Social Work, 5*(2), 53–66.

Morrow, D. F. (2006). Gay, lesbian, bisexual and transgender adolescents. In D. F. Morrow and L. Messinger (Eds.), *Sexual orientation & gender expression in social work practice: Working with gay, lesbian, bisexual & transgender people* (pp. 175–195). New York: Columbia Press.

Morrow, D. F. (2006). Gay, lesbian, and bisexual identity development. In D. F. Morrow and L. Messinger (Eds.), *Sexual orientation & gender expression in social work practice: Working with gay, lesbian, bisexual & transgender people* (pp. 81–104). New York: Columbia Press.

Morrow, D. F., and Messinger, L. (2006). *Sexual orientation & gender expression in social work practice: Working with gay, lesbian, bisexual, & transgender people*. New York: Columbia University Press.

Moss, J. F. (1994). The heterosexual bias inventory (HBI): Gay, lesbian and bisexual clients's perceptions of heterosexual bias in psychotherapy. (Doctoral dissertation, Michigan State University). *Dissertation Abstracts International 55*(12), 5571–B.

Mucklow, B. M., and Phelan, G. K. (1979). Lesbian and traditional mothers' responses to adult response to child behavior and self-concept. *Psychological Reports, 44*, 880–882.

Nagel, J. (2000). Ethnicity and sexuality. *Annual Review of Sociology, 26*, 107–133.

National Association of Social Workers. (1996). *Code of ethics*. Washington, DC: Author.

National Association of Social Workers National Committee on Gay, Lesbian, and Bisexual Issues (2000, January 21). *Position Statement: "Reparative" and "conversion" therapies for lesbians and gay men*. Retrieved August 28, 2006 from http://www.naswdc.org/PRAC/LBG/reparative.html

Neisen, J. H. (1990). Heterosexism: Redefining homophobia for the 1990's. *Journal of Gay & Lesbian Psychology, 1*(3), 21–35.

Nelson, J. B. (1978). *Embodiment: An approach to sexuality and Christian theology*. Minneapolis, MN: Augsburg.

Newman, B. S., Dannenfesler, P. L., and Benishek, L. (2002). Assessing beginning social work and counseling students' acceptance of lesbians and gay men. *Journal of Social Work Education, 38*(2), 273–288.

Ossanna, S. M. (2000). Relationships and Couples Counseling. In R. M. Perez, K. A. DeBord, and K. J. Bieschke (Eds.), *Handbook of counseling and psychotherapy with lesbian, gay, and bisexual clients* (pp. 275–302). Washington, DC: American Psychiatric Association.

Pagelow, M. D. (1980). Heterosexual and lesbian single mothers: A comparison of problems, coping and solutions. *Journal of Homosexuality, 5*, 198–204.

Parker, B. A. (2007). Orientations: GLBTQ. In Tepper, M.S. and Owens, A.F. (Eds.) *Sexual health, Volume 1, Psychological foundations*, (pp. 231–262). Westport, CT: Praeger publishers.

Patterson, C. J. (1994a). Children of the lesbian baby boom Behavioral adjustment, self-concepts, and sex-role identity. In B. Greene and G. M. Herek (Eds.), *Contemporary perspectives on lesbian and gay psychology: Theory, research and applications* (pp. 156–175). Beverly Hills, CA: Sage.

Patterson, C. J. (1994b). Lesbian and gay families. *Current Directions in Psychological Science, 3*, 62–64.

Patterson, C. J. (1995a). Families of the lesbian baby boom: Parents' division of labor and children's adjustment. *Developmental Psychology, 31*, 115–123.

Patterson, C. J. (1995b). Lesbian mothers, gay fathers, and their children. In A. R. D'Augelli and C. J. Patterson (Eds.), *Lesbian, gay and bisexual identities across the lifespan* (pp. 262–290). New York: Oxford University Press.

Patterson, C. J. (1996). Lesbian and gay parenthood. In M. H. Bornstein (Ed.), *Handbook of parenting* (pp. 255–274). Hillsdale, NJ: Lawrence Erlbaum.

Pauling, M. L. (1999). *A conceptualization of transgender issues: Research and treatment ideas*. Poster presented at the 107th Annual Convention of the American Psychological Association. Boston, MA.

Payne, A. (1978). Law and the problem patient: Custody and parental rights of homo-sexual, mentally retarded, mentally ill, and incarcerated patients. *Journal of Family Law, 16*, 797–818.

Pfohl, A. H. (2004). The intersection of personal and professional identity: The heterosexual supervisors' role in fostering the development of sexual minority supervises. *The Clinical Supervisor, 23* (1), 139–164.

Phillips, J. C., and Fischer, A. R. (1998). Graduate students' training experiences with lesbian, gay, and bisexual issues. *Counseling Psychologists, 20*(3), 712–734.

Rand, C., Graham, D. L. R., and Rawlings, E. I. (1982). Psychological health and factors the court seeks to control in lesbian mother custody trials. *Journal of Homosexuality, 8*, 27–39.

Riddle, D. I., and Sang, B. (1978). Psychotherapy with lesbians. *Journal of Social Issues, 34*(3), 84–100.

Roskoff, A. (2008, May 2). ENDA Origins. *The New York Blade, 12*(18), 35.

Rubin, A. (2008). *Practitioner's guide to using research for evidence-based practice*. Hoboken, NJ: John Wiley & Sons, Inc.

Rust, P. C. R. (2007). The construction and reconstruction of bisexuality: Inventing and reinventing the self. In B. A. Firestein (Ed.), *Becoming visible: Counseling bisexual across the lifespan* (pp. 3–27). New York: Columbia Press.

Ryan C., and Futterman, D. (1997). *Lesbian and gay youth: Care and counseling*. Philadelphia, PA: Hanley & Belfus.

Satterly, B. A. (2006). Therapist self-disclosure from a gay male perspective. *Families in Society, 87*(2), 240–248.

Satterly, B. A. and Dyson, D. A. (2007). Sexual identities of gay men and lesbians: Cultural foundations and controversies. In Tepper, M. S. and Owens, A. F. (Eds.) *Sexual health, volume 3: Moral and cultural foundations* (pp. 315–342). Westport, CT: Praeger Publishers.

Sausa, L. A. (2003). The HIV prevention and educational needs of trans youth: A qualitative study. *Dissertation Abstracts International, 64*(04), 1186. (UMI No. 3087465)

Savin-Williams, R. C. (1994). Verbal and physical abuse as stressors in the lives of lesbian, gay male, and bisexual youths: Association with school problems, running away, substance abuse, prostitution, and suicide. *Journal of Consulting Clinical Psychology, 62*, 261–269.

Schidlo, A., Schroeder, M., and Drescher, J. (2001). *Sexual conversion therapy: Ethical, clinical and research perspectives*. Binghamton, NY: Haworth Press.

SIECUS (1993). Sexual orientation and identity. *SIECUS Report, 21*(3), 19–20.

Signorile, M. (1997). *The Signorile report on gay men: Sex, drugs, muscles, and the passages of life.* New York: HarperCollins.

Silverstein, C. (2003). The religious conversion of homosexuals: Subject selection is the voir dire of psychological research. *Journal of Gay and Lesbian Psychotherapy, 7*(3), 31–53.

Spitzer, R. (2003). Can some gay men and lesbians change their sexual orientation? 200 participants reporting a change from homosexual to heterosexual orientation. *Archives of Sexual Behavior, 32*(5), 403–417.

Tharinger, D., and and Wells, G. (2000). An attachment perspective on the developmental challenges of gay and lesbian adolescents: The need for continuity of caregiving from family and schools. *School Psychological Review, 29*(2), 158–173.

Thompson, N., McCandless, B., and Strickland, B. (1971). Personal adjustment of male and female homosexuals and heterosexuals. *Journal of Abnormal Psychology, 78,* 237–240.

Trebay, G. (2000, February 2). *Homo thugz blow up the spot.* Village Voice. Retrieved January 14, 2006, from http://www.villagevoice.com

Troiden, R. R. (1988). Homosexual identity development. *Journal of adolescent health, 9,* 102–112.

Van Wormer, K., Wells, J., and Boes, M. (2000). *Social work with lesbians, gays, and bisexuals: A strengths perspective.* Boston: Allyn & Bacon.

Vancouver Board of Education (2004). *Policy manual.* Retrieved from http://www.vsb.bc.ca/districtinfo/policies/a/ACG-Lesbian_Gay_Bisexual.htm

Weinberg, G. (1972). *Society and the healthy homosexual.* New York: St. Martin's Press.

Wisniewski, J. J., and Toomey, B. G. (1987). Are social workers homophobic? *Social Work, 32,* 454–455.

Zucker, K. J. (2003). The politics and science of "reparative therapy", *Archives of Sexual Behavior, 32*(5), 399–402.

GENERALIST PRACTICE WITH ABUSED AND NEGLECTED CHILDREN AND THEIR FAMILIES

Paula Silver and Beth Barol

Mira/Alamy

Chelsea R. is a MSW student completing her first-year internship at a public child welfare agency. She had worked at the same agency for 4 years as a child protective services worker conducting investigations and assessments of reports of abuse and neglect. Although Chelsea had learned a great deal while doing her job, she was very happy to have been selected by her agency to pursue her MSW degree under the agency's education leave program.

In the 4 years that Chelsea had been a child welfare caseworker, she had felt both challenged and gratified by her job. She felt challenged by the extraordinary unmet needs of the children and families with whom she has worked, but also gratified by the many opportunities she found to make a big difference in their lives by helping them to access resources and making sure that children were safe. Chelsea was aware that she had relied on her "gut feelings" and innate empathy to guide her in her work. With MSW education, Chelsea looked forward to learning the theories, techniques, and skills to make more informed assessments and decisions. She was also eager to learn about new methods that might provide more effective services for the children and families she had encountered.

When Chelsea arrived at her internship on Monday morning, she could feel the tension in the air. She soon learned from coworkers that over the weekend 14-year-old Daniella Patrick had died as a result of dehydration and malnutrition. Although the girl was living with her mother and three younger siblings at the time of her death, the family had been known to the agency for over 3 years as a result of repeated reports from family and friends alleging neglect and abuse of Daniella and her siblings. A protective services worker, assigned to the family when the initial reports were received, was responsible for assessing the safety of the Patrick children and making recommendations regarding needed services.

The family had also been referred for services from a private provider agency under contract with Chelsea's agency. The role of the provider agency was to deliver intensive supervision and supportive services for the Patrick family in their home. It is routine practice to assign a public agency caseworker to monitor the provision of services of provider agencies to make sure that appropriate support was available to the family. Accordingly, a second caseworker from Chelsea's agency was responsible for visiting the family monthly to evaluate the situation and to review the reports of the provider agency regarding the family's status.

Chelsea was horrified, and the mood among the staff at the agency was one of depression and anxiety. The media and the public already viewed child welfare workers negatively. This would only make it worse. Two agencies—one public and one private—were responsible for ensuring the welfare and safety of Daniella. Three caseworkers had been involved in and charged with responsibility to make sure that Daniella was safe. Yet she was found dead in her home, a victim of extreme neglect. How could this happen?

Chelsea already knew that her job required her to make decisions about the safety of vulnerable children in potentially high-risk situations. She was working with several families who could be considered "high-risk." Could one of the children on her caseload die? Was she assessing safety and risk accurately? Was she using effective interventions in working with the parents or caregivers of the children for whom she was responsible? Are the current policies in place sufficient for protecting children from maltreatment and supporting families? If not, what changes in policies should be considered to prevent something like this from happening again? Should she reconsider the field of practice in which she had chosen to specialize?

No! Chelsea was determined to devote her energy to helping vulnerable children and their families—even if the risks were high. However, she was fully aware that there was so much she needed to know to feel confident in her role as a child welfare case manager. By the end of this chapter, you should be able to help Chelsea better understand:

- The scope and nature of the problem of child maltreatment in the U.S.
- The debates surrounding public child welfare policy
- The roles and tasks performed by child welfare social workers
- Generalist social work skills to support child welfare practice at specific points of intervention
- Some of the evidence-based "best practice models" in child welfare practice.

CHILD WELFARE AS A FIELD OF PRACTICE

As a field of practice, social work child welfare practice involves organizing, planning, and implementing strategies to help families at risk of disruption due to neglect or abuse of their children. The roles played by child welfare social workers are varied and require a strong grasp of generalist social work principles. More often than not, child welfare social workers work with families at a point of crisis or transition. In order to be effective, they must have the ability to engage clients in a productive helping relationship, even when they are viewed as unwelcome intruders in the clients' lives. They must be knowledgeable about resources; they must understand child welfare policy mandates; they must be keen observers; they must be critical thinkers; they must keep up to date on "best practices" in the field; they must be able to promote collaboration; and they must understand and be able to work effectively across racial and ethnic differences. Whatever functions a child welfare social worker performs— understanding how child maltreatment is defined, the scope of the problem, and the social policy mandates that govern the field of practice are important foundations.

CHILD MALTREATMENT DEFINED

Our nation's values and ideas about children's rights, childrearing practices, and the very nature of childhood have evolved over time as a consequence of shifts in dominant values and socioeconomic conditions. In a country as a culturally diverse as the U.S., it is challenging to achieve consensus about where to draw the line between culture-based child discipline practices and child maltreatment.

The Child Abuse and Prevention Act of 1974 (CAPTA) was an initial attempt by the federal government to establish national standards for definitions of child abuse and neglect. According to the most recent CAPTA amendments included in the Keeping Children and Families Safe Act of 2003, the term "child abuse and neglect" is, at a minimum,

- Any recent act or failure to act on the part of a parent or caretaker which results in death, serious physical or emotional harm, sexual abuse or exploitation; or

- An act or failure to act which presents an imminent risk of serious harm

The act specifically defines sexual abuse to include:

- The employment, use, persuasion, inducement, enticement, or coercion of any child to engage in, or assist any other person to engage in, any sexually explicit conduct or simulation of such conduct for the purpose of producing a visual depiction of such conduct; or
- The rape, and in cases of caretaker or interfamilial relationships, statutory rape, molestation, prostitution, or other form of sexual exploitation of children, or incest with children

Within these minimum standards, each state enacts its own legal definitions. While states' definitions vary, four major categories of abuse or neglect are generally addressed: physical abuse, neglect, sexual abuse, and emotional abuse:

- **Physical Abuse** – nonaccidental physical injury that is inflicted by a parent, caregiver, or other person who has responsibility for the child. Nonaccidental injury is considered abuse regardless of whether the person inflicting the injury intended to do harm. Physical discipline is not considered abuse as long as it is "reasonable and causes no bodily injury to the child."
- **Neglect** – failure of a parent, guardian, or other caregiver to provide for a child's basic needs. This can include physical neglect, medical neglect, educational neglect, abandonment, and emotional neglect.
- **Sexual Abuse** – activities by a parent or caregiver such as fondling a child's genitals, penetration, incest, rape, sodomy, indecent exposure, and exploitation through prostitution or the production of pornographic materials.
- **Emotional Abuse** – a pattern of behavior that impairs a child's emotional development or sense of self-worth.

In recent years, most states have also recognized substance abuse in their definitions of abuse and neglect. Two main areas or concern regarding substance abuse are addressed by the states: (1) the harm caused by prenatal drug exposure and (2) the harm caused to children of any age by exposure to illegal drug activity in the home. (Child Welfare Information Gateway, 2008).

PREVALENCE OF CHILD MALTREATMENT

In 2006, the total population of children in the U.S. was 73.7 million. According to the U.S. Department of Health and Human Services National Child Abuse and Neglect Data Systems (NCANS), approximately 12 out of every 1,000 children were victims of child maltreatment. Figure 15.1 highlights of the 2006 NCANS report.

Many child welfare experts believe that the documented incidence of child maltreatment represents only a small proportion of the actual victimization of children. Many incidents of child abuse or neglect are likely to go unreported for a variety of reasons, including the general public's distrust of public authority, reluctance to interfere in the privacy of neighbors, and confusion over what might be legitimately considered abuse or neglect.

In 2006,

- 3.3 million referrals were made to child protective services (CPS) agencies alleging maltreatment of approximately 6 million children
- 3.6 million children were the subject of CPS investigations or assessments
- 905,000 children – 30% of all investigations – were substantiated to have been victims of maltreatment
- 1,530 children died from causes attributed to abuse or neglect.

FIGURE 15.1 | U.S. CHILD MALTREATMENT STATISTICS – 2006

Source: U.S. Department of Health and Human Services, Administration of Children, Youth and Family Services (2006).

THE EVOLUTION OF CHILD AND FAMILY WELFARE POLICY

Very often, the roles and responsibilities of the generalist social worker are both supported and constrained by the social policy provisions that apply to the field of practice and the population served. This is especially true in the field of child welfare. It is very important for the child welfare social worker to understand the origins of evolution of child welfare social policy in order to appreciate present day policy provisions.

Social forces, dominant values, economic trends, and the willingness of the public to fund the costs of protecting children have shaped the evolution of child welfare policy. Underlying social tensions can be discerned as one traces this evolution. These tensions can be described as a set of competing emphases:

- Parental rights and family support versus child protection
- Voluntary services versus public mandates
- Child neglect and abuse as a function of family dysfunction versus social forces
- Family reunification versus permanence for children

Where the emphasis has been placed in addressing the needs of children at risk can be seen to play out throughout the evolution of child welfare social policy.

CHILDREN AS PROPERTY (1600S–1700S)

During the first two centuries of the nation's history, emphasis was placed squarely on parental rights, and the needs of the family far outweighed concerns about the protection of children. In keeping with English common law, children were considered to be the personal possession of their parents and did not have independent rights. Corporal punishment—both at home and in school—was generally accepted as a legitimate means of ensuring obedience to authority. The fate of children depended almost entirely on the situation of their families.

Parents who could not adequately provide for their children were socially condemned and seen as having forfeited their rights as parents. Indigent parents and their children were thought to require instruction in the values of work and self-sufficiency. All of the provisions for families and dependent children during the first two centuries of American history, as McGowan (2005) states, "can be characterized as meager arrangements made on a reluctant, begrudging basis to guarantee a minimal level of subsistence" (p. 12).

EMERGENCE OF PUBLIC CONCERN FOR CHILDREN (1800s)

Several economic shifts in the U.S. economy and social relationships influenced provisions for children during the 1800s. During the first half of the century, the practice of indenturing indigent and orphaned White children declined as the availability of slave labor reduced the need for indentured White children. At the same time, growing numbers of social "reformers" began to publicize the miserable conditions of dependent children confined to almshouses and call for new solutions. Over the next several decades, residential institutions for children, such as orphanages and poor farms, and church-based organized efforts to provide foster care began to appear around the country.

Beginnings of Organized Foster Care.   One of the most ambitious efforts to champion foster care as a solution to the problem of homeless children was the work of Charles Loring Brace, a New York minister. In 1864, Brace found the Children's Aid Society of New York City, dedicated to finding families in the West to house and care for the city's homeless children. Over the next 75 years, the Society sent over 150,000 children to live with farm families in the Western part of the country (DiLorenzo and Cairns, 2005). Although many of these "farmed out" children ended up with loving and nurturing families, inadequate screening and no oversight left many prey to exploitation and maltreatment.

Emergence of State-mandated Child Protection.   A broader notion of public responsibility for child protection began to take shape toward the end of the 19th century. In 1874, the tragic story of "Little Mary Ellen" in New York captured the attention of the country. Abused and neglected, Mary Ellen came to the attention of New York's Society for the Protection of Animals (SPCA). With no existing laws for the protection of children to turn to, the SPCA used New York's laws for the protection animals to file suit on behalf of Mary Ellen. The result was a highly publicized trial that revealed the need for greater legal protections for children.

In response to the Mary Ellen story and increasing numbers of orphaned and abandoned children in cities growing rapidly through immigration, organizations began to appear throughout the country addressing the plight of homeless and abused children. Over 300 anticruelty societies were organized in the U.S. by the early 1900s (DiLorenzo and Cairns, 2005). These societies were typically voluntary and operated without governmental sanction, oversight, or funding.

Types of Services During The 1800s.   Toward the end of the 19th century, as care for homeless and indigent children in almshouses or through "outdoor relief" fell into disfavor, foster homes and institutional care, administered by voluntary organizations, emerged as the preferred alternatives. At the same time, state governments began to take a greater role in oversight of these efforts. Increasingly, state governments adopted legislation mandating some sort of provision for the needs of homeless and indigent children. Legislation took various forms in different states, but generally local communities were increasingly held responsible either directly or through purchase of services from private organizations for the care and well-being of dependent children.

Children of African Descent.   It is important to point out that, however meager the provisions for White children, the needs of children of African descent went totally unrecognized by White society until well into the 20th century. During the days of slavery, enslaved children were the sole property of the slave owner. They were routinely separated from their families and traded just as adults. Freed slaves and/or those Africans able to escape to nonslave-holding territories did not have access to even the meager provisions available to indigent White families.

After abolition, both public and private provisions for children systematically excluded Black children. Consequently, a separate child welfare system, funded and administered by voluntary organization, evolved in the Black community alongside the "official" system for White children. The emergence of a federal mandate on behalf of the needs of children gradually ended the exclusion of Black children from the public system. However, even today many historically Black voluntary child welfare organizations continue to address the needs of children of African descent.

The Federal Mandate to Protect Children in the 20th Century (1900s)

For the first three centuries of the nation, protection and care for at-risk children and their families were dispensed primarily by private and voluntary organizations. States and/or local communities provided whatever public oversight existed. The 20th century began a period during which provisions for the welfare of children became primarily driven by governmental mandate. The major legislative mandates and provisions are described below.

The early decades (1900s–1950s).   Recognition of a role for the federal government in the protection of children began to evolve in the early 1900s. The first White House Conference on Children was held in 1909 and called for an organized federal effort to address the needs of the nation's children. In 1912, as a result of the pressure of a coalition led by Jane Addams, Lillian Ward, and other organized groups, the U.S. Children's Bureau was established. The new agency was charged with responsibility for investigating and reporting on all matters related to the welfare of children.

> What was most significant about the passage of this law was that it represented the first congressional recognition that the federal government has a responsibility for the welfare of children. It also introduced the concept of public responsibility for all children, not just groups of poor, neglected, disturbed, and delinquent children served by public and private agencies. (McGowan, 2005, p. 20)

The U.S. Children's Bureau continues today, as an arm of the Department of Health and Human Services Administration for Children and Families, to carry federal responsibility for investigation, regulation, public education, advocacy, research, and the development of best practices.

The Social Security Act of 1935 provided the first federal funding for child welfare services. Title IV of the act established Assistance to Dependent Children (ADC), the first federal program to attempt to support children in poverty. Title V of the act provided grants to states for establishing child welfare agencies and developing services for dependent children. The size of the federal expenditure authorized under the Social Security Act increased steadily throughout the first half of the century.

1960s and 1970s.   The 1961 Amendments to the Social Security Act expanded funding to states to establish child abuse protection programs and protective services and created a formula for matching funding for state programs. Notably, the act tied the need for income maintenance—renamed as Aid to Families of Dependent Children (AFDC)—to a presumption of the family's need for social service support. Heralded at the time as an advance in social policy, this provision could be viewed as reminiscent of the belief that poverty was, at its root, the result of personal dysfunction rather than economic conditions. The 1961 amendments led states to significantly expand state public-administered child welfare services, including child protective services, social service supports for families receiving public income maintenance, and foster home care for children deemed to be living in unsuitable housing. The latter provision led to a steady increase in the number of children residing in foster care over the next decades. Figure 15.2 lists the years of important benchmarks of child and family policies.

The Child Abuse Prevention and Treatment Act of 1974 (CAPTA) represented another major advance in federal involvement in the protection of children. As previously described, CAPTA set minimum standards for the definition of abuse and neglect. The act required states to pass child abuse and neglect laws identifying mandated reporters. It also provided funding, at a very modest level, for research and demonstration projects for addressing the needs of children at risk of abuse and neglect.

The 1975 Title XX Amendment to the Social Security Act reflected a political willingness to increase investment in and public provision of child welfare services. The legislation significantly expanded federal funding and placed responsibility for the needs of dependent children squarely on the shoulders of the states. Among its provisions were requirements that states assume direct responsibility for social service planning and program development, develop comprehensive and integrated service plans, and track the costs and benefits of programs. The amendment also introduced the idea of "minimal level of care and protection" as a guide for child welfare decision-making. The determination of abuse or neglect would now be based on whether a child was receiving "minimal care and protection." Although this standard was loosely defined, and highly vulnerable to subjective assessment, it dominated to practice of risk assessment well into the 21st century.

Together, CAPTA and the Title XX amendments represented a major shift in child welfare policy by expanding the roles of the federal and state governments in

1909	First White House Conference on Children
1912	Creation of U.S. Childrens Bureau
1935	Social Security Act, Title IV, ADC; and Title V, Child Welfare Services Program
1961	Social Security Amendment, AFDC (foster care)
1962	Social Security Amendment providing 75% federal matching funds to states for child welfare services for current, former and potential AFDC recipients
1967	Social Security Amendments: Title IV-B authorizing the use of funds to purchase services from voluntary agencies
1974	Child Abuse and Protection Act (CAPTA)
1975	Title XX of the Social Security Act
1978	Indian Child Welfare Act
1980	Adoption Assistance and Child Welfare Act (Title IV-E)
1993	Family Preservation and Support Services Program
1994	Multi ethnic Placement Act
1996	Personal Responsibility and Work Opportunities Act (TANF)
1997	Adoption and Safe Families Act (AFSA)
1999	Foster Care Independence Act
2000	Child Abuse Prevention and Enforcement Act
2001	Promoting Safe and Stable Families Amendment
2003	Keeping Children Safe Amendment

FIGURE 15.2 | THE EVOLUTION OF THE FEDERAL ROLE IN CHILDREN, YOUTH, AND FAMILY SERVICES

Source: McGowan, B.G. (2005).

welfare of children. These federal mandates focused on protecting children, physically removing children from abusive and neglectful situations, and foster home care as the preferred out-of-home placement option. It should be noted that services to support a family's capacity to provide minimally adequate care and protection was not emphasized.

The 1980s. The next several decades of child welfare policy development can best be described as an era of shifting emphases. Each new piece of legislation was an effort to respond to the prevailing public view of the failings of child welfare policy and services. The tensions of family preservation versus child protection, the public costs of child protection, and beliefs about the underlying causes of child abuse and neglect would play out in each new piece of legislation.

As a result of CAPTA and Title XX, the numbers of children in foster care significantly expanded. Along with increasing numbers came increased length of stay in care. Research studies identified the problem of "foster care drift," the common experience of children left in limbo in temporary foster homes for years—and even worse—moved multiple times from one temporary foster home to another. Studies demonstrating the negative impact on healthy child development of such instability, as well as the mounting public cost of foster care, sent a strong alarm out to policy-makers, and calls for reform were heard both from the politicians and the social work profession.

The Adoption Assistance and Child Welfare Act of 1980 was a response to the phenomenon of "foster care drift" and encouraged a planning approach to estab-lish permanent living situations for children in the child welfare system as quickly as possible. The act introduced the concept of **permanency planning** into the lan-guage of child welfare, and it remains one of the explicit goals of child welfare intervention to the present day.

> Two overriding philosophies emerged from the act. The first was permanency planning, which assumed that prompt and decisive action to maintain children safely in their homes, or to place them quickly as possible in permanent homes with other families was the most desirable goal of child welfare services. The second philosophy was embodied in the words reasonable efforts ... (Gelles, 1996)

The term "reasonable efforts" meant that states were *first* to try to keep fami-lies together by providing both prevention and family reunification services. What constituted "reasonable efforts" would become a matter for ongoing public and professional debate.

If children could not be reunified with their families, the act also provided new funding to encourage adoption planning and placement for children in foster care. Finally, the act gave the court system a role in monitoring planning for children by requiring regular court review for all children in care.

The 1990s.   This decade was marked by a dramatic increase in social legislation affecting the child welfare system. The Family Preservation and Family Support Services Program, adopted in 1993, was, in part, an effort to encourage "reason-able efforts" activities called for by 1980 legislation. Most observers agreed that the "reasonable efforts" mandate was only given "lip service" throughout the 1980s. Services to help families avoid placement were minimal and poorly funded. The new legislative program provided increased funding for community-based child abuse and neglect prevention programs and increased services for families at risk of child placement.

The Multi-Ethnic Placement Act of 1994 (MEPA) was an effort to expand adoption efforts for children in long-term foster care. The act was also a response to several highly publicized and controversial cases of Black children being re-moved from White foster families with whom they had established strong bonds and adoptable Black children languishing in foster care because of the shortage of Black adoptive families. MEPA prohibited states from denying adoption and foster care placements on the basis of race or ethnicity, but at the same time permitted states to consider race and ethnicity in making placement decisions. States were also required to increase their efforts to recruit foster and adoptive families from diverse racial and ethnic groups to expand the number of homes available to chil-dren of color.

The Personal Responsibility and Work Opportunity Reconciliation Act of 1996 introduced Temporary Aid to Needy Families or TANF to replace the income maintenance provisions of the AFDC provisions of the Social Security Act of 1961. The significance of TANF for child welfare had to do with the restrictions placed on family eligibility for income support. First, families would have a 5-year lifetime limit on eligibility for benefits. Strict work requirements were placed on parents, regardless of access to appropriate childcare. Parents convicted of drug-related offenses were to be deemed ineligible for life to receive either TANF or food stamps. Finally, under the act states could choose to deny additional benefits for children born into families already receiving TANF support. The provisions of TANF promised to dramatically increase the numbers of families that would be disrupted due to poverty, alone.

> ...the passage of [TANF] marks the first time in U.S. history when federal law mandates efforts to protect children from maltreatment, but makes no guarantee of basic economic supports for children. (Coulter, 1997, as quoted in McGowan, 2005, p.39)

The Adoption and Safe Families Act of 1997 (ASFA) was yet one more effort to address perceived failings of the child welfare system and represented another swing of the pendulum of child welfare policy. Concerns that child welfare legislation to date had done little to curb "foster care drift" and at the same time had created a bias toward family preservation at the cost of child safety were widely discussed by child welfare professionals and policymakers. The provisions of AFSA addressed these concerns and represented a definitive shift away from an emphasis on "reasonable efforts" to one of focusing on permanency planning and safety. AFSA mandated that

- Child safety, permanency, and well-being be the first concern in planning for children at risk
- States were to expedite permanency planning for children in foster care
- States increase the number of children placed for adoption
- States be given funding incentives to promote adoption
- States meet outcome and performance standards and
- Financial penalties be imposed on states that fail to demonstrate improvements in outcomes

ASFA intensified the mandate for permanency planning and introduced the practice of "concurrent planning" for children in temporary placement. Concurrent planning requires social workers to begin consideration of a permanency plan (e.g., termination of parental rights, adoption, kinship care, etc.) for children as soon as they enter care, while at the same time make reasonable efforts to achieve family reunification. Concurrent planning was intended to shorten the stay in temporary care should family reunification prove unworkable within an identified time period. ASFA imposed a time limit on out-of-home placement—15 consecutive months or 22 nonconsecutive months of out-of-home placement. The public child welfare agency was responsible for providing a child with a permanent living situation when the time limit on out-of-home placement elapsed.

The Promoting Safe and Stable Families (PSSF), included in the AFSA legislation, was an attempt to support efforts to reduce the length of placement and encourage adoption as a permanency planning option. Its provisions also expanded funding for family support services in an effort to bolster "reasonable efforts" to reunify families. The program put even more "teeth" in the idea of permanency planning by mandating specific time limits for temporary foster care placement. If a child remains in foster care longer than 15 consecutive months or 22 nonconsecutive months, the public child welfare agency is mandated to pursue legal termination of parental rights.

CHILD WELFARE IN THE 21ST CENTURY (2000S)

The child welfare legislative initiatives of the 1980s and 1990s represented major advances in child welfare social policy. At the same time, many argued that the result was an inflexible bureaucratic public child welfare system, insensitive both to the families and children served and its workforce. The challenging client population and often unrewarding work environment created high worker turnover and low job satisfaction. Bureaucratic rigidity also made it nearly impossible for the system to test and incorporate new approaches to helping children and families. Tragedies like the one faced by Chelsea occurred regularly and captured the public's attention, just as the case of Little Mary Ellen at the end of the 19th century.

The first major child welfare legislation of the new century was the 2001 Amendments of the Promoting Safe and Stable Families program. With the increase in adoptions resulting from permanency planning and time limits on temporary foster care came an increasing number of failed adoptions and recognition that children adopted through the child welfare system often had special needs. The 2001 amendments provided federal funding to the states to promote postadoption services. The problem of substance abuse had long been recognized by child welfare social workers as one of the major causes of child maltreatment and family dysfunction and disruption. The legislation specifically directed funding for substance abuse programs to prevent placement and promote family reunification.

The Keeping Children and Families Safe Act of 2003 reauthorized the CAPTA and included additional funding through grants for projects to improve states' child protective services system infrastructures. It also attempted to stimulate innovation in the public child welfare system by making grant funding available for research, program demonstrations, training, and community-based prevention efforts.

Pending before Congress is the Keeping Families Safe Act of 2008. The bill, an amendment to title IVE of the Social Security Act, proposes an initiative to support families affected by substance abuse. If adopted, the act would allow children in foster care to be reunified with their parents in residential family treatment centers that provide safe environments for treating addiction and promoting healthy parenting.

In general, the beginning of the 21st century was greeted across all social service systems with calls for greater accountability and evidence that services provided were effective. Child welfare was no exception. In an effort to assess efforts and identify weaknesses, the Department of Health and Human Services Administration of Children and Family Services began to implement a program of systematic review of state child welfare systems in 2000. The first Children and Family Service Reviews (CFSRs) were conducted in 14 states with disappointing results.

Not a single state met the outcome benchmarks set by DHHS. By 2004, 52 CFSRs had been conducted with similar results (Di'Lorenzo and Cairns, 2005).

In summary, the evolution of child welfare social policy reflects continuous effort to address the needs of vulnerable children and families. Each new approach represents an effort to fix the failings of the previous approach. Clearly, "getting it right" in child welfare policy has been elusive. McGowan writing over 20 years ago, remains applicable today.

> … the history of American child welfare suggests that many of the dilemmas confronting the field today reflect the solutions devised to address the problems of the past, and we can anticipate that although current proposals for change will resolve some issues, they will create still others. (McGowan, 1983, p. 44)

CHILD WELFARE: GENERALIST PRACTICE SKILLS

The social work generalist practitioner carries an especially valued role in child welfare. Families experience the entire range of issues and stressors that affect our society today. They struggle with sociopolitical issues including poverty, poor education, eroding communities, and victimization, as well as the wide array of interpersonal and intrapersonal issues including maltreatment, mental and physical illness, differing abilities, substance abuse, and stigmatized life choices. We rely heavily on the generalist social worker's breadth of knowledge, skills, and familiarity with the multiple systems that affect the lives of their clients. The well-trained generalist practitioner is prepared to work with a wide variety of individuals, using well-developed practice skills to build a trusting relationship as they work collaboratively to understand and solve the issues at hand.

STRENGTHS-BASED PRACTICE—AN OVERARCHING PARADIGM

Social workers have moved away from traditional worldviews that are judgmental and controlling and are continuously moving toward richer models of empowerment and strengths-based approaches. The 21st century heralds a new era in child welfare. Promising practices, such as the family connection model, parent-child interaction therapy (PCIT), multisystemic therapy (MST), parent management training (PMT), The Incredible Years (Chaffin and Freidrich, 2004), and solution-focused interventions (Berg and Kelly, 2000; DeJong and Berg, 2001), are guiding progressive state child welfare agencies to combat the public perception that social services need to be punitive to be effective. Instead, grounded in evidenced-based practice, they are actively promulgating the strengths-based approach as the paradigm that underlies the services that are provided.

> Better outcomes can be achieved "if families are active in decisions and intervention planning (Corrigan & Bishop, 1997; McWilliam, Tocci, & Harbin, 1998). Individuals are seen as capable partners in the change process (Christensen et al., 1999) with strengths with which to build (Powell & Batsche, 1997). Family focused casework addresses a full range of barriers and strengths for the family and promotes practices that focus on successes and natural community partnerships (Brun & Rapp, 2001; Kutash, Duchnowski, Sumi, Rudo, & Harris, 2002; Skiba & Nichols, 2000). Such integrated agency services require believing

in family strengths, sharing control, and calling on the community to collaborate in strengthening families (Jehl, 1999)." (Huebner et al., 2006, p. 695)

CRITICAL THINKING

In response to this positive shifting of practice paradigms, the generalist practitioner has to hone her critical and creative thinking skills in order to meet the needs of her clients. Child welfare workers are faced with very complex and urgent situations on a daily basis. They have to make decisions regarding the safety and well-being of children and the capacities of families to meet the core needs of their children. Workers can feel pressured due in part to the volume of cases referred to the worker and the short time frames often required for decision-making and paper work filing. Often a worker will respond to this pressure by resorting to making snap decisions and relying upon stereotypes in order to finish their assign tasks in an expeditious manner. This approach, however, has yielded disastrous results for their families, and their communities. Quick decisions are often overly simplistic, inaccurate, and lead to overlooking key strengths and resources within the family and the family's support system.

The well trained and effective generalist practitioner uses a mode of thinking that is committed to thorough information gathering and open-minded examination of all aspects of a situation in order "to get to the bottom" of the issues at hand, rather than making superficial, stereotypical, and "snap" judgments (Paul and Elder, 2005).

We safeguard families and children at risk most effectively when we conscientiously:

- **Collect all the available data,** including a thorough review of the available records, interviewing all involved parties, making careful, professional on-site observations of the family's interactions and the home and community environment as it relates to the identified issues at hand.
- Seek additional information such as interviewing neighbors, teachers, friends, and family on how they have witnessed family interactions over time, carefully reviewing all information to add to what we know.
- **Engage in careful monitoring** of our own speculations, remembering that the "map is not the territory" and that the available information might not be giving us the full picture. We have an obligation to work against our own tendencies to be judgmental, biased, or to make assumptions without a factual basis.
- **Foster our multicultural sensibilities,** discerning the difference between differences in worldview and interaction style, and risk to the child.
- Dedication ourselves to transparency, a state in which nothing is hidden or camouflaged. As we coalesce all of the information that we have collected, and write a description of the case, the client should be able to recognize him or herself in the description, agree to the accuracy of the facts, even if they might not agree with the workers' conclusions regarding the disposition of the case.
- **Ground all of our decision-making in the factual material collected,** when making decisions regarding the level of risk and the motivation and capacity of

individuals and families to remediate the current situation as required. In other words, it is vital that we allow the facts of the case, the results of our careful investigation, to draw our conclusions rather than work by trying to validate our foregone conclusions with our data collection and selection.

- **Utilize the most promising, strengths-based, person-centered practice wisdom available** to inform the disposition of the case and to drive practice decisions, interventions, and referrals for additional services.

As we have seen in earlier chapters in this book, generalist social work practitioners utilize their ability to think critically and creatively with each person or family that they are working with, seeing him or her as a valuable human being, full of potential, who, with the help of person-centered supports can find the solution to the problems that threaten their well-being.

SOLUTION-FOCUSED APPROACHES

Solution-focused approaches are being promoted by many child welfare agencies, because they identify and build upon the strengths of each person in the family. This change in practice perspective and its concurrent change in practice tools has generated considerable evidence showing that long-lasting positive change occurs most frequently when we look at ourselves as partners, or power-sharers with our clients. When we work together to identify problems, issues, and struggles that *they* feel the need to solve, they become activated and invested in improving their life situations. The solutions to current challenges are derived from the skills, strengths, interests, and capacity of the client. Locating the power to change within the client's own history and capacity is much more likely to promote a helping relationship that incorporates "doing with" and "power sharing" as opposed to "doing to" and "power over."

The power-sharing or "power-with" model is not, as some detractors would suggest, a matter of abdicating responsibility for the situation. Neither is it a naive approach that pretends that abuse and neglect are not the issues that may have brought the client to the attention of public child welfare in the first place. Rather, it is aimed at transforming a mandated or involuntary relationship into one that is respectful of client's strengths and places the client in control of identifying relevant solutions. Restoring control for the change process to the client supports client self-esteem, self-efficacy and self-responsibility—all qualities that child welfare workers seek to help their clients to strengthen.

The solution-focused approach is an example of a power-sharing model that has been applied effectively in the context of child welfare practice. The solution-focused approach "emphasizes the co-construction of solutions" generated from dialogue between the client and the social worker in response to the worker's skillful questioning and active listening (Dielman and Franklin, 1998). The worker facilitates the client's recognition of prior successes and solutions. The worker encourages clients to do more of those behaviors that have yielded successful results.

Solution-Focused Brief Therapy is a future focused, goal directed approach to brief therapy designed to identify *exceptions* (times when the problem does not occur, or could occur less in the client's real life), *solutions* (a description of what life will be like when the problem is gone or resolved), and *scales* which are used to both measure the client's current level of progress towards a solution and reveal the behaviors needed to achieve or maintain future progress. Solution-Focused Brief Therapy has often been identified with innovative techniques, but doing so only tells half the story. Underlying the search for solutions .... (is) an abiding belief in the client's ability to know what is best for them and to effectively plan how to get there. Many techniques can be integrated into SFBT as long as they do not violate this fundamental principle. (Trepper et al., 2006, p. 134.)

After an initial exploration of the presenting issues and how the client has approached the problem to date, emphasis is placed on the description of the behaviors, attitudes, and feelings that one wants to promote rather than on the absence of these behaviors (Dielman and Franklin, 1998). Taylor (2005) points out that teaching the client to reframe her thought processes and communication is a vital aspect of SFBT. Moving from a focus on what isn't wanted to one of what is wanted is one of the treatment techniques. Shifting to solution-focused language sets the stage for the search for solutions. Figure 15.3 compares problem language and solution language.

Techniques such as using the **miracle question**, "suppose that one night while you are sleeping, a miracle happens, and the problem that brought you here today dissolved. How would you find out in the morning that the miracle had happened?", help the worker and the client articulate the goal.

Taylor (2005) describes the five lines of inquiry that flow from the shift toward solution-focused language: "What is the goal? When do little pieces of that happen? How do you do that? What good things result from that? What's next?" (p. 29).

ENGAGEMENT: WORKING WITH THE INVOLUNTARY OR MANDATED CLIENT

While engaging the client in the planning and decision-making process is important in all fields of social work practice, it is essential in child welfare practice. The quality of social worker–client engagement is one of the most critical factors in successful outcomes in child welfare (Altman, 2003; Karski, 1999; Littell, 2001; Sieppert, Hudon, and Unrau, 2000). Successful client engagement in the context of child welfare practice has some inherent challenges. Power and authority are inherent tensions in the helping relationship in child welfare practice. The child welfare social worker carries a public mandate to protect children from maltreatment and has the power to intervene.

Problem Language	Solution Language
What I don't want	What I do want
When things go wrong	When things go right
Forces beyond my control	Forces Within my control
I'm stuck	I'm progressing
More troubles to come	I see some possibilities

FIGURE 15.3 | SHIFT FROM PROBLEM LANGUAGE TO SOLUTION LANGUAGE

Source: (Taylor, 2005. p. 28).

Establishing a mutually respectful "power-sharing" relationship is the challenge of every field of practice in social work. The challenge is magnified when the client is mandated or court ordered to accept our interventions. At the point of intervention, the child welfare social worker represents implicit or explicit threat to the family and the parent's continued custody of the child or children. Most parents will react by resisting and protect themselves against this intrusion in their lives. The challenge for the social worker in child welfare practice is to establish a helping relationship that moves beyond threat and reaction to threat.

The keys to this transformation are establishing rapport and trust between the worker and the client. Congruent with our person-centered strengths-based philosophy, social workers must see the client as an individual, with their own needs and wants and mitigating circumstances. As we saw in Chapter 8, each person has a need to be *seen* for whom they really are, *heard* when they are communicating, and *known* in their full context. The worker who is mindful of this need moves to address these needs from the start of the first contact with the client. Rather than set forth for themselves the task of telling the client what he or she should do, or trying to establish herself as a powerful person at the expense of the client, the worker needs to empower the client, and show that she respects her as a human being and wants to hear what she has to say, understand her in her context, and work with her to figure out solutions. The resistant client wonders, "what is in this for me and for my family? How could an intervention with this emissary from the system that is threatening me possibly add anything positive to my life? All they will do is add more work and demands to my already overburdened life. And if I don't go along they will come and take my kids." Again, the need here is for the worker to hear the concerns of the client, validate them, and employ their critical thinking skills to the situation at hand.

Under the strengths-based paradigm, we also employ a solution-focused orientation (DeJong and Berg, 2001) when presented with a client who is neglecting or abusing a child. The worker's mandate is, of course, to end the child maltreatment or other issue that led to the system's intervention. However, before taking action, the worker must ask herself many questions including, "who is this person and what has brought him or her to the point that they would behave in this manner?" The Case 15.1 illustrates how one might employ a solution-focused approach when working with an involuntary client.

The social worker and Marie are off to a good start. Marie has moved from being overtly hostile to being able to talk to the worker and to start working on solutions to meet her own goal of a more enjoyable, less conflict-ridden life with her son. The worker joined with the mother during the course of the visit, she was nonjudgmental toward the mother, open to hearing her side of the story, validated her experience of the situation, and while not validating the violent confrontations, validated that the mother was doing what she could at that time. She then helped the mother develop some hope, based on a positive past experience, that things could indeed change. The rapport was beginning to be established, and through this process the mother could see the worker as an ally to the family to help them become independent of the service system rather than as a vehicle for the system to intrude into her life. Once the rapport was established, the mother could then become interested and energized in working with the worker.

CASE 15.1 | **WORKING WITH AN INVOLUNTARY CLIENT**

Marie was referred to child protective services when her son, Michael, repeatedly came to school with bruises on his face. One day, he even had a handprint on his cheek from his mother's slap. Michael, a 13-year-old boy, reported that his mother yelled at him every day "for no reason." They would get into screaming fights and his mother would end up slapping and hitting him.

After receiving the Child Hot Line report made by the school social worker, Janet, a CPS social worker, made a visit to the family's home. Upon their first meeting, Marie showed a great deal of hostility toward Janet. She sat with her arms crossed and would rarely make eye contact. When she did make eye contact it was to glare at Janet. She said that it was "none of her damn business how she disciplined her son." When Janet asked Marie to tell her about what was going on at home, Marie said that her son had an "attitude" and that she was not going to take it from him, she had taken too much from Michael's father before he left them, and she was not going to be walked on by Michael as well.

Janet realized that this mother was not eager to work with her and was wary of her potential interventions. Using a strengths-based approach, Janet understood that the first step was to develop a rapport with the mother. She said, "sounds to me as if Michael is a handful for you and that you are trying to teach him how behave in a more respectful way toward you. You don't want him to end up like his father, treating you and other people badly. Do I have that right?"

Yes," said Marie, "I see him becoming more like his old man every day."

"When do these problems typically occur?"

"It starts the minute he comes home from school. He walks in the house, slams the door and throws his jacket on the floor. I tell him to pick it up and he says 'no' and goes to sit in front of the TV. I turn off the TV and tell him to hang up his jacket. He says 'make me,' and then I start getting worked up and next thing I know we are yelling at each other and I am slapping him. I would have gotten a lot worse if I had ever talked back that way to my mother, believe me!"

"Wow", said Janet, "I would start dreading the end of the school day if I were you! How frustrating this must be for you. Stressful too I would think. Is that right?" "Yes! Marie said. "I am completely worn out by him. I work very hard to support both of us. I get up early to go to work so that I can be home when he gets back from school. If I am not home he gets in trouble in the neighborhood, so I have to be here. But I am already tired from work and then he starts all of this. And now you are here and what are you going to do? Take away my son?"

"You have a lot on your shoulders Marie, I really appreciate that. You are really working hard to take care of Michael and to survive financially, and it must seem that all of this is being taken for granted. Is that right?"

"Yes," Marie said, softening, "no one cares about me."

At this point Janet had a clearer picture of what is going on between Michael and Marie. Marie is trying to be a good mother. She also needs to feel respected. She is tired of the daily struggle with Michael. She might even be lonely, needing a sense of warmth and connection from Michael and other adults. Child rearing is hard enough on a single parent without having to struggle with these types of interactions on a daily basis. Additionally, she is afraid that Michael will grow up to be like his father. Michael's behaviors seem to bring up feelings in Marie that were brought us be his father. Michael then might get an even angrier response from Marie than the situation warrants because of all of the emotion that his behavior triggers in his mother. It is also apparent to the worker that Marie's parenting model that she adopted from her own parents might also have been a punitive one. Marie is doing the best she can with what she knows and under these circumstances.

Janet then asked, "Marie, has there ever been a day when there hasn't been a struggle? Is it ever fun with Michael?"

"Oh Yes", said Marie. "Michael has his wonderful side as well. Maybe that is why I get so mad at him, because I know he can be better."

Janet: "Really? That's great to hear! What happens when it is going well? Can you describe a good day to me?"

(Continued)

CASE 15.1 | *Continued*

Marie: "Well, a few weeks ago, I had a day off from work and Michael was at school. I usually only have a day off when Michael is at home, but I got up with him in the morning and made his breakfast and then I went back to bed for a while and rested some more. I guess I was feeling pretty good by the time Michael came home. It was a beautiful day so I met him at the bus stop and asked if he wanted go for a walk and get some ice cream or something? He was glad to do it with me, very glad. We walked and talked. Michael has a good sense of humor when he is in a good mood. We laughed a lot. Then we both came home, and hung up our jackets together and then made dinner together. It was a great evening. I wish it could be like that all of the time."

Worker: "Marie, it sounds to me as if you have a clear picture of how it could be with Michael. You have had some great success with him. What would life be like if most days were like the one you described, fun and warm between you, no fighting and so on?"

Marie: "Well for one thing, no offense, but I wouldn't have to have you or other inspectors in my house any more."

Janet: "No offense taken, I wouldn't want intrusions into my life either. How about we work together to make this rare occurrence of getting along well to become more of a constant experience so that you and Michael don't have violent fights any more, and you can get me and the system out of your hair?"

Marie: "Sounds good to me."

Janet: "Great. Let's go back to the example you gave me about the great day you had? What was going on that was different from your normal troublesome day?......"

Notice that the worker helped the mother articulate what needed to be done to have her case closed, without ever making false promises to the mother. It is very important that the worker remains transparent about the process, and the natural consequences of the solution, rather than make assurances that all will be well at the start of the intervention that might imply that the client doesn't need to work toward the solution.

The worker would then help the mother identify changes in her daily life that would continue to foster a better relationship between the mother and child, such as welcoming Michael when he comes home and offering an alternative to be engaged with her rather than starting off their afternoon with a power struggle over the jacket. The worker will support the mother in enhancing her skills through encouraging her to repeat and further develop the successful interventions that she has tried. Next, together they will set up goals to see how well the ideas are working with the promise to come back together regularly to tweak their ideas or to brainstorm again if the plan is not working. A date will be set for a follow-up visit the next week. The worker's agenda will also be met in that this will assure that Michael is safe from further abuse.

Of course the above example, while true, is more simple and straightforward than many clients that the social work practitioner will encounter. Clients with longer histories with the service system, more complex issues such as poverty, substance dependence, trauma histories, and so forth, may take longer to develop a sense of trust in the worker. They may also need more support to be able to articulate their goals and to develop a sense of hope toward achieving their goals. The worker must take in the context of the client's experience, in order that she not lose hope and remain resilient as she continues to work to engage this individual.

The steps and tools used in solution-focused and other evidence-based practices are effective with even the most resistant clients, given enough time and supports.

For many clients in the child welfare system, there is a need to bring many agencies together to help provide the supports to meet the solutions identified by the clients with their workers. Addressing poverty, mental health concerns, educational needs, job training, as well as parenting skills training might require that many separate services are necessary to solve the issues at hand. It is very easy for the client to become overwhelmed by the differing requirements and expectations and sometimes contradictory requirements of the various services. Clients who started out hopeful and energetic can become dispirited and demotivated when faced with the multisystem abyss. It is a vital role of the social worker to help the client and the agency representatives create a seamless integration of the various support systems in order that positive outcomes can result.

CHILD WELFARE: GENERALIST PRACTICE FUNCTIONS

Child welfare social policy mandates that the child welfare system perform the following functions (NAPCSW, 1999):

- Assess the safety of children
- Intervene to protect the children from harm
- Strengthen the ability of the family to protect their children or
- Provide an alternative safe family for the children

Public child welfare systems are directly responsible for assessment and initial intervention to protect children from harm. Services aimed at strengthening families' ability to protect children and/or providing alternative safe families for children may be provided by the public child welfare agency or by private agencies. Child welfare services provided by private agencies are usually monitored and funded, at least in part, by the local public child welfare agency.

Regardless of the service being provided, the child welfare social worker must have the generalist skills and knowledge to support effective engagement of children and families in a helping relationship, accurate assessment of risk of child maltreatment and family functioning, use of appropriate interventions, and culturally competent practice.

SAFETY AND RISK ASSESSMENT

The initial assessment of child safety is conducted as a result of a report of suspected child abuse and/or neglect having been filed with the local public child protective services. Legislation requires that public child protective services (CPS) investigate such reports within a specific time period. In a few locations, provisions have been adopted to enable local police to conduct initial investigations. Most states have a "triage" system of response to reports of suspected child maltreatment. The CPS worker responsible for screening reports must make a decision regarding whether the information does indeed suggest abuse and/or neglect, whether the information suggests imminent risk. How quickly a report is investigated will depend on the severity of maltreatment and risk implied by the information provided. Reports suggesting imminent and severe risk of harm generally require an immediate investigatory visit, and public child welfare agencies are required to have staff available 24 hours each day to respond to such reports.

If a report of suspected neglect or abuse requires CPS assessment, it is assigned to a CPS intake worker. The CPS intake worker's tasks at the point of initial contact are to

- Engage the family in the initial assessment process
- Determine whether child maltreatment has occurred
- Determine the risk of future maltreatment
- Determine whether continuing service is needed
- Identify and implement an immediate safety plan, if needed

Case 15.2 illustrates the functions of a child protective services worker.

CASE 15.2 | **CHILD PROTECTIVE SERVICES**

Kelly R. has been a child protective services (CPS) intake worker for 4 years. She is one of the few workers in her unit with a BSW degree. Most of the case managers in her agency, while college graduates, did not have the advantage of social work education and were not as well prepared as she for working in the field.

Although Kelly confronts many challenging situations as she responds to reports of suspected child abuse and/or neglect, she feels satisfaction in her role of protecting or rescuing children from harm. In Kelly's experience about 2 out of 3 of her investigations result in finding no evidence to substantiate abuse or neglect. Nevertheless, based on her assessments Kelly knows that many of the children, for whom abuse or neglect is not substantiated, still need lots of help. Kelly has often used her generalist practice skills and relationship with the family to help them to accept supportive services.

This new report of suspected neglect had Kelly very worried. The report was filed on the Child Hot Line by the principal of the school attended by the two oldest Jackson children. It is not unusual for reports to be made by professionals. *As mandated reporters, professionals file more than half of all reports of alleged child abuse or neglect (NCCANS 2006).*

According to the principal, the children had not been in school for over 8 days. Phone calls to the Jackson home were unanswered. When the home and school visitor went to the home, she could hear sounds inside but no one came to the door in response to her knocking on the door and calling out. For the last

month, teachers at the school had reported that the Jackson children had spotty attendance at best and generally came to school hungry, dirty, and inadequately clothed. The principal stated in her report that the family had four children ranging in age from 2 to 9 years old. She also knew that Mr. Jackson, father of the children, was a factory worker and had recently lost his job as the result of the closing of his plant.

The situation described by the school principal sounded like one of serious neglect. From Kelly's experience, neglect situations were often the most challenging with regard to risk and safety assessment. More often than not, child neglect was in large part the result of circumstances beyond parental control—extreme poverty, mental illness, family crisis, and so forth. She also knew resources were limited to address these family challenges and avoid removal of the children. Nevertheless, Kelly's task as a CPS worker was to make a determination of whether neglect and/or abuse had occurred and to assess the safety of the Jackson children and to what degree they may be at-risk of future harm.

The hot line screening assessment had marked the report "high risk" and needing an urgent response. This meant that Kelly was required to visit the home within 24 hours of the report. Kelly arrived at the Jackson home early the next morning. She had reviewed her agency's new CPS risk and safety assessment instrument prior to her visit to make sure that she remembered to note all of the factors she was required to rate.

Continued

The Jackson home was located on a block of dilapidated row homes in a very run-down, impoverished neighborhood. Kelly was cautious to look around as she left her car to walk to Jackson address. She used all of her "street smarts" to assess whether the setting posed a risk for her own safety. Several of the homes on the block appeared to be abandoned. Kelly noted signs that some of the abandoned properties were likely being used by "squatters" or perhaps as "crack houses"—not uncommon for this neighborhood well known to be a haven for drug addicts, but it was early enough in the day that the addicts were likely to be sleeping. Addicts were generally too ill or disorganized to pose much of a threat anyway, and the drug selling "action" wouldn't start up until later in the day. Kelly could see some people out on their stoops tending to young children. They looked at her with curiosity, but nothing set off any major alarm bells for her. So for now, Kelly felt safe.

The Jackson row home was one of the most run-down of the occupied homes on the block. Torn trash bags with rotting garbage were piled up in front of the house, even though this didn't appear to be trash day. She noticed that a couple of the front windows were broken, and all were covered from the inside with what appeared to be newspaper. Kelly thought to herself that this situation didn't look good. The broken windows alone would pose a hazard to young children.

There was no response to Kelly's loud banging on the front door, but after a few minutes she noticed a little boy, about 8 or 9 years old, peeking out from behind the covering on one of the windows. Kelly called out to the child and asked him to please open the front door for her. After several minutes the boy opened the front door. Kelly noted that he was very dirty, his clothes were ill fitting and torn and he appeared to be very frightened. She asked if his mother was at home. He shook his head "yes" and turned to go back in the house, gesturing for her to follow him.

What Kelly found took her breath away. The smell was overpowering – a combination of odors, the most identifiable of which seemed to be that of excrement. Kelly entered what she guessed was the living room. Although it was dark because the windows were covered with newspaper, she could discern a woman,

probably the mother, sitting on a broken couch. The woman was staring into space, rocking back and forth and making unintelligible song-like sounds. She was tightly holding a toddler—about 2 years old—clothed only in a diaper. The floor of the room was covered with debris, mostly torn newspapers, empty food containers, candy wrappers, soiled diapers, and what Kelly recognized as either human or animal excrement. Several cats were lying around the room. Kelly noted three children in the room, the boy who had opened the door, the child on the mother's lap, and what appeared to be a 4-year-old sitting in a corner eating from a box of crackers. She said hello to the woman, who glanced briefly at her and began to rock faster in her seat, still clutching the young child.

Kelly was deeply alarmed. She made a few quick assumptions. She wasn't sure what was wrong with the woman, but it was clear that she was sufficiently unresponsive to provide adequate care for the children. Kelly suspected she was suffering from serious mental illness. The condition of the living room itself posed a threat to the health and well-being of the children. The situation she faced would definitely merit a rating of "high risk" and "low level of safety" on her assessment instruments. Kelly considered this to be a crisis that needed immediate action.

Kelly explained calmly to the woman, even though she remained unresponsive, and to the little boy who she was and why she was there. She reassured them that she was there to help and that it appeared to me that they needed help quickly. Kelly asked the little boy his name. He shyly responded, "my name is Christopher."

KELLY: Is this your mom?

CHRISTOPHER: Yes (nodding).

KELLY: Is your mom not feeling well?

CHRISTOPHER: Yes (nodding).

KELLY: Where is your daddy?

CHRISTOPHER: Dunno.

KELLY: How long has he been gone?

CHRISTOPHER: I dunno. Long time.

(Continued)

CASE 15.2 | *Continued*

KELLY: Are you worried about your
mom?

CHRISTOPHER: (tears welling up and nodding) Yes.

KELLY: Has mom been feeling like this for
a long time?

CHRISTOPHER: (more tears). Yeah . . . long time.

KELLY: I understand. I am going to help
you and your mom.

Kelly stepped outside and called her supervisor on her mobile phone. She quickly reported the situation. In Kelly's opinion, this situation called for immediate intervention. In consultation with her supervisor, Kelly determined that following immediate actions needed to be taken

1.   A mobile psychiatric assessment team would be called in to assess the mother's mental health status
2.   A search for the father and other relatives and/or friends would be conducted to determine if care could be found for the children among family's support system
3.   If no one could be found to care for the children, they would be placed in emergency temporary foster care

Kelly waited at the Jackson home for about an hour for the mobile mental health team to arrive. She used the time to gather all of the children in the living room and attempt to engage and reassure them. All of the children appeared hungry, dirty, and frightened. From Kelly's observation, Christopher had taken over the parenting role for his younger siblings. They huddled around him as Kelly explained that she had called for people to come and help their mother. Despite Ms. Jackson's lack of responsiveness, Christopher spoke to her, stroked her hair, hugged her and brought her a glass of water.

Kelly tried to gather information from the children about potential family supports. Christopher told her that they didn't have any relatives in the neighborhood; his father had been gone awhile and he didn't

know how to contact him; he had an aunt, but didn't know her phone number or address; and that some of the neighbors would bring the family food on occasion, but their mother didn't want them to open the door.

While the mobile emergency team was evaluating Ms. Jackson, Kelly knocked on neighbors' doors. While no one was in a position to take the children in, they were cooperative and provided some information. They seemed relieved that the Jackson family might get some help. Kelly learned that up until about 3 months ago, the Jackson family seemed to be doing just fine. The parents took good care of the children and they were good neighbors. Apparently, Mr. Jackson was laid off about 3 months ago. He recently went back to Selma, Alabama, where the Jackson family had lived until about 2 years ago. Ms. Jackson had told neighbors that Mr. Jackson was going to get a job and send for the family. Not long after her husband left, Ms. Jackson began to behave strangely. She became very suspicious, covered her windows in newspaper, wouldn't let the children out to play, stopped going to the store for food, and appeared generally to stop functioning. Several neighbors tried to talk with her, but they found her increasingly irrational. The neighbors didn't have contact information for any relatives or other friends who might be able to help the children, but they thought that a paternal aunt lived somewhere in the city.

The mobile emergency psychiatric team diagnosed Ms. Jackson as likely experiencing an acute psychotic episode and needing emergency hospitalization. The most heart wrenching part of the day was when Kelly took the 2-year-old from Ms. Jackson's arms. The child had been dozing comfortably and seemed to be soothed by her mother's continuous rocking motion. Ms. Jackson began to wail "my baby, my baby." This triggered crying and screaming among all of the children. Christopher, whose own reaction was more stoical, helped Kelly to comfort the sobbing younger children, even though tears were streaming from his eyes. The children called out to their mother as she was taken from the home.

Later that day, Kelly documented her contacts and interventions with the Jackson family. Ms. Jackson had been involuntarily committed to a local psychiatric hospital unit. Kelly had tried to find out something about the paternal aunt, but could not locate an address or phone number. The five Jackson children had been placed together (a miracle in Kelly's experience) with a nurturing and experienced foster mother.

A follow-up commitment hearing would take place before a juvenile court judge. Each state determines the speed in which the hearing must occur. Kelly would not need to appear at that initial hearing, but she might have to appear at subsequent hearings to support the initial findings in the case. Accurate and complete documentation of this initial phase of intervention is critical. This had been a very hard and sad day for Kelly. At the same time, she knew that what she had done had been necessary for the protection of the Jackson children and was hopeful that it would be the first step toward restoring the family to normal functioning. She had done her job. She had assessed the threats to the safety of the Jackson children (high risk). She had developed a safety plan (temporary placement). She had begun the initial step toward reunification (psychiatric services for Ms. Jackson). Kelly's contact with the Jackson family and the actions taken demonstrate several generalist practice skills needed at the point of initial contact.

Initial Engagement.   The CPS intake worker usually walks into situations about which little is known. More often than not her visit is unannounced and very rarely is it welcomed. The CPS social worker must understand that inevitably she is seen as an intruder by almost everyone involved. Nevertheless, she is performing a vital function of carrying out of the public mandate to protect children. Even though the family may perceive the social worker as a threat, her challenge is to engage the family in the assessment process. Effective engagement with the family at this stage of the process sets a tone for any interventions that follow. The child protective services social worker initial engagement with a family should reflect:

- Strengths perspective
- Nonjudgmental stance
- Transparency

Strengths Perspective.   Engaging a family in the assessment process is possible when the worker approaches the family from strengths perspective. Every family has inherent strengths, despite the crisis in which the CPS social worker might find the family. There were many observable positive indicators about the Jackson family's strengths, even though they were in crisis. Christopher's care of his younger siblings and gentle comforting of his mother suggested to Kelly that the family had a close bond. The children, while hungry and dirty, did not seem to be suffering from long-term malnourishment and had no observable bruises or injuries. Despite Ms. Jackson's unresponsiveness at this time, the children gathered around her and hung on to her, suggesting that they were accustomed to viewing their mother as a source of comfort and safety. There were family pictures on the wall and toys scattered around. All of these things suggested to Kelly that Ms. Jackson had probably functioned quite differently as a mother when not in the clutches of serious mental illness.

Kelly allowed herself to feel empathy for the confusion, fear, and trauma the children and Ms. Jackson were experiencing. However, she was careful not to become immobilized by her own feelings for the family's plight. She was certain that Ms. Jackson would not want her children to go hungry and dirty. She knew that her intervention, if the appropriate services were provided, was the only way to help this family be restored to its earlier level of functioning.

Kelly understood that she entered the Jackson home with a public authority to take action to ensure the welfare of the Jackson children. A great deal of power is associated with this authority and is unavoidably viewed as a threat by the client. In her practice, Kelly recognized that in order to successfully engage her new client, she must convert the implied threat of authority to one of collaboration in a process to resolve whatever presenting problems brought the family to the attention of the public agency.

Nonjudgmental Stance.   The social worker should strive to present a nonjudgmental tone to reduce the family's sense of threat and intrusion. Throughout her time with Ms. Jackson and the children, Kelly remained calm and supportive. She spoke soothingly to Ms. Jackson. Even though she was uncertain how much Ms. Jackson understood, Kelly told her everything that she was going to do. She complimented Ms. Jackson on her beautiful children and praised Christopher as a wonderful helper. She commented to Ms. Jackson that it must feel very comforting to her to hold her baby.

Transparency.   The social worker should be transparent about the engagement process, providing the client with complete information about what is happening and why it is happening. With the children, Kelly did her best to be reassuring that their mother would be well cared for and they would see her again soon. She was careful not to usurp Christopher's role as caregiver and allowed him take the lead in comforting the younger children and prepare them to leave the house. She did her best to explain to Ms. Jackson, despite her unresponsiveness, and the children what was happening and what was going to happen next.

Making a Determination.   The CPS social worker has two essential assessment tasks in response to a report of suspected child maltreatment. The first is to determine whether the report is substantiated or founded, indicated, or not substantiated or founded. The second is to develop and implement a safety plan if a positive determination of maltreatment has been made and/or if the child is at risk of future harm.

A determination of substantiated abuse and/or neglect is one in which evidence of neglect and/or abuse was found. When no evidence of neglect or injury is found, a report is determined to be unsubstantiated. A determination of "indicated" is made when evidence of abuse and/or neglect is found, but there is no evidence the person responsible for providing care for the child inflicted the injury and/or abuse.

Kelly completed the agency's safety and risk assessment instrument and made a determination of "substantiated" with regard to neglect. Even without the instrument, it would have been clear to Kelly that the Jackson children were suffering from severe neglect and the situation was one of high risk. However, the instrument provided documentation to support the agency's request for emergency protective custody of the Jackson children authorizing their placement.

Making determinations of current threats and future risks to child safety can be a life or death decision, but often, the evidence upon which to base a determination is confusing, inconclusive, and ambiguous. To assist CPS workers, most states have adopted formal risk and safety assessment instruments. These instruments generally take the form of a rating checklist of indicators or factors that have been identified as strongly associated with current threats to a child's safety and/or risks of future harm.

The instruments are quite varied but generally require the child welfare worker to rate indicators of risk that fall into six categories (Popple and Vecchiolla, 2007):

* Nature and type of maltreatment - severity, nature, and extent of neglect and/ or injury(ies)
* Child's vulnerabilities - e.g., age, developmental level, child's behavioral characteristics, special needs, health status
* Parent/caregivers' characteristics - e.g., age, history of previous child abuse or neglect, history of substance use, mental health status, history of domestic violence
* Family characteristics - e.g., number of children, number of adults in household, status of relationship among adult caregivers, history of domestic violence, availability of social support
* Socioeconomic and environmental characteristics - e.g., financial stressors, condition of physical environment, level of neighborhood safety
* Service-related characteristics - e.g., family known/not known to CPS, previous history of child placement, family involvement with social services

There is much debate in the child welfare literature about safety and risk assessment instruments. Research suggests that instruments currently have low "interrater reliability" and questionable "validity." Low "interrater reliability" means that different workers are more likely to rate the same situation differently depending on the workers' life experience, cultural perspective, and subjective judgment. Concerns about "validity" address whether the factors used to rate the level of safety and risk are predictive of actual risk and safety outcomes. Despite these problems, safety and risk assessment instruments are widely used in CPS, and researchers are working hard to improve both interrater reliability and validity.

In the Jackson case, Kelly has ample evidence to *substantiate* child neglect. The condition of the household, the absence of adequate food, and the children's poor hygiene were all indicators of serious neglect. Given the number of children in the household and their age, the Jackson children would be considered highly vulnerable. Ms. Jackson's apparent acute mental illness represented a serious threat to the safety of the children. As far as Kelly knew, the family had no history of neglect or abuse; however, the current situation was sufficient to substantiate neglect. Having made her determination of child neglect, Kelly had to take the next step to develop an initial safety plan. Having been unable to identify friends or relatives who could assist that family, Kelly moved the children into temporary foster care placement.

THE PLANNING PHASE

After the initial crisis is stabilized, the social worker and family collaborate in a more thorough assessment of the family's situation and needs in order to develop a plan of action. Building on the relationship established at the point of initial investigation, the social worker and the family work together to identify family strengths and potential supports, the family's needs, and risk and safety factors. The planning phase is an extended, but time-limited, process that involves gathering additional information, identifying appropriate resources, making contacts with collateral resources, and providing an appropriate and supportive context for the development of a plan of action.

CASE 15.2 | **CHILD PROTECTIVE SERVICES** *Continued*

The day after the Jackson children were placed, Kelly made contact with the psychiatric social worker at Ms. Jackson's hospital. Kelly was able to interview Ms. Jackson at the hospital about 1 week later. The psychiatric social worker sat in on the interview. When Kelly walked into the interview room, she was shocked to see a different Ms. Jackson. The disheveled, expressionless, muttering, unkempt woman of one week ago, was well groomed, alert, and very eager to talk to Kelly.

When Kelly introduced herself, Ms. Jackson smiled apprehensively and immediately asked about her children. Kelly was able to reassure her that the children were together, being cared for by an experienced and nurturing foster family. Ms. Jackson asked questions about each of the children and gave Kelly information specific to each of the children's needs that Kelly knew would be helpful to the foster mother. Kelly noted that Ms. Jackson seemed insightful about her children and anxious that others understand their unique personalities and needs. Ms. Jackson asked about seeing the children, and Kelly reassured her that they would plan a visit before Kelly left the interview.

The psychiatric social worker explained that Ms. Jackson was making a rapid recovery. She had been diagnosed as suffering from "psychotic depression" and had responded very quickly to psychotropic medications. Although she remained anxious and depressed about her situation, she was now well oriented, able to care for herself, and was eating and sleeping well. In fact, Ms. Jackson's recovery was proceeding so smoothly that she was scheduled for discharge at the end of the week. Kelly registered

alarm at this, indicating that there was much to be done to help Ms. Jackson be able to resume the care of her children. The psychiatric social worker shared the concern but explained that Ms. Jackson was no longer a threat to herself or others, and her psychosis was under control. Medical insurance would not extend her hospitalization beyond 10 days. She would be discharged by the end of the week.

In response to Kelly's questions, Ms. Jackson reported that the family's problems began when Mr. Jackson was laid off from his job at a local plant about 6 months ago. Unable to find a job, he began to "change." He was often angry, drank too much, and gambled what little money they received from his unemployment insurance. Their relationship became very strained. About 2 months ago, Mr. Jackson announced he was going back to Selma, Alabama to look for work and he would send for the family as soon as he could. Ms. Jackson had not heard from him since.

The family's situation rapidly deteriorated. Ms. Jackson was able to get Temporary Assistance to Needy Family (TANF) funds and food stamps, but it was barely enough to feed the family, let alone pay rent. She feared eviction and that she and the children would end up in a homeless shelter. Having to seek public support had been a major blow to Ms. Jackson's self esteem. She felt she had hit bottom. She had always believed "God helped those who helped themselves." Now, she couldn't even help herself. Neighbors tried to help her, but she was too embarrassed to take their charity and tried to hide the family's situation. She couldn't take a job because she had no one to care for the little ones. She did have relatives—cousins and an aunt—who lived in another

(Continued)

CASE 15.2 | *Continued*

neighborhood, but she was too ashamed to reach out. Who could take on the burden of a family with five children? She didn't know how she would survive. She felt abandoned by her husband. Ms. Jackson remembered that she had began to have thoughts about killing herself but knew that she couldn't leave her children alone. She had no memory of the last few weeks, probably corresponding to the time that her psychiatric condition became acute.

Kelly listened carefully to Ms. Jackson's story about how the family had slipped into crisis. At several points, she asked questions for clarification and made comments to reassure Ms. Jackson that Kelly was following her story closely. Kelly also expressed empathy for the struggle Ms. Jackson has experienced over the last several months and how difficult it must have been to feel all alone. She stated that it was not surprising that the stressors had finally taken their toll on her ability to "hold it all together." Ms. Jackson appeared to relax as the conversation progressed, and Kelly felt that Ms. Jackson was sensing that Kelly was "on her side" and not judging her as a failure.

After gathering as much information as she could, Kelly explained the need to develop a "family service plan" that would support the return of the children to their mother's care. Kelly reassured Ms. Jackson that they would work closely together to reunify the family as quickly as possible. However, they both had much work to do to establish a stable and safe living situation for the Jackson children.

Kelly expressed understanding for Ms. Jackson's reluctance to reach out to others, but stressed that in a crisis everyone needs the support of friends and family. Ms. Jackson acknowledged that she realized now it had been a mistake to isolate herself and her family from people who could help. Kelly asked Ms. Jackson if she would allow Kelly to contact people—relatives and friends—who might be interested in helping the family. Ms. Jackson readily agreed.

Ms. Jackson and Kelly spent some time on brainstorming the supports that Ms. Jackson felt the family might draw on at this time of crisis. Together, they came up with a list that included several relatives, the school social worker, people from the church the Jackson family attended, and the psychiatric social worker. They agreed that Kelly would set up a meeting, pulling together as many of the people on the list as she could. At the meeting, a plan would be developed for assisting the family in reunification.

Given the time frame, Ms. Jackson would most likely be discharged before the meeting could be arranged. A plan was already in place to discharge Ms. Jackson to one of her cousins, who had quickly come to visit after learning about Ms. Jackson's hospitalization from neighbors. A date was set for the planning meeting. It would be held at Kelly's office in 2 weeks. Ms. Jackson would be responsible for identifying the participants. Kelly would be responsible for making all of the contacts. In the meantime, the Jackson children would remain in temporary foster care, and Kelly would arrange for Ms. Jackson to visit with the children in the office as soon as she was discharged from the hospital. Ms. Jackson would write down a little information about each of the children that Kelly could share with the foster mother to help the children adjust to their new surroundings.

Kelly's interview with Ms. Jackson reflects many of the important generalist practice skills essential to the planning phase:

- *Engagement* – involves the family in a power-sharing process that is respectful of the family's self-efficacy and integrity
- Strengths-based – identifies aspects of family's adequate functioning as well as family's challenges
- *Cultural sensitivity* – respects the family's cultural traditions and identify ways in which cultural factors may influence the situation and the social worker–client relationship
- *Critical thinking* – is grounded in available information and draws appropriate inferences

- *Collaboration* – maximizes participation of family members and other social supports to the greatest extent possible
- *Supportive stance* – maximizes efforts to support parental roles and family bond

Engagement. Kelly understood that engaging the parent or caregiver fully in the planning process was essential to achieving permanency for the Jackson children. She also understood that engaging the Ms. Jackson would require setting a tone of "partnership" in the goal of permanency for the children and reducing the threat to Ms. Jackson inherent in Kelly's role as CPS worker.

When a child is taken out of the home, regardless of the reason, the parent experiences a major blow to her or his self-esteem. In asking Ms. Jackson to provide detailed information about her children for the foster mother, Kelly was conveying her appreciation for Ms. Jackson's parental role. Again, not only would the information be helpful, it would support Ms. Jackson's sense of herself as an effective and caring mother and help restore her self-esteem.

Kelly understood that Ms. Jackson's depression must have involved her feeling that she had no control over what was happening to her family. She felt alone and helpless. In engaging Ms. Jackson, Kelly would stress that Ms. Jackson had control over what would happen in the future. Restoring Ms. Jackson's sense of personal effectiveness would not only support reunification of the family, it would also support Ms. Jackson's recovery.

Strengths Perspective. In her meeting with Ms. Jackson, Kelly consistently looked for evidence of Ms. Jackson's strengths—her parenting capacity prior to the current crisis and potential for adequate parenting with appropriate supports. Ms. Jackson's sensitivity to the needs of each of her children was a sign of parenting skill and attachment. Her expressed concern about the welfare of her children and desire to see them quickly were additional signs of strong parent–child bonding.

Cultural Sensitivity. Kelly listened carefully to Ms. Jackson's statements about not wanting to be a burden to others, not wanting charity, and shame at her predicament. Kelly did not understand the origins of these feelings. Perhaps, they arose from her family of origin or her faith. Although these feelings did not serve the family well in this situation, they reflected a sense of independence and responsibility that could be strengths to build on. Nevertheless, Ms. Jackson was going to need help, and Kelly knew that she would have to be sensitive to Ms. Jackson's feelings about dependency, privacy, and receiving help. As they worked together, these feelings would need to be acknowledged and understood.

Critical Thinking. At the end of the day, Kelly critically evaluated the information she had collected so far about the Jackson family. This information, although preliminary, would provide a starting point for developing a plan of action. In assessing family functioning, Kelly had to be careful to accurately distinguish between conclusions based on evidence and inferences or speculation. Based on the data she had collected, Kelly drew some *tentative* conclusions and made some inferences.

Kelly's conclusions were tentative because she knew that she was just beginning to get to know the family, and there was still much information that needed to be gathered: (1) Kelly *tentatively concluded* that the Jackson family had been functioning adequately up until Mr. Jackson lost his job. The family was not known to the agency through any prior report. The school had reported that the children had been doing well until recent months. (2) Kelly *tentatively concluded* that the family's decline had likely begun as a result of financial crisis and that neglect of the children had begun relatively recently. (3) Kelly *speculated* that Mr. Jackson deserted because he could not emotionally cope with his inability to support his family. She *speculated*, however, that the relationship might have been strained prior to this crisis, given Mr. Jackson's lack of contact with the family for several months. (4) Since Ms. Jackson had no prior history of mental illness, Kelly *tentatively concluded* that Ms. Jackson had slipped into an acute psychotic depression, likely brought on by the many stressors in her current situation— abandoned by her husband, financially stressed, and very limited social support. (5) Kelly *tentatively concluded* that reunification was a reasonable planning goal for this family.

Collaboration. Kelly took care to fully disclose to Ms. Jackson all of the steps that they would need to take in working toward reunification. She was respectful of Ms. Jackson's competence as a parent and made room for her participation. She asked Ms. Jackson to help her children with their adjustment in temporary care by providing helpful information for the foster mother. Kelly supported the family's attachment by arranging for speedy visitation. Kelly gave Ms. Jackson responsibility for identifying potential family supports to participate in the planning meeting. Kelly assumed responsibility for organizing the planning meeting and for ensuring that Ms. Jackson would have frequent visitation with her children to maintain the parent–child attachment and support Ms. Jackson's role of "mother." Kelly hoped their collaboration at this point would set the tone for their helping relationship.

Supportive Stance. Supporting Ms. Jackson and the children during this phase required Kelly to find ways to maintain the family's bond, despite the separation. This required providing Ms. Jackson with opportunities to spend "quality time" with her children. The agency did not permit parental visits in temporary foster homes. Kelly would bring the children to the office to see their mother. Despite the time involved, Kelly viewed these visits as further opportunity to engage and support the family, observe Ms. Jackson's interaction with the children, and gather more information.

CASE 15.2 | **CHILD PROTECTIVE SERVICES** *Continued*

By the time the planning meeting took place, Kelly had brought the children to the office for two visits with their mother. The reunions were very touching and gratifying to Kelly. The children were apprehensive when they saw their mother for the first time. Although Kelly had explained that their mother would probably seem like her "old self," the children were not sure

what to expect. After about 5 minutes, the children's anxiety visibly subsided. Ms. Jackson obviously went through a range of emotions. She cried, laughed, and cried again. She hugged and kissed them all, inspected their little bodies, complimented them on how pretty and handsome they looked. With Kelly's help, Ms. Jackson had decided on how to explain to the

(Continued)

CASE 15.2 | *Continued*

children, particularly Christopher, what had happened and what she hoped would happen now.

Ms. Jackson demonstrated appropriate parenting skills in her interaction with her children. She appropriately set limits when the younger children became rambunctious. She was fully engaged and supportive, asking the children appropriate questions and encouraging them to listen to their foster mother. Christopher seemed quite relieved at his mother's resumption of the parent role. The visits supported Kelly's earlier impressions about the Ms. Jackson's strong parenting skills.

THE FAMILY SERVICE PLAN

A family service plan is completed after the disposition of a report of child maltreatment and is guided by the legislative mandates described earlier. The plan outlines a set of specific set of tasks for (1) implementing "reasonable efforts" to restore or support the family's capacity to provide a safe and stable living situation and (2) ensuring permanency for the children within a mandated time limit. The plan sets time limits and should identify "who" is to do "what" and "when" the task is to be completed. As required by AFSA legislation, if a child(ren) is in temporary placement, the plan must specify a strategy of "concurrent planning"—working toward reunification and permanency simultaneously.

Prioritizing Needs. An important aspect of the family service plan is prioritizing family needs. Many frameworks for family assessment were discussed in Chapter 7. Popple and Vecchiolla (2007) proposes Abraham Maslow's "hierarchy of needs" as a useful model for assessing and prioritizing a family's needs in the context of child welfare practice. Maslow (1970) suggests that all humans share a common set of needs. However, some needs are more fundamental to survival and must be met before other needs can be addressed. Maslow's hierarchy of need begins with basic *physiological* needs required for survival, such as adequate food and shelter. *Safety* needs are the second level in the hierarchy and refer to the need for protection from harm or the risk of harm. The third level of need, *belongingness*, refers to a child's sense of attachment to his/her family and he/she is central in the parent's affection. It also refers to the social support network that is available to the family. *Esteem* needs, the fourth level, applies to the sense of satisfaction and pride each family member feels about his/her family unit and role in the family unit. The final level, only reached after each of the lower level needs is met, is self-actualization. The need for *self-actualization* refers to the opportunity and "luxury" to develop self-awareness and freedom to make choices to maximize personal happiness and satisfaction.

Planning Meetings. A successful planning meeting that brings all relevant parties "to the table" requires a great deal of preparation by the social worker. The social worker must be thorough in contacting all potential participants; conducting pre-meeting interviews; collecting relevant information from collateral resources; ensuring accessibility with regard to time, location and transportation; and structuring the meeting to address the family's relevant needs.

Kelly used Maslow's framework to develop the agenda for the planning meeting that would set the priorities for the Jackson family service plan. The highest priorities for the Jackson family would be to address the family's *physical* and *safety* needs. The family needed safe and secure housing. The children needed caregiving that ensured their *safety* and well-being. The third level of the hierarchy—*belongingness*—would be considered once the first two were met. It was Kelly's impression that the children felt a strong family bond. However, it was unclear how they were reacting to the disappearance of their father. Also, Ms. Jackson clearly had suffered a major emotional blow as a result of the dissolution of her relationship with her husband and the support that relationship may have provided her at one time. If Mr. Jackson were not going to return, Ms. Jackson would need support in assuming the role of single parent for four children and in establishing herself as a single parent. Undoubtedly, her self-esteem had been assaulted by the decline in the family's situation and her inability to cope with it all. Although the physical environment and safety needs were highest in the hierarchy, Kelly knew that the family service plan would have to address the next levels on the hierarchy of needs to ensure lasting stability.

Engaging Families and Resources in the Planning Process.   Most families rely on a network of support systems to cope with the challenges encountered in life. Family support systems usually include both informal and formal resources. Informal resources, such as extended family (kin), friends, work colleagues, or faith-based communities can provide both material and emotional support in times of need. Many families access formal support systems such as schools, healthcare professionals, counselors, and social service organizations when informal supports are insufficient.

Families that come to the attention of child protective services often have inadequate informal and formal supports or are unable to access supports for one reason or another. Parents or caregivers may become isolated from relatives and friends due to mental or physical illness, poor interpersonal skills, or reluctance to accept help. They may be unable to access formal supports due to fear, distrust, or lack of knowledge of available resources.

One of the tasks of the social worker at the planning phase is to pull together informal and formal resources to establish a "community of support" around the family in crisis. The "family group decision-making" model has recently received a great deal of attention as an effective approach to establishing a "community of support" for the family in crisis (DeMuro, 1999; Macgowan and Pennell, 2001; Pennell and Burford, 2000; Ribich, 1998). The term "family group decision-making " refers to a number of approaches in which family members and other interested parties are brought together to make decisions about how to care for the family's children and develop a plan for services. The literature describes a number of different approaches, including family team conferencing, family team meetings, family group conferencing, family team decision-making, family unity meetings, and team decision-making. These approaches differ in various aspects. For example, the "family unity" model provides a structured time for the participants to share information about family strengths and concerns. The principal feature of the "family group conference" is *private time* for the family, excluding all professionals, to consider the information, deliberate, and develop a plan that is then presented to the professionals. All of the models generally involve several phases and the use of a trained facilitator or coordinator to organize and lead the meeting (Child Welfare Information Gateway, http://www.childwelfare.gov/famcerntered/overview/approaches/family_group.cfm, retrieved 9/20/08).

In response to the mounting evidence of the effectiveness of family group decision-making, child welfare agencies are beginning to incorporate the model in developing initial family service plans. Rick, a second-year MSW student, completed his field internship at a county public child welfare agency. His county child welfare agency had been selected as a pilot county for gathering data on the efficacy of the family group decision-making model. Rick used the model in his work with Marisol and her son, Juan. Case 15.3 describes this process.

CASE 15.3 | FAMILY GROUP CONFERENCING

By Rick Vukmanic, MSW Student

Over the course of several days, Child Protective Services received numerous referrals regarding Marisol and her eleven-year-old son, Juan. According to the referral information, the mother was in the last stages of terminal brain cancer, often confined to a hospital bed. The cancer had metastasized throughout her body and was not responding to treatment. Marisol was becoming increasingly forgetful as a result of the repeated chemotherapy and radiation treatments, was physically weak, and emotionally overwhelmed.

Juan had been born with Fragile X Syndrome and was diagnosed with mental retardation that presented intellectual as well as developmental challenges. He was recently withdrawn from school as the family had initially planned to move to Oregon to live with the mother's sister. These plans fell through after the mother admitted to using marijuana to combat the side effects of her medical treatment. In addition, due to her forgetfulness, Marisol often failed to give Juan his prescribed medications. Marisol was given an ultimatum by her family to cease using marijuana, but refused.

Marisol and Juan were left with no money, little family support, and were living in a one-room apartment with a known drug dealer. The most recent report stated that Marisol had left Juan with a friend from church with a small bag of clothes asking that he care for Juan until her condition improved. Both Marisol and her friend were advised by Juan's case manager from the county's Mental Retardation department to have Juan placed in a residential program.

Marisol had been placed in a children's home as a child and remained there until she finished high school, craving contact with her extended family. After ending a physically abusive relationship with Juan's father, Marisol raised Juan by as a single mother. She was adamant that Juan not be placed in an institution. Fearing involvement of Child Protective Services and the very real potential that Juan would be removed from her care, Marisol dodged the caseworker's attempts at contact for several weeks. During this time, her physical condition continued to deteriorate, but she also began to gain the support of neighbors and community members who learned of her plight. An informal support network slowly embraced both Marisol and Juan, but it became apparent that more formal plans would need to be made for Juan's ongoing care in the future.

Following a conversation with a supervisor from Child Protective Services, Marisol's friends were able to convince her to consider having a family group conference, a meeting in which they could plan, with the support of the formal agencies, for Juan's future. Marisol remained fearful of the intentions of the formal agencies, but strongly desired to be involved in planning for her son's future. The visiting nurse and her attending physician advised against the meeting, due to Marisol's compromised condition, but after being assured that the meeting would be kept within a 2-hour limit, they reluctantly agreed.

Going against protocol, the family group conference was held in the mother's apartment rather than on "neutral ground." Representatives from the Mental Retardation Case Management Unit, the school, the church, and Child Protective Services were invited. Also present were 10 friends and neighbors. Additionally,

CASE 15.3 | *Continued*

friends arranged for an attorney from Legal Aid to be present.

Marisol was placed on the couch by her hospice worker and made as comfortable as possible. Her breathing was heavy and the nurse prepared an oxygen mask. Prior to the family group conference, it was agreed that the purpose of the meeting would be to develop a plan to provide a safe and stable home for Juan for a time when his mother would no longer be able to do so herself. Almost immediately some of the service providers expressed their concern that the purpose was not realistic and that Child Protective Services would need to take custody of Juan in order for any plan to be successful. Marisol was assured that while this was an option, she and her "family" could also plan around other options.

Wanting to save time, the nurse and hospice worker requested that the group forego the discussion about strengths and move directly into a discussion about the "grave" concerns facing both Marisol and Juan. With Marisol's approval, however, the group facilitator followed the conference protocol and initiated a discussion about strengths. Throughout the discussion, the nurse and hospice worker continued to point at their watches offering Marisol medication and suggesting that she lie down. At the same time, Marisol became more involved in the conversation, moving to a sitting position and became increasingly engaged in the discussion. She expressed her surprised that in her "hopeless" situation, the group was able to identify over 30 strengths.

When the discussion turned to concerns, the service providers quickly interjected that the situation could be quickly resolved if Marisol simply allowed Child Protective Services to assume custody of Juan. Marisol reminded the providers that according to the model, she would be given the opportunity to express her concerns first. Two main themes surfaced. Marisol acknowledged that she was often unable to care for Juan and herself and identified that persons would need to be available to assist on a daily basis. Secondly, and just as important, an identified guardian had not been established for Juan, and clear steps would need to be taken to accomplish this task. The group was shocked at her honesty as well as the passion with which she expressed herself.

Although the first phase of the meeting lasted well over an hour and a half, Marisol remained committed to the process over the objections of her nurse. After listening to the resources available through all of the formal systems, Marisol and her friends met in private for another hour and a half to address the concerns. After several interruptions regarding the length of the meeting, Marisol requested that her nurse and hospice worker leave the main room of the home and wait in the hallway with the service providers.

Unexpectedly, a detailed plan emerged, including an emergency contact list and a 24-hour schedule of support to maintain Marisol in her home. It was agreed that Juan would remain in the family home as long as possible. When the need arose to move him, a family friend was identified as his permanent caretaker. Respite caregivers were also identified. The plan included detailed steps outlining how the legal transfer of custody would take place. In presenting their plan, it became apparent that Marisol and her family had addressed almost all of the potential problematic issues that could arise in the future regarding Juan's care. At the end of the meeting, Marisol addressed the group, thanking them for the opportunity to plan for her son's future. Marisol explained the importance of being able to admit to herself that she was no longer able to care for Juan independently, a fact she refused to acknowledge when questioned in the past.

Following Marisol's death a month later, Juan's mental retardation case manager contacted Child Protective Services requesting that the agency assume custody of Juan. The case manager was referred to the family group conference plan, which is currently being implemented. Juan's well-being was being assured by his family friend and other members of the "family group" as previously arranged. Over the next several months, similar calls were received. Each concern was addressed by referring back to the plan that continued to work well for Juan.

Several years later, the plan still remains in place and has been used to answer each question that arises. Marisol's desire to effectively plan for her son's future has been accomplished. He continues to have permanency and loving care in his home community.

CHILD WELFARE SERVICES

As discussed earlier, the cumulative child welfare legislation of the 1990s requires states to make "reasonable efforts" to preserve families by avoiding disruption, *consistent with safety*, and to reunify families as quickly as possible when placement is unavoidable. Various legislative packages have extended funding to support the development of programs aimed at offering in-home services that support families in providing safe and adequate care for their children. The funding led to a profusion of home-based services aimed at supporting families.

IN-HOME FAMILY SERVICES

In-home family services refer to a range of in-home supports provided by public and private agencies designed to support and bolster the family's capacity to care adequately for its children. The services may vary with regard to the frequency of contact and level of involvement with the family. In-home services are classified as either **preventive** or **postinvestigative**. Preventive services are voluntary and aimed at improving parenting skills. Families engaged in preventive services may or may not have come to the attention of child protective services. *Postinvestigative* in-home services can be either voluntary or court ordered and focus on ensuring child safety (Popple and Vecchiolla, 2007). Postinvestigative services are provided for families that have become known to child protective services.

Postinvestigative in-home family services can vary with regard to the intensity of the intervention. The term "family support service" generally refers to interventions that offer low to moderate family contact and intervention. The services are usually designed to enhance the strength and stability of the family and increase parents' confidence and competence in parenting, and promote healthy child development (Tracy, 2000).

Research evidence suggests that well-implemented and well-designed family support services can have a positive impact on prenatal outcomes, parent–child interactions, child development, and parenting skills (Comer and Fraser, 1998). The outcomes of family support appear to depend on the intensity of the service, the timing of the delivery of services, and the degree to which the services are tailored to specific family needs (Tracy, 2000).

The term **family preservation** designates programs that offer more intensive services generally to families that have had a history of child neglect and/or abuse or are at high risk. Based on the presenting problems, the services may include frequent visitation, homemaker services, home health aids, in-home instruction on household management, intensive parenting education, medical monitoring, and so forth. Family preservation services are generally home based and time limited. They require low worker caseloads and in most programs, 24-hour emergency availability of professional staff.

Components of intensive family preservation services typically include:

- **Clinical services** - family treatment approaches (e.g., cognitive-behavioral, systems theory, structural, crisis intervention, etc.) aimed at strengthening family coping capacity, relationships, and functioning

- **Concrete services** - an array of in-home supports (e.g., home health aids, childcare, homemaker services, transportation for medical care, etc.) aimed at improving the physical environment, health status of the family, and household management

- **Case management services** - assistance with prioritizing and implementing actions aimed at alleviating immediate crisis and family stressors (e.g., housing problems, health access problems, financial problems, etc.), securing supportive services, and ensuring the safety and well-being of the children

Social Work Skills In-Home Services.   Social workers who provide home-based services may be involved in providing any or all of the services described above. When delivering clinical services, the social worker must well trained in the models of intervention she is employing and have a good grasp of family dynamics. Chapter 7 provides an introduction to the knowledge base and skills for providing social work services for families in the context of home-based services.

When providing case management services, social workers must employ many of the skills already discussed—strengths perspective, engagement skills, cultural sensitivity, critical thinking, collaboration, transparency, and a supportive stance. In addition, the social worker must take an active role in coordinating the services provided for the family. The intervention of multiple services systems can often overwhelm and confuse a family, exacerbating problems instead of providing the intended support. Coordinating the efforts of multiple service systems can be a critical part of in-home family services and of preventing family disruption.

Jill, an experienced child welfare social worker, had been assigned to the In-home Family Services Unit. She enjoyed her role of engaging multiple supports to help families better meet their children's needs and avoid the disruption of placement. When Jill began work with the Walker family, among the problems faced by the family were substance abuse, mental illness, household management, poor school attendance by the children, and poor parenting skills. Several different formal resources became involved with the family, including individual counseling, family therapy, and substance abuse rehabilitation. Case 15.4 shows how each of these systems had multiple staff involved with the Walkers.

CASE 15.4

WORKING WITH THE WALKER FAMILY: A MULTISYSTEMS COLLABORATIVE APPROACH

By Jill Albright, MSW Student

Mr. Walker's mental health case manager contacted Jill to inform her that Mr. Walker had been missing his individual and family therapy sessions. According to the information, when Mr. Walker would attend his individual and family sessions, he appeared to be under the influence of drugs or alcohol. Mrs. Walker was recently discharged against medical advice from a drug and alcohol rehabilitation center. Mrs. Walker signed herself out of treatment as she felt that her chil-

dren's care was more important than her own, and she planned to seek outpatient treatment after she assured her children's safety. Mr. and Mrs. Walker have three children under the age of 8. In the past, Mr. Walker commented about "kicking their (children) asses," and their youngest child revealed during an individual play therapy session that Mr. Walker hits him with a belt as a form of punishment. Both Mr. and Mrs. Walker have mental health and criminal histories. The parents'

(Continued)

CASE 15.4 | *Continued*

criminal history includes multiple charges related to bad checks. These charges occurred during periods of relapse that created further financial stressors for the family.

During the assessment, Mr. and Mrs. Walker accurately identified their strengths and supports, accepted responsibility for their previous behaviors, and agreed to cooperate with interventions to lower the risk to their children. This was a gradual process that helped to evolve due to the trusting and mutually respectful relationship that was established. Empathetic listening was vital to rapport building, and the Walkers' confidence and sense of control seemed to increase as the social worker validated their concerns and highlighted their achievements. A strengths-based focus served as the social worker's foundation and helped to encourage the family's present/future focus perspective. Based on the parents' insight, goal negotiation was encouraged and the social worker assisted the family to concentrate on potential solutions. This approach focused toward the positive, toward the task, and toward the solution. Voluntarily, Mr. and Mrs. Walker enlisted extended family members to care for the children while they sought supportive and counseling services to improve their overall family situation. Mr. and Mrs. Walker were candid with their children regarding their personal needs, and the children's enthusiasm seemed to strengthen the parents' commitment.

Multiple systems including child welfare professionals, mental health providers (psychiatrists, mobile therapists, therapeutic staff supports, case managers), drug and alcohol counselors, parent educators, and extended family members became involved with the Walker family and their pursuit to secure services and complete their goals. Unfortunately, the services were not coordinated, and Mr. and Mrs. Walker were reluctant to voice their frustrations because they did not want their feelings to be interpreted as lack of cooperation. Instead, they withdrew from services through nonattendance and missed appointments. When Jill was finally able to contact Mr. and Mrs. Walker, they refused further service.

Jill began to receive information from family members and service providers that Mr. and Mrs. Walker had relapsed into their addictions, and the children were again neglected and at risk. In preparation for the court hearing to petition for commitment of the

children to the custody of the child welfare agency, Jill collected the various service providers' contracts, the mental health providers' treatment plans, and the parent educators' progress notes. The number of goals established in the six different treatment plans and the demands placed upon them by these plans amazed Jill. Based on these plans, Mr. and Mrs. Walker were expected to commit to a minimum of 15 hours of services on a weekly basis. Jill created a grid to further illustrate Mr. and Mrs. Walker's expected level of commitment to these services. It became apparent to Jill that services had overwhelmed the Walkers, rather than helped them. Instead of pursuing the custody hearing, Jill decided to hold a team conference meeting.

Jill invited child welfare social workers, mental health providers, parent educators, extended family members, social service providers, and the Walker family to the meeting. Collectively, these people met to end the "tug-of-war" battle and re-determine the purpose and the need for each service. If a need was identified, specific rather than redundant goals were established. Action steps were created using the collaborative model as its basis to stay solution focused and driven. Monthly cross-systems meetings were maintained to assure accountability and limit the number of home visits and reviews conducted by the various agencies. Initially, the Children and Youth Services' social worker coordinated the meetings; however, as Mr. and Mrs. Walker became empowered by this process, they requested and independently coordinated the meetings. The Walkers regained control and direction of their lives, and they were able to proactively plan their future success. As a result of Mr. and Mrs. Walker's dedication to their children and the cross-systems meetings, the Walker family completed their goals and is no longer monitored by Child Protective Services. In addition to Mr. and Mrs. Walker maintaining their sobriety, they have stable housing and employment, and they continue to meet and exceed their personal goals. Their eldest child recently graduated from high school, and their younger children earn honor roll grades. Ultimately, due to this cross-systems approach, the family learned how to monitor and evaluate its own needs. Presently, the Walkers provide their children with care, supervision, and support without the involvement of any mandated social support agencies.

Efficacy of In-Home Family Services.   Legislation of the 1990s had envisioned that in-home family services would significantly reduce the number of children entering placement due to neglect and/or abuse and the length of stay in placement for those children in temporary care. Recent studies on the efficacy of in-home family services for preventing family disruption and improving child safety have revealed mixed results (U.S. Department of Health and Human Services, 2001). There is some evidence to suggest that certain program models may be more effective than others and that certain program models work better for some problems rather than others (Nelson, 2000). For example, programs serving families coping with children with behavior problems or mental illness appear to significantly reduce the number of out-of-home placements and improve parenting skills for managing challenging behaviors (Fraser, Nelson, and Rivard, 1996). On the other hand, Littell and Schuerman (2002) found no reduction in the percentage of out-of-home placement resulting from family preservation services in 7 of the 11 programs they studied. Fraser et al. (1997) conclude that intensive, short-term family preservation services may be most appropriate for addressing child behavior problems and inappropriate for situations involving young children or serious child maltreatment. Gelles (1996) argues that the legislative emphasis of the 1990s on family preservation services and keeping a child with a family that has a history of serious abuse or neglect have shifted child protective services away from its most paramount responsibility to protect children from harm.

Child welfare experts caution that there are many constraints to empirically evaluating the outcomes of in-home family services, and much more research is needed before "throwing the baby out with the bath water." According to Pecora et al. (2007), "studies have been confounded by a number of administrative and evaluation problems; however. Problems in administration include referral, staff training, and community resources. Evaluation problems include the use of non experimental designs, small samples, poor case targeting, underuse of qualitative designs, and inappropriate assessment measures" (p. 290). Families that are served by the child welfare system typically have multiple challenges reflecting social problems that reach far beyond the family itself—poverty, failing communities, underfunded education systems, and so forth. Pecora et al. (2007) argue that the expectation that single services, such as in-home family services, be expected to produce dramatic changes in complex social problems is unreasonable.

FOSTER CARE

Each year thousands of children are removed from their homes to protect them from abuse or neglect. Foster care is the term used for any supervised out-of-home placement, whether it is with nonrelated foster families, relatives, neighbors or agency-sponsored group residential care. According to the U.S. Children's Bureau, in 2005 approximately 513,000 U.S. children were residing and over 800,000 children had spent some time in foster care during the year (U.S. Department of Health and Human Services, 2008). Currently, the vast majority of children in out-of-home placement reside either with nonrelated foster families or with relatives. Foster care provided by relatives is referred to as "kinship care." Whether the placement is with a nonrelated family or in kinship care, care is monitored by public child welfare directly or by a private agency designated by the public agency. Several challenges plague the services for children requiring out-of-home care.

Challenges of the Foster Care System.   Public perception of foster care has historically been highly negative. Over the years, horrific stories of child neglect and abuse by foster parents captured by the media have understandably promoted sentiments that indict the entire system. Generally not portrayed by the media are the thousands of foster parents who provide nurturing and competent substitute care for children unable to remain with their birth parents.

Length of Placement.   As discussed earlier, the policies governing foster care have evolved over time to address a number of concerns. The most important of which was the phenomenon of children "adrift" in the foster care system for years, moved from one temporary home to another, and getting "lost" in the system. Concern about "foster care drift" led to the legislation of the 1980s and 1990s aimed at promoting "permanency" for children and the practice of "concurrent planning." Currently, the official time limit for temporary out-of-home placement is 15 consecutive or 22 nonconsecutive months. When the time limit has expired, a plan for permanency must be ready to be implemented. The preferred plan is family reunification consistent with the safety and well-being of the child. If reunification cannot be accomplished, then permanency is sought through termination of parental rights to pave the way for adoption, transfer of legal custody to relatives, emancipation, long-term foster care, or some other arrangement that assures a nurturing and permanent living situation for a child.

Despite permanency planning mandates, concurrent planning, in-home services to support family reunification, and increased numbers of adoptions for children in foster care, the length of time children remain in foster care has remained relatively stable since 2000 (U.S. Department of Health and Human Services, 2008). Implementing concurrent planning and meeting time limits on temporary out-of-home placement are hampered by high worker caseloads; too few resources to meet birth families' basic needs for housing, childcare, and employment; and limited numbers of adoptive homes for children of color and children with special needs.

Racial and Ethnic Disparities in Foster Care.   Policymakers have long been concerned about the overrepresentation of children of color in the foster care system. Of the 513,000 children in foster care in 2005, 50% were children of color, even though children of color represent only 39% of the U.S. child population. African-American children are by far the most overrepresented group in foster care, constituting approximately 32% of the children in care, while representing only 15% of the U.S. child population (U.S. Department of Health and Human Services, 2008).

The literature suggests that the overrepresentation of children of color in foster care is not due to their being at higher risk of neglect or abuse (McRoy, 2005).

> Yet children and youth of color experience disproportionately higher rates of maltreatment investigation and of abuse and neglect substantiation (Fluke, Yuan, & Edwards, 1999). Children of color are more likely to be removed from their parents and placed in foster care, they stay in foster care for longer periods of time, and they are less likely to be either returned home or adopted. (McRoy, 2005, p. 624)

The literature further suggests that the poorer outcomes for children of color with regard to foster care may be due to inequities in service delivery (Courtney et al., 1996; McRoy, 2005). According to McRoy (2005) a variety of factors contribute to these inequities in service delivery, including racially biased assessments, limited or ineffective cultural competency training for child welfare workers, underrepresentation of people of color in the child welfare workforce, and the inability of the child welfare system to retain experienced workers.

Stability of Foster Home Placement.   There is general agreement that multiple placements are damaging to children. Research supports that multiple changes in a child's primary caregiver can lead to compromised ability to form healthy attachments, learning problems, serious mental health disorders, and problems functioning in adulthood (D'Andrade, 2005).

According to D'Andrade (2005), approximately half of all foster children experience only one or two placements. Not surprisingly, children who are in foster care placement for short periods of time experience better stability than children in care for longer periods of time. According to Usher et al. (1999), approximately 60% of children in care for longer than 3 years experienced three or more placements. Research further indicates that children placed with relatives experience greater placement stability than children placed with nonrelatives (Berrick, Needell, Barth, and Jonson-Reid, 1998). Certain child characteristics appear to be associated with greater placement instability. Males, older children, and children and youth with emotional or behavior problems tend to have greater placement instability (D'Andrade, 2005).

Caseload Size and Worker Training.   The goals of foster care are to provide children with safe, permanent, and nurturing substitute care. In order to achieve these goals, out-of-home placements must be monitored and supervised closely. The overtaxed child welfare system and large worker caseloads have compromised child welfare systems' ability to adequately meet these responsibilities. Workers typically have insufficient time or foster home resources to make well-thought-out child/foster family matches, to closely monitor the child's adjustment, or to provide guidance for foster parents in helping a child to minimize the trauma associated with the disruption in the child's life.

PROMISING APPROACHES IN ADDRESSING THE CHALLENGES OF FOSTER CARE

Reducing placement instability, greater supervision of and support for foster parents, professionalizing the role and skills of foster parents, and extending kinship care represent promising directions for improving outcomes for children in out-of-home placements.

Kinship Care.   As mentioned earlier, placements with relatives or kin have greater stability than nonrelated foster care placements. In recognition of this fact, child welfare agencies see kinship care as the preferred option for children in need of out-of-home placement. As a result of legislative mandates of the 1990s, kinship care providers receive the same benefits and supervision as nonrelated foster care providers.

Therapeutic Foster Care.   Child abuse or neglect can occur when parents or caregivers are unable to cope with a child who has behavioral, emotional, or mental health problems or developmental disabilities. Until recently, residential treatment facilities and group homes—both large and small—were the only placement options for children and youth needing care because of social, emotional, or developmental challenges. Currently, therapeutic foster care (TFC) is the most widely used placement option for such children (Chamberlain, 2000).

TFCs generally use treatment teams composed of foster parents, therapists, case managers, and respite caregivers. TFC foster parents receive special training, support, and close supervision from the professional staff. When compared with residential treatment placements, TFCs have shown promising results in achieving placement stability for children with severe behavior problems and improved post-placement adjustment (Chamberlain, 2000).

Improved Supports for Foster Parents.   Recruiting, retaining, and supporting competent foster parents are major challenges for the child welfare system. Among the reasons former foster parents give for quitting are lack of agency support, poor communication with the child welfare worker, foster child behavior problems, and lack of participation in planning (U.S. Department of Health and Human Services, 1993).

Many states have initiated reforms and programs to better support foster parents, improve foster parent retention, and enhance outcomes for children in placement (Christian, 2002). Among the initiatives are

- **Enhanced training** – intensive preservice and in-service training
- **Information sharing** – routinely providing foster parents with information about the child's case plan, educational and medical status, placement history and treatment history
- **Inclusion in planning** – foster parents considered members of the child's case planning team
- **Agency oversight** – adequate agency supervision, monitoring and consultation
- **Mutual accountability** – opportunity for foster parents to provide feedback to the agency without fear of reprisal
- **Foster parent rights** – clear articulation of foster parents' roles, rights, and responsibilities
- **Ancillary services** – agency provision of supports including childcare, respite care, liability insurance, and healthcare
- **Mentoring and peer support** – agency support for foster parents to establish peer support mechanisms

Professionalization of Foster Care.   The term "professional foster parent" is applied to foster parents who are considered trained employees and who receive compensation and benefits in addition to a foster care subsidy. Proponents of professional foster care argue professionalization of foster care reduces the financial burden of foster care, increases the supply of foster homes in socioeconomically depressed areas, and keeps children closer to their communities of origin.

Professional foster parent programs have been initiated in a number of locations, including Chicago, Florida, and Boston (Christian, 2002). One such program is Chicago's Neighbor to Neighbor program that provides professional foster parents with an annual salary, intensive training, childcare, respite care, and other ancillary services. Preliminary evaluations of outcomes of professional foster care programs have been promising. For example, Testa and Rolock (1999) compared the placement experience for children placed in Chicago's Neighbor to Neighbor "professional" foster home model with kinship care and nonrelated foster care. They found that "professional" foster homes consistently performed better than kinship care and nonrelated foster care with regard to stability, keeping sibling groups together, and placing children near their homes of origin.

Family to Family Initiative.   The Annie E. Casey Foundation has spearheaded efforts to reform the foster care system through a variety of strategies. The Family to Family program model is aimed at building community capacity to provide temporary substitute care for children while also supporting the family. The model embraces four strategies (Anne E. Casey Foundation, 2001):

* **Building community partnerships** – establishing a network of community organizations and leaders in neighborhoods with high rates of CPS referrals to create an environment to support families involved in the child welfare system
* **Team decision-making** – in addition to birth parents, relatives and foster parents, involving all relevant community resources in placement decisions and in developing a network of support for the children and their families
* **Resource family recruitment, development, and support** – recruiting and supporting foster and kinship homes that will allow children in need of out-of-home placement to remain in their communities of origin
* **Self-evaluation** – systematic assessment of Family to Family model outcomes to determine efficacy and identify improvements needed

In 1992, the Foundation awarded planning grants to five state child welfare agencies (Alabama, New Mexico, Pennsylvania, Maryland, and Ohio) to pilot the implementation of the Family to Family model. Usher's (1998) preliminary evaluation of program outcomes suggest that the model has had a significant impact on foster care policies, placement stability, family reunification rates, and promotion of family-focused and strengths-based practice.

SUPPORTING CHILDREN IN TEMPORARY FOSTER CARE

In most cases, the role of monitoring and supporting a foster family is assigned to a worker who specializes in foster home service. The foster home social worker is usually a different person from the intake social worker who conducts the initial investigation and who enters the children in placement. This separation of roles has advantages and disadvantages. It allows for a social worker to have the opportunity to develop and focus on the specialized knowledge and skills required to support foster parents and children in care. On the other hand, unless the foster home social worker collaborates closely with the social worker responsible for developing and implementing the permanency plan, it can result in confusion and poor outcomes for children and families.

While employing all of the social work skills discussed above (e.g., strengths perspective, engagement, collaboration, critical thinking, transparency, etc.), the social worker assigned to supporting foster parents and children in temporary foster care has several critical tasks. A few of the most important tasks are discussed below.

Addressing the Impact and Trauma of Separation.   Attachment theory has taught us that all children require a nurturing and consistent primary caregiver to ensure healthy psychological development. While the need for secure attachment to a primary caregiver is greatest in early childhood, the need is present throughout childhood. The loss of the primary caregiver is traumatic for the child.

Children who must be separated from their primary caregiver due to neglect or abuse experience a "double dose" of trauma. The need for placement itself suggests failure on the part of the caregiver to consistently and adequately meet the child's basic survival needs. By definition, the child who enters placement has already experienced the trauma of a disturbed attachment to the primary caregiver. The degree of that trauma will, of course, be related to the extent of the threat to the child's basic survival and the child's developmental stage. The second traumatic injury is the loss of the primary caregiver. Regardless of how inadequate the primary caregiver's parenting skills may have been, she was all the child had. Thus, the child who enters foster home placement can be expected to be experiencing the effects of trauma.

Supporting the Foster Parent in Meeting the Child's Unique Needs.   The task of the foster home social worker is to help foster parents create a "holding environment" in which the child can begin to heal. The social worker assists the foster parent in gaining insight about the child's unique needs and behaviors and how these unique needs and behaviors can be understood in light of the child's life experience. By sharing all available and relevant information, the foster parent can be helped to understand the context of the child's behavior and the factors that might have shaped his personality. If and when problematic behaviors arise, the social worker helps the foster parent understand these behaviors as manifestations of the child's learned coping mechanisms. The goal is for the foster parent to be able to use this insight and empathy about the child's specific uniqueness and needs to guide her daily interactions with and reactions to him, as well as help others with whom the child comes into contact.

Maintaining Continuity of Family Ties.   No matter how compromised a primary caregiver's parenting may have been, the parent–child bond is an essential factor in the lives of the parent and the child. As discussed earlier, concurrent planning requires the development and implementation of a family reunification plan, if possible, along with an alternative plan for long-term, permanent out-of-home care, should reunification efforts fail. The parent's motivation to accomplish the difficult tasks required for reunification is fueled by the parent–child bond and the longing for her child to be returned to her. The child's ability to tolerate separation from the parent is, in large part, supported by the hope that the parent will be able to meet his needs and that the family can be reunited. Strategies for maintaining the family tie during separation are essential to support concurrent planning.

Essential to maintaining the family bond is helping the foster parent to create a nonjudgmental and strengths-based "climate" both for the child and the birth parent. The social worker sets the tone for this stance in the way she frames and presents information about the child and the family and promotes respect for the parent–child bond. The social worker also helps the foster parent to avoid "triangulating" the child's affections during the separation. In other words, the child must not be made to feel as though he must choose between the foster parent and his birth parent. The foster parent understands that she is a "substitute" caregiver and not a "competitor" for the child's affections.

The social worker helps the foster parent to adopt a nonjudgmental and strengths-based perspective toward the birth parent. A birth parent who has lost physical custody of her children due to neglect and/or abuse suffers a major injury to her self-esteem. When the parent is overwhelmed by this injury, her reactions may take a variety of forms, including shame and depression, anger, defensiveness, criticism of the foster parent's care of the child, hostility to the social worker, etc. It is important for the social worker to help the foster parent understand how the birth parent is coping with the loss and collaborate on strategies to help bolster the birth parent's sense of competence with regard to her parental role. This can be very challenging for the foster parent, but at the same time extraordinarily powerful in helping the family. Anyone experienced in foster care has witnessed the amazingly positive impact a supportive and encouraging foster parent can have on the birth parent during the period of separation.

Supporting Visitation.   Decisions about where, when, and how often visits take place will be a function of the nature of the circumstances that required placement, consistent with the safety of the child, and the needs and functioning of the parent. Decisions about visitation should a collaborative effort, taking into consideration the child's age, needs, and safety; the birth parent's wishes; the foster parent's recommendations and observations about the child; and the recommendations of other relevant partners in the planning process.

The rule of thumb is that visits should be at consistent regular intervals and in the "least restrictive setting." In other words the child should be able to "count on" seeing her parent and other important family members to promote the child's confidence in the possibility of stability in her life and the constancy of her connection to her family. Consistent with consideration of safety, the setting should be comfortable, conducive to relaxed and quality interaction, and private.

SUMMARY

The magnitude of the number of children and families involved in the child welfare system makes the safety and well-being of families one of the primary concerns on the social agenda. After centuries of at best ambivalent and at worse coercive and punitive practices, the promising trend in the new century is toward building an empowering and healing partnership between families at risk, their communities, and the social work generalist practitioners. Together, they can forge successful alliances and strengthen families on the behalf of their children.

Promising practices geared toward helping families achieve economic and social stability as well as positive parenting skills have a growing evidence base. In-home and out of home supports have also evolved to be increasingly effective. The effective child welfare worker needs to be well versed in the variety of solution-focused strategies, generalist social work tools, and resources available on the behalf of their clients.

Case example 15.2 concludes with an example of how the many supports involved in the Jackson family are coordinated on the behalf of the family. The social workers work in concert to maintain a seamless continuum of care. Workers recognize the need for education, skills building, recognition, and solution-focused supports when helping the foster parent maintain the often complex middle road between offering the physical and emotional care children need and respecting and encouraging the connection with the birth parents.

CASE 15.2 | **CHILD PROTECTIVE SERVICES** *continued*

The planning meeting for the Jackson family was held 3 weeks after the children were initially placed in foster care. Kelly was very pleased by the number of people who attended and the support it demonstrated for Ms. Jackson. Ms. Jackson was there, along with several members of her extended family. They included her maternal aunt, the cousin with whom she was staying temporarily, the cousin's husband, and two other female maternal cousins. Also, attending the meeting were the pastor of Ms. Jackson's church and two friends from the church. Among the professionals at the meeting were Kelly, the outpatient psychiatric social worker, the social worker from the school the Jackson children had attended, the court-appointed child advocate, and Ms. Jackson's legal aid attorney who would represent her at the next dependency court case review.

Family reunification within 6 months was the goal identified by the group. Cleaning and fixing up the family's home and stabilizing Ms. Jackson's psychiatric status through continued psychiatric supportive counseling and medication monitoring were the two principal tasks required for reunification. Ms. Jackson expressed that she wanted to find employment so that she could have a viable means of support for her family. She had been a licensed practical nurse (LPN) in Selma, but had not returned to work after the family moved north. She felt strongly that being able to work would not only help the family financially, but it would help sustain her emotionally. However, she would need to take a refresher course to renew her license and she would need childcare for the younger children. One of Ms. Jackson's friends from church, a retiree, offered to provide childcare for the younger children and after-school care for the school-aged children. Since she lived in the neighborhood, the children would be able to walk to her house after school.

Kelly agreed to refer Ms. Jackson for vocational counseling to help her negotiate the process of regaining her LPN. They estimated that this process would take about 6 months, leading to the 6-month time frame for reunification. Other details of the plan included weekly visitation for Ms. Jackson and the children in the foster home, Ms. Jackson's participation in her church's weekly fellowship meetings (something she had enjoyed prior the crisis), and Ms. Jackson's consultation with legal aid interns to set up a payment plan for the family's debt (e.g., unpaid rent and utilities). Ms. Jackson's extended family expressed their commitment to helping her fix up the house and lending her money for needed repairs and purchases. They would also work alongside her in the clean up effort. Once the children were returned, the family would be referred for in-home family support services to help the family during the transition period and solidify the gains made by Ms. Jackson.

Tom Y., the social worker assigned to support the children in placement, had already been collaborating closely with Kelly from the very beginning. He was thorough in reviewing the intake information gathered by Kelly. He followed up with contacts with the school the children had attended and the school they would attend while in foster care to facilitate the transition. He collected developmental and medical information on each of the children, which he shared with the

CASE 15.2 | *Continued*

medical providers who would be following the children while in care. Most importantly, Tom visited the foster home weekly, meeting both with the foster mother, Ms. Tyler, and the children. Tom was thorough in sharing all pertinent information with Ms. Tyler and encouraging her to identify any concerns she had or challenges she encountered in meeting the children's needs.

During Tom's second visit to the foster home, Ms. Tyler reported that the younger children appeared to be making a good adjustment to the transition to care. Ms. Tyler commented that it was obvious to her that the mother must have provided "solid" parenting before her illness, because the children seemed basically trusting and easily comforted when their needs for food, play, and attention were met.

Ms. Tyler's primary concern was about Christopher. He was moody and uncommunicative. He was unresponsive to her efforts to relate to him and at times, he was blatantly hostile to her, particularly when she was attending to the younger children. Ms. Tyler admitted that she was close to losing her patience with him, felt hurt by his rejection of her, and his lack of gratitude for her efforts to make him and his siblings comfortable.

Tom, an experienced foster home social worker, knew that Christopher's behaviors described by Ms. Tyler were common reactions to the trauma of separation and loss and probably indicative of an unique emotional dilemma Christopher was experiencing in the transition to foster care. Tom's job was to engage Ms. Tyler in a process of insight development about Christopher's behavior so that her feelings of rejection and resentment might be replaced by empathy for Christopher's emotional dilemma.

TOM:	I've told you about how Christopher had assumed the role of caregiver for his younger sisters and brother and his mother when his mother became depressed. He must have been doing this for a couple of months.
MS. TYLER:	Yes, I remember. He must have been very frightened.
TOM:	Frightened, but maybe he was also proud of his role. It is also possible that he may have had a caregiving role even prior to his mother's illness. That often happens in families with many young children. The older child may become a surrogate parent.

MS. TYLER:	Oh, yes. I understand that. I was the oldest of five children and from an early age, I was like a second Mama.
TOM:	Really. How would you have felt, if someone who didn't really know you stepped in and took over your role when you were Christopher's age.
MS. TYLER:	Well, I guess I wouldn't like it much. I suppose little Christopher might be a little bit resentful. But I just want him to be able to be a little boy. He is only 9 years old after all.
TOM:	Yes. You and I know that would probably be best for him in the long run. But he is going through so many changes now that must be very confusing for him. When we are threatened by change, we often cling to what we know best.
MS. TYLER:	Yes. I suppose he wants to hold on to being the "little man" and he resents it when I don't let him.
TOM:	So what do you think you might do to help him with this transition?
MS. TYLER:	Well, maybe I can give him some space to help with the care of the little ones—not too much, but just enough to let him feel he is still the "little man."
TOM:	I think you were also right that he should be able to be a little boy, too. Are there ways that you can help him to do that?
MS. TYLER:	Let me think about that. Hmm. I think it would be good for him to get away from the little ones for a while. My son would like to take him out to play ball. He has been reluctant to leave the house, but I think I should continue to encourage him to do things that little boys might like to do.

Discussion Questions

1. Why is it important to be aware of the historical context of child welfare services? Cite two examples where knowing the history would be helpful in current practice.
2. Discuss the relevance and value of generalist practice to the field of child welfare. What is the contribution of the social work perspective?
3. What are the primary issues surrounding our work with an involuntary or mandated client? What steps and considerations would a generalist practitioner take in building a supportive helping relationship?
4. What are the tasks of the child welfare worker at the point of investigation?
5. How would you apply solution-focused processes in each phase of social work intervention in the field of child welfare?
6. What is the meaning behind the paperwork and time frames so prevalent in child welfare practice today? Do you think that these requirements add or detract from client care and supports? Discuss your response.

References

Altman, J. (2003). A qualitative examination of client participation in agency-initiated services. *Families in Society, 84,* 471–479.

Annie, E. Casey Foundation (2001). *Family to family: Tools for rebuilding foster care.* Baltimore, MD: The Annie E. Case Foundation.

Berg, I. K., and Kelly, S. (2000). *Building solutions in child protective services.* New York: Norton.

Berrick, J., Needell, B., Barth, R., and Jonson-Reid, M. (1998). The tender years: Toward developmentally sensitive child welfare services for very young children. New York: Oxford University Press.

Chaffin, M. and Friedrich, B. (2004) Evidence-based treatments in child abuse and neglect. *Children and Youth Services Review, 26,* 1097–1113.

Chamberlain, P. (2000). What works in treatment foster care. In M. Kluger, G. Alexander, and P. Curtis (Eds.), *What works in child welfare* (pp. 157–162). Washington, D.C.: Child Welfare League of America.

Child Welfare Information Gateway (retrieved September 20, 2008). http://www.childwelfare.gov/famcerntered/overview/approaches/family_group.cfm (retrieved 9/20/08).

Child Welfare Information Gateway (retrieved September 29, 2008). http://www.childwelfare.gov/systemwide/laws_policies/statutes/drugexposed.cfm

Christian, S. (2002). Supporting and retaining foster parents. *National Conference of State Legislatures Legislative Report, 27*(11), 1–11.

Comer, E. and Fraser, M. (1998). Evaluation of six family-support programs: Are they effective? *Families in Society, 79*(2), 134–148.

Courtney, J., Barth, R., Berrick, J., Brooks, D., Needell, B., and Park, L. (1996). Race and child welfare services: Past research and future directions. *Child Welfare, 75,* 99–137.

D'Andrade, A. (2005). Placement stability in foster care. In G. Mallon and P. Hess (Eds.), *Child welfare for the 21st century* (pp. 608–622). New York: Columbia University Press.

DeJong, P., and Berg, I. K. (2001). Co-constructing cooperation with mandated clients. *Social Work, 46,* 361–374.

DeMuro, P. (1999). *Team decisionmaking: Involving the family and community in child welfare decisions.* Baltimore: Annie E. Casey Foundation.

Dielman, M., and Franklin, C. (1998). Brief solution-focused therapy with parents and adolescents with ADHD. *Social Work Education, 20*(4).

Di'Lorenzo, P., and Cairns, J. (2005). Public child welfare: A history of challenge and opportunity. In A. Giardino and R. Alexander (Eds.), *Child Maltreatment.* (pp. 261–268). St. Louis: C.W. Medical Publishing Inc.

Fraser, M., Nelson, K., and Rivard, J. (1997). Effectiveness of family preservation services. *Social Work Research, 2*(2), 138–153.

Gelles, R. (1996). *The book of David: How preserving families can cost children's lives.* New York: Basic Books.

Huebner, R., Jones, B., Miller, V. P., Custer, M., and Critchfield, B. (2006). Comprehensive family services and customer satisfaction outcomes. *Child Welfare, 85*(4), 691–714.

Karski, R. (1999). Key decisions in child protective services: Report investigation and court referral. *Children and Youth Services Review, 21,* 643–656.

Littell, J. (2001). Client participation and outcomes of intensive family preservation services. *Social Work Research*, 25, 103–114.

Littell, J., and Schuerman, J. (2002). What works best for whom? A closer look at intensive family preservation. *Children and Youth Services Review*, 24, 673–699.

Macgowan, J., and Pennell, J. (2001). Building social responsibility through family group conferencing. *Social Work with Groups*, 24(3/4), 67–87.

Maslow, A. (1970). *Motivation and personality*. New York: Harper & Row.

McGowan, B. (1983). Historical evolution of child welfare services. In B. McGowan and W. Meezan (Eds.), *Child welfare: Current dilemmas, future directions* (pp. 44–90). Itasca, IL: Peacock Publishers.

McGowan, B. (2005). Historical evolution of child welfare services. In G. Mallon and P. Hess (Eds.), *Child welfare for the 21st century* (pp. 10–43). New York: Columbia University Press, 10–43.

McRoy, R. (2005). Overrepresentation of children and youth of color in foster care. In G. Mallon and P. Hess (Eds.), *Child welfare for the 21st century* (pp. 623–634). New York: Columbia University Press.

National Association of Public Child Welfare Administrators (NAPCSW) (1999). *Guidelines for a model system of protective services for abused and neglected children and their families*. Washington, DC: American Public Human Services Association.

Nelson, K. (2000). What works in family preservation services. In M. P. Kluger, G. Alexander, and P. A. Curtis (Eds.), *What works in child welfare* (pp. 11–22). Washington, D.C.: Child Welfare League of America.

Paul, R., and Elder, L. (2005) *The thinker's guide to the nature and functions of critical & creative thinking*. Dillon Beach, CA: The Foundation for Critical Thinking.

Pecora, P., Whittaker, J., Maluccio, A., and Barth, R. (2007). *The child welfare challenge* (2nd ed.). New Brunswick, N.J.: Aldine Transaction.

Pennell, J., and Burford, G. (2000). Family group decision making: Protecting children and women. *Child Welfare*, 79(2), 131–58.

Popple, P., and Vecchiolla, F. (2007). *Child welfare social work*. Boston: Pearson.

Ribich, K. (1998). Origins of family decision making: Indigenous roots in New Zealand. *Protecting Children*, 14(4), 21–22.

Sieppert, J., Hudon, P., and Unrau, J. (2000). Family group conference in child welfare: Lessons from a demonstration project. *Families in Society*, 81, 382–391.

Taylor, L. (2005). A thumbnail map for solution-focused brief therapy. *Journal of Family Psychotherapy* 16(1/2), 27–33.

Testa, M., and Rolock, N. (1999). Professional foster care: A future worth pursuing? *Child Welfare*, 78(1), 108–124.

Tracy, E. (2000). What works in family support services. In M. P. Kluger, G. Alexander, and P. Curtis (Eds.), *What works in child welfare* (pp. 3–9). Washington, D.C.: Child Welfare League of America.

Trepper, T., Dolan, Y., McCollum, E., and Nelson, T. (2006). Steve De Shanzer and the future of solution-focused therapy. *Journal of Marital and Family Therapy* 32(2), 133–139.

U.S. Department of Health and Human Services, Administration of Children, Youth and Family Services (1993). *National survey of current and form foster parents*. Washington, DC.: U.S. Government Printing Office.

U.S. Department of Health and Human Services, Administration of Children, Youth and Family Services (2006). *Child maltreatment. 2006: Reports from the states to the national child abuse and neglect data system*. Washington, DC: U.S. Government Printing Office.

U.S. Department of Health and Human Services, Administration of Children, Youth and Family Services (2008). *Adoption and foster care analysis and reporting system*. http://www.acf.hhs.gov/programs/cb/stats_research/afcars/trends.htm, retrieved 9/25/08.

Usher, L. (1998). *Evaluation of family to family*. Chapel Hill, NC: Health and Social Policy Division, Research Triangle Institute.

Usher, C., Randolph, K., and Gogan, H. (1999). Placement patterns in foster care. *Social Services Review*, 73, 22–36.

16 GENERALIST PRACTICE WITH PEOPLE WHO HAVE EXPERIENCED TRAUMA

Barbara Gilin and Mimi Sullivan

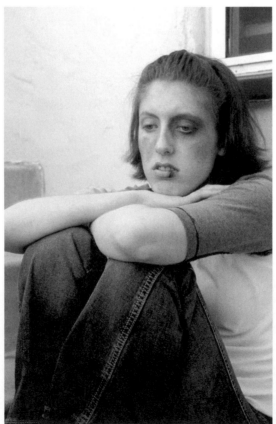

Bill Aron/PhotoEdit

Jamal L., a senior BSW student who had a field placement in the counseling office of a primarily African-American inner-city school, was at home reading the trauma chapter from this book, when he noticed that he had just read three full pages without remembering any of what he had read. He also noticed feeling weird—agitated and numb at the same time—and also slightly nauseous and lightheaded. Jamal analyzed the situation and realized that he had been reading a "symptoms-of-trauma" section that talked specifically about numbing out at times and becoming overaroused (physiologically excited and overactivated) at others. Jamal remembered feeling that way when he was growing up, especially when he was 8 years old, after having witnessed a neighborhood shooting in which a friend was accidentally shot. Jamal had never understood why he had felt so numbed out and unable to concentrate in school back then, or why people thought he was hyperactive and had labeled him as ADHD. At this moment, Jamal felt a sense of relief and validation when he realized that his childhood symptoms had been misunderstood by the people around him and that the symptoms had actually been a natural response to what he had witnessed.

Jamal doubled back on the three pages he did not remember reading, and he noticed that they contained diagrams of the physiological process of dissociation (spacing out in the face of an overwhelming stress). He wondered if looking at the diagrams in the textbook had made him mentally "go away." The next morning Jamal felt agitated, stuck, and numb again—the same feelings he had experienced as a child. He wondered if his present state was some sort of an emotional flashback.

Jamal wanted to talk to his practice teacher, Dr. Washington, about his feelings, but he was afraid. He thought the fact that he was affected by the trauma material might make Dr. Washington think that Jamal was unfit to be a counselor. After all, weren't people who were going to be counselors supposed to have it "all together"? Jamal did, however, decide to write about his feelings in his class journal. The next week, when Dr. Washington handed Jamal's journal back, there was a validating note from the instructor. "Fantastic journal, Jamal. I find that most students who take my class have experienced some sort of trauma that is not fully processed, and when they are exposed to this chapter on trauma, they have certain revelations. It's not always easy. It is normal to have the kinds of feelings that you are having, and it shows great strength that you are willing to explore your reactions in your journal. Throughout your career you will have revelations based on what you are learning. It never ends. Embrace the process. It will make you stronger and wiser. Don't hesitate to talk with me further on this subject."

By the end of this chapter Jamal will be able to:

1. identify the symptoms of trauma
2. understand the biological causes of symptoms
3. be familiar with the three phases of trauma counseling
4. be capable of assisting clients with Phase 1 psychoeducation, stabilization, and coping skill tasks
5. understand and develop ways to handle the impact of trauma work upon himself (the social worker).

PSYCHOLOGICAL TRAUMA

A widely accepted definition of trauma was provided by van der Kolk (1987), "**Trauma,** by definition, is the result of an exposure to an inescapably stressful event that overwhelms a person's coping mechanisms" (p.6). van der Kolk and others emphasize that it is an individual's *subjective* experience that determines whether or not an event is traumatic. Pearlman and Saakvitne (1995) wrote that psychological trauma is a unique individual experience in which "the individual's ability to integrate his/her emotional experience is overwhelmed, or the individual experiences (subjectively) a threat to life, bodily integrity, or sanity" (p. 60). Many trauma experts agree that two different people can actually undergo the same traumatic event, and one might be traumatized while the other is not.

For instance, an individual with a fairly healthy upbringing and no previous trauma, who survives a traumatic earthquake without a complicated aftermath, will generally heal relatively quickly. However, an individual seeking help for traumatic stress, who throughout childhood was emotionally abused by a controlling, neglectful parent, would likely exhibit many more symptoms and would likely have a more protracted recovery time than the previously mentioned one-trauma-incident individual. The above examples illustrate the "**DOSE–RESPONSE**" relationship in working with clients who have experienced trauma. The higher the dose of trauma, the more potentially damaging the effects; the greater the stressor, the more likely the development of PTSD. Everyone has an ability to absorb a certain amount of trauma/overwhelming experience and to keep going without exhibiting trauma symptoms; however, at some point an individual may accumulate too much of a "total trauma load" and begin experiencing the effects of the trauma.

TYPE I AND TYPE II TRAUMAS

Terr (1992), in her studies of traumatized children, first made the distinction between "single blow" (**Type I**) and "repeated" (**Type II**) traumas. Classen and Koopman (1993) noted that examples of Type I would include: natural disasters, plane crashes, car accidents, school shootings, and single incidents of criminal violence such as a robbery or rape. Examples of Type II repeated traumas are: domestic violence, child abuse, sexual abuse, and war and political violence. Giller (n.d.) wrote, "Prolonged stressors, deliberately inflicted by people, are far harder to bear than accidents or natural disasters" (p. 7). Psychological effects are most likely to be severe if the trauma is: "human-caused, repeated, unpredictable, multifaceted, sadistic, undergone in childhood, and perpetrated by a caregiver" (pp. 7–8).

DIAGNOSTIC CATEGORIES IN THE DSM-IV-TR (DIAGNOSTIC AND STATISTIC MANUAL)

Posttraumatic stress disorder (Figure 16.1) and acute distress disorder (Figure 16.2) are the two *currently* recognized diagnoses that apply to trauma. In 1980 the American Psychiatric Association first included PTSD in its *Diagnostic and Statistical Manual of Mental Disorders* (DSM-III). At that time, there was no diagnosis

A. The person has been exposed to a traumatic event in which both of the following were present:

1. the person experienced, witnessed, or was confronted with an event or events that involved actual or threatened death or serious injury, or a threat to the physical integrity of self or others.
2. the person's response involved intense fear, helplessness, or horror.

B. The traumatic event is persistently reexperienced in one (or more) of the following ways:

1. recurrent and intrusive distressing recollections of the event, including images, thoughts, or perceptions
2. recurrent distressing dreams of the event
3. acting or feeling as if the traumatic event were recurring (includes a sense of reliving the experience, illusions, hallucinations, and dissociative flashback episodes, including those that occur on awakening or when intoxicated)
4. intense psychological distress at exposure to internal or external cues that symbolize or resemble an aspect of the traumatic event
5. physiological reactivity on exposure to internal or external cues that symbolize or resemble an aspect of the traumatic event

C. Persistent avoidance of stimuli associated with the trauma and numbing of general responsiveness (not present before the trauma), as indicated by three (or more) of the following:

1. efforts to avoid thoughts, feelings, or conversations associated with the trauma
2. efforts to avoid activities, places, or people that arouse recollections of the trauma
3. inability to recall an important aspect of the trauma
4. markedly diminished interest or participation in significant activities
5. feeling of detachment or estrangement from others
6. restricted range of affect (e.g., unable to have loving feelings)
7. sense of a foreshortened future (e.g., does not expect to have a career, marriage, children, or a normal life span)

D. Persistent symptoms of increased arousal (not present before the trauma), as indicated by two (or more) of the following:

1. difficulty falling or staying asleep
2. irritability or outbursts of anger
3. difficulty concentrating
4. hypervigilance
5. exaggerated startle response

E. Duration of the disturbance (symptoms in Criteria B, C, and D) is more than 1 month.

F. Disturbance causes clinically significant distress or impairment in social, occupational, or other important areas of functioning.

The diagnosis of Posttraumatic Stress Disorder applies to the individual who has exhibited symptoms for more than one month. If the symptoms are still present for more than 3 months, specify "Chronic." If the onset of symptoms is at least 6 months after the stressor, specify "Delayed Onset."

FIGURE 16.1 | DIAGNOSTIC CRITERIA FOR PTSD (309.81)

A. The person has been exposed to a traumatic event in which both of the following were present:

(1) the person experienced, witnessed, or was confronted with an event or events that involved actual or threatened death or serious injury, or a threat to the physical integrity of self or others

(2) the person's response involved intense fear, helplessness, or horror

B. Either while experiencing or after experiencing the distressing event, the individual has three (or more) of the following dissociative symptoms:

(1) a subjective sense of numbing, detachment, or absence of emotional responsiveness

(2) a reduction in awareness of his or her surroundings (e.g., "being in a daze")

(3) derealization

(4) depersonalization

(5) dissociative amnesia (i.e., inability to recall an important aspect of the trauma)

C. The traumatic event is persistently reexperienced in at least one of the following ways: recurrent images, thoughts, dreams, illusions, flashback episodes, or a sense of reliving the experience; or distress on exposure to reminders of the traumatic event.

D. Marked avoidance of stimuli that arouse recollections of the trauma (e.g., thoughts, feelings, conversations, activities, places, people).

E. Marked symptoms of anxiety or increased arousal (e.g., difficulty sleeping, irritability, poor concentration, hypervigilance, exaggerated startle response, motor restlessness).

F. The disturbance causes clinically significant distress or impairment in social, occupational, or other important areas of functioning or impairs the individual's ability to pursue some necessary task, such as obtaining necessary assistance or mobilizing personal resources by telling family members about the traumatic experience.

G. The disturbance lasts for a minimum of 2 days and a maximum of 4 weeks and occurs within 4 weeks of the traumatic event.

H. The disturbance is not due to the direct physiological effects of a substance.

FIGURE 16.2 | DIAGNOSTIC CRITERIA FOR ACUTE STRESS DISORDER (308.3)

---

that could describe the painful and debilitating imbalances experienced by returning soldiers from the Vietnam War. Until there was a "name" for what they were suffering, they could not access benefits from the VA for treatment. That first PTSD diagnosis was built on Dr. Abram Kardiner's (1941) work in which he described symptoms of "war neuroses" seen in World War II veterans. His work had, in turn, been built on the observations of Dr. Charles Samuel Meyers, who first used the term "shell shock" in 1915 to describe symptoms presented by returning WWI veterans (Lasiuk and Hegadoren, 2006, p. 17).

In 1990, the DSM-IV expanded the original criteria for PTSD, and then again, in 1994, the DSM-IV-TR clarified further the distinctions between PTSD

(Figure 16.1) and acute stress disorder (Figure 16.2). It is important for social workers to be aware of the criteria listed for each of these diagnoses because, at sometime, all workers will meet clients who are suffering from "untreated" PTSD or complex PTSD (described below). Clients who are viewed through the lens of being "trauma survivors" may end up being treated more sympathetically by other professionals and thereby receive more effective interventions than clients with other diagnoses. Hodges (2003) wrote that "women diagnosed with borderline personality disorder are often considered mentally unstable and are therefore subject to institutionalization, forced medication, and loss of parental rights. In a similar vein, they are also discredited as court witnesses in cases involving sexual assault. This contrasts significantly with the manner in which women diagnosed with PTSD are treated" (p. 9).

In order for social workers to have the necessary credibility when suggesting to other professionals that clients' problems may, to some extent, be the result of trauma(s) they suffered, those workers must demonstrate a good understanding of the criteria listed below. According to Hodges (2003), "Posttraumatic stress disorder (PTSD) is one of only a few diagnoses in the DSM-IV whose symptoms are attributed to situational causes alone" (p. 2). Therefore, the PTSD diagnosis is more consistent with the professional values and the systems thinking used by social workers.

The criteria for acute stress disorder (listed below in Figure 16.2) are the same as those for PTSD, except for the length of time that the individual has exhibited symptoms. A diagnosis of **acute stress disorder** applies to the individual who has exhibited symptoms **for less than one month**.

AN EXPANDED DIAGNOSIS: COMPLEX PTSD

Since its inception in 1980, the diagnosis of PTSD has described only a limited number of posttraumatic symptoms. The current DSM-IV-TR criteria for PTSD still do not accurately or fully describe the symptoms of many trauma survivors, because the PTSD diagnosis was originally formulated for the specific purpose of ensuring that Vietnam War veterans qualified for benefits. For the 2 years leading up to the DSM-IV-TR (1994), a group of trauma experts recommended the addition of another diagnostic category that was called either complex PTSD, or disorders of extreme stress not otherwise specified (DESNOS) (Figure 16.3). Their proposed diagnosis was built on the understanding that prolonged trauma that first occurs at an early age, and/or is of an interpersonal nature "can have significant effects on psychological functioning above and beyond PTSD symptomatology" (van der Kolk, et al., 2005, p. 394). An expanded diagnosis would have included symptoms that are more specific to victims of child abuse, sexual assault, and domestic violence.

The proposal was defeated in 1994, but experts in the field of traumatic stress are already building a case for the complex PTSD diagnosis to be added to the upcoming DSM-V. An expanded diagnosis could "stimulate the development of relevant and effective treatment approaches to clients with complex trauma over the course of development" (van der Kolk et al., 2005, p. 387).

I. Alteration in Regulation of Affect and Impulses, including suicidal preoccupation, and difficulties controlling anger.

II. Alterations in Attention or Consciousness, including amnesia and dissociation.

III. Somatization of Emotions, including digestive problems.

IV. Alterations in Self-Perception, including beliefs that one is responsible for the abuse or that one is permanently damaged.

V. Alterations in Perception of the Perpetrator, including the victim's acceptance of the perpetrator's negative beliefs about the victim.

VI. Alterations in Relations with Others, including inability to trust or victimizing others.

VII. Alterations in Systems of Meaning, including loss of previously sustaining beliefs.

FIGURE 16.3 | PROPOSED NEW CATEGORY: COMPLEX PTSD OR DESNOS (DISORDERS OF EXTREME STRESS NOT OTHERWISE SPECIFIED)

THE PLASTIC BRAIN: THE NEUROBIOLOGY OF ATTACHMENT VERSUS NEGLECT

Popular psychology often preaches that the emotional attitudes and verbal behaviors of others can affect individuals only to the extent that they allow. For instance, if a boss bullies an employee and tells that person that he or she is worthless, it is popularly thought that it is up to the employee to filter out the boss's incorrect statements and to maintain positive self-esteem and a positive mood, even in the face of such abuse. In other words, "sticks and stones may break one's bones, but words will never hurt one." Research into the neurobiology of attachment and into mirror neurons has debunked that thinking. It is true that we can use cognitive techniques to filter and control a certain amount of the impact of others upon us, but the moods and opinions of others will still, to some degree, affect and imprint upon us.

In order to understand the physical impact of others' behaviors upon our minds and bodies, it is necessary to go over some fundamentals regarding the neurobiology of attachment: in other words, the ways in which the brain is shaped by attachment experiences.

The Neurobiology of Attachment.   Infants are born with more than 100 billion brain cells (neurons), and with the potential for trillions of connections to be made among the billions of neurons (Amen, 2008; Perry, 2000). The infant brain is a fairly undifferentiated, unconnected mass of brain cells. The outside of the newborn brain looks like a smooth, rounded lump of clay. It does not yet have the external, squiggly appearance of the developed, adult brain.

Nurturing Attunement.   The infant brain rapidly begins to organize, structure, and shape itself by growing connections between neurons. Unique connections are developed and imprinted on the baby's brain through soothing and attuned interactions with primary caregivers (Amen, 2005; Romano McGraw, 2004). Although the brain is plastic and can be patterned via interactions with significant others throughout life, the younger a person is, the more plastic and impressionable the brain. Therefore, the brains of new babies are very malleable (Perry, 1997) and are quickly shaped and influenced by caregiver interaction. Much of early caregiver programming helps the infant to develop a capacity for later self-regulation, for instance, the ability to soothe oneself when one is upset (Ainsworth and Bowlby, 1991; Amen, 2005, 2008; Romano McGraw, 2004; Schore, 1994, 2001a, 2001b).

Consider the case of Da and her new infant, Sing. Da has never been a mom before and Sing is crying. Da is not sure what to do. Sing doesn't know what he needs, just that he is distressed. Da tries feeding Sing, but he still cries. Then she tries to burp him, but he continues crying. Finally she wraps him in a blanket. He stops crying. He was cold!

In the moment of attunement, during which Sing feels soothed by the blanket, Sing and Da gaze at each other and the pupils of both become large and dilate. A "flashbulb" moment of synchronized connection and imprinting occurs during the pupil dilation (Romano McGraw, 2004; Schore, 1994, 2001a, 2001b). Sing's neural connections have just been set up to recognize that the particular distressed feeling that he just experienced required delivery of a blanket by his mom. Now he can start to develop a particular cry that will signal Da when he needs a blanket. Later in life, he will be able to identify when he is cold and needs to find a way to get warm. Da is a good mom and she rarely fails to attune to Sing, so in a few months Sing's brain is rich with imprinted neural connections, and thus his brain begins to get the squiggly appearance of an adult brain.

Neglect, a Lack of Attunement.   Children who experience early neglect (for instance, children who are in orphanages in which they receive little attention or attunement) may fail to develop the neural programming and associations that allow them to interpret and respond appropriately to distressing feelings. It is hard to initiate the appropriate action to take care of oneself, when one cannot label the distress that one is feeling. In examining the brains of adults who have been neglected in their youth, the external appearance of the brain is often smoother and less "squiggly" than individuals who experienced good attunement in early life (Amen, 2005). Individuals for whom inappropriate coping skills have been modeled often use inappropriate means to calm and soothe (i.e., aggression towards others or substance use, Amen, 2005; Perry, 1997). It is important to realize that the brain is plastic and is constantly building and changing throughout life.

Plastic throughout Life: The Impressionable Brain.   While the adult brain is not as plastic and impressionable as the newborn brain, the adult brain does retain plasticity and is affected by attunement. For example, when an employee is belittled by her boss, she may tell herself that her boss's behavior is incorrect and inappropriate, yet the angry demeanor of the boss causes the employee to be affected by his angry emotion through the action of "mirror neurons" in the brain. If someone is angry with us or is abusing us, our mirror neurons cause our brains and bodies to register the abuser's emotional state (Enticott, Johnston, Herring, Hoy and Fitzgerald, 2008). The misattunement by the boss affects attachment imprinting and imprints the employee with a message that she is inadequate. If she is exposed to many negative messages from her boss, over time her neural circuitry will change, and she will be imprinted with the message that she is inadequate and, on some level, she will begin to feel that way about herself. Likewise, if the boss really "hears out" the employee's good ideas and offers positive feedback, the employee's brain will be imprinted with more positive messages, and new positive neural connections will be made.

Neuroplastic Implications.   What are the implications of the neurobiology of attachment and the phenomenon of mirror neurons for us as social workers?

- It is important to help clients to avoid abusive situations. Emotional and verbal abuse causes physical alterations to the brain, in the way described above, and through a steady release of cortisol that may bombard and shrink important areas of the brain (Carrion, Weems, and Reiss, 2007).
- It is important for our clients to be in relationships with others who are positive influences. Safe and trustworthy friends as well as groups like Alcoholics Anonymous that attune to the individual's experiences and that teach excellent coping skills, are tremendously healing. A person who has been emotionally wounded through neglectful or abusive relationships can generally experience healing through the repaired neural circuitry that occurs from appropriately attentive, positive relationships.
- It is important for us to make sure that, in our own relationship with our clients, we foster authentic and positive connection. Many studies have been conducted to look at what types of help are most effective, but the studies seem to show that, regardless of the technique used by a counselor, it is the relationship between the worker and the client that is the primary healing factor (Omer and London, 1989). Through our attunement with clients, they will heal.

The neurobiology of attachment provides an explanation why a good, attuned connection with one's client can reciprocally contribute to the social worker/counselor's own brain health and sense of well-being.

STATE-DEPENDENT LEARNING

An understanding of state-dependent learning is crucial when working with trauma survivors. State-dependent learning explains, in part, why survivors cannot remember significant elements of traumatizing events when they are calm, and/or cannot remember how to use coping skills to protect themselves when under stress.

Simply described, if a person learns something in a one state, she may not be able to remember or retrieve what she has learned when in another state. For instance, if a person has learned a fact while drunk, she may not be able to recall that fact until she is drunk again (CommunityWorks, 1998). Consider the following example.

CASE 16.1	**APPLICATION OF KNOWLEDGE ABOUT STATE-DEPENDENT LEARNING**

Lyndsey F. had an internship in a middle school that was that was experiencing an outbreak of violent schoolyard fights, so Lyndsey and her supervisor developed a program to teach the kids better conflict management skills. Lyndsey taught the new program in all of the seventh-grade health classes. The kids were receptive and eager to learn the new techniques, which they appeared to fully understand; however, subsequent to the training, Lyndsey was disappointed to realize that the incidence of fighting at the school did not decrease.

While reading this textbook for her practice class, and while learning about state-dependent-learning, a *light bulb* went off for Lyndsey. She realized that when she was teaching conflict management techniques to the kids, they were in a relaxed state, and although they understood the techniques while in the relaxed state, when they were in an aroused, fighting state, they could not retrieve or remember the conflict management skills learned in class. Lyndsey remembered her practice instructor saying that sometimes it was a good idea to

have people do jumping jacks when learning conflict management techniques, so that their heartbeat and their physiologically aroused state, during the jumping jacks, would approximate the fight or flight arousal of the conflict situation, thus facilitating state-dependent retrieval during an actual conflict.

Lyndsey came up with the idea of posting her conflict-management techniques on posters in the gym, so that kids would receive reinforcement of the new conflict management principles while in the physiologically aroused state of playing sports (Follmer, 2006). Lyndsey hoped that reinforcement of the techniques, while kids were engaged in hard play, would facilitate state-dependent recall of those skills when the kids were aroused and getting ready to fight. A month after Lyndsey put up her gym posters, fighting in the school significantly declined. Lyndsey and her supervisor published an article in an academic journal on their gym poster program, and soon other schools and social work agencies began to replicate the program successfully.

Imagine that we are studying a group of students who are all required to eat chocolate while studying for a test. Chocolate interacts with serotonin, dopamine and endorphin neurotransmitter systems, producing a pleasurable state (Parker, Parker, and Brotchie, 2006). Although all of the students eat chocolate while studying for the test, only half eat chocolate while taking the test. The students who eat chocolate while taking the test will theoretically do much better than the students who are abstaining, because they are in the same chocolate-elevated state of well-being as they were while studying. The students who are not allowed to eat chocolate while taking the test will not do as well, because they are in a different state than the chocolate-elevated state they were in while studying. (CommunityWorks, 1998; Rothschild, 2000)

Information learned in a particular state may only be able to be retrieved or remembered while in that same state. How does state-dependent-learning affect our clients? Consider the following, based on an example provided by psychiatrist Sandra Bloom (CommunityWorks, 1998).

Imagine that, in the calm setting of an office, a counselor and a domestic-abuse client develop an effective escape plan for the client to use when the client's husband starts to become abusive. The client feels secure with the plan of action. That night the client hears her husband coming up the stairs to their apartment, and she can tell from the noises that he is making that he is drunk. Immediately her body transitions out of a calm state into a flight, fight, freeze state. Her husband comes in and abuses and berates her. As the woman undergoes the violent abuse, she does not once remember that she had composed an escape plan earlier in the day. Later, after the woman calms down, she remembers the escape plan, and she cannot understand why she did not recall it during the abusive incident.

It is important to teach clients about state-dependent learning and to help the client figure out ways to remember the skills calmly learned in the counseling office when the client is actually aroused (meaning when the person's body is physiologically excited and activated). See how Lyndsey F., described below, developed a way to overcome the limitations of state-dependent learning with the kids at her field placement.

SYMPTOMS OF TRAUMA

At the outset of this section, the most important point to be made is that the "symptoms" seen in trauma survivors are, in fact, *adaptations* that have enabled individuals to survive the overwhelming experience of being traumatized (Ford, Courtois, Steele, van der Hart, and Nijenhuis, 2005; Pearlman and Saakvitne, 1995). The below description of trauma symptoms will be followed by a case example that illustrates the decades-long fallout of a traumatic event originally experienced in childhood.

THE BIOLOGICAL IMPACT OF TRAUMA ON THE BRAIN AND BODY

A key to understanding, predicting, and treating the "stuck" symptoms and patterns of trauma lies in obtaining an understanding of how trauma symptoms are biologically generated when a person is confronted with an overwhelming experience. The physiological changes caused by a prolonged and intense fear state (traumatization) cut across cultures. In fact, the physiology of traumatization is the same for most mammals (Levine, 1997a, 1997b; Rothschild, 2000).

The Survival Response: Flight, Fight, and Freeze. The body's physiological flight, fight, and freeze responses to overwhelming stress are central to the formation of trauma symptoms. When a person faces a physical or psychological threat, adrenalin (ephinephrine/norepinephrine) is released by the adrenal glands to prepare the individual to flee or to fight. As adrenalin surges, blood flows away from the stomach and from other organs of the body that are not essential for flight or fight. Blood courses towards the arms and legs, so that the limbs have additional power. Blood also leaves the part of the brain that is involved in finer thinking and reasoning, and it infuses the part of the brain that is involved in rougher, "black and white" survival responses. If an individual is trapped and does not have the option of fleeing or fighting, then the body will release cortisol, which partially numbs the individual's brain and body against pain. Because of the numbing effect of cortisol, the trapped person will not mentally or physically feel the full impact of any emotional or physical injury as it is occurring. If enough cortisol is released, the person will experience a floppy kind of "tonic immobility" (including the inability to fully move his muscles) and will appear inert (Levine, 1997a; Rothschild, 2000).

The release of the numbing cortisol may block the formation of explicit memory, so that in the future the individual may experience a kind of amnesia, or partial amnesia, when trying to recall the fearful, traumatic situation. For example, in attempting to remember a traumatic situation, individuals may not be able to remember what happened to them in words, but instead may recall a few surreal images and may experience a wave of nausea (a body memory).

After the danger is over and the threat has passed, the body produces another surge of cortisol. The second cortisol surge causes the individual's body to reset, by causing the person to literally shake (or quake) out of the survival state and back to a calm state and to a feeling that he or she is again safe.

As mentioned previously, other mammals have the same fear and survival responses as humans. Peter Levine's 1997 book, *Waking the Tiger*, offers an excellent explanation of this phenomenon, as described below.

A cat catches sight of a mouse and chases it (Rothschild, 2000, p. 49). The mouse freezes for a moment to assess the situation, and then the mouse experiences a flight or fight response, as its adrenal glands (glands sitting above the kidneys) release adrenalin. The mouse flees (since it is too tiny to fight the cat). The cat captures the mouse in its mouth. Then the adrenal glands of the trapped mouse release the numbing cortisol. As cortisol surges, the mouse becomes floppy and inert in "tonic immobility" (Gallup and Maser, 1977; Levine, 1997a). Some people call this the mouse "playing dead." The surge of cortisol anesthetizes the mouse against pain, in case the cat eats the mouse, but if the cat is not hungry, he will lose interest in the mouse and will drop it.

In our scenario, the cat is not hungry, so he becomes bored with the floppy mouse and runs off to chase something else. Once the cat goes away and the danger has passed, the mouse starts to revive. A second, big surge of cortisol is released, which allows the mouse to reset itself back into its normal, relaxed state. As it starts to reset, the mouse trembles and shakes uncontrollably. Once reset, the mouse seems oblivious to its recent brush with death, and it resumes calmly frolicking in the woods with fellow mice.

How does the mouse model relate to humans? If a person does not experience a second, resetting cortisol surge, his/her body will not be released from the fight, flight, or freeze state back to a relaxed state. The person may then be perpetually and simultaneously stuck in a state that causes him/her to feel both aroused *and* numb. Two reasons why individuals do not experience a cortisol surge sufficient enough to reset the body are: that the person remains stoic and prevents himself/herself from shaking following a brush with a fearful situation, or that the person has been in danger so consistently that their cortisol has been depleted, and as a result, there is not enough cortisol left to provide the surge necessary to reset the body.

Biological Changes and Trauma Symptoms.   Many of the traumatized clients seen by social workers are individuals whose survival systems have been overtaxed. The case of Nadia, below, illustrates a number of typical, long-term psychobiological consequences of trauma on an initially healthy child who has been psychologically held captive, and who has repeatedly defended herself against overwhelming stress. Nadia's case illustrates the fallout (through adulthood) of constantly defaulting to the use of survival-system defenses. As her survival system becomes depleted in childhood, Nadia's body develops a habitual pattern with which she begins to handle *all* stress. (*Most* everyday stresses do not require the mobilization of the full-fledged flight, fight, freeze defense system.) A commonly seen cascade of symptoms and ineffective patterns of behavior develops for Nadia. Her body ends up feeling as if it is "jammed" with "one foot on the accelerator and one foot on the brake" (Levine, 1997b).

In preparation for Nadia's story, some of the symptoms that occur as a result of the psychobiological fallout of being chronically traumatized are introduced below.

Van der Kolk and Courtois (2005, p. 386) maintain that, "at the core of traumatic stress is the breakdown in the capacity to regulate internal states." When van der Kolk assesses traumatized clients, he looks for the following elements, all of which originate as an attempt to manage overwhelming stress (many of which will be explored in Nadia's story):

Intrusive Reexperiencing—Examples of reexperiencing include flashbacks, strong feelings, bodily sensations, nightmares, and repeating, destructive patterns in relationships.

Autonomic Hyperarousal—The sympathetic nervous system stays "on alert" even after the trauma has passed.

Numbing of Responsiveness—In order to control their emotions, traumatized people avoid distressing internal sensations. Examples of this avoidance include, "feeling dead to the world" or "just going through the motions." Numbing may be expressed as depression; dissociation; lack-of-feeling, pleasure, or motivation; or psychosomatic symptoms.

Intense Emotional Reactions—Traumatized people lose the ability to regulate their emotions. For, example, "they tend to experience intense fear, anxiety, anger, and panic in response to even minor stimuli." Their emotions may escalate very quickly—similar to a car that accelerates from 0 to 60 miles-per-hour in seconds. Addictions, eating disorders, and other self-harming behaviors may result.

Learning Difficulties—Chronic "hyperarousal" makes it difficult to concentrate and to learn from experience. One consequence for children is poor academic performance at school.

Memory Disturbances and Dissociation—Clients "who learn to dissociate in response to trauma are likely to continue" to use dissociation (which causes a form of amnesia) when exposed to new stresses.

Aggression against Self and Others—Traumatized people "are likely to turn their aggression against others or themselves." Examples of this are: self-injurious behaviors (like cutting), substance abuse, negative self-talk, road rage, oppression of others, and intimate partner abuse.

Psychosomatic Reactions—Many traumatized people have difficulty translating physical sensations into words. They experience much of their distress in terms of their organs, and in terms of body pains, physical symptoms (like shaking or tremors), or physical illness, rather than as psychological states (van der Kolk, 1996, 420–423).

Case 16.2, "Nadia's Story" illustrates the effects and process of trauma. The "Nadia's Story" will continue in sections throughout the remainder of the chapter.

CASE 16.2 | **NADIA'S STORY**

Nadia is 7 years old. For some reason, it seems that her teacher, Ms. Gray, does not like her. One day, when the other children go to lunch, Ms. Gray walks Nadia into the coat closet, and backs her into a corner. In a quiet and intense manner, Ms. Gray tells Nadia that she is a "f———, useless, little slut, who would be better off dead" and tells Nadia that if she tries to escape the coat closet, or if she tells anyone else what Ms. Gray has said, Ms. Gray will find and kill Nadia's baby sister (Figure 16.4).

Immediate Changes Caused by Trauma
A Disrupted Sense of Safety in the World. Nadia previously held the unquestioning belief that teachers were supposed to protect kids. Now her view of the world as an ordered, safe place has been turned upside down. She no longer feels that she can safely predict whom she can trust.

The Initiation of the Survival Response in a Healthy Child. When Ms. Gray starts to berate her, Nadia is momentarily frozen in shock, as she recognizes the fact

Ms. Gray takes Nadia to the coat closet at the back of the classroom.

FIGURE 16.4

(Continued)

CASE 16.2 | *Continued*

that she is in danger (Figure 16.5). Then adrenalin surges, and her limbs are flooded with blood so that she can flee or fight. Blood flows away from the parts of her brain (Figure 16.6) involved in fine reasoning (the cerebral cortex), and blood pervades the brain's seat of the survival instincts (the limbic system). Nadia assesses that she can neither run away from her teacher, nor can she successfully fight Ms. Gray, because she will "get in trouble." She is trapped.

Overwhelming Threat That Creates "Dissociation" via a Cortisol Surge. A human being who is trapped, and whose survival is under threat, can actually be frightened to death or can become mentally disturbed if adrenalin continues to surge unchecked, without successfully being able to flee or fight (Community Works, 1998). As Ms. Gray holds little Nadia hostage in the closet, Nadia's survival system appropriately defends against the consequences of unchecked adrenalin, by releasing cortisol (Figure 16.7). Nadia becomes somewhat anesthetized by the cortisol

release. If Ms. Gray were to strike her, Nadia would not feel it, just as she no longer feels the sting of Ms. Gray's words.

As Nadia's body and mind become numbed by cortisol, she experiences tonic immobility and she "goes away" (Figure 16.8) into what is called a "dissociative state." (Sometimes people missay this word as *disASsociative*, but the term is *dissociative*.) Following her body's initial release of cortisol, Nadia feels emotionally separated from herself. She almost feels as though she is viewing herself and Ms. Gray from a seat on the ceiling. While the dissociative state protects Nadia from the full impact of the abuse, the state also causes Nadia's experience to be fragmenting into a scattered distribution within her psyche. It is as if the scary experience were being bundled into smaller, more manageable components. Although the "cracking apart" of the whole of the experience into its separate components, like physical sensations, emotions, thoughts, smells, and visual images,

Nadia is stunned as Ms. Gray starts screaming at her, for seemingly no reason.

FIGURE 16.5

CASE 16.2 | *Continued*

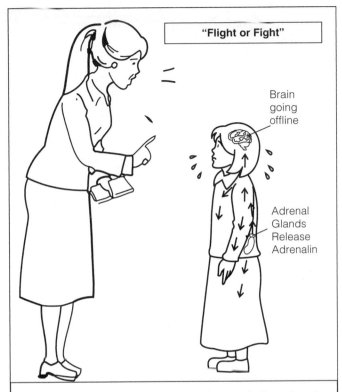

"Flight or Fight"

Brain going offline

Adrenal Glands Release Adrenalin

Nadia's adrenal glands send a surge of adrenalin throughout her body. Blood flows away from her intellectual functions and away from her thinking brain (which goes somewhat "offline"). Blood courses to her limbs, so that she can flee or fight her attacker.

FIGURE 16.6 |

effectively defends Nadia against a fully felt impact, the dissociative state will later cause difficulty when she tries to remember what happened. When she tries to recall the experience, she may only be able to retrieve a fragment or two. For instance, when she tries to remember what happened, Nadia may only be able to retrieve a feeling of distress and the smell an old orange that had rolled out of someone's pocket. She may recall very little of what Ms. Gray actually said.

Dissociation Causes an Altered Sense of Time. After she is finished abusing Nadia, Ms. Gray orders Nadia outside to play with the other children, and she instructs Nadia to pretend that she is happy.

Nadia has no idea how long she was in the closet, because when one is in flight, fright, freeze mode, one loses an accurate sense of the passage of time.

Symptoms That Come from Not Allowing the Body to Reset. When Nadia is released to the safety of the playground, she begins to shake, yet she is afraid that if she allows herself to shake, people will know something is wrong and then Ms. Gray will kill her little sister, so Nadia stops herself from shaking and pastes a smile on her face. The threat has passed for now, but because Nadia does not let herself shake, she has disallowed her body from producing the cortisol surge that would reset her body back to a

(Continued)

CASE 16.2 | *Continued*

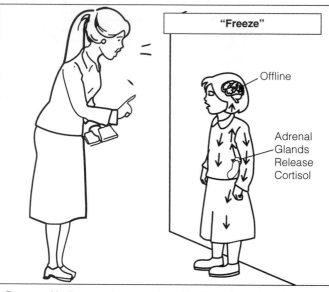

Because Nadia cannot escape from Ms. Gray, her adrenal glands release numbing cortisol, so that she will not feel it if she gets hurt. Cortisol also disables the part of the brain that allows experiences to be encoded with language.

FIGURE 16.7

calm state. Thus, Nadia's body continues along a constantly aroused, anxious, and numb track.

Prolonged Stress That Causes Habitual Survival-System Defenses. Since Ms. Gray is able to feel better about herself by abusing Nadia, she frequently takes Nadia to the closet. Nadia never knows when Ms. Gray will strike. Nadia's body constantly produces adrenalin and also a slightly numbing level of cortisol, so that Nadia is able to tolerate the constant stress of wondering, "When the other shoe will drop," and of wondering when she is going to be dragged back to the closet again.

Habitual Defenses and Symptoms That Result from Ongoing Trauma
Tonic Immobility and Dissociation as Habitual "Default" Defenses. Nadia's body has learned that there is no escape from the coat closet, so she has instinctively developed a new defensive habit. As soon as

Nadia intuits that Ms. Gray is going to abuse her, Nadia's body briefly spikes with adrenalin, and then immediately and habitually switches to a cortisol surge that quickly results in tonic immobility and dissociation. Because of the effectively protecting dissociative habit created to deal with the overwhelming, unpredictable stress of Ms. Gray's abuse, dissociation becomes Nadia's automatic default defense for all of life's stresses, big and small.

Hypervigilance and the "Hyper-Startle Response." Nadia keeps alert and aroused enough to perpetually scan the environment for Ms. Gray's threat. To maintain an alert state, a constant level of adrenalin streams through her body. A continuously aroused state is referred to as a "hypervigilant" state. Because of Nadia's hypervigilant state, her sleep quality is poor. If Nadia's brother approaches her from behind while she is seated watching TV, Nadia will jump up "startled" at his approach. Nadia jumps up startled

CASE 16.2 | *Continued*

As cortisol continues to surge and to numb Nadia's fear, Nadia experiences "tonic immobility," and she begins to "dissociate." She feels as if she is watching everything from a somewhat removed spot on the ceiling (which is one way to experience the feeling of dissociation). She feels calm and sleepy.

FIGURE 16.8 |

when she hears almost any loud or surprising noise, or if anyone approaches her from behind. Trauma sufferers who are hypervigilant often have the symptom of a hyper-startle response.

Foot on the Accelerator and on the Brake. Nadia's body simultaneously surges with adrenalin and cortisol. Her body feels as if she is racing as fast as she can, while simultaneously, she has the feeling that someone is holding her down and trapping her motionless. Over time, Nadia's body becomes habitually stuck in the "accelerator/brake" mode. She is activated and hypervigilant most of the time—and also strangely numb, inert, and emotionally flat.

Learning Difficulties. Nadia used to be an "A" student, but her grades are sliding. She cannot focus or concentrate in school. She has a hard time sitting still. She seems always to be daydreaming. The school psychologist thinks that she has attention deficit disorder (ADD)...or maybe attention deficit hyperactivity disorder (ADHD, Perry, 1997, 2000); however, Nadia's fidgety inability to remain attentive is really a symptom of her hypervigilant, traumatized state. (When one is in flight, fight, or freeze mode, blood has moved away from the higher intellectual centers in the brain in order to fuel the survival system, so the higher intellect is effectively "offline.")

Intense Emotional Reactions and Flashbacks: The 90/10 Reaction. Because Nadia is always ready for flight, fight, or freeze, she often over- or underreacts when confronted. One morning, a friend of Nadia's notices that Nadia has accidentally put on mismatched socks. When the friend jokingly mentions this, Nadia feels confronted and interprets the confrontation as a serious threat—as if her survival were at stake.

The feeling of a confrontation (even an insignificant confrontation) is a trigger that creates a type of a flashback for Nadia. The mismatched sock

(Continued)

CASE 16.2 | *Continued*

confrontation in the present triggers an emotional "affect bridge" to the trauma of confrontation with Ms. Gray. The overwhelming feelings of unresolved fear and threat that surround past confrontations with Ms. Gray flood forward and superimpose upon the lighthearted confrontation regarding mismatched socks. Lewis, Kelly, and Allen (2004), in their excellent book, *Restoring Hope and Trust* (p. 34), call this the 90/10 reaction. The 90/10 reaction happens when 10 percent of the emotional response to a conflict comes from the present, and 90 percent comes from the past. But Nadia does not know that this is a 90/10 reaction. She feels that she is currently under threat. Nadia's 90/10 reactions cause her friends to drift away from her and cause her to become socially isolated.

Dissociation and the Fragmenting of Memory. Nadia's mother is worried. She cannot get Nadia to tell her what is wrong, so she sends Nadia to a clinical social worker. The social worker wins Nadia's trust, so Nadia discloses the fact that Ms. Gray has been abusing her. When she tells the social worker what she recalls, her telling is flat, emotionally unconvincing, disorganized, and full of holes. Nadia cannot tell her counselor the worst parts of the abuse, because she cannot recall them in words. Because Nadia's body was producing the numbing chemical cortisol at the time of Ms Gray's attack, the part of Nadia's brain that would have stored the experience in a language "file" was essentially turned off. Because the abuse memory was not encoded and "filed" with language, Nadia cannot recall the experience with language and thus cannot verbally communicate the experience to the social worker.

Nadia's story about Ms. Gray is so flat, disjointed, and absent of critical information, that the clinical social worker does not get the feeling that the abuse really occurred. As a result Nadia is not treated for past abuse, nor is she protected against future abuse. Her story is not believed, and Nadia's belief that she deserves protection from Ms. Gray is invalidated.

Harming Oneself and/or Others: Traumatic Reenactment/Completion Tendency. One of the most heart-wrenching dynamics that trauma survivors experience as a result of being traumatized is the dynamic of traumatic reenactment. Hardly anyone would purposely choose to reenact his/her victimization over and over again; however, the habitual defenses utilized by trauma survivors, and the 90/10 reactions they experience, often cause individuals to unconsciously repeat the dynamic of their original trauma in a variety of concrete and symbolic ways. The compulsive repetition of unsolvable trauma dynamics, in an attempt to master, complete, and solve the dynamic, is called *traumatic reenactment syndrome* (Miller, 1994, 2003; Miller and Guidry, 2001) or *completion tendency* (Sullivan, 2002).

The Unsolvable Problem. People find unsolved problems to be intolerable because human beings are instinctively programmed to solve all problems. The instinctive drive toward completion is typified by the expression, "If at first you don't succeed, try, try again."

Consider the value of the problem-solving drive as it applies to everyday life. Rothschild (2000, p. 52) gives the example that a small child will make many attempts to learn how to tie a shoe. The child will make many mistakes, but true to the adage, "If at first you don't succeed, try, try again," he/she will finally master the tying of the shoe. The compulsion and the instinct to persist and solve all problems generally work in a person's favor.

The exception to the rule is when an individual continues to work on unsolvable psychological problems. Trauma survivors often find themselves in an unsolvable-problem scenario that replicates the dynamics of their original traumatization. Survivors may experience a compulsion to stay in the replicated scenario until the problem is solved, completed, and mastered. Yet too often the dynamics of the problem scenario are not solvable, and the survivor ends up trapped in and unable to master a "groundhog day" parallel of his/her original traumatization.

The Victim, Abuser, Bystander Unsolvable Problem. One way to understand traumatic reenactment/completion tendency is to apply a commonly encountered unsolvable-problem dynamic, the *victim, abuser, bystander triangle* (as identified by Miller, 1994, 2003; Miller and Guidry, 2001), to Nadia's story (Figure 16.9), and then to examine the ways in which Nadia repeats the unsolvable victim, abuser, bystander problem over the next decades of her life.

CASE 16.2 | *Continued*

If the actors in a conflict dynamic are locked into one of the three roles in the unsolvable-problem dynamic—victim, abuser, or bystander—the conflict can never be solved. It is literally unsolvable. It is important for the trauma survivors to be able to identify the unsolvable pattern as "unsolvable," even though there will be a compulsion to solve the pattern by futilely taking on one of the ascribed roles. Then the survivor must step outside of the problem dynamic and, instead, apply a solvable dynamic to the issue (e.g., "win–win"). If the other actors in the dynamic refuse to abandon their victim, abuser, or bystander roles, the trauma survivor must make the decision to abandon the unsolvable scenario.

Let us take a look at how the unsolvable victim, abuser, bystander dynamic was set up in Nadia's life.

In childhood, Nadia tried every strategy she could think of to keep Ms. Gray from abusing her. Nothing worked. Ms. Gray was the abuser, Nadia was the victim, and the clinical social worker, whom Nadia had trusted, was a bystander who did not believe Nadia and so did nothing to protect her (Figure 16.10).

Nadia, in Adulthood

Fifteen years later, Nadia's body is still physiologically rutted in the habitual pattern of hyperarousal and numbing that was initiated during her second-grade abuse. She has not been able to solve the victim, abuser, bystander conflict dynamic.

Substance Abuse as Reenactment. Nadia finds it difficult to calm her mind sufficiently to study for her college classes, so she starts to drink in a substantial fashion, in order to keep her hyperaroused state from sabotaging her grades. Soon she is dependent on alcohol. The victim, abuser, bystander triangle is internally manifested (Figure 16.9). Nadia is the abuser, abusing herself with alcohol. She is the victim being victimized by the alcohol, and she is also the bystander, bystanding her abuse of herself with alcohol. As long as she continues to drink, she will be stuck in the unsolvable dynamic, as she to tries to control alcohol. But, because she is addicted, she will never be able to control it (Miller and Guidry, 2001). She will instead need to step out of the victim, abuser, bystander triangle, and completely give up

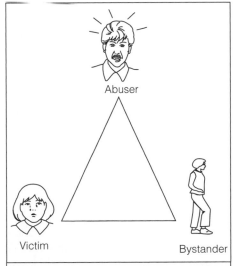

In childhood, Nadia is unable to escape from the "victim, abuser, bystander" unsolvable problem.

FIGURE 16.9

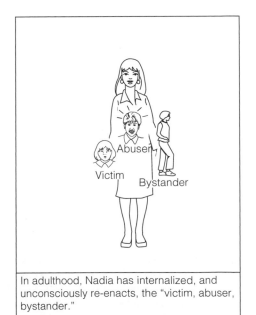

In adulthood, Nadia has internalized, and unconsciously re-enacts, the "victim, abuser, bystander."

FIGURE 16.10

(Continued)

CASE 16.2 | *Continued*

alcohol. She will need to engage in a 12-step program that will nurture her. (Twelve-step programs are excellent pathways to healing from traumatization.)

Negative Self-Talk as Reenactment. Nadia's internal narrative/self-talk also creates an internalized victim, abuser, bystander triangle. When Nadia makes a mistake, she calls herself an idiot and calls herself derogatory names. She abuses herself, she is a victim to herself, and she bystands the abuse of herself. Nadia fails to realize that emotional and verbal abuse, including abusive self-talk, causes a cascade of trauma hormones (adrenalin/cortisol) that shrink and damage the brain.

Relationship Abuse as Reenactment. Nadia falls in love with a man who seems perfect for her. He wants to be with her all of the time. He appears to treasure her and to be kind. Once or twice during their courtship he yells at Nadia, but as soon as her body starts to feel stressed by his yelling, Nadia is triggered into the habitual, unconscious coping skill of cortisol release and numbing dissociation, so she does not feel the attacks. Once they are married, Nadia's husband becomes jealous and isolates Nadia from her family and friends. He will not allow her out alone. When they are home together, he tells her that she is an awful and worthless person (even though she is not). He does not allow Nadia to spend money, and he puts her on a small allowance (even though she earns a full salary). Nadia wants to go back to school so that she can advance in her career, but he will not let her go. No matter what Nadia does, she cannot get her husband to change his behavior. It feels as if she is in the abusive childhood incident with Ms. Gray again. Her husband is the inescapable abuser, and she is the victim. Although her husband's parents know that he is abusing Nadia, they are bystanders who say nothing. Nadia feels trapped, inert, and helpless to leave the marriage with a husband who alternates between loving behavior and abusive behavior.

Changing Roles in Reenactment. Individuals who have been victims may change their role in a reenactment. They may move from the victim role to the abuser role, or to the bystander role.

Soon Nadia has children. Because Nadia is always hyperaroused, when her children challenge her, she does not react with patience, but with anger, as if her children truly are malicious and mean to hurt her.

When Nadia's very kind boss, Charles, questions why Nadia has made a particular choice, Nadia takes the challenge as an attack and strongly and rather abusively retaliates against him. Nadia then sends a somewhat defensive e-mail to Charles "documenting" their confrontation. She copies the whole office, because she feels that her boss no longer "has her back" and she wants others to "be informed of what is going on." Nadia's boss and fellow workers are beginning to feel that Nadia is a problem, since she frequently overreacts to challenges with aggressive attacking behavior and with defensive, paranoid, broadly broadcast e-mails. Next time the company lays off workers, it is likely that Nadia's name will be on the layoff list. When anyone challenges Nadia, she funnels all of her attention to the challenge. Sometimes she get so distracted by a tunnel vision focus on a "perceived threat" that she becomes blind to truly threatening elements in her environment.

Rupture of Trust

Because supposedly trustworthy people have violated Nadia's trust, she no longer knows whom to trust. Because adrenalin and cortisol are always running in Nadia's system, she can no longer feel who is safe and who is unsafe. Sometimes she decides to trust everyone, and sometimes she decides to trust no one. Because of traumatic reenactments in which she has engaged, and feelings that she is paranoid, she no longer trusts her own judgment. She says, "My trust sensor is off."

Summary

Nadia is a good person, who is trying to do the best she can, yet at the age of 35, she is on the verge of being out of work, is in a bad marriage, is isolated with few friends, and is having parenting difficulties. Because she is not able to negotiate life well, because she feels that her judgment is not good, and because her self-esteem is low, she feels anxious and depressed. She feels that she is not in control of her life. She does not understand why bad things keep

CASE 16.2 | *Continued*

happening to her and why everyone is against her. She cannot figure out why she consistently encounters highly unproductive interpersonal conflict at work. She wonders why God has abandoned her (and she wonders if there is a God). She does not trust anyone. She has migraines. She is always getting a cold or flu, and her sense of time is "all messed up." She is always late for everything. Nadia would never kill herself, because it would affect her parents and her children too much, but she often thinks that if a truck just came along and hit her one day, it would all be over, and that would be OK.

Nadia's own parents are confused and do not know what to do. They hardly ever see Nadia, because her husband keeps her isolated from anyone who supports her. Nadia's parents do all they can to support her, but they are being vicariously traumatized by knowing about the difficulty their daughter encounters in negotiating the world, knowing about the abuse that she is suffering in her marriage, and knowing that their grandchildren are being affected by witnessing their father's cruelty to their mother.

Despite her negative experience with counseling in childhood, Nadia finally reaches out to a local family service agency for help. She bonds with an effective MSW student intern there named Awilda P. In the pages ahead, we will return to Nadia's case as Awilda educates Nadia about trauma and domestic violence

and as Awilda teaches Nadia the foundational skills for recovery.

Nadia's story makes it clear that childhood trauma, in particular, can affect all aspects of the self. According to Saakvitne, Gamble, Pearlman, and Lev (2000, p. 19), "The specific impact on a child is influenced by several factors: the child's genetic makeup, developmental stage at the time of the abuse, his or her relationship with the perpetrators, the quality of his/her attachment to caregivers, and the social and cultural context in which s/he grows up." Survivors of trauma, particularly of early trauma, often continue to utilize the same protective defenses and strategies used during the original traumatization, on virtually every stress or conflict that arises. Unfortunately, the protective, adaptive strategies used to survive past experiences can interfere with the ability to live a healthy and satisfying life in the "here and now." It is important for survivors to love the defenses that protected them from harm at the time of the trauma and to preserve those defenses should they be needed again, but also to develop a wide variety of additional defenses that may be appropriately applied to lesser magnitude issues. The social worker can help the survivor to understand the genesis of survival-system defense strategies and can help the survivor to evaluate whether he or she should continue to pervasively apply those defenses.

RECOVERY FROM TRAUMA

Many expert trauma workers have observed the phases that clients pass through as they recover from the effects of traumatic stress (Courtois, 2004; Ford, Courtois, Steele, van der Hart, and Nijenhuis, 2005; Herman, 1992; Rosenberg, 2000). van der Kolk and Courtois (2005) wrote that the "consensus model" for helping clients "with complex trauma histories is sequenced and progressive" (p. 387). It is important for workers at all levels of professional development and in many different settings to recognize the signs and specific tasks for each of these phases. There is general consensus that Phase 1 involves **stabilization** *and* **skill-building**, followed by Phase 2, which consists of **remembering** the details of the traumatic memories, *only after* the client has learned skills to manage his/her reactions to their memories. Phase 3 is called either **self** *and* **relational development** (Courtois, 2004; Rosenberg, 2000), **reconnection** (Herman, 1998), or **enhancing daily living** (Ford, Courtois, Steele, van der Hart, and Nijenhuis, 2005.)

In many social work settings, there will not be the opportunity or the necessity to move beyond Phase 1. Nonetheless, it is important to delineate elements of Phases 2 and 3 so that a worker will be able to recognize when their interventions with a client may be "out of phase" with what a client wants or needs or is capable of handling at a particular time. All three phases of work with traumatized clients are described below, focusing particularly on Phase 1, which, according to Herman (1998), "may last days to weeks with acutely traumatized people or months to years with survivors of chronic abuse" (p. 147). A set of interventions known as "Psychological First Aid," which may be used with clients who have experienced a recent trauma, including a natural disaster, will be described in a later section.

Even if the worker never *intends* to work directly or in prolonged way on the actual content of the traumatic memories, there will still be occasions when detailed memories will come up in Phase 1 work. However, Ford, et al. (2005) wrote that workers "do not encourage deeper delving into the details of trauma memories, but instead assist the client in self regulation" (p. 439). It *is* important to respond empathically to the client's distress and suggest that they may choose to reconnect with more of the strong feelings and images about the trauma at a later point. In a respectful way, generalist social workers should explain that the reason for moving away from the intensity of their memories is to assess their current coping methods, supports, and strengths (Rothschild, 2000).

PHASE 1—STABILIZATION AND SKILL BUILDING

There are a number of tasks associated with Phase 1 of the recovery process. The following briefly summarize the major tasks to be accomplished.

Restoration of Safety.   The most important goal is to restore a client's sense of safety, both internally and externally. According to Ford et al. (2005), work with clients should

> first involve a primary emphasis on safety—real and perceived— along with skills-building and psychoeducation within the broader context of a relational approach. A critical challenge involves enabling the client to gain control of overwhelming affect, impulsive behavior, and self destructive thoughts and behaviors and replacing them with self-management strategies. (p. 438)

In addition, Herman (1998) wrote that "establishing safety begins by focusing on control of the body and moves outward toward control of the environment... including the establishment of a safe living situation, mobility, financial security, and a plan for self protection" (p. 147).

Attention should be focused on reducing any current threats to the client, as in the case of clients who are still living with abusive partners. For example, if the client is currently in a situation involving domestic violence, it is important to immediately develop a written safety plan. Included in such a plan would be: routes of escape, details regarding avoiding being trapped in rooms that contain weapons (like kitchens, in which there is fire and there are knives), a list of safe places that the client and any children might go to receive confidential shelter, a packed bag with car keys and important papers hidden somewhere outside of the house, and a way to call for help and alert the police or authorities that abuse is occurring. A good source to consult for safety planning is: The National Center for Victims of Crime's Domestic Abuse Safety Plan: http://www.ncvc.org/ncvc/main.aspx?dbName= DocumentViewer&DocumentID=41374.

Assessment.   It is important to realize that *clients who come to an agency setting do not always volunteer information regarding a past trauma*, for example, whether they were sexually abused as a child.. If the client had a more recent "Type I" traumatic experience and if the trauma did not involve an experience that the client viewed as "shameful," he or she may be more likely to volunteer information about the experience. Otherwise, trauma clients often seek social work services for other issues, such as, depression, substance abuse, anxiety, problematic relationships, parenting problems, and self-harming behaviors. They may have been given any number of diagnoses *other than PTSD* throughout their lives. Therefore, as part of most assessments, particularly in mental health settings, a worker should routinely ask about possible traumatic experiences. Clients do not often link their current difficulties with the aftermath of past traumatic experiences, and they do not often see their "symptoms" as the result of their efforts to manage overwhelming experiences in the recent or distant past.

As part of the assessment process, workers should routinely ask about:

- History of abuse including sexual abuse
- History of trauma
- Drug and alcohol use/abuse
- Suicidality of self and family members (if a family member has committed suicide, it is more likely that your client will try suicide than an individual from a family where no one has committed suicide.)
- Self-injury
- Ongoing abuse
- Abuse, oppression, and/or trauma experienced by the clients or by the clients' extended family

Because it takes a while for many trauma survivors to develop trust, they may not accurately answer all of the above questions upon first meeting you. Be sure to ask "sensitive" assessment questions again at a later time, after knowing the client better and after having established safety in the helping relationship.

Building a Relationship.   For clients who have been repeatedly harmed by others, building a trusting and collaborative relationship can take a long time and may, in fact, prove to be the *most* beneficial "intervention" to help clients regain feelings of trust in others and in the world. Trauma survivors, particularly those who suffered interpersonal violence, abuse or neglect, may test the trustworthiness of the worker more than once in order to determine whether the worker will harm them as others have done. According to Pearlman and Courtois, (2005) "experiences at the hands of inconsistent, neglectful, and abusive attachment figures" are often "at the heart of chronic and pervasive trauma" (p. 450). Therefore, the helping relationship often "provides a secure base from which the client can make necessary changes" in his or her life (p. 457). This relationship can provide "an opportunity to rework attachment difficulties," and to "take in" a new image of a trustworthy and caring person to offset other internal images of people who were abusive or neglectful (p. 457). In their books, Solomon and Siegel (2003) and Cozolino (2002) describe the current state of research into positive brain changes that may result from receiving empathy and attunement in the context of a helping relationship.

When starting a relationship with traumatized survivors, it is especially important to keep the following points in mind:

- The worker should hold the client in positive regard and always appear happy to see the person. This does not mean that the client is not confronted to the appropriate degree, when counseling-interfering behaviors occur.

- Listen carefully to the client's description of what they need from you, and convey the sense that they are "in charge" of the agenda. The clients' own needs and concerns and goals should be respected.

- Avoid telling clients what they *should* do or feel, since they have likely experienced coercion from those who previously abused or harmed them.

- Inquire about past relationships that the client has had with other social workers or helping professionals.

- Let the client know you care. Remember that it is not always necessary maintain a "neutral" facial expression with traumatized clients. For example, a client may feel validated if a worker appears saddened or alarmed by the client's story, and the worker's feedback may assist the client in finally trusting his or her own reactions or perceptions.

- Check out whether or not you have understood what the client is trying to communicate. The client needs to see that you are really "attuned" to his/her feelings, state, and the content of what the client is saying. (This is the type of interaction that may, in fact, help build new and needed connections in the client's brain.)

- Know the laws and civil procedures pertaining to domestic violence and child abuse.

- Do not overpromise what you can do, because it is important to *follow through* on what you say you will do in order to build trust.

- Maintain professional boundaries so that clients feel safe with you. This includes: avoiding self-disclosure in the beginning of the relationship, sticking to the time set for your meeting, not touching the client without their permission (other than a handshake), and clarifying the rules of confidentiality.

- If client is engaged in any self-harming behaviors as a way to cope with difficult feelings or memories, tell them with compassion that you understand that the behaviors have probably helped them to cope, but that you will help him or her find other options.

- Hold hope for the client. The physiology of posttraumatic stress often causes individuals to believe that there is no hope for the future and that things will never be better (the DSM criteria for PTSD calls this inability to feel optimistic, "a sense of a foreshortened future"). It can be helpful to say something like, "I know that you can't feel hopeful right now and that it doesn't feel like things are ever going to be better, but I'd like to ask you if you can let me hold the hope for you, and let me have the belief that one day you will be able to hold hope for yourself."

NADIA, PHASE 1: ASSESSMENT

During Nadia's intake assessment at the family service agency, the worker Awilda informed Nadia that she was an MSW student intern. Nadia was not quite sure how she felt about being taken care of by a student, but Awilda seemed capable and very pleasant. Awilda's thorough bio/psycho/social assessment took about an hour and a half. Nadia described her symptoms, her abusive relationship with her husband, and her background of abuse with Ms. Gray. Nadia had been ashamed of being abused as a child and had not mentioned Ms. Gray, since she had originally disclosed the abuse to her unbelieving childhood counselor.

Awilda did not seem to judge Nadia, and in fact Awilda expressed the hypothesis that many of Nadia's present symptoms appeared to be a normal (although terribly annoying and unpleasant) outcome of having been repeatedly abused and then disbelieved in childhood. Awilda said that she understood when Nadia said, "Sometimes I feel as if it would just be easier if a truck were to hit me, and then it would all be over—even though I would never do anything to hurt myself." Awilda understood! Nadia felt validated and felt a great sense of relief. Awilda then said, "Nadia, I know that you can't feel hopeful for the future right now, but will you allow me to hold the hope for you, until you can feel it for yourself? Nadia said, "Yes."

When Awilda asked Nadia how much she drank, Nadia was not ready to tell her that she had at least three drinks every day, so she decided to withhold that information. Instead Nadia told Awilda that she had a couple of drinks on Sundays with dinner.

Nadia's hope, for the moment, was that she would have the chance to work further with Awilda, since Awilda seemed to really understand her. Maybe then she would tell Awilda about the drinking.

Psychoeducation and Skill Building.   One of the most effective ways to begin helping a client suffering from trauma is through psychoeducation. According to Courtois (2004), "Education of a client involves de-mystification of the helping relationship and education about trauma and its impact. Education is also the foundation for teaching life skills in many domains: self care, identifying and regulating emotional states, and more" (p. 418). It is important for generalist social workers to educate their clients (and the supportive people who are close to them) about posttraumatic stress. This is critical since clients and their family members may not understand the symptoms of trauma.

For instance, when an individual is incapacitated and immobilized by fear (even when there is no longer a danger present), concerned family members may want the individual to just "get over it" and "get on with life." It can be helpful to understand that the individual's symptoms are a normal (although frustrating) response to the past stressor and that it is necessary to be patient as the person slowly recovers with the assistance of a competent social worker. Symptoms are the a result of a stuck survival state that came about because the person had protected herself well against "going crazy" or being "frightened to death" at the

CASE 16.3	**"I FROZE"**

Sixteen-year-old Tamika was raped in a park on her way home from school. She was very confused and upset with herself that she did not try to escape when the rapist walked away from her for a few moments. She was instantly relieved when her social worker described how a "freeze" reaction occurs when people conclude that they do not have the physical strength to fight or flee. She no longer believed that she was partly responsible for being raped and she was able to tell her mom and received much-needed support from her.

time of the trauma (CommunityWorks, 1998). The following example illustrates the use of psychoeducation.

Education of the client allows him/her to view symptoms with greater understanding, and enables him/her to develop his/her own unique and creative strategies to dismantle the "default" use of coping skills that are not appropriate to the person's current life. It is important for clients to love and appreciate the "pesky" hypervigilant and dissociative coping skills that protected them during the trauma. As social workers, we don't want to completely eliminate those effective coping skills. The skills that manage serious threat are important to hold on to, but they are not appropriate to apply to everyday life. It is important to help the client to develop a large repertoire of *additional* coping skills, so that he or she may have many skills from which to choose when addressing the wider range of life circumstances.

The value and necessity of educating clients about the posttraumatic stress information contained in this chapter cannot be sufficiently emphasized. Education that provides a logical framework for understanding the effects of trauma allows the individual to become free from shame and self-blame. Greater knowledge also provides the person with the ability to design his or her own interventions aimed at outwitting and overcoming the posttraumatic symptoms. Pertinent educational pieces should be delivered at a pace that is cautious, comfortable, and safe for the client.

Relevant, initial educational topics often include:

- The ways in which an individual may become traumatized
- Symptoms of traumatization
- The importance of dwelling on the positive and of engaging in enjoyable activities (hobbies, spiritual practices, etc.)
- Calming and soothing practices and coping skills (including meditation, mindfulness, grounding techniques, exercise, proper diet, sleep hygiene, etc.)
- The biology of PTSD (i.e., in order to answer the question "Why am I numb sometimes and overanxious at other times?")
- Boundary setting and staying safe
- The skills to assess trustworthiness in others in order to develop the ability to trust again (Aphrodite Matsakis' 1998 book, *Trust After Trauma* is a wonderful resource)
- Ways in which to find other resources (e.g., support groups for particular issues)

CASE 16.1 | *Continued*

Nadia, Phase 1: Psychoeducation and Skill Building

Awilda greeted Nadia with a smile each time they met. Nadia felt that Awilda was "in her corner." As Awilda established a safe, authentic, and trusting relationship with Nadia, she began very slowly to (over many weeks in small, digestible pieces), teach Nadia about the psychobiology of being traumatized and about the resulting symptoms. Sometimes Awilda drew diagrams to help Nadia understand; however, Awilda was very conscious of making sure that Nadia did not get too aroused by what she was learning. Awilda explained to Nadia that, in the first phase of counseling, it was best to keep the client's distress level low, so Awilda and Nadia devised a plan whereby, if Nadia started to get fairly anxious or aroused, Awilda and she would switch subjects for a while to talk about Nadia's gardening hobby. Nadia found it instantly calming to talk about the flowers she was planting, the feeling of the sun on her skin, the feeling of her hands in the soil, and the smell of a freshly mown lawn.

Through Awilda's psychoeducational efforts, Nadia learned that her symptoms were a normal result of having been exposed to an overwhelming stressor, and she began to understand the nature of her reactions. Because of her new understanding, she was able to create some unique and innovative coping methods.

Awilda was reading this book in her MSW social work practice class. She copied the boxed-in self-soothing exercises from this chapter and provided copies to Nadia, which they went over and practiced in counseling sessions. Nadia was able to use many of the exercises to deal with, and to begin to heal from, her trauma.

Awilda explained to Nadia that the first step in counseling someone suffering from traumatization was to help them to self-soothe and to feel safe. Nadia found the flashback protocol particularly helpful, and she made sure to do the light stream meditation every day at lunch, which provided her with a little "mental vacation" and a sense calm at the office. Nadia's "paranoia" at the office melted away. Awilda also composed a domestic-abuse safety plan with Nadia, so that she would be ready, and could keep herself safe, should she and her children need to flee from Nadia's abusive husband. Awilda also hooked Nadia up with a support group at a local domestic-abuse agency.

After Nadia had been working with Awilda for several months, Awilda subtly reasked Nadia some of the more intimate/delicate questions that had been part of the initial assessment. Awilda knew that clients were not always ready to divulge their most personal information during intake, so it was her practice to revisit those questions.

When Awilda reasked Nadia about her drinking pattern, Nadia admitted that she was drinking way too much. Awilda said she understood and that it made sense that Nadia had utilized drinking as a coping skill. Awilda suggested that it might be time to replace that coping mechanism with other skills. Awilda provided some basic education on the effects of substances on the brain and then suggested that she and Nadia sit in on an open Alcoholic Anonymous (AA) meeting hosted by the Family Service Agency. Nadia subsequently decided to join AA. She realized that, in order to stop drinking, she needed the support of a positive recovery community.

Self-Care and Self-Soothing Exercises.   Herman (1998) wrote that "self care is almost always severely disrupted for survivors of prolonged trauma … the client's capacity for self care and self soothing must be painfully reconstructed" (p. 147). Examples of self-care and self-soothing exercises for clients, along with other skill-building instructions are provided below.

1.   **Calming Your Nervous System ("Reducing Hyperarousal")**
    When talking with traumatized clients it is important to pay attention to how aroused their nervous systems are becoming. Signs of moderate to severe hyperarousal include: rapid breathing and heart rate, becoming pale, and cold

sweating. At times like these it is very helpful to insert an "anchor" that you and the client have identified earlier. "It is preferable that anchors be chosen from the client's life, so that positive memories in client's mind and body can be utilized" (Rothschild, 2000, p. 93.) Examples of anchors include a special person, an animal, an object, or an activity. An anchor should provide a client with a feeling of relief and a sense of well-being. Applying the anchor is very straightforward. When the hyperarousal gets too high, the worker can say, "Let's stop for a moment. Tell me more about [insert their anchor]" (Rothschild, 2000, p. 94).

2. **Safe Place Exercise**

    The safe place is a "specialized anchor" and was defined by Jorgenson as "a current or remembered site of protection" (Rothschild, 2000, p. 95). The following script is adapted from Saakvitne and Pearlman (1996):

    "Now imagine that you are in a very pleasant and protected place. This may be a place you have been before, perhaps a time you spent at the ocean, a lake, a special room, or it may be a place you have imagined before. Whatever you imagine it is a very safe and comfortable and pleasant place for you to be. In your mind's eye, you can vividly see yourself there now, and you can sense all that is around you including the colors and sounds and smells of this lovely place. Take some time now to just enjoy being in this place as you continue to breathe in and out, in and out, feeling relaxed and grounded and comfortable, supported by your breathing, feeling a sense of well being and freedom from fear. Remember that you can always return to this pleasant protected place you've imagined and focus on your gentle breathing to stay relaxed and comfortable" (p. 121).

3. **Relaxing Breath**

    You may do this sitting or lying or even standing or walking. Exhale completely through your mouth. Then close the mouth and inhale quietly through the nose to a (silent) count of 4. Then hold the breath for a count of 6, and then exhale through the mouth to a count of 8. Repeat for a total of four times, then breathe normally. What is important is the ratio: 4 in, 6 hold, 8 out, to ensure that the out breath is always longer than the in breath. If you would like, you could imagine breathing in relaxation and exhaling tension as well. (Weil, 1995, pp. 204–205)

4. **Flashback-Halting Protocol**

    A first step in helping individuals who have acute stress disorder or PTSD is to teach them how to stop their flashbacks. Clients may need help in knowing that they are not in danger now, even though they may be experiencing the same feelings of helplessness and terror as if the trauma were occurring in the present. In this case, the following "flashback-halting protocol" (Rothschild, 2000) may be taught:

    *   Right now I am feeling _____.
    *   And I am sensing in my body _____.
    *   Because I am remembering _____.
    *   At the same time I am looking around where I am now _____.
    *   Here_____.
    *   And I can see _____.

- And so I know that [the traumatic event]
- Is not happening now. (pp. 133–134)

This approach to stopping flashbacks is an example of a "grounding technique." Saakvitne, Gamble, Pearlman, and Lev (2000) wrote, "The goal of any grounding technique is to reconnect the person to the present .... orienting him to the here and now, connecting him to his body and his sense of personal control, and connecting him to the worker and the safe context of the present setting" (p. 119).

5. **"Light Stream Exercise" (Shapiro, 2001)**

   This guided imagery is used when a client reports uncomfortable physical sensations that arise in a session with you, possibly in response to a difficult subject. Provide the following instructions, which are taken, *almost verbatim*, from Shapiro (2001):

   - *Concentrate on that feeling in your body. If the feeling had a shape, what would it be?*
   - After the client responds, s/he is asked, *If the feeling had a size what would it be?*
   - *If it had a color, what would it be?*
   - The client is then asked, *Which of your favorite colors do you associate with healing?*
   - Once the client provides a color, you say:

   Imagine that this favorite colored light is coming in through the top of your head and directing itself at the shape that you identified in your body. You can pretend that the more of the light you use, the more you have available. The light directs itself at the shape and permeates it, moving through and around it. As it does, what happens to the shape and color?

   Repeat the above until the shape is gone or has assumed the same color as the light. Change in the image usually correlates with the disappearance of the unpleasant physical sensation. You can continue by saying:

   As the light continues to direct itself to that area, you can allow the light to gently fill your entire body (beginning with your head and slowly moving down to your feet.)

   You can end the imagery by suggesting that this feeling of peace and calm will stay with them for a while. (Shapiro, 2001, pp. 244–246)

Managing Self-Injurious Behaviors.   Traumatized clients have often developed self-destructive behaviors as a way to manage the experiences that overwhelmed their abilities to cope. According to Saakvitne, Gamble, Pearlman, and Lev (2000), "Self-injury is a fundamentally adaptive and life-preserving coping mechanism. It enables people struggling with overwhelming...affect, intense arousal, intrusive memories, and dissociative states to regulate their experiences and stay alive" (p. 93). Examples of self-injury include cutting, addictions, and suicidal gestures. A useful framework for understanding and helping clients identify safe and more effective coping methods is described in Figure 16.11.

Step 1: To discover how the behavior (such as cutting or alcohol abuse) attempts to solve a problem.

   Assessment: How does the destructive behavior help?

   Intervention: List three **other** ways to achieve all or part of that goal.

Step 2: To discover what self skills need development.

   Assessment: Assess client's current skills for managing strong feelings, staying connected to positive people, and increasing feelings of self-worth.

   Intervention: Develop specific ways to practice each skill and talk about them. Plan your intervention following four goals:

   1. Separate past from present
   2. Increase control
   3. Regain connections
   4. Gain insight (Saakvitne et al., 2000, p. 90)

FIGURE 16.11 | PLAN FOR MANAGING DESTRUCTIVE BEHAVIORS

Dialectical Behavior Therapy. Dialectical behavioral therapy (DBT) is a broad-based cognitive-behavioral approach that was originally developed to work with people who have the diagnosis of borderline personality disorder (BPD) (Linehan, 1993). Linehan (1993) summarized the difficulties of people diagnosed with BPD into five categories: difficulty regulating emotions, unstable or chaotic relationships, impulsive and problematic behaviors that include self-injury, lack of a sense of a solid self, and dissociation. She found that *75% of clients diagnosed with (borderline personality disorder) have experienced childhood physical, sexual, or emotional abuse.* In fact, Wagner, Rizvi, and Harned (2007) remind us that the majority of criteria for BPD overlap with the leading descriptions of complex PTSD (p. 392), and, therefore, the skills taught in DBT are often useful for trauma survivors. Linehan (1993) wrote that "a belief in the client's essential desire to grow and progress, as well as a belief in her inherent capability to change" underlies the DBT approach (p. 5), a view that is consistent with social work values. Studies have shown that DBT can be helpful in reducing self-mutilation, suicidal feelings, depression, anger, and substance abuse, and admission to hospitals (Koerner and Dimeff, 2000; Scheel, 2000; Wagner, Rizvi, and Harned, 2007).

The skills taught in DBT are linked to the main difficulties presented by survivors of chronic interpersonal trauma, many of whom received a BPD diagnosis at some time in their lives. To deal with each of the categories listed above, Linehan (1993) identified the following skills:

- **Emotion regulation skills** to help regulate emotional expression.
  - Treat physical illness and take care of your body.
  - Balance your eating by not eating too much or too little.
  - Avoid mood-altering drugs, including alcohol.
  - Balance your sleep.

- Get some sort of brief exercise every day.
- Do one thing every day that makes you feel competent and in control. (p. 154)

- **Interpersonal effectiveness skills** to improve relationships.
  A way to remember these skills is to think of the term **"DEAR MAN,"**
  Describe, Express, Assert, Reinforce, Mindful, Appear Confident, Negotiate:
  - Describe the current situation. Tell the person what you are reacting to.
  - Express briefly YOUR feelings.
  - Assert yourself by asking for what you want or saying no clearly.
  - Reinforce the person ahead of time by telling them the positive effects of getting what you need or want.
  - Stay mindful of your objectives, and when necessary repeat yourself.
  - Appear confident by appearing effective and competent and using a clear, firm voice.
  - Negotiate by being will to give a little if the other person seems willing to solve this problem with you. (p. 12)

- **Distress tolerance skills** to reduce impulsive and self-destructive behaviors.
  A way to think of these skills is to think of soothing each of the **five senses**:
  - With **vision**: Buy a beautiful flower; light a candle and watch the flame; look at beautiful pictures in a book; look at nature around you.
  - With **hearing**: Listen to music that you enjoy; hum a tune; sing along to a favorite song; just notice the sounds around you, imagining them coming in one ear and going out the other.
  - With **smell**: Spray a fragrance in the air; light a scented candle; bake cookies; smell flowers; boil cinnamon.
  - With **taste**: Have a favorite soothing drink like tea or hot chocolate (no alcohol); suck on a piece of peppermint candy; chew your favorite gum; really taste the food you eat.
  - With **touch**: Soak your feet; put lotion on your body; put a cold compress on your forehead; take a bubble bath or warm shower; pet your dog or cat. (pp. 168–169)

- **"Mindfulness" skills** to increase self-awareness and self-knowledge, and to reduce dissociation:
  - Just notice the experience without getting caught in it. Experience without reacting.
  - Have a "Teflon mind", letting experiences, feelings, and thoughts come into your mind and slip right out.
  - Watch your thoughts coming and going, like clouds in the sky.
  - **Describe**: Put words on an experience. When a feeling or thought arises, acknowledge it, such as: "My stomach muscles are tightening" or "I notice sadness coming up in me".
  - **Participate**: Actively practice your skills as you learn then until they become part of you. Practice: (1) Changing harmful situations, (2) changing your harmful reactions to situations.
  - Act intuitively from "wise mind." Do just what is needed in each situation. (p. 111)

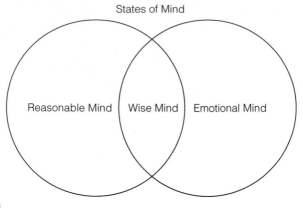

States of Mind

FIGURE 16.12 | STATES OF MIND

- As shown in Figure 16.12 "Wise mind" is the integration of "emotion mind" and "reasonable mind." You are in "emotion mind" when your emotions are in control. You are in "reasonable mind" when you are thinking and planning and evaluating things logically. "Wise mind" integrates your emotions with your reasonableness. (pp. 65, 109)

Other Cognitive Therapy Approaches.   Survivors of cumulative trauma typically develop cognitive distortions (faulty thinking) about themselves, their worth in relationships, and the motivation of others. A client's beliefs about self and others involve negative perceptions and "expectations of maltreatment or abandonment by others" (Briere, 2005, p. 402). These beliefs are "easily evoked by later stimuli that are somehow reminiscent of the original abusive experience" (Briere, 2005, p. 402). One of the tasks of the social worker is to help clients become more aware of their automatic negative thoughts and their longstanding "core beliefs" such as: being unlovable, or helpless, or responsible for mistreatment they receive from others.

One approach used by cognitive-behavior therapists is called "weighing the evidence." Clients are assigned the task of writing down events or incidents that do NOT support a core belief of theirs. For example, if their belief is "I am unlovable," they would be asked to notice when someone treated them nicely, A second task would be to identify their "preferred" core belief, such as "I am deserving of good treatment" and to write down times when they were acting on the basis of their preferred belief. It is important to keep in mind that clients need compassion and understanding from social workers regarding the origins of their cognitive distortions and core beliefs, instead of negative judgments or impatience regarding the persistence of these lifelong habits of thought. Workers need only to notice how hard it has been for *them* to change beliefs about themselves and others in order to develop the patience and compassion for their clients' struggles to change their faulty thinking.

A second technique in CBT is to help clients become more aware of the connections between their thoughts, feelings, and resulting behaviors. For example,

Time	Distressing incident	Internal distress (1–10)	Thoughts and emotions (that preceded or followed the incident)	Resulting action ?or behavior	Consequences

Possible alternative responses:

FIGURE 16.13 | DAILY SELF-MONITORING FORM

---

they may notice how their thoughts ("My boss is frowning and therefore wants to fire me") influence their feelings (anger or sadness) and their resulting actions (hiding in their office or exploding in anger towards their boss.) The form shown in Figure 16.13 is an adaptation of the "Dysfunctional Thought Record" commonly used by workers employing CBT. The goal of the homework, better described as "work to be done between sessions" (Curran, Machin, and Gournay, 2006, p. 48) is to help clients identify the triggers (their thoughts and/or their feelings) that precipitated the action they took so that they identify alternative responses in the future when faced by a similar distressing event.

Prolonged Exposure (PE) has been used to treat PTSD for approximately 20 years. It was developed by Edna Foa (Foa, 1998; Foa, Dancu, Hembre, and Jaycox, 1999; Foa, Hembree, and Olasov, 2007) and was originally used to treat obsessive compulsive disorder. "Exposure" is defined as "facing something that has been avoided because it provokes anxiety" (Curran, Machin, and Gournay, 2006, p. 46). Exposure therapy should be:

- *Graded*: People list all situations that make them afraid in order, identifying those that make them least afraid to those that make them most afraid. They begin facing the situations that make them least afraid.
- *Repeated*: People must face the feared situation many times in order to successfully reduce their anxiety.
- *Prolonged*: People remain in the presence of the feared situation until their fear subsides. "If we remain in the presence of something that frightens us for around 50 minutes, the fear response is likely to lessen" (Curran, Machin, and Gournay, 2006, p. 46).

Exposure therapy has been shown to be effective in reducing distressing symptoms associated with PTSD (Foa, 1998). Studies indicate that in order for PE to be effective, the strict protocol for PE must be followed, without mixing it with other therapies (Foa et al., 1999; Foa, Keane, and Friedman, 2000). Critics express concern that the continuous requirement for the individual to relive the details of the trauma is unduly uncomfortable and may cause individuals who cannot tolerate the level of discomfort to become more traumatized (Pitman, et al., 1996).

PHASE 2—REMEMBERING

There are recognizable signs that a client has achieved the important tasks of Phase 1 and may be ready to move on to the work of Phase 2. Herman (1998) wrote that the survivor may "now be ready to tell the story of the trauma, in depth and in detail" (p. 147). *Whether or not a client and worker enters into Phase 2 depends on the training and experience of the worker, the agency mission, the amount of time available to work with the client, and finally, on the client's full and informed consent to proceed with a more direct and planned exposure to traumatic memories.* The second phase of trauma work is more directly "trauma focused," actively involving the client in recalling traumatic memories as well as related body states, emotions, and perceptions in amounts and at a pace that is safe and manageable (Ford, Courtois, Steele, van der Hart, and Nijenhuis, 2005, p. 439). Herman (1998) wrote, "As the survivor summons memories, the need to preserve safety must constantly be balanced against the need to face the past" (p. 147). It is important for the worker and client to be confident that the client has learned enough skills to be able to handle intense emotions and images and physical sensations that may arise in the course of Phase 2 work. In Rothschild's (2000) words, "client and therapist must be confident they can 'apply the brakes' before using the 'accelerator' "(p. 99).

Safely Telling the Trauma Story.   Rothschild (2000) recommends the following outline to aid clients in telling the story of their traumatic experience. In order to pace the telling of the "Trauma Narrative," she suggests that they:

• Name the trauma
• Outline the trauma by designating titles to the main incidents
• Fill in the details of each incident, one at a time, using "braking strategies" to slow down or stop a "runaway" traumatic process, and reduce uncomfortable symptoms of "hyperarousal" (pp. 114–115)

EMDR.   Eye movement desensitization and reprocessing (EMDR) was developed by Francine Shapiro in the late 1980s (Shapiro, 2001). EMDR utilizes elements of various therapies including psychodynamic, cognitive, and somatic (body sensation) therapy and integrates those elements with bilateral stimulation. Bilateral stimulation is any form of physical sensation that is delivered to both sides of the body, while the therapeutic process is occurring. For instance, bilateral stimulation can be delivered through the client's movement of his/her eyes side to side during processing, or by a tonal sound being delivered first to one ear and then alternating to the other, or by having a part of the body (like the hands) tapped on one side of the body and then on the other.

Although EMDR has been proven to work, no one is quite sure why it works. Put very simply, it is theorized that trauma memory is fragmented in the brain and that traumatic memories generally activate the side of the brain that handles negative thoughts (leaving the other "positive" side of the brain inactive). So, when a person is processing trauma with EMDR, stimulation on both sides of the body will stimulate both the negative *and* the positive side of the brain. The trauma memory then synthesizes together as a more balanced "reconsolidation" of past negative and new positive thoughts (Donovan, 1999; Shapiro, 2001). It is thought that reconsolidated memories cannot be reconstituted or made traumatic again by exposure to future trauma (Suzuki et al., 2004). When a memory is reconsolidated, the person does not forget what has happened. He maintains the wisdom gained from the experience, but he is no longer ruled or controlled by the memory. The person develops a feeling that the trauma is over, and the individual becomes free to move on with life. The web links for the eight phases of the EMDR protocol and for training in EMDR can be found at the end of the chapter.

EMDR is thought to be very efficient, in that the therapist can select one early, vivid, "target" memory that is representative of a number of traumas, and by clearing that one trauma it is possible for like traumas to be diminished or cleared. In EMDR, although the client talks about some of the disturbing elements of the traumatic experience, the client is not required to discuss all of the details. EMDR appears to access and clear dissociated, nonverbal memory in a way that most talk therapies cannot. EMDR is considered a therapeutic "power tool." As with any powerful therapy, it must be utilized carefully and cautiously, and at the appropriate pace for the client. In 2004 the American Psychiatric Association found that EMDR was an effective treatment of trauma. Also in 2004, the Department of Veterans Affairs and Department of Defense (2004) placed EMDR in the "A" category as "strongly recommended" for the treatment of trauma. Research studies in the United States and around the world have found that: EMDR and CBT were treatments of choice for PTSD (Bisson and Andrew, 2007; Bisson, Ehlers, Matthews, Pilling, Richards, Turner, 2007; CREST, 2003; Dutch National Steering Committee, 2003; National Institute for Clinical Excellence, 2005). EMDR was effective in children with PTSD (Ahmad, Larsson, and Sundelin-Whalsten, 2007; Fernandez, Gallinari, and Lorenzetti, 2004). EMDR was found to be superior to a group receiving Prozac alone, and the EMDR group continued to improve after the treatment ended (van der Kolk, Spinazzola, Blaustein, Hopper, E., Hopper, J., Korn, and Simpson, 2007). A link to these and other studies can be found at www.emdria.org.

NADIA, PHASE 2: REMEMBERING

Six months after starting to work with Nadia, Awilda was finishing with her first-year field placement, and it was time to transfer Nadia to another social worker for Phase 2 of counseling. Nadia felt that she might never have a counselor who was as effective as Awilda again. It was difficult to believe that Awilda was "just" a student.

Nadia felt that Awilda really believed in her. Every time Nadia had difficulty taking a step forward she remembered that Awilda unquestioningly felt that she was equal to the challenge. Awilda had taught Nadia to "trust her gut" when her trauma symptoms confused her. Awilda had attuned well to Nadia, and as a result, Nadia had internalized Awilda's positive assessments of her. Eventually, Awilda's positive view of Nadia became Nadia's view of herself.

Awilda found an accomplished clinical social worker at the Family Services Agency to whom she could transfer Nadia. Awilda wanted to encourage a smooth transition, so Nadia, Awilda, and the new therapist, Amy, met to create a treatment plan together. The three decided that Nadia would begin to process her past trauma with EMDR. Awilda sat in on the first few sessions with Amy. Awilda's presence in those initial sessions helped Nadia to feel safe enough to bond with Amy.

On Awilda's last day at the agency, Nadia and she exchanged poems that symbolized what they had accomplished together. Awilda wanted to provide Nadia with a transitional object that would help her to feel grounded while moving forward. Nadia kept Awilda's poem in her dresser drawer for many years, and would look at it when she needed inspiration.

PHASE 3—RECONNECTION

Phase 3 has been titled differently by various trauma experts. It has been called: "self and relational development" by Courtois (2004) and Rosenberg (2000), "reconnection" by Herman (1998), and "enhancing daily living" by Ford, Courtois, Steele, van der Hart, and Nijenhuis (2005). Here we will use the term "reconnection." According to these authors, tasks of this final phase include:

- Continued strengthening of self-management skills
- Applying these skills more broadly
- Envisioning new possibilities for the future
- Developing healthier and more trustworthy relationships, exploring resistance or fears to making additional positive changes
- Achieving a deeper understanding of what the traumatic experiences have taught them, and
- Possibly engaging in political or educational actions to prevent others from being victimized in the future

It is important to note that clients begin completing each of these tasks in Phase 1. Indeed, one of the reasons that a client is able to eventually form healthier relationships in the world is because of the role played by the social worker in Phase 1. Many clients are able to accomplish the tasks of Phase 3 *without* needing to undertake the deeper memory work that can take place in Phase 2. *Phase 3 becomes a time for deepening and refining and practicing new knowledge and skills originally gained in Phase 1.*

By Phase 3, the survivor is ready to engage more actively in the world. She can establish an agenda. Herman (1998) stated that she can "recover some of her aspirations from the time before the trauma, or perhaps for the first time she can discover her own agenda" (pp. 148–49). Ford et al. (2005) wrote that in this phase the "quality of the client's life is the focus as he or she brings a fresh and wise perspective to his personal, occupational, relationship, and spiritual goals" (pp. 440–441). The client is now in a more powerful position to "forge relationships founded on trust and intimacy rather than on insecurity and repetition" (Rosenberg, 2000, p. 68).

NADIA, PHASE 3: RECONNECTION AND TRANSFORMATION

After EMDR with her new therapist, Amy, Nadia decided to leave her abusive husband (with the assistance of the domestic abuse agency that had provided her with a support group). Nadia made sure that her children had a good trauma counselor, so that they could get over the trauma of having witnessed domestic abuse, and so that they would not experience the same long-term consequences of abuse that Nadia had suffered. After 5 years of recovery and counseling, Nadia was no longer troubled by trauma symptoms, or by negative interpersonal or work relationships. She felt free to pursue her dreams, and she was back in school studying for a new career. Nadia developed many rewarding friendships and was a sponsor at her AA meeting. She was remarried to a kind, loving, well-balanced man. She became a volunteer "mentor" at a domestic abuse agency in order to help other women in abusive relationships. When she helped others who were suffering, Nadia realized that they were not to blame for having been victimized, which further served to release Nadia from shame and blame regarding what had happened in her own life.

Later, when she looked back, Nadia could not believe how many years had been lost to the fallout from the miserable Ms. Gray, but in a strange way Nadia was grateful for what she had suffered. Nadia felt that overcoming her challenges had made her a better, more understanding, wiser, and more grateful person than she would have been had the trauma never happened to her. She often thought about how proud Awilda would have been of her.

Substance Abuse and PTSD

Nadia's case reflects the fact that trauma survivors frequently abuse substances including alcohol, illegal drugs, and prescription drugs as a way to manage the distressing aftereffects of trauma. According to the National Institutes of Health (2006), at least 30%–60% of substance abusers meet criteria for the PTSD diagnosis. That percentage would be much higher if all people with a significant history of traumatization were included (instead of only those who meet the stricter DSM-IV-TR criteria for PTSD). In individuals who are traumatized, substance use usually begins as a way to cope with overwhelming feelings, with numbing, and with hypervigilance. In the past, counseling programs insisted that substance abusers be clean and sober before beginning therapeutic work on traumatic experience. That thinking has changed, because to avoid relapse, clients must be counseled on ways to handle uncovered trauma symptoms as they are becoming "clean and sober." Traumatic experience must be acknowledged and contained as it arises. The TARGET (Trauma Adaptive Recovery Group Education and Therapy) Program (Ford and Russo, 2006) and the Seeking Safety Program (Brown, Najavitz, Cadiz, Finkeistein, Heckman, and Rechenberger, 2007; Najavitz, 2002a) are two good trauma/substance counseling approaches. In four studies, conducted in three different settings, the Seeking Safety program showed significant reductions of trauma symptoms, substance use, family functioning, problem-solving, depression, anxiety, hostility, and feelings and thoughts related to safety (Najavitz, 2002b). Further research may be accessed at www.seekingsafety.org

Trauma Interventions for Children

All forms of child maltreatment have the potential to be traumatic. Falasca and Caulfield (1999) wrote, "Some of the events that have been shown to have a 'high likelihood' of producing trauma in children are: natural disaster, the loss of a significant attachment figure, a serious threat to the child's life, physical and sexual abuse, and community and family violence' (p. 214). Nadia's story makes it clear that childhood trauma, in particular, can affect all aspects of the self. However, children's responses to trauma vary widely from child to child. According to Saakvitne, Gamble, Pearlman, and Lev (2000):

> The specific impact on a child is influenced by several factors: the child's genetic makeup, developmental stage at the time of the abuse, his or her relationship with the perpetrators, the quality of his or her attachment to caregivers, and the social and cultural context in which s/he grows up. (p. 19)

Other factors include the level and duration ("dose") of the trauma, supports available to the family, and previous level of functioning.

Eliana Gil, a well-respected play therapist who has specialized in working with traumatized children for over 20 years, observed that children seem to use two basic drives to cope with their emotional injuries: "The first drive is to master what is painful or confusing, restoring a sense of control and mastery: the second drive is to avoid painful emotions..." (Gil, 2006, p. 8). An example of mastery can be found in the following case:

CASE 16.4 | **RESTORING MASTERY**

Derek, age 6, had witnessed his mother being repeatedly beaten by her boyfriend. His mom was concerned about some of the "games" that Derek had been playing since she had ended the relationship with her boyfriend. For example, he liked pretending that he was trapped in some way and then he would "break free" like a super hero who suddenly had found great strength. He also liked to pretend that he was hiding from a burglar and would call to his mom to "find" him and give him a hug. The worker helped the mom to understand that children often work through their fears by playing out scenes such as these, which have an "ending" that brings them feelings of safety and comfort. As the worker predicted, Derek's needs to play these games decreased as he became more convinced that his mom had taken the necessary steps to keep herself and him safe from the former boyfriend.

According to Gil (2006), the second drive is to avoid or suppress what is painful. Children can do this in various ways: by refusing to think or talk about the abuse, by withdrawing from interactions with people, and by refusing to play with materials that remind them of traumatic experiences. These two drives of mastery and avoidance can appear together or separately, and a child can alternate between the two. In addition, children can display a wide assortment of other "symptoms" in order to cope with trauma. According to Falasca and Caulfield (1999), symptoms can be grouped into affect, memories, and behaviors.

- **Affect:** Expressions of anger, rage, irritability, excessive worry, social and and emotional withdrawal, loneliness, fear of retraumatization, feelings of helpessness.
- **Trauma-related memories:** Traumas that occurred once are more likely to be remembered in their entirety, while memories of prolonged or repeated trauma "seem to be retained in a spotty, incomplete, fragmented manner." (p. 215)

- **Behaviors:** Nightmares, sleep disturbances, intrusive thoughts, compulsive repetitions, suicidal thoughts or actions, rebelliousness, dissociation which may take the form of detachment/numbing, physical aggression towards others. (pp. 214–215)

Sgroi (1982) may have been the first trauma author to describe **behavioral indicators seen in children** who could be suffering from abuse or neglect. Recognizing these indicators is still an important part of the assessment process. Although the presence of these indicators may indicate abuse, *they are not conclusive.* However, it can probably be said that the more of these signs that a social worker observes, the more he or she should suspect that a child is being physically or sexually abused, or neglected. The following are behavioral indicators of abuse.

- Overly compliant behavior
- A pattern of acting out or aggressive behavior
- "Pseudomature" behavior, that is, acting always like a young adult and never "just like a child"
- Persistent and inappropriate sexual play with peers or toys or with themselves, or sexually aggressive behavior with others
- Detailed and age-inappropriate understanding of sexual behavior (especially by young children)
- Consistently arriving at school early and leaving late
- Inability to make friends or poor peer relationships
- Lack of trust, particularly with significant others
- Inability to concentrate in school
- Sudden drop in school performance
- Extraordinary fear of males seen in girls
- Running away from home
- Sleep disturbances, sometimes manifested in falling asleep in class
- Regressive behavior
- Withdrawal
- Depression
- Heightened anxiety
- Suicidal feelings or thoughts (Sgroi, 1982, p. 110)

When reading this list, it is equally important for social workers to remember that most children are very resilient and to believe that "traumatized individuals are not inevitably doomed to succumb to the stressors in their lives" (Gil, 2006, p. 15).

Play Therapy.   Gil (2006) wrote that, "It is best to avoid pressuring children into talking about abuse when they don't feel ready to do so" (p. 10). In fact, pressuring them may only increase their level of avoidance. According to her, it is important to "allow children ample room to unfold their stories (verbally or nonverbally) at their own speed and through various types of communication (behavior, play, or verbal and nonverbal language" (p. 10). Some children *do* prefer to speak with words, but Gil and other child therapists found that they needed to find *other* ways of communicating and making contact with many children. Therefore, she and others who work with traumatized children use "expressive therapies" that include play therapy, art therapy, sand tray therapy, storytelling, dance, and music so that children have other ways of communicating their inner world to outsiders.

For example, in play therapy, children can choose certain toys or miniature figures and project their own thoughts and feelings onto those objects and eventually work through painful thoughts or feelings in "a protected and safe way" (Gil, 2006, p. 11). A child is more likely to talk about "the scared boy" in a dollhouse than to speak directly about his or her own fears, or to use a puppet to express certain feelings "for" him or her Similarly, a child can draw a figure, such as an animal, and the worker can ask about the "animal," knowing that the child will reveal something about *themselves* in the process. Gil provides a good example of a boy who drew a squirrel next to a rock. Instead of asking any "why" questions or making any interpretations (such as "That squirrel must be feeling very scared"), the worker should ask more open-ended questions or make statements such as the following: "What's it like for the squirrel to be behind the rock?" (p. 14).

In addition to these expressive therapies, Gil utilizes cognitive-behavioral therapy with traumatized children. This approach encourages workers to identify and address cognitive distortions or thinking errors that may, in turn, lead to negative behaviors. A very common example of a cognitive distortion in a child who was sexually abused is that the abuse was somehow their fault. This thought may lead them to conclude that they are "bad" and to then behave in ways that flow from this faulty thinking, such as physically harming themselves or others. Another cognitive distortion in children who have been abused is "no adults are to be trusted," a thought that could lead to withdrawal or physical aggression around adults, including teachers at school or foster parents.

Some of the cognitive-behavioral strategies that are used include: identifying the child's current thoughts and beliefs, understanding the reasons for their beliefs, and over time, replacing the cognitive distortions with accurate ones (Gil, 2006). This final step can be accomplished in multiple ways: through books, worksheets, games, stories, videos, and through the expressive therapies described earlier. In addition, children can be taught to identify their emotions and to recognize the connection between certain thoughts and feelings and behaviors; to learn and practice ways of calming and soothing themselves; identify thoughts that will help them to behave in ways that bring fewer negative consequences; to engage them in role plays to practice new ways of thinking and behaving; and to provide praise and recognition for the slightest evidence that they view themselves in a more positive light (Gil, 2006). Gil and others also believe that counseling with children *must include, when possible, collaboration with parents and/or caregivers, parent–child counseling, and family therapy.*

Trauma-focused cognitive behavioral therapy is an empirically tested treatment for abused children. According to Cohen and Mannarino (2006), "TF-CBT was originally developed for sexually abused children, but was then tested in multiply traumatized children, for children exposed to terrorism after September 11, 2001 and is currently being evaluated for children exposed to domestic violence and

Childhood Traumatic Grief" (p. 739). The TF-CBT treatment components are summarized by the acronym PRACTICE: Parenting skills, Psychoeducation, Relaxation skills, Affective modulation skills, Cognitive processing, Trauma narration, In vivo desensitization, Conjoint child–parent sessions, and Enhancing safety and future development. TF-CBT has been tested in six randomized controlled trials against other active treatments. These studies have included children from 3 to 17 years of age, as well as those with a wide variety of sexual abuse experiences. In all six studies, children who received TF-CBT demonstrated significantly greater improvements, and some of the studies demonstrated improvement in parents' functioning as well (Cohen and Mannarino, 2006).

Information about a web-based training in TF-CBT can be found at the end of the chapter.

PSYCHOLOGICAL FIRST AID: IMMEDIATE POSTTRAUMA INTERVENTIONS

Here we provide an overview of guidelines and principles for assisting adults who have suffered a recent trauma that falls under the category of a "single incident" or "Type I" event, including natural disasters, physical assaults such as rape, car accidents, or witnessing acts of violence such as a school shooting.

Fortunately, most people who suffer this type of traumatic stress go on to recover without difficulties that last beyond the first weeks. As described earlier in the Definition section, people who do go on to suffer from ongoing posttraumatic symptoms or from full-blown PTSD most likely received a "fuller dose" of the trauma (such as being in close proximity to someone who was shot) or were victimized at earlier points in their life (such as adult survivors of child sexual abuse.) Those individuals will probably require interventions beyond those that fall under the general category of **psychological first aid (PFA)**, which is intended to offer only short-term support, including counseling, education, advocacy, and assistance with problem solving. As you will see, a number of the PFA interventions overlap with those already described for survivors of chronic or multiple incidents of trauma.

According to Ruzek, Brymer, Jacobs, Layne, Vernberg, and Watson (2007), "Psychological first aid consists of a systematic set of helping actions aimed at reducing initial post-trauma distress and supporting short- and long-term adaptive functioning" (p. 17). It was designed for delivery anywhere that trauma survivors can be found. PFA is designed around eight core actions: (1) contact and engagement, (2) safety and support, (3) stabilization, (4) information gathering, (5) practical assistance, (6) connection with social supports, (7) information about coping, and (8) linkage with other collaborative services. "PFA for adolescents and children focuses on these same core actions, with modifications to make them developmentally appropriate" (p. 17). The web link to the complete psychological first aid manual can be found at the end of this chapter. Rusek et al. (2007) acknowledge that the process of evaluating the effectiveness of PFA "is currently in a very early stage" (p. 37). The National Institutes of Mental Health and the World Organization both recommend PFA as a set of interventions to improve psychological outcomes in "first responders" and the general public (McEvoy, 2005, p. 66).

Ruzek et al.'s (2007) "eight core actions" overlap with those identified by Hobfall et al. (2007). Hobfall et al. (2007) assembled a worldwide panel of experts on the "treatment" of those exposed to disaster and mass trauma to gain consensus on intervention principles. They identified "five empirically supported intervention principles that should be used to guide and inform intervention efforts at the early to midterm stages" (p. 284). The following intervention principles *can* be adapted to help survivors of Type I traumatic experiences:

1. **Sense of safety**
   Ensure people's physical safety, teaching people "grounding" techniques, providing balanced information, gather information about safety of friends and relatives, limit exposure to news coverage of the traumatic event, use cognitive techniques such as reminding people of current reality to prevent thoughts such as "the world is completely dangerous place" do not become encoded in people's memories.

2. **Calming**
   Teach anxiety management techniques such as relaxed breathing and deep muscle relaxation and exercise, normalize clients' stress reactions, eliminate watching or reading information that promotes negative emotional states, assist people to break down problems into small, manageable units, review sleeping patterns, encourage involvement in uplifting activities, discourage use of alcohol or other nonprescription drugs.

3. **Sense of self- and community efficacy**
   Provide people with outside resources to promote empowerment, involve victims in individual and community decision-making efforts, include children in community recovery when necessary, teach individuals to set achievable goals, teach people emotional regulation skills when faced with trauma reminders, gather people together who have all been affected by the same trauma to identify common problems and possible solutions

4. **Connectedness**
   Target social support via psychoeducation and skills building, including identifying potential sources of support, helping people identify and link with loved ones, identify and assist those who lack strong support or whose support system may undermine their recovery.

5. **Hope**
   Instilling hope is critical because trauma (especially mass trauma) is often accompanied by a "shattered worldview" (Hobfall et al., p. 298). Provide necessary resources, normalize people's reactions and tell them that most people can recover, highlight already-existing strengths, reduce catastrophic thinking (when appropriate) by focusing instead on facts, plan community meetings when there have been others affected by the same trauma.

In an earlier article, Pynoos and Nader (1988) described some elements of providing psychological first aid to children exposed to community violence. They believe that whether or not the violence occurred on or near the school, that the "school setting can be an ideal place for screening, classroom consultation, and individual counseling and support" (p. 457). If there is an incident that affected all the children, the "counseling and nursing offices should be open to students"

(p. 458). In the following weeks, the classroom itself is an ideal location "for a group consultation" and is the "best site to address children's fears of recurrence" and their distorted thinking. The aim of classroom consultation is to "provide permission to express feelings, clarify cognitive confusions, screen children for exposure, traumatic response, and risk factors, to promote classroom cohesion and ongoing learning, and to encourage help-seeking" (p. 458). It is important to provide ongoing support to the teachers since "children carefully observe their teacher's responses to an event" (p. 459). Parents need to be provided information about posttraumatic responses in large- or small-group settings.

Specific "first aid strategies" for different age groups are as follows:

- **Preschool through second grade:** Provide support, rest, comfort, play, food. Reestablish "adult protective shield". Provide accurate information. Provide emotional labels for common reactions. Provide consistent caretaking (e.g., assurance of being picked up from school), tolerate regressive behaviors in a time-limited fashion.
- **Third through fifth grades:** Help to express secret beliefs about the event. Help to identify reminders of the event and how to handle their reactions. Encourage them to let parents and teachers know their thoughts and feelings. Support them in reporting dreams. Offer to meet with children and parents, to help children express what they are feeling and guide parents in how to respond. In case of injury or death, encourage constructive activities on behalf of the injured or deceased.
- **Sixth grade and up:** Help normalize their feelings. Help them to understand their acting out behavior as an effort to numb themselves, or to express anger. Address and normalize impulse toward reckless behavior while searching for other ways to express distress. Elicit any plans of revenge they may have. Link attitude changes to the traumatic event. (pp. 461–463)

Group work outside of a classroom is also a useful modality in helping children recover from trauma. An interesting group model for children who experienced community violence was developed in Northern Ireland and was entitled the "Face Your Fears Club." Stewart and Thompson (2005) described the group structure as well as the benefits of the group. According to the parents, some of the benefits of the group for the child participants include fewer nightmares, more interest in playing with friends, less fear, and realizing that not all people are bad. The parents also identified benefits for themselves including: how to help their child, understanding that children do not show their feelings in the same way as adults, understanding why their child is acting as they are. The benefits of group work for adult survivors will now be described.

GROUP WORK

Group counseling is a powerful force for recovery. Individuals who have experienced trauma often feel isolated and as if they are "the only one" who has experienced a particular problem or dynamic. In the group setting, when a client hears a story very much like his/her own (only the details are different) coming out of another client's mouth, the resulting feeling of normalization can facilitate tremendous healing.

Homogenous trauma groups are particularly effective (for instance, groups that focus on one type of trauma, such as groups of: domestic abuse survivors, war veterans, sexual abuser survivors, or disaster survivors). It is often effective to identify a topic and to provide an educational handout for each group, and then to invite discussion of the topic as it relates to group members' personal experiences.

Screening and Preparing Potential Members.   It is important to think about the timing of the group experience in each client's recovery. As discussed in Chapter 16.8, groups, like individuals, move through certain phases. Therefore, the group leader needs to consider the topics and issues that are discussed in the beginning versus the middle or ending phases of group counseling. Clients who participate in group counseling need to feel a strong sense of safety in the group, and in their lives, before they are asked to disclose more painful information. The group leader, similar to an individual counselor, must make certain that clients have gained a repertoire of skills and healthy coping methods that can be used when they encounter distressing feelings as a result of hearing others' stories or sharing their own story. Many leaders prefer that clients receive individual counseling before, and possibly during, the time that they are participating in a survivors' group.

Potential group members must be screened to assess their stability, support systems, and their ability "to give as well as to receive" in a group setting. Also during screening, potential members should be advised of the general activities and process that they will encounter within the group. If a group is filled with members who have never had individual counseling, the leader must ensure that the initial topics and activities are aimed at providing educational material that creates feelings of safety in the group. The Trauma Recovery and Empowerment program is one of the available models for conducting groups with trauma survivors (Harris, 1998).

CASE 16.5 | "I'M NOT THE ONLY ONE!"

Angela O. was attending the domestic abuse support group for the first time. As she observed the 12 other women seated around the table, she was apprehensive. The group counselor opened the session by providing educational material on the *cycle of abuse* (Walker, 1979, 1994). The counselor said that the "cycle of abuse" (Figure 16.14) was present in almost every domestic abuse relationship, and that the cycle consisted of: a tension-building phase that was rather long, then a relatively short, acute abuse phase in which the abuser behaved extremely abusively, and then a brief "honeymoon" period, during which the abuser appeared to go back to being the good person that he or she had seemed to be during the courtship.

Angela could not believe it! This was exactly the cycle that she had been experiencing from the moment she got married. Why wasn't this cycle of abuse thing

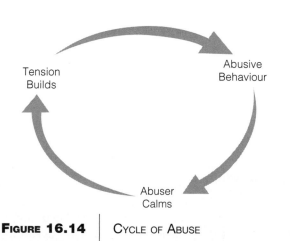

FIGURE 16.14 | CYCLE OF ABUSE

Source: Minister of Public Works and Government Services Canada, 2006

CASE 16.5 | *Continued*

taught in high school? ... If Angela had learned about it back then, she might have recognized that she was being abused years ago, instead of just now!

After the group counselor's presentation on the cycle of abuse, another group member, Gina F., expressed just what Angela had been thinking. Gina wanted to know why everyone had not been educated about the cycle of abuse, since it was a phenomenon that caused such misery and destruction. Gina then began to open up about the ways in which cycle of abuse had manifested itself in her own home. She talked about how she could feel the insecurity and tension building up in her life partner, until finally her partner would come home from work and vio-

lently explode, using "something about the dinner" as an excuse for her violence. For instance, Gina said that her partner would complain that the food was not "hot and waiting" when she walked in the front door.

This was exactly the same dinnertime abuse nonsense that occurred in Angela's house! The only difference was that Gina's partner was a woman and Angela's a man. Angela could see that Gina was a good person and that the abuse was based on nothing but the abuser's desire to be controlling. All of a sudden Angela felt better about herself, and she realized that neither she, nor Gina, was to blame for her partner's abuse cycles.

Tips Specific to Running a Trauma Group.   There is a great deal of excellent material on running groups in general, so those basics will not be replicated here; however, below are some caveats, specific to running trauma groups, that may not be found elsewhere.

It is a good idea to type up a list of group rules to be reviewed by the entire group at the beginning of each session. The articulation of group boundaries assists clients in feeling safe. During the session, the group leader should support clients in following the rules.

Traumatized individuals often have difficulty being on time. Obviously the group counselor's explicit expectation will be that everyone will be punctual, but the fact of the matter is that it will be impossible for some traumatized clients to be on time. So what will the policy be? Will the meeting door be closed after 15 minutes, or will late clients simply be asked to do their best to be punctual next time, in light of the fact that late arrivals are disruptive to the group?

When people are sharing their trauma stories in the group setting, instruct them to provide only the outline of what occurred, absent the details. For instance, an individual can outline the fact that he was molested by his mother's boyfriend over a period of years, in the family bathroom, but he should not give the details of what the boyfriend did, since that might trigger and cause overwhelming feelings and flashbacks for others (disturbances that are beyond containment by a group). The group counselor should let it be known that she/he will help clients by gently guiding them away from providing too much detail. While it is not appropriate to share details (like the smell of a dead body), in a support group, counselors do not want to make clients feel that their experiences are so toxic that they cannot be shared. It is generally best for trauma survivors to receive individual counseling at the same time that they are in a group. In the safe environment of individual counseling, the traumatized individuals can divulge whatever details they wish, so that they will no longer be alone with the toxic material.

It is important always to scan everyone in the group to get a read on how each person is feeling and to keep all individuals safe (it is difficult to anticipate when any one person might be triggered). If someone becomes very upset or aroused in the group, it is not unlikely that others will be triggered by that person's upset state. The triggering of others in the group is normal, and sometimes it helps to acknowledge the phenomenon of contagious upset to the group. The counselor should try to make sure that she/he continues to scan the entire group for reactions, rather than having a tunnel vision focus on handling the one individual who is overaroused.

Often when individuals appear to be falling asleep, they are actually dissociating as a defense to having been triggered by the material. When a person dissociates, his/her eyes generally roll up to an outside corner, and then he/she seems to fall asleep quickly. One way to help individuals to stay present is for the group facilitator to move around the room. If clients orient to a moving facilitator by shifting their eyes and body positions, it keeps them grounded, and it keeps them from going into a dissociative state. It is also helpful to vary the pace and rhythm of the group material, and to interweave lighter elements into the group process.

Understand that it is generally easy for beginning counselors to help people to "get in touch" with their traumatic experiences and feelings, but it is much more difficult to get clients to return to a calm state by the time that they go home. Beginning counselors should always allow for a chunk of time at the end of the group session to help clients reorient and calm down before leaving. Reading and reflecting on an uplifting, calming, and inspiring poem is an example of a reorienting ending task.

Some traumatized clients can be very fragmented and tangential when they speak. These individuals often get stuck in endless, looping, and repeating explanations of seemingly unimportant details and do not appear to be able to stop talking. They are often "stuck in time" and stuck in the traumatic experience. While it is important to give people a chance to share what they need to say, it is also important for the group leader to prevent any one person from dominating or taking over the group, or from using excessive time. It is best gently and firmly to impose a time limitation on individuals who overly encroach upon group time.

Group members should refrain from advice giving and from using "you" statements. Individuals should instead talk about their own experiences and should use "I" statements. For instance, rather than addressing another group member by saying, "You have to stop calling your father, because you know he's just going to victimize you," it is preferable to say, "I can understand how hard this is for you, and I can relate, because I had great difficulty disconnecting from an abusive friend. Here's what I had to do, etc."

Any bullying or abusive behavior of one member of the group to another must not be tolerated. Bullies must be removed from the group and provided with another treatment opportunity, until they can cease unacceptable bullying behavior. It is essential that individuals who are recovering from trauma not be revictimized by the group dynamic.

Some trauma recovery groups will contain aggressive individuals who will challenge the leader. (Substance abuse groups and abuser groups are examples.) It is important to disarm and befriend challengers by validating the truth in their challenges (and gratefully accepting the gift of valid criticism) and by drawing firm but kind boundaries around the part of their challenges that are harmful and not valid.

Studies have shown that support groups in which individuals simply vent their problems are unproductive (Hayslip and Kaminski, 2005; Strom and Strom, 2000). Venting can actually make individuals feel worse. Imagine sitting in a group for two hours as everyone in the room tries to top one another in a series of rants regarding how unfair the world is, how everyone is being terribly and hopelessly victimized, and why that awful dynamic will never change! Venting groups provide negative brainwashing that may cause group members to feel even more powerless and inert. It is important that traumatized people be allowed to discuss what distresses them, but with the positively focused goals of identifying solutions, providing active support, providing empowerment, and providing education.

Much of the research on groups for trauma survivors appears to have been done with adolescent and adult victims of child sexual abuse. Four of those studies found a number of benefits of group participation including better psychosocial functioning, reduced psychological distress, fewer behavior problems, and better coping strategies. (Hebert, 2007; Stalker and Fry, 1999; Tourigny, Hebert, Daigneault, and Somoneau, 2005; Zlotnick, Shea, Rosen, Simpson, Mulrenin, Begin, and Pearlstein, 1997). Another study found that group participation minimizes the impact of trauma in the following specific ways: normalizes stress reactions and PTSD symptoms, teaches helpful ways to cope with and manage intrusive and disruptive symptoms, assists in recognizing and working through distorted perceptions of self and others, assists in developing a stronger sense of self because members' feelings and experiences are validated, and provides support and understanding and sense of connection. (Knight, 2006, p. 23)

WAR VETERANS

Since Vietnam, studies have shown that about 15% of soldiers returning from war have suffered from PTSD (Kulka, 1990; Spollen and Labbate, 2008). Soldiers also suffer from additional mental health consequences, including anxiety, depression, and substance abuse disorders (Spollen and Labbate, 2008). In 1990, as many as 75% of Vietnam veterans who met criteria for PTSD also met criteria for alcohol abuse or dependence (Kulka, 1990).

A recent study of the Iraq war indicated that only 23%–40% of soldiers who needed mental health treatment received treatment, and only half of the soldiers needing treatment said that they were willing to seek it (Hoge and Terhakopian, 2007; Spollen and Labbate, 2008). Many soldiers express concern about the stigma associated with receiving professional help (Stecker, Fortney, Hamilton, and Ajzen, 2007); those who are most in need of help are also the most likely to report concern about being stigmatized (Stecker et al., 2007). Soldiers who do not recover from PTSD often experience great difficulty in their interpersonal lives. For instance, because of a perpetual state of hyperarousal and a resulting misperception of threat during even small conflicts at home, many soldiers with PTSD are at high risk for engaging in domestic abuse (Sherman, Sautter, Jackson, Lyons, and Han, 2006). The website of the National Center for PTSD, found at the end of the chapter, publishes a rich range of training materials, military tip sheets, and counseling guides that are helpful in working with members of the military.

THE REWARDS AND CHALLENGES OF WORKING WITH TRAUMA SURVIVORS

Many people have described the difficulties of listening to the stories of client survivors. In undergraduate and graduate school, it can also be difficult and painful to hear other students describe their own or their clients' traumatic experiences. There are important strategies for workers to learn in order to avoid "burn out" as a result of helping traumatized clients or hearing other students describe their clients' stories. In this section, we will summarize those strategies so that you can continue to offer the best care to your clients *and* to yourself.

At the same time, it is important to recognize how deeply rewarding and meaningful this work can be. The good news is that workers *are* often able to help clients by offering them a safe place to understand their symptoms, to learn new methods for coping, to learn new relationship skills, and to gain self-respect and a new appreciation for their strengths, and to move beyond an identity which has been defined too often by their trauma experiences. Along the way, you will be inspired and touched by your clients' resilience and efforts to recover, as well as challenged and deeply saddened by what they have suffered. You too *will* change as a result of working with trauma survivors.

DEFINITION OF VICARIOUS TRAUMATIZATION

The negative effects of working with trauma survivors were originally included under the broader topic of "**countertransference**" until the late 1980s. In the 1990s, Saakvitne and Pearlman first used the term "**vicarious traumatization**" to refer to the specific ways that trauma work impacts helping professionals. It is their belief that "vicarious traumatization is an inescapable effect of trauma work" (Saakvitne, Gamble, Pearlman, and Lev, 2000, p. 157). Since then, others have written about similar processes and used terms that include secondary traumatic stress and compassion fatigue (Courtois, 1988; Figley, 1995; Herman, 1992). Vicarious traumatization is:

> the transformation or change in a helper's inner experience as a result of responsibility for and empathic engagement with traumatized clients (including witnessing the signs of abuse and neglect, and vivid descriptions of traumatic events, reports of intentional cruelty (Saakvitne et al., 2000, p. 157).

Vicarious traumatization is a process that occurs over time, rather than just being one event. "The single most important factor in the success or failure of trauma work is the attention paid to the experience and needs of the helper…. We cannot meet the needs of clients when we are ignoring or overriding those of the helpers" (Saakvitne et al., 2000, p. 157). The preceding statement has implications for individuals, organizations, and for those who fund programs and services for trauma survivors.

SIGNS OF VICARIOUS TRAUMATIZATION

Saakvitne and Pearlman (1996) described a number of ways that vicarious traumatization can change the helping professional. Fortunately, there are many steps that can be taken to counteract negative effects. According to Saakvitne and Pearlman (1996), the changes in the worker's life and beliefs can include the following:

- The worker's own identity and sense of who he/she is.
- Beliefs about the world, for example, the belief that parents are always protectors of their children.
- Beliefs about spirituality, including questions about God and faith.
- Workers struggling with feeling more negative emotions and having to learn how to handle these feelings.
- Workers staying busy to avoid noticing their feelings.
- Core beliefs about safety (both their own and the safety of loved ones) can change.
- Difficulty believing that people are basically trustworthy as we hear stories of exploitation and abuse.
- A heightened need to exert control over significant others in their lives.
- Feelings of disconnection from others in their life who do not understand what this work entails.
- Intrusive images about clients' traumatic experiences. (p. 40)

STRATEGIES TO MINIMIZE VICARIOUS TRAUMATIZATION

While each of the preceding changes *can* be challenging, the following provide examples of how to minimize the negative impact that this important work may have on social workers. The more prepared a worker is to recognize these signs, the more he or she will be able to address any signs of vicarious traumatization that may appear. Throughout your work with clients, it is important to regularly assess whether or not you are experiencing any of the preceding feelings or beliefs, and to be prepared to add new strategies to those you are already using to counteract any negative effects.

Self-Care.   The first set of strategies for minimizing vicarious traumatization falls under the general category of "self-care." Workers must use the same coping mechanisms that they teach their clients for calming down their nervous systems and restoring balance to their lives. It is important to consider the advice that is given to parents who are traveling on an airplane with their children. As the flight attendants remind everyone, adults must first put on their own oxygen masks before attending to their children, since parents will be unable to help their children if they lose consciousness! Self-care strategies for social workers involve attention to physical, emotional, and spiritual needs.

Physical Self-Care.   The second includes good nutrition, physical movement or exercise, getting enough sleep, and practices such as yoga or meditation or deep breathing that will elicit the body's own natural relaxation response (the parasympathetic nervous system). It is important to attend to these needs throughout the day as well as during time away from work. One consequence of listening to painful client stories is that your muscles often store a lot of tension that may not even enter your awareness. Therefore, it is important to take a few moments whenever possible to stretch, walk a few steps, take a few "cleansing breaths," sip some water or tea, and possibly focus on a photo or object that reminds the worker of something good in life.

Emotional Self-Care.   The third involves any strategy for managing the range of emotions that can arise when working with people who have suffered traumas. It is imperative for workers to have opportunities to be able to express their *own* feelings—to a supervisor, or to colleagues who understand the toll of the work, in journals, or to their own therapist, to good friends or family members. Understanding the concept of "vicarious traumatization," and the signs listed above, can help normalize emotional reactions such as anger, hopelessness, disbelief, sadness, frustration, and anxiety, and can point workers in the direction of how to take good care of themselves. For workers who have their own histories that include neglect and abuse, it is recommended that they undertake their own personal counseling in order to prevent being retraumatized by client stories and to be able to stay focused on their clients' needs.

In terms of emotional self-care, there is also no substitute for building in activities that provide total respite from the images and emotions that can arise, and provide a different focus for our mental and physical energies. Rothschild (2000) used the term "oases" to describe activities that provide valuable distraction, space, and distance from the difficult stories workers may hear in any given day (p. 92). Oases can range from planned vacations to pleasure reading to a good night's sleep to hobbies such as knitting to watching comedies on TV. Like clients, workers need to know when to take "breaks" as well. And like clients, workers need to realize that it will be necessary at some point to return to difficult emotions and not be overwhelmed by them.

In her book, *Help for the Helper*, Rothschild (2006) offers wise and practical recommendations about the self-protection of workers. First, she attempts to eliminate the myth that being empathic requires workers to fully visualize the experiences of abuse and neglect that their clients have suffered. *It can be particularly harmful to workers to picture themselves or someone that they love experiencing the same traumas that a client endured.* Many workers mistakenly think that it is their duty to consciously visualize the details of a client's trauma, or even worse, to visualize the traumas as if it were happening to them. In fact, doing so increases the risk that workers will suffer from intrusive images later. Second, brain research has shown that workers are more likely to experience the same emotions as their traumatized clients when they "mimic" the facial expression or physical posture of their clients. Conscious "mirroring" of a client's expression or posture can provide information about how a client is feeling, but unconscious mirroring throughout a session can cause harm to workers, who may then identify too strongly with what clients are feeling. Rothschild (2002) suggests that workers become more aware in sessions of whether they *are* imitating client expressions or postures, and to occasionally change posture or facial expression so that they are not automatically the same ones as their client's.

Spiritual Self-Care   This form of self-care focuses on taking care of one's "spirit" and varies widely from person to person and culture to culture. Spirituality, as defined by each person, is an important dimension in anyone's life. Some people pray, others meditate, some seek balance in nature, some attend regular religious services, and more. Working with traumatized individuals forces many workers to confront very hard questions for which there are no easy answers. For example, a question such as "How can someone cause so much physical harm to a child?" can be answered in psychological terms but also requires many to seek answers through spiritual beliefs and practices, including but not limited to organized religions.

Trying to make sense of the traumatic experiences suffered by clients is a difficult task, but coming up with answers that are meaningful for each worker—and helping clients to do the same—takes many into a more spiritual realm. Many social workers come to understand their own personal motivations for doing this work and to recognize that "it is more than just a job." In a quiet moment, workers can write down the reasons they have chosen to work with clients who have painful stories to tell, as well as the rewards they have experienced in their work. Reminding themselves of why they have chosen this profession can help them maintain their spirit during difficult times in their professional life. Many workers end up transforming their experiences with clients by engaging in meaningful actions to eliminate the causes of some traumas and by: advocating for new programs, laws, attitudes, and social policies to help those who are suffering.

Professional Self-Care   Workers can and should continue to seek the knowledge needed to help their clients. Attending conferences can provide ideas about new interventions and can counteract feelings of being "drained" by this work. Attending professional training with others who do similar work with trauma survivors is a powerful antidote to vicarious traumatization. Keeping up with new readings, seeking out peer supervision groups, and seeing a consultant who has a particular specialty on a one-time basis can all help to keep professional "batteries charged." In addition, workers can advocate for opportunities within their settings for the organizational and supervisory support that they need—such as in-service trainings, half-day retreats, reasonable caseloads and work hours, monthly group meetings to talk about the challenges and rewards of working with traumatized clients, and participation in employee assistance programs that can provide short-term counseling and referrals.

GUIDELINES FOR THE WORKPLACE

Administrators should always convey to their staff an attitude of respect for the difficulty of working with trauma survivors as well as a commitment to address the potential for harm to them. As Saakvitne and Pearlman (1996) wrote,

> Organizations that serve traumatized individuals must acknowledge the impact of vicarious traumatization on their employees and identify strategies for protecting and healing workers.... Making time to address vicarious traumatization is important symbolically and pragmatically. (p. 82)

A particularly promising set of **guidelines for creating healthy workplaces** is the Sanctuary Model of Organizational Change, developed by Sandra Bloom (1997). This model "represents a comprehensive trauma-informed method for creating or changing an organizational culture in order to more effectively provide a cohesive context within which healing from psychological and social traumatic experience can be addressed." (*Description of the Sanctuary Model, n.d.*). The Sanctuary Model is presently being applied to a number of settings including adult inpatient and outpatient mental health settings, residential and acute settings for children and adolescents, substance abuse programs, shelters for victims of domestic violence, and others. According to this model,

> Interactions occur between traumatized clients, stressed staff, pressured organizations, and hostile economic and social forces in the larger environment. As a result, our systems can inadvertently recapitulate the very experiences that have proven to be so toxic for the people we are supposed to help. Not only does this have a detrimental effect on clients but it also frustrates and demoralizes staff and administrators, a situation that can lead to worker burnout or vicarious trauma. (*Description of the Sanctuary Model, n.d.*)

The Sanctuary Model aims to increase democratic decision making, increase sense of community and cohesion, improve client satisfaction, and reduce staff turnover. There have been studies done to demonstrate the effectiveness of the model in achieving those goals. Links to those studies, and to other article and books about the Sanctuary Model, can be found at www.sanctuaryweb.com.

SUMMARY

A widely accepted definition of trauma was provided by van der Kolk (1987), "Trauma, by definition, is the result of an exposure to an inescapably stressful event that overwhelms a person's coping mechanisms" (p.6). The higher the dose of trauma, the more potentially damaging the effects; the greater the stressor, the more likely the development of PTSD. Psychological effects are most likely to be severe if the trauma is: human-caused, repeated, unpredictable, multifaceted, sadistic, undergone in childhood, and perpetrated by a caregiver.

A key to understanding, predicting, and treating the symptoms and patterns of trauma lies in obtaining an understanding of how trauma symptoms are biologically generated when a person is confronted with overwhelming experience. The body's physiological flight, fight, and freeze responses to overwhelming stress are central to the formation of trauma symptoms. Many of the traumatized clients seen by social workers are individuals whose survival systems have been

overtaxed. Van der Kolk and Courtois (2005, p. 386) maintain that, "at the core of traumatic stress is the breakdown in the capacity to regulate internal states." Symptoms include intrusive re-experiencing of the traumatic event, hyperarousal, including rapid heart rate and breathing, numbing of responsiveness, intense emotional reactions, memory disturbance and dissociation, aggression against self and others, and addictive behaviors.

The "symptoms" seen in trauma survivors are, in fact, *adaptations* that have enabled individuals to survive the overwhelming experience of being traumatized. The "consensus model" for helping clients with complex trauma histories is "sequenced and progressive." (Courtois, 2005, p. 387) **Phase 1** involves *Stabilization and Skill-Building*, including the tasks of restoration of safety, psychoeducation about trauma, self care and self soothing exercises, and managing self-injurious behaviors, and most important, building a trusting relationship. The neurobiology of attachment provides an explanation for how an empathic, attuned connection to a worker contributes to a client's healing from trauma. The helping relationship often provides a secure base from which the client can make necessary changes. **Phase 2** consists of *Remembering the Details* of the traumatic memories, after the client has learned skills to manage his/her reactions to their memories. **Phase 3** is called either *Self and Relational Development Reconnection*, or *Enhancing Daily Living*.

For children, some of the events that have been shown to have a 'high likelihood' of producing trauma are: natural disaster, the loss of a significant attachment figure, a serious threat to the child's life, physical and sexual abuse, and community and family violence. Their symptoms can be grouped into specific affect, memories, and behaviors. Children seem to use two basic drives to cope with their emotional injuries "The first drive is to master what is painful or confusing, restoring a sense of control and mastery: and the second drive is to avoid painful emotions. (Gil, 2006) Practice recommendations include avoiding pressuring children into talking about abuse when they don't feel ready to do so, and using "expressive therapies" that include play therapy, art therapy, sand tray therapy, storytelling, dance and music so that children have other ways of communicating their inner world to outsiders.

Vicarious traumatization is a term for changes in the worker's life as a result of working with traumatized clients. These include profound changes in the worker's identity, beliefs about the world, sense of safety, and belief in the trustworthiness of others. Strategies to minimize vicarious traumatization involve different forms of self care, including: expressing strong feelings to colleagues and supervisors; taking care of one's physical self; attending to one's spiritual needs; advocating for healthier workplaces; and fighting to change societal conditions that lead to abuse of others. At the same time, it is important to recognize that working with trauma survivors is often deeply rewarding and meaningful. Workers are typically inspired and moved by their clients' resilience and efforts to recover.

Other important topics covered in the chapter were: Psychological First Aid, an approach that provides immediate post-trauma interventions, Substance Abuse, Group Work with Trauma Survivors, and PTSD in war veterans.

CASE EXAMPLE

The final case example in this chapter illustrates how past trauma effects the victim's functioning and psychological well-being long after the abuse. It also illustrates the positive consequences of purposeful interventions.

| CASE 16.6 | THE RECOVERY OF MS. P |

History and Assessment

Ms. P. was a 50-year-old African-American woman who sought counseling at a mental health center for recurrent depression and anxiety. She was employed part time as a home health aide. She had been married for 25 years and was the mother of two teenage daughters. She was finding it difficult to function in her job, and she described chronic marital unhappiness. Ms. P. was a diabetic who would not follow her diet or take her prescribed medication when she would become depressed, sometimes leading to life-threatening medical consequences. She described numerous physical complaints, including stomach pain, headaches, and a feeling of "pressure" in her chest.

Ms. P. had a history of earlier psychiatric hospitalizations for suicidal ideation and debilitating anxiety and

(Continued)

CASE 16.6 | *Continued*

had once been incorrectly given the diagnosis of "paranoid schizophrenia" due to "hallucinations." She was unable to complete college due to a "breakdown" that led to her first lengthy hospital stay. During her intake, Ms. P. mentioned that she had been "molested" by her three older brothers throughout her childhood. She had never told her parents about this abuse because she was afraid that her father, who was a violent man, would seriously harm or kill her brothers.

One of the counseling goals with Ms. P. was to identify the precipitants to episodes of depression, poor self-care, and anxiety. Through this exploration, it became clear to the worker and to Ms. P. that the current situations, which led to depression and poor self-care, were ones that contained reminders of her earlier experiences of sexual abuse. In her prior mental health treatment, she had not made the connection between her current "symptoms" and her history of molestation. Psychoeducation regarding the link between her current difficulties and her history of child sexual abuse helped Ms. P. not to feel "crazy" as she had felt during most of her life. It was important for her to understand that her depression, anxiety, forgetfulness and difficulties with concentration (due to dissociation), and some physical symptoms were probably a result of the trauma and neglect she experienced in her family. She even came to understand that earlier "visual hallucinations of a presence in the room" were actually flashbacks to images of her earlier abuse, rather than being indicators of schizophrenia.

Present "Triggers"

Ms. P.'s worker helped her feel hopeful that she could experience relief from distressing emotions, thoughts, and self-harming behaviors, now that the original causes of her "symptoms," along with present-day "triggers" (reminders of the abuse), had been identified. Examples of more recent "triggers" that had led to a decrease in her functioning included the following:

- Her teenage daughter began to ask her more detailed questions about sexuality and reproduction.
- One of her brothers who had abused her became physically ill with cancer, and she was in the position at times of having to take care of him,

including the responsibility of helping him with his toileting needs.
- A neighbor kept parking his car on her property, and she was extremely upset that he would not respect the boundaries of her property.
- Her dentist spilled liquid all over her face, and then angrily blamed her for not sitting still.
- Her husband brought home a used mattress that he had gotten from a friend but she would not allow him to bring it into the house. She began to shake and cry and then said to him, "How do you know what happened on that mattress?"

Interventions

The elements of each of these incidents that were reminiscent of earlier experiences are probably obvious to the reader but were *not* obvious to her. Her social worker helped her to understand how and why these events triggered current anxiety, depression, difficulty concentrating, and self-harming behaviors. She also learned to predict when a certain situation may cause a "flashback" to earlier abuse, and to plan for how she would handle her emotions and thoughts. In sessions with her worker, she learned "grounding" techniques such as relaxed breathing and the "safe place" imagery, along with assertive communication skills, to help her manage distressing feelings and impulses.

Other interventions that were helpful to Ms. P. in reducing depression, anxiety, and self-harming behaviors were:

- Teaching and practicing other skills for coping with negative feelings, including finding "oases," engaging in physical exercise.
- Helping her to be aware of how many of her physical symptoms were, in fact, actual "stored memories" of sensations she experienced while being abused. She began to take better care of her physical self.
- Including her husband in some sessions to provide support as she articulated her own needs and limits more clearly. Educating him regarding the origin of many of her troublesome symptoms.
- After she had built up a repertoire of skills for calming herself over the course of a year, she was encouraged to tell more stories about the

CASE 16.6 | *Continued*

actual sexual abuse she suffered, allowing her to express the full range of her feelings—from loyalty to shame to fear and more. To assist with telling her story, she would bring in different photographs of her family members. She was able to recount certain incidents while connecting with her emotions, without becoming numb or overwhelmed. *(In this outpatient mental health setting, this particular worker did have the time and the experience, and Ms. P.'s consent, to undertake some of the Phase 2 work.)*

Ms. P.'s Own Description of Interventions That Helped Her

In her own words, Ms. P. described what had helped her to become less anxious and depressed, more hopeful about her future, and better able to function in her roles as mother, worker, and wife:

It helped me to talk to someone, to cry and take deep breaths, to read books about what I went through, to have family sessions, to fight back verbally, to write down what I would do if I got upset, to find a better medical doctor, to read my bible, to have a therapist who "maintained professionalism," to see my psychiatrist regularly and take the medicine he prescribed, to watch my "sugar," to remember when an "anniversary" of an upsetting event was coming up, and to see a physical therapist to get stronger.

Discussion Questions

1. If you knew you only had four meetings with Ms. P., what would you see as the most important tasks for your time together?
2. Ms. P. wondered if she should tell her daughters, who were young teens, about the abuse she suffered. How would you help her to make this decision?
3. How exactly might you help Ms. P. deal with any of the situations that had triggered memories of earlier abuse?
4. If this were your first experience in working with a survivor of child sexual abuse, what do you think you would need to do to prepare yourself, personally and professionally, for working with her?
5. If the social worker had also been a victim of earlier abuse, should she or he disclose this experience to the client? How could this worker avoid being retraumatized and to stay attentive to the client's needs?
6. What might be societal solutions to the ongoing abuse and exploitation of children by their caregivers?
7. How could a worker be helpful to Ms. P. in settings other than an outpatient mental health center, for example, at the diabetes clinic or an inpatient unit?

References

Ainsworth, M. S., and Bowlby, J. (1991). An ethological approach to personality development. *American Psychologist*, 46, 333–341.

Ahmad, A., Larsson, B., and Sundelin-Whalsten, V. (2007). EMDR treatment for children with PTSD: Results of a randomized controlled trial. *Nord J. Psychiatry*, 61, 349–54.

Amen, D. G. (2005). *The brain and behavior: A comprehensive clinical course on the neurobiology of everyday life.* Newport Beach, CA: Mindworks Press.

Amen, D. G. (2008, May 20). *The incredible brain.* Retrieved August 28, 2008, from Amen Clinics Web site: http://amenclinics.com/ac/bitn/bitn_detail.php?articleID=182

Bisson, J., and Andrew, M. (2007). Psychological treatment of post-traumatic stress disorder (PTSD). *Cochrane Database of Systematic Reviews 2007*, Issue 3. Art. No: CD003388. DOI: 10.1002/14651858. CD003388.pub3

Bisson, J. I., Ehlers, A., Matthews, R., Pilling, S., Richards, D., and Turner, S. (2007) Psychological treatments for chronic post-traumatic stress disorder. Systematic review and meta-analysis. *British Journal of Psychiatry, 190,* 97–104.

Bloom, S. L. (1997). *Creating sanctuary: Toward the evolution of sane societies.* New York: Routledge.

Briere, J., and Spinazzola, J. (2005). Phenomenology and psychological assessment of complex post-traumatic states. *Journal of Traumatic Stress, 18* (5), 401–412.

Brown, V., Najavitz, L., Cadiz, C., Finkeistein, N., Heckman, J., and Rechenberger, E. (2007). Implementing an evidence-based practice: Seeking safety group. *Journal of psychoactive drugs, 39*(3), 231–240. Retrieved August 27, 2008 from EBSCOhost database.

Carrion, V., Weems, C., and Reiss, A. (2007). Stress predicts brain changes in children: A pilot longitudinal study on youth stress, posttraumatic stress disorder, and the hippocampus. *Pediatrics, 119*(3), 509–516.

Classen, C., and Koopman, C. (1993). Trauma and dissociation. *Bulletin of the Menninger Clinic, 57*(2), 1–17. Retrieved March 7, 2008 from Academic Search Premier database.

Cohen, J. A., and Mannarino, A. P. (2006). Psychosocial interventions for maltreated and violence-exposed children [electronic version]. *Journal of Social Issues, 62*(4), 737–766.

Courtois, C. (1988). *Healing the incest wound: Adult survivors in therapy.* New York: Norton & Co.

Courtois, C. (2004). Complex trauma, complex reactions: Assessment and treatment. [electronic version]. *Psychotherapy: Theory, Practice, Research, Training, 41*(4), 412–425.

Cozolino, L. (2002). *The neuroscience of psychotherapy: Building and rebuilding the human brain.* New York: W.W. Norton and Company.

CommunityWorks (1998). [Producer]. In *Overcoming the tyrany of the past: The psychobiology of violence and recovery - Sandra Bloom interview.* [DVD].

Curran, J., Machin, C., and Gournay, K. (2006). Cognitive behavioral therapy for patients with anxiety and depression [electronic version]. *Nursing Standard, 21*(7), 44–52.

CREST (2003). *The management of post traumatic stress disorder in adults.* A publication of the Clinical Resource Efficiency Support Team of the Northern Ireland Department of Health, Social Services and Public Safety, Belfast.

Description of the Sanctuary Model (n.d.) Retrieved June 6, 2008, from http://www.sanctuaryweb.com/main/the_sanctuary_model.htm.

Donovan, F. (1999). [Producer]. In *Looking through hemispheres [DVD].* [Available through the store of the EMDR Humanitarian Assistance Programs]. Retrieved September 1, 2008, from http://www.emdrhap.org/osCommerce/product_info.php?products_id=76

Dutch National Steering Committee Guidelines Mental Health Care (2003). Multidisciplinary Guideline Anxiety Disorders. Quality Institute Heath Care CBO/Trimbos Intitute. Utrecht, Netherlands.

Enticott, P., Johnston, P., Herring, S., Hoy, K., and Fitzgerald, P. (2008). Mirror neuron activation is associated with facial emotion processing. *Neuropsychologia, 46*(11), 2851–2854.

Falasca, T., and Caulfield, T. J. (1999). Childhood trauma. *Journal of Humanistic Counseling, Education, and Development, 37*(4), 212–314. Retrieved on April 18, 2008 from EBSChost database.

Fernandez, I., Gallinari, E., Lorenzetti, A. (2004). A school-based EMDR intervention for children who witnessed the Pirelli Building airplane crash in Milan, Italy. *Journal of Brief Therapy, 2,* 129–136.

Foa, E. (1998). *Treating the trauma of rape: Cognitive-Behavioral therapy for P.T.S.D.* New York: The Guilford Press.

Foa, E. B., Dancu, C. V., Hembree, E. A., and Jaycox, L. H., Meadows, E. A., and Street, G. P. (1999). A comparison of exposure therapy, stress inoculation training, and their combination for reducing post-traumatic stress disorder in female assault victims. *Journal of Consulting and Clinical Psychology 67*(2), 194–200.

Foa, E. B., Hembree, E. A., and Olasov R. B. (2007). *Prolonged exposure therapy for PTSD: Emotional processing of traumatic experiences: therapist guide: Treatments that work* (Oxford ed.). New York: Oxford University Press.

Foa, E. B., Keane, T., and Friedman, M. (2000). *Effective treatments for PTSD: Practice guidelines from the International Society for Traumatic Stress Studies.* New York: Guilford.

Figley, C. R. (1995). *Compassion fatigue: Coping with secondary traumatic stress in those who treat the traumatized.* London: Brunner/Routledge.

Follmer, L. (2006). State-dependent learning via gym posters in a partial-hospital setting. Paper delivered in a Widener University trauma-treatment class session.

Ford, J. D., Courtois, C. A., Steele, K., van der Hart, O., and Nijenhuis, E. R. S. (2005). Treatment of complex posttraumatic self-dysregulation. *Journal of Traumatic Stress, 18*(5), 437–447.

Ford, J., and Russo, E. (2006). Trauma-focused, present-centered, emotional self-regulation approach to integrated treatment for posttraumatic stress and addiction: Trauma adaptive recovery group education and therapy. *American Journal of Psychotherapy, 60*(4), 335–355.

Gallup, G. G., and Maser, J. D. (1977). Tonic immobility: Evolutionary underpinnings of human catalepsy and catatonia. In Seligman, M. E. P. and Maser, J. D. (Eds.), *Psychopathology: Experimental models* (pp. 334–357). San Francisco: W.H. Freeman Press.

Gil, E. (2006). *Helping abused and traumatized children: Integrating directive and non-directive approaches.* New York: The Guilford Press.

Giller, E. (n.d.). What is psychological trauma? *Sidran Institute.* Retrieved June 6, 2008, from http://www.sidran.org/sub.cfm?

Harris, M. (1998). *Trauma recovery and empowerment model.* New York: The Free Press.

Hayslip, B., and Kaminski, P. (2005). Grandparents raising their grandchildren: A review of the literature and suggestions for practice. *Gerontologist, 45*(2), 262–269.

Hebert, M. (2007). Efficacy of a group intervention for adult women survivors of sexual abuse [electronic version]. *Journal of Child Sexual Abuse, 16*(4), pp. 37–61.

Herman, J. L. (1992). *Trauma and recovery.* New York, NY: Basic Books.

Herman, J. L. (1998). Recovery from psychological trauma [electronic version]. *Psychiatry and Clinical Neurosciences, 52*, 5145–5150.

Hobfall, S. E., Watson, P., Bell, C. C., Bryant, R. A., Brymer, M. J., Friedman, M. J., et al. (2007). Five essential elements of immediate and mid-term mass trauma intervention: Empirical evidence [electronic version]. *Psychiatry, 70*(4), 283–303.

Hodges, S. (2003). Borderline personality disorder and post-traumatic stress disorder: Time for integration? [electronic version]. *Journal of Counseling and Development, 81*(4), 409–417.

Hoge, C. W., and Terhakopian, A. (2007). Association of posttraumatic stress disorder with somatic symptoms, health care visits, and absenteeism among Iraq war veterans. *American Journal of Psychiatry, 164*, 150–165.

Ironson, G. I., Freund, B., Strauss, J. L., and Williams, J. (2002). Comparison of two treatments for traumatic stress: A community-based study of EMDR and prolonged exposure. *Journal of Clinical Psychology, 58*, 113–128.

Kardiner, A. (1941). *A traumatic neurosis of war.* New York: Hoeber.

Knight, C. (2006). Groups for individuals with traumatic histories: Practice considerations for social workers. *Social Work, 51*(1), 20–30.

Koerner, K., and Dimeff, L. A. (2000). Further data on dialectical behavior therapy. *Clinical Psychology: Science and Practice, 7*(1), 104–112.

Kulka, R. A. (1990). *Trauma and the Vietnam War generation: Report of findings from the National Vietnam veterans' readjustment study.* New York: Brunner/Mazel.

Lasiuk, G. C., and Hegadoren, K. M. (2006). Post traumatic stress disorder part I: Historical development of the concept [electronic version]. *Perspectives in psychiatric care, 42*(1), 13–20.

Levine, P. A. (1997a). *Waking the tiger: Healing trauma: The innate capacity to transform overwhelming experiences.* Berkeley, CA: North Atlantic Books.

Levine, P. A. (1997b). *The body as healer.* Retrieved September 6, 2008, from Foundation for Human Enrichment Web site: http://www.traumahealing.com/art_Chapter1.html

Lewis, L., Kelly, K., and Allen, J. G. (2004). *Restoring hope and trust: An illustrated guide to mastering trauma.* Baltimore, MD: Sidran Institute Press.

Linehan, M. (1993). *Skills training manual for treating Borderline Personality Disorder.* New York: The Guilford Press.

Matsakis, A. (1998). *Trust after trauma: A guide to relationships for survivors and those who love them.* Emeryville, CA: Publishers Group West.

McEvoy, M. (2005) Psychological first aid: Replacement for critical incident stress debriefing? [electronic version]. *Fire Engineering*, 63–66.

McCann, I. L., Pearlman, L. A. (1990). *Psychological trauma and the adult survivor.* Philadelphia, PA: Bruner/Mazel.

Miller, D. (1994). *Women who hurt themselves: A book of hope and understanding.* New York: Basic Books.

Miller, D. (2003). *Your surviving spirit: A spiritual workbook for coping with trauma*. Oakland, CA: Publishers Group West.

Miller, D., and Guidry, L. (2001). *Addictions and trauma recovery: Healing the mind, body, and spirit*. New York: W.W. Norton.

Minister of Public Works and Government Services (2006). *Abuse is wrong in any language*. Retrieved September 20, 2008, from Pubic Health Agency of Canada Web site: http://www.phac-aspc.gc.ca/ncfv-cnivf/familyviolence/html/femviolang_e.html

Najavitz, L. (2002a). *Seeking Safety: A treatment manual for P.T.S.D. and substance abuse*. New York: The Guilford Press.

Najavitz, L. (2002b). "Seeking safety": Therapy for trauma and substance abuse [electronic version]. *Corrections Today*, October, 2002, 136–141.

National Center for PTSD (n.d.). *Returning from the war zone: A guide for families of military personnel*. Retrieved December 10, 2007, from National Center for PTSD. Web site: http://www.ncptsd.va.gov/ncmain/ncdocs/manuals/nc_manual_return-warz_gp.html

National Child Traumatic Stress Network (2007, July). *Creating trauma-informed child-serving systems*. Retrieved August 28, 2008, from The National Child Traumatic Stress Network Web site: http://www.nctsnet.org/nctsn_assets/pdfs/Service_Systems_Brief_v1_v1.pdf

National Institute for Clinical Excellence (2005). *Post traumatic stress disorder (PTSD): The management of adults and children in primary and secondary care*. London: NICE Guidelines.

Omer, H., and London, P. (1989). Signal and noise in psychotherapy: The role and control of non-specific factors. *British Journal of Psychiatry, 155*, 239–245.

Parker, G., Parker, I., and Brotchie, H. (2006). Mood effects of chocolate. *Journal of Affective Disorders, 92*(2–3), 149–159.

Pearlman, L. A., and Courtois, C. A. (2005). Clinical applications of the attachment framework: Relational treatment of complex trauma. *Journal of Traumatic Stress, 18*(5), 449–459.

Pearlman, L. A., and Saakvitne, K. W. (1995) *Trauma and the therapist*. New York: Norton.

Perry, B. D. (1997). Incubated in terror: Neurodevelopmental factors in the "Cycle of Violence." In Osofsky, J. (Ed.), *Children, yout,h and violence: The search for solutions*. New York: Guilford Press.

Perry, B. D. (2000, January). *Maltreated children: Experience, brain development and the next generation*. Retrieved August 29, 2008, from Child Trauma Academy Web site: http://www.child-trauma.org/CTAMATERIALS/brain_i.asp

Pitman, R., Orr, S., Altman, R., Longpre, R., Poire, M., Macklin, M., et al. (1996). Emotional processing and outcome of imaginal flooding therapy in Vietnam veterans with chronic posttraumatic stress disorder. *Comprehensive Psychiatry, 37*(6), 409–418.

Pynoos, R. S., and Nader, K. (1988). Psychological first aid and treatment approach to children exposed to community violence [electronic version]. *Journal of Traumatic Stress, 1*(4), 445–472.

Romano McGraw, P. (2004). *It's not your fault: How healing relationships change your brain & can help you overcome a painful past*. Wilmette, IL: Bahâi Pub.

Rosenberg, L. G. (2000). Phase oriented psychotherapy for gay men recovering from trauma [electronic version]. *Journal of Gay and Lesbian Social Services, 12*(1/2), 37–73.

Rothschild, B. (2000). *The body remembers: The psychophysiology of trauma and trauma treatment*. New York: Norton.

Rothschild, B. (2002). The dangers of empathy. Understanding the keys to vicarious traumatization. *Psychotherapy Networker*, July/August, 61–69.

Rothschild, B. (2006). *Help for the helper: The psychophysiology of compassion fatigue and vicarious trauma*. New York: W.W. Norton.

Ruzek, J. I., Brymer, N. J., Jacobs, A. J., Layne, C. M., Vernberg, E. M., and Watson, P. J. (2007). Psychological First Aid [electronic version]. *Journal of Mental Health Counseling, 29*(1), 17–49.

Saakvitne, K., and Pearlman, L. A. (1996). *Transforming the pain: A workbook on vicarious traumatization*. New York: W.W. Norton and Company.

Saakvitne, K. W., Gamble, S., Pearlman, L. A., and Lev, B. T. (2000). *Risking connection: A training curriculum for working with survivors of childhood abuse*. Baltimore, MD: The Sidran Press.

Scheel, K. R. (2000). The empirical basis of dialectical behavior therapy: Summary, critique, and implications. *Clinical Psychology: Science and Practice, 7*(1), 68–86.

Schore, A. N. (1994). *Affect regulation and the origin of the self: The neurobiology of emotional development*. Mahway, NJ: Erlbaum.

Schore, A. N. (2001a). The effects of a secure attachment relationship on right brain development, affect regulation, and infant mental health. *Infant Journal of Mental Health*, 22(1–2), 7–66.

Schore, A. N. (2001b). The effects of early relational trauma on right brain development, affect regulation, and infant mental health. *Infant Mental Health Journal*, 22(1–2), 201–169.

Sgroi, S. (1982). *Handbook of clinical intervention in child sexual abuse*. New York: The Free Press.

Shapiro, F. (2001). *Eye movement desensitization and reprocessing (EMDR): Basic principles, protocols, and procedures* (2nd ed.). New York: Guilford Press.

Sherman, M. D., Sautter, F., Jackson, M. H., Lyons, J. S., and Han, X. (2006). Domestic violence in veterans with posttraumatic stress disorder who seek couples therapy. *Journal of Marital and Family Therapy*, 32(4), 479–490.

Solomon, M. F., Siegel, D. J. (2003). *Healing trauma: Attachment, mind, body, brain*. New York: The Guilford Press.

Spollen, J., and Labbate, L. A. (2008). Posttraumatic stress disorder in veterans. *Psychiatric Times*, 25 (2), 37–40.

Stalker, C. A., and Fry, R. (1999). A comparison of short-term group and individual therapy for sexually abused women [electronic version]. *Canadian Journal of Psychiatry*, 44, 168–174.

Stecker, T., Fortney, J. C., Hamilton, F., and Ajzen, I. (2007). An assessment of beliefs about mental health care among veterans who served in Iraq. *Psychiatric Services*, 58, 1358–1361.

Stewart, D., and Thomson, K. (2005). The FACE YOUR FEAR Club: Therapeutic group work with young children as a response to community trauma in Northern Ireland. *Child Care in Practice*, 11(2), 191–209. Retrieved August 23, 2008 from EBSCO host database.

Strom, R., and Strom, S. (2000). Meeting the challenge of raising grandchildren. *International Journal of Aging & Human Development*, 51(3), 183.

Sullivan, M. (2002). *Completion Tendency [Brochure]*. Willingboro, NJ: Providence House Domestic Violence Services.

Suzuki, A., Josselyn, S. A., Frankland, P. W., Masushige, S., Silva, A.J., and Kida, S. (2004). Memory reconsolidation and extinction have distinct temporal and biochemical signatures. *The Journal of Neuroscience*, 24(20), 4787–4795.

Terr, L. (1992). *Too scared to cry: Psychic trauma in childhood*. New York: Basic Books.

Tourigny, M., Hebert, M., Daigneault, I., and Simoneau, A. C. (2005). Efficacy of group therapy for sexually abused adolescent girls [electronic version]. *Journal of Child Sexual Abuse*, 14(4), 71–93

van der Kolk, B. A. (1987). *Psychological trauma*. Washington, DC: American Psychiatric Press.

van der Kolk, B. A. (1996). *Traumatic Stress: The effects of overwhelming experience on mind, body, and society*. New York: The Guilford Press.

van der Kolk, B. A. (2001). The psychobiology and psychopharmacology of PTSD. *Human Psychopharmacology: Clinical & Experimental*, 16(S49–S64).

van der Kolk, B. A., and Courtois, C. A. (2005). Editorial comments: Complex developmental trauma. *Journal of Traumatic Stress*, 18(5), 385–388.

van der Kolk, B. A., Roth, S., Pelcovitz, D., Sunday, S., and Spinazzola, J. (2005). Disorders of extreme stress: The empirical foundation of a complex adaptation to trauma. *Journal of Traumatic Stress*, 18(5), 389–399.

van der Kolk, B. A., Spinazzola, J., Blaustein, M. E., Hopper, J. W., Hopper, E. K., and Korn, D. L. (2007). A randomized clinical trial of eye movement desensitization and reprocessing (EMDR), fluoxetine, and pill placebo in the treatment of posttraumatic stress disorder: Treatment effects and long-term maintenance. *Journal of Clinical Psychiatry*, 68, 1–10.

Wagner, A. W., Rizvi, S., and Harned, M. S. (2007) Applications of dialectical behavior therapy to the treatment of complex trauma-related problems: When one case formulation does not fit all. *Journal of Traumatic Stress*, 20(4), 391–400.

Walker, L. E. (1979). *The battered woman*. New York: Harper & Row.

Walker, L. E. (1994). *Abused women and survivor therapy: A practical guide for the psychotherapist*. Washington, DC: American Psychological Association.

Zlotnick, C., Shea, T. M., Rosen, K., Simpson, E., Mulrenin, K., Begin, A., and Pearlstein, T. (1997). An affect-management group for women with post traumatic stress disorder and histories of childhood sexual abuse [electronic version]. *Journal of Traumatic Stress*, 10(3), 425–436.

Web Resources

Adolescents

- Download the "Integrated Treatment for Complex Trauma for Adolescents," at www.JohnBriere.com

Attachment

- Association for Treatment and Training in the *Attachment* of Children: www.attach.org/

Childhood Trauma

- www.childtrauma.org

EMDR

- http://www.emdr.com/briefdes.htm
- www.emdria.org

General Trauma Information and Seminal Articles

- http://www.trauma-pages.com

Gun Control

- www.bradycampaign.org

National Association of Social Workers

- Political Action for Candidate Election: http://www.socialworkers.org/pace/default.asp

National Coalition against Domestic Violence: www.ncadv.org.

National Child Traumatic Stress Network

- Creating trauma-informed child-serving systems: http://www.nctsnet.org/nctsn_assets/pdfs/Service_Systems_Brief_v1_v1.pdf

National Health Insurance

- Physicians for a National Health Program: www.pnhp.org

National Institute of Mental Health

- Information sheets and pamphlets on trauma: http://www.nimh.nih.gov/health/publications/topics/index-ptsd-publication-all.shtml

Psychological First Aid

- The complete manual can be downloaded at http://www.ncptsd.va.gov/pfa/PFA.html

Rape

- www.mencanstoprape.org
- www.rainn.org

Sanctuary Model for Organizations: www.sanctuaryweb.com

Self-Injury

- SAFE (Self Abuse Finally Ends): www.selfinjury.com

Substance Abuse

- For first-rate information on drug and alcohol use and treatment, go to: the National Institutes of Health's National Information on Drug Abuse (NIDA) website, www.nida.nih.gov; and the United States Department of Health and Human Services, Substance Abuse & Mental Health Services Administration SAMHSA website, www.samhsa.gov.
- Psychiatrist Daniel Amen offers an excellent video targeted at teenagers (but it is good for all populations) that utilizes neuroimaging (scans of substance users' brains) to show the physical impact of drug and alcohol use on the brain. The video is called, "Which Brain Do You Want" and may be ordered from www.amenclinics.com.
- Seeking Safety group program for co-occurring PTSD and substance abuse: www.seekingsafety.org

Trauma-Focused Cognitive Behavioral Therapy

- Web-based training: http://tfcbt.musc.edu/
- General Information: http://www.childwelfare.gov/pubs/trauma/trauma4.cfm

Traumatic Stress Education and Advocacy

- www.sidran.org

van der Kolk, Bessel A.: www.traumacenter.org

Veterans

- For the National Center for PTSD's guide on working with the military, go to: www.ncptsd.va.gov/ncmain/ncdocs/manuals/nc_manual_iwcguide.html

INDEX

AB design, single-system evaluations and, 92–93
ABA design, single-system evaluations and, 92
ABC design, single-system evaluations and, 93
abuse and poverty, 392
abused/neglected children and generalist practice
  case examples, 543–544, 546–548, 552–553, 555–556, 558–559, 561–562, 570–571
  and child welfare as field of practice, 528–530
  critical thinking and, 539–540
  and evolution of welfare policy, 530–538
  and family service plan, 556–559
  foster care and, 563–569
  and in-home welfare services, 560–563
  and planning phase, 552–556
  safety/risk assessment and, 545–551
  solution-focused approaches and, 540–541
  strengths-based practice and, 538–539
  trauma and, 587–595, 611–615
  and working with involuntary/mandated client, 541–545
accent response, 112
acceptance, importance of, 110
action plan/outcome evaluation, 182–183
action stage of change, 10–11
acute stress disorder, diagnostic criteria for, 578

addicted people and generalist practice
  addiction defined, 427–429
  adolescence and, 426–427
  adolescent treatment programs and, 443–444
  agonist maintenance treatment and, 439
  assessments and, 422–426
  case examples, 445–446
  counseling and, 441–442
  court-mandated treatment and, 439
  and cycle of addiction, 431–432
  detoxification and, 438–439
  disease model/psychological model and, 433–434
  drug classification/drug effects, 418–421
  elderly and, 471–472
  general information, 416–418
  interventions for, 434–435
  moral model and, 432–433
  motivation interviewing and, 436–438
  neurobiology and, 429–431
  nonstep support groups and, 443
  online support and, 442–443
  outpatient treatment and, 441
  residential treatment programs and, 439–440
  self-help groups and, 442
  sociocultural model and, 433
  therapeutic communities and, 440–441
addiction cycle, 431–432
additive empathy, 117
administration, organizations and, 264

Administration on Aging (AoA), 453
adolescent and addictions, 426–427, 443–444
adolescent treatment programs, addictions and, 443–444
Adoption and Safe Families Act of 1997 (ASFA), 536
Adoption Assistance and Child Welfare Act of 1980, 535
adoption/substitution, cognitive restructuring (CR) and, 155
advocacy. See also client advocacy
  case management and, 163
  communities and, 344
  elderly and, 480–482
affirmative practice and GLBT populations, 512–515
Agency Assessment Tool (appendix), 303–316
agonist maintenance treatment for addiction, 439
Aid to Families with Dependent Children (AFDC), 383, 533
alcohol dependency. See addicted people and generalist practice
Alcoholics Anonymous, 443
alternating, case management and, 160
alternative explanations, critical thinking and, 38
ambivalence check as intervention skill, 128
American Association of Retried Persons (AARP), 481–482
American Psychological Association's Division44, 515
Annie E. Casey Foundation, 567

635

anti-discrimination laws, 386
Area Agency on Aging (AAA), 458–459, 465
articulate tasks
    collaborative model and, 60–61
    and intervention phase of collaborative model, 120–124
ask tasks, collaborative model and, 60–61
asking for story of client, 109–114
assessments
    addicted people and, 422–426
    assessment tools for organizations, 273–274
    assessment variables of organizations, 259–263
    boundaries (family subsystems), 204, 211–213
    cognitive restructuring (CR) and, 155
    common organization constituencies and, 257–259
    communication patterns (family subsystems), 204, 209–211
    and disengagement phase of collaborative model, 129–130
    elderly and, 461–469
    emotional climate (family subsystems), 204, 208–209
    ethnicity/culture (family subsystems), 204–206
    family subsystem types, 203–204
    family system, 203
    focus groups for organizations, 274–275
    and internal organizational considerations, 263–272
    legal/policy environment of organizations, 272–273
    life-cycle stages (family subsystems), 204, 206–207
    observational performance ratings for organizations, 274–278
    strengths-based, 56–59
    structure (family subsystems), 204–205
assets assessment, communities and, 338–340
Attachment History Questionnaire, 38
attachment theory, 36–38
authority, 267
avoidant model of attachment, 37
awareness, cognitive restructuring (CR) and, 155

Barol, Beth. See groups and generalist practice
baseline, 91
behavioral observations, as measurement tool of strength-based assessments, 81–84
behavioral therapy, client change through, 47

bi-negativity, 494
biopsychosocial assessment, 178–179
Brace, charles Loring, 531
brain functions. See neurobiology and addiction
brainstorming, and intervention phase of collaborative model, 122
by-laws and foundation policies, 263

Care Manager Certified (CMC), 483
caring as basic human right, 36. See also ethics
case advocacy, 163
case management
    individual client systems and, 159–161, 163
    micro/macro client systems and, 4–5, 8
case study design, single-system evaluations and, 93
cementing strategies, case management and, 160
Certified Advanced Social Worker in Case Management (C-ASWCM), 483
Certified Case Manager (CCM), 483
Certified Social Work in Case Manager (C-SWCM), 483
chain of command, 267
challenging as intervention skill, 126–128
chaos/struggle stage, group practice and, 231–232
checkback strategy, case management and, 160
Chester, Pennsylvania, 406–408
Child Abuse and Prevention Act of 1974 (CAPTA), 528, 533–534
Children and Family Service Reviews (CFSRs), 537
Children's Aid Society of New York City, 531
Childress, Anna Rose, 430–431
Circle for Change, 67–68
clarify tasks, collaborative model and, 60–61
CLASS Program, group practice and, 245–246
client advocacy
    case management and, 163
    micro/macro client systems and, 5
client logs, as measurement tool of strength-based assessments, 80–81
client system, 3–4
client system level, 4
clients, 110. See also economically disadvantaged peoples
    and articulation of focus/plan of action, 120–124
    asking for story of, 109–114
    assessing strengths of, 56–57
    bisexual, 509–510
    clarification of working with, 118–119

client progress evaluation in collaborative model, 54–56
    and client's culture/value/beliefs/environment, 107–109
    cognitive restructuring (CR) and, 155–157
    consequence of poverty for, 390–392
    cultural/ethnic diversity and, 13–14
    definition, 9–10
    after disengagement, 132–133
    effect of prior experiences on, 12–13
    employability factors of, 385
    empowerment in collaborative model, 53–54
    expectations of, 13
    gay/lesbian, 508–509
    importance of collaboration with, 35–36
    importance of helping relationship for change of, 46–49
    and importance of trust, 46, 49–51
    listening for meaning/feelings of, 114–117
    mistrust of professionals by, 46–47
    and perseverance of relationship, 124–129
    reluctant, 11–14
    skills/knowledge of, 15
    stages of change in, 10–11
    strength in collaborative model, 51–53
    transgender, 510, 516
    types in generalist social work practice, 8–11
    worker-client transactions in ecosystems perspective, 32
Clinical Assessment for Social Workers (Jordan and Franklin), 89
clinical significance, 94
closed family systems, 212. See also families
coalition building, 343–344
cognitive restructuring (CR), 155–157
cognitive therapy (CT), 155
cognitive-behavioral therapy
    client change through, 47
    elderly and, 485
    GLBT and, 516–518
    trauma and, 606–607
    trauma-focused, 614–615
collaboration
    definition, 52
    and principles of strength-based practice, 35–36
collaborative model. See also intervention phase of collaborative model; pre-engagement phase of collaborative model
    case examples, 106–107
    client change in helping relationship as theoretical proposition of, 46–49

client empowerment as practice principle, 53–54
client mistrust of professionals as theoretical proposition of, 46–47
client progress evaluation as practice principle, 54–56
client strength as practice principle, 51–53
disengagement phase of, 129–133
Helping Relationship Inventory (HRI) and, 62–65
inputs of, 60–62
intervention phase of, 120–129
outputs of, 60, 62
phase of, 60–61
pre-engagement phase of, 107–119
skills of, 60, 62
strengths-based assessment and, 56–59
tasks of, 60–61
trust in relationships as theoretical proposition of, 46, 49–51
common ground processing (as tool), group practice and, 239–243
communication
and client's culture/value/beliefs/environment, 107–109
elaboration skills and, 110–114
importance of respect/acceptance, 110
as workers' use of self in, 6–7
communities. See also economically disadvantaged peoples
assets assessment (pre-engagement) and, 338–340
case examples, 340–341, 350–353
collaborative model and, 326–327
community development (engagement), 343–344
Community Organization Resource Inventory (appendix), 364–369
consequence of poverty for, 392–393
data collection (pre-engagement) and, 334–338
definition, 323–324
education/training (engagement), 344–345
elderly and, 459
Evaluating the Participation of Traditionally Marginalized Groups (appendix), 371
evaluation/termination (engagement), 347–349
focus groups (pre-engagement) and, 334–335
general information (pre-engagement) and, 327–329
GIS (pre-engagement) and, 341
group practice and, 223
individual capacity assessment (pre-engagement) and, 340
interventions (engagement), 343
as level of macro client system, 4–6

needs assessment (pre-engagement) and, 329–331
observation (pre-engagement) and, 331
organizational capacity assessment (pre-engagement) and, 340–341
Planning Document Template (appendix), 370
population/resource data (pre-engagement) and, 331–333
poverty causes in, 381, 388–390
and principles of strength-based practice, 35
program planning (engagement), 344–347
research literature (pre-engagement) and, 331
resource mapping (pre-engagement) and, 340–342
social work practice with, 323–326
surveys (pre-engagement) and, 333–334, 336
Tools for Community Assessment and Development (appendix), 355–363
working stage and, 232–234
community development
communities and, 343–344
micro/macro client systems and, 4
Community Organization Resource Inventory, 364–369
community practice, 324
community-based participatory research (CBPR), 347–349
concurrent baseline, definition, 91
concurrent validity, strengths-based assessments and, 77–78
Conference on Aging, 453
constitution, 263
construct validity, strengths-based assessments and, 78
contemplation stage of change, 10
content validity, strengths-based assessments and, 77
contradictions, critical thinking and, 38
convergent validity, strengths-based assessments and, 78
cooperative intentions, collaborative model and, 119
coordinator role, service coordination and, 160–161
Cornell Scale of Depression in Dementia, 469–470
cortisol, 588–591. See also trauma-experienced people and generalist practice
Council for Social Work (CSWE), 456–457
counseling
addictions and, 441–442
family group, 558–559
micro/macro client systems and, 4–5, 8

supportive, 154–157
trauma and, 617–621
countertransference, 622
court-mandated treatment for addiction, 439
critical incident recording, 81
critical thinking
abused/neglected children and, 539–540
EST and, 39
generalist social work practice and, 38
cultural mores
abused/neglected children and, 554
and client engagement, 15
and client reluctancy, 11
collaborative model and client's, 107–109
diversity and, 13–14
elderly and, 456–457
families and, 191, 204–206
individual client systems and, 137

data collection, communities and, 334–338
data collection/organization. See also evaluations
sharing of, 123–124
strengths-based assessments and, 75–81
Defense of Marriage Act (DOMA), 505–506
deficit model, 188
delivery systems, values and, 16–19
demographics, 137–138, 331–333. See also economically disadvantaged peoples
elderly and, 450–453, 486
foster care and, 563–565
depressants, 418–420
detoxification, 438–439
Diagnostic and Statistical Manual of Mental Disorders (DSM-III), 576–577
Diagnostic and Statistical Manual of Mental Disorders (DSM-IV-TR), 56, 189
Diagnostic and Statistical Manual of Mental Disorders (DSM-IV-TR), 427–429
dialectical behavior therapy (DBT), 604–606
direct observation, behavioral observations and, 83
direct practice, 3
Disability benefits (SSD), 395–396
discrete time sampling, behavioral observations and, 82–83
discriminant validity, strengths-based assessments and, 78

discrimination, 386. *See also* economi-
    cally disadvantaged peoples; gay/
    lesbian/bisexual/transgender people
    baby boomers and, 452
    nondiscrimination policies, 506–507
disease model and addiction, 433–434
diseases and poverty, 392
disengagement
    group practice and, 227, 230
    reactions to termination, 165–166
    types of termination, 163–165
disengagement phase of collaborative
    model, 60–61, 129–133
disorders of extreme stress not otherwise
    specified (DESNOS), 579–580
disorganized model of attachment, 37
distress tolerance skills, 605
drugs. *See also* addicted people and
    generalist practice
    classification/effects of, 418–421

Earned Income Tax Credit, 400
ecological theories, organizations and,
    270–271
ecomaps, 474–476
economically disadvantaged peoples
    case examples, 406–409
    cash assistance (policy issues),
        395–398
    and client needs, 390–392
    and consequences of community
        poverty, 392–393
    engagement issues and, 400–405
    food/nutrition (policy issues), 375,
        398–399
    general information (policy issues),
        393–394
    health (policy issues), 394–395
    housing/energy (policy issues),
        399–400
    poverty causes (communities/large
        groups) and, 381, 388–390
    poverty causes (individuals/families)
        and, 379–388
    pre-engagement issues and, 400–401
    problem of poverty in, 374–378
    taxes (policy issues), 375, 400
    welfare and, 378–379
ecosystems perspective of social work,
    description, 31–33
Eden Alternative, 481–482
education, micro/macro client systems
    and, 4–5, 7
education/training
    communities and, 344–345
    foster care and, 566
    individual client systems and, 159
    psychoeducation, 599–601
elaboration skills, 110–114
elderly and generalist practice
    advocacy for, 480–482
    assessments, 461–469

case examples, 463, 466–467, 479,
    486–488
case management and, 482–483
cognitive-behavioral therapy and, 485
demographics and, 450–453, 486
engagement strategies for, 478–479
GLBT, 505
life review and, 483–484
policy issues and, 453–455
resources for, 469–478
social work practice with, 455–461
supportive counseling and, 484–485
e-mail groups and addictions, 442
emotion regulation skills, 604–605
empathy, importance of, 115–117
empirical practice movement, 30
empirically supported treatment (EST),
    39
Employment Non-Discrimination Act
    (ENDA), 506–507
empowerment of clients, 53–54
emptying/resolution stage, group prac-
    tice and, 232
ending. *See* disengagement phase of
    collaborative model
engagement phase of collaborative
    model, 60–61
    economically disadvantaged peoples
        and, 400–405
    group practice and, 227, 230
environment
    assessment axis and, 57–58
    collaborative model and client's,
        107–109
    immediate, 387
    person-in-environment concept,
        58–59
    resources in, 36
ethics
    and advocacy for the elderly,
        480–481
    caring as basic human right, 36
    dilemmas, 19–22
    generalist social work practice and,
        19–25
    NASW Code of Ethics, 3, 16
    NASW ethical standards and,
        19–20
ethnic diversity, 13–14, 137–138, 324
Evaluating the Participation of Tradi-
    tionally Marginalized Groups, 371
evaluation design, 89
evaluations. *See also* assessments
    and analyzing single-system data,
        93–97
    behavioral observations, 81–84
    case examples, 100–103
    client logs, 80–81
    collaborative model and, 54–56
    communities and, 347–349
    designing of, 89–93
    goal attainment scales, 86–88

and intervention phase of collabora-
    tive model, 124
measurement guidelines, 74–79
measurement tools, 79
process of, 73–74
rating scale, 84–86
single-system data analysis, 93–97
single-system data components,
    90–93
standardized measures, 88–89
and statistical significance, 97–99
evidence, critical thinking and, 38
Evidence-Based Practice (EBP)
    definition, 39
    GLBT and, 516–519
expertise power, 53
eye movement desensitization and re-
    processing (EMDR), 608–609

face validity, strengths-based assess-
    ments and, 77
faith-based organization (FBO),
    262–263
families
    assessments with, 198–199
    assessments with family system, 203
    boundaries (subsystem assessment)
        and, 204, 211–213
    and caregiving tips for elderly,
        459–460
    case examples, 213–216
    communication patterns (subsystem
        assessment) and, 204, 209–211
    emotional climate (subsystem assess-
        ment) and, 204, 208–209
    ethnicity/culture (subsystem assess-
        ment) and, 204–206
    family development plan, 199–203
    family group conferences, 193–194
    family systems approach, 196–198
    family-centered programs, 194–195
    foster care and, 563–569
    GLBT youth and, 501
    in-home services and, 560–563
    interdependence and, 187–190
    life-cycle stages (subsystem assess-
        ment) and, 204, 206–207
    with multiple challenges, 192
    structure (subsystem assessment) and,
        204–205
    types of, 186–187
    working with strengths of, 190–191
family
    as level of micro client system, 4–5
    and principles of strength-based
        practice, 35
family development plan, 199–203
family preservation, 560
Family Preservation and Family Support
    Services Program, 535
family service plan, abused/neglected
    children and, 556–559

family subsystem assessments. *See* assessments
family systems approach, 196–198
Family to Family Initiative, 567
family-centered programs, 194–195
flight/fight/freeze, 585–586
focus groups
  communities and, 334–335
  organizations and, 274–275
focused listening, 116
Food Stamps, 375, 398–399
food stamps, 400
formal evaluation, 55
formal organizations, 260–261
for-profit organizations, 261
foster care, abused/neglected children and, 563–569
foundation policies, 263–264, 288–290
front line workers, organizations and, 264
functional family therapy (FFT) team, 7
gay/lesbian/bisexual/transgender people
  best practice recommendations for, 515
  biased/inadequate/inappropriate practices with, 511
  bisexual clients and, 509–510
  case examples, 494–495, 503, 518–520
  elderly and, 505
  evidence-based practice and, 516–519
  and forces of oppression, 493–494
  and GLB identity development, 496–501
  GLBT people of color, 502–503
  GLBT youth, 501–502
  homophobia and, 493, 508–509
  Kinsey Scale and, 495–496
  marriage equity and, 505–506
  nondiscrimination policies and, 506–507
  and oppression in practice, 508
  orientation-behavior-identity and, 494–495
  parents/children, 504–505
  sexual orientation terms, 493
  strengths perspective and, 510–514
  theological stances and, 514–515
  transgender clients and, 498–501, 510, 516
  and transgender identity development, 501

Gay-Straight Alliances (GSA), 518–519
gender identity, 498–501
Gender Identity Disorder (GID), 510
general anchor descriptions, 86
generalist social work practice
  attachment theory and, 36–38
  attachment/attachment models and, 36–38
  definition, 3

ecosystems perspective of social work, 31–33
ethics and, 19–25
modern approach to social work, 29–31
postmodern approach to social work, 29–31
and principles of strength-based practice, 35–36
reluctant clients and, 11–14
strengths-based, 2–3
types of, 3–6
types of clients in, 8–11
values and, 16–19
geographic information system (GIS), communities and, 341
Geriatric Depression Scale, 469–470
geriatrics. *See* elderly and generalist practice
goal attainment scales (GAS), as measurement tool of strength-based assessments, 86–88
goal determination, individuals and generalized practice and, 147–151
goals/objectives and helping relationship
  economically disadvantaged peoples and, 401–403
  organizations and, 263–265, 278–282
grant writing as intervention, organizations and, 282, 286, 288–290
group
  as level of micro client system, 4–5
  and principles of strength-based practice, 35
group conferences (families), 193–194
group dynamics
  chaos/struggle stage and, 231–232
  community/working stage and, 232–234
  emptying/resolution stage and, 232
  group control and, 234–235
  group influences and, 230–231
  process versus content in, 235
  pseudocommunity/initiation stage and, 231
  stage models of, 229–230
  termination and, 235–236
groups and generalist practice
  case examples, 222–225, 227–229, 237, 241–243, 245–251
  CLASS Program, 245–246
  common ground processing (as tool) in, 239–243
  defense mechanisms and, 226
  first introductions for, 236
  and group dynamics, 229–236
  group intervention models and, 244
  group resistance, 221–222
  leaders/facilitators of, 227–229
  and needs of humans, 223–225

pre-engagement/engagement/disengagement phases and, 227
process versus content (as tools) in, 236–237
and reduction of group anxiety, 225–226
Second Step Program, 245
successful, 222–223
Talking Paper (as tool) in, 238–239
types/purposes groups for, 220–221

hallucinogens, 420–421
Handbook of Attachment, The (Cassidy and Shaver), 38
hardshipes, and principles of strength-based practice, 35
haunting strategy, case management and, 160
Help for the Helper (Rothschild), 624
helpfulness, NASW Code of Ethics on, 16–19
helping relationship. *See also* communication
  and clarification of working with client, 118–119
  client change in helping relationship as theoretical proposition of, 46–49
  effect of cultural mores on, 15
  Helping Relationship Inventory (HRI) and, 62–65
Helping Relationship Inventory (HRI), 62–65
heterosexism, 493–494
history of child/family welfare. *See* welfare
homophobia, 493, 508–509
hopefulness
  diagnostic labeling and, 56
  and intervention phase of collaborative model, 120–121
Housing Acts, 399
Hudson, Walter, 89
human dignity as value, 17–18
human relationship importance as value, 18–19
Human Rights Campaign (HRC), 507
hunger/nutrition, consequence of poverty as, 390

identity developmental model, 497
immediate environment, 387
implications, critical thinking and, 38
implicit underlying feelings, 117
Indian Housing Authorities (IHAs), 399–400
individual
  as level of micro client system, 4–5
  and principles of strength-based practice, 35
individual capacity assessment, communities and, 340

individual rating scales, evaluations and, 55–56
individualized rating scales, 84–86
individualizing, case management and, 160
individuals and generalized practice
assessment forms for, 139–142
case examples, 140–142, 144, 159, 162–163, 168–169
case management and, 159–161, 163
and clients' reactions to terminations, 165–166
education/training and, 159
goal determination and, 147–151
goals/objectives and helping relationship, 151–152
goals/objectives defined, 148–149
graphic displays and, 145–147
input/output checklist and, 144–145
intervention/evaluation plan development and, 152–153
interventions with, 153
mental health evaluations and, 142–144
mental status evaluation and, 142–144
pre-engagement and, 136–139
problem-solving therapy and, 157–159
purpose of goals/objectives, 148
and selecting/defining objectives, 149–151
supportive counseling and, 154–157
and types of termination, 164–165
informal evaluation, 55
informal organizations, 260–261
information retrieval skills, collaborative model and, 108–109
inhalants, 421
input/output checklist, 144–145, 181
inputs, collaborative model and, 60, 62
institutional theories, organizations and, 270–271
insurance, diagnosis required for, 56
interdependence, 187–190
internal consistency reliability, strengths-based assessments and, 77
Internal Revenue Service (IRS), organizations and, 261
interpersonal component, 448–449
interpersonal effectiveness skills, 605
interpersonal practice, 3
interpersonal therapy, client change through, 47
interval sampling, behavioral observations and, 82
intervention phase of collaborative model
and articulation of focus/plan of action, 120–124
and perseverance of client relationship, 124–129

interventions
addictions and, 434–435
advocacy for, 480–482
case examples, 479
case management and, 482–483
cognitive-behavioral therapy and, 485
communities and, 343
engagement strategies for, 478–479
grant writing as, 282, 286, 288–290
life review and, 483–484
micro/macro client systems and, 4
productivity improvements as, 282–284
resource development as, 282, 286–287
staff development as, 282, 284–285
strategic planning as, 282, 285–286
supportive counseling and, 484–485
interviews. See also communication
elaboration skills and, 110–114
motivational, 436–438
involuntary clients, definition, 10

Kardiner, Abram, 578
Keeping Children and Families Safe Act of , 2003, 528–529
Keeping Families Safe Act of 2008, 537
Kinsey, Alfred, 495
Kinsey Scale, gay/lesbian/bisexual/transgender people and, 495–496
kinship care, 565–566

LAAM, 439
labeling, diagnostic, 56
leadership
group practice and, 228–229
organizations and, 266–270
legal/policy environment of organizations, 272–273
legitimate power, 53
Levine, Peter, 585
Likert-type scales, 62–63
line authority, 267
listen tasks, collaborative model and, 60–61
listening for meaning/feelings, 114–117
live chat groups and addictions, 442
logical positivism, 30

macro social work practice, aspects of, 4–5
maintenance stage of change, 11
marriage equity, 505–506
Maslow, Abraham, 378
Maslow's hierarchy of needs, 378, 556–557
Measures for Clinical Practice (Fischer and Corcoran), 89
Measures of Personality and Social Psychological Attitudes (Robinson, Shaver, and Wrightsman), 89

Medicade, 375, 394
Medicare, 350–353, 394
Medicare and You, 458
mental illness and poverty, 392
mental status form, 180
message boards and addictions, 442
methadone clinics, 439
Meyers, Charles Samuel, 578
mezzo-level direct practice, definition, 3–4
micro social work practice
aspects of, 4, 6
definition, 3
Microsoft MapPoint, 341
Miller, Bill, 436
mindfulness skills, 605–606
Mini-Mental Status Examination (MMSE), 467–468
minorities. See ethnic diversity
mission and foundation policies, 263–265
models of attachment, 37
modern approach to social work, description, 29–31
monitoring design, single-system evaluations and, 93
moral model and addiction, 432–433
motivation interviewing, 436–438
Multi-Ethnic Placement Act of 1994 (MEPA), 535

naltrexone, 439
NASW Code of Ethics, 3. See also ethics
National Association of Professional Geriatric Care Managers (NAPGCM), 482–483
National Association of Social Workers (NASW), 456–457
National Association of Social Workers (NASW) Code of Ethics, 16
ethical standards and, 19–20
GLBT and, 507
National Child Abuse and Neglect Data Systems (NCANS), 529–530
National Institute of Mental Health, on client change, 47
National School Lunch Program, 398–399
network intervention, 133
neurobiology
attachment versus neglect, 580–582
and impact of trauma, 585–587
neurobiology and addiction, 429–431
nongovernmental organizations (N.G. O.s), definition, 260–263
nonjudgmental attitudes, importance of, 18
nonprofit organizations, 261
nonstep support groups, addictions and, 443
nonvoluntary clients, 10

observation, communities and, 331
observational performance ratings, organizations and, 274–278
Older American's Act of 1965 (OAA), 453
online support, addictions and, 442–443
open family systems, 212. *See also* families
operating core, organizations and, 264
opiods, 419–420
organizational adaptation theories, organizations and, 270–271
Organizational Capacity Assessment (appendix), 299–302
organizational capacity assessment, communities and, 340–341
Organizational Evaluation/Objective Attainment Tracking Form (appendix), 321
Organizational Goal Planning Form (appendix), 317–319
Organizational Intervention Planning Form (appendix), 320
organizational level of macro client system, 4–5
organizational theory, definition, 259
organizations and generalist practice
  Agency Assessment Tool (appendix), 303–316
  assessment tools for, 273–274
  assessment variables of, 259–263
  case examples, 284–285, 293–295
  engagement phase, 278–282
  evaluation and, 291–293
  focus groups and, 274–275
  grant writing as intervention, 282, 286, 288–290
  and internal organizational considerations, 263–272
  legal/policy environment and, 272–273
  observational performance ratings and, 274–278
  Organizational Capacity Assessment (appendix), 299–302
  Organizational Evaluation/Objective Attainment Tracking Form (appendix), 321
  Organizational Goal Planning Form (appendix), 317–319
  Organizational Intervention Planning Form (appendix), 320
  pre-engagement phase, 257–259
  productivity improvements as interventions, 282–284
  resource development as intervention, 282, 286–287
  staff development as intervention, 282, 284–285
  strategic planning as intervention, 282, 285–286
  termination and, 290–291

orientation-behavior-identity and sexuality, 494–495
outpatient treatment and addiction, 441
outputs. *See also* pre-engagement phase of collaborative model
  collaborative model and, 60, 62
overlearning, 132

parents/children, lesbian/gay, 504–505
partializing, and intervention phase of collaborative model, 121–122
partnership with client, 121
  families and, 190, 213
Patient Self-Determination Act, 460–461
people with addictions. *See* Addicted people and generalist practice
permanency planning, 535
persever tasks, collaborative model and, 60–61
persevering task, 124–129
Personal Responsibility and Work Opportunity Reconciliation Act of 1996 (PRWORA), 262, 397, 535–536
person-in-environment concept
  definition, 32–33
  identification/analysis of, 58–59
Philadelphia Area Research Community Coalition (PARCC), 348
Planning Document Template, 370
play therapy, 613–614
policy issues and economically disadvantage people, 393–400
postinvestigative in-home services, 560
postmodern approach to social work
  definition, 31
  description, 29–31
posttraumatic stress disorder (PTSD)
  complex, 579–580
  diagnostic criteria for, 576–577
  Prolonged Exposure (PE) and, 607
  war veterans and, 621
poverty. *See* economically disadvantaged peoples
power
  collaborative model and, 53–54
  organizations and, 266–267
PRACTICE, 615
precontemplation stage of change
  and client reluctancy, 11
  definition, 10
predictive validity, strengths-based assessments and, 78
pre-engagement phase of collaborative model, 60–61
  and asking client to tell story, 109–114
  case examples, 133–134

and clarification of working with client, 118–119
and client's culture/value/beliefs/environment, 107–109
economically disadvantaged peoples and, 400–401
group practice and, 227, 230
and listening for meaning/feelings, 114–117
pre-engagement phase of communities
  assets assessment and, 338–340
  data collection and, 334–338
  focus groups and, 334–335
  general information and, 327–329
  GIS (pre-engagement) and, 341
  individual capacity assessment (pre-engagement) and, 340
  needs assessment and, 329–331
  observation and, 331
  organizational capacity assessment (pre-engagement) and, 340–341
  population/resource data and, 331–333
  research literature and, 331
  resource mapping (pre-engagement) and, 340–342
  surveys and, 333–334, 336
pre-engagement phase of organizations, common constituencies and, 257–259
preparation stage of change, definition, 10
preventative in-home services, 560
prior experiences, clients and, 12–13, 15
private geriatric case managers (PGCM), 482–483
problems, and principles of strength-based practice, 35
problem-solving skills, 132
problem-solving therapy (PST), 154–157
  individual client systems and, 157–159
productivity improvements as interventions, organizations and, 282–284
professionals
  foster care and, 566–567
  mistrust of, 47
  worker attributes of, 47–48
program planning
  communities and, 344–347
  micro/macro client systems and, 4–5, 7
Prolonged Exposure (PE), 607
Promoting Safe and Stable Families (PSSF), 536–537
pseudocommunity/initiation stage, group practice and, 231
psychoeducation, 599–601
psychological first aid (PFA), 615–621

psychological model and addiction, 433–434
public housing authorities (PHAs), 399–400

questionnaires, attachment and, 38

random family systems, 212. *See also* families
rating scale, as measurement tool of strength-based assessments, 84–86
rational emotive therapy (RET), cognitive restructuring (CR) and, 155
reappraisal, cognitive restructuring (CR) and, 155
Reciprocal Attachment Questionnaire for Adults, 38
recording at preset time periods, client logs and, 80
referent power, 53
reflective empathy, 116–117
reframing, 114
rehearsal as intervention skill, 128–129
relabeling, 114
relationships
    economically disadvantaged peoples and, 403–405
    importance of, 18–19
    after trauma, 597–599
relevance, strengths-based assessments and, 76
reliability
    of HRI scale, 63
    strengths-based assessments and, 77
religious organizations, 260–261
reluctancy of clients, 11–14
Replacing Aid to Families with Dependent Children (AFDC), 397
residential treatment programs for addiction, 439–440
resistant model of attachment, 37
resource development as intervention, organizations and, 282, 286–287
resource identification skills, collaborative model and, 109
resource mapping, communities and, 340–342
resource mobilization
    case management and, 161, 163
    micro/macro client systems and, 5
resources in environment, 36
    organizations and, 271–273
respect, importance of, 110
retrospective baseline, definition, 91
Richmond, Mary, 30
rights. *See* ethics
risk
    continuum of, 50–51
    definition, 50
Rollnick, Stephen, 436

Sanctuary Model of Organizational change, 626

sandwiching, case management and, 160
Second Step Program, group practice and, 245
secure model of attachment, 37
self
    collaboration and, 52
    cultural/ethnic diversity and, 14
    self-worth as value, 17–18
    strengths-based generalist practice and, 3–8
self-anchored rating scales, definition, 84
self-care/soothing exercises, 601–603, 623–625
self-help groups, addictions and, 442
self-worth as value, 17–18
sensitivity, 107
sensitivity to change, strengths-based assessments and, 76–77
service coordination
    case management and, 160–161
    micro/macro client systems and, 5
service linkage
    case management and, 159–160
    micro/macro client systems and, 5
service negotiation
    case management and, 161
    micro/macro client systems and, 5
service to others as value, 16
Sexual Behavior in the Human Female (Kinsey), 495
Sexual Behavior in the Human Male (Kinsey), 495
sexuality. *See also* gay/lesbian/bisexual/ transgender people
    elderly and, 472
shelter, consequence of poverty as, 391–392
significance
    clinical, 94
    standard deviation and, 98–99
    statistical, 97–99
    visual, 94–97
single-system designs, 89–90
single-system evaluation designs
    data analysis and, 93–97
    data components of, 90–93
skills, collaborative model and, 60, 62
social diagnosis, definition, 30
Social Diagnosis (Richmond), 30
social isolation of elderly, 473
social justice as value, 16–17
Social Security Act of 1935, 533
Social Security Old Age, Survivors, and Disability Insurance (OASDI), 395–396
social work clients. *See* clients
Social Work Consultation Services (SWCS), 408–409
sociocultural model and addiction, 433
soft skills, 387

solidify tasks, collaborative model and, 60–61
solution-focused approaches, abused/ neglected children and, 540–541
span of control, 267
staff authority, 267
staff development as intervention, organizations and, 282, 284–285
stages of change in clients, 10–11
standard deviation, significance and, 98–99
standardized measure, evaluations and, 55
standardized measures
    as measurement tool of strength-based assessments, 88–89
    strengths-based assessments and, 88–89
state-dependent learning, 582–584, 601
statistical significance, 97–99
stimulants, 420
strategic apex, organizations and, 264
strategic planning as intervention, organizations and, 264, 282, 285–286
strengths and obstacles worksheet, 173–177
strengths perspective of social work
    attachment theory and, 36–38
    critical thinking and, 38
    description, 33–34
    evidence-based practice and, 39
    principles of, 34–36
    versus traditional deficit approach, 40–42
strengths-based assessments, 56–59. *See also* evaluations
strengths-based generalist practice
    description, 2–3
    ethics and, 19–25
    generalist social work practice and, 3–6
    reluctant clients and, 11–14
    self and, 3–8
    and types of social work clients, 8–11
    values and, 16–19
strengths-based practice, abused/neglected children and, 538–539
stress. *See* posttraumatic stress disorder (PTSD)
study tasks, collaborative model and, 60–61
substance abuse, 427. *See also* addicted people and generalist practice
successive intervention design, single-system evaluations and, 93
summarization during interviews, 112–114
Supplemental Security Income (SSI), 375, 395–396
support staff, organizations and, 264
supportive counseling
    elderly and, 484–485

individual client systems and, 154–157
micro/macro client systems and, 5
surveys, communities and, 333–334, 336
Survivors benefits (SSS), 395–396

Talking Paper (as tool), group practice and, 238–239
TARGET (Trauma Adaptive Recovery Group Education and Therapy) Program, 611
target system, 8–9
tasks
  and articulation of focus/plan of action, 120–124
  asking client to tell story, 109–114
  clarification of working with client, 118–119
  client's culture/value/beliefs/environment, 107–109
  collaborative model (general) and, 60–61
  listening for meaning/feelings, 114–117
  and perseverance of client relationship, 124–129
taxes (policy issues), 375, 400
team authority, 267
Temporary Assistance to Needy Families (TANF), 375, 393, 395, 397–398, 535–536
termination, individual client systems and, 164–165
test-retest reliability, strengths-based assessments and, 77
therapeutic communities and addiction, 440–441
therapeutic foster care (TFC), 566
Thomas, William, 481–482
time sampling, behavioral observations and, 82–83

Title XX, 533–534
Tools for Community Assessment and Development, 355–363
training. *See also* education
  micro/macro client systems and, 4–5, 7
transgender clients, 498–501, 510.
  See also gay/lesbian/bisexual/transgender people
Transgender Emergence, 501
trauma, and principles of strength-based practice, 35
trauma-experienced people and generalist practice
  case examples, 583, 587–595, 600–601, 612, 618–619, 627–629
  and categories in DMS-III, 576–584
  for children, 611–615
  immediate posttrauma interventions, 615–621
  psychological trauma, 576
  and reconnection/transformation as recovery, 610–611
  and remembering as recovery, 607–610
  rewards/challenges of working with survivors, 622–626
  and stabilization/skill building as recovery, 596–607
  substance abuse and PTSD, 611
  and symptoms of trauma, 584–595
  war veterans, 621
triangulation, 75
true validity, strengths-based assessments and, 77
trust in relationships
  importance of, 46, 49–51
  and solidifying task of disengagement, 130–132
  strengths assessment and, 57
Twelve Step program, 433
Type I/II traumas, 576

understanding
  definition, 107
  importance of, 115–116
Unemployment benefits (UI), 395–396

validity
  of HRI scale, 63
  listening for validation, 117
  strengths-based assessments and, 77–78
values. *See also* ethics
  collaborative model and client's, 107–109
  generalist social work practice and, 16–19
vicarious traumatization, 622–626
video/voice chats and addiction, 443
vision and foundation policies, 263–265
visual significance, 94–97
voluntary clients, 10

Waking the Tiger (Levine), 585
WALMYR, 89
War on Poverty, 383
war veterans, 621. *See also* posttraumatic stress disorder (PTSD)
welfare, 378–379, 408–409
  children as property (1600s-1700s), 530–531
  evolution of, 530–538
  and federal mandate to protect children (1900s), 532–537
  in-home services, 560–563
  and pulbic concern for children (1800s), 531–532
worker-client transactions, ecosystems perspective and, 32